CORNERED TIGERS

A history of Pakistan's Test cricket

ADAM LICUDI

with Wasim Raja

HANSIB

First published in 1997 by Hansib Caribbean
PO Box 2773, St John's, Antigua, WI

Distributed in the United Kingdom by Readers Book Club
Tower House, 141-149 Fonthill Road, London N4 3HF
(Fax: 0171-263 9656)
Printed in the United Kingdom by Martins the Printers Ltd
Berwick Upon Tweed

Photos courtesy of Allsport & Allsport/Hulton Getty
Tiger illustration by Stefan Brazzo

British Library Cataloguing in Publication Data.
A catalogue record for this book is available from the British Library

ISBN 1-807518-31-4

Publisher's note
Readers unfamiliar with Hansib's publications may note the use of
'Westindies' (not 'West Indies'). This has been used in all Hansib
publications since 1973 in a tribute to the formation of the Caribbean
Community (CariCom) at Chaguaramas, Trinidad, on 4 July 1973
and as an appropriation of the name given by the "discoverers" to
assert the region's united, unique and distinctive identity.

Contents

—————— *The Players* ——————

Preface

The sport of cricket in Pakistan enjoys a rich legacy, emanating from their historic Test match victory against England in 1954 at the Oval - the first side to win a Test on their first tour to England - through to the 1992 World Cup victory over the same opponents and the 1996 Test series.

Nearly forty-five years after joining the International Cricket Conference, Pakistan is still producing cricketers who are deservedly regarded as being of the highest calibre. At the start of the 1996/7 season, several exciting new prospects have emerged to join the established stars who will be leading the side into the 21st century. They include teenager Shahid Alfridi - the scorer of the fastest-ever century in one-day cricket - and Hassan Raza, who was credited with being the youngest-ever Test cricketer. Two other players made sensational Test debuts: Mohammad Wasim, the captain of the under-19s, by scoring a hundred against Zimbabwe, and Mohammad Zahid, who took 11 wickets in his first match against New Zealand. These youngsters continue Pakistan's tradition of introducing youth at the earliest opportunity, which was started in the 1950s with the likes of the Mohammad brothers, Hanif and Mustaq.

Cornered Tigers is named after the famous quote by the former Pakistan Test captain, Imran Khan, during the 1992 World Cup which he used to rally the side, and this book is intended to be a document for inspiration as well as one of sporting record.

The initial idea came in the Spring of 1988 at the launch of Hansib's *100 Great Westindian Cricketers* in Antigua, when I sought the advice of Pakistan's tour manager Intikhab Alam. This event, which was hosted by the Antigua & Barbuda Prime Minister VC Bird, was attended by both the Westindies and the Pakistan teams, who were at the time contesting a three-match series. The idea received the immediate support of the Pakistan cricket team management.

Special acknowledgement must go to Adam Licudi for his diligent work, Wasim Raja for his cooperation throughout and to Bobby Ayyub Syed for his assistance in the promotion and marketing of *Cornered Tigers*.

Arif Ali
Hansib Caribbean

Arif Ali with Intikhab Alam in Antigua, 1988 - discussing the idea of a book on Pakistan's Test cricket history

Foreword

I am delighted to be able to write the foreword to Cornered Tigers, a definitive history of Pakistani cricket. Having been involved with my country's Test cricket since its inception in 1952, I realise how far the game has come since then.

With a host of recent Test victories against all comers and with the 1992 World Cup triumph still a happy memory, the Pakistan side of the nineties is on a high, and possesses some of the finest players in the world, with a host of talented batsmen and the likes of Wasim Akram and Waqar Younis fronting the bowling.

They are building on the success achieved by the Test team of the seventies and eighties, which proved to be a match for anyone. Imran Khan and Sarfraz Nawaz established a great fast bowling heritage, while Abdul Qadir continued the country's tradition of discovering magical leg-spinners. Some glorious batsmen have been produced, such as Majid Khan, Asif Iqbal, Zaheer Abbas and Wasim Raja, each of whom played throughout the seventies, to Javed Miandad and Salim Malik in the 1980s.

A project of this kind is long overdue and provides a welcome insight into many Pakistani players, from the greats of the fifties, such as Abdul Hafeez Kardar and Fazal Mahmood, the early captains, through to the present, as well as discussing the domestic and international scene.

As I know from my own family, which has provided five Test cricketers to Pakistan - three of my brothers, Wazir, Mustaq and Sadiq, as well as my son, Shoaib - cricket seems to be in the blood of most Pakistanis. So this is a cricket document that any Pakistani or cricket lover should gain pleasure from, as well as providing an invaluable source of reference.

Coming out in the 50th anniversary year since Independence, this book is a fitting tribute to 45 glorious years of Pakistan's Test cricket, which announced itself as a force in world cricket with that now famous victory over England at the Oval in August 1954, when the tourists became the first team to win a Test on their first visit to England - a match I remember with affection.

Hanif Mohammad
Karachi 1996
Pakistan Test cricketer 1950-70 (Captain 1964-7)

Khan Mohammad takes Pakistan's first wicket in Test cricket when he bowls Pankaj Roy, Delhi, October 1952

Hanif Mohammad hits Wardle to the boundary at Old Trafford on Pakistan's first tour to England, July 1954

Early development

Pakistan's fight for Test status

It was a remarkable feat that within five years of partition Pakistan was involved in its first Test series. Differences with its neighbour were not fully resolved and the new Muslim state - Jinnah's brain-child - was geographically divided into two separate regions, namely West Pakistan and East Pakistan. The West wing had a population of some 35 million and had a fine tradition of cricketers and sportsmen, with hockey, squash and polo being very popular. The influence of British colonial rule was clear to see, inheriting cricket grounds belonging to the military and the colleges which were quintessentially English. Servicemen on leave from the North-West Frontier garrisons played cricket regularly in Lahore. The University had a history of good players and it was they who formed the nucleus of the first representative sides for Pakistan.

The more populous East Pakistan - now the independent state of Bangladesh - had a population of 40 million who had yet to see first-class cricket when Dacca staged Pakistan's first Test on home soil. Although Dacca continued to host a number of the early Tests, this was a tenuous link to the main cricket playing region which has produced almost all of Pakistan's Test cricketers. East Pakistan's occasional representative teams did not fare well; the 1955/6 Marylebone Cricket Club (MCC) tourists bowled the side out for 103 and 55 to win by an innings, yet within a week the MCC were losing by an innings to the full Pakistan XI. Indeed in 24 years only one Test player, Niaz Ahmed, a seam bowler who played two Tests in the sixties, came from East Pakistan.

Before Partition the Northwest region of India produced many first-class cricketers who went on to play Test cricket for India. From Jullundar came Baqa Jilani (one Test), Nazir Ali (two Tests) and his brother Wazir Ali (seven Tests) whose son Khalid Wazir was soon to be playing Test cricket for Pakistan against India in 1954, and Jahangir Khan (four Tests) whose son, Majid Khan, was to captain Pakistan in the seventies. From Hoshiarpur came Mahomed Nissar (six Tests); from Karachi, Naoomal Jeoomal (three Tests) and from Lahore, Dilawar Hussain (three Tests). All

but the first and last named played in India's inaugural Test match against England in 1932. There were three other cricketers from Lahore who played for India before 1947 and went on to represent Pakistan. These were Gul Mahomed (eight Tests for India) Amir Elahi (one Test for India) and Pakistan's first Test captain A H Kardar, who played three Tests for India under the name of Abdul Hafeez. The great fast bowler Fazal Mahmood was selected for India's tour to Australia in 1947 but decided to pin his allegiance to Pakistan on the formation of the new state. Two others Gogumal Kischenchand and "Jenni" Irani, who were born in Karachi, made their debuts on that tour for India. Kischenchand, a middle-order batsman, later played against Pakistan in their second ever Test.

India played just ten Tests - all against England - before Partition. As each Indian side included several players from the area that was to become West Pakistan, that region can be credited with contributing significantly to establishing India's Test cricket as well as Pakistan's. Indeed Lala Amarnath, who captained India against Pakistan in 1952/3 was, like Kardar, born in Lahore. Gulabrai Ramchand, who played under Amarnath in that inaugural Test, was born in Karachi and later captained India against Australia in 1959/60. Others such as Salim Durani and Panamal Punjabi, both from Karachi, and Man Mohan Sood from Lahore played for India later in the fifties and sixties.

The rapidity of separation left great holes in the administration of cricket in Pakistan. There was no gradual handing over of control and many Hindu players and administrators left the region. The country was in a parlous state financially, that it regrouped so quickly and effectively under such adverse circumstances was a minor miracle.

In the summer of 1948 the Board of Control for Cricket in Pakistan (BCCP) was formed to try and re-establish cricket in the four main regions, namely Sind, Punjab, Bhawalpur and North-West Frontier. Much of the early work was conducted under the auspices of Justice 'Bobby' Cornelius who set up the BCCP and succeeded in popularising cricket and securing some early funding. Within six months he invited the Westindies, who were touring India, to visit

Pakistan. Against a strong Westindies side captained by John Goddard, and including George Headley, Clyde Walcott, Everton Weekes, Jeff Stollmeyer and Allan Rae, Pakistan secured a draw in their first "unofficial" Test staged in Lahore thanks to a second-wicket stand of 205 between Imtiaz Ahmed and Mohammad Saeed, who both scored centuries.

Earlier in the year the Westindies had been captained for the first time by a black player, the great George Headley, albeit for only one Test to abate the growing clamour to end the run of white captains. The same desire for independence that Pakistan had felt was soon to spread through the Caribbean.

The Board was suitably encouraged by the results against the tourists and sent three prominent players, Khan Mohammad, Imtiaz Ahmed and A R Dinshaw, to England for coaching at Alf Gover's, in Wandsworth, south-west London. The first two named were to play a prominent part in Pakistan's early Test teams.

The next year (1949/50) a Commonwealth team, managed by the former England wicket-keeper George Duckworth, visited the sub-continent, playing five matches in Pakistan, and remaining undefeated, winning the "unofficial" Test in Lahore. Duckworth brought sides back the following year and in 1953/4.

The domestic game still required much attention and a concerted effort was made in 1950 with School and University Tournaments being arranged as well as inter-provincial matches. The MCC tour in 1951/2 was a great fillip to the game in Pakistan. Although the MCC only included a handful of well-known names, it was clear that they had underestimated the progress that had been made. The MCC played five games and left without a win. Nazar Mohammad hit 140 and Fazal Mahmood took 5 for 58 for Punjab against them. In a slow-scoring first "Test" Pakistan gave a good account of themselves. After Khan Mohammad had bowled with plenty of pace and hostility, taking 5 for 84 to help bowl MCC out for 254, the sixteen year old Hanif Mohammad, who made 26 in two and three-quarter hours, added 96 for the first wicket with Nazar Mohammad, who made 66. Mohammed Ghazali, with 86, and Maqsood Ahmad, who made 137, put together a partnership of 168 to set up a big lead for Pakistan, who declared at 428 for 8. MCC fared much better in their second innings now that the track was completely lifeless, and Graveney and Spooner secured a draw as each hit not out hundreds.

Even the Universities showed great fighting qualities. After being bowled out for 88 in their first innings, Shakoor Ahmad (104 not out) and Shujayuddin (112 not out) ensured a draw. Bahawalpur ran up a big score, 348 for 9 declared, with Imtiaz Ahmed making 99, Hanif Mohammad 71, and Wazir Mohammad 67, then bowled out MCC for just 123 and made them follow-on.

The final game was the second "Test" played at Karachi and it proved to be one of the most significant in Pakistan's history. On a coir matting wicket Fazal Mahmood took 6-40 as MCC collapsed to 123 all out. Pakistan fared little better in their first innings but nudged to a seven run lead. Thanks to a fine hundred by Tom Graveney MCC set a difficult target of 285 in the fourth innings. They had been kept in check by Khan Mohammad's five for 88. Pakistan were not going to let their chance slip; Hanif Mohammad led the way with a 64, made in four hours, showing remarkable concentration for his age. At 178 for 5 the game was in the balance but the captain, Abdul Hafeez Kardar, saw the side through to a four wicket victory with 50 not out, adding 83 for the 6th wicket with Anwar Hussain. The 1953 *Wisden* records: "The Pakistan authorities were highly delighted at their success and regarded it as a great help towards their claims for inclusion in the Imperial Cricket Conference."

Kardar wrote a letter to *The Times*, in London, presenting Pakistan's case for Test status. At the next meeting of the Imperial Cricket Council (ICC), on 28th July 1952, the notion was put to the vote. Pakistan, on the proposition of India and seconded by MCC, was unanimously accepted. Thus all the forthcoming unofficial tours now became official and Pakistan would start playing Test cricket in India that winter.

In preparation the BCCP sent a youth team, the Pakistan Eaglets, to England for coaching at Gover's and to witness some first-class and Test cricket, watching England's series with India. The Eaglets were organised by Mohammad Saeed, whose son Yawar played for Somerset and whose son-in-law was Fazal Mahmood.

Pakistan's Test history begins

The selectors' faith remained largely with youth for the tour to India, picking some players who had yet to play for their provincial associations and setting a precedent matched by no other country for throwing players in at the deep end, to make them "fight like cornered tigers" as much then as now.

As there was just one warm-up match - a game against West Zone in which Hanif Mohammad scored a hundred in each innings - selections for the inaugural Test were based as much on trials held in Pakistan a month before.

Abdul Hafeez Kardar led his side out to field at the Feroz Shah Kotla Stadium, Delhi, on 16th October 1952, as a Test playing nation for the first time. The team list read, in batting order:

1. Nazar Mohammad, 31, Karachi; he was to be the first player to score a hundred for Pakistan, "carrying his bat" in the second Test victory, and finished the series with an average of nearly 40. However his Test career was prematurely ended by a serious arm injury. He became a National coach, teaching his Test playing son Mudassar Nazar.

2. Hanif Mohammad, 17, Bahawalpur; he became the cornerstone of the batting for the next 17 years, missing only two of Pakistan's first 57 Tests, hitting 12 hundreds including the highest Test score by an Asian, 337. In 1958, he set the highest first-class score, 499, a record which stood until 1994, when Brian Lara made 501 not out. Hanif kept wicket for the first three Tests.

3. Israr Ali, 25, Multan and Bahawalpur; a left-handed batsman and fast-medium bowler, whose Test career was a short one, playing in Pakistan's first and third Tests, and then two more in 1959/60 against Australia.

4. Imtiaz Ahmed, 24, Services; another stalwart of the side, who played in 41 out Pakistan's first 42 Tests. He took over the 'keeping from Hanif and was to make the highest score by a keeper, 208, when batting at No 8.

5. Maqsood Ahmed, 24, Bahawalpur; a stylish right-handed batsman, who entertained the crowds with his strokeplay, he was a regular in the side for the first few years of Pakistan's Test history.

6. Abdul Hafeez Kardar (captain), 27, Services; Pakistan's captain for the first 23 Tests, he also played three Tests for India before Partition. He led his side with calm authority, producing a most impressive string of results.

7. Anwar Hussain, 32, Karachi; a right-hand bat and fast-medium bowler, he played in four of Pakistan's first five Tests, but was not called upon again.

8. Waqar Hassan, 20, Karachi; a fine right-handed strokemaker who was a regular in the side until 1960. His brother, Pervez Sajjad, also distinguished himself for Pakistan during the sixties.

9. Fazal Mahmood, 25, Punjab; one of Pakistan's finest-ever bowlers. He was often instrumental in his side's success, a match-winner who took 65 wickets in the seven Pakistani victories in which he played. He turned down selection by India in 1947 in order to play for Pakistan.

10. Khan Mohammad, 24, Bahawalpur; a fine opening bowler who took 50 Test wickets in just 11 Tests. Injury prevented him playing more and establishing himself as one of the best bowlers in the world.

11. Amir Elahi, 44, Bahawalpur; amongst the oldest Test players, he also played in a Test for India before Partition. Because of his age this was his only Test series, but he was a most useful leg-spinner and shared in a tenth-wicket stand of 104 with Zulifqar Ahmed in the 4th Test.

Considering the itinerary, which had been rapidly drawn up, the results were most encouraging. Although the first Test was lost, by an innings and 30 runs, Pakistan's first Test victory came in the very next game, on a matting wicket at Lucknow, reversing the result with an innings victory of their own. Fazal Mahmood took 12 wickets in the match.

No other new member of the Imperial Cricket Conference had achieved a Test win so soon, and their record over their first fifty matches was to prove to be exceptional, winning ten and losing only 14 matches. [The chart on page 16 shows when each country achieved its first Test win and the results over the first fifty Tests].

Although the series was eventually lost 2-1, Pakistan had an excellent chance of squaring the series in the 4th Test at Madras when heavy rain washed out the last two days. They were also hampered by the loss through injury of Khan Mohammad, their experienced opening bowler, and the loss of form in the Tests of Imtiaz Ahmed.

Pakistan still lacked any proper domestic structure. The only first-class games tended to be those against touring sides. However in 1953/4 an inter-provincial championship, the Quaid-e-Azam Trophy, was set up, and a number of trial games before selection for the tour to England were played.

The early years brought several surprise victories, the most famous of which was beating England at the Oval in 1954, when Pakistan bowled England out in the fourth innings to win by 24 runs, thus becoming the only team to have won a Test on their first tour to England, and squared the series in the process. The side had shown great fighting qualities; the last two wickets in the second innings had doubled Pakistan's score, giving Fazal Mahmood just enough to bowl at. Some of the fielding on the tour was sub-standard, illustrating a general lack of experience, but despite the weather Pakistan still managed to win nine of their games and lost only three.

The prestige of that success and an intensifying rivalry with India meant that matches between the neighbours precluded risk by either side. In the first series on Pakistan's own soil (1954/5) all five Tests were drawn and the scoring rate was often less than two runs per over. At Dacca only 710 runs

Fazal Mahmood leads the side from the field after bowling Pakistan to victory at the Oval in 1954

were scored in total over the four days; at Peshawar the scoring was even slower, with just 638 runs. Five more draws were played out in the next series in 1960/1, after which the two countries fought each other more often on the battle ground than the cricket field.

Pakistan continued to produce good results at home, recording a first series win in only their fourth series by beating New Zealand (1955/6) 2-0. In the same season a strong MCC side was defeated 2-1 though the first signs of animosity between the two countries were evident when umpire Idris Begh was dowsed in cold water by some of the MCC players who had been aggrieved by his umpiring. Begh was understandably upset by this ill-mannered prank and Lord Alexander of Tunis, the President of the MCC, offered to cancel the rest of the tour. It is difficult to envisage such behaviour by the MCC against more established opponents. The final three matches of the tour were played out in a frosty atmosphere, and in the final Test at Karachi Imtiaz Ahmed felt it necessary to complain about further abuse of the umpires on the field by the visitors.

The next year, Pakistan won convincingly, by nine wickets, in a one-off Test against Australia (1956/7), who stopped off on their way back from England. Although the first day of that Test produced only 95 runs, by all accounts it was a fascinating duel on a virtually unplayable pitch.

Pakistan travelled to the Westindies in 1957/8 and by drawing the first Test in Barbados, had stretched their unbeaten sequence to 12 Tests spread over three-and-a-half-years. They were saved from defeat in that Test by Hanif Mohammad, whose epic innings of 337 - the longest-ever in first-class cricket - took them to safety. However in the remaining Tests Roy Gilchrist proved too quick for some of the players while Garry Sobers set a new highest Test score, 365 not out (since beaten by Brian Lara's 375), and was in prodigious form for the rest of the series. Although the next three Tests were lost, Pakistan salvaged some pride with a well deserved victory in the last Test, by an innings.

Pakistan had its revenge too winning the return series in the following season, 1958/9. Fazal Mahmood had taken over the captaincy from Kardar and led by example with 19 wickets in the first two Tests, which brought comfortable wins on matting wickets. The third Test, on turf, was lost.

Pakistan's first home series defeat came at the hands of the Australians in 1959/60. Pakistan had grown used to playing on coir matting up until then but this was the first series scheduled to be played exclusively on grass wickets, which had been encouraged, ironically, to improve results abroad and to attract more touring sides. In fact, neither eventuated.

After heavy rain the first Test at Dacca had to be played on matting rather than the new grass pitch, and represented Pakistan's only defeat on that surface. Admittedly coir had served them well in their early years, but no more than normal home advantage in other countries, but the switch was to put Pakistan at a disadvantage for several seasons.

There had been a general lack of grass wickets in the country as a whole as well as of stadia, though more were being built. The limitations of first-class cricket were also beginning to tell and consequently the sixties were a bad time in Pakistan's cricket history. Several of the leading players such as Kardar and Fazal Mahmood, who had done so much to get Pakistan Test status and just as importantly Test credibility, had retired and the Test side was struggling to live up to the high expectations of it.

The nucleus of players who had learned their cricket in the Ranji Trophy was now exhausted and Pakistan was struggling to produce players of Test match quality. Opportunities arose for a few highly talented individuals to come through quickly, though the likes of Mustaq Mohammad appearing in a Test at the age of fifteen reflected a dearth of more experienced talent. It was the quality of schools' cricket that helped sustain the game during this period. For instance, many future Test players appeared in the Rubie Shield, which was contested for by schools in the Karachi/Sind area, and matches often attracted bigger crowds than first-class matches.

After a home series defeat to England in 1961/2 followed by a drubbing on the return tour in 1962, Pakistan's horizons became very limited. The bland nature of the new grass wickets hid deficiencies in technique which were cruelly exposed in England. Javed Burki, at 24, was too young when he took over for that tour. He had made his Test debut only eighteen months before, was somewhat reclusive by nature and had trouble knitting the side together. Only Mustaq Mohammad came away with an enhanced reputation and indeed was signed up by Northamptonshire to play county cricket after that tour.

Burki's replacement as captain, Hanif Mohammad, had a similar approach to captaincy as he had to batting, though with limited resources at his disposal it was often the only way. Pakistan's version of the grass wicket did not help; the pitches were terribly slow and produced 15 draws in the first 20 Tests on them.

Progress was hindered by a lack of Test cricket, for there were two long periods without a single Test, from August 1962, to October 1964, and from February 1965 to July 1967, yet a glut in 1964/5

A group shot from the 1962 touring side to England

when eight Tests were played. It meant that in Hanif Mohammad's first Test in charge in 1964 he had six new caps in a totally changed side from the one that had played in Pakistan's last Test against England 26 months before. All things considered, results were fairly encouraging. Pakistan drew the single Test played against the Australians, on their way home from England, and the two sides played out another draw in Melbourne as the Pakistan team made its way to New Zealand for a three match series, which was closely contested but finished 0-0.

New Zealand's return tour brought Pakistan their first Test win at home for over six years with a most convincing innings victory at Rawalpindi. It also ended a barren spell of 22 Tests without a win. They out-played the tourists in the drawn second Test at Lahore, where Hanif Mohammad scored a double-hundred, and won the third Test to secure Pakistan's only series win between 1958/9 and 1972/3. Those two wins were the only two at home between 1959 and 1976.

After a joyous childhood, Pakistan's cricket was going through its difficult teenage years but talent was beginning to shine through. Some of Pakistan's greatest players were coming into the side - Asif Iqbal, Majid Khan and Mustaq Mohammad and soon Imran Khan - perhaps before they were really ready yet it was they that formed the nucleus of the side throughout the seventies.

Because of the lack of official Tests, a number of unofficial Tests and tours were undertaken. The Eaglets toured England in 1963, a full representative side travelled to Sri Lanka (Ceylon) in 1964 and there were tours to Pakistan by various international teams, including the Cavaliers and the Commonwealth. Certain players also, appeared for the Commonwealth team; Hanif Mohammad and the Nawab of Pataudi, captains of Pakistan and India respectively, whose countries were at odds with each other, played in the same side on a tour to Rhodesia.

The MCC sent an under-25 side for the first time to Pakistan in 1966/7, and many of the players who featured in that series also appeared in their respective full Test sides in England in 1967. Asif Iqbal captained the under-25 side and scored a marvellous hundred to save the second "Test" at Dacca. Majid Khan, who had made a hundred not out and 57 in the first Test at Lahore, helped out with 95. Mustaq Mohammad demonstrated his all-round ability with 120 and 57 in the first Test and seven wickets for 73 in the third at Karachi. All three Tests were drawn.

That summer in England, in the first Test at Lord's, Hanif Mohammad batted for 542 minutes, scoring 187, to prolong his unbeaten record as captain. However the next two Tests were lost. The third Test, though, produced a remarkable ninth-wicket partnership of 190 between Asif Iqbal and

Intikhab Alam but it was not quite enough to avoid defeat.

Domestic cricket had seen a major re-structuring through the efforts of Abdul Hafeez Kardar who had got the main Banks and companies such as Pakistan International Airways (PIA) and Pakistan Automobile Corporation (PACO) involved in supporting the game. However the stadia built to reflect the success of the early years now struggled to attract big crowds. Prices were inflated to keep out troublemakers associated with the growing political factions in Pakistan at a time when the country was yearning for a direction that had only been half-satisfied in 1947. Student demonstrations, war with India, civil disruption over the East wing, which was soon to become Bangladesh - this was the back-drop to which cricket was being played. It was a wonder that it kept going at all. The series with England in 1968/9, a late replacement for the cancelled tour to South Africa, was constantly interrupted by crowd invasions and little meaningful cricket could be played.

The next year the series against New Zealand in 1969/70 was also affected, though to a lesser degree. The series saw a rare home defeat and the end of an era, Hanif Mohammad's last Test which

was played alongside his brothers Mustaq and Sadiq for the first and only time.

The 1971 tour to England, which initially was in doubt because of various political problems, heralded the arrival of two more superstars. Imran Khan played his first Test with a marked lacked of success but Zaheer Abbas announced himself with a brilliant innings of 274 at Edgbaston, a game Pakistan would surely have won but for the rain. Zaheer and Sadiq Mohammad were soon to be signed up by Gloucestershire. Still all-square going into the final Test, Pakistan's batting cracked under pressure, as it has been prone to do, and they slipped to defeat by just 25 runs.

Mustaq Mohammad and Intikhab Alam were amongst those invited to play for the Rest of the World that winter in Australia for a full programme of matches, and Alam led Pakistan on the tour there the following year (1972/3). Although well beaten in the first Test at Adelaide the side should really have won the next two. They made 574 for 8 declared at Melbourne but lost, and chasing only

An XI from the 1971 tour to England

Pakistan's squad for the 1982 tour of England, led by Imran Khan for the first time

159 to win at Sydney collapsed to 106 all out.

There was much bickering within the squad but once certain individuals had been sent home, the team began to play to its potential. Pakistan at last, in its 21st year of Test cricket, came of age by winning a first overseas series, in New Zealand. Victory there ended another poor run of 16 games without a win but also began a similar sequence of 15 Tests unbeaten, which lasted until 1976/7.

Overall the seventies proved to be an unsettled time in Pakistani cricket. Greater expectations and professionalism brought their demands for results, and for better renumeration. By now many of the players were establishing themselves as world class and helped produce the best string of series in Pakistan's history. Drawn rubbers at home and away with England, a draw at home with Westindies, victory against New Zealand, a draw for the first time in Australia, narrow defeat in the Caribbean: these were results to match any other team in the world, at a time when Westindies and Australia had some of their best players too, and in certain respects it was fitting that World Series should come along and bring them all together, paying them what they were worth for playing the world's summer sport to such a high standard. Seven Pakistanis eventually played for Packer - others were invited - and that number reflected the quality of the national side. It also reflected the level of dissatisfaction with the terms they were getting from the BCCP, which had caused a players strike before the tour to Australia and Westindies in 1976/7 and evidently had not been fully resolved as a number of the players signed up for World Series during the series in the Caribbean.

There was an ever-increasing number of Pakistanis playing county cricket in England and demand for more in the Northern Leagues. However the Packer defections did highlight a lack of strength in depth, though certain players such as Abdul Qadir and Mudassar Nazar did get the chance to come through. Although drawing at home to England in 1977/8, Pakistan were easily beaten in England a few months later when the Packer players were again excluded. When cricketing relations were resumed with India the following winter, after a seventeen year break, the Board of Control for Cricket in Pakistan ensured special clearance from Packer - prompted by President Zia-ul-Haq - so that they could field a full strength side, and duly beat India 2-0.

Unfortunately Pakistan probably did not quite fulfil their potential in that golden period, occasionally hindered by the old caution or trouble under pressure, which was evident in the return series in India in 1979/80, where the home team had the upper hand and several players suffered a loss of form as a result of the tension. Pakistan's progress was not helped by a less than full schedule of Test series in the seventies and results were also hindered by divisive pay disputes and by the occasionally insensitive handling of players and, in particular, of the captaincy.

For instance, despite victory in New Zealand in 1972/3, Majid Khan was announced as captain as Intikhab Alam's replacement for the forthcoming home series with England before the New Zealand tour was even over, yet Intikhab was re-instated for the next tour to England in 1974. Factions appeared within the side, which were only exaggerated by the clash with Kardar and the BCCP, and the defections to Packer. Team spirit was lacking though there were some magnificent individual performances, such as the batting of Majid Khan and Wasim Raja in the Caribbean and the bowling of Sarfraz Nawaz, who took seven wickets for one run in a 33-ball spell against Australia at the Melbourne Cricket Ground in 1978/9.

Certainly Pakistan underachieved in the World Cups in which their blend of brilliant strokemakers and all-rounders, most of whom had plenty of experience in England (where the first three tournaments were held), suggested they would make at least the semi-finals each time.

Javed Miandad's first tenure of the captaincy brought in spirit as well as some fighting qualities but also brought in some fights; he squared up to Dennis Lillee on the pitch, then fell out with his team who refused en masse to play under him after he had blamed his senior players for the team's performances in Australia 1981/2.

It was left to Imran Khan, who took over the leadership for the tour to England in 1982, to harness that spirit while instilling confidence and ambition in the side. Believing that "ambition should be made of sterner stuff" he did not suffer fools lightly, demanding high standards, commitment and loyalty, and fitness in his bowlers to ensure the flesh was not weak. He knew the type of player he wanted and insisted on the final say in selection.

Pakistan's performances in the dozen years from 1982/3 to 1994 were bettered only by the Westindies, who remained unbeaten in any Test series in that period. Significantly, Pakistan held Westindies to three one-all series draws and whenever the two sides met the contest was invariably billed as "the best in the world" decider.

Pakistan went unbeaten for 12 Tests again between 1982/3 and 1983/4 during which they whitewashed Australia 3-0 and beat India by the same margin in a six Test series. Imran Khan was at his peak as a bowler and took an unparalleled 40 wickets in the last mentioned series. Pakistan's progress was checked by his serious shin injury which kept him out for two years. It allowed for certain internal squabbles to resurface again, often over the captaincy.

Shortly after Imran Khan's return to the side Pakistan enjoyed their best run, remaining undefeated for 16 Tests (1986-88), during which they beat both India and England in away series for the first time, and England at home in the infamous, acrimonious series of 1987/8. Just prior to that, Pakistan had produced its best World Cup performance in four starts, though a semi-final defeat, in fact, was a bitter disappointment for the co-hosts.

During the next eight years, Pakistan lost only one home Test, to the Westindies. The side shared two series with them, in the Caribbean (1987/8) and at home (1990/1), beat the Australians in Pakistan (1988/9) then lost narrowly away in a curtailed series (1989/90), won the Nehru Cup in India (1989), whitewashed New Zealand (1990/1) and beat England convincingly in England (1992).

The pinnacle came just before that series, when they won the 1992 World Cup, playing like "cornered tigers" when they were on the verge of going out of the competition. That rallying call reflected Pakistan's struggle for Test status and credibility, their backs-against-the-wall situation in the sixties, their anger in the seventies and fighting qualities in the eighties. It is their motto for the nineties.

With expectations following the World Cup running so high, 13 one-day defeats in 16 matches since that victory were most disappointing and prompted an inevitable change of captaincy, with Wasim Akram replacing Javed Miandad. Ironically a splendid victory in a one-off Test in New Zealand had made Miandad his country's most successful captain, level with Imran with 14 victories but from far fewer matches (34 compared with 48). High hopes in the Westindies in 1992/3 were quickly crushed. Akram, whose performance was vital to his side if it was to succeed, was out of form while other key players were injured.

An easy series win at home to Zimbabwe was not enough to save him or his vice-captain, Waqar Younis, as dissatisfaction within the team reappeared. However, when both are fully fit they remain the most feared bowling duo in the world, and they combined to help the new captain, Salim Malik, to record comfortable series wins in New Zealand in 1993/4, and in Sri Lanka the following summer. The side held its nerve brilliantly in a thrilling series at home to Australia, which was won by virtue of a classic one-wicket win at Karachi. Perhaps Pakistan has never performed so well under pressure. It made their results in 1995 all the more surprising, with performances fluctuating wildly, though off-the-field disputes and injuries to key players did not help. The enchanting - and enfuriating - thing about Pakistan is that they can be the best and the worst side in the world in the same

The 1996/7 Pakistanis rejoice after beating Australia in a one-day international

week! They lost heavily to both South Africa and Zimbabwe, yet came back to take the series against the latter. It was only the third time a side has come from behind to win a three-match series after losing the first Test, and the first to do so away from home. But, incredibly, they suffered the same fate themselves against Sri Lanka in their very next series. It was Pakistan's first series defeat at home for fifteen years and the first time they had lost two matches in a home rubber since 1959/60. Two further defeats followed in Australia, as Pakistan equalled their worst losing sequence, but just as the position of their third captain in as many series, Wasim Akram, looked in jeopardy, the side bounced back to win convincingly at Sydney and produced a solid performance to beat New Zealand.

That the team is beginning to blend under Akram, who has learned a lot since his last tenure in office, was evident on the tour to England, which was highly successful both on and off the field. Positive batting at Lord's and the Oval set the stage for some brilliant bowling on the last day to win both matches.

With the likes of Mustaq Ahmed at last realising his potential as a match-winning bowler, and the batting really taking shape around the consistency of the likes of Saeed Anwar, Ijaz Ahmed and Inzamam-ul-Haq, Pakistan cricket has never looked healthier. They again look a side that could beat anyone. They need Wasim and Waqar to remain fit, and to find greater stability in their batting, and this highly talented side could yet develop into one of the strongest in Pakistan's history.

First Test win for each Test cricketing nation and record in their first 50 Tests

| | First Test | First 50 mtch | | | First win |
		W	L	D	
England	1876/7	30	14	6	2nd Test
Australia	1876/7	18	26	6	1st Test
South Africa	1899	9	32	9	12th Test
Westindies	1928	16	17	17	6th Test
India	1932	4	18	28	25th Test
New Zealand	1929/30	2	25	23	40th Test
Pakistan	1952/3	10	14	26	2nd Test
Sri Lanka	1981/2	4	22	24	14th Test
Zimbabwe*	1992/3	1	7	8	11th Test

16 Tests played

16

Results

Pakistan's Test results every 50 Tests

	W	L	D
Tests 1-50	10	14	26
Tests 51-100	9	12	29
Tests 101-150	14	11	25
Tests 151-200	15	6	29
Tests 201-231	16	10	5

Pakistan's Test results every 10 years

	P	W	L	D
1952/3-1962	42	8	14	20
1962/3-1972	20	2	5	15
1972/3-1982	61	14	15	32
1982/3-1992	79	25	10	44

Pakistan's Test results by decade

	P	W	L	D
1950s	29	8	9	12
1960s	30	2	8	20
1970s	46	9	11	26
1980s	79	23	13	43
1990s	46	22	12	12

(to 1996)

Most consecutive matches without defeat

16 Karachi 1986/7 to Port of Spain 1987/8
15 Wellington 1972/3 to Adelaide 1976/7
12 Manchester 1954 to Bridgetown 1957/8
12 Karachi 1982/3 to Nagpur 1983/4

Most consecutive matches without victory

22 Lahore 1958/9 to Christchurch 1964/5
16 Lord's 1967 to Wellington 1972/3

Most consecutive wins

4 Karachi 1989/90 (v NZ) to Karachi 1989/90 (v WI)
3 Port of Spain 1957/8 to Dacca 1958/9
3 Lahore 1978/9 to Christchurch 1978/9
3 Karachi 1982/3 to Lahore 1982/3
3 Karachi 1982/3 to Hyderabad 1982/3
3 Sialkot 1985/6 to Kandy 1985/6
3 Colombo 1994/5 to Karachi 1994/5
3 Bulawayo 1994/5 to Peshawar 1995/6
3 Sydney 1995/6 to Lord's 1996

Most consecutive defeats

4 Faisalabad 1995/6 to Hobart 1995/6
4 Leeds 1971 to Sydney 1972/3
3 Port of Spain 1957/8 to Georgetown 1957/8

Most consecutive draws

9 Auckland 1972/3 to Karachi 1974/5
8 Faisalabad 1988/9 to Sialkot 1989/90
6 Karachi 1959/60 to Delhi 1960/1
5 Dacca 1954/5 to Karachi 1954/5
5 Karachi 1964/5 to Christchurch 1964/5
5 Lahore 1982/3 to Nagpur 1983/4
5 Karachi 1986/7 to Ahmedabad 1986/7

Chronology of events

Date	Event
1930-1	Chodary Rahmat Ali determines name of Pakistan for chiefly Moslem states in the north-west of the continent at the Round Table Conference
1940	Demand for separate Moslem state, after fears of recriminations should largely Hindu India gain self-rule from Britain
1947	October - Partition creates two separate dominions India and the formation of East and West Pakistan, capital in Karachi
1952	July - Voted into the ICC, thus giving Pakistan Test match status
1952	October - Inaugural Test match v India at Delhi First Test victory, in only 2nd Test, by an innings and 43 runs at Lucknow
1955/6	First series win at home to New Zealand
1956	Pakistan is proclaimed an Islamic Republic
1958	Ayub Khan becomes President
1959	Capital is changed to Rawalpindi
1965	At war with India over disputed Jammu and Kashmir regions
1967	Capital changed once more to Islamabad Pakistan People's Party founded by Zulfikar Ali Bhutto
1969	Yahya Khan takes over as President
1971	Disputes between West and East Pakistan lead to civil war, and eventual formation of two separate states, Pakistan and Bangladesh respectively
1972	Pakistan leave the Commonwealth under President Zulfikar Ali Bhutto, who becomes Prime Minister the following year; Bangladesh recognised as an Independent state
1972/3	First overseas series win, v New Zealand
1977	Martial law imposed followed by a military coup led by General Zia-ul-Haq, who becomes President
1977	October World Series Cricket begins
1979	Execution of former PM Bhutto
1982/3	First series win in India
1987	First series win in England
1987	October Co-hosted 4th World Cup with India, losing in semi-final to Australia
1989	November - First major one-day tournament win - Nehru Cup in India
1991	Death of President Zia-ul-Haq in plane crash
1992	March World Cup victory, beating England in the final by 22 runs, in front of over 87,000 spectators at the Melbourne Cricket Ground
1992	October 40 years of Test cricket completed
1994	40th anniversary of first Test win over England
1996	February - Co-host of sixth World Cup November - Benazir Bhutto sacked as Prime Minister
1997	February - Nawaz Sharif elected as Prime Minister

Domestic cricket

The first-class cricket structure in Pakistan was based on the skeleton left behind at Partition, with three main associations namely Punjab (formerly Northern India), Sind and North-West Frontier Province. A fourth, Bahawalpur, produced what was in effect a private team selected by the Amir of Bahawalpur, whose influence soon declined. East Pakistan played some cricket but was insignificant in terms of the standard or the players it provided to the representative side; the inaugural first-class match there was in fact a Test match and Pakistan's first on home territory.

Much of the early first-class cricket was played against touring sides, giving it instant appeal and kudos. The first national representative side played against the Westindies as early as November (26-29) 1948, drawing the game at Lahore. A tour to Ceylon (Sri Lanka) was undertaken in March 1949, where both unofficial Tests were won by Pakistan, but cricket was soon tottering in the wake of economic, social and political problems. It needed the Marylebone Cricket Club's tour of 1951/2 to sustain it.

Despite the victory over that MCC team in December 1951, and election to the Imperial Cricket Conference in July 1952, most of the players who went on Pakistan's first Test tour in the winter of 1952/3 had played only a handful of what could be considered first-class matches.

Although the Karachi Quadrangular Tournament had been revived, Pakistan did not have a domestic cricket competition until after the country had started playing Test cricket. The Quaid-e-Azam Trophy was first played in 1953/4 and was named after Mohammad Ali Jinnah, the founder of Pakistan, who was known as "The Great Leader" (the translation of Quaid-e-Azam). It was organised on the same lines as India's Ranji Trophy, which had zonal knock-out or league champions competing in a final, though several changes have been made to its structure over the years.

The country lacked cricket stadia that could accommodate spectators, and had only six cricket centres, namely Karachi, Lahore, Peshawar, Sialkot, Punjab and Bahawalpur. Of these only three could offer grass wickets. Finances were limited and cricket purely as an amateur sport was going to be difficult to sustain, as it depended on the goodwill of employers to grant leave. A H Kardar himself almost missed the tour to England in 1954 because he could not be certain of getting leave from the Pakistan Air Force.

Kardar led with great authority - both on and off the field - and he instilled a steely determination in the side in its early years. He was very much a figurehead in Pakistani cricket but when he retired, a bungling bureaucracy stepped in and domestic cricket suffered as a consequence. That Pakistan has risen to the top of world cricket is all the more remarkable for this. Imran Khan has always been scathing of the system and wrote a damning invective against domestic cricket in Pakistan in his book *All Round View*,

"The history of Pakistan cricket is one of nepotism, inefficiency, corruption and constant bickering. It is also the story of players who rise above the mire. A cricketer needs immense talent, belief in himself and sheer luck to survive the political maze of our cricket. There have been brief periods when the BCCP [Board of Control for Cricket in Pakistan] have tried to promote cricket, but by and large its function has been to assert mindless authority and blunder through...Our present first-class structure is a fair indication of the BCCP's inability to understand the game." No wonder Imran played no cricket in Pakistan, other than for the national side, after 1981. It is debatable whether his course of action, or inaction, can have benefited Pakistan's cricket, as surely just by playing he would have improved its standard.

However he explained his decision thus: "The nature of domestic cricket is non-competitive. The standard is low, and I didn't play on principle, which I told the Board. I played until 1981 but in the end I discovered it was just a strain on me. I didn't want to play on awful wickets and there was no pressure and no crowd. There was no interest in that cricket. Why should I want to play in that? I tried to explain this to the Board - if you had proper regional cricket I wouldn't mind playing it. Why should I play for an organisation like a bank, who hired me first. Imagine playing for Barclay's against Lloyd's or NatWest. I would only have been playing for the money but I had no interest in the money so I stopped."

By comparison, perhaps only Australia is satisfied with the nature of its domestic cricket and Pakistan should restructure on similar lines. They play four-day matches on good wickets and remain competitive as the fixture list is limited. Many of the criticisms of Pakistan's cricket have been levelled at English first-class cricket too and this is often offered as an excuse for poor results. It is not the right model for Pakistan's game. The standards in the Westindies have also declined; for instance, even top club cricket in Barbados used to be virtually of first-class quality. Westindies have been criticised as much as most for political and parochial selections in their Test team, while the regional influence in Indian cricket has become too strong.

Imran was getting intrinsically involved in the restructuring of domestic cricket in Pakistan as an advisor to the Board, but since he resigned from the ICC in May 1994 because of his ball-tampering "revelations" he has let it be known that his involvement in cricket is likely to diminish. He may still look out for young talent and do his level best to get promising players to be taken on by English counties. The great players of the seventies were largely groomed in England but opportunities are scarce now and may be withdrawn altogether. Wasim Akram and Waqar Younis are established, Aqib Javed has had one season but is not a front runner at the moment for another chance. The young pace bowler Mohammad Akram has an excellent opportunity with Northamptonshire, where he takes over from the legendary Curtly Ambrose in 1997. Mustaq Ahmed has been highly successful since his arrival at Somerset in 1993, and secured a new contract with them during the 1996 tour. The batting opportunities, however, are likely to be scant. Salim Malik was the last and he was released by Essex after his second season with the county in 1993.

Imran believes Pakistan did not produce one world-class batsmen in the eighties. His personal disagreements with Salim Malik are probably why he does not rate him in this category, but the essence of what he was saying was true. However, the situation recently is much improved with the likes of Saeed Anwar and Inzamam-ul-Haq both proving shining examples of the batting talent that is now being produced.

The BCCP (now the Pakistan Cricket Board) is a governmental body and thus appointments to it are usually politically motivated. The old Board was dissolved by the state president and patron of the Board, Farooq Ahmed Khan Leghari, during the 1993/4 season, replaced temporarily by an ad hoc committee, and then by the PCB.

A number of former players have served the board as chairmen or selectors, but all too often the administration has been done by people with a less than full knowledge of cricket. There is one story of General Safdar Butt, the former Board president, who while watching Pakistan playing the Westindies, suggested that Abdul Qadir would be more successful if he took a long run-up like the Westindian bowlers did! Others have assumed megalomaniac tendencies when in office, paying little regard to the players' considerations. Many of the jobs are sinecures and there is little accountability just a shuffling around when the team loses. Instead each association needs a democratically elected committee.

Abdul Hafeez Kardar saw the need to restructure cricket in Pakistan. His theory was sound - to bring in commercial organisations (such as Pakistan International Airlines, Habib Bank, National Bank, United Bank and the Pakistan Automobile Corporation) to sponsor cricket, running teams in a prestigious competition and at the same time providing employment for the players. The companies have done a great service in many respects and players appreciate the career opportunities afforded them after they retire from playing. However the system has at times become so open to abuse that it proved a hindrance, as commercial considerations got in the way of the cricket.

The companies were supposed to own and maintain their own grounds, but shirked this responsibility and instead the same municipal grounds were hired time and again by different sides resulting in their over-use and deterioration. Imran Khan objected strongly to this. "You could get eight matches played non-stop on one wicket which would be under-prepared. The spinners would open the bowling with me and I thought 'What am I doing running all that distance?'"

This lack of a "home" venue only compounded the absence of any parochial attachment to the companies for the players or the spectators, who are not numerous anyway. Consequently there has been no real pressure or competitive edge in these matches and so players getting into the Test side have been susceptible under stress.

At least from the 1996/7 season a new rule has come in, which stipulates that all departmental teams must own and maintain at least two grounds.

Many cricketers can end up playing for many different teams, while some companies have signed up players just to prevent them turning out for someone else. "There were players being paid by these organisations who still didn't play," Imran said. This happened at the start of the 1990/1 season when United Bank contested ADBP's signing of Saeed Anwar without obtaining a "No Objection" certificate. The BCCP ruled against Habib Bank as they had not included Anwar on their list of the 25 players each side is allowed, despite his being in the Test squad. Before the 1992 World Cup there was the ridiculous situation of Mustaq Ahmed, who was about to play a crucial part in Pakistan's win in that tournament, not being played by his first-class side. Now, with relegation and promotion, you can get the situation where Test players appear mainly in Grade II cricket.

It is no coincidence that most of the players featured in this book have relations who have played first-class cricket. Such favouritism has usually been eradicated at a more senior level though Javed Miandad's younger brother, Anwar, once found himself 12th man for a one-day international though he was not even in the original squad. However this is a mere peccadillo compared with the friends and relations of various bank managers and the like who have a first-class game to their name. Not surprisingly a number of scores and records are regarded as meretricious. The situation became ridiculous when a recent Lahore captain was told that five players had to play but he could pick the remaining six. Lahore, thus, were relegated to the second division despite being the major cricketing centre. Captains nurse certain players; Imran Khan benefited from this when playing under the captaincy of his cousin Javed Burki. Some players have been more concerned with securing patronage than runs or wickets. Consequently there is often an unhealthy rivalry within sides, leading to internal bickering, self-interest and back-stabbing.

The big companies invariably operate from the two main centres, Lahore and Karachi, and cricket in between had almost died though the location of Test venues was spreading. Regional cricket lost much of its status and any aspiring young players from the regions know they must move to stand a chance of playing for the top teams. Performances have been difficult to judge and compare because, for instance, a batsman may have played all his cricket on the blandest of wickets, as in Karachi, and score stacks of runs while other pitches, as in Lahore, are left a bit greener, as Imran explained:

"The records of players were meaningless and not an accurate indication of ability. You can't even gauge a player's performances. In England you can because they have home and away matches, so if half your matches are on easy-paced pitches at least the others won't be. But in Pakistan a player can play the whole of his first-class matches on one wicket and that can be a batting paradise, while someone else could be playing on a completely under prepared wicket - you cannot compare the performances at all."

The machinations of this are best illustrated by some of the players who have been given little or no chance at international level despite consistently good performances in domestic cricket. For instance, Shafiq Ahmed has been quite comfortably the most prolific batsman in first-class cricket, nine times making over a thousand runs in a season for National Bank and United Bank and finishing with nearly 20,000 runs in his career at an average of over 50. Yet he played in only six Test matches for Pakistan and three of those came in 1977/8 when several batsmen were absent because they had signed up for Kerry Packer's World Series Cricket. Few players have scored a thousand runs in a season more than twice in domestic cricket but for those that have it has not been reflected in selection. Neither Arshad Pervez, who made a thousand runs four times for Habib Bank, nor Mansoor Rana, who did the same for Agricultural Development Bank of Pakistan, have played Test cricket and have just two one-day international caps each to show for their efforts. Shajit Ali (United Bank/National Bank) is another with three "thousands" who has played ten one-dayers but has no Test caps to his name and only Rizwan-uz-Ziman amongst this prolific bunch (four "thousands" for PIA/Karachi) has been given any sort of chance, winning 11 Test caps albeit thinly scattered.

The same situation occurs amongst the most successful bowlers. Sajjad Akbar took 104 wickets in 1989/90 for Pakistan National Shipping Corporation/Sargodha and 96 for Lahore in 1985/6; his reward, just two one-day internationals. Shahid Mahboob has taken over 70 wickets in a season three times yet has played in only one Test. He shares, with Imran, the record partnership for the sixth wicket in the World Cup, adding 144 against Sri Lanka in 1983. Ijaz Faqih, an accomplished all-rounder, set a record of 107 wickets with his off-spinners in 1985/6 for Karachi and in the following season made a hundred in only his third Test, some five years after his second cap. Against a strong Indian attack, he reached both his fifty and his century with sixes and shared a record 7th wicket partnership with Imran Khan. He played just twice more.

The domestic structure has been continually tinkered with; over the years the Quaid-e-Azam has been decided by league, or by zonal leagues and knock-out, and between different groups of teams. Now a second division exists, which is not first-class but does afford the opportunity for the champions to be promoted. The BCCP Trophy for a while just became a qualifying tournament and lost its first-class status (1979/80-1982/3).

There still remain elements of high farce; recent events in the Quaid-e-Azam and Patron's trophies demonstrate a range of endemic weaknesses in domestic cricket. For instance the 1991/2 competitions were played very much in the shadow of the World Cup and so only a handful of (former) Test players were available. An extra team was involved in the Quaid-e-Azam because an unresolved relegation dispute from the year before meant the BCCP could not demote the bottom club. Thus with nine teams in the competition two were relegated and one promoted at the end of 1991/2, to bring the number back to eight. Those demoted included Peshawar, who had their victory against Faisalabad overturned, and Karachi Blues, who finished bottom and so left the other premier cricket city with only one first-class team for the 1992/3 season.

For the Patron's Trophy, an eight team league determines the four semi-finalists, with the top of the league playing the fourth side and the second and third teams playing each other. However the semi-finals were strangely scrapped because the Domestic Tournament Monitoring Committee decided that they should not be played during Ramadan, yet there were still two weeks to go to play out the matches. After losing in the Grade II final, Pakistan Customs accused the winners, the House Building Finance Corporation, of unfair tactics, time-wasting and having the support of both the umpires. The year before HBFC had been relegated after conceding walkovers to PNSC and Combined Universities after they had been refused a change of venue for those games. Initially the BCCP scratched them from the competition though their later reinstatement did them no good.

The amount of first-class cricket in any given season can vary enormously according to the international schedule, as can its quality. Co-hosting the World Cup in the winter of 1987/8 reduced the number of games to 54 from 126 the previous season. At least the staging of the World Cup in 1995/6 was less intrusive as it was staged later in the season.

Also the demands on the international players are so great that they may not be able to play any first-class cricket at all in Pakistan which can only diminish the overall standard of the competition. However domestic cricket received a boost in 1990/1 when, for a number of unforeseen reasons, various international commitments were cancelled. The under-23 tour to Sri Lanka was called off because of civil unrest there. Then Pakistan pulled out of the Asia Cup and the proposed tour to India that was to follow it, because of the political tension with her neighbour, while with anti-west feeling running high during the Gulf War, the England A tour was abandoned after just three matches.

It meant all eyes were on the most significant change in domestic cricket for many years; the Quaid-e-Azam Trophy was to be played on a regional basis again with one side each from Faisalabad, Bahawalpur, Sargodha, Peshawar, Rawalpindi, Multan and two sides from Karachi (the Blues and the Whites). Meanwhile the commercial organisations competed for the Patron's Trophy, with the top five sides also playing in the Pentangular Trophy, which had been suspended for five years.

The vast region between Karachi and Lahore had only produced seven Test cricketers in Pakistan's first 35 years (up to 1987). Now there are a few more players coming from outside those two main centres, with the likes of Waqar Younis, Inzamam-ul-Haq and Mustaq Ahmed all playing for Multan (and United Bank) and Aamir Sohail for Sargodha. However Imran Khan believes this a superficial improvement: "Still players from outside have to move to Lahore and Karachi to play cricket, even established players like Waqar, Mustaq and Aqib. If you come from outside the two main centres you can't compete."

With Pepsi-Cola's sponsorship of youth cricket the net has again been cast earlier too, drawing on the enthusiastic and generally well-organised schools' cricket. The under-19 side has always been a good feeder to the Test team and since its introduction in 1970/1, has increased in importance as an essential nursery for first-class cricket and indeed Tests. The team that competed in the youth World Cup Final of 1987/8 included four current Test players, while none of their opponents have yet to play for Australia. The under-19 championship in Pakistan now supports two grades consisting of ten teams each. The 1992/3 competition included all three Karachi teams, who should soon replenish the senior sides.

That such good players are still being produced is encouraging and the interest in the game remains extremely high as was clearly evident by the euphoria following the 1992 World Cup triumph, while television is now widely available, helping to spread the game. Indeed too popular and too widely according to some; during the series between Pakistan and India (1982/3) a protest group formed to try and ban cricket from the TV as they felt it was responsible for the sudden, sharp decline in mosque attendance. The group petitioned the President, and asserted that the purpose of the media was to implement and propagate Islam and not give mileage to "a game more British than Asian."

Cricket is played and followed with a religious fervour, affecting the mood of the nation. If a structure could be devised to best utilise this enthusiasm and the lurking talent of natural ball players, Pakistan will have a high-class Test team for many years to come, indeed may begin to enjoy the same sort of domination which the Westindies produced in the 1980s, when they too were quick to pick and nurture raw talent.

Although there is a move towards more consistency in selection, there is a great waste of ability. Because Pakistan tend to introduce players at such a young age, they may appear on the scrap heap by the time they are in their early twenties. There's always the question being asked, "What ever happened to so-and-so?" A player such as Aftab Baloch had started and finished his Test career by the time he was 21. He made his debut at the age of 16 years and 221 days, against New Zealand at Dacca in 1969/70 and had to wait five years for his next Test, against the Westindies at Lahore (1974/5). In between he made the seventh highest first-class score (428) for Sind v Baluchistan in 1973/4, and despite averaging 48.50 in his two matches, those remained his only caps.

Others include three Khalids; Khalid Hassan made his debut in the 2nd Test against England at Trent Bridge in 1954, thirteen days before his 17th birthday but never played again. Khalid Wazir, the son of Wazir Ali who played Test cricket for India, made his debut in the previous Test to Hassan at Lord's at the age of 18 years and 44 days and returned for the third Test at Old Trafford but he, too, never played again. Khalid Ibadulla was only 17 when he first toured with Pakistan, playing one match on the tour to India in 1952/3. However it was not until 1964/5 that he made his Test debut, marking the occasion with 166 against Australia at Karachi, the fifth highest score on debut, but only played in three more Tests.

Good players can be lost through selectorial aberrations, or cricket politics. This becomes evident when one looks at how many players have played in only one Test match. Between 1952/3 and 1993/4, there were 24 which represents 18.3 per cent of the 131 Pakistani Test cricketers to that point. Another nine had played only twice, five more just three times, eight others had four caps, and seven had played five Tests. Thus 55 players had played in five Tests or fewer, and over fifty percent in eight or under.

England was thought to be bad on this point, yet had 14 per cent of "one cap wonders" at that time. Since then, a club has even been formed to commemorate them! Their selectorial problems stem from having the widest pool of players many of whom are much of a muchness. First-class cricket in England has also become largely non-competitive, the wickets are bland and the crowds are sparse, and the national team has declined as a consequence. At least in Pakistan young players are not made to go through the system, working their way up through a county hierarchy.

It would be a travesty if Pakistan, who have seemed on the verge of becoming a great side at times during the nineties, did not realise their potential because of poor administration. However, even Imran Khan saw some hope before he bowed out of cricket altogether: "We haven't had a cricket set-up, though I've been fighting for this now since 1980. For 14 years I've been saying it but nothing happened, but we are hoping that something will happen now. It looks now that the ad hoc committee are making the right proposals."

Pakistani cricket has recently received massive sponsorship from Coca-Cola, which will certainly help in improving the game there. It is up to the recently formed Pakistan Cricket Board, which took over from the ad hoc committee, to implement change and put those proposals into action. They need some continuity. Arif Ali Abbasi, the Chief Executive of the Board, was replaced shortly after the 1996 World Cup by Majid Khan. He was ready to disassociate himself from the game after Abbasi had him removed as manager after the series with Sri Lanka, 1995/6, but he has been tempted back into the fold. A former player of his standing and temperament is an ideal man to run the game and he may well be the man to lead Pakistan's cricket forward. He has already implemented changes and seems determined to tackle any problems head on.

One-day wonders

For many victory in the 1992 World Cup was the pinnacle of Pakistan's cricketing achievement, in the country's 40th year of international cricket. In the later stages of the competition the country had come to a virtual standstill as everyone seemed to be watching or listening to the broadcasts from Australia.

Yet it was a wonder that Pakistan had never reached the World Cup Final before 1992, which represented a marked underachievement. Indeed, Pakistan's first major one-day trophy did not come until 1986 when the side beat India in an epic final of the Austral-Asia Cup in Sharjah, though it took a six, struck by Javed Miandad, off the last ball of the final over to win the tournament. That was the first sign that the team's potential was coming to fruition. Pakistan's one-day form has been sketchy,

Imran with the Nehru cup

particularly in the World Series Cup competitions in Australia in 1983/4, 1989/90 and 1992/3, but elsewhere in recent years the side has produced a fine string of results, dominating the Sharjah tournament with six wins in a row there until losing in the final in 1993/4 to the Westindies, reaching the semi-final of the 1987 World Cup, winning the Nehru Cup in 1989, and capping them all by taking the 1992 World Cup. Yet England beat Pakistan convincingly in the one-day series in England after the World Cup and perhaps Graham Gooch's comments best summarise Pakistan in one-day cricket: "If they click as they did [in the final], they can be a very classy side." At other times, though, they have seemed to be playing well below their potential.

The squads sent to the first three World Cups in England looked to be well-suited to make a serious challenge. The side was packed with glorious strokemakers, many of whom could also bowl effectively, yet the teams of the seventies tended to be full of mercurial, individual talent without the strength of unity.

The squad for the 1975 World Cup was highly regarded and all but Pervez Mir had been on the tour to England the previous year. In 1979 the whole team had played in England the year before, either for Pakistan or in county cricket, while in 1983 only Ijaz Faqih, Rashid Khan and Shahid Mahboob were new to English conditions.

In 1975 Pakistan were in much the tougher of

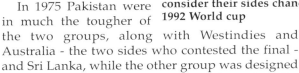

Graham Gooch and Imran Khan consider their sides chances in the 1992 World cup

the two groups, along with Westindies and Australia - the two sides who contested the final - and Sri Lanka, while the other group was designed to ensure the hosts an easy passage through to the semi-finals, and included England, New Zealand, India and East Africa.

Pakistan lost to Australia in the opening game by 73 runs, but later were to amass 330 against Sri Lanka in an emphatic win by 192 runs. The crucial game was their second match, which was against the Westindies. With every team playing only three matches each, no side could afford more than one defeat. Pakistan made a challenging score of 266 for 7 from their 60 overs with Majid Khan, Mustaq Mohammad and Wasim Raja each making fine fifties. Westindies then collapsed against Sarfraz Nawaz who took the first three wickets, and were only kept in the game by a half-century from Clive Lloyd. The lower-order had managed to take the score from 99 for 5 to 203 when the ninth wicket fell with Westindies still needing 66 to win. Majid Khan, who was deputising for Asif Iqbal, had a difficult task taking over the captaincy for such a crucial match. He had gambled by using up the overs of his front-line bowlers in trying to push home the advantage, but this backfired as the last-wicket pair of Deryck Murray and Andy Roberts saw their side home with three balls to spare. The official captain, Asif Iqbal, was ill in hospital and sorely missed; he had made a sparkling fifty against Australia and his bowling was important to the balance of the side.

The defeat was no disgrace in a classic encounter but going out at that stage, after just one win, was a disappointment for a team with such tremendous all-round ability; Asif Iqbal, Mustaq Mohammad, Wasim Raja, Imran Khan and Sarfraz Nawaz all finished their Test careers with at least 1000 runs and fifty Test wickets, while Majid Khan and Javed Miandad also bowled reasonably well early in their careers.

In 1979 the format of the competition again allowed no margin for error; comfortable wins over Canada and Australia meant that the game against England would decide who would qualify top, and so play the runners-up in the other group in the semi-final thus avoiding the favourites the Westindies. On a typical seaming pitch at Headingley and under grey skies, the bowlers dominated. England made only 165 but in reply Pakistan collapsed to 34 for 6 against Mike Hendrick and Ian Botham. However with Asif Iqbal, Wasim Raja and Imran Khan at seven, eight and nine in the batting order, all was not lost and they inched the side ever closer. Eventually, though, Pakistan lost by 14 runs as Geoff Boycott surprised everyone by picking up the last two wickets, leaving Imran stranded with 21 not out and four overs unused.

In the semi-final Westindies' 293 was too stiff a target to chase, though Majid Khan (81) and Zaheer Abbas (93) made a marvellous attempt in a thrilling partnership of 166, but unfortunately once they were separated the chase lost momentum as no one else got to twenty.

In 1983 every side played each other twice in their qualifying group, which ensured the best four teams in the semis. Pakistan squeezed through on run rate just ahead of New Zealand by virtue of the 338 they had made against Sri Lanka and by making enough runs in their final game against New Zealand, thanks to some brilliant batting by Zaheer Abbas and Imran Khan who shared a partnership of 147 in 75 minutes.

Once again it was the Westindies that put Pakistan out; a total of 184 from 60 overs was not enough to put their opponents under pressure. Yet, to make matters worse, India defended a similar total in the final against the Westindies to take the Prudential World Cup.

If Pakistan were going to win the Cup, it seemed that 1987 would be the time and the place as Pakistan played all its games at home in a tournament co-hosted with India. Pakistan were enjoying their best period in Test cricket having just beaten India and England in away series for the first time, and had won that dramatic victory in Sharjah the year before. The team was full of confidence with a well balanced side playing in front of partisan crowds. Again they had genuine all-rounders with Imran Khan, Wasim Akram, Abdul Qadir and Salim Yousuf in the side, each of whom was to do the "double" of a thousand runs and a hundred dismissals in Tests, while Imran, Akram and Mudassar Nazar are amongst a very select few to have done the double in one-day internationals.

Pakistan finished top of their qualifying group, losing only one out of six games, which included a thrilling victory over Westindies when Abdul Qadir managed to score 13 off five balls in the last over from Courtney Walsh. However in the semi-final the 267 Australia made was just beyond them. The Australians managed to score 18 off their last over, the eventual winning margin. Javed Miandad had had to keep-wicket after Salim Yousuf had been injured early in the match and later on, when he batted, he began to tire just as he was trying to force the pace. Defeat left the whole country distraught.

Pakistan went into the Nehru Cup (1989/90) in India full of confidence, having just won the Champions Cup in Sharjah, against India and Westindies, in convincing style. The Nehru Cup included all the Test nations apart from New Zealand, and Pakistan played some superb cricket, especially in the semi-final and final. They chased 195 in 30 overs against England, winning with nine balls to spare, to get to the final where they beat Westindies by getting the 274 required with just one ball to spare in the fiftieth over, when Wasim Akram smote the first ball he received, bowled by Viv Richards, over mid-wicket for six.

Pakistan's fine one-day form prior to the fifth World Cup saw them just behind the favourites, Australia, in the betting. Yet before the competition had even started the side was having troubles. Waqar Younis, who had taken 61 wickets in just nine Tests in the previous 15 months, had been ruled out with a stress fracture of his back before the competition started. Abdul Qadir, too, was injured and his replacement Mustaq Ahmed was out of form as his first-class team in Pakistan did not always include him. Pakistan's form slumped in the warm-up matches but the worst moment came two days before the first World Cup match when Imran Khan felt a twinge in his shoulder while he was warming up. He kept practising, not accepting that something was seriously wrong, but as soon as he stopped and the muscle cooled down, he could hardly move it.

Yet Imran Khan had been so fit at that stage, having trained rigorously for three months. It distracted his whole approach and made him somewhat aloof at practice, as he contemplated how fate seemed to be ruining what he considered to be his and the team's destiny to win the World Cup.

One-day cricket is very much a "method" game and he had also planned his tactics meticulously, considering the strengths and weaknesses of the team, to come up with what he thought would be a winning formula. He said during the competition, "One-day cricket revolves around combinations. You usually don't have to have a team full of good players to win. Look at India in 1983 - they got it right with their combinations."

Imran decided to sit out the opening game hoping that the injury would settle and allow him to play later. Javed Miandad had not captained the side for a while and had not fully tested his way of doing things. Pakistan were over-cautious, batting too slowly to start with. Ramiz Raja made a not out hundred but it was not until Miandad came in that he began to cut loose. The pair put on 123, taking 81 from the last ten overs, but after their allotted fifty overs they remained only two wickets down and the acceleration should have started much earlier after a solid start. Westindies cruised home without losing a wicket, passing Pakistan's 220 with 19 balls to spare.

Imran thought he had better play in the next game, against Zimbabwe, to try and ensure Pakistan's first win. They won comfortably by 53 runs as Aamir Sohail this time scored a hundred and Miandad, who was warming to the competition, made 89 from 94 balls. Imran mused, "It was the perfect match for me - no batting, no bowling and no catches."

Again he sat out the next, against England at Adelaide, where Pakistan seemed to be in a bit of a shambles, bowled out for 74 on a green wicket under overcast skies; the batsmen tried to hit their way out of trouble against a side used to playing in such conditions, who took some excellent catches to support their bowlers. The rain though intervened and the match was abandoned eventually but not before the ridiculous new rule regarding stoppages for rain proved how ill-conceived it had been. The rule stated that if there was a stoppage then the number of overs left to the side batting second, in this instance sixteen, was taken and a new target total calculated on the basis of the best 16 overs from the first innings. So here Pakistan's best 16 overs produced most of their runs, 63, and England were suddenly left with a tricky task. Rain interrupted again to wash out the game with England 24 for 1 from eight overs and in danger of losing. Imran, watching from the sidelines, admitted, "It was a very lucky break for us." This farcical rule was to rear its ugly head again to Pakistan's disadvantage next time.

Worse was to follow; Pakistan lost to arch-rivals India by 43 runs. Imran Khan was run out for nought as he reached a personal nadir, while Javed Miandad, who spent 34 overs accumulating 40 runs, only got going after a verbal exchange with the Indian 'keeper Kiran More, who had appealed for an improbable leg-side catch. Miandad leapt up in down in mock imitation of More. Tensions were beginning to fray and the captain could see the heads going down, the enthusiasm wane at

Javed Miandad mimics the frustration of India's 'keeper Kiran More

practices, and the belief and confidence of the side drain away.

The team were at a low ebb and it got worse against South Africa , a game in which the fielding fell apart in stark contrast to that of the South Africans, whose sharpness in the field was epitomised by Jonty Rhodes' acrobatic run out of Inzamam-ul-Haq. It appeared that "the wheels had come off" for Pakistan, as they gave away perhaps twenty runs in the field. Wasim Akram could not control the swing he was getting from the white ball and bowled a handful of wides. To add injury to insult, Moin Khan lobbed the ball back to the bowler, Aqib Javed, who was not watching and was struck on the forehead and had to leave the field, because of a rudimentary error. He joined a casualty list which already had Javed Miandad, Ramiz Raja and Wasim Haider on it.

To make matters worse as they chased 212 to win in 50 overs a light shower stiffened Pakistan's target to 194 in just 36 overs. Imran decided to stay on the field at first when the rain started to fall hoping to be able to play through and not incur the ramifications of a stoppage on the required rate, but this adversely affected the wicket, making the bounce uneven and stopping the ball coming on.

The team were under so much pressure by now, with great expectations back home and everything apparently going wrong. Pakistan were above only Zimbabwe and had to win all their remaining games to have a chance of qualifying for the semi-finals. To take the pressure off his young team Imran just tried to get them to relax, saying the worst that could happen is that they lose but reminded them that in the recent past they have always pulled through in adversity and reacted well under pressure. The crunch match was that against Australia who had also started the competition badly. As hosts they had really felt the pressure just as Pakistan had done in 1987 and the Australian captain Allan Border made a point of this before the very first match, putting his excuses in place, and so taking away the confidence of the team with his negative thoughts.

In the dressing room at the WACA, Perth, before that game, Imran Khan made his now famous speech. He told the team, "Just fight like a cornered tiger, you've got nowhere to go, just go all out. Forget all these worries about no-balls and wide balls and just go out and fight." It had the same sort of rousing theme for the team as Shakespeare's Henry V before Agincourt.

One could sense fate changing as the luck turned Pakistan's way. Aamir Sohail was caught behind off a Bruce Reid no-ball before he had scored and went on to top-score with 76. Sohail and Ramiz Raja got the side off to a good start and Miandad

again played an important hand. The lower-order faltered but Australia got off to a poor and slow start, with Aqib Javed taking two quick wickets, as the home side chased 221 to win. The only threat came when Dean Jones and Mark Waugh were together, but Mustaq Ahmed accounted for both of them and Allan Border in a telling mid-innings spell. He was just starting to bowl beautifully and should have had Mike Whitney caught behind too but he was given not out. This led to a heated exchange of words between Whitney, the 'keeper Moin Khan and Aamir Sohail. Each was fined $250. It did not affect the result as the Australian tail was not good enough to score quickly off Wasim Akram and Pakistan, who won by 48 runs, had survived.

A four-wicket win against Sri Lanka, after an at times nervous but generally controlled chase, saw the winning runs come in the final over. It was set up by Miandad and Salim Malik, who each made fifties and shared a century partnership, and meant that Pakistan could still qualify if they beat the previously undefeated New Zealand in Christchurch, and provided Australia beat the Westindies in Melbourne. It ensured an intolerably long and tense day, in which the team would have to endure the anxieties of two matches in a row. Pakistan did their part in style, containing New Zealand to just 166, despite Mark Greatbatch's impressive assault on Aqib Javed's first over which contained two fours and a six, thanks largely to Mustaq Ahmed who bowled his ten overs for 18, and took two wickets.

With Pakistan struggling at 9 for 2, Ramiz Raja rescued the side with his second not out hundred of the World Cup to record a comfortable seven wicket win with 32 balls to spare. The side then had to sit and watch the outcome of the game broadcast live from Melbourne, but Imran Khan was happy as soon as Australia won the toss and batted. The home team had at last found the right combination of bowlers and Westindies were always going to be under great strain knowing, 45 minutes into their game, that Pakistan had already won. He was right as the Westindies' batting crumbled as they slipped to a 57-run defeat. So Pakistan qualified and would play New Zealand again in the semi-final four days later, this time in Auckland.

The way Pakistan had had to hang on got them used to the cauldron. New Zealand had cruised through to the semi-finals, just as Pakistan had done in the 1987 World Cup, and had not been exposed to the sudden tension and weight of expectation that had built up amongst the home media and crowds.

Again Greatbatch got New Zealand off to a flying start but Aqib Javed had learned his lesson and after being hit for a huge straight six, he deceived the big left-hander with a superb slower ball, an off-break which pitched outside leg stump and spun to hit middle - one of the best deliveries of the competition.

However, Martin Crowe played what Imran thought was the best innings of the tournament, a controlled assault on the bowling. Unfortunately he damaged a hamstring and could not lead the side in the field, a crucial blow as he had been the inspiration throughout to a side lacking world class players, and whose shrewd bowling changes had got the most out of a limited attack.

Still the 262 they made was a more than challenging target. Imran Khan was out of touch and got bogged down, in what he concedes was one of his worst innings. Eventually he was caught at deep-square for 44 as he tried to hit out and when Salim Malik followed shortly after, Pakistan were left needing 123 from 15 overs. Inzamam-ul-Haq, who was a doubtful starter for the game because of food poisoning but played on his captain's insistence, came in to join Javed Miandad. The 21 year-old from Multan blazed away, hitting the ball to all parts in making 60 off just 37 balls with some magnificent clean hitting. Akram and Moin Khan continued the assault while at the other end Miandad was inspired, nudging and deflecting and coaxing the most from his partners.

In the other semi-final England beat South Africa though the ending was highly unsatisfactory with the rain-rule again turning the game into a farce. England were booed as they left the field though it was not their fault. It was a Pyrrhic victory; the side did not have the boost to their confidence that a tight semi-final victory should have brought and one could sense a certain embarrassment when the team arrived at the Melbourne Cricket Ground for the final.

Imran could tell Graham Gooch, his opposite number, was tense. Gooch and Ian Botham had walked out of a dinner the night before because they took exception to a comedian's parody of the Queen.

However for Imran and his young tigers it was an occasion they were determined to enjoy. He was more confident before this game than for any other in the tournament and told his side that this was his first final in five attempts and that they might not play in another saying, "just enjoy yourself, enjoy the atmosphere and forget about everything else."

Imran was already revelling in the atmosphere himself when he went out for the toss in front of 87,000 people. Relaxed and wearing a T-shirt with a cornered tiger motif on the front as he went out to the middle before the start, he was asked by Ian Chappell about his team and the new sobriquet. "We really have been through the fire, we looked like being knocked out and suddenly to have

comeback has given me the greatest pleasure and satisfaction," Imran reflected.

Chappell continued, "You want them to play like cornered tigers?" The proud Khan answered, smiling quizzically, "That's the motto recently and they've done a great job, especially the young boys, you know. They haven't been overawed by anything and as long as they play like tigers, I don't mind if we win or lose today."

The strategy was set. Pakistan must get off to a solid start, after winning the toss, knowing that the England attack lacked the variety or penetration to contain Pakistan's strokemakers later on. However Aamir Sohail and Ramiz Raja fell in a tight opening spell from Derek Pringle; Imran again decided to bat at three despite batting less than fluently in the semi-final. He and Miandad made slow but steady progress. A crucial moment came in the 21st over when Khan took a chance trying to hit Phil DeFreitas to leg and skied the ball towards mid-wicket; Neil Fairbrother slipped as he set off and so Gooch had to run across from square-leg, but the ball just eluded his grasp as he dived for the catch. Pakistan would have been in a lot of trouble if that chance had been taken as there was not enough time for the next batsman to be so watchful yet too long to go to be able to throw caution to the wind.

It was the turning point. Imran had become becalmed again and Pakistan were only on 56 at the time, but he is a great believer in fate and this was part of his conviction that Pakistan were destined for the Cup. Khan and Miandad, the senior pros in World cricket who, uniquely, had each played in all the previous World Cups - each were appearing in their 28th match - used their collective experience to get the scoreboard moving. At times, they batted as though they expected rain later on, and that all these low-scoring overs would be removed from the equation. Yet soon one realised that they were completely in control, assured of their own ability, confident of the side's game plan. Between them they had played in more than 400 one-dayers and scored 11,000 runs - they knew what they were doing. Although the score stood at only 70 at the half-way mark, their acceleration was perfectly paced, and their partnership realised 139 in 31 overs. Both were tiring and got out at the right time, Imran for 72 and Javed for 58, allowing Inzamam-ul-Haq and Wasim Akram a free rein to attack the bowling in the last few overs. Without the pressure of thinking about their wickets, they added 52 in six overs. Inzamam was again impossible to contain, making 42 off 35 balls, mixing fierce strokes with finesse, while Akram's 33 came from just 18 balls.

England did not get the start they wanted, with Botham and Alec Stewart falling to the new ball. Mustaq Ahmed was introduced early on and

picked up two quick wickets, trapping Hick with a googly that he did not spot and Gooch, as he tried to sweep, to an excellent diving catch by Aqib Javed at deep square leg.

Neil Fairbrother, England's most successful batsman in the competition, and Allan Lamb, their most experienced, threatened in a stand of 72 which took the score to 141 but two deliveries from Wasim Akram effectively sealed the match. From around the wicket he swung the ball in and then straightened it off the pitch to bowl Lamb and with the very next ball beat Chris Lewis for pace.

England's last four batsmen all got to double figures to keep the game alive but Pakistan's fielding rose to the occasion, Ramiz Raja taking a fine running catch to dismiss Reeve and Salim Malik running out DeFreitas from the deep, and when Richard Illingworth hoisted Imran Khan to deep extra cover in the 50th over, Ramiz's catch secured the marvellous triumph by 22 runs.

In what proved to be his final match for Pakistan, Imran Khan received the Benson and Hedges World Cup, a Waterford Crystal trophy, and cheque for $50,000 from Sir Colin Cowdrey. He has been criticised for the egotistical nature of his acceptance speech; he had not meant to ignore his team but he was just expressing the relief that he felt now that he was sure the hospital project, the first of

its kind in Pakistan to which he had dedicated every spare moment of his non-cricketing life in recent years, would definitely go ahead.

It had been very much a team effort and each wicket was greeted with unrestrained joy and enthusiasm on the field. Back home it seemed that everyone in the whole country had been awake since the early hours of the morning. It was as though there was a curfew during the match until they won when everyone came out onto the streets to celebrate in the middle of the working day.

Some have tried to take the gloss off Pakistan's victory by saying they were lucky to qualify, having lost three of their first four games, and that they would have lost and gone out but for the intervention of the rain against England at the round robin stage. In fact England finished as Pakistan had started losing three out their last four games. This included an embarrassing defeat to Zimbabwe and probably they would have gone out but for the intervention of the rain. in the semi-final against South Africa. Pakistan played well when it mattered, were the only side to beat New Zealand, which they did twice, and finished strongly while England wilted. For Pakistan it was a triumph of talent over professionalism. At last they had fulfilled their potential and won the grandest prize in cricket.

any believed that the squad for the 1995/6 World Cup in Pakistan, India and Sri Lanka was strong enough to defend the title. After all, they had nine of the players that contested the 1992 final in their squad. However, it must be remembered that no side had ever won the trophy on their own soil, and only the Westindies had ever defended their title or won it twice, winning at Lord's in 1975 and 1979. There was enormous pressure on Pakistan to do extremely well in the competition. So much so that manager Intikhab Alam admitted on the tour to Australia that preceded it that the team were using the series as preparation for the World Cup. The signs were not good as they did not even qualify for the World Series final against Australia and Sri Lanka, the two sides which subsequently were to contest the World Cup final.

Perhaps the side never hit upon a winning formula that they could trust for the later rounds. Saeed Anwar and Aamir Sohail gave them the classiest opening pair in the competition, who got the team off to some great starts and finished the tournament with averages of 82 and 45 respectively.

However, Pakistan did not utilise the experience of Javed Miandad and Ramiz Raja, both of whom had averages of over 50 in World Cup competitions. Miandad, in his sixth World Cup, should have batted at No 3 and anchored the innings to allow the other strokemakers to play around him. However the incumbent batsmen from the tour to Australia and New Zealand expressed that they wanted to keep the batting order as it was, thus ensuring that Miandad's return was to an unfamiliar position. He needed to get in early as he had not played international cricket for over two years and was never going to be as effective in the final ten overs when powerful hitting is required.

Pakistan's early form was much better than in 1992, recording comfortable wins over the United Arab Emirates, Holland, England and New Zealand, but losing to South Africa. Unfortunately, the quarter-finals saw Pakistan pitted against India - the pair everyone had wanted to see in the final. Pakistan were dealt a cruel blow when Wasim Akram had to pull out on the morning of the match after straining his side in the previous game against the Kiwis. India got off to a good start through Sachin Tendulkar and Najvot Sidhu, who made 93. However, the crucial impetus to the innings was provided by Ajay Jadeja, who treated Waqar Younis as though he was an ordinary medium-pacer, hammering 45 off only 25 balls. Sohail (55 off 46 balls) and Anwar (48 off 32 balls) were undaunted by India's challenging total of 287 as they set about attacking the new ball, racing to 84

off the first ten overs. Sohail, the acting captain, got carried away. Just after reaching fifty, he smashed Prasad for another boundary and exchanged words with the bowler, but was bowled next ball as he attempted to repeat the stroke.

Pakistan lost their way. They needed a steady partnership and the two most experienced one-day players in the world, Malik and Miandad, attempted to provide it, but could not find the boundaries they needed. At times Miandad's selection looked like one owing more to sentiment than pragmatism, but he tried valiantly to try and conjure something from his prime to win the match.

Pakistan eventually lost by 39 runs, leaving the whole nation distraught, but out with them at the quarter-final stage were all the other semi-finalists from the last competition: South Africa, New Zealand, England.

World Cup Squads 1975-1995/6

1975 (in England): Asif Iqbal (capt), Majid J. Khan, Sadiq Mohammad, Mustaq Mohammad, Zaheer Abbas, Wasim Raja, Imran Khan, Javed Miandad, Sarfraz Nawaz, Wasim Bari, Asif Masood, Naseer Malik, Pervez Mir, and Shafiq Ahmed.

1979 (in England): Asif Iqbal (capt), Majid J. Khan, Sadiq Mohammad, Zaheer Abbas, Javed Miandad, Haroon Rashid, Mudassar Nazar, Imran Khan, Sarfraz Nawaz, Wasim Bari, Sikander Bakht, and Wasim Raja.

1983 (in England): Imran Khan (capt), Mudassar Nazar, Mohsin Khan, Zaheer Abbas, Javed Miandad, Wasim Raja, Ijaz Faqih, Tahir Naqqash, Wasim Bari, Sarfraz Nawaz, Abdul Qadir, Mansoor Akhtar, Shahid Mahboob and Rashid Khan.

1987/8 (in Pakistan and India): Imran Khan (capt), Javed Miandad, Ramiz Raja, Mudassar Nazar, Salim Malik, Ijaz Ahmed, Shoaib Mohammad, Mansoor Akhtar, Wasim Akram, Salim Yousuf, Abdul Qadir, Saleem Jaffer, Tauseef Ahmed and Manzoor Elahi.

1991/2 (in Australia and New Zealand): Imran Khan (capt), Javed Miandad, Ramiz Raja, Aamir Sohail, Inzamam-ul-Haq, Salim Malik, Wasim Akram, Moin Khan, Mustaq Ahmed, Aqib Javed, Wasim Haider, Zahid Fazal, Iqbal Sikandar.

1995/6 (in Pakistan, India and Sri Lanka): Wasim Akram (capt), Aamir Sohail, Saeed Anwar, Ijaz Ahmed, Inzamam-ul-Haq, Salim Malik, Javed Miandad, Ramiz Raja, Rashid Latif, Mustaq Ahmed, Waqar Younis, Ata-ur-Rehman, Aqib Javed, Saqlain Mustaq

Future prospects

There is every chance that when Pakistan celebrates its fiftieth anniversary of Test cricket in October 2002, the side will have just enjoyed their most successful decade. Unfortunately Pakistani teams are never that predictable. The team that is developing in the mid-nineties is highly talented and has a happy mix of youth and experience, with several outstanding players and others potentially reaching their peaks. The team is also playing plenty of international cricket all over the world, achieving good results at home and abroad, albeit with the occasional surprise defeat.

Pakistan's first decade of Test cricket was most impressive for a side in its formative years, though not many Tests were won, but for the next ten years, as the side rebuilt, results were poor and few opponents granted Pakistan full Test series. In the seventies, the team had brilliant players but never quite fulfilled their potential, mainly because Pakistan still did not play enough Test cricket, while during the eighties, the results became more consistent though the side relied very much on players who had established themselves earlier. For most of the current players, their best days in Test cricket could still be to come.

Many of the current squad had virtually no first-class experience when they first came into the Test side. Akram was selected after only a couple of matches, while Younis was chosen at a training camp, to which he was invited by Imran Khan, who had been impressed when watching him play for the first time on television. Aqib Javed and Inzamam-ul-Haq were also selected on the evidence of a net session, while Aamir Nazir, who toured Westindies in 1992/3, had yet to play first-class cricket when he arrived in the Caribbean. While this would suggest that Pakistan is unique in assessing ability quickly, in fact for every discovery there are probably several lost in the mire of domestic cricket. Their chief talent spotter in recent years, Imran, has retired and is unlikely to be involved in cricket very much in the future. Although Pakistan has a history of picking players from obscurity, such as Tauseef Ahmed, whose second first-class game was a Test match, it is too ad hoc a way to pick the national side.

The prospects for the Pakistan team for the rest of the nineties still depend much on the "cornered tigers" who won the 1992 World Cup, in which they showed brilliant glimpses of their talent and collective will to win. In fact, Pakistan are much better-suited to Test cricket as their bowling is so attacking and offers such variety, and this real quality was even more apparent on the subsequent tour to England in 1992, when the likes of Wasim, Waqar and Mustaq Ahmed were a joy to watch. That summer, Robin Marlar wrote in *The Sunday Times;*

"They seem to recognise that, at the moment, no other team can match the sum of their individual skills. They know too that only by winning can this be demonstrated."

However, there is no Test equivalent of the World Cup and Pakistan has not been consistent enough over any length of time to be considered a great side. Since then they hammered Sri Lanka away from home but lost the return series. They suffered an embarrassing innings defeat to Zimbabwe, yet came back to take the series. They beat Australia at home, yet were totally out played for two Tests over there, only to look the better side in the final Test, which was won, and followed by a fine victory over New Zealand.

Imran Khan believes that the current side has the most ability of any since the seventies: "The batting is getting to that level. All of them are very talented batsmen." They showed this in the summer of 1996, when five batsmen averaged over 60 in the series, giving Wasim Akram more scope to attack in the field.

In the seventies the side had under performed, mainly through a lack of Test cricket and then the occasional glut. Now with a more consistent spread - albeit constant - the side has the chance to develop into the best that Pakistan has ever had. For as well as their array of batsmen they have the most versatile fast bowlers in the world in Wasim Akram and Waqar Younis, who between them have the best strike-rate of any new ball duo in Test history, and they have been ably supported by the likes of Aqib Javed and Mustaq Ahmed, as well as plenty of up-and-coming youngsters.

Imran Khan has been delighted by what he has seen: "There is incredible talent in the country. I used to think that the Westindies had the most talent but now I think Pakistan has the greatest talent. Nowhere else in the world do you have under-19 cricketers jumping into Test cricket. I organised an under-15 and under-16 clinic in

Pakistan and I couldn't believe the quality of talent. After 21 years I can spot talent."

Whether this talent ever fulfils its true potential, we shall have to wait and see, but the signs are encouraging. It is amazing to think that Pakistan is now a breeding ground for fast bowlers while most other countries are struggling. Even the Westindies' production line seems to have dried up; injuries to Curtly Ambrose and Ian Bishop in recent years have revealed a sudden lack of replacements, such as the typical raw 20-year-old expresses which were so plentiful in the Caribbean and who could be moulded into great bowlers once in the Westindies side. It was ironic that for Pakistan's home series with Australia in 1994/5, Pakistan had the fast bowling strength and the visitors the edge in spin bowling. The most recent additions to the squad, Mohammad Akram and Shahid Nazir, have genuine pace, while Mohammad Zahid made a remarkable start to his Test career, taking 11-130 on debut against New Zealand at Rawalpindi (1996/7). A heritage has been created and now everyone wants to bowl fast like their heroes in the Test team.

The Pakistan XI has always been full of mercurial talent. On their day, they can beat any side in the world, in either Test or one-day cricket yet the side is prone to inconsistencies, best illustrated by the fifteen-month period from the start of the World Cup to the end of the tour to Westindies (1992/3). Even during the World Cup Pakistan's form went from woeful to wonderful. In the subsequent sixteen one-day internationals they won only three times, yet in the meantime were beating England in England, more convincingly than the 2-1 scoreline suggested and the "sultans of swing," Wasim and Waqar, rescued Pakistan from dire straits in New Zealand to turn around the Hamilton Test.

However, they suffered a real set-back in the Westindies, where everything seemed to go against them. At times they were a bit of a shambles. In what was billed as a decider for the "world's best" title, they were comprehensively beaten 2-0. Nevertheless, losing to the Westindies had been avoided longer - 12 years - by Pakistan than any other Test playing nation and was no disgrace. Pakistan's performance in the Caribbean was unfortunate. The side was plagued by injuries, poor form from key players, ill-luck with half-chances and umpiring decisions and they were not helped by irrational selectorial decisions, which chose to leave Salim Malik and Shoaib Mohammad behind. Added to this were the unsettling effects of the drugs charges in Grenada. Pakistan were desperately unlucky with injuries as these exposed their collective inexperience as they had to field players with little or no first-class

cricket behind them. They lost Aqib Javed for the whole series, Mustaq Ahmed during the first Test, Aamir Sohail for the last one, and Rashid Latif until the last one, while both Wasim Akram and Waqar Younis seemed jaded and were below their best.

Leaving out Salim Malik and Shoaib Mohammad did at least give Inzamam-ul-Haq and Basit Ali a chance to establish themselves. In the Westindies, Basit won great admiration for the way he approached each innings, and it is significant that he had not been involved in the surfeit of limited-overs internationals that the rest of the side had been playing around the world in the previous 15 months. In that time, Inzamam-ul-Haq played in 44 such games travelling from Pakistan to Australia and New Zealand, to England, back to the Antipodes, to Southern Africa, to Sharjah and finally to the Caribbean. Indeed, the national side were away on tour for 212 days in 1992, far more than any other Test side and played 55 one-days in total in 1992 and 1993, as well as thirteen Test matches. The dangers of players getting burnt out are enormous, while the excess of limited-overs cricket can affect technique and application in Test matches. A fresher side would have given the Westindies a good fight.

Potentially, Pakistan could produce their strongest-ever side between now and the turn of the century depending on the development of the current players in the side and the need for probably one more batsman and one more bowler to establish themselves. While the team misses Imran Khan's ability as a player and authority as a leader, Wasim Akram is gradually winning back the confidence of his players, while his own form has remained good.

Most of those likely to feature strongly in this period are covered in detail elsewhere. Wasim Akram and Waqar Younis are the quickest and most lethal opening bowlers in the world and barring injury should remain so. They could have more than 650 wickets between them by the year 2000. In Mustaq Ahmed, Pakistan has a potential match-winner, who really grew in stature and confidence over the winter of 1995/6, which showed on the 1996 tour to England, where all his hard work paid off.

A bowler of the quality of Aqib Javed, a worthy third seamer, has been ousted by bowlers of greater potential, though his last series, against Sri Lanka in 1995/6, was his best to date. Among the strong bowling reserves are Ata-ur-Rehman and Aamir Nazir, each of whom created a good impression in the Caribbean in 1992/3, even though the latter was very raw, having no first-class experience before that tour, and struggled with routine details such as his run-up but he showed that he could swing the ball late into the right-handers. He made a bizarre return to the side in South Africa in 1993/4, when he was flown in from Pakistan on the morning of the match as a late replacement for the injured Waqar Younis. He bowled well enough taking two wickets, though was twice struck down by cramp. He bowled well on the rest of the tour, helping Pakistan to get back into the series in Zimbabwe, by taking 11 wickets in the final two Tests at only 15.54 each to top the bowling averages. He has been unlucky to play in only one Test since.

Rehman was not originally selected for the tour of England in 1992, but was called in when Wasim Akram was injured and made his debut just a few days later in the first Test at Edgbaston, at the age of 17 years and 69 days. He bowled impressively, dismissing Alec Stewart, Mark Ramprakash and Allan Lamb for 69 runs. Also from Lahore, Imran Khan rated him then as "the most promising pace bowler in Pakistan," and was surprised Rehman was not in the original squad. Rehman made his first-class debut less than a year before playing for Pakistan A in Sri Lanka. He had the edge over the others as Pakistan's third seamer behind Akram and Younis, but he has been in and out of the side since his debut, chipping in with wickets against Westindies, Zimbabwe and New Zealand (1993-1994), but losing his place during the 1994/5 season. He returned for one match against Sri Lanka and for the World Cup in 1995/6. He was chosen for the 1996 tour to England and played in the first two Tests, taking four wickets in the first innings at Lord's, but did not really establish himself.

Mohammad Akram made his debut at the age of 21 against Sri Lanka in 1995/6 and went on the tour to Australia and New Zealand. He bowled well on tour without much luck, having four relatively easy chances dropped off his bowling at Brisbane. He could be the pick of the up-and-coming quickies. Chosen for the 1996 England tour, he had some experience of the conditions from playing club cricket in Bristol and for Gloucestershire second XI. There, he was given advice by Courtney Walsh, whose action his resembles. He has genuine pace, on a par with Waqar's, and could develop into a very fine fast bowler. He took seven for 51 against county champions, Leicestershire, and shortly after the tour he was signed by Northamptonshire as Curtly Ambrose's replacement. His spell in county cricket should be very beneficial. Shahid Nazir was also picked for the tour after just four first-class matches in which he took 16 wickets at a cost of only 20 apiece. He played only three matches in England, but topped the averages with

12 wickets at 13.67 and looks a fine prospect.

Others fast bowlers have been tried; Ashfaq Ahmed was the leading wicket-taker in domestic cricket in 1993/4, while Kabir Khan is a promising left-arm seamer. Both were selected for Pakistan's tour to Sri Lanka in the summer of 1994, while Mohsin Kamal won a surprise recall against Australia (1994/5), adding an eighth cap more than seven years since his last, against England in 1987.

Off-spinner Saqlain Mustaq is rated by England's John Emburey as the best slow bowling prospect around. He took 52 wickets at 18.23 apiece in his first season in domestic cricket in 1994/5 for PIA and Islamabad and made his Test debut the following season against Sri Lanka when he was just 18. He toured Australia and New Zealand and was in the World Cup squad, but did not play in the competition. His form subsequently in one-day internationals suggests that was an error, for has proved to be remarkably economical and a wicket-taker. He seems to have ousted Akram Raza as the first choice off-spinner and looks good enough to become Pakistan's best of his genre. He was unfortunate not to play in a Test on the tour to England, after taking 29 wickets at only 15.72 apiece against the counties.

The squad is well-blessed with wicket-keepers. Rashid Latif is crucial to the balance of the side, as the tail is unreliable. As well as being an accomplished wicket-keeper, who has proved more consistent behind the stumps than Moin Khan, his batting is composed and stylish, and could develop into a wicket-keeper-batsman in the Jeffrey Dujon mould. It was originally his batting superiority that got him the call-up. However, recently Moin has proved a revelation with the bat and so Latif has had to rely on his tidier 'keeping to gain selection. After nine Tests Latif was averaging over forty, while Khan had an average of just 13 from his 11 Tests, but the situation has changed markedly. When called up as a replacement for the injured Latif against Australia (1994/5) at Karachi, he marked his return with a fighting hundred when his side most needed it and he did the same against Sri Lanka at Sialkot in 1995/6. Incredibly, he did it a third time on the tour to England, making a hundred at Headingley, even though he only found out he was playing on the morning of the match. The competition between the two is a healthy one and they are likely to be in contention for some years to come.

The batting line-up is just beginning to make the runs it should. Saeed Anwar and Aamir Sohail are the most exciting opening batsmen in Test cricket, while Ijaz Ahmed is a classy No 3 enjoying a second lease of life, who has a very important role as the anchorman. Inzamam-ul-Haq is very consistent and if he can just convert a few more of his fifties into three figures, Pakistan will have a top four to match any in the world. Salim Malik's experience could be utilised for the next two or three years as the balance of the team is important - to mix the side with youth and experience, strokemakers and accumulators, attacking bowlers and steady performers. The competition for the final batting slot is the most exciting. Two teenagers were introduced at the start of the 1996/7. Shahid Alfridi marked his second one-day international with a remarkable hundred against Sri Lanka, scored from only 37 balls which was an incredible 11 balls faster than the previous quickest, scored by Sanath Jayasuriya. Also, in October 1996, Pakistan gave a Test debut to Hassan Raza, who a few months earlier had been opening the batting for the under-15 side in the junior World Cup. He was reportedly only 14 years and 227 days, though subsequently it has been proved that he was probably a few months older. Still, he looked wonderfully composed in making 27 against the touring Zimbabweans. The success of Mohammad Wasim, who scored a hundred on his Test debut against New Zealand at Lahore (1996/7), demonstrates the abundance of talent.

Other recent batting selections include Asif Mujtaba, who played two Tests against the Westindies in 1986/7 and one against England the following season but he was discarded and left in the wilderness for five years. He kept producing fine performances in domestic cricket, including over fifteen hundred runs and 57 wickets in 1989/90. He won selection for the England tour in 1992 through Javed Miandad's insistence and batted with a calm assurance through the series. He was again steady in the Caribbean and was Pakistan's vice-captain on the next two tours, to New Zealand and Sri Lanka in 1994, but lost his place and that role. Shear weight of runs (1367 with eight hundreds in the 1995/6 domestic season) earned him a recall for the tour to England in 1996, and he made a valuable fifty in the second Test at Headingley. Though his front-foot method is better suited to domestic cricket than Tests, he is still young enough (born November 1967) to make his mark and is an intelligent cricketer. After 23 Tests, though, his average is only in the mid-twenties. He has looked composed at the crease, with some classy looking shots in his repertoire, but he has yet to make a century, and despite eight fifties his top-score is only 65. He has been a useful performer in one-day cricket, with a one-day hundred against Sri Lanka to his name, and he once tied a match with Australia (WSC 1992/3) by hitting the last ball from Steve Waugh for six. He is the type of player who could have been lost completely through selectorial whims in the past, but could still have a useful international future.

Imran Khan thought that Zahid Fazal would put the icing on the cake in the batting line-up but has yet to come through. Fazal has a precocious talent, coming into the Test side at the age of 17, against the Westindies in 1990/1, following some brilliant form for the under-19 side and for Pakistan B. Born in Sialkot in November 1973, he resembles that city's most famous son, Zaheer Abbas, playing with the same ease off his legs, sending the ball to the boundary with a flick of the wrists, and loves to drive especially off the back-foot. He made his first-class debut for Pakistan Automobile Corporation in 1989/9, toured England with the under-19 squad in 1990, making 99 in the third Test, and went to Zimbabwe with Pakistan B, where he made three hundreds in consecutive matches against their B team. Consequently he was drafted in to face the Westindies, making his debut at Karachi, but had a disappointing series. He played a match-winning innings against Sri Lanka in the third Test at Faisalabad (1991/2) just prior to the World Cup and he seemed a certainty for the No 3 slot in that competition especially after the way he batted in the Wills Trophy Final against India in Sharjah a few months before, making 98 before having to retire because of cramp.

However, he played in only two games, against India and South Africa, without success. He toured England, South Africa and Westindies with Pakistan in 1992-3 but was given few opportunities on any of the tours, though he did play an amazing innings of 190 in a 48-over game against Bermuda on the way home from the Caribbean. The danger of being on the fringes of the side on tour is the lack of cricket and Fazal could suffer because of this. He already has some useful experience and was still only twenty when he played the last of his nine Tests against Australia in 1994. He is waiting patiently for another opportunity.

Pakistan introduced two uncapped batsmen for the tour to England in 1996, Shahid Anwar and Shadab Kabir. The former has been a consistent performer in domestic cricket, who captained Pakistan A against England A in the winter of 1995/6, a season in which he averaged over 50 for Lahore. At 27, he is old by Pakistani standards but may still develop. Kabir looks a very exciting prospect, who was picked entirely on his potential after modest returns with the bat during the domestic season. Just 18, he is an elegant left-hander, who has a full range of strokes, though on his debut at Lord's he played a fine defensive innings when asked to open in the second innings because of an injury to Aamir Sohail. He batted for over three hours for his 33 but helped Saeed Anwar add 136 to shut England out of the game.

While the future of Pakistan is with such young guns, there are several vastly experienced players who still have a part to play and it is important to the balance of the side that the selectors do not waste the experience of such players. Ramiz Raja and Javed Miandad were both recalled during 1995/6, Raja to captain against Sri Lanka, Miandad to play in his sixth World Cup. Raja put together a good sequence of scores that winter but was a surprise omission from the tour to England.

There have been some fine players who have disappeared long before their careers should have been over. Ijaz Ahmed appeared to be one such player who was on the brink before his surprise but highly successful return to the side during for the 1994/5 series with Australia. He replaced 31-year-old Aamer Malik, another experienced player who had appeared in the previous Test after a four year absence. A fine player, in just 13 Tests he had scored two Test hundreds, against India in 1989/90, and a 98 not out during his second Test against England in 1987/8, made in over seven hours to earn a draw. He made a hundred in each innings on his first-class debut, one of only three people to have done so, but never quite fulfilled his potential, which Imran thought was enormous.

There are some brilliant cricketers coming out of Pakistan but the domestic structure makes it difficult to gauge the depth of this talent, with players often having to be tested at international level to judge their temperaments. A handful of injuries could devastate the side; Waqar, Aqib Javed, Mustaq Ahmed and Rashid Latif have all had back trouble, while Wasim Akram has had a recurrent groin injury and problems with his shin. The selectors could fill such gaps by making better use of those players who have had an introduction to Test cricket but not been allowed to blossom.

One-day cricket has become of disproportionate importance in Pakistan, with results often determing selection. As defending champions, this was compounded as the World Cup in 1996 drew closer, with the team turning their attention to the competition while on tour in Australia.

Pakistan has been playing against the weaker opponents recently - New Zealand, Zimbabwe and Sri Lanka - which has allowed some of the younger players to get established and others to be tried for the tougher challenges ahead. The side is beginning to show great steel under pressure, where once they were suspect. The series against Australia in 1994/5 should have proved to be a watershed. Pakistan won the first Test by one wicket, after Inzamam-ul-Haq and Mustaq Ahmed shared a tense, match-winning last wicket stand of 57, and fought back superbly in the next two Tests to earn draws when defeat was looming large, inspired by their captain Salim Malik, who finished the series with a record 577 runs. However, there have been some lacklustre performances since.

Another potential hindrance to Pakistan's progress is the haphazard nature of domestic cricket, which is partly to blame for inconsistencies in performance. The lack of competitive edge meant that the eighties were fallow years compared with the halcyon days in the seventies when several batsmen might have been in contention to play in an eclectic World XI. However, in the last few years the talent has really come to the surface.

By comparison, England have also suffered, since wickets have been universally covered and with the decrease in overseas players in county cricket, and has had to rely increasingly on batsmen who learned their game elsewhere, such as Allan Lamb, Robin Smith and Graeme Hick.

There has been much concern that with domestic cricket in such a parlous state and with overseas opportunities limited to a few highly sought after places in county cricket, Pakistan will struggle to maintain their highly regarded status in world cricket, yet at the moment they are blessed with an array of gifted young batsmen. That such talent is still coming out of Pakistan is despite the system not because of it. With the sponsorship of Wills, Coca-Cola and of Pepsi, who have started a number of youth coaching projects, efforts are being made to build from the ground up, though a major restructuring at first-class level is needed to get the edge back into domestic cricket. Matters do seem to be improving slowly and it is encouraging that some of the new talent is coming from outside the two main centres, and having the Quaid-e-Azam and under-19 tournament on a more regional basis now should continue to encourage this, though players still find it necessary to come to Lahore and Karachi to progress in the game.

Pakistani players often start learning when they come into the national squad. They are thrown in at the deep end, picked on promise and potential yet often have technical flaws. Some are given only one chance and are then discarded, being unable to develop their game sufficiently afterwards. There is a terrible natural wastage of this kind, as over half of all Pakistan's Test players have played fewer than ten Tests and many players have found themselves on the scrap-heap by the time they are in their early twenties. Thus it makes it very difficult to predict who will feature through to the end of the decade. Already some of the "Future greats" may be out of the reckoning.

If the improvements can be made to domestic cricket, which help to harness the enormous enthusiasm and affinity for the game that exists in Pakistan, the Test side will be unstoppable. Pakistan has the potential to be the pre-eminent force in Test cricket.

Dispute and disrepute

Pakistan have been castigated as the bad boys of Test cricket, with allegations of ball-tampering, unsportsmanlike conduct, biased umpiring and pitch doctoring. The next few chapters will endeavour to examine the allegations, try and separate fact from fiction, and make comparison with the records of other countries. The media of Pakistan's opponents love to blow up events out of all proportion, creating a build-up of bad feeling between both the players and nations.

One cannot claim that Pakistani cricket has a blemish free record but it is by no means the only Test playing country to fall foul. There are a host of incidents that perhaps could not happen anywhere else; Tests have been held up by dust storms, rain storms, fog, on-field disputes, off-field disputes, protests, pitch invasions, by an umpire arriving at the ground and realising he had forgotten his coat. There have been hiccoughs, but most of these have been part of the game's rich pageant.

Often Pakistan are forced to play their home Test series at the most uncomfortable times of the year, September or March, because Australia tends to get the pick of the tours as they are so much better off financially. No wonder Ian Botham did not want to send his mother-in-law there! By choice, the Pakistanis themselves would not be playing cricket at that time of year.

Touring sides who go to Pakistan and complain about the facilities do not appreciate the nature of the country and its culture, or the difficulties that it has gone through in its short history since Partition. Pakistan is a fast developing young country straining under the pressures of a rapidly growing population [currently 130 million] that is stretching the infrastructure to the limit. Yet every effort is made to accommodate touring sides with the best facilities available and warm hospitality, something many of the Pakistani players do not feel is adequately reciprocated when they travel overseas.

Pakistan touring sides have suffered shoddy treatment, been put up in indifferent hotels, and been given over-demanding schedules. In the Westindies in 1987/8, for instance, one Pakistani player lost his meal ticket and did not get any food at one ground and while the home team had mineral water with their meal, the Pakistani players had none - minor but irritating points.

On the team's arrival in England in 1987, instead of being granted the courtesy of some sort of diplomatic status as you would expect, it was forced to wait behind at customs while all the luggage was searched by sniffer-dogs. On the 1993 tour to the Westindies it went one step worse when Wasim Akram, Waqar Younis, Aqib Javed and Mustaq Ahmed were arrested and charged for being in "active possession" of drugs - some reefers were found close to where they had been sitting on the beach. The allegations proved ill-founded and were a great embarrassment to both the Pakistani team and the Grenadian government. The manager, Khalid Mahmood, felt that this incident had left his side without the "mental and physical strength" to play the series, while the newly appointed captain, Wasim Akram, was bitter about the whole experience saying, "We are accused of things wherever we go. In England in 1992 it was ball-tampering, and now this which was 20 times worse. We are not bad human beings. We don't make trouble. All we are is good cricketers. Why are some people jealous of that?"

On field disputes

International cricket has seen a sharp increase in the number of incidents that only a few years ago would be considered simply "not cricket." Unfortunately old values are rarely applicable these days. The rising media attention, indeed constant scrutiny of TV and the press, plus the higher and higher stakes that are being played for have heightened the pressure on international players.

I will not attempt to justify poor sportsmanship or unsavoury behaviour on Pakistan's behalf but will at least offer some mitigation, show that other teams are hardly exemplary and that on occasions incidents do occur in the heat of the moment which, if not forgivable, at least make them understandable. It must be remembered also that Pakistan has played more than half its Test cricket in this modern - post Packer - era when standards of sportsmanship worldwide have been at their lowest.

The way matters are reported can cloud the issue; too often the tabloids sensationalise a minor on the field dispute, by concentrating on the controversy especially, it seems, when Pakistan is involved, yet rather less so when other countries transgress. This was particularly so in 1992 when sections of the press took up the slack from the last acrimonious series in 1987/8.

It was then that undoubtedly the worst incident in recent years took place - the Gatting-Rana fiasco - but as shown in more detail in the sections on umpiring and Faisalabad, a sequence of events led to this. Gatting on reflection has said that he should not have taken Rana on and probably should have been sent home for doing so. The Press tried to paint the incident at Old Trafford with Aqib Javed in 1992 in the same light, but this time came down on the side of the umpire even though Aqib Javed's gesturing was much less aggressive than that of Gatting.

Javed Miandad never seems to be too far away from any of the recent controversies but it would be unfair to always blame him as the instigator. For instance in the clash with Dennis Lillee in 1981/2 it was the Australian who was fined and suspended for two one-day internationals. Lillee deliberately obstructed Miandad as he was running between the wickets. Words were exchanged after which Lillee kicked at Javed, gently hitting him on the bottom. Miandad swirled around, bat raised threateningly at Lillee. There was no serious intent to clobber Lillee but it did make the great fast bowler back off sharply, something he was not used to doing, before the umpire stepped in. It was Miandad's first overseas Test as captain and Lillee was testing his mettle. Although Greg Chappell defended Lillee, shifting the blame onto Miandad by saying his action "was the most disgraceful thing" he had seen on a cricket field, most thought Lillee had gone too far. Tony Greig summed it up "Javed Miandad is no angel...but its a bit of a joke Greg Chappell complaining about people who bait." Ian Chappell, in *Australian Cricket,* said "to kick a batsman when he wasn't looking was the act of a spoiled, angry child." Keith Miller and Bill O'Reilly, two Australian cricketing legends, went further saying Lillee should have been suspended for the rest of the season.

Merv Hughes tried a similar tactic against Wasim Akram, deliberately standing in his way when he went for a single during the Adelaide Test in 1989/90. They clashed and angry words were exchanged; Wasim ended up waving his bat at Hughes and shouting, "What's your problem?" This was generated entirely because Hughes was trying to intimidate Wasim, all part of his idea of being a macho fast bowler.

Perhaps the most unsporting act was when Greg Chappell told his brother Trevor to bowl under-arm for the last ball of a World Series Cup final match at the Melbourne Cricket Ground against New Zealand in 1980/1 to give the batsman Brian McKecknie no chance of hitting it for the six runs required. Earlier in the same game Greg Chappell refused to go when an out-fielder Martin Snedden claimed a low but apparently fair catch. The umpires, who were watching for short runs and so did not see it, had to give it not out.

Both incidents were indicative of the way Australian cricket has gone. They are now notorious for sledging and swearing on the field, without the hint of humour of earlier years, and for adhering to a policy of not walking. They sold their souls to Packer and have got wrapped up in their idea of professionalism. Since losing the Ashes in 1985 and 1986/7, sides under Allan Border have socialised with the opposition off the field less and less, while increasing their verbal aggression on it. This came to a head in the Westindies (1990/1) where their slurs were often racist and markedly offensive. Not surprisingly Viv Richards, who at times lost his cool during the series, ranks that victory over Australia as his sweetest.

There are always going to be words exchanged on the field especially from quick bowlers; Fred Trueman and Dennis Lillee were known for their quips, glares, stares and strong language directed at the batsmen. It is now part of cricket. Waqar Younis has shown some fiery displeasure, though the verbal he once got back from Robin Smith made him back off sheepishly. One of the best calls of recent times, attributed to Aamir Sohail, was to Ian Botham as he departed after being out for nought in the World Cup Final. Sohail suggested, "You should have sent your mother-in-law." (alluding to a remark Botham once made, saying that he wouldn't even send his mother-in-law to Pakistan).

Botham can get away with a derogatory remark such as that, yet at a celebratory dinner on the eve of the Final the shoe was on the other foot when he took offence to a comedian who was mocking the monarchy. Botham and Gooch stormed out in protest.

Most Pakistani players at some time or other have played a fair amount of street cricket, though fair is not usually the word best suited to it; usually anything goes. The games tend to be hectic with everyone appealing all the time and trying to run the batsmen out in a show of youthful exuberance. Similar enthusiasm is shown with beach cricket in the Westindies where bouncer after bouncer is bowled to a cordon of slips stretching into the sea. Not surprisingly some aspects of each have come through in the way their respective first-class games are played.

Imran Khan recounts one such example when Miandad ran out Rodney Hogg when the batsman left his crease in a Tests to do some "gardening".

Imran felt it quite amusing at the time as it was just the sort of thing that might happen in a street match in Karachi. Rodney Hogg smashed the stumps down in disgust. His captain Graham Yallop said afterwards, "I was surprised that he left one stump standing." However that was only after Mustaq Mohammad, the Pakistan captain at the time, had had his request to the umpire to withdraw the appeal rejected. Umpire Clarence Harvey's amazing refusal had its repercussions throughout the rest of the series and sparked a number of retaliatory acts.

In the next Test Sikander Bakht, who was at the non striker's end, was run out by the bowler Alan Hurst as he backed up. Bakht was helping Asif Iqbal add important runs for the last wicket and Iqbal was understandably furious, demolishing the wicket at his end in the manner of Hogg in the first Test. Consequently the Pakistanis were out for revenge at the first opportunity so when Andrew Hilditch, at the non-striker's end, picked up a wayward return to the bowler and in a helpful gesture handed it to Sarfraz Nawaz, the bowler, he promptly appealed for "handled the ball" against Hilditch. Surprisingly, the appeal was upheld.

Had Mustaq Mohammad's request to revoke the decision been granted as it should have been by Harvey (the elder brother of the Test batsman Neil), the subsequent bad sportsmanship may well have been avoided. As with England's tour after the World Cup in 1987, this series was ill-conceived with little public interest after the World Series cricket and staged at the back-end of the 1978/9 season. However with strong umpiring all such trouble could have been avoided. It was totally inflammatory to reject the Pakistan captain's request. On a similar occasion, when Dilip Doshi was run out at Delhi (1979-80) when he left his crease to ask the umpire about the shadow of a tree that was encroaching onto the pitch, the batsman entreated Majid Khan, the acting captain, to withdraw the appeal and the matter was closed as soon as he did.

Miandad's running out of Hogg is not a unique occurrence or one exclusive to Pakistan. England's Tony Greig once ran out Alvin Kallicharran as he walked off the field after the last ball of the day in the first Test at Port of Spain in 1973/4. The batsman had to be reinstated to avoid a major crowd disturbance. Similarly, Dean Jones was run out in the Westindies in 1990/1 when he left his crease to return to the pavilion, thinking he had been dismissed, as he had not heard the no-ball call that should have gained him a reprieve. However neither the players nor the umpires knew the law that prevents such a dismissal. Ramiz Raja has also been out in this manner, along with his dismissals for "handling the ball" and

"obstructing the field" to complete a unique treble.

In a fit of pique Sikander Bakht once kicked down the stumps in a Test match, against India at Kanpur (1979/80), though on a day when just over a hundred runs had been scored in over four hours, *Wisden* described it as "the highlight of the day". Following the Hogg and Asif Iqbal examples with the bat, it did start a bit of a trend of bowlers kicking the stumps at a time when the wicket was more in danger from the tantrums of the bowlers or batsmen than from the ball. The first reported stump-kicking was back in 1922 when the Hampshire bowler, Jack Newman, sat down on the ground and refused to bowl after four successive appeals for lbw were turned down (Newman had the habit of running across in front of the umpire in his follow-through). When his captain Lord Tennyson ordered him from the field, Newman's parting gesture was to kick down the stumps.

Michael Holding picked up the stump-kicking trend at Dunedin against New Zealand in 1980/1 after an appeal for a catch behind off John Parker had been turned down. By most accounts it was a disgraceful act but carried out with typical Holding grace. On that tour the players also staged a lock-in and Colin Croft deliberately barged into umpire Goodall after having another appeal rejected.

Jeff Thomson was another to take out his frustration on the stumps, in 1982/3 at Lahore, after he had been no-balled by Shakoor Rana. Sikander Bakht, who always aspired to being a quick bowler, must have been pleased that the two quickest bowlers in the world followed his lead! Neil Foster kept the habit alive in a county match in 1993.

Foster's former county captain, Keith Fletcher, gave the stumps a tap when he was in charge of England against India in 1981/2, and probably lost the captaincy as a result; Chris Broad completed a rather more obvious demolition, at Sydney v Australia in 1987/8, when he flattened the leg stump after he had been bowled off his body by Steve Waugh, and was fined £500. Worse has occurred in India when the bowler, Rashid Patel, actually used a stump as a weapon to attack the batsman, Raman Lamba, during the 1991/2 final of the Duleep trophy.

Much was made of the catches claimed by Salim Yousuf during the third Test at Headingley in 1987. The action replays showed that both had been grounded. The first one Yousuf scooped up on the half-volley though, as occasionally happens he may well have been unsighted. With the team charged up no one doubted the catch, off the unlucky Chris Broad, who had taken the offending hand off the bat at the point of contact and so should not have been given out on two counts.

Later in the innings Yousuf took a fine catch down the leg-side, spilled it as he tumbled over but managed to retrieve it on the bounce. He still claimed the catch though he had clearly dropped it. The batsman Ian Botham gave him a piece of his mind and the umpire, who had given it not out, had to intervene. Imran Khan was furious and gave Yousuf a good dressing down, though again he was retaliating because of a bad decision in favour of Bill Athey.

It is something like this that can bring the whole integrity of a nation's cricket into question and tends to get brought up as a "typical" example. Yet this was a one-off occurrence when Yousuf got carried away as Pakistan pushed for victory. Plenty of other similarly false claims for catches have been made by other players. David Gower revealed in his biography that Bob Taylor, the Derbyshire and England 'keeper, who had an impeccable reputation, once claimed a catch against the Australians in 1978/9, though the ball appeared to have bounced a foot in front of him. No one thought of calling the batsman back when the umpire called him back. Gower admitted, "Because it was Bob Taylor, it did not develop into an issue, but when a Pakistani player becomes involved in something similar, he is labelled a cheat." The same was true in 1996 when Graeme Hick claimed a catch against India at Edgbaston. The replay showed clearly that the ball had not carried.

In the 3rd Test match between South Africa and India (1992/3), David Richardson claimed two dubious catches which showed up on replay as not having hit the bat. In the first Test at Brisbane against Westindies 1992/3, Ian Healy also claimed a stumping when he clearly did not have the ball in his hand when he broke the wicket. Brian Lara was the unlucky batsman and was well set on 58 - who knows how many he would have gone on to make. That is certainly not the first dubious claim made by an Australian wicket-keeper.

It is very difficult to repair a feeling of ill-will between two sides especially when there is constant suspicion of the umpires. This came to a head in the 1992 series between England and Pakistan. Aqib Javed misinterpreted the umpire's actions after he had bowled a succession of short-pitched deliveries at Devon Malcolm. After being spoken to earlier in the over Umpire Ken Palmer warned Aqib Javed for intimidatory bowling. The last ball had been short but not a bouncer and Aqib assumed that that was what he was being warned for as he had already bowled his one bouncer for the over. Aqib Javed took offence when the umpire gave him his jumper back, which could just about have been construed as rude, though in fact only looked that way because the jumper had caught in the umpire's coat and required a sharp tug to extricate it.

Aqib Javed is a hot-headed young man who was fined for his actions and has since been suspended for his poor conduct in a one-day game in New Zealand. Although in no way an excuse, one must remember how young Aqib was at the time, just 19. Because of the nature of domestic cricket many Pakistani players coming into international cricket have had very little first-class experience. Some probably do not even know the laws fully; something that is given out or a law that is not enforced in a school match may well be interpreted differently at senior level. To be thrust

Aqib Javed and Javed Miandad, Old Trafford 1992

upon such an unfamiliar stage, under the spotlight, in front of big crowds in a foreign land (often for the first time in their lives) whilst still in one's 'teens must be quite some experience. One can understand the occasional transgression.

Most cricketers of a similar age in England would just be breaching the gap between school and club cricket. To rise so quickly to international stardom requires a certain arrogance, confidence and impetuosity to go with one's talent but it does not come ready made with experience and worldly wisdom. Other young and talented players in other countries have shown similar signs of petulance. Compare the track records of England's Mark Ramprakash, Nasser Hussain and Phil Tufnell all of whom have missed out on selection because of a poor disciplinary record.

Although Miandad was quick to jump in to protect his young fast bowler at Old Trafford and showed his old predilection for a scrap, in the rest of the series he was much more avuncular, quick to stem any such over-excitement. Indeed in the very next Test his conduct was commended when he stepped in quickly when Moin Khan and Rashid Latif began to show dissent when a bat-pad decision was turned down. Both were fined, yet an almost identical incident occurred the following summer against Australia. Just as Moin Khan had, England's Alec Stewart ran towards the umpire in expectation of a decision in the fielding side's favour. Graham Thorpe, the bat-pad catcher, began the premature celebrations, just as Latif had done, and then threw the ball down in disgust when it was given not out. The only difference was that Latif, who was on as a substitute, through his cap down instead. Yet the two Pakistanis were each fined, the two Englishman just cautioned.

Allan Border and Merv Hughes have been frequently spoken to about their conduct, such as after the Brisbane and Perth Tests against Westindies (1992/3) for dissent. Many felt they should have been suspended. Then on the tour to New Zealand that followed Hughes was not even fined for spitting at Mark Greatbatch during a Test, for gesticulating at the crowd, or for making unsavoury jibes at Martin Crowe. Border and Hughes were cautioned once again during the Ashes series with England for over-zealous appealing and dissent at the umpires' decisions. Eventually Hughes and Shane Warne were both fined for their behaviour in the series against South Africa in 1993/4. Yet Hughes, who would have earned around A$60,000 for the 15 Tests he played covering the three warnings, was fined a mere A$800. Peter Kirsten, of South Africa, was fined twice for dissent in the same match against the Australians at Adelaide in 1993/4, totalling 40 per cent of his match fee, but a local radio station

had a phone whip-round and he actually made a profit! He had been fined the year before as well, in a one-dayer against India.

There have been worse shows of petulance; Viv Richards' appeal for a catch off Rob Bailey at Bridgetown 1989/90 was described by *Wisden Cricket Monthly* as "a manic, arm-waving ceremonial dance". Richards' actions were completely over the top and indeed it was suggested at the time that he had intimidated the umpire, though this statement was withdrawn and an apology made by Christopher Martin-Jenkins, to avoid legal action being taken by the offended umpire, Lloyd Barker.

In the next Test, Richards was certainly intimidating, seeking out a British journalist, James Lawton, in the press box when he should have been on the field, and also gesticulated rudely at his own crowd.

The Westindies have often over-done short-pitched bowling and there is no doubt that the bouncer barrage Brian Close and John Edrich got at Old Trafford in 1976 was intimidation. Lillee and Thomson have expressed that their much-favoured use of the bouncer was to intimidate, while there was general condemnation of Bob Willis' tactic to bowl short from round the wicket at night-watchman Iqbal Qasim. This is one area where Pakistan have set a fine example; there is no "Bodyline" skeleton in their closet. The bowling of Wasim Akram and Waqar Younis has demonstrated how to use the bouncer, as a surprise, while generally bowling a full length allowing the ball to swing as in the days of yore. Admittedly Imran Khan and Akram both used to over-do the bouncer when they were young and it is true for some time Pakistan had no one much above medium pace to bowl bouncers, but now they are demonstrating the art of fast bowling moving it into new and exciting dimensions.

Crowd trouble

There have been several disturbances and unsavoury interactions with the crowd. It seems, though, that when these take place in places like Pakistan they are described as riots, but rather demurely referred to as "incidents" in England.

Both Javed Miandad and Abdul Qadir have been involved in altercations with spectators. Miandad was in Sri Lanka, 1985/6, when someone in the crowd started throwing little stones at him. He saw who and went into the stand after him and had to be restrained by his team-mates. Qadir was in Barbados, 1987/8, and during the closing stages of a very tense Test match was being mercilessly heckled. He eventually cracked and threw a punch at the spectator. Both of these pale in comparison with Sylvester Clarke's reaction to being constantly pelted with fruit during a Test in Multan. The Westindian pace bowler picked up a boundary marker brick and flung it into the crowd, scoring a direct hit on the head of the leader of a local students' union, Shafiq Ahmed, who had to be taken to hospital. Play was held up for twenty minutes and only resumed after a plea on bended knee from Alvin Kallicharran.

There have been other fruit peltings and worse. For instance, India's semi-final against Sri Lanka in the 1996 World Cup had to be abandoned when the Eden Gardens crowd, knowing that their team was about to lose and disappointed with the performance, threw bottles and debris onto the pitch. The players were led from the field by the umpires and the match referee Clive Lloyd awarded the game to Sri Lanka when a resumption proved impossible.

Ray Illingworth was forced to lead his team from the field when a spectator grabbed at a player, John Snow, on the boundary after the fast bowler had hit Australian batsman Terry Jenner with a bouncer during the 1970/1 series.

Touring sides have had to contend with pitch invasions, demonstrations and political activity at grounds in Pakistan. It got particularly bad on England's tour in 1968/9, at a time of social unrest in the country. There was similar trouble in 1977/8 when the protesters spilled on to the pitch and threatened the pavilion. However, when the situation calmed down the protesters helped clear the outfield of debris!

Cricket is such a public stage that it is prone to such demonstrations. On India's last tour to Pakistan in 1989/90, a spectator ran on during the first Test with the intention of assaulting an Indian player, in protest against recent killings of Moslems in Bihar in India. He menaced Kapil Dev and scuffled with Srikkanth, who had his shirt ripped.

Yet similar disturbances have occurred in Australia, India, Sri Lanka and Westindies. England is hardly blemish free; there was bomb scare at Lord's in 1973, the pitch was dug up at Headingley in 1975 and during the Centenary Test of 1980 the umpires were physically assaulted as they returned to the pavilion by, of all people, MCC members, after a prolonged stoppage for rain. There have been pitch invasions too, though mainly good-natured such as when Geoff Boycott completed his hundredth hundred in a Tests at Headingley (1977), but also disruptive such as in the 1975 World Cup Final when the crowd thought it was all over when the last wicket was taken but off a no-ball. Similarly the crowd ran on as the last

ball was bowled during the deciding one-day international in Guyana 1992/3. The match was declared a tie as the Pakistani fielders were hindered by the converging crowd.

There has been not much worse than when unruly English spectators ran onto the pitch at Perth 1982/3. The Australian seamer Terry Alderman tried to apprehend the intruders only to dislocate his shoulder as he tackled one of them, which for a while threatened his career. In New Zealand in 1993/4, Pakistan fast bowler Ata-ur-Rehman had to be led from the field at Eden Park, Auckland, during a one-day international after being hit on the head by a bottle thrown by a spectator. Salim Malik felt it necessary to take his players from the field to allow the crowd to settle down.

There has been nothing as unsavoury as the racist taunts of so-called "fans"at Headingley in 1992 which culminated in someone throwing a pig's head into a section of Pakistani spectators, or the assault on a supporter who had his throat slashed at Trent Bridge in 1987. Again in 1996, the Western Terrace at Headingley brought shame to the ground as yobs taunted Pakistani supporters.

Taking the rough with the smooth

Things are seldom what they seem

Suspicions of ball-tampering have been simmering just below the surface throughout the nineties, coming to a head twice on the field, in the summers of 1992 and 1994, and twice in the court room in 1993 and 1996.

Ironically, after all the allegations levelled at Pakistan, it was Michael Atherton, the England captain, who was the first to be censured in a Test match. During the third afternoon of the first Test against South Africa at Lord's in 1994, he was seen on television apparently tampering with the ball. The TV cameras focussed in on Atherton just as he was reaching into his pocket, and then proceeded to take out a substance in his fingertips and then rub that substance into the ball. As it transpired this was only some dirt which he had in his pocket to dry his hands, and the umpires were happy that he had not altered the condition of the ball. When asked to explain his "unfamiliar action" to the match referee, Peter Burge, Atherton was economical with the truth, failing to mention the dirt in his pocket. Consequently the England manager, Ray Illingworth, fined Atherton £1,000 "for giving incomplete information to the match referee" and another £1,000 "for using dirt."

Burge warned Atherton to be on his guard, and perhaps regretting that he had not taken stronger action himself at Lord's, later that summer fined him at the first opportunity, for showing dissent at an umpire's decision after being given out lbw first ball in the third Test at the Oval.

At least the media were consistent and called for the captain's head. Nearly two years before, Pakistan had stood accused of ball-tampering during the fourth one-day international against England at the same ground, and one can only imagine the furore that the media would have made had, for instance, Javed Miandad been caught taking similar action. The scenario was very similar to that in 1992 - alleged ball-doctoring followed soon after

by a fast bowler, in this case Darren Gough, achieving reverse-swing and taking wickets with the old ball.

Intikhab Alam, the manager when Pakistan were accused, also called for Atherton to go. "Atherton has been caught red-handed. He has to be replaced. We have suffered for two years after [the alleged tampering], being called cheats, but this is totally different. Atherton has been found out admitted it and it's clean cut."

Asif Iqbal was angered by the inconsistencies. He told the London *Evening Standard*, "If an

Atherton attends to the ball

ICC [International Cricket Council] referee knows he [Atherton] has lied to him on as big an issue as this, then all referees should forgive all cricketers when they apologise! The Pakistanis were branded cheats on far less visual evidence than has been produced in Atherton's case.

"One more criticism, many of the people defending Mike say it's common practice for bowlers to rub their hand in the dust, therefore it was OK for Mike to do so. Bowlers use the dust to give themselves a better grip but Mike isn't a bowler. It's an insult to the common man's intelligence that this explanation was accepted."

Jonathan Agnew, the BBC cricket correspondent and a close friend of Atherton's, and Geoff Boycott, the former England opener and BBC commentator, both felt that Atherton should have resigned or been sacked as his position was untenable.

The recent ball-tampering controversy started when the ball that Pakistan were using in the morning session of the 4th Texaco Trophy match with England at Lord's, was changed during the lunch interval. In their wisdom, the Test and County Cricket Board [TCCB] failed to make any sort of announcement as to why the ball was changed which only fuelled speculation, especially after Allan Lamb claimed he had asked the umpires to have a look at the ball and then in a *Daily Mirror* exclusive three days later alleged ball-tampering, in an article under the banner headline "How Pakistan cheat at cricket." He was suspended by his county Northamptonshire and fined £2,000 (originally £5,000) and *The Asian Times* replied with "Lamb roasted for his bleating." Lamb had named former team-mate, Sarfraz Nawaz, as the instigator of the ball-tampering trend; an allegation for which Nawaz took him to court in November 1993, a case that ended in an inconclusive draw with both sides claiming victory. However, it was a hollow, Pyrrhic victory for both men for although Nawaz was satisfied that his name had been cleared when he dropped the libel action against Lamb, the whole controversy was thrown under the spotlight once more. For Lamb, who was accused in court of having double-standards as if one plays on the same side as him, "you can cheat because he isn't going to complain about it." [Jonathan Crystal, counsel for Nawaz], while in effect the article spelt the end of Lamb's international career.

His revelations appeared to be the last throes of a player on the brink of losing his place after culpably failing to work out the swing of Akram and Younis, especially the relatively new phenomenon reverse-swing. Robin Smith had given evidence in court, explaining that a batsman could not determine which way the ball was going to swing by looking at the ball in the bowler's hand as it contradicted the norm. However, once reverse-swing is occurring the ball does not suddenly go back to swinging in the conventional manner.

The TCCB's silence was anything but golden. There are two rules governing changing the ball. The first (5.5) refers to when the ball is lost or becomes out of shape, stating that an equivalent alternative be found and the batsmen informed of the change. The second (42.5) refers to foul play and illegally tampering with the ball. It does not specify that the batsmen have to be told of the change. As they were told on this occasion there is an implication that the former law was being applied. However, subsequently the reserve umpire at the match, Don Oslear, has revealed that the latter law was invoked. The change of ball did the trick; the replacement swung all over the place and England were bowled out.

The English press, of course, sensationalised the story; there had been murmurings all summer and this was the opportunity many had been looking for, on the "Champs or cheats" theme. What was so galling was that ball-tampering was being offered as the only reason why England lost, which ranked alongside the excuses offered by Ted Dexter the next winter of the smog, the prawn curries and the stars being in the wrong firmament, as amongst the weakest excuses of our time.

Wasim Akram and Waqar Younis said as much in the statement they issued to the press after the allegations.

"We have played in this country for both Lancashire and Surrey County Cricket clubs and have bowled hundreds of overs for both counties.

We have played in numerous county and Test games on a variety of grounds throughout the world; we have taken hundreds of wickets on all different times of surfaces. At no time has any umpire, official or administrator had cause to allege anything illegal.

These people are specifically given a job of making sure that the rules are obeyed and they have never accused us of doing anything wrong.

It is significant that these allegations are only now being made after we have beaten England in a Test series. When we have been on the losing side in county or Test cricket nothing has been said.

It is very convenient to blame the failure of the English players' batting techniques on us. The simple truth is that we have both bowled extremely professionally throughout the last series against England.

We are amazed that a fellow professional has stooped so low as to make such unfounded comment s in the papers. We can only guess as at Allan Lamb's motives for his article in the *Daily Mirror,* but we hope that they are nothing so base as money or even worse our nationality.

The upset and damage which has been caused to us by these articles is an extremely serious matter. We are taking legal advice and our rights to sue for damages are fully reserved."

The ball-tampering file was reopened at the start of the 1994 season after Imran Khan admitted in a candid interview with his biographer, Ivo Tennant, that he had tampered with the ball on one occasion, when in an unimportant county match he scratched the ball with a bottle-top. *The Daily Mirror* again chose to sensationalise the issue, as they had in 1992. Yet Imran Khan had made almost exactly the same "revelations" in an article he had written in *The Daily Telegraph* (20 November 1993) six months before.

The Daily Mirror used the three back pages to portray him as a cheat, yet devoted space on the gossip pages of the paper to calling him a sex symbol and the game's most eligible bachelor. Imran Khan slammed the tabloid, "I can't believe it. It's so racist, it's so racist."

He was incredulous that such a storm had blown up. "I certainly wasn't expecting this reaction. I wrote almost an identical piece to what appeared in this book [his biography] in *The Daily Telegraph* last year. I wrote exactly the same thing, saying it [ball-tampering] goes on all the time. Is there a bowler that doesn't do it? I asked that same question then but it was ignored by the *Mirror*. They could have made a big issue out of it then but ignored it. Derek Pringle wrote exactly the same thing [in *The Independent*] that it goes on all the time and he too did it. David Lloyd, the Lancashire captain and batsman wrote the same, in the *Telegraph*, two years ago and it was again ignored."

There was no lurid back-page story then. Asked why he thought that there had been no such headlines when Pringle made his confession, Geoff Boycott told Darcus Howe (on the Channel 4 programme *Devil's Advocate,* in which Imran Khan was answering the criticisms), "He's white, from Essex, and not much good." Imran Khan feels that while few bowlers, in their heart of hearts, would deny tampering most are "too scared to tell the truth, as they are worried about the repercussions."

Imran Khan only raised the issue again as he felt it was still unresolved and that there were inconsistencies in the interpretation of what was "above board and acceptable." Some sections of the media do not fully understand what is meant by ball-tampering and reverse-swing, and that one does not go hand in hand with the other.

"No cricket body has come out with anything. The ICC hasn't said anything. The TCCB hasn't done anything - it's hanging in the air - and the umpiring body hasn't come up with anything. So the issue is still there and I feel terrible that two of the finest bowlers in world cricket, Wasim and Waqar, have this big question mark over them. Are they being successful because they are cheating? This is why the issue has to be addressed.

"In my career the longest of all fast bowlers - 21 years - I found that some sort of tampering went on - not all the time by every bowler - but every bowler, at some time or other in his career, has tampered with the ball. If that is cheating then the implication is that every fast bowler that ever bowled, and a lot of good spinners - because a lot of them lift the seam - cheat."

Boycott has never been one to mince his words and confirmed that ball-tampering was an accepted part of the English game, "I can put my hand on my heart and say that I have seen it done in my own teams," and said that he was sympathetic to Imran Khan because he "had seen it done by a lot of players," though would not divulge who for legal reasons though admitted, "they knew it was wrong or they wouldn't have done it secretively. But they do it like we all do it when we drive our cars and go 75-80mph and, if we can get away with it, a bit faster."

Younis Ahmed, a former team-mate of Imran's then tried to jump on the band-wagon, selling his story to *The Mail on Sunday* alleging that Khan had confided in him, admitting that he had achieved his success by illegal means, taking a screwdriver out on to the field. Ahmed, who played in just three Test matches for Pakistan with a seventeen-year gap in between the first and the second, was known to be impecunious, after the collapse of several business ventures, and was thought to have phoned round all the national newspapers in England to try and sell his story for £20,000. It is rumoured that the eventual buyer paid no more than £2,000 for the exclusive.

Khan was dismissive of the allegations, "Look at the credibility of the man. He was sacked by two counties, he bet against his own team..." Ahmed's financial worries have stemmed from his restaurants in Hampstead, North London, and Johannesburg, South Africa, going bust. He has also been prosecuted for fraud and once before made headline-grabbing claims about Imran Khan, after being left out of the squad to England in 1987, alleging that Imran had been selling drugs and holding lascivious parties on the just completed tour to India!

Imran was mystified by Ahmed's motives: "Clearly he needed the money. The biggest question is which bowler, or which sportsman, would ever tell anyone who he doesn't know very well "this is the only reason for my success, because I used these tools." The most laughable thing is that I would tell him. Whoever respected Younis Ahmed? He was the most disgraceful player. Ask any cricketer, any county where he played. He was someone of the lowest integrity."

Most cricketers realise that if one side is doctoring the ball, the other will not be far behind. Indeed most countries realise it goes on and are looking to address the problem. Mudassar Nazar, the Pakistan B coach in 1991, has made a public statement (quoted in *Wasim and Waqar*) saying: "The outlawed practice of roughing up one side of the ball to enhance swing must be eradicated in Pakistan. It's got to stop; it will be hard to enforce, but we will be firm."

English umpires have been scrutinising recently. Indeed the ball was changed in the last Test against the Westindies in 1991, because it had been tampered with. One of the umpires, John Holder, consequently fell foul of the establishment and has been taken off the Test panel for his diligence. In

India a new scheme was put in place for the start of the 1993 season to try and eliminate it.

In the series against New Zealand in Pakistan in 1990/1, the tourists were suspicious of what was going on, again because the opposition had no answer to the pace of Akram and Younis. When they got home New Zealand's team manager, Ian Taylor, accused Pakistan of doctoring the ball - an allegation Intikhab Alam dismissed as "rubbish." - but also admitted to tampering with it themselves in the Third Test where Chris Pringle took career best figures, seven for 52. Willie Watson, the New Zealand medium-pacer, has revealed subsequently that Martin Crowe, the captain, instigated the use of a bottle top, while team-mate Mark Greatbatch was in charge of "scratching duties." Rumour has it that the New Zealanders left a letter of warning in the team hotel for Des Haynes, who was soon to be leading the touring Westindies.

The same accusation was levelled during that series. Imran Khan replied, "It's a ridiculous charge, the Pakistan bowlers play in county games and have never been accused by any player or umpire. They played under the close scrutiny of John Hampshire and John Holder in the series against India [1989-90] and not a finger was raised. I am surprised at the allegations."

As it transpired the ball used by the Pakistanis in the first Test was shown to the Westindies' team manager, Lance Gibbs, by Arif Ali Abbasi, the secretary of the Pakistan Board at the time, along with the one used by the Westindies. Abbasi said "The manager agreed that the ball used by the Westindians was in a much worse condition than the one used by Pakistan."

The truth is that Wasim Akram and Waqar Younis are superb bowlers, whose Test records stand comparison with any in the game. Matthew Engel, the editor of *Wisden,* wrote of them in the 1993 edition as "two brilliant fast bowlers" and commissioned an article by Jack Bannister to consider their methods. He concluded in favour of the bowlers.

Since the allegations in 1992 studies at the University of Keele have looked into the phenomenon of reverse swing. In wind tunnel experiments it has shown that, contrary to earlier thinking about the optimum speed to swing the ball (about 70 mph), above a certain speed, 85 mph, different drag and air-resistance forces come into operation. Thus the very fastest bowlers who pitch the ball right up can make the ball dip in the last few feet of its flight before pitching so producing the staggering swinging yorkers that were the feature of the summer of 1992. England had no one of that pace, accuracy, stamina and with the correct technique to do the same. It was notable that Aqib Javed only swung the ball intermittently; he is well

Ramiz Raja and Waqar Younis discuss the condition of the ball

below the 85 mph required. Other bowlers from around the world have achieved reverse swing. Two fine exponents, Danny Morrison of New Zealand and Darren Gough, both have similar actions to Waqar.

It must be remembered too that in Pakistan the ball gets roughened up after a few overs and they have perfected the art of polishing the ball to preserve the shine on one side. With the whole team aware of it, no one touches the shiny side except to polish it. They have also experimented with wetting one side of the ball to make it heavier, and thus give it a bias, which produces reverse-swing. This is what Sarfraz Nawaz was particularly adept at doing. Imran Khan, too, was an expert at it, though he found in England that the ball did not roughen enough until later in the season when the pitches and outfields were harder.

There are tales of ball-tampering from the past, which have never been frowned upon, suggesting that it is an accepted practice. Jonathan Agnew has said that not too many bowlers, who knew how to gain some benefit, would not give it a go. There is a story about Imran (divulged in *Wasim and Waqar*) that an umpire once told him to stop picking the seam and he told the umpire he did not want to. Simon Hughes, the Middlesex and Durham seamer, said in an interview on Sky Sports at the time of the 1992 controversy that Imran had shown him a trick in the nets at Lord's in the early eighties; "by slightly raising the quarter seam he could swing the ball prodigiously," though Hughes stressed that he had no evidence of Imran doing this in a match. He also added that he thought the gentle scuffing of the ball (the most that has been going on) should not be illegal.

Surrey were fined for ball-tampering in two county games in 1991, in one of which Waqar played. Also when the issue came to a head, in the same programme on Sky Sports, Ian Greig (Surrey) and David Hughes (Lancashire) recounted a tale of how at the captains' meeting at the end of 1991 season, a ball that had been tampered with was being passed around. It came to Hughes and he quickly passed it on, but when it got to Greig he said, "Ah, this is one of ours, Waqar will have had that." Hughes remained sheepishly quite, thinking that it looked for all the world like one of his from Lancashire.

To deny completely using any of the fast bowlers tricks of the trade is dangerous and provocative. A lot of people have prevaricated; Mickey Stewart the departing England manager in 1992 said, "I know how they do it but I won't comment on whether it's fair or unfair," which is really quite a pointless remark. Charles Colville, the Sky cricket presenter, asked Ian Greig directly, Did Waqar ever do anything with the ball at Surrey," to which he answered, "I'd rather not say."

On the same programme John Lever, the former Essex and England bowler, readily admitted to it and went much further saying, "I don't think there's a bowler in the country who hasn't." He was amazed that Lamb had gone to the press calling him, "a silly boy" because it just made it look like sour grapes after England's defeat. Lever was adamant, "I don't think there's a story there, I really don't. Wasim and Waqar are the two best swing bowlers I've seen in a long, long time. I've sat in front of the television and thoroughly enjoyed it [their bowling] and if you want to stop that swing by saying it's illegal I think it's all wrong."

The rumours have encouraged photographers to snap away whenever Wasim and Waqar have the ball in hand and one or two photos tell a tale. Indeed New Zealand television crews were offered a reward equivalent to about £330 if they caught the Pakistanis at it in the Hamilton Test in New Zealand 1992/3. After the Atherton incident at Lord's, it became a new sport for the photographers to try and catch surreptitious scratching of the ball, and there was certainly as much evidence of the South African bowlers using "an unusual grip" on the ball as they walked back to their marks as there had been against the Pakistanis in 1992.

However a slight scuffing with the finger nail is hardly serious. Compare the antics in baseball, where players have been known to have a little bit of sand-paper concealed under their tongues with which to scuff the ball. It is all considered part of the gamesmanship.

Other bowlers have come on line admitting to picking the seam, or doing anything to redress the imbalance between bat and ball. David Lloyd, the former Lancashire and England batsman, one time umpire, commentator and now England coach, relates a story about his former team-mate Peter Lee, who twice took a hundred wickets in a season in the mid-70s. Lee was once caught in the act by an umpire, who himself had been a master of the art in his own playing days. "I would have been proud of that myself," he told Lee, "If you don't get seven wickets with it in that condition, I will have to report you!"

For swing bowlers the surface of the ball is more important. Up until 1980, the Law allowed rubbing the ball on the ground to roughen it, though this tactic was usually employed only by spinners to help them grip a shiny ball. There were suspicions in 1982 when Pakistan did not take the second new ball until the 118th over, because the old one was still swinging. Then the accusation was that they were putting something on the shiny side.

The way cricket balls are made these days seems to have changed their properties. They tend to be heavily lacquered and so only swing for a few overs to start with until the gloss has gone, but the lacquer remains. It can then take forty of fifty overs before this has come off and the bowler can really work on the shine on one side. Also, there is a difference between makes. During the 1996 series between England and Pakistan, the captains tossed for the choice of make to be used. Akram kept winning and kept choosing Reader's, which are more inclined to reverse-swing, rather than Duke's which swing more when new but less later.

The fad used to be more towards trying something to enhance the shine, using anything from brylcream, to lip salve to Vaseline, now roughing one side seems to be in vogue. There were those that thought Australia's Terry Alderman was up to something, because his lips were always covered with white zinc and he kept getting England players out. Many observers asked why Allan Donald had to cover his face with quite so much sun-block in 1994. John Lever was accused of putting Vaseline on the ball in India; as mentioned he has admitted that during his career he has tampered with the ball, but on that occasion at Delhi on his debut, he reckoned it was just a "rogue" ball which was unevenly weighted.

Peter Roebuck, writing in *The Cricketer* (December 1992), called all the talk "sanctimonious poppycock," suggesting that bowlers have always done it. Certainly most teams at whatever level could tell a tale or two about ball-tampering. There was a well-known club cricketer called Oliver

Babcock who used to enhance the seam to such an extent that no one would field at mid-off to him as the fielders feared being lacerated by the protruding seam!

As Wasim Akram showed in the World Cup, he can swing the ball all over the place, indeed he sometimes had trouble controlling it when it was new, bowling dozens of wides, yet as two white balls were used per innings, one from each end, the umpires could examine the ball at the end of each over, yet they found nothing wrong. Wasim is a great swing bowler; he bowled one delivery in the World Cup Final at Derek Pringle from around the wicket, the line of which started wide of off stump yet dipped almost at right angles to home in on leg-stump at yorker length. The inference that ball-tampering is the raison d'etre for Wasim's success is ridiculous. It is much more a mastery of the techniques required, a perfect synchronisation of finger, wrist and arm action. The ball that he dismissed Allan Lamb with in that same final curved in and then cut away off the seam. The ability to swing the ball has baffled scientists, so if Akram has found a a way to scar the ball to make it swing in and then cut away like that, good luck to him. Roebuck again defended Pakistan in *The Sunday Times*, saying that their sleight of hand was magic not trickery.

Geoff Boycott summed it up; "Pakistan would have bowled England out with an orange." Certainly Wasim and Waqar bowled plenty of jaffas.

There are two other bones of contention surrounding Pakistan's cricket, neither of them worth losing much sleep over. Firstly pitch doctoring - the practice of preparing a wicket to suit the home team's strengths. Providing the wicket is safe to play on, there is nothing wrong with this; it is only England who do not produce the wickets to suit themselves, probably because no one knows what they are best on. England tried to get a traditional English seamers wicket at Headingley against Australia in 1993 but got a wicket which was ideal for the opposition. That is the whole point of home advantage and is why so few sides win away from home. The wicket at Trent Bridge used to be tailor-made for Sir Richard Hadlee and Clive Rice's seam bowling and they helped Nottinghamshire win two Championships because of it. The groundsman who prepared the wicket in Barbados when Michael Holding bowled that famous opening over at Geoff Boycott in 1981 told me that the pitch was "like glass" for that match, the quickest he has prepared.

The other matter is age; because of the plethora of teenage Test cricketers in Pakistan there is some scepticism about a few of the 'youngest' records that have been chalked up. Certainly to think that

Mustaq Mohammad played Test cricket at fifteen and that Aqib Javed was twelve when he made his first-class debut does seem remarkable. However there is no reason why not; look at the age of Pakistan's squash players or on a broader scale the age some tennis players are beginning to play professionally. Their ages are feasible and accepted as such. Admittedly the Surrey physio had never seen anyone as strongly developed as Waqar Younis for his age when he first arrived at the Oval but this does not mean his purported age is wrong.

There are a couple of reasons given why the ages should be inaccurate. In the years preceding and just after Partition, the keeping of such records was a little haphazard, quite understandably at a time of such fundamental change, and many births were not registered immediately. More recently some parents have not registered births until their children attend school for the first time. Others may be registered as a year or two younger than they really are to help gain entry to a school, or perhaps with a view to helping a young boy get into the under-9 team when he is really ten. There is nothing heinous about this, it is just as peccadillo; most of us would pretend to be a little younger if we could get away with it. Indeed, the editor of *Wisden*, Matthew Engel, said as much after doubts were raised over the true age of Pakistan's Hassan Raza, who was thought to be the youngest-ever Test cricketer at 14 years and 227 days when he made his debut against Zimbabwe in October 1996: "Lying about your age has a long and honoured tradition." Pakistan has looked to address the problem by having all youth team players screened electronically at Imran Khan's Shaukhat Khanum Memorial Hospital. Queries were raised because Raza's x-ray before the under-15 World Cup showed him to be around 15 in June 1996. He may still have been the youngest but not by as much as originally stated. Six of the 22 World Cup probables were older than they said and did not go to the competition and others have been banned. Everyone knows the importance of getting established at an early age in Pakistani cricket, and this is why there are inaccuracies.

In any case it makes little real difference in adult cricket. Indeed it may prove to be a hindrance; Basit Ali, for instance, was not that highly rated when he got into the Pakistan under-19 side because it was rumoured that he was older than he claimed.

Umpiring

Allegations of poor umpiring around the world have been made ever more stridently during the last fifteen years. Increasing television and press coverage has put the umpires under more and more pressure as any mistakes are highlighted and their significance blown out of all proportion. Players who got a bad decision thirty years ago would only have had their team-mates to moan to and they probably would not have paid much attention but now, with television in most dressing rooms, they can scrutinise any decision for their own peace of mind. Consequently it does not take long for a sense of injustice to pervade a team's thinking.

Pakistan, above all other Test nations, has tried to address the problem of poor standards of umpiring. Most recently in domestic cricket, the PCB decided that, as of 1996/7, there would be a fixed age limit for their umpires and those receiving bad reports for two seasons would be taken off the panel. More importantly, in international cricket Imran Khan advocated neutral umpires from the day he became captain in 1982. Recognising that Pakistani umpiring, too, was not always up to standard he sought an improvement in his own country, though the problem is just as prevalent in other countries.

Before he became captain Imran was able to sympathise with opponents who got bad decisions. Des Haynes recounts (in *The Lion of Barbados*) that after the 1980/1 series Imran said to him, "Desi boy, you had a rough time." Khan wanted impartiality, preferably through neutrals, as this was the only way - in home Tests at least - that Pakistan would get the recognition they deserved as a Test playing nation.

Wasim Akram makes this clear in his biography (*Wasim and Waqar* by John Crace); "All Pakistan's umpires unofficially admit that Imran has been the one captain who has never asked them to help him out." On one occasion the umpires walked into the Pakistani dressing-room and asked him for instructions. "You do your job, and we'll do ours," was the reply."

Not surprisingly there have been far fewer complaints about the umpiring in Tests in Pakistan when Imran Khan has been in charge. He made his views known from the outset. In his first home series in charge, against Australia 1982/3, he upheld a request from the tourists for the umpires that were used in the first Test to be retained for the second. He did so despite a similar request on Pakistan's tour to Australia the previous season when their request for a change of umpires was refused.

So many of the controversies in modern Test cricket could have been avoided by using either neutral umpires or umpires whom both captains found acceptable. Pakistan's requests in the past not to have a particular umpire were totally reasonable, yet invariably these were ignored by bloody-minded administrators. Why risk an area of possible disharmony when there is such a simple solution?

Pakistan was the first to instigate changes; they started the experiment of using international umpires in the series with the Westindies in 1986/7, when V K Ramaswamy and P D Reporter stood in the 2nd and 3rd Tests, an experiment that Imran Khan felt worked very well. Pakistan won the first Test convincingly so it was not in their interests to get neutrals but was instigated for the benefit of the game. The Pakistan v India series in 1989/90 was the first to be umpired throughout by neutrals, England's John Hampshire and John Holder, and was incident free.

Dickie Bird joins Khizer Hyat on Test duty in Pakistan

The Board of Control for Cricket in Pakistan continued to use independent umpires intermittently though the goodwill they were showing by doing this was broken by Martin Crowe's egregiously undiplomatic remarks. When the New Zealand captain heard of the BCCP's plan to offer neutral umpires for the 1990/1 series, he was reputed to have said, "We don't know anything about the two guys appointed, but we believe they will be better than having two Pakistani umpires." He strongly denied the claim but the Pakistan Board strongly withdrew the offer.

Remarkably, considering the hostility that has existed between the two countries, Pakistan chose umpires from India to preside over them. The same could be said of the English umpires they have asked. It shows to what lengths they were prepared to go to avoid umpiring controversy.

Originally rejected on grounds of cost, neutral umpires should eventually do away with the necessity for costly match referees, who are respected as they are usually famous former Test players, but in reality the post is little more than a sinecure. Indeed, there is just a hint that referees are reluctant to use their full powers of fines and in particular suspensions in case they are struck off the referees' list. There is too much timidity amongst the games administrators.

England has generally been regarded as having the best umpires but in recent years standards have been slipping. This was highlighted by the two series in 1992 and 1993 - the last to be umpired by two home umpires - when the England captain, Mike Atherton, said he felt it was "not as good" as in the past.

There was one appalling decision made by umpire Ken Palmer at a crucial stage of the 1992 fourth Test at Headingley where the England captain, Graham Gooch, was clearly run out by about a yard, yet given not out. It appeared that Palmer was looking in the wrong direction. Photographs of the margin of error were duplicated and displayed on buses in Pakistan with the lampooning legend "English professional umpires - the best in the world."

It was an even worse decision than the one made by umpire Johnson to the benefit of John Dyson at a crucial moment in the 5th Test of the Ashes series of 1982/3. The umpire said he did not know whether the batsman was six inches in or six inches out - in fact he was about two foot out. There was grave suspicion of Johnson in the England camp after that, yet it seems that England cannot countenance a similar loss of faith in the umpiring from their opponents. Had such an incident occurred in Pakistan benefiting Javed Miandad, it would have been reported as cheating.

Indeed one Pakistani journalist said as much of the umpiring at Headingley, though more to echo the words of an English journalist who accused the Pakistanis for their conduct in the previous Test (for which he was sued). In fact the majority of English writers were on the Pakistani side in this instance. Mike Selvey writing in *The Guardian* gave the most accurate account, emphasising that "hardly any of the appeals were frivolous, and most of them marginal, but only five of 34 wickets were leg-before and even those were of an apparently arbitrary nature: those given seemed to have no more merit than many that were not."

Scyld Berry, in *The Independent on Sunday,* wrote thus: "There was a smell during the fourth Test which I had never detected before in a Test in England. There was something in addition to the inevitable, unconscious, bias which umpires have towards home teams and in particular home captains. Tight-lipped and highly formal, the umpiring at Headingley generated the impression that, come what may, judgments were not going to be delivered in Pakistan's favour until England were safely established in both their innings."

This somewhat blows out of the water the notion that English umpires go out of their way to accommodate touring sides. Once the breakthrough was made in the first innings of that match, Waqar Younis destroyed the middle-order as the last eight wickets fell for 28, with batsmen six to 11 mustering just two runs among them. By then though, England's lead was already a telling one.

It was a difficult Test to adjudicate. The bounce was uneven and often low, with much lateral movement, leading to plenty of appeals in a tight match, all of which were reasons cited in the press as excuses for umpiring errors in this game. Imagine the same scenario and then throw in 40,000 noisy, partisan spectators, 100 degree heat, the dust, much less experienced umpires who could have been dropped by the BCCP at any moment and you have got a typical Test in Pakistan. The difficulties of umpiring at the latter are many times more difficult than at Headingley.

I believe the the margin of error in the Gooch run out at Leeds prompted the early introduction of the third umpire in the pavilion using a TV monitor as tried in South Africa in 1992/3 against India and in the Ashes

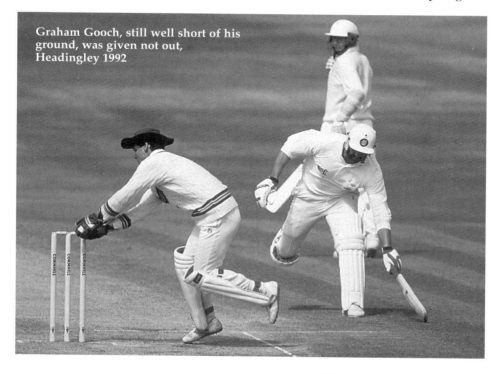

Graham Gooch, still well short of his ground, was given not out, Headingley 1992

series of 1993 to help adjudge matters of fact (i.e. run outs and stumpings) - certainly a large number of close decisions have been checked since. Although not yet universal, no one now should get away with the "benefit of the doubt" (perhaps batsmen will stop venturing from their creases!) though Steve Bucknor, one of the outstanding umpires of the World Cup, decided not to use the third umpire for a run out decision in the South Africa-India series (1992/3). Yet the batsman, Jonty Rhodes, who was given the benefit of an unnecessary doubt was shown to be just out. Other umpires have failed to call upon the technology, one even used it incorrectly, illuminating the wrong light and so bringing the unfortunate batsman's innings to a premature end. In South Africa in the 1995/6 series against England, the South African players pressed the umpire to check whether Graham Thorpe had made his ground after rumbles from the crowd, who had seen a replay, hinted that he was out. He was, and that decision changed the course of the Cape Town Test. In view of the Test at Headingley in 1992, adjudging lbws and bat-pad catches as well must have been considered. With super slow-mo replays now available, the time may come sooner rather than later.

The 1992 England-Pakistan series may also have prompted the introduction of neutrals. At last, in the autumn of 1993, the International Cricket Council opted for one home umpire and one independent umpire to become the norm where possible for officiating at all Tests. This was tried out in the 1992/3 series between the Westindies and Pakistan - again at Pakistan's instigation. Ironically there were a record number of lbws in the 1st Test (17) but nobody complained as Bird and Bucknor are well respected. However in the next Test Pakistan were on the receiving end of a couple of poor lbw decisions. Dickie Bird gave Inzamam-ul-Haq out though he looked to be outside the line of off-stump (and well forward), but the one by the Westindian umpire Lloyd Barker against Asif Mujtaba, to Winston Benjamin bowling around the wicket, was described by *Wisden Cricket Monthly* as "quite outrageous". Pakistan's team manager on that tour, Khalid Mahmood, accused the home umpires of cheating calling some of the decisions "atrocious." Why allow the opportunity for such animosity which two neutrals would have removed? Barker allegedly apologised to Mujtaba later for making "a rank bad decision" against him, though even such apologies are frowned upon; Umpire Meyer did likewise after giving a decision against Viv Richards at Lord's in 1984, and was advised to keep such matters to himself.

There is as much media pressure now on umpires as there is on players and they will always be the easiest scapegoats for players mistakes from club to Test level. Good umpires make mistakes just as

players do - there is rarely conscious bias. Gone are the days, though, of reserved appealing. Now, as often as not, appeals seem orchestrated and are invariably histrionic. All countries are at it, Pakistan included. All I can say in Pakistan's defence is that much of the appealing does seem to stem from a total enthusiasm for the game; in street, school or club cricket everyone appeals, whether they are in the slips, down at third man or stood at square leg. It is not entirely a direct ploy to put pressure on the umpires. Many of the players are young and it takes a while for them to settle down - admittedly one or two never quite do - but one should not condemn the passion with which they play the game as the reverse is the staid approach that is festering in county cricket. Waqar Younis and Mustaq Ahmed are both a fine sight in full voice, beseeching the umpire for a decision in the affirmative.

You cannot blame the umpires when players put pressure on them with continual appeals and by no longer walking if they get an edge if one occasionally gets a bad decision. Geoff Boycott, commentating on television about an lbw decision when a batsman indicated to the umpire that he thought he had hit the ball, said "Don't read anything into that, its an old pro's trick we used to use all the time." Australians are known not to walk even if the edge is blatant. For instance in South Africa's opening game of the 1992 World Cup, Allan Donald's first ball found the edge of Geoff Marsh's bat, deflecting high and wide to the wicket-keeper's right, yet the batsman did not walk and amazingly umpire Aldridge did not give him out.

Many allegations have been levelled at Javed Miandad receiving an unrealistic benefit of the doubt from umpires in Pakistan and certainly the facts at first glance seem to bear this out. His first lbw in a home Test came after more than ten years of international cricket when he was trapped in front by Ravi Ratnayeke of Sri Lanka in 1985/6 and indeed fell lbw in the next Test as well.

To set the record straight Miandad as a player (as distinct from as captain) had never been given out lbw in a Test by a Pakistani umpire until the series with Zimbabwe in 1993/4 when he was dismissed twice in that manner. He has only been lbw on one other occasion and that was at the hands of a neutral in 1989/90 against India when Manoj Prabhakar won the decision. Contrary to popular opinion, however, as captain his figures are quite normal, with five lbws in 29 completed innings in Pakistan representing 17.2 per cent of his dismissals. This is marginally below his overall figure in Tests, 19.6 per cent (33 lbws in 168 dismissals) and not much below the comparison with overseas Tests, 23.9 per cent (23 in 96 innings). Yet it is generally believed that Miandad as captain would never be lbw. Even his overall percentage at home, 8.8 per cent, is not totally disproportionate for the best player on his own pitches in the world.

Compare Miandad's figures with those for Graham Gooch since he came back into the England side in 1985 after his ban for going to South Africa. In the 37 innings he had at home as a player (1985-89) he was lbw 14 times (37.8%), yet in 39 innings as captain of England (1988-93), he was given out only seven times lbw (17.9%). No one has drawn attention to this disparity.

Anyway, Miandad was on the receiving end of one of the worst lbws I have seen when he was given out in a one-day match at the Sydney Cricket Ground. On a slow pitch that had been saturated by torrential rain, Javed Miandad was batting at least two feet out of his crease. He moved further down as he played forward to Terry Alderman, the ball striking him on the front pad. He was amazed to be given out and, as he returned to the pavilion, turned round to watch the action replay on the big screen at the Sydney Cricket Ground and pointed at it to the umpire in disbelief.

Umpires all around the world tend to benefit the home captain. Their livelihood is often dependent on the captain's report. A BBC documentary, "The men in white coats," screened in August 1993 showed that English county captains are given out [lbw] 25 per cent less often than other players and this is no happy coincidence. It is the captains who mark the umpires' cards at the end of the match.

Originally umpires were employed by the amateurs who ran the game. The famous English umpire Frank Chester, standing in his first first-class game, was warned by his colleague after he had given both the captains out, that his career was likely to be a short one if he carried on like that. Some years later in 1953, the Australians took exception to his umpiring which had become somewhat cantankerous. At first their objection to his standing in the final Test was refused but Lindsay Hassett, the touring captain, dug his heels in and Chester was replaced though officially he was "indisposed."

When a side loses confidence in an umpire like that it is perfectly reasonable to ask for a change yet historically this has rarely been done. In the build up to the Faisalabad fracas such requests had been turned down, allowing tensions to simmer and eventually boil over. Pakistan had not been happy with the umpiring of Ken Palmer or David Constant during the 1982 series in England. Palmer gave what Imran Khan described as "one of the poorer decisions in Test cricket" when he upheld an lbw appeal against Mudassar Nazar at Edgbaston and Constant, who they felt did not live up to his name, made what on replay looked like a major error at a crucial stage in the final Test when he adjudged Sikander Bakht caught behind though there appeared to be a lot of daylight between bat and ball.

Because of their good track record and professional status, coupled with the fact that most of them have played first-class cricket, English umpiring has a fine reputation. The "best in the world" tag is largely accurate, but as the 1987 Pakistan manager, Haseeb Ahsan, pointed out they cannot all be the best. Nevertheless it has meant that the Test and County Cricket Board has adopted the moral high ground. Whereas England expects the umpires they choose when they go on tour, sides touring England have had their objections to certain umpires refused dismissively without thought. On occasions recently some of the appointments by the TCCB have seemed almost provocative.

The Pakistan Board made a perfectly reasonable request before the start of the 1987 series for umpire Constant to be chosen in only one Test, if at all. (Apparently the Indian touring side had objected to his appointment the year before as well). The TCCB poured oil on the flames by leaking the objection to the press. The cooperative and by all accounts charming Ahsan - a man who used to whistle merrily as he came up to bowl - confirmed that he had not been happy with the appointments and was attacked mercilessly in the press for saying so. To make matters worse Constant and Palmer were the only umpires to get two Tests that summer. It was these events that led to Faisalabad. Ahsan was in charge again that winter and there was no way he was going to do England any favours.

Its amazing that the TCCB did not learn the lesson; in 1992 they used eight umpires, and inevitably mistakes were made, especially in that crucial fourth Test at Headingley. Most international captains probably could not name eight umpires in the world that they would be happy with. However there was a wide enough choice to have a panel exclusively of umpires that Pakistan trusted. These included John Holder and John Hampshire, who had umpired the Pakistan v India series, Dickie Bird, the most experienced umpire in the world, who stood in the 1987 World Cup, and David Shepherd who had earned a good reputation for himself in the previous two World Cups. Instead Roy Palmer (Ken's brother) stood in the third Test, which produced the row with Aqib Javed, and Ken Palmer in the fourth in another controversial match.

It appears, however, that the home side can object to an umpire but not visiting teams. For instance John Holder, one of England's best umpires, was struck off the Test panel, allegedly because Holder objected to the England side tampering with the ball in the final Test at the Oval against the Westindies in 1991. The previous summer, Holder had given Graham Gooch out caught behind during the Old Trafford Test against India, a decision to which the outgoing batsmen showed obvious disgruntlement.

As the stakes have increased some of the charm

has gone out of the game. Errors of umpiring are no longer accepted with good grace. On MCC's first tour to Pakistan (1951/2) it was noted in *Wisden*, in a most matter of fact way, that the tourists did not think much of the umpiring during the final "Test". It recorded, "MCC were still below their best, but it must be said that they were very surprised at some of the umpiring decisions in the match, not one of the thirty lbw appeals being granted in their favour." However Pakistan only received two themselves, Nigel Howard being lbw to Khan Mohammad in each innings. If there was a hint of bias towards the home side it seemed to be in a good cause, as that victory helped secure Pakistan Test status! (Compare Headingley 1992; 34 appeals and five decisions in the affirmative).

On the next tour in 1955/6, during the third unofficial Test, MCC suffered four lbws against them on the first day and made some undiplomatic remarks about the umpiring. After the third day's play the MCC players, led by Donald Carr, took it upon themselves to teach one of the umpires, Idris Begh, a lesson - again assuming that they were right - by dowsing him with a bucket of cold water. It was a schoolboy-type prank but a little more menacing when perpetrated by several grown men. The President of the MCC, Lord Alexander of Tunis, offered to cancel the tour and pay Pakistan compensation for loss of revenue. The press had a field-day with the story though it was quickly papered over. Certainly it soured relations between the two sides and though the tour continued, by the last match Imtiaz Ahmed felt that the MCC players were abusing the umpires openly on the field. Imran feels it is something that had gone on unreported since, and it was only the Gatting-Rana incident that subsequently highlighted the problem. "People don't know what happened in our country, with touring teams openly abusing our umpires," he said.

Until recently, at least, teams have been more accepting of poor decisions. For instance Mike Brearley, the England captain on the tour to Pakistan in 1977/8, could recount in good humour, if slightly aggrievedly, that one of the umpires at Lahore sent him a note at the end of the day's play explaining his decision to give Brearley out "caught" off his pad-strap, after a big appeal had been echoed by the 40,000 voices in the crowd. His charmingly innocent and sincere apology read that he was "very sorry about his decision, but he felt his arm going up and couldn't stop it".

In the previous Test, at Hyderabad, the umpire actually asked Brearley for advice saying he had only done a handful of first-class games and none in the last six months. Geoff Boycott had the good sense to call him "sir" every time he checked his guard, and apparently got away with about three lbws and two nicks behind.

Pakistan has made the effort to improve matters. Occasionally there has been a bit of tit for tat in the umpires chosen but only in response to the non-cooperation of other countries. Some of the umpiring has been bad but has there really been anything worse than the New Zealanders umpiring against the Westindies in 1980/1, or against Pakistan in 1988/9, or the Sri Lankans against Pakistan in 1985/6? Individual decisions are usually what are highlighted; each country can offer some bloomers, which have seemed, biased, bad or incompetent: Johnson's run out decision benefiting John Dyson; Aldridge benefiting Marsh; Ken Palmer's in favour of Gooch; Bucknor's in favour of Jonty Rhodes. There are those that have gone against the batsman: Richards suffering at the hand of Meyer; Sikander Bakht to Constant; Mudassar Nazar to Ken Palmer; Miandad to Evans; Mujtaba to Barker.

Some appointments have been totally insensitive, choosing umpires specifically objected to. Even the refereeing selections have been badly handled with some totally insensitive choices. Donald Carr was appointed for the Sri Lanka series against Pakistan 1991/2 while, Tom Graveney who had said after the Faisalabad incident that "Pakistan have been cheating us for 37 years," was originally picked for the 1992/3 tour to the Westindies. He was later replaced, after obvious objections, by Raman Subba Row, who in fact played a significant mediating role after Faisalabad.

One can but wait to see what the outcome of the independent umpires experiment is but the early examples have proved a success. They are not the panacea for all of cricket's ills, and some of the umpiring has been of a poor standard, but at least the feeling of bias has gone.

Imran Khan was delighted when they came in. "It was long overdue, but I'm so pleased. I think you'll find all sorts of problems in cricket being solved as a result of it." Umpires should not, on the whole, be blamed for mistakes, after all they are only judging upon errors made by the cricketers themselves. The players and media put them under so much pressure, but if "neutral" or "international" umpires are used from now on (as in most other sports), this will remove the ill-feeling that has crept into the game, and there is no reason why cricket cannot be revered once more as the paragon of sporting conduct and fair play.

And so to Faisalabad

The incident between England captain Mike Gatting and Pakistani umpire Shakoor Rana is probably the most notorious episode in cricket history. It reflects badly on both English and Pakistani cricket, causing as much controversy as anything since the "Bodyline" series of 1932/3.

However, it was an accident waiting to happen given the increasingly poor relations between the two sides, that got off on the wrong foot with MCC's first tour in 1951/2, through the showering of Idris Begh in 1955/6, to the non-co-operation of the Test and County Cricket Board to meet Pakistan's umpiring requests a few months before.

The controversy must also be put in context. The 1987/8 series was ill-advised coming just after the highs and lows of the World Cup, which left England as beaten finalists, and the whole of Pakistan in virtual mourning after they lost in the semi-final to Australia. The nation was crying out for a morale boosting victory. The players were still on edge after that hectic competition played in front of packed crowds, yet for the Tests the fans stayed away and the series started in front of just 200 people in the 50,000 capacity stadium at Lahore.

The Board of Control for Cricket in Pakistan reverted to using home umpires after the experiment with independent umpires against the Westindies, and as such was Pakistan's first series using BCCP umpires since the debacle in Sri Lanka 1985/6, where the umpires seemed to be part of a conspiracy. Pakistan had benefited from only one lbw compared to Sri Lanka's 11 in the series, while Arjuna Ranatunga apparently had about three edges to the 'keeper not given during his hundred in the 2nd Test. The Pakistan team was so upset that they almost came home early and only stayed at the request of President Zia-ul-Haq.

It did not help that Javed Miandad was back in charge for the series with England in place of Imran Khan, who had retired temporarily. It meant it pitted

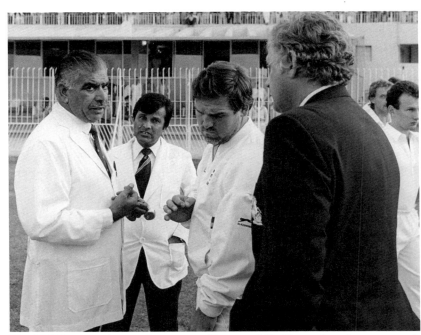

The 1987 Test reaches an impasse as Rana and Gatting refuse to compromise

two aggressive captains against each other; Gatting and Miandad had already had an altercation in the World Cup match when Miandad, who was lingering after being given out lbw (by a neutral umpire Tony Crafter), took exception to Gatting's invitation to leave. Miandad's RSVP included some reasonably strong vernacular and a punch aimed (but not thrown) at Gatting.

There were three pointless one-dayers between the World Cup and the Tests which again produced niggles. England appealed successfully against Ramiz Raja for "obstructing the field," when he blocked the throw while completing a second run that would have taken him to his hundred off the last ball of the game. The game was safe and no harm would have been done had the fielders allowed Ramiz a well deserved century. In the game before Salim Yousuf had his thumb dislocated in the first over of the game. Gatting refused a specialist substitute, yet he had benefited only the year before from two in one match thanks to the magnanimity of New Zealand's captain, Jeremy Coney, who allowed first Bob Taylor then Bobby Parks to keep-wicket in place of the injured Bruce French. Gatting was not trying very hard to endear himself to the opposition.

The umpiring, unquestionably, was poor in the first Test; whether it was biased is a matter of conjecture. Certainly matters were not helped by the way Pakistan was treated in England that summer and it was even reported in Pakistan that "puppet" umpires were being used, while three respected Pakistani umpires from the World Cup sat on the sidelines. One of the umpires appointed for the first Test, Shakeel Khan, stood despite England's objections to him. Following the refusal of Pakistan's requests concerning Constant and Palmer this was understandable, if a little inflammatory.

England felt they got several bad decisions against them in the first innings, while Pakistan got the benefit of the doubt, but matters came to a head in the second innings when Chris Broad was adjudged caught behind by Shakeel Khan. He stood his ground for over a minute, half in protest half in disbelief, and had to be ushered from the crease by the non-striking batsman, Graham Gooch. His delay was unjustifiable, however convinced, as he was, that he did not hit the ball. He was "severely reprimanded" by the tour manager, Peter Lush, whose sympathies were obviously with Broad as he criticised the umpiring at the same time, calling for neutrals, as had been used in the World Cup. Gatting too was strong in his criticism, given leave to air his grievances: "We roughly knew what to expect but never imagined it would be quite so blatant. They were desperate to win a Test match, but if I was them I wouldn't be too happy about the way they did it." England thought that as many as nine decisions went against their batsmen.

None of the committee cared to mention England's poor batting which *Wisden* described as "woefully sub-standard," at the mercy of Abdul Qadir on a pitch offering generous assistance to the spinners. However distraught Broad was he should have departed more smartly. Had, for instance, Sikander Bakht delayed as long when he was given out at Edgbaston in 1982, when he received a similarly bad decision, he would have been hounded by the press, and the incident blown up. Broad was known for having a short fuse - indeed he smashed down the stumps after being dismissed just two months later in Australia - and the Pakistan Board felt that the reprimand was totally inadequate.

The England management stayed in Lahore after the Test in order to try and learn who would be umpiring in the next Test. However their request for a private disclosure was ignored, and they discovered the appointments by reading about them in the local press.

The choice of Shakoor Rana may well have been opposed; he had driven the 1984/5 touring New Zealanders to distraction. Jeremy Coney lead his team from the field in the final Test after Rana turned down an appeal for caught behind against Javed Miandad. On the lighter side he once delayed a Test match because he had forgotten his coat; Gatting could empathise about something like that, as he once turned up late for a tour match after over-sleeping.

In Faisalabad, the general atmosphere at first was better, though there was one heated moment when a bat-pad appeal by Bill Athey against Ijaz Ahmed was turned down; Gatting at slip muttered, "One rule for one and one rule for another," which unfortunately was picked up by the pitch microphone, which had been turned full on, and broadcast across Pakistan. The game was three balls away from getting through the second day without further controversy. Gatting, with a few minutes left to play, had been moving the field to try and prevent a single. He waved at the fine leg fielder, David Capel, to stop him coming up any further. Video does not determine whether he had informed the batsman, Salim Malik, but Gatting insists he did. Anyway he was still signalling to the fielder as the bowler was coming in to bowl, presumably not to gain any surreptitious advantage, but because he was not quite where he wanted him to be. Rana construed this as sharp practice on Gatting's part and called a halt to proceedings declaring that it was "unfair play." Gatting asked what was and Rana replied, "You're waving your hand - that's cheating. You're cheating." Both expressed their opinion on the matter vehemently. Then Rana, provoked or unprovoked - it is uncertain - let forth a blast of strong language, which prompted more finger pointing and verbal exchanges.

Rana should have had a few quiet words after the ball was bowled, but instead was confrontational in his rebuke of Gatting. To call the touring captain a cheat was unprecedented. Rana's action was not one of a neutral administrator trying to rule out unfair play (indeed he was portrayed mischievously in the English press wearing a Pakistan cap). He should have said something like "you must not move your fielders without informing the batsman" - end of comment - but was much more accusatory in his words. Both camps were so on edge after the first Test that any comment could have been misconstrued.

Gatting, for his part, should have just backed down but the exchange became a heated one, with each cursing the other. It was not beyond the realms of possibility that the aggressive finger pointing and arguing could have lead to blows being exchanged.

One of England's senior players should have lead Gatting away immediately. Both he and Rana acted like spoilt children, with neither backing down; Gatting was at breaking point after a Test and a half of suspicion of the umpiring and Rana, for his part, was merely reacting to what he saw as sharp practice and as the umpire, was in the right. However it is doubtful whether he would have confronted Miandad in similar fashion for a similar action.

The moment seemed to have past but the next morning Rana refused to umpire unless he received an apology. He had done this before at Faisalabad in 1978 when the Indian captain Sunil Gavaskar used abusive language after Rana warned Mohinder Amarnath for following through onto the danger area of the pitch. That was resolved early the next morning. Similarly Arthur Fagg requested an apology from Westindies' captain Rohan Kanhai, who showed continued dissent after Fagg turned down an appeal at Edgbaston in 1973, and did not come out at the start of the next day though he did return after only one over.

However on this occasion what followed was deadlock. The whole of the third day was lost while a compromise solution was sought, both parties refusing to give an inch. By mid-afternoon it appeared a mutual apology would allow the game to restart, but Rana changed his mind, rumour has it at Javed's recommendation, and stayed in his hotel room. Javed was quizzed on his influence by an English journalist but shrugged his shoulders, smirked and said he did not understand the question. Rana's superiors at Lahore Railways sent him a telegram telling him not to continue until he received an apology from Gatting.

At this new crisis point, finding a solution was not helped by the elusiveness of various Pakistani officials. The BCCP secretary, Ijaz Butt, disappeared in mid-afternoon to go to Lahore and in the end Peter Lush had to undertake the journey that evening himself to try and discuss the matter with the Board's President.

Just as he was leaving, there was a tap on the window of his car. There was Javed asking for a lift to Lahore in perfect English. The journey must have seemed somewhat surreal as the two protagonists exchanged polite conversation for the next two-and-a-half hours.

Having dropped Javed off, Lush reached Lt-General Safdar Butt's house only to find that he was out to dinner and had to stay overnight in Lahore in order to meet Safdar and Ijaz Butt, and Haseeb Ahsan the next day (the rest day in the Test). Meanwhile it was decided by the TCCB in London that if no solution could be struck then Gatting should be told to apologise to allow the game to restart. The statement read thus:

"It was unanimously agreed that the current Test match in Faisalabad should restart today after the rest day. The Board manager in Pakistan, Peter Lush, was advised of this decision immediately and asked to take whatever action was necessary to implement it. In reaching their decision the members of the Board recognised the extremely difficult circumstances of the tour and the inevitable frustration for players arising from those circumstances, but they believe it to be in the long-term interests of the game as a whole for the match to be completed. The Board will be issuing a statement on the tour when it is finished, but in the meantime the chairman and chief executive will be going to Karachi for the final Test next week."

In Faisalabad, the team manager was put in an invidious position as the voice of both the team and of the TCCB and issued a statement of his own:

"The Test and County Cricket Board has instructed me as manager of the England team to do everything possible to ensure that this Test match continues today and that we honour our obligations to complete the tour of Pakistan. We have tried to resolve amicably the differences between Mike Gatting and umpire Shakoor Rana following their heated exchange of words which took place on the second day. We all hoped this could have been achieved in private and with a handshake. Umpire Shakoor Rana has stated he would continue to officiate in this match if he received a written apology from Mike Gatting. The umpire has made it clear he will not apologise for the remarks he made to the England captain. In the wider interests of the game Mike Gatting has been instructed by the Board to write an apology to Shakoor Rana, and this he has now done."

That note was somewhat curt and written on a scrappy piece of paper, but allowed the match to continue on the fourth day. It read; "Dear Shakoor Rana, I apologise for the bad language used during the 2nd day of the Test match at Fisalabad (*sic*). Mike Gatting, 11th Dec 1987."

The England players in turn issued a statement; they had determined that they would not continue if presented with such an ultimatum.

"The England players deplore the fact that it was not possible to effect a compromise solution between Mike Gatting and umpire Shakoor Rana. We would have expected the governing bodies of both countries to use their influence and authority to resolve the problem.

"What is beyond dispute is that the umpire was the first to use foul and abusive language to the England captain. This was clearly heard by England players close to the incident. Mike Gatting was ready to apologise two days ago for his response, provided the umpire would do the same.

"We also wish to register a unanimous protest that the TCCB should consider it necessary to issue instructions through our manager, Peter Lush, to order the captain to make an unconditional apology to the umpire. By doing so, the captain, in the "wider interests of the game," felt he was forced to act against his own free will."

There were also some outside considerations to re-starting the match; concern was being shown by the Foreign Office in London, and most of the guaranteed tour purse had yet to be paid. The chairman and chief executive of the TCCB, Raman Subba Row and Alan Smith respectively, flew to Karachi to settle the situation.

With Gatting ready to resign and the England team still fuming, Subba Row examined the evidence and was satisfied that Rana, unjustifiably, had started the swearing and had called Gatting a cheat. The chairman backed the players to the tune of £1,000 each by way of a "hardship bonus" which was meant to be kept a secret.

On the whole, the incident was reported parochially. However, Simon Barnes, writing in *The Times*, wrote thus, "By open dissent, and by implicit support of open dissent from captain and tour management, England abandoned the principles of fair play they claimed they were defending. In effect, they said that if a Pakistani refuses to walk, he is a cheat; when an Englishman refuses to walk, it is because the umpire is a cheat. In the immortal words of Mike Gatting: 'One rule for them, one for us,' while *The Nation* admitted, "The standard of umpiring witnessed in the current series is deplorable." Clive Lloyd, the former Westindies captain who lives in England, was appalled, "I do not think British sport could sink any lower. How I bitterly regret what Mike Gatting has done." An editorial in *The Guardian* was also despondent at Gatting's actions, "National prestige, cultural tradition, class and racial prejudices play their irrepressible parts. They affect this Test match as they have affected every match between black and white cricketers, and perhaps also every match involving either the world's only Islamic cricketing nation or the representatives of the most snobbish and hypocritical sports administration."

Gatting, in fact, had received a conciliatory note from Rana during the third Test but chose to keep it to himself as it did not include a direct apology. The whole episode was a shameful chapter in cricket's history. Gatting for his part has said, on his biographical video, *Gatt*, that he should not have acted the way he did, taking on Rana on the pitch, and that he probably should have been sent home for doing so. Though he did not lose the England captaincy then, he was sacked soon after for a minor misdemeanour. The BCCP did not choose Shakoor Rana to officiate in a Test match again until the 3rd Test against Sri Lanka in 1991/2.

The ramifications continued into the next series with Australia, who thought they would get a positive backlash. However they were so suspicious that trouble flared almost immediately.

The next series with England had its problems, with Aqib Javed at Old Trafford and with umpiring mistakes at Headingley, as well as the ball-tampering allegations against Wasim Akram and Waqar Younis which the press often concentrated on rather than some excellent cricket in a tight series. Although Asif Iqbal said after the third Test that you could be sure that Pakistan would not get a "hardship bonus", in fact, with the growing pressure in the series, the Board did award an extra payment with a certain amount of irony, to echo and parody that made in 1987/8 to England by the TCCB. The BCCP treasurer, Arif Abbasi, awarded the bonus "because of the hardship they [the players] have had to withstand and because they were able to withstand the pressures of the British tabloid press."

The cricket relations between England and Pakistan have been sour and it seemed unlikely that England would tour Pakistan for some time. Certainly, Imran Khan could not envisage a tour being arranged but Arif Abbasi, when he became PCB Chief Executive, did offer an invitation to the TCCB to tour saying that, with the new set up in Pakistan, it was time to forgive and forget. The England A team had a happy tour there in 1995/6 and the build up to the 1996 tour to England was much more conciliatory, suggesting relations are on the mend.

The whole Faisalabad affair was an embarrassment to both sides, though the way it was presented in the press in the respective countries portrayed two very different stories. In truth, the actions of both Gatting and Rana were appalling, though really were the manifestation of the lingering animosity between the countries. Hopefully, a couple of friendly series could bury the hatchet for good. After 1996, they were half way there.

A place to play

Pakistan's Test match grounds

Pakistan played 103 Test matches at home between 1952 and December 1995, winning 36 of them, losing only ten and drawing the remaining 57. The Tests have been spread around 15 grounds in 11 centres, with Karachi and Lahore dominating, as you would expect, hosting 62 Tests between them. Three of the other centres - Bahawalpur, Multan and Gujranwala - have had only one Test each, while Peshawar has staged only two and more than forty years apart. Many of the grounds benefited from major investment prior to the 1996 World Cup, seeing a marked improvement in facilities all round.

Bahawalpur has not been used since Pakistan's first home series, against India at the beginning of 1955. **The Dring (now Bahawal) Stadium** belonged to the Amir of Bahawalpur, and has a princely splendour to it, remaining largely as then, tree-lined and with temporary stands. Bahawalpur won the first domestic tournament (the Quaid-e-Azam in 1953/4 and once again in 1957/8. However as the Amir's influence declined so did the cricket in this region, though first-class cricket is still played there. Pakistan's second-ever Test was played at the stadium in January 1955 against India, producing a very slow-scoring draw.

The Gymkhana (Services Club) Ground, Peshawar, Pakistan's fourth Test venue, offers a neat, compact, ground a cricket ball's throw from the Khyber Pass. Its first first-class match was in November 1949, between the North-West Frontier Province Governor's XI and the touring Commonwealth team. Its only Test saw Pakistan draw with India in 1954/5. It has since been superseded by a new stadium, the Arbab Niaz Stadium, which was used for a one-day international against

England in 1987/8, and hosted its first Test match in September 1995 - cricket's 75th Test venue - against Sri Lanka. That match was Ramiz Raja's first in charge and was won by an innings.

The last Test against the Westindies in 1980/1 is the only one to date to be played at the **Ibn-e-Qasim Bagh Stadium,** Multan. It was marred by an ugly incident when the Westindian fast bowler Sylvester Clarke, who was being pelted with oranges, lobbed a brick boundary marker into the crowd, scoring a direct hit on the president of a local students' union, which sparked a minor riot. The start of the game had been delayed when the umpire, Shakoor Rana, arrived at the ground only to discover that he had forgotten his umpires' coat, and the last two days were largely washed out by torrential rain.

The use of the **Municipal Stadium**, Gujranwala, for the 1991/2 Test against Sri Lanka, was part of an attempt to bring Test cricket to new regions. It is an industrial town 40 miles north of Lahore but its only match to date was ruined by bad weather, with only 36 overs being bowled in the match. It became the 65th Test match venue across the world.

The Pindi Club Ground, Rawalpindi, witnessed Pakistan's first home Test win for six years, when Hanif Mohammad's side recorded an innings victory over New Zealand in the first Test there in

March 1965. It is steeped in colonial history. Indeed, Queen Victoria's grandson, Christian Victor, played a game there scoring a double-hundred, the first such score in what was to become Pakistan.

The ground is now known as the Pindi Cricket Stadium and is part of a fine multi-sport complex, much favoured by the military. It was used for Pakistan's 1987 World Cup match against England, which the home team won, and although it is a little too small really to play Test cricket there, it was used for the second Tests against Zimbabwe in 1993/4, and Australia in 1994/5. In the latter, Salim Malik scored a superb double hundred to earn a draw after Pakistan had been forced to follow-on for only the second time in a home Test.

Uniquely, the same location is considered to both the 43rd ground used for Test match cricket and the 71st. It is a popular venue for touring sides as they are usually well entertained by their country's embassy in nearby Islamabad.

The Jinnah Stadium, Sialkot, has been used four times since the first Test there in October 1985

against Sri Lanka, which Pakistan won by eight wickets. Traditionally it is one of the faster wickets in Pakistan and it seemed likely that it would be used more often to suit the likes of Wasim Akram and Waqar Younis. However, the pitch used for the match against Sri Lanka in September 1995, had been re-laid and was slow and low. The selectors completely misread it, picking four fast bowlers, and Pakistan lost by 144 runs and in so doing lost their first home series for 15 years. Sialkot is the home town of Zaheer Abbas, and is famous for the production of sports equipment.

Hyderabad is 120 miles north of Karachi across the Sind desert. Its ground, **the Niaz Stadium**, first hosted a Test in March 1973, against England, but has not been used since staging the 1,000th Test in cricket history (its fifth) in November 1984 against New Zealand. Two years earlier Javed Miandad and Mudassar Nazar shared a record partnership there, putting on 451 for third wicket against India.

Dacca was the site of Pakistan's first ever Test, against India in January 1955, but since 1971, when East and West Pakistan became two independent states, it has been part of Bangladesh. That year the stadium witnessed cricket, riots, killings, rallies and finally celebrations of independence.

The Dacca Stadium saw the last of its seven Test matches against New Zealand in November 1969. The previous Test there against England earlier in the year was policed by student leaders, and passed without incident. Its newly laid grass wicket could not be used as intended for Australia's match there, in November 1959, because of heavy overnight rain so the old matting wicket had to be used again.

The National Stadium in Karachi is like no

other ground in the world as, despite being Pakistan's most used Test venue with 31 Tests, the home side has never lost there. In this respect it surpasses even the Kensington Oval in Bridgetown, Barbados, where Westindies were invincible between 1935 and 1994, until England ended a 29-match unbeaten run. Consequently the decision to use the Defence Stadium instead, in uptown Karachi, to stage the inaugural Test against Zimbabwe in December 1993 caused quite some controversy. It was the first time it had hosted a Test, which was won by 131 runs, to maintain the city's unbeaten record.

The National Stadium, though, is Pakistan's premier venue. Located ten miles outside Karachi on the fringes of the Sind desert, it produced 15 of Pakistan's first 36 wins at home. The last of those was the epic one-wicket win over Australia in 1994/5 - the closest the venue has come to witnessing defeat.

Coir-matting wickets were used there until England's tour of 1961/2, when sufficient irrigation became possible to turn to grass. Generally the wickets are little more than baked mud and can be terribly low and slow. The arid climate can cause the problem of dust storms, which held up play during the 1972/3 Test against England.

The ground is in a huge concrete bowl, oval in shape, whose largely uncovered terraces are broken by the occasional "shamianas" that are similar to the canopy roof covering the Mound Stand at Lord's.

It has seen its fair share of crowd disturbances, with the match against England in 1968/9 having to be abandoned before even the first innings of the match had been completed, while Karachi, as the domicile of the deposed Bhutto family staged angry protests against General Zia-ul-Haq. The fourth day's play of the 1982/3 Test v India had to be abandoned in mid-afternoon when protesters ran onto the ground and tried to damage the pitch.

Another ruckus erupted after a crowd invasion to celebrate Wasim Raja completing his hundred against the Westindies in March 1975, causing two-and-a-half hours to be lost.

Karachi's original ground, **the Gymkhana**, first staged first-class cricket in 1926/7 when a combined side of Parsis and Muslims played the MCC. The first "international" was also played there when the first representative side for Pakistan played the Westindies in November 1948. However it was never given a Test match.

The first three matches at Lahore were played on matting wickets at **Lawrence Gardens** named after the Raj ruler of Punjab, John Lawrence. It is a quintessentially English-looking ground, tree-lined and reminiscent of the Parks at Oxford University. It is situated just off the famous Mall. It was later renamed the **Bagh-i-Jinnah** (after the founder of Pakistan), meaning "Jinnah's gardens." The last Test there was against the Westindies in March 1959 and resulted in Pakistan's first defeat on home soil. However, the ground is still used regularly for club cricket and for the occasional first-class match.

The Board of Control for Cricket in Pakistan, which was based in Lahore, felt they should have a new stadium. Thus the **Lahore Stadium** was built, another massive concrete bowl capable of holding some 50,000 people. A perfect circle in shape it has one of the largest playing areas of any cricket ground in the world and is also used for other

sports, such as hockey, in the off-season. It, too, was later renamed, becoming known as the **Gaddafi Stadium** after the Libyan leader.

It was first used in November 1959, against Australia and has become another Pakistani stronghold with just one defeat there since 1970. It offers one of the few wickets that can be prepared with a bit of pace, when it is left slightly green. However when it is left bare it is a batting paradise, and it provided the pitch on which Pakistan made its highest score at home, amassing 699 for 5 declared against India in 1989/90.

There have been several stoppages because of crowd trouble at Lahore. There were several interruptions in the Test against England in March 1969, in which Aftab Gul made his debut. Gul, an

influential student leader at the time, suggested - half in jest - that had he been left out of that side there would not have been a Test match played because of the protests. Then, against the same opponents in December 1977, there was a major disturbance when the crowd invaded in premature celebration of Mudassar Nazar's hundred. As it was the slowest in Test history perhaps they were driven to distraction. The pitch invaders were chased by police but when one of them was belaboured, a running fight began with the crowd turning and chasing their pursuers. Four policemen ended up seeking sanctuary in the England dressing-room. The trouble-makers stormed the VIP enclosure and dressing-rooms with stones and bricks, yet after 45 minutes (which included twenty minutes for the scheduled tea interval) play resumed allowing Mudassar Nazar to make the single he required to complete his hundred. Oddly enough the pitch invaders helped clear up all the debris and returned to their seats as though nothing had happened.

The Test there against Zimbabwe in 1993/4 - the 26th to be held at the ground - was badly hit by fog, which allowed only 21 minutes play on the third day.

Faisalabad, an old mill town, has become an increasingly popular venue in recent years, with 17 Test matches in all since 1978, when its first match was played, seeing the resumption of Test cricket with India after over 17 years. The town, formerly known as Lyallpur, was named after a king (Faisal) and the ground after a national poet, Iqbal. The venue achieved notoriety through the Rana-

Gatting row in 1987/8. From Pakistan's point of view it is better remembered for the 674 for 6 declared made against India in 1984/5 and for the bowling out of the Westindies there for just 53 in 1986/7.

The ground in **Sharjah** is set in the Great Arabian Desert in the United Arab Emirates yet has become a second home to Asian and, in particular, Pakistani cricketers since cricket was first played there in 1981, between a Javed Miandad XI and a Sunil Gavaskar XI. It was the brainchild of Arab businessman Mr Abdulrahman Bukhatir, who raised the £2 million required to build the stadium. He wanted to bring cricket to the three-quarters of a million Pakistani and Indian population, most of whom emigrated to UAE to meet the labour shortage there.

Originally it seemed that Sharjah might become a breakaway organisation but since 1984/5 it has had the official backing - and blessing - of the various Test-playing countries' Boards of Control. The stadium, on the outskirts of the city, can now accommodate some 18,000 people. The playing area is like a mirage in the desert; tons of soil had to be transported to the site to produce an even, firm surface and the pitch, though slow, is true and very good for batting.

The Sharjah competition has attracted an array of sponsors for the Sharjah Trophy, Champions Trophy and Austral-Asia Cup, such as Rothmans and Wills, and has always offered lucrative prize money as well as raising significant funds for the Cricketers' Benefit Fund Series. A number of players are nominated as beneficiaries at each tournament, and those named now receive $35,000 each. The fund is organised by former Pakistan captain, Asif Iqbal, who has been intrinsically involved in the running of Sharjah cricket since his retirement. The players nominated are usually Asian cricketers who are coming to the end of their careers or who have recently retired. So far over 50 players have picked up substantial cheques for their services to cricket.

There have been some classic matches none more so than when Javed Miandad hit a six off the last ball of the 1985/6 final to beat India. He was showered with gifts worth tens of thousands of dollars and was even given a Mercedes. In another game in October 1991 against the Westindies a spectator died in the excitement as Pakistan snatch a one run victory.

Pakistan has been virtually invincible there in recent years winning six competitions in a row, before losing to the Westindies in November 1993. UAE, who won the ICC Trophy in 1993 which is contested amongst non-Test playing countries, were invited to enter their national side in April 1994 and gave a good account of themselves. The team, in fact, usually has five or six players of Pakistani origin.

Pakistan's Test Match Grounds (15)

(chronological order)

City	Ground	First Test	Opp.	P	W	L	D
Dacca*	Dacca Stadium	1.1.1955	(v I)	6	1	1	4
Bahawalpur	Dring Stadium	15.1.1955	(v I)	1	0	0	1
Lahore	Lawrence Gardens (Bagh-i-Jinnah after 1959)	29.1.1955	(v I)	3	1	1	1
Peshawar	Services Club Ground	13.2.1955	(v I)	1	0	0	1
Karachi	National Stadium	26.2.1955	(v I)	31	15	0	16
Lahore	(Gaddafi) Stadium	21.11.1959	(v A)	27	7	4	16
Rawalpindi	Pindi Club Ground	27.3.1965	(v NZ)	1	0	0	1
Hyderabad	(Sind) Niaz Stadium	16.3.1973	(v E)	5	3	0	2
Faisalabad	Iqbal Stadium	16.10.1978	(v I)	17	5	3	9
Multan	Ibn-e-Qasim Bagh Stdm	30.12.1980	(v WI)	1	0	0	1
Sialkot	Jinnah Stadium	27.10.1985	(v SL)	4	1	1	2
Gujranwala	Municipal Stadium	20.12.1991	(v SL)	1	0	0	1
Karachi	Defence Stadium	1.12.1993	(v Z)	1	1	0	0
Rawalpindi	Pindi Cricket Stadium	9.12.93	(v Z)	2	1	0	1
Peshawar	Arbab Niaz Stadium	8.9.95	(v SL)	1	1	0	0

Until 16.12.1971, part of East Pakistan, now in the People's Republic of Bangladesh

Pakistan at other grounds

INDIA	P	W	L	D
Madras	4	0	1	3
Calcutta	4	0	0	4
Delhi	3	0	1	2
Bangalore	3	1	0	2
Brabourne*	2	0	1	1
Kanpur	2	0	0	2
Wankhede*	1	0	1	0
Nagpur	1	0	0	1
Jullundur	1	0	0	1
Ahmedabad	1	0	0	1
Jaipur	1	0	0	1
*Bombay				

ENGLAND				
Lords*	10	3	2	5
Headingley	8	1	4	3
The Oval*	7	3	2	2
Birmingham	6	0	3	3
Manchester	3	0	0	3
Nottingham	3	0	2	1
*London				

WESTINDIES				
Port of Spain	5	1	3	1
Bridgetown	4	0	2	2
Georgetown	3	1	1	1
Kingston	2	0	1	1
Antigua	1	0	0	1

AUSTRALIA	P	W	L	D
Melbourne	7	2	3	2
Adelaide	4	0	1	3
Sydney	5	1	3	1
Perth	3	0	3	0
Brisbane	3	0	2	1
Hobart	1	0	1	0

NEW ZEALAND				
Auckland	6	1	1	4
Wellington	5	1	0	4
Christchurch	4	2	1	1
Dunedin	2	1	1	0
Napier	1	0	0	1
Hamilton	1	1	0	0

SRI LANKA				
Colombo(PSS)	3	1	1	1
Kandy	2	2	0	0

SOUTH AFRICA				
Johannesburg	1	0	1	0

ZIMBABWE				
Harare	2	1	1	1
Bulawayo	1	1	0	0

Uneasy lies the head that wears a crown

Pakistan's Test match captains

The tale of the accession to the captaincy of Pakistan has all the intrigue of a Shakespearean play, all the squabbles of a TV soap opera. After a relatively stable period from 1985 to 1992, when Imran Khan and Javed Miandad in effect shared the honour, the fall from grace of the latter precipitated as tumultuous a period as there has ever been in Pakistan's cricket history, as the national side was led by four different captains in the space of twelve months. In the four years between the two tours of England (1992 and 1996), the position became a poisoned chalice with as many as eight different players captaining Pakistan in internationals during that period.

When Imran Khan retired after the World Cup in 1992, it appeared that, at last, Miandad would enjoy a long tenure in charge. Despite five previous terms in office, he had never had more than eleven Tests consecutively and even as he led Pakistan to victory over England in 1992, there were still rumours abounding that Imran Khan, as soon as he was fit, might turn up and take over. As it transpired, though, with feeling in the side running against him for the first time in his career, Imran may not have been welcome.

In the World Cup Khan had, eventually, been the driving force behind Pakistan's triumph. However, early on the captain seemed preoccupied with thoughts of his cancer hospital project and with his injured shoulder, believing fate was against him. Even Wasim Akram felt he was unusually remote and introverted, and Imran would often leave net practice straight after he had batted for treatment on his shoulder, which did not help engender team spirit. Despite injuries and poor early form, he rallied his young tigers when they were on the verge of going out and forged a powerful team out of the disparate bunch. Unfortunately the captain failed to mention his team when he received the World Cup, instead speaking of his personal relief as the victory, he felt, would ensure the completion of his worthy project. Overjoyed as he received the Waterford Crystal trophy from Sir Colin Cowdrey, he said, "I would just like to say that I want to give my commiserations to the English team. But I want them to know by winning this World Cup, personally it means that one of my greatest obsessions in life, which is to build a cancer hospital...I'm sure that this World Cup will go along way towards completion of this obsession. I would also like to say that I feel very proud that at the twilight of my career finally I have managed to win the World Cup. Thank you." This was an oversight for which Imran was soon to apologise for publicly, but it had come across badly.

However, that there was an undercurrent of resentment in the team became evident when there was a misunderstanding over the allocation of funds presented to Imran at a reception given in honour of the team in Singapore, on the way back from the World Cup, the players believing the money raised was for them rather than the Cancer Hospital Appeal. Also, others felt that the individual's opportunity to benefit from the team's success - in the way that, for instance, Javed Miandad had benefited after one famous victory in Sharjah where he was bestowed with gifts of great value for hitting the last ball of the game for the winning six - were being diminished by the appeal. An independently organised tour of the main cities was arranged so that the players could receive their due recompense.

So Miandad had the full backing of his young side and led them astutely in England, forming a good relationship with Salim Malik, who had been discontented during the World Cup and declared on the team's arrival that the team was happier "with no superstars in the team." That disenchantment stemmed from the manner in which the vice-captaincy had been taken away from him after the warm up matches for the competition.

During the 1992 series, Imran Khan wrote in his column in *The Daily Telegraph* that he felt that Wasim Akram would, in time, make a good captain. So, naturally, when Miandad was replaced by Akram after the tour to New Zealand, 1992/3, the deposed leader was sure that Imran had pulled some strings to get rid of him, knowing that he favoured the young all-rounder. Imran explained that it was entirely down to results, as the one-day champions of the world had only won three out of 16 games since that victory over England in the World Cup.

"Of course it is very flattering to be thought of as that powerful...but had Javed won even half of those games there would have been no change. It was nothing to do with me. I have very little to do with cricket anymore. The truth is, if you perform no intrigue can work against you."

Ironically, as the table shows, Miandad was Pakistan's most successful captain in Test cricket at the time. He had taken the rubber against England in 1992 - winning two Tests in a series against them for the first time - and had led the side to a superb victory against New Zealand in Auckland. He had been relatively willing to make way for Imran Khan in the past, who was the first choice captain for a decade, though Javed had enjoyed several interregnums, but was most upset to have to stand down for the sixth time.

The appointment of Akram to the post, at the age of 26 in January 1993, represented a move by the Board of Control for Cricket in Pakistan to find a man to lead the side well into its fifth decade of Test cricket. Waqar Younis, just turned 21, was his vice-captain, ahead of the more experienced Salim Malik and Ramiz Raja, the men who had the job on the previous tours to England, and Australia and New Zealand respectively. In so doing, the BCCP put their two main match winners in charge of Pakistan. It seemed an inspired move at first, though by the end of the year the two great fast bowlers had fallen out.

The one-day results improved immediately with Akram's appointment, with victory by 114 runs over Sri Lanka in the Sharjah Final, and a sterling fight back in the Westindies to level the series. Akram seemed to have patched up the rift with a disconsolate Miandad, saying "it's not your fault and not my fault that I am captain so let's get on with it." However, the Test series in the Caribbean proved a disaster. The unfounded drugs charges in Grenada unsettled the young captain, who found the pressures of leading from the front much greater than he thought, while several key players were injured. As his own form slipped, Akram's leadership became grouchy.

Akram broke his hand in another competition in Sharjah and so missed the inaugural Test with Zimbabwe in November 1993 and in his absence his vice-captain and great friend, Waqar Younis, took over. He led the side astutely and bowled with inspiration. Akram returned for the final two Tests but as the series progressed the level of dissatisfaction with him increased. At the end of the series, ten senior players, led by Younis of all people, made a stand against Akram. They protested against the non-selection of Javed Miandad, Ramiz Raja and Aqib Javed for the tour to New Zealand, 1993/4, and more importantly against Akram's brash style of leadership and his use of strong language at his own players on the field.

Consequently, Akram was replaced for the tour to New Zealand by Salim Malik, who had just returned to the side after being "rested" against the Westindies. Akram's demise was most unexpected. Imran Khan's recommendation was on the basis that Akram was the "most popular player in the team" and "the best all-rounder in the world." Surprisingly the pressures of captaincy had got to him; he is not the first, especially against the Westindies, who adopt a deliberate policy of specifically trying to limit the influence of the skipper. The part that Younis played in leading the players' stand has caused a rift between the two new ball bowlers and ruled him out of contention as captain. Initially Malik proved to be a shrewd choice as a stopgap leader, both on and off the field. His batting was inspired against Australia in 1994/5, averaging nearly a hundred for the series, yet there were still rumours circulating of an impending coup, especially after Wasim Akram and Waqar Younis pulled out on the eve of the final match of the series.

Events in Southern Africa, at the start of 1995, did not help. Salim and his vice-captain, Rashid Latif, disagreed over tactics in the Mandela Trophy matches, when Salim went against the wishes of his team after winning the toss. Pakistan were beaten by an innings in their inaugural match against South Africa and when the first Test against Zimbabwe was lost by a similar margin, Malik's days in charge seemed numbered. Yet Pakistan fought back to become only the third team in history to come from behind to win a three-match series and the first to do so overseas. This was all the more remarkable as, during the decider, Malik was accused in an Australian newspaper of trying to bribe the Australian spinners Shane Warne and Tim May to throw the first Test between the sides at Karachi a few months earlier. Malik was stripped of the captaincy, pending further enquiries. It will be ironic if he has played his last Test as captain; he has an excellent record of seven wins in twelve matches and his batting average as captain is bettered only by Hanif Mohammad.

The changes did not stop there. The side needed someone to at least go and toss up during the Sharjah tournament that followed. Moin Khan was chosen but was struck down with chickenpox before the end of the tournament. Saeed Anwar took over temporarily, but Pakistan failed to make the final. Ramiz Raja, who had not played Test cricket for nearly three years was asked to captain the side against Sri Lanka as a happy compromise, being an experienced player who had not been involved in the dressing room squabbles of the previous winter. He started brilliantly with an innings victory but without Akram and Younis for the final Test, Sri Lanka recovered to take the series.

Inevitably, Raja lost the captaincy, and the Board reappointed Wasim Akram. Although the side started badly in Australia, losing the first two Tests, Pakistan came back well to win in Sydney and then beat New Zealand. There were calls for his head when Pakistan lost to India in the World Cup quarter-final, though thankfully the PCB kept faith. Even still, injury to Wasim precipitated a temporary change, with Aamir Sohail taking over for two one-day tournaments in Singapore and Sharjah. Wasim was appointed for the tour to England in 1996 and completed a hat-trick of wins, when the side won the first Test at Lord's. With victory at the Oval to ensure the series, Akram confirmed his progress as a captain, especially as the team appear to be gelling and fulfilling their potential.

The events of this troubled three year period, with so many different captains and vice-captains, exemplifies a recurrent problem in Pakistan's cricket history. Perhaps only Abdul Hafeez Kardar and Imran Khan have felt fully secure in leading the national side. Kardar, as the first captain, had no other obvious candidates vying for the position and led the side with calm authority and a certain austerity for the first five-and-a-half years of Pakistan's Test history. His sequence of 23 consecutive Tests in charge remains the national record and he is considered by many to be Pakistan's best captain to date. Imran Khan's early tenure was considered at the time to be a temporary measure and he accepted it only because he felt he could produce a better team spirit than that which existed before. Because he was sure of his place in the side and as the leadership was not that important to him, he could afford to be more attacking as a captain, not scared to risk defeat, and had the confidence to challenge the BCCP over selection in which he was determined to have the final say. He could not avoid the politics, however, that has always haunted the position. In fact, early on, he became just as embroiled as others had done. It was not

until he came back from injury in 1985 that he became totally assured and could start being more forthright with the Board. Both Imran Khan and Kardar had a strong influence on selection, but most of the other captains have suffered and felt that their hands were tied. Although the number of Test captains, 18, is not excessive in 44 years of Test cricket (1952-96), Wasim Akram's second appointment was the 32nd change of leadership in that time, though a couple of those changes were one-offs because of an injury to the incumbent captain. It must be remembered that just three players, namely Imran Khan, Javed Miandad and Abdul Hafeez Kardar, share virtually half of Pakistan's Tests among them as captain.

Kardar led the side during its difficult beginnings to a most successful inauguration into Test cricket. Although losing the first series to India, Pakistan won the second Test by an innings and on the first tour to England won the final Test to draw the series, which is a unique achievement. The side held India to a draw at home, beat New Zealand convincingly and defeated Australia in a one-off Test.

On Kardar's retirement, after defeat in the Westindies in 1958, the captaincy proved problematic. The side could not match their early success and signs of the nepotism and class prejudice that have blighted the history of Pakistan's cricket came to the fore. Results fell away as several leading players retired and as they lost the advantage of playing on matting wickets at home. A whole generation had to adapt to the newly prevalent grass pitches.

The results suffered; Pakistan won just one series - at home, to New Zealand in 1964/5 - between 1959/60 and 1972/3, and consequently there was quite a stream of captains, as the selectors tried to produce some positive results. In the sixties, there were six different captains in just nine series.

Fazal Mahmood, who had won his first series in charge at home to Westindies but lost the following year (1959/60) to Australia, was widely criticised during his last series in charge, a dull 0-0 draw with India in 1960/1. Various factions had developed within the team because of Mahmood's suspected favouritism. Such divisions were to blight Pakistani cricket for the next few years. Imtiaz Ahmed inherited a troubled side and was given just one series at home to England, which was lost 1-0.

Strong parochial feeling was increasingly being expressed in the newspapers and indeed within the BCCP, with two clear factions developing from Lahore and Karachi. Not surprisingly captains became more and more uncertain of their position and overly concerned about not losing and this, coupled with the bland pitches, produced just four positive results in 18 home matches spread over 15 years.

Javed Burki, an aristocrat from Lahore, had made his debut only 18 months before being given the captaincy and was probably too young at 25 to take charge, but he presented the selectors with the opportunity once again to have a captain of Kardar's social status. After suffering Pakistan's worst defeat, 4-0 to England, he too was replaced.

When Hanif Mohammad, the one player of international standing in the side at the time, took over he became the first captain from Karachi. Although he was criticised for being over-cautious, Pakistan beat New Zealand at home and held them to a draw away, while also drawing one-off Tests at home and away to Australia. The captaincy helped him double his resolve when he batted, and several stonewall innings ensured that Pakistan were still unbeaten after his first ten Tests in charge. His batting average surged to 58.73 compared with 43.98 as a player, but when Pakistan lost the final two Tests of the series in England (1967), he was pressurised to stand down and played his last full series back in the ranks.

Saeed Ahmed, from Lahore, who had had his differences with the Board, was a surprise choice as captain. He enjoyed the briefest of tenures, just three matches, and not surprisingly was replaced, despite drawing with England in the trouble-hit series at home in 1968/9.

Thus Intikhab Alam became the third captain in as many series and took over at the worst possible time. The team were divided as was the country and the affable Inti' was to be poorly treated by the Board. Narrow defeats against New Zealand (1969/70) and England (1971) were followed by a three-nil defeat in Australia. There were disagreements within the team, mainly between the captain and the man he had replaced, Saeed Ahmed. Consequently the latter and Mohammad Ilyas, who had a disagreement with Kardar, were not required when the rest of the team travelled on to New Zealand, but the Board had already decided to replace Alam, which produced the most undiplomatic of situations. Majid Khan was appointed while still on tour under Intikhab, much to Inti's and the team's chagrin. Ironically Intikhab was in the middle of

leading Pakistan to their first series win overseas and his own form was instrumental to that success.

As a result M J Khan, the new captain - through no fault of his own - never received the full support of the team in his one series in charge, at home against England in 1972/3. Alam was reappointed for the tour to England in 1974 and the side began, at last, to play to their full potential yet he was not included in the squad for the World Cup the following year, as it was assumed that leg-spinners could not play a part in one-day cricket. The designated captain, Asif Iqbal, was taken ill though after just one match and so Majid Khan took the reins once more.

The leadership issue was not helped by the lack of Test cricket being played by Pakistan at the time. The next series was not until 1976/7, at home to New Zealand.

By then the incumbent Test captain, Intikhab Alam, had not only lost the captaincy but had been dropped from the squad as well. He was recalled to the side as a player at the eleventh hour and performed most creditably with the ball. He was then used as a sacrificial pawn in a dispute between the team and the Board over pay and conditions. He was reinstated temporarily as captain for the tour to Australia and Westindies when Mustaq Mohammad, the new captain, and other senior players refused to play. Eventually the matter was settled and Intikhab stood down graciously on the understanding that he would tour Australia and the Caribbean. However, he found himself being ostracised for the purportedly Machiavellian nature of his accession, and played next to no part on the tour. Mustaq was restored and led a highly talented side on the arduous four-month tour.

The team was beginning to blossom again as

Waqar and Wasim, vice-captain and captain in 1993

more and more players came to England to play county cricket, giving the nucleus of the side more experience and knowledge of different types of wicket. This paid dividends and results improved. Not surprisingly, the county players dominated the captaincy stakes, with only Wasim Bari (in charge because of Packer absentees) the sole captain of Pakistan between 1969/70 and 1995 not to have played county cricket.

With as many as seven playing first-class cricket in England, this brought greater professionalism on the field and behind the scenes and a sequence of pay disputes culminated in several defections to Packer.

Mustaq Mohammad was past his best as a Test batsman against the quickest bowling, which adversely affected his confidence and therefore his captaincy. His last series was an acrimonious one against Australia but he had united the side, making the team more competitive and laying the foundations of Pakistan's success in the future.

The political pressures of captaincy remained though, and are best illustrated by the demise of Asif Iqbal. He had proved himself one of the finest batsmen in the world in the late seventies and surpassed himself in Packer's "Super Tests" yet retired from the game after leading the side to defeat in India. Born in India himself, he could not face the criticism that was sure to follow on his return home, and so retired from international cricket despite being in his prime as a player.

Mustaq Mohammad, who was now managing the side proposed Javed Miandad, who was just 21 and not yet mature enough to lead a squad containing several senior players and the odd awkward customer. Miandad's first tenure in office ended with a players' revolt, when the team he had led to Australia in 1981/2 refused en masse to continue to play on under him after he had criticised the players for the defeat in that series. He remained in charge but of a completely different team against Sri Lanka and the "first XI" only returned, after missing two Tests, when he agreed to stand down for the forthcoming series in England, in 1982.

Factions had developed within the team as they had done in the sixties, with individuals quite happy to see the team lose so long as it would advance their own cause as player or captain. The appointment of Imran Khan - incidentally the fourth Pakistan captain educated at Oxbridge - was initially considered a stopgap measure. He took on the responsibility only because he felt he must be able to engender a better team spirit, and he handled the side astutely on and off the field in England, and was inspirational against India in 1982/3. In effect, he became the first choice captain whenever he was fit and available for the rest of his career, leading the side in all but three of his last 51 Tests.

However, when he was injured and unable to play at the start of the 1983/4 season the captaincy again became an issue. Zaheer Abbas, who yearned for the leadership, stood in and played out a dull drawn series in India, but Imran Khan's continued absence at the start of the tour to Australia, allowed the press to extol the virtues of their parochial favourites. Imran Khan had been reappointed for the tour to Australia but when he could not play in the first two Tests, Zaheer Abbas, his vice-captain, let it be known that he wanted the job permanently. Yet when he was offered the captaincy for the rest of the tour he refused, saying he was leading on a caretaker-only basis and that it was not the side he would have chosen. His obsession with the captaincy caused a lot of tension within the team. He promoted his cause publicly after that tour and got the job officially when Imran's shin injury became chronic, preventing him from playing for two years. Ironically the pressures of the leadership became too much for Abbas and within a year he had resigned.

Javed Miandad was reinstated but after two three-Test series he too stood down saying, just after making a double-hundred, that he wanted to concentrate on his batting. Pakistan had just lost three important one-day internationals in a row to India and he may well have been replaced soon anyway. Imran Khan, who had just returned to the side, was the only realistic candidate, but he too had to contend with an awkward first series back in Sri Lanka, where the team felt the umpiring was openly biased.

As Miandad had resigned voluntarily it made for a fairly harmonious transfer of power. For the next half-a-dozen years the two, in effect, shared the job, Miandad always taking over if Khan was unavailable, while on the field, he still had a great influence and was often seen to be making field changes and offering tactical advice. Because of this, Imran was able to concentrate fully when he was bowling, leading from the front - his forte - and being the eloquent figure-head off the field. Between them they were to lead Pakistan to 28 out of their first 50 Test victories, sharing the wins evenly.

Since Imran Khan's return to Test cricket in October 1985 and the announcement of his retirement in 1992, Pakistan lost only one Test series - a curtailed rubber away to Australia in 1989/90 - and the side achieved several excellent results, including holding the Westindies to draws at home and away, and beating England and India abroad for the first time, all under Imran, and thrashing New Zealand 3-0 in Pakistan and beating England at home and away under Javed. In addition there were six triumphs in Sharjah in seven attempts, and victory in the 1992 World Cup and in the Nehru in 1989.

Imran's influence is best illustrated by the fact that his retirement from the game was delayed by some four years almost by parliamentary decree - President Zia-ul-Haq persuading him to take the side to Westindies in 1988 - as Javed did not want to captain at that point. Miandad, too, was persuaded out of retirement, by Benazir Bhutto, and has the best record of any of Pakistan's captains, with 14 wins from 34 Tests. It must be remembered, too, that for most of his time as captain, he was without his leading player, Imran, who only played in 21 of those 34 matches. Who knows what he may have achieved with Mr Khan in the side? On the whole Miandad was content to be, in effect, Imran's permanent understudy.

Imran's crowning glory was winning the World Cup in 1992, cajoling his side to greater performance with his famous "fight like cornered tigers" battle cry. His self-belief has often carried Pakistan, but his victory speech seemed so egotistical (misconstrued, as he explained later), that there was growing support within the team for Miandad to take the reins once more. Miandad, who was captaining one of the youngest full Test touring sides, which had an average age only 23, led a united side to the series win in England, but his sacking after victory in New Zealand in January 1993, sparked another tempestuous period in the continuing saga that has surrounded the battle for the captaincy.

Now that he has settled back in, Wasim Akram hints at a rare permanency in the position.

Salim Malik walks out to toss with Australia's Mark Taylor, during a controversial series which ultimately cost him the captaincy

Most consecutive Tests as captain

	Tests	Dates
Abdul Kardar	23	1952/3-1957/8
Imran Khan	16	1985/6-1987
Javed Miandad	13	1979/80-1981/2
Imran Khan	12	1982-1982/3
Intikhab Alam	12	1969/70-1972/3
Salim Malik	12	1993/4-1994-95
Hanif Mohammad	11	1964/5-1967
Mustaq Mohammad	11	1976/7

Javed Miandad and Imran Khan have both had six tenures in office. There have been 18 captains but Wasim Akram's appointment was the 32nd change.

Captains in one-day internationals

Imran Khan	(175)	139
Javed Miandad	(233)	62
Wasim Akram	(201)	38
Salim Malik	(229)	34
Zaheer Abbas	(62)	13
Aamir Sohail	(101)	9
Ramiz Raja	(171)	8
Asif Iqbal	(10)	6
Abdul Qadir	(104)	5
Wasim Bari	(51)	5
Mustaq Mohammad	(10)	4
Intikhab Alam	(4)	3
Majid Khan	(23)	2
Waqar Younis	(128)	1
Saeed Anwar	(98)	1
Sarfraz Nawaz	(45)	1

Record of Pakistan's Captains 1952/3-1996

	M	W	L	D	Pts	%
Waqar Younis	1	1	0	0	3	100.00
Salim Malik	12	7	3	2	16	66.00
Javed Miandad	34	14	6	14	42	61.76
Mustaq Mohammad	19	8	4	7	23	60.52
Zaheer Abbas	14	3	1	10	16	57.14
Imran Khan	48	14	8	26	44	56.25
Wasim Akram	12	5	4	3	13	54.17
Abdul Kardar	23	6	6	11	23	50.00
Hanif Mohammad	11	2	2	7	11	50.00
Fazal Mahmood	10	2	2	6	10	50.00
Saeed Ahmed	3	0	0	3	3	50.00
Majid Khan	3	0	0	3	3	50.00
Intikhab Alam	17	1	5	11	13	38.23
Wasim Bari	6	0	2	4	4	33.33
Asif Iqbal	6	0	2	4	4	33.33
Ramiz Raja	3	1	2	0	2	33.33
Imtiaz Ahmed	4	0	2	2	2	25.00
Javed Burki	5	0	4	1	1	10.00

Two points for a win, one for a draw. % of possible points.

Personal performances as captain of Pakistan

CAPTAIN	M	I	NO	Runs	HS	Avg	100s	Balls	Runs	Wkts	5wi/10wm	Avg	BB	Ct/st
A.H.Kardar	23	37	3	847	93	24.91	-	2712	954	21	-	45.42	3-35	15
Fazal Mahmood	10	15	1	116	18	8.28	-	2402	785	41	5/1	19.14	6-34	4
Imtiaz Ahmed	4	8	0	174	86	21.75	-	-	-	-	-	-	-	8/3
Javed Burki	5	10	0	252	140	25.20	1	12	14	0	-	-	-	2
Hanif Mohammad	11	18	3	881	203*	58.73	4	2	4	0	-	-	-	16
Saeed Ahmed	3	4	0	109	39	27.25	-	591	224	9	-	24.88	6-64	1
Intikhab Alam	17	30	3	608	68	22.51	-	376	1714	54	5/2	31.74	7-52	6
Majid Khan	3	5	0	214	99	42.80	-	162	67	2	-	33.50	2-51	4
Mustaq Mohammad	19	33	2	1035	121	33.38	3	2557	1125	38	2/0	29.60	5-28	20
Wasim Bari	6	8	1	45	17	6.42	-	-	-	-	-	-	-	8/-
Asif Iqbal	6	10	1	267	64	29.66	-	218	72	2	-	36.00	1-3	4
Javed Miandad	34	51	4	2354	211	50.09	5	114	72	0	-	-	-	31/1
Imran Khan	48	64	18	2408	136	52.34	5	9211	3790	187	12/4	20.27	8-60	17
Zaheer Abbas	14	21	4	773	168*	45.47	1	134	56	3	-	18.66	2-21	3
Wasim Akram	12	20	2	273	40	15.17	-	2826	1268	50	2/0	25.36	5-53	8
Waqar Younis	1	1	0	13	13	13.00	-	336	135	13	0/1	10.38	7-91	-
Salim Malik	12	21	1	1047	237	52.35	3	36	26	0	-	-	-	2
Ramiz Raja	3	5	0	208	78	41.60	-	-	-	-	-	-	-	4

THE PLAYERS

Pakistan's greatest players
from 1952 to the present

Zaheer Abbas

Zaheer Abbas is Pakistan's most prolific scorer in first-class cricket with nearly 35,000 runs at an average of over 50. He is one of only four non-English players with a hundred hundreds - and the only Asian - the others being Don Bradman of Australia, Glenn Turner of New Zealand and Viv Richards of Westindies. Zaheer was a ruthless run-scorer who would take full advantage when on form, with a Boycott-like determination. Yet he was no accumulator but a masterful timer of the ball, full of graceful strokes. His career figures are very similar to those of Viv Richards and he was much more in his mould as an entertainer, less powerful but more likely to late cut or ease the ball through the field with pure timing, which was the hallmark of his batting.

Born in Sialkot months before Partition, he was brought up in Karachi, where he was educated at Jahangir Road Secondary School and Karachi University. His father, a locust controller, was not so keen for any of his six sons to play so much sport, though each excelled at either hockey or cricket. As well as Zaheer, Tatheer (PWD) and Sagheer (Karachi) also played first-class cricket. Zaheer made his debut for Karachi Whites in 1965/6 and he was soon signed up by PIA.

He modelled his technique on Colin Cowdrey and Tom Graveney who both toured with England in 1968/9 and each made Test hundreds in that series. That same season Zaheer helped set a new record for the 6th wicket in Pakistan's first-class cricket, making 197 as he added 353 with Salah-ud-Din who got 256, for Karachi against East Pakistan.

Zaheer made his Test debut the following year against New Zealand in his home town, and got 12 and 27, but did not play in the rest of the series. He secured his place for the tour to England with five hundreds in six matches - four in successive innings - in 1970/1, including a double hundred against Karachi A to remind Intikhab Alam, Pakistan's captain, of his ability.

That form continued on tour. Hundreds against Worcestershire and Kent maintained his remarkable record of scoring a hundred every five knocks and were the prelude to a brilliant innings in the first Test at Edgbaston. Coming in for the fourth ball of the match, after Aftab Gul was forced to retire hurt after being struck on the head by a delivery from Alan Ward, Zaheer totally dominated proceedings for the next nine hours and ten minutes. He caressed his way to 159 at close of play on the first day, and started the next with 14 off Ken Shuttleworth's first over of the morning. He cruised past 200 and on to 274, then the second highest score for Pakistan after Hanif's 337. He added 291 with Mustaq Mohammad for the 2nd wicket, a national Test record, out-scoring his senior partner by 2 to 1. His superb innings, which included 38 fours, took him past 1,000 runs for the season achieved as early as 4th June.

He averaged just under a hundred in that series and made over 1,500 runs on the tour and thoroughly deserved to be named among *Wisden's* Five Cricketers of the Year. His magnificent innings in Birmingham also earned him selection for the World XI, which toured Australia that winter. Not surprisingly, a flood of offers came from the counties too. He decided to sign for Gloucestershire, as did his team-mate Sadiq Mohammad.

He struggled in his next couple of Test series in 1972/3, not coming to terms with the extra bounce in the Australian wickets, nor with an experiment using him as an opener in New Zealand, and was dropped for the first Test at home against England. He was recalled to the side for the last two Tests without success, hidden down the order at number seven. However, when the lean patch continued for Gloucester, he went to an optician who prescribed a new pair of glasses, with his now characteristic gold-rims. Six foot tall and willowy, if he ever donned an umpire's coat he would be mistaken for a doctor. The new glasses seemed to do the trick; that winter he broke the domestic record for the most runs in a season, with 1,597 at 84.05.

Returning to England in 1974 with the national side, he made another brilliant double-hundred, this time on a slow Oval track, batting for just over nine hours and hitting twenty-two fours. Again he shared in a record partnership (since beaten) with Mustaq, putting on 172 for the third wicket. Strangely, Zaheer had scored just two fifties in his 21 Test innings between those double-hundreds.

He was not "at home" at home against the Westindies (1974/5), and he played just one innings of substance in the inaugural World Cup in England, 97 v Sri Lanka. Still not consistent at international level, he was phenomenal in county cricket for Gloucestershire. In all he was to pass a thousand runs in a season eleven times but he was in his prime in a memorable summer of 1976, as he made 2,554 runs at an average of 75.11, the highest aggregate for 15 years, including 11 hundreds (one before lunch). Twice in that season he scored a double hundred and a hundred in a match without being dismissed, a feat he was to repeat once the following summer and again in 1981 (see page 73). When playing against Kent, against whom he made 230 and 104, he told Derek Underwood, who was to finish with 297 wickets in Test cricket, that he liked his bowling! He explained to a deflated "Deadly" later that he liked it, because he thought he was a very good bowler, who made him have to concentrate. Gloucestershire achieved their best results for a hundred years, finishing third in 1976 and 1977, the year they won the Benson and Hedges, in which Zaheer made 70 in the final against Kent, Underwood and all.

Yet his form remained very sketchy when he returned to Test cricket in the series against New Zealand (1976/7), failing to reach twenty in the three Tests. However, on tour in Australia he regained his touch and put together scores of 85, 101 at Adelaide, and 90 and 58 at Melbourne. Then in the Caribbean, he missed the first two Tests because of a toe injury, sustained while playing football on the beach, but made 95 in his first match back against Guyana, and 80 in the Test there, where he shared a stand of 159 with Majid Khan.

It was his county form of recent years that made him an straightforward choice for Kerry Packer's World Series Cricket, though he had never been at his best against high pace, and he took until the 2nd year to make much of an impact against the plethora of fast bowlers.

He had flown back to Pakistan with Imran Khan and Mustaq Mohammad in order to play against England in 1977/8, but in the end the Packer players were not chosen.

Zaheer relished being back for the renewal of contests with India in 1978/9. Scores of 176, 96, 235 not out, 34 not out, and 42 - 583 runs at an average of 194.33 - confirmed his reputation as "the king of spin". In the first Test at Faisalabad he dominated a stand with Javed Miandad of 255 for the fourth wicket, at the time the highest partnership for any wicket between the countries. He was savage on anything short and drove majestically, hitting two sixes and 24 fours in a stay of 315 minutes. He fell four runs short in the 2nd innings of a hundred in each innings to a rather ignominious dismissal, when he became the only Test victim of Sunil Gavaskar's very occasional bowling. At Lahore, Zaheer hit a brilliant double hundred made in 375 minutes, with 29 fours and two sixes, which was scored at such a rate that Pakistan had plenty of time to bowl India out and so set up the series win.

He dominated the bowling to such a degree that he disrupted completely the great Indian spin quartet of the time. The series finished Erapalli Prasanna's career, Bishan Bedi lost the captaincy, while Bhagwat Chandrasekhar lost confidence for the series which followed, against the Westindies, which proved to be his last. He wrote of Zaheer in his biography *The Winning Hand* (with Rajan Bala); "If one batsman really gave me the stick it was this Pakistani strokemaker. There was a point when I felt helpless enough to want to throw the ball back to my captain and ask him to get somebody else to bowl. He gave me the feeling he knew everything about my bowling." Chandra' felt that Zaheer Abbas had more shots against spin bowling than all the best batsman he had bowled to.

A return to WSC meant Zaheer missed the first Test in New Zealand in 1979, but in the third at Auckland he made his sixth Test hundred after being dropped first ball. He moved smoothly to his hundred in under four hours but then got bogged down, taking two and half hours to add 35 more. He was back in Australia in March for the ill-tempered two-Test series, and made an important fifty in victory at the MCG.

His reputation as one of the best one-day players was enhanced by an innings of 93 in the semi-final of the 1979 World Cup against Westindies, in which he shared an exhilarating partnership of 166 with Majid Khan in a narrow defeat. Zaheer's timing and placement were such that he was very difficult to contain and he could out-score anyone when on song, though he was not always such a good judge of a run, getting run out more than most.

The following winter, 1979/80, he had an unhappy time in Tests. Always a little highly-strung, the pressure of playing in India got to him despite the weight of his scoring in the previous series against them. By the fifth Test, in which he got a duck in the first innings, he was convinced that someone had put a curse on him. He was dropped from the final match, having scored just one fifty in the series. Although re-called against Australia, he lost his place again after two matches for the final game at Lahore on a whim of Javed Miandad's that did nothing for team morale.

He was below par for Gloucester in the summer too, and made no impression on the home series with Westindies in 1980/1, though Colin Croft made an impression on him, putting a two inch dent in his helmet with a bouncer. Zaheer had pulled out of the first Test, ostensibly with a shoulder injury, but knowing he was out of form he seemed to have lost his nerve against the quicks even before Croft hit him, as he developed a tendency not to stay in line.

Imran Khan feels he was never the same batsman after that series. In the past he used to hook and pull with aplomb, but word soon gets round when a player is thought to be suspect against the short stuff. Zaheer had a high back-lift and his first movement was onto the front foot, and he had to change his grip to facilitate playing quick bowling. India's captain, Mohammad Azharuddin, had a similar problem in the late eighties and went to Zaheer for advice.

Yet in domestic cricket he was superb, making over a thousand runs at an average in the nineties. He made 100 not out in each innings for PIA against Railways, and captained his side to victory in the PACO cup and to second place in the Quaid-e-Azam Trophy. He took that form with him to Gloucester in 1981. He scored 2,305 runs at an average of 88.69, hit ten more hundreds (to add to his five in the winter), twice hitting a hundred in each innings, which each included a hundred before lunch. He was the first to a thousand runs that season, despite not playing a first-class innings in April or May (because of the weather), as he amassed 1,016 runs in June at an average of 112.88.

In Australia, in 1981/2, he missed the first Test through injury, after being hurt whilst fielding in the game against Victoria, but he made a classy 80 in the second Test at Brisbane and 90 in the third at the MCG to finish top of the averages. He was also Pakistan's top batsman in the limited-overs triangular competition with Australia and Westindies, making a fine hundred against the former.

He captained on a few occasions in the one-day games and sought the job on a permanent basis. He had been in open conflict with Javed Miandad in the players' dressing room and was quick to join the stand against his captaincy after that tour.

Consequently he missed the first two Tests v Sri Lanka, but celebrated his return with a fine hundred in Lahore. He was bitterly upset to be overlooked for the captaincy of the 1982 tour to England, perhaps because of his feud with Javed, as they each refused to play under the other. The captaincy issue was to mar his outlook for at least the next three years.

Considering his experience of English conditions and a tour average in the seventies, he was a disappointment in the Tests, though he did make an important 75 at Lord's. His partnership there of 153 with Mohsin Khan set up a match-winning score.

He had a superb winter at home in 1982/3, making 919 Test runs at an average of 114.87, to end a long lean patch in which he had scored only 528 runs in his previous 23 Test innings. The Australians imagined him to be vulnerable against the new ball, but the success of the top order meant he was only ever subjected to the second new ball of the innings! In the first Test at Karachi he benefited from three dropped chances to top-score with 91, and in the next, on a turgid Faisalabad pitch, he made a fine hundred sharing a stand of 155 for the 4th wicket with Mansoor Akhtar. Again he took advantage of misses at 57 and 119. His innings of 126 included 19 in an over from Peter Sleep in an otherwise watchful innings. A brilliant hundred followed in the one-day international, and he made another fifty in the final Test, to complete a sequence of seven scores in a row over fifty.

He was at his best in the home series with India that started two months later. He made his 99th first-class hundred, for the Patron's XI against the tourists, a few days before the first Test at Lahore which gave him the chance of emulating Geoff Boycott in 1977, by scoring his 100th first-class hundred in an international. Like Boycott, he made sure it was a big one, going on to his fourth Test double hundred - only Don Bradman, Javed Miandad and Walter Hammond have more. He batted for only five and half hours, facing 254 balls, and hit 23 fours and two sixes as he took the attack apart, recording the fourth fastest 200 in Test history off only 241 balls.

He was the first and, as yet, only Pakistani to the landmark, which was achieved in only his 658th innings: only Bradman (295), Len Hutton (619) and Boycott (645) have taken fewer innings to complete the feat. Curiously, Viv Richards took the same number.

In the one-dayer at Multan between the Tests, he made another glorious hundred and shared in a record stand of 205 with Mohsin Khan in only 27 overs. Then in the Test, with Pakistan struggling at 18 for 3, he put on 110 with Javed Miandad, and 213 with Mudassar Nazar to set up an innings victory, as he made 186 in his home town. By now the Indians did not know where to bowl at him.

Another hundred followed in an overs game at Lahore (reduced to 33 per side, because of a delayed start), in which Pakistan amassed 252, and Zaheer made a third consecutive Test hundred, at Faisalabad, where he added 287 in partnership with Miandad for the 4th wicket. Salim Malik and Imran Khan also made hundreds in a total of 652.

That was Zaheer's sixth hundred in a row in all cricket against India, and he was only denied the chance of another by a record partnership of 451 between Mudassar and Miandad in the 4th Test, that delayed him from getting to the crease but for a brief 25 not out before the declaration. Still not satiated, he made his sixth one-day international hundred in the next game, in Karachi, making 113 from 99 balls with three sixes and 11 fours, dominating a 2nd wicket partnership of 170 with Mudassar Nazar.

In all cricket against the touring sides that season his scores read: 26, 91, 126, 109, 52, 5 not out (v Australia) and 10, 108, 215, 118, 186, 105, 168, 25 not out, 113 (v India). At last the bubble burst in the final two Tests, scoring 13 and 43. Among them Zaheer, Mudassar and Miandad had scored over 2,000 runs in the series - a unique contribution with each averaging over a hundred.

Pakistan again reached the semi-final in the World Cup in 1983, but then the batting let them down against Westindies, collapsing after Zaheer had played on to Larry Gomes in the over before lunch. To reach the semis, Pakistan had had to make a big score in their last game against New Zealand. Zaheer responded with a marvellous hundred in a dazzling partnership of 147 in 75 minutes with Imran to bring victory and improve their scoring rate sufficiently. Earlier Zaheer had made scores of 82 against Sri Lanka and 83 not out against England.

In a shortened season with Gloucester, because of the World Cup and preparation at home for India, "Zed" (his usual sobriquet) played two remarkable one-day innings. He made 158 as his side chased over 300 against Leicester, and another hundred in the Sunday League against Middlesex to chase 271.

Zaheer's amazing form the previous winter had been pivotal in Pakistan's best-ever sequence in Tests, winning six out of seven, so when Imran Khan was sidelined with a stress fracture of the shin, Zaheer was the obvious replacement even

Zaheer had a distinguished county career with Gloucestershire

though his first assignment was to take the side to India, where he had failed last time.

His captaincy proved to be tactically weak and he was inclined to avoid risks. Imran called it "too cautious and self-absorbed." Zaheer made sure the series with India was not lost - he was under instructions from the Board to do so - which gave his side the moral victory as they were playing away. However, he missed the opportunity to push home an advantage at Jullundar and Nagpur.

Imran made himself available as a batsman only for the tour to Australia - as he had done successfully in the World Cup - and was re-instated as captain much to Zaheer's chagrin. However, when a selectorial dispute cropped up, a Karachi-biased pressure group formed, and sought to appoint the more malleable Zaheer.

When Imran discovered that he would not be able to play immediately because of his injury, Zaheer (who was vice-captain) took over but he issued a disclaimer, saying that it was not the team he would have chosen, though he did not elucidate on his choice. Zaheer was obviously unhappy with the situation, which soured the whole tour, but surprisingly he turned down the captaincy when the BCCP felt obliged to appoint him officially.

Imran did return for the 4th and 5th Tests, drawing one and losing the last, and Zaheer, who was dissatisfied with the whole affair, left the tour early to work on his benefit season, missing the one-day competition. When this went disastrously badly, with Pakistan winning just one game in ten, Zaheer pressed his case for the captaincy in his newspaper column of the Karachi-based paper, *Dawn.*

In fact, Imran's injury prevented him playing for some tim, and so Zaheer took over again for the home series with England, which was won 1-0 by virtue of a 3-wicket win in a tense 1st Test at Karachi. It was Pakistan's first win in 13 matches with England in Pakistan and gave the home team their first series win over England. In the third Test at Lahore a groin injury meant Zaheer had to bat with a runner in both innings, but he was fit enough to make 82 not out in the first knock.

He left Gloucestershire half way through the 1984 season, jaded after eleven Tests the previous winter and the imbroglio over the captaincy issue. A strict Moslem, Zed was very much the quiet family man and was happy to return early to be at home with his wife and daughters.

With Imran Khan still out of action, Zaheer remained in charge. Always at his best at home to India he started the 1984/5 series by making his 12th and final Test hundred, equalling Hanif Mohammad's record for Pakistan (since beaten by Javed Miandad), and sixth against India. It was his only Test hundred in 14 Tests as captain, though his

Zaheer comes unstuck against a short ball

average remained constant. His 168 was his third in a row against India at Lahore. Typically, he cashed in once he reached three figures. Indeed, his average three figure score was nearly 180 and only Bradman and Brian Lara average more among those with more than half a dozen Test centuries to their name. Unfortunately the series, which was drawn, was marred by umpiring controversy, and more importantly by the assassination of Indira Ghandi during the 2nd one-dayer. That game was abandoned on hearing the news, and the rest of the series was cancelled.

A few weeks later Zaheer led the side against New Zealand to a comfortable 2-0 home win, but again the umpiring caused concern. During the 1st Test at Lahore and Zaheer's 72nd match, he became the first Pakistani to pass 5,000 runs in Test cricket, though generally he had a poor series. Strangely, he had an indifferent overall record against New Zealand, and Javed Miandad took over for the return leg there, as Zaheer stood down citing mental stress as the reason. Consequently, he joined the tour late and had an unhappy time once he got there; again out of touch with the bat, he also had an altercation with Abdul Qadir, who was subsequently sent home.

Zaheer's demise was unexpectedly rapid. He played just one more Test innings, in the series against Sri Lanka in 1985/6. In the first Test he sat with his pads on while 397 were added for the third wicket and never got in. He announced during the 2nd Test at Sialkot - his birthplace - that he would retire at the end of the series. He made just four in his only innings there and withdrew on the eve of the final Test, to be played in his home town of Karachi, claiming he had been forced to stand down by certain senior players. He went to Sharjah shortly after but he did not play.

It was not the finale Zaheer deserved. He was a most gifted batsman of enormous charm; his high-back lift, sound technique and wristy strokes gave him unsurpassed timing. However, when this was slightly out he could struggle, and being a perfectionist who was not happy unless he was scoring heavily. Consequently he could become introspective which only compounded any loss of form or confidence.

At his best he was a complete player with shots all round the wicket, masterful in one-day cricket, and though thought to be suspect against high pace, this is not fully substantiated in his figures. He did not score particularly well against the Westindies, it is true, but had a good record against Australia; oddly it was New Zealand that was his real bogey team.

Zaheer certainly scored most heavily at home, particularly against India, whose spin attack he mastered, and he tended to make his large scores on good batting tracks. One cannot criticise him for cashing in on favourable conditions though. He certainly made the most of them, going on to make big hundreds, and like no other, taking that form into the second innings; uniquely he has scored a hundred in each innings eight times in first-class cricket.

Unlike other batsmen with a love of records and averages, he batted with a carefree spirit, determined to score runs by dominating rather than accumulating. Zaheer once said, "I have the same ideas about making runs as Boycott," yet his immense concentration was geared towards textbook, flowing strokeplay rather than defence. John Thicknesse, of the London *Evening Standard*, wrote of him that "he was from that select band of batsmen incapable of a boring innings."

Somerset's Dennis Breakwell will testify to that as he found to his cost, conceding 30 in an over (466626) in an amazing Zaheer hundred in 1979. In all he hit nine sixes and 11 fours in his innings of 147, made in two and a quarter hours of brilliant strokes, and with little support from the other end - the next highest score was Sadiq Mohammad's 24.

His record in one-day cricket was phenomenal, indeed unsurpassed amongst players who played more than 20 games. Although he played before the era when limited-overs cricket was commonplace, he made over 2,500 runs in 62 games at an average of 47.63, which included seven hundreds and 13 fifties.

The captaincy proved a millstone around his neck; he was not really suited to it nor to the ramifications of its pursuit in Pakistani cricket - being a quiet family man - and Imran's shadow put unfair pressure on him. This probably exaggerated his defensive approach to the job, drawing ten of his 14 matches in charge, but losing only one, in Australia, when he had neither Imran Khan or Sarfraz Nawaz to bowl for him. He scored well as a captain and recorded a first series win over England.

Overall Zed was a magnificent batsman, peerless when on the top of his form, a record-breaker, yet always an entertainer.

Zaheer's record sequence of scores

(hundreds in each innings)

216* & 156* v Surrey, The Oval, 1976
230* & 104* v Kent, Canterbury, 1976
205* & 108* v Sussex, Cheltenham, 1977
100* & 100* v Railways, Lahore, 1980/1
215* & 150* v Somerset, Bath, 1981
135* & 128 v Northants, Northampton, 1981
162* & 107 v Lancashire, Gloucester, 1982
125 & 101 v Karachi, Karachi, 1982/3
* indicates not out

Career Details

Born: Sialkot, 24 July 1947
Role: right-hand, middle-order batsman, right-hand off-break bowler
Clubs: Karachi (1965/6-1975/6), Public Works Department (1968/9), PIA (1969/70-1986/7), Gloucestershire (1972-85), Sind (1975/6-1976/7) and Dawood Club (1975/6)
First-class record: (1965-86) 34,843 runs (51.54) including 108 centuries (HS 274), 28 wickets (37.82) and 262 catches
Tests: 78
Test debut: v New Zealand, Karachi, 1969/70
Test record: 5,062 runs (44.79), 3 wickets (44.00) and 34 catches
Best Performance: HS 274 v England
Tours: England 1971, 1974, 1982
Australia; 1972/3, 1976/7, 1978/79, 1981/2, 1983/4, 1984/5 (World Championship of cricket)
New Zealand; 1972/3, 1978/9, 1984/5
Westindies; 1976/7
India; 1979/80, 1983/4
Overseas Test; 45
One-day Internationals; 62
World Cups: 1975, 1979, 1983
Sharjah; 1983/4
Rest of the World: Australia (1971/2)

Imtiaz Ahmed

Imtiaz Ahmed was an automatic selection for the first decade of Pakistan's Test history. He played in 39 consecutive Tests - then a record - and thus outlasted all the others who played in his country's inaugural Test match in 1952 (though Hanif Mohammad played on longer). He played a significant part in helping to establish the side's credibility as a Test playing nation.

Imtiaz was a stylish right-handed batsman, who was particularly fond of the pull and the sweep, and developed into a most dependable wicket-keeper. He started his first-class career at the age of sixteen playing for Northern India from 1944/5 until Partition and then for the Punjab in the newly formed Pakistan.

The quality of his batting was soon evident as he scored 300 not out for the Prime Minister's XI against the Commonwealth at Bombay in 1950/1 - to register the first triple hundred by a Pakistani. The following winter he played against the MCC for a combined Bahawalpur-Karachi side, making 99 in two hours 20 minutes, and he top-scored for Pakistan in the first innings of the last unofficial Test, which was won and ultimately helped secure Pakistan full Test status.

Imtiaz was an obvious choice for Pakistan's first official Test against India at Delhi in October 1952, batting at number four, but was unfortunate to make three ducks in his first four innings. He kept his place in the side, partly because by the fourth match he had taken over the wicket-keeping from Hanif Mohammad, and also because of his outstanding form in the other matches on the tour. He made 213 not out out of 356 against Central Zone, 96 v Bombay Cricket Association and 103 v East Zone, and finished with a tour average of over 40. At last he showed some of that form in the Tests, making 57 in the final Test at Calcutta.

Imtiaz proved to be a most reliable wicket-keeper, taking the spinners and Fazal Mahmood's sharp leg-cutters without fuss. As well as making over a thousand runs, he made a record 86 dismissals for a tourist on Pakistan's first visit to England in 1954. These included 59 catches when 'keeping and 21 stumpings, and another six catches as a fielder. In the fourth Test he took seven catches, all off Fazal, in the historic win at the Oval. "Caught Imtiaz bowled Fazal" became a most familiar end for batsmen, that was to claim 29 victims in all.

Although moving around in the order, his batting was beginning to show more consistency, with three fifties in the 1954/5 home series with India, and another in the first Test against New

Zealand at Karachi (1955/6). No one though could have expected what happened in his next (26th) innings against the same opposition in his home town of Lahore. Coming in at 111 for 6, with Pakistan still requiring 37 to avoid the follow on, he and Waqar Hassan put on 308, a Pakistan record for the seventh wicket.

Hassan made 189, the highest score for Pakistan, but that record lasted only about an hour as Imtiaz became the first Pakistani to score a Test double hundred, batting for 680 minutes and hitting 28 fours. His 209 was the highest in all Tests by a wicket-keeper until beaten by his compatriot Taslim Arif, who made 210 not out against Australia in 1979/80. Imtiaz's brilliant effort was also the highest innings made batting at No 8.

Later that winter Imtiaz played against the MCC touring side and, after after some appalling off-the-field behaviour by the English players towards umpire Begh during the previous Test, he felt obliged to complain that the MCC players continued this abuse of the umpires on the field during the final "Test" at Karachi.

For the tour to Westindies in 1957/8, he began to open the batting, though still keeping wicket, and made 91 in the first Test at Bridgetown, putting on 152 with his opening partner Hanif Mohammad, who went onto his epic 337. Imtiaz scored a fine 122 in the third Test at Kingston, dropping anchor after Hanif had been dismissed early, though his ton was somewhat overshadowed by Garry Sobers' 365 in the same match. Imtiaz, who had had to keep wicket for over 200 overs after his long first innings knock, could be forgiven for getting a duck in the second innings. However, he still finished the series with 344 runs at an average of 38.22.

He kept well but made little impression with the bat when Westindies toured Pakistan in 1958/9. The following season he got the chance to captain the side against Australia for one Test, at Lahore, when Fazal Mahmood was injured which, without the team's best bowler, was lost by seven wickets. However, as well as leading the side Imtiaz opened the batting, making 18 and 54, and then took four catches and made a stumping.

The tour to India in 1960/1 produced a dull sequence of draws though one of the highlights of the series was the record opening stand of 162 between Hanif Mohammad and Imtiaz at Madras,

Imtiaz made Pakistan's first double-hundred in Tests

at Edgbaston. His record sequence of 39 consecutive matches for Pakistan ended when he missed the third Test. In the fifth Test at the Oval, he became only the second batsman after Hanif Mohammad to pass 2,000 runs for Pakistan, making 49 and 98 in his final Test appearance. As he had done in 1954, he ended the tour with over a thousand runs and made over fifty dismissals.

Imtiaz finished his Test career with 93 Test dismissals and thus was close to joining an elite group of just seven wicket-keepers who have made 2,000 runs and 100 dismissals. Only Wasim Bari and Salim Yousuf have made more dismissals behind the stumps for Pakistan.

He led Pakistan against Ceylon and the Commonwealth side the following year and toured Ceylon in 1964/5. He was a squadron leader in the Pakistan Air Force and later became the Commander of the Pakistan Air Force School for Physical Fitness.

He continued to play first-class cricket until 1974 and later that year he managed the under-19 side on their tour to England. He has enjoyed several spells working for the BCCP, becoming chairman of the selectors, 1976-8. He was the assistant manager to Mahmood Hussain on Pakistan's tour to England in 1978, had another period as chairman of the selectors in 1980, and rejoined the cricket committee under Javed Burki in January 1994.

where the wicket-keeper went on to score 135. When Fazal Mahmood was dropped after that series, Imtiaz was appointed captain for the three-Test series against England in 1961/2. A quiet, shy man, who has had his reflections published in a book of poems, Imtiaz was not ideally suited to the task at a time when growing nationalism demanded results. He had a disaster with the bat, getting three ducks in a row, and only made amends with 86 in his final innings in charge, at Karachi. Yet in domestic cricket he had his most successful season with the bat in which he scored 1,142 runs, including 251 - his 4th double-hundred - for Services against Karachi Blues, and averaged almost fifty.

The 1-0 defeat was not a bad scoreline in retrospect, considering how Pakistan were to be outplayed that summer in England, losing 4-0 under the new captain, Javed Burki, whom the selectors thought ideal for the job. Imtiaz went on the tour and, despite his disappointment at losing the captaincy, scored well and continued to keep impeccably. He let through only 11 byes in four Tests and none when England rattled up over 500

Career Details

Born: Lahore (India), 5 January, 1928
Role: right-hand, middle-order or opening batsman; wicket-keeper
Clubs: Northern India (1944/5-46/7), Punjab (1947/8-1948/9), Services (1953/4-1964/5), PAF (1969/70-1972/3)
First-class record: (1944-74) 10,383 runs (37.21) including 22 centuries (HS 300 not out), 391 dismissals (315 catches, 76 stumpings)
Tests: 41
Test Debut: v India, Delhi, 1952/3
Test record: 2,079 runs (29.98), and 93 dismissals (77 ct, 16 st)
Best Performances: HS 209 v New Zealand, Lahore, 1955/6
Tours: India; 1952/3, 1960/1
England; 1954, 1962
Westindies; 1957/8
Overseas Tests; 23
Ceylon; 1948/9, 1964/5

Saeed Ahmed

Saeed Ahmed, along side Hanif Mohammad, was Pakistan's star batsman in the sixties when the side on the whole was weak. He served Pakistan with distinction for 15 years, playing in 38 consecutive Tests, toured seven times, and finished with a Test batting average bettered by only a handful of Pakistani players. A stylish, elegant right-handed batsman, with a powerful drive and full range of strokes, he was also a useful off-spinner, though he bowled only occasionally in Tests.

Saeed, who was born in Jullundar in 1937, was brought into the Test side after some fine performances for Punjab. His early Test record was a model of consistency and made a phenomenal impact on his first series, against the Westindies in 1957/8, which proved to be his most productive one, with scores of 13, 65, 11, 64, 52, 44, 150, 12 and 97 to give him over 500 runs at an average 56.44.

That fine sequence of scores allowed him to establish a remarkable record of sharing a century stand in each of the five Tests. He was one of the four partners in a row to add a hundred with Hanif Mohammad to help save the first Test at Barbados, where he put on 154 for the third wicket on his debut. In the next Test, at Port of Spain, he shared a stand of 130 for the 2nd wicket with Hanif and in the third, at Kingston, helped add 118 in a 2nd wicket partnership with Imtiaz Ahmed. During his brilliant innings of 150 at Georgetown, Saeed again paired up with Hanif, to put on 136 (for the 3rd). Then to complete the set and keep the Mohammads involved, he added 169 for the third wicket in partnership with Wazir to set up an innings victory in the final Test back in Trinidad. It was a brilliant start to his Test career.

The Westindies must have been sick at the sight of Saeed and Hanif batting together because in the first Test of the return series (1958/9), at Karachi, they took Pakistan well beyond the tourists' first innings score with a 2nd wicket partnership of 178, which helped Pakistan to win the game. Saeed finished with the most runs in the series though injury to Hanif in the first Test precluded the chance of any more centuries together.

Saeed's form remained impressive as he averaged over fifty in the next two rubbers. Against Australia in 1959/60, he made 166 (a Pakistani record against them until 1979/80) at Lahore - the first time the new grass pitch there had been used - and 91 at Karachi. A retrospective Coopers and Lybrand rating at this stage of his career would earn him 874 points, which only Javed Miandad has bettered for Pakistan.

The following season he made two more Test hundreds - one dour, the other stylish - in the drawn series in India. Needless to say, the first of those came in tandem with one from Hanif as this dynamic duo set a 2nd wicket record for Pakistan of 246 in the 1st Test at Bombay. This was a crucial stand as once they were parted with the score at 301, the side collapsed to 350 all out. His second hundred was made in the high-scoring draw at Madras.

In home and away series against England (1961-2) his form was competent rather than spectacular, but he still made five fifties in eight Tests. He scored 1,294 runs on the tour, an aggregate only exceeded by Mustaq Mohammad.

Pakistan went for over two years without Test cricket but he soon found his touch when matches resumed in 1964/5, making an eighty at both Melbourne and Christchurch. When New Zealand toured Pakistan, Saeed made his highest Test score, a superb 172 not out (out of 307 for 8 declared) at Karachi, which turned the match around and secured Pakistan the series. He shared a stand for the 3rd wicket of 114 with Javed Burki, of which Burki made only 29, the innings' next top score. Saeed batted for five hours 40 minutes, playing splendidly throughout, and so dominated the scoring that he finished with 64 per cent of the total runs off the bat, which is among the highest proportions of any Test innings.

Again Pakistan was without Test cricket for two years, though Saeed played some games for the MCC in 1966. He returned to England in 1967 and in the 2nd Test held the innings together on a difficult pitch at Trent Bridge, where he top-scored in each innings, with 44 out of 140 and 68 out of 114.

Although he was an experienced captain, leading both Punjab University and Lahore, Saeed was a surprising choice as captain of his country considering his individual style and frequent differences with the

Board of Control for Cricket in Pakistan. He was in charge for just one series, against England in 1968/9, which was marred by social unrest and eventually cut short by student demonstrations, which forced the last two days of the third Test at Karachi - and of his tenure as captain - to be abandoned.

His career came to a disappointing end for he lost his place for the next series against New Zealand, in Pakistan in 1969/70, despite his good record against them, which included his highest score in the last Test between the two sides (1964/5). His brother, Younis Ahmed, in effect took his place, playing in the first two Tests of that series, making 62 on his debut.

However, Younis had to wait 17 years and 111 days for his next Test appearance, against India in 1986, when Imran Khan called him up for two more matches, as he wanted a left-hander in the side and a man of proven experience. He did quite well in the second of those, making 40 and 34 not out, batting slowly but after 17 years he was not going to throw his wicket away. However, he reacted angrily when he was left out of the squad to tour England in 1987. Prior to that he had a distinguished county career, for Surrey (262 matches, 1965-78), Worcester (85 matches, 1979-83) and then for Glamorgan (58 matches, 1984-6) and was capped by each, though left the first two counties under acrimonious circumstances. He went to court claiming unfair dismissal after being sacked by Surrey, and left Worcester after making a £100 bet against his own team during a Sunday League match against Leicester. At one stage during his long absence from Test cricket he considered qualifying, by residence, for England. He finished his career with over 26,000 first-class runs, fifth among Pakistanis and behind only Zaheer Abbas, Mustaq Mohammad, Javed Miandad and Majid Khan, scored at an average of above 40. His career figures are almost identical to those of David Gower.

His name hit the headlines again in May 1994 when he alleged that Imran Khan had shown him how to doctor a cricket ball, in a story he sold to the *Mail on Sunday*.

Saeed Ahmed had his best domestic season in 1970/1, making over a thousand runs at an average of 56.22, including a double-hundred for Karachi against Public Works Department, which earned him a re-call for the tour to England that summer. Despite the experience of two previous tours there, he never really found his form and only played in the last Test, at Headingley, because Majid Khan was unavailable. He was the senior player on the tour, but when he had to share a room with Imran Khan, a cocky 18-year-old on his first trip, he encouraged him to go out partying. Hoping to get his own room Saeed then reported Imran for consistently waking him up, which he cited as the reason for his poor form. In a county game he was reduced to tears after several catches had gone down off his bowling.

He was also an unhappy tourist in Australia in 1972/3, where he was constantly feuding with Intikhab Alam (who had replaced him as captain). In the first Test at Adelaide (where, incidentally, Younis Ahmed was playing his cricket that winter), he was promoted to opener after Dennis Lillee had broken Talat Ali's thumb in the first innings. He made 39 and then scored a fine, if unorthodox, fifty in the second Test at Melbourne, but had several heated exchanges with Lillee, who let it be known that he was going to go after him on the fast, well-grassed pitch at the Sydney Cricket Ground, where the next Test was to be played.

Saeed withdrew on the eve of the Test, complaining of a back injury, and on the second day of the match was told that he and Mohammad Ilyas would not be required for the second half of the tour, to New Zealand, technically for a "lack of fitness". Saeed went home in disgrace, while Ilyas stayed on in Australia and applied for citizenship; neither played Test cricket again.

Saeed's cricketing career was effectively over, too, though he did appear against the England touring side as late as 1977, for the North-west Frontier Governor's XI. He had finished with a solid career batting average of over 40, and had taken 332 wickets at 24.75 apiece.

He was a difficult, maverick character, like his half-brother Younis, and never far from controversy. While his exit from Test cricket was inglorious, this belies a fine cricketing ability for he scored nearly three thousand Test runs at a commendable average and often held the batting together at a time when the side was frequently at a low ebb during the sixties.

Career Details

Born: Jullundur, India, 1 October 1937
Role: right-hand, middle-order batsman, slow-medium off-spinner.
Clubs: Punjab (1954/5-1957/8), Railways (1955/6), Lahore (1959/60), PIA (1961/2-1962/3), Karachi (1961/2-1971/2) and Public Works Department (1971/2)
First-class record: (1954-78) 12,847 runs (40.02) including 34 centuries (HS 203 not out), 332 wickets (24.75) and 122 catches
Tests: 41
Test Debut: v Westindies, Bridgetown, 1957/8
Test record: 2,991 runs (40.41), 22 wickets (36.45) and 13 catches
Best Performances: HS 172 v New Zealand, Karachi, 1964/65
BB 4-64 v England, Lahore 1968/9
Tours: Westindies; 1957/8
India; 1960/1
England; 1962, 1967, 1971
Australia; 1964/5, 1972/3
New Zealand; 1964/5
Overseas Tests; 25
International XI; Rhodesia 1961/2
Rest of the World; England 1968

Tauseef Ahmed

Tauseef Ahmed's progression to the Test side is one to match every schoolboy's dream. Having played just one first-class match, and even that of dubious status, Tauseef was chosen to play for Pakistan on the strength of an hour long net just prior to what proved to be his maiden Test match. He played on and off for the next fourteen years, establishing himself as his country's most successful off-spinner with 93 Test wickets.

Born in 1960 in Karachi, he originally aspired to being a batsman who could bowl a bit of medium pace. However he never grew beyond 5 foot 5 inches tall and he was persuaded by friends to take up bowling off-breaks, which were immediately successful. He could turn the ball prodigiously given a little encouragement from the pitch. Imran Khan heard about Tauseef from a friend who had seen the little off-spinner bowl with great success in a local league. Imran took the recommendation with a pinch of salt as he knew the quality of the wickets in such leagues was poor, offering generous assistance to the spinners. However Tauseef was called up just to satisfy Imran's insistent friend.

It did not take long for the captain Javed Miandad and the manager Mustaq Mohammad to realise that he was indeed better than the off-spinner already chosen in the XII for the match. So Tauseef, who had never even seen a Test, was plucked from obscurity to play for Pakistan while still just a teenager of nineteen. He had a dream start too. On a Karachi pitch taking spin, he returned slightly better figures than his more experienced partner, Iqbal Qasim, finishing with four for 64 from 30.2 overs, as each took four wickets.

In the second innings Iqbal came into his own, but Tauseef played his part with three more wickets, including Kim Hughes for the second time in the match and the Australian captain, Greg Chappell. In the next Test, with Australia making a huge total on a placid Faisalabad pitch, he was the pick of the bowlers, taking three for 77 from 33 overs, and finished the series with 12 wickets at 29.66.

Both Ijaz Faqih and Mohammad Nazir Junior were used ahead of Tauseef in the next series against Westindies, but at least he was now playing first-class cricket regularly and finished the winter with 61 wickets for United Bank. Another excellent domestic season in 1981/2, in which he took 87 wickets at 18.22, ensured his re-call to the national side, albeit because of the players' revolt, which had seen most of the side who had toured Australia refuse to continue under Javed Miandad. Tauseef kept his place for the third Test at Lahore despite the return of the rebels, and his four top-order wickets in the second innings helped ensure an innings victory.

Surprisingly he was not selected for the tour to England that summer and with Abdul Qadir and Iqbal Qasim becoming firmly established as the two front-line spinners, he slipped out of contention. After a couple of tidy domestic seasons (1982-4) in which he took over 100 wickets in all at 20 runs apiece, he had an outstanding season in 1984/5, with 83 wickets at 15.83, including 15 wickets for 148 for United Bank in the Quaid-e-Azam trophy group match against Railways, and then seven for 61 in the final against them. One would have thought that that would have put him back on the right track with the selectors yet he played in only one Test against India and one against New Zealand that winter and with limited success.

Recalled for the third Test at Karachi against Sri Lanka (1985/6), he took five for 54 in the second innings, as Pakistan won by ten wickets. It ensured his place on the reciprocal tour at the end of the season, and in the first Test at Kandy he produced a match-winning performance. After an important last wicket stand of 39 with Akram, Tauseef took six for 45 in the second innings, his Test best, to give him nine for 77 in the match. Yet he was out of the side by the third Test, dropped in favour of Qadir.

He played in three Tests at home against Westindies (1986/7), chipping in with some useful wickets, as well as playing a couple of gutsy innings in the first Test. In the series that followed against India, he finished as Pakistan's leading wicket-taker. In the first Test at Madras he helped Imran Khan in an unbroken stand of 81 for the tenth wicket and then sent down 67 overs on the docile pitch. He was ill and could not play in the 4th Test, but he came back with a superb performance in a thrilling match at Bangalore. In Pakistan's first innings of just 116 he made a useful 15 not out, but really came into his own with the ball on a rapidly deteriorating pitch. He bowled the first three batsman and then had Dilip Vengsarkar and Ravi Shastri caught to finish with five for 54 to restrict India's lead.

He played another crucial innings second time round; although he made only ten, he and Salim Yousuf added 51 for the 9th wicket which was to make all the difference later. Tauseef opened the bowling and bowled virtually unchanged, sending down 45.5 overs, largely in tandem with Iqbal Qasim, and each finished with four victims. In a nail-biting finish Tauseef took the last wicket to secure Pakistan victory by just 16 runs to give his side their first series in India. It was his ninth wicket of the match in his 73rd over at a cost of only 139 runs.

He was an automatic choice for the tour to England in 1987, but struggled at first to come to terms with the English wickets in a wet start to the summer. However, he bowled tidily in the rain-ruined first Test at Old Trafford but broke a finger catching David Capel in the county match against Northamptonshire that followed. He returned in time for the fifth Test at the Oval even though he had played no first-class cricket in between. He did a creditable job considering, bowling nearly 70 overs in support of Abdul Qadir.

Tauseef's ill-fortune continued in the winter. He split a finger attempting a return catch which required two-stitches in the World Cup semi-final, and then in the first one-day international on the tour to Westindies (1987-88), he was injured again and had to be sent home. In between, he played in the unsavoury series with England but had been dropped for the final Test to make way for another seamer despite bowling well in tandem with Qadir in the previous Tests. Indeed, his one first innings wicket at Lahore prevented the leg-spinner taking all ten in the innings.

Pakistan played three specialist spinners in their next home series (1988/9), with Tauseef being chosen to provide the off-breaks against an Australian side which usually contained three or four left-handers. In the first Test, after playing a determined innings of 35 as night-watchman, in which he out-scored Javed Miandad in a 4th wicket partnership of 67, he bowled with remarkable economy, sending down 47.4 overs to take three for 44 in the match to help towards Pakistan's innings victory. He bowled steadily throughout the rest of the series, finishing with 11 wickets at 24 runs apiece, and again showed signs of his new found batting talent with another 35 (not out) in the next Test at Faisalabad. That was to remain his top Test score but in the last Test he was again called upon to defend stoutly, blocking out the last five overs to prevent Pakistan slipping to defeat.

He went on the tour to New Zealand that followed in the Spring, but played only in the last Test at Auckland where he bowled with his usual economy, wheeling down 69 overs for 106 in the first innings, to provide useful support for Abdul Qadir.

With the emergence of the likes of Waqar Younis and Aqib Javed to support Imran Khan and Wasim Akram, Tauseef's opportunities have been limited of late. He did not play against India (1989/90) but bowled creditably as the senior spinner on the following tour Australia, after Abdul Qadir had returned home early.

Injuries to the faster bowlers and Imran Khan's absence allowed him a place in the side for the series with New Zealand (1990/1) but when Pakistan looked to fight fire with fire against Westindies he was excluded again; Qadir and Mustaq Ahmed were preferred as the spinners to support Imran, Wasim and Waqar. Tauseef was unlucky not to play for the next three years, after all he was just behind Qadir in the Coopers and Lybrand ratings after their last series together in 1990, and in his 70 one-day internationals he always proved to be a reliable and tight bowler.

However, he did get a surprise recall for one Test against Zimbabwe at Karachi in 1993/4 but unfortunately he did not manage to add to his 93 Test wickets in that, his 34th match. He was only 33 at the time and finished the 1994/5 domestic seasons second in the averages with 45 wickets, including a hat-trick, so it is just possible that his experience will be called upon again, though Saqlain Mustaq is establishing himself fast. Tauseef deserves the chance of completing 100 Test, for his wickets have come at a better average than even Qadir's, and it would be a shame if he were to slip out of Test cricket as rapidly as he entered it.

Career Details

Born: Karachi, 10 May 1960
Role: right-hand, lower-order batsman, right-hand off-break bowler
Clubs: Public Works Department (1978/9), United Bank (1980/1-1994/5), Karachi (1983/4-1989/90)
First-class record: (1978-95) 1627 runs (15.06) HS 77; 631 wickets (22.27), 42 x 5w, 7 x 10w, BB 8-52, and 66 catches
Tests: 34
Test Debut: v Australia, Karachi, 1979/80
Test record: 318 runs (17.66), 93 wickets (31.72) and 9 catches
Best Performances: HS 35 v Australia, Karachi, 1988/9, & 35 not out v Australia, Faisalabad, 1988/9
BB: 6/45 v Sri Lanka, Kandy, 1985/6
Tours: Sri Lanka; 1984/5
India; 1986/7
England; 1987
Westindies; 1987/8
Australia; 1988/9, 1989/90
Bangladesh; 1988/9
One-day Internationals; 70
World Cups; 1987/8

Wasim Akram

Wasim Akram is generally regarded as the most difficult bowler in the world to play against. As well as extreme pace, he has remarkable versatility, able to swing and cut the ball, old or new, whether bowling over or around the wicket. As an all-rounder, he is perhaps peerless amongst his contemporaries, succeeding the era of great all-rounders such as Imran Khan, Richard Hadlee, Ian Botham and Kapil Dev. As such, the selectors chose him to captain Pakistan into its fifth decade of Test cricket. As their key player it was a risk and a challenge, but as with Imran Khan, it was hoped that the extra responsibility would bring the best out in him especially his batting, which had promised so much, but after 53 Tests had brought just over a thousand runs. Instead the gamble backfired; as a player, Wasim had been thoroughly popular, very much a team man and respected for his talent, but found that his form and popularity both waned rapidly once he took on the captain's mantle. Wasim had to wait nearly three years for another chance to show he was the right man for the job, and despite losing his first two Tests back, Pakistan recovered to win the next two. Most importantly, Wasim's form remained unimpaired. The tour to England was a great success, both off and on the field. Wasim showed how much his leadership and man management had improved, and dare I say it, he could be in charge for some time to come.

Wasim has run into more than his fair share of controversy, but such matters though are a total misrepresentation of the man, who is likely to be without peer as an all-rounder in Tests in the nineties, and is already regarded by many as the finest left-arm fast bowler of all time. In the one-day game, he can turn a match in a couple of overs with bat or ball, and is on the point of becoming the first player to score 2,000 runs and take 300 wickets in limited-overs internationals.

Wasim was born in Lahore in June 1966 to a well-to-do family, who lived in the district of Model Town. His father, Choudhry Mohammad Akram, who runs a spare parts business, sent him first to be educated at the private, English-speaking Cathedral School, where he soon made his mark in the school team, playing in the first team from the age of 12 and captaining in his last year there, aged 15. He used to play cricket all the time, practising in the nets and playing in many an impromptu street competition, played with a tennis ball around Mazang Adda in the old part of Lahore, where Wasim was popular as well as successful as there was usually a winner-takes-all kitty. He was somewhat rebellious, skiving off school to go biking with friends or to play cricket, rather than settling down to his studies.

When he changed schools to go to Islamia College, he did not get a regular place in his new school's side in his first year, but playing club cricket for Ludhiana he turned in some strong performances and he was invited to the traditional close season talent camps. He won immediate selection for the National under-19s, where Khan Mohammad took a liking to him and worked on his pace, getting him to throw his front arm higher. He also impressed Javed Miandad in the nets, who got him selected to make his first-class debut for the Patron's XI against the touring New Zealanders a few weeks later. He made an auspicious start, taking seven for 50 in the first innings and added two more wickets in the second. When Sarfraz Nawaz announced his retirement after the first one-dayer Wasim was drafted in for his first international, albeit for a curtailed game in which he bowled four expensive overs.

He did not make the Test side that series but had to wait only until the tour to New Zealand for his opportunity. He was so naive then that he did not even know that players got paid for going on tour, and when he asked his captain how much spending money he should take he was shocked by Javed's quip of $50,000. Miandad had to fight hard for Wasim's inclusion but Wasim soon vindicated the decision, coming in for the second Test at Auckland to spearhead an attack that had been relying on the medium pace of Mudassar Nazar to open the bowling. In the next Test at Dunedin Wasim became the youngest bowler, at 18 years and eight months, to take ten wickets in a Test, with figures of five for 56 and five for 72, and almost bowled Pakistan to a victory that would have squared the series. Towards the end he hit Lance Cairns with a bouncer that fractured the batsman's skull, and forced him out of Test cricket. He was also warned for intimidatory bowling. Although he overdid the short-pitched ball early in his career - something many bowlers have resorted to in Pakistan when there is no movement - he has now perfected its use as a shock tactic.

Despite his inexperience, unfamiliarity with conditions and lack of decent kit (he had to borrow some proper pads from Miandad), his ability to swing the ball at pace was apparent and he was soon to learn to keep the ball up to maximise movement, like the great bowlers of old. However he found it difficult settling into the side with senior players treating him like a new boy in a school and took awhile to feel comfortable in the side. After two quiet series at home and away to Sri Lanka and a plethora of one-day internationals in 1985/6, Wasim began to show his all-round worth in a hectic year and a half (starting in October 1986), which saw him playing in 19 Tests, the World Cup and nearly 30 other one-dayers, before playing in his first full season in county cricket with Lancashire. Not surprisingly all this cricket began to take its toll on him physically. A tall, wiry man, standing 6 foot 3 inches tall, he weighs only twelve and a half stone and the aches and strains of fast bowling began to tell.

Imran Khan had already pronounced Wasim to be "easily the most promising young player in the world" and he soon began to show why he was rated so highly. In the first Test at Faisalabad against the Westindies (1986/7), he took 6-91 and scored 66, including sixes off Malcolm Marshall and Tony Gray, to set up his side's victory. Unfortunately he twisted his ankle while fielding

in the next game at Lahore and missed the last Test of the series, but by now felt part of the team and confident in his own ability. He was fit again for the tour to India, where he helped Pakistan to their first series win there. Despite the hostile crowds and the generally bland nature of the wickets, he still bowled some telling spells, taking five wickets for 96 in the 1st innings at Calcutta, and producing a four for 10 burst at Ahmedabad, knocking over the last three batsmen in five balls. In the first Test he had made a thrilling fifty, which included five sixes, adding a record 112 for the 8th wicket with Imran Khan, helping take Pakistan to their highest score in India, 487 for 9 declared.

Soon after Wasim was signed by Lancashire on a unique long term contract. David Hughes, the Lancashire captain, had seen him during the Perth Challenge matches at the beginning of 1987, and he was signed later in secret in Sharjah, just before Pakistan's tour to England. Wasim had spent the previous summer playing League cricket for Burnopfield in Durham on Imran's recommendation, to give him experience of English conditions, but found it very cold and a bit lonely, despite sharing a flat with his compatriot Mohsin Kamal.

In a badly rain-affected series Wasim shouldered the attack when Imran Khan could not bowl in the first Test and ensured his side a draw

Wasim has great untapped potential as a batsman

in the fourth when England had the chance of squaring the series by chasing 124 off 18 overs at Edgbaston, bowling all the overs from one end. He also played some swashbuckling innings, hitting 43 off 41 balls including four sixes on a tricky Headingley wicket. He was struck down with appendicitis during the final Test, which probably cost Pakistan the chance to push for victory but by that stage Pakistan had secured there first series win in England.

With their good recent record and as co-hosts, Pakistan were favourites in the 1987 World Cup; their unexpected defeat in the semi-final to Australia caused a grievance that spilled over into the home series against England. Wasim missed the notorious match at Faisalabad with a groin injury, and was not fully fit for the final Test, but played and bowled a few overs with the new ball.

Wasim had to have minor surgery on his groin and hernia injuries and was still recuperating when the squad left for the Westindies in the Spring of 1988. Imran Khan, who had been persuaded out of retirement, insisted that Wasim travelled with them and trained back to fitness during the early part of the tour. Though still carrying niggling injuries he played an important supporting role in the first two Tests, and in the third at Barbados, Wasim bowled with great heart and stamina, keeping going almost throughout in the second innings as Westindies just scraped home by two wickets. It was an extremely hard fought and fiercely competitive series. Some important decisions seemingly went against Pakistan in the third Test, one of which led to an altercation between Wasim and Viv Richards who, after an exchange of words, suggested in the heat of the moment that they settle it outside the ground later.

Straight after the tour Wasim went into his first county season with Lancashire, when really he should have rested his groin injury, for it proved to be a persistent problem and he broke down seven weeks before the end of the season, requiring further remedial surgery. He played in just ten out of 22 Championship matches but put in some excellent performances, including a century in his first match at Old Trafford, and against Surrey scored 58 and 98 (off 78 balls) and took eight wickets in the match including a hat-trick.

His injury meant that he missed Pakistan's next two Test series, though he managed a one-day tournament in Australia in between. He also played in the 1989 Sharjah competition just before the next English season, where he bowled in tandem with Waqar Younis for the first time. Again Wasim played in only half of Lancashire's Championship matches because of injuries, but was an integral part of the county's winning of the Sunday League, taking over 40 wickets.

The following winter he established himself as a world class all-rounder, the ramifications of which - added pressure and recognition - were to have a bearing on his next season at Lancashire. He helped Pakistan win a thrilling Nehru Cup final against the Westindies; with three runs required from the last two balls of Richards' over, he swung his first ball high into the crowd at mid-wicket for an astonishing six. Then Pakistan played in a typical stalemate against India, but Wasim gave the home side its few moments of supremacy, finishing with 18 wickets in the series, the best on either side. He accounted for Srikkanth, the Indian captain, six times in a row early on, and consistently posed problems, especially with the new ball.

In Australia, Akram came into his own as an all-rounder of the highest class, indeed he was mooted for the first time as the world's best. Despite being let down by poor close to the wicket catching he still took half his side's wickets in the three Tests, including his best figures at the time, 6-62, in the first innings at the Melbourne Cricket Ground, which took him to 100 wickets in his 30th Test (78 of those had come in the last 14 Tests). He would have had more but for four dropped catches off his bowling. He followed this with 5-98 in the next innings, to give him match figures of 11-160 from 71.4 overs.

In the second Test Wasim came of age as a batsman, having spent much of his Test career lurking as low as ten or eleven in the order. He made a fine fifty off 89 balls in the first innings, though he exchanged angry words with Merv Hughes who deliberately stood in Wasim's path when he was running between the wickets. Umpire Crafter, who had "refereed" the Miandad-Lillee clash, once again had to step in.

In the second, with Pakistan struggling to save the game at 90 for five which was in effect 6 for 5, as they were 84 behind on 1st innings, Akram came out to join Imran Khan in one of the finest partnerships I've seen, sharing in a record stand of 191. The latter played the sheet-anchor role, while Wasim, with the encouragement of his captain, went for his shots. He played an innings comparable to either of Ian Botham's hundreds against Australia in 1981. His shot selection was so good, and his power and timing so impressive that he conjured memories of the likes of Garry Sobers or Graeme Pollock in their pomp. He finished with a six and 18 fours, many to Adelaide's long, straight boundaries. In a stay of just over four hours - half his captain's - he made Imran feel like a novice. It transformed the game, allowing for a challenging declaration.

In between those fine innings he had taken another five wicket haul, the third time in a row, bowling 43 overs to finish with 5-100, to join

Mustaq Mohammad and Imran as the only Pakistanis to score a hundred and take five wickets in a Test. Not surprisingly he was man-of-the-match again, later man-of-the-series, should have been in the World Series finals too, and was voted International Cricketer of the Year. Towards the end of the tour he was severely hampered by his old groin injury, requiring pain-killing injections to get him through the one-dayers. He stayed on in Australia to have another operation, this time through a top sports injuries expert, Neil Halpin, who advised that the muscle should be cut away from the bone. Within weeks he was playing again and in the Sharjah final against Australia smashed 49 not out, including 18 of the last over, and wrapped up the game with his second hat-trick over there.

The rigours of the winter and his perennial groin problem meant that he could play only seven championship matches for Lancashire in 1990. This began to niggle some of the members and committee at his county, but Wasim did play in both the one-day final victories, being instrumental in their success in the Benson and Hedges, with a rapid 28 off 21 balls which included a huge straight six into the Pavilion, and taking 3-30. The way he unsettled Graeme Hick with his pace raised the first real doubts about Hick's ability at the top level.

That winter Wasim once again suffered problems with his leg. After taking eight wickets in the first Test against New Zealand at Karachi the groin injury recurred in the 2nd game and Wasim could bowl only a few overs. He flew back to England to see a Harley Street specialist, who recommended a programme of weight-training for his left-leg which had become 50 per cent weaker than his right, since his operation to cut the four adductors away from the pelvis.

Wasim was fit again in time for the series with Westindies and played a key part in securing a draw in the contest, finishing as comfortably the leading wicket-taker on either side with 21 wickets at just 14.19 runs apiece. In the final Test, as well as making important runs in both innings, he bowled a remarkable spell to end Westindies second innings. He had Jeff Dujon caught behind, and bowled Malcolm Marshall first ball, then to his disbelief saw Ian Bishop get a leading edge to the hat-trick ball, only for Imran Khan to drop the straightforward catch at mid-off, and the batsman steal a single. However, with his next two balls he had Ambrose and Walsh lbw, to become only the third bowler to take four wickets in five balls in a Test.

His new found status, on top of the demanding schedule of the winter and his leg injury again caused problems at Lancashire. There was some resentment that Wasim did not give his all to his county. In some respects this is fair - top players often give of their best on the big occasion - but it was not as though he was not trying. Wasim's action puts a lot of strain on his body as is evident by the amount of surgery he has had to have. Fast bowlers have to pace themselves throughout a season but as counties pay very high wages to players like Wasim and Waqar Younis, this can mar their judgment on such matters.

Wasim was also involved in a clash with umpire Plews that season that led to a somewhat excessive fine of £1,000, which he paid begrudgingly, with some help from his team-mates, but it almost resulted in his leaving the club. Wasim had been warned for short-pitched bowling by both umpires, and got a final warning from Plews, which meant he could not bowl again in the innings. Wasim swore mildly under his breath, saying "shit umpiring," which Plews obviously overheard and reported the matter. Wasim knew he would be reprimanded, but thought the fine too much and was upset with the committee for not replying to his letter of explanation.

Nevertheless Wasim's return for that season was his best so far, taking 56 wickets at 22.33, seven times taking five wickets in an innings (the rest of the side managed just two such hauls among them), and hitting a fine hundred against Hampshire. His value to the side was illustrated by Lancashire's record in his absence because of injury (a broken bone in his foot). He played in just one of the last eight games, six of which were lost, and his side slipped from second in the Championship to eighth.

Wasim had a sensational year in 1992, starting with the third Test in an otherwise rain-affected and somewhat pointless series with Sri Lanka, where he was man-of-the-match for his five wickets in the game and fine fifty which helped his side to a three-wicket win. The World Cup in Australia and New Zealand followed. With Imran Khan struggling with a shoulder injury and Waqar out with a stress fracture of his back, Wasim was under considerable pressure but kept Pakistan afloat in the early stages of the competition when his team was in difficulty, and although he was having trouble with no-balls and wides, swinging the new (white) ball too much, he concentrated on attack, which proved vital later.

In the Final he gave the innings the impetus it needed with 33 off 18 balls, dismissed Ian Botham early on, for nought, and then produced a devastating mid-innings spell, to turn the game. He bowled Allan Lamb, who was well set, with an unplayable ball, bowled from around the wicket that was angled in on middle stump and straightened off the pitch to hit off. No wonder Lamb cannot believe Akram's bowling is fair! The next ball he beat the hard-hitting Chris Lewis for pace with an in-swinger, to end England's challenge and ensure himself the man-of-the-match award.

In England Wasim suffered a stress fracture of his left shin during the first one-day international, and missed the first Test as his leg had to be put in plaster for two weeks. In the four remaining Tests though, he was devastating as he and Waqar Younis cut through the heart of England's batting time and time again. At Lord's he also played a crucial innings, making 45 not out to steer Pakistan to a two-wicket victory in a partnership with Waqar that took his side from 95 for eight to 141, to record one of the narrowest Test wins in history.

After the rain-ruined game at Old Trafford, where Wasim took five wickets in England's only innings, he found Headingley's helpful wicket too much of an assistance, moving the ball too much to find the edge, but on the hard true pitch at the Oval, showed the full range of his skill, changing his length, line and angle and moving the ball both ways, to take five wickets in an innings for the 12th time in Tests. His six for 67 included a spell of five for 18 in 7.1 overs to wrap up England's innings. Three more wickets in the second innings brought him the man-of-the-match award and took him to 21 wickets for the series. Fittingly he shared the man-of-the-series award with Waqar, with whom he shared 43 of the 70 wickets to fall to Pakistan's bowlers in the series.

Despite being out for three weeks because of his shin, Wasim took 82 wickets at 16.21 on the tour, finishing second in the national averages, and was instrumental in Pakistan picking up a £50,000 bonus from the sponsors, Tetley Bitter, by winning nine out of their 12 games against the counties, the best record since the legendary 1948 Australians.

During the winter of 1992/3 Wasim played across the globe. He started in domestic cricket, took part in the Hong Kong international sixes, and then went onto Australia and New Zealand. In the latter, Pakistan played a one-off Test at Hamilton, where Wasim and Waqar combined to destroy the Kiwis on the last day just as victory appeared to be theirs. Requiring only 127 to win, Wasim bowled throughout the innings from one end. Bowling with notable pace and aggression, he made the inroads on the third evening to give Pakistan a chance by taking the first three wickets, and then helped Younis complete the demolition as the last seven wickets fell for only 28. His five for 45 earned him the man-of-the-match award.

In the WSC in Australia, Pakistan were a shadow of the side that had won the World Cup less than a year before and despite Miandad's solid Test record they thought it expedient to replace him. With Imran Khan's backing, Wasim's recent form swayed the captaincy his way. Immediately, Pakistan started winning again, taking the Wills Trophy - and the man-of-the-series award - in Sharjah, albeit against the lesser lights of international cricket, Zimbabwe and Sri Lanka, and played reasonably well in a triangular tournament in South Africa, against the host nation and Westindies.

Pakistan travelled to the Caribbean with confidence and started well by fighting back in the one-dayers to square the series. However, on the evening of the day they arrived in Grenada, Akram, Waqar Younis, Aqib Javed and Mustaq Ahmed were arrested on a charge of "constructive possession" of marijuana. Some reefers had been found in the sand nearby to where the four main bowlers on the tour were sitting on the beach. The allegations were completely unfounded and the charges were later dropped, but the incident threw the side off their stride.

The side never lived up to expectations in the Tests, losing 2-0. For Wasim it was a disaster; the signs had been there early on as he struggled with bat and ball in the build up to the Tests and was so obviously jaded and below his best form that he was reluctant to run in as of old. He was not helped by the lack of experience in the side and injury to key players, while it is rumoured that injured pride led to Miandad's dismissal in the 2nd Test when Pakistan were struggling to save the game; in a fit of pique he tried to hit the last ball of the day for a second consecutive six.

Tactically Wasim was improving but his man management under stress was poor. His authority diminished with his form, and at the end of the series he had only taken nine wickets, of which only two were front-line batsmen, at nearly 40 runs each, while averaging under ten with the bat. However, it must be remembered that Westindies have a unique ability - and deliberate policy - to limit the influence of the opposition captain; only Imran Khan and Graham Gooch in the previous twelve years had enhanced their reputations when leading against the Westindies. Ian Botham suffered in a similar

way when he took over. His form deteriorated, and he found it difficult to find a happy medium between commanding respect and staying "one of the lads."

Wasim's incongruous habit of courting controversy continued in England. As Lancashire were on their way to Lord's for the 1993 Benson and Hedges Final against Derbyshire, he pleaded in *The Daily Telegraph* on the morning of the match for the rumours to stop. Two weeks earlier in a Championship match, Derbyshire had made renewed claims of alleged ball-tampering after Wasim had bowled them out with a spell of six for 11 in 49 balls. The ball was inspected regularly by the umpires but Derbyshire insisted it be sent to the TCCB, who also found nothing untoward. It was a wonder they did not send his bat as well as he had scored a fine hundred against them too. Wasim found it necessary to state in the paper that there would be no sour grapes and that he would let his cricket do the talking but when, early in the final, Akram hit Chris Adams on the back of his shoulder with what could only be described as a beamer, this just stoked the fire for those wishing to keep the focus on anything other than Wasim's cricketing genius, perhaps because they realise that he is sensitive to such criticism. The papers were less than impressed by this incident calling the beamer "a disgrace" to the bowler's art. Wasim had been the match-winner in the semi-final against Leicestershire with a spell of five for two in nine balls, yet this error, which was not intentional, clearly unsettled Wasim, affecting his bowling in the rest of the match.

Wasim remained in charge of Pakistan, but had the misfortune to break his hand when hit by a full-toss from Champaka Ramanayake of Sri Lanka during the Champions Trophy in Sharjah. In his absence, after six consecutive victories in Sharjah tournaments, Pakistan lost in the final to Westindies. He missed the first Test against Zimbabwe, which was won convincingly under the leadership of Waqar Younis. Akram was fit in time for the 2nd Test and took a wicket in his first over back. He dismissed Grant Flower again with the first ball of the second innings and then, just when Zimbabwe threatened first to win the game and then to save it, Wasim took vital wickets during his 13th five wicket haul in Tests to complete his first win as captain and secure the series.

After the final Test, which was drawn, ten players - led by Waqar Younis - refused to play on under Wasim's captaincy, citing his "domineering" behaviour, repeated foul language on the field, and influence in the non-selection of Javed Miandad, Aqib Javed and Ramiz Raja for the tour to Bangladesh and New Zealand as the reasons. Akram was replaced by Salim Malik to appease the

protesters but there was no recall for Miandad, who had lost the captaincy under similar circumstances back in 1981/2. Wasim agreed to tour New Zealand saying, "If the boys are not happy with me as a captain then I'll tour as a player. It's my job to play cricket."

The same has happened to many a good player when given the captaincy, but it was a surprise that it happened to Wasim. The leadership had come unexpectedly soon. Less than a year before Imran Khan had led Pakistan to the World Cup triumph and then retired, and Javed Miandad was in charge for the series win in England and then a remarkable victory in the one-off Test against New Zealand (1992/3). Yet it was Wasim Akram who was the raison d'etre for those successes, being the man-of-the-final, -the-series and -the-match respectively. With Pakistan suffering a disastrous run in one-day cricket after the World Cup, winning just three of their next 16 games, and with Miandad below par with the bat and advancing in years, Akram was rewarded with the captaincy for the Sharjah tournament in February 1993 and then the tour of South Africa, for a triangular one-day tournament, and the Test series in the Caribbean.

Despite being only 26, he was the third oldest in the tour party to the last named, in one of the youngest-ever full international squads, average age just 23. It was thought that Wasim's age would help him relate to the younger players but as it transpired some obviously felt it difficult to cope with his new found authority. In a side already lacking experienced players it did not help that Javed Miandad was known to have been most upset by being sacked, suspecting some intrigue on behalf of Imran Khan who had, in an unofficial capacity, recommended Wasim for the captaincy. Yet Wasim, who has always looked up to Miandad and was sympathetic to his plight, reassured him that he still wanted him in the side and told him in South Africa, "It's not my fault what has happened and it's not yours," which seemed to help.

Back in the ranks in New Zealand, he got on with that job in some style. In his 51st Test, at Auckland, he took his 200th Test wicket in the first innings and then, with Pakistan trailing by 27, he bowled throughout New Zealand's second innings to record his best Test figures, six for 43, and set up his side's victory. He improved on those figures in the next Test at Wellington, taking seven for 119 to ensure an innings victory, and give him eleven wickets in the match. The deposed captain finished with 25 wickets in the series at 17.24 apiece.

He was even more devastating against Sri Lanka, where Pakistan recorded two big wins. Wasim was the pick of the bowlers with 13 wickets at 13.46 each. At Kandy, he combined with Waqar, bowling unchanged to dismiss Sri Lanka for just 71 in 28.2 overs.

At home to Australia, his eight wickets in the first Test at Karachi proved decisive in Pakistan's narrowest of wins. He triggered a dramatic collapse in the second innings which saw the tourists plummet from 171 for 2 to 232 all out. Wasim played two useful hands with the bat in the series, but missed the final Test through injury, though rumours were rife that he and Waqar had withdrawn because of a dressing room row. Certainly there was disharmony on the tour to Southern Africa, which was not helped by the heavy defeat in the inaugural Test against South Africa and an embarrassing innings defeat to Zimbabwe. Wasim led the fightback at Bulawayo. Early on, he bowled Grant Flower, a double-century maker in the previous match, to give him his 250th wicket in his 60th Test, and he destroyed Zimbabwe in the second innings, taking 5-43 from 22.3 overs with a menacing display of fast bowling.

Wasim had an excellent season with Lancashire, who won the Benson and Hedges and finished fourth in both the Championship and the Sunday League. Putting the troubles of the winter behind him, Wasim put all his efforts into his cricket, taking 81 wickets at 19.72 in only 14 matches. Perhaps most telling were his performances in three matches as captain in Mike Watkinson's absence. Lancashire won all three, with Wasim shining in each. In his first match in charge against Somerset, he made 61 and Lancashire won inside two-and-a-half days. Against Hampshire he took 7-52 and ten in the match, then against Leicester, he produced what *Wisden* described as a "superb one-man show," taking 6-72 and 6-93, and then hitting 50 not out off only 35 balls to see his side home from a precarious position.

He flew straight from England into a Test match against Sri Lanka and even surprised himself with his performance. Bowling within himself, he took five for 55, including a spell of four wickets in 21 balls, and was later named man-of-the-match, with Pakistan winning by an innings. Wasim strained his left shoulder in the next Test, was unable to bowl in the second innings and had to withdraw from the series-deciding third Test. Without him or Waqar Younis, Pakistan slipped to defeat. As a consequence, Ramiz Raja was sacked as captain, and Wasim was handed the reins once more.

Wasim was determined to get it right this time and his leadership style had matured greatly since his previous tenure as captain, and though the team, which included a handful of ex-captains, was still unsettled in Australia, he gained plaudits for his handling of the side both on and off the field, leading to an harmonious series. He bowled brilliantly at times, too, though with little luck but still finished top of the averages with 14 wickets at 19.50. Following victory in Sydney, in the one-off Test against New Zealand he took five wickets in an innings for the 20th time.

There were calls for Wasim's head after Pakistan's quarter-final defeat to India in the World Cup - a game Wasim missed because of a side injury, he had incurred whilst batting in the previous game - but there should have been no doubts that he was the right man for the job.

Before the tour to England his stated intention was to address the bad press that Pakistan has received, restoring the side's reputation by playing the game hard but fair. Older and wiser, he has mellowed since his first tenure as captain - perhaps his marriage at the end of the 1994 season has helped - and he has learned from his mistakes.

Wasim never quite looked as threatening with the ball as in 1992, but he still bowled some telling spells, mixing his pace and angle of delivery. However, when it really mattered, he bowled the most thrilling overs of the whole summer in a short sharp blast against Alec Stewart and his opposite number and Lancashire colleague, Mike Atherton, in the second innings at the Oval. The England pair did well to survive, but it produced the kind of unsettling experience in the England dressing room that can weaken resolve. On the final day, with Pakistan requiring a coup de grace, Wasim raced in to pick up the three wickets he required to take him to 300 in Test cricket. He demolished Alan Mullally's stumps first ball to enter the record books as only the 11th player to reach the landmark, as well as being the first left-armer and only the second Pakistani after Imran Khan. It had been just 19 matches since he reached 200.

After the bad blood which has surfaced between the two sides in recent years, Wasim must be praised for the pleasant nature of the tour and the spirit in which the series was played. This side could go a long way under Wasim.

Akram has a unique action, sprinting in off a dozen paces; he collapses his front leg as he delivers (usually the leg is braced) which has caused the pressure on the inside of his rear leg, and this is exacerbated by his rear-foot which points towards mid-off, rather than square to the popping crease or pointing more towards the batsman which is more common. He generates his pace from a blurringly fast arm-action, which enables him to bowl as quickly as anyone in the world. Mike Atherton, his team-mate at Lancashire, reckons that only Waqar Younis, Patrick Patterson and Allan Donald are quicker, though Wasim appears to be able to bowl the occasional ball a yard faster (about 5mph) - usually his bouncer or yorker - with a little more flick of the

Wasim shows Alec Stewart that he can still
generate plenty of pace - Oval, 1996

Wasim's team-mates rush to congratulate
him on taking his 300th Test wicket

wrist. Imran Khan described him in 1989/90, in Australia, as the best left-arm fast bowler since Alan Davidson, who took 186 wickets in 44 Tests for Australia. No one though has bowled as effectively from both over and around the wicket.

When operating from the latter he has bowled some of the most memorable balls seen in international cricket, big inswinging yorkers, whose trajectory appear to start from as wide of the crease as Colin Croft used to bowl from, and others that curve in only to straighten off the pitch - the sort of delivery Derek Underwood used to bowl at half the pace. All the batsman sees as Wasim gathers, is him looking over his right shoulder and then a blur of arm, wrist and ball coming from behind the bowler's body.

This versatility makes it like having two bowlers in one, while his variety of swing and cut, length and line, has meant that he has often left batsmen transfixed. He once beat Tom Moody, the Australian batsman, six times in an over. Wasim has hit batsmen from top to toe because his action makes his length so difficult to pick. He is tall but does not always bowl with a high action, especially when bowling around the wicket and consequently often skids the ball on to the batsman.

If there is a flaw in his bowling it is in the number of no-balls he bowls, which probably come from the amount of variety he uses, mixing up his point of delivery; sometimes he seems to just turn and run in, ignoring his run-up marker. He also favours the old ball and perhaps, therefore could be more effective with the new ball than he has been. Strangely he tends to be less attacking in his opening spell.

Akram's ability with the bat is not reflected in his Test figures, which are slightly disappointing, averaging under 20, some way below that of the great modern day all-rounders, though his bowling figures stand comparison with them. He has a good eye and there are few more dangerous hitters in the game. However, in Test cricket, his technique has suffered from playing so much one-day cricket, tending to slog and play away from his body rather than trusting himself to play the sort of quality strokes he played during his century against Australia.

In fact Wasim's eyesight is not very good and occasionally he cannot be bothered to put in his contact lenses before going out to bat. In many of his early games he batted at ten or eleven, but now Pakistan needs consistent runs from him in a tail that can look very fragile. He has often scored runs though when it has mattered most, showing he does have the temperament, and he should become more productive with the bat before his career is over, as he leads from the front.

His ability is such that he is unlikely to have any long lean periods with the ball. Barring injuries, which may take their toll, he seems certain to spearhead the Pakistan attack for the rest of the decade, by which time he will have surpassed Imran Khan's record number of wickets for Pakistan, and perhaps even challenged Kapil Dev's world record.

Career Details

Born: Lahore, 3 June 1966
Role: left-hand, lower middle-order batsman, left-hand fast bowler
Clubs: PACO (1984/5), Lahore 1985/6, Lancashire (1988-95)
First-class record: (1984-95) 4,679 runs (21.76) including 4 centuries, 747 wickets (21.51) and 56 catches
Tests: 70
Test Debut: v New Zealand, Auckland, 1984/5
Test record: 1652 runs (19.21), including 1 hundred and 4 fifties, 300 wickets (22.91) 20 x 5wI, 3 x 10wM, and 26 catches
Best Performances: HS 123 v Australia, Adelaide, 1989/90
BB 7-119 v New Zealand, Wellington, 1993/4
11-160 (6-62 & 5-98) v Australia, Melbourne, 1989/90
Tours: New Zealand; 1984/5, 1992/3, 1993/4, 1995/6
Sri Lanka; 1985/6,
India; 1986/7, 1989/90 (Nehru Cup)
Westindies; 1987/8, 1992/3
Australia; 1984/5 (WSC), 1986/7 (Perth Challenge), 1988/9 (WSC), 1989/90, 1991/2, 1992/3 (WSC), 1995/6
England; 1987, 1992, 1996
South Africa; 1992/3 (one-day), 1994/5
Zimbabwe; 1992/3 (one-day), 1994/5
Overseas Test; 45
One-day Internationals; 201
World Cups; 1987, 1992, 1996
Sharjah; 1984/5, 1985/6, 1986/7, 1988/9, 1989/90, 1991/2, 1992/3, 1993/4, 1994/5

Intikhab Alam Khan

Intikhab Alam was a highly talented all-round cricketer, who batted pugnaciously and bowled leg-spin, but always with a jovial air. However, he had the misfortune of establishing himself in the side during Pakistan's weakest decade, the sixties, when often the sum of the side's ambition was to draw matches, and pitches at home were prepared to serve that end. He took over the captaincy when both the cricket and the country were in a state of flux, and has not been credited with the great strides that Pakistan made under his guidance. Subsequently, he has had a major influence in his country's most successful decade, the eighties, as the first-choice manager.

He was born in 1941 in the northern Punjab town of Hoshiarpur, where his father was a senior engineering contractor, and useful fast bowler in club cricket. Intikhab, too, started as a seamer, until his solid frame filled out rather than up and he turned to the leg-spinners and googlies that were to bring him more first-class wickets - 1,571 - than any other Pakistani before or since. His stocky stature, amiable demeanour and jolly outlook belied a certain shyness off the field and a steely determination on it.

Two years after first playing for Karachi, for whom his brother Aftab also played, Intikhab's Test career began as no other's has done for Pakistan, as he took a wicket with his first ball - that of Australian Colin McDonald with his flipper. He was just 17 years and 341 days old and the game was the first to watched by an American President, Dwight D Eisenhower, who was at the National Stadium for the 4th day of the game, which unfortunately was the second slowest day's play in Test history. Pakistan have always blooded their talented youngsters early - Mustaq Mohammad had made his debut nine months before at the age of fifteen - and Intikhab's early introduction would have stood him in good stead later in his career for dealing with youngsters as captain or tour manager.

It took him a couple of seasons to establish himself in the Test side, but he had hinted at his all-round potential as early as his second match, scoring 56 and taking two wickets in each innings against India at Calcutta. He played in the last three Tests of that tour (1960/1) and the first two against England the next season, though with limited success. He was in and out of the side on the tour to England in 1962, but by playing in the last two Tests he started a sequence of 39 consecutive Tests spread over the next fourteen and a half years.

Pakistan went for over two years without any Test cricket, though "Inti" toured England again in 1963 with the Pakistan Eaglets, finishing with the most wickets (19 at 23.15), as well as touring Ceylon with Pakistan, and East Africa with PIA in 1964. In his next batch of Tests in the busy season of 1964/5, he made fifties in both the home and away one-off matches against Australia, and set a ninth wicket record against them with Afaq Hussain at Melbourne. However, he was still short of wickets, having taken just two wickets in the four Tests in Australasia, but changed all that in the 3rd Test at Karachi against New Zealand, when he took seven for 92 in 50.4 overs in the match.

Again Pakistan went over two years without internationals, and Intikhab joined the West of Scotland club as their professional in the interim, where he developed the accuracy he needed for the slow wickets of the time. He toured England again in 1967 with the national team and finished top of the bowling averages with 35 wickets, including eight for 61 and four for 58 against the Minor Counties, seven for 52 and four for 51 v Gloucestershire, and seven for 58 against Lancashire. In the final Test at the Oval, which was to be his home ground for 12 years (1969-1981), he put on the highest 9th wicket partnership in all Tests. Coming in at 65 for 8, with Pakistan still requiring 159 to make England bat again, he made 51 as he helped Asif Iqbal add 190 at more than a run a minute to save face if not the match.

That winter "Inti" had an excellent domestic season playing for Karachi and Public Works

The young leg-spinner sends down another delivery

Department, taking 77 wickets at 21.89 runs each. After his first year at Surrey in 1969, the captaincy of Pakistan came to him but it could not have come at a more fractious time. Hanif Mohammad, the last of the "founding fathers" of Pakistan cricket, had been ousted as captain after the trip to England, and the eccentric Saeed Ahmed had seen his one series in charge perpetually disrupted by the student demonstrations that were commonplace in the country at the time.

The side, not unlike the country, was going through a difficult period. Pakistan had won only two Tests in the sixties, and were playing with little ambition beyond drawing games. Intikhab's first match in charge - Hanif's last Test - was drawn, but a further setback came when Pakistan lost the next in Lahore and with it the series to New Zealand for the first time, despite Intikhab's fine efforts to square the rubber. In the third Test, the last to be played in Dacca, he took ten wickets in the match, unusually recording the same figures (five for 91) in each innings, bowling nearly a hundred overs in all, and was only denied a push for victory by bad light, minor disturbances in the crowd and a pitch invasion.

However, the team was beginning to blend under his astute leadership. He took the side to England in 1971, where the previous year he produced some useful performances in five "Tests" playing for the Rest of the World, and for whom he was to be vice-captain for their winter tour to Australia (1971/2). Both series were arranged in place of scheduled tours by South Africa.

He was desperately unlucky to lose the series against England. In the first Test at Edgbaston Pakistan made over 600, and following on, England was still 71 behind with only five wickets in hand when rain washed out most of the last day. After a rain-affected draw at Lord's, Pakistan's batting let them down as they chased 231 at Headingley. They lost their last six wickets for 45, leaving them 26 runs short of victory.

This was an unfortunate trait that continued in Australia in 1972/3, where the batting twice collapsed under pressure when victory was in sight. Intikhab played several captain's innings though, helping to double the score from 104 for 7 to 208 in a record 7th wicket partnership with Wasim Bari at Adelaide, making 64 in the 1st innings at Melbourne to build a big lead, and top-scoring, with 48, in the 2nd as he tried to hold the tail together.

The tour had not been a happy one; the 3-0 defeat was not a true reflection of the relative skills of each side, though Pakistan's out-cricket had been poor. The schedule was not fair to the tourists, giving them little time to acclimatise against decent opposition. Indeed their first match was in Sri Lanka and prior to the first Test they played only two games against weak sides in Tasmania.

Most importantly, various factions had developed in the side, leading to two players, Saeed Ahmed and Mohammad Ilyas, being sent home from Australia, and the BCCP had already decided to replace Intikhab with Majid Khan before the end of the trip to New Zealand. This caused further resentments, and came at a most inappropriate time.

For Intikhab was in the middle of leading Pakistan to its first overseas series victory and was at his best with bat and ball. A not out fifty in the first Test at Wellington was followed by a match-winning performance in the 2nd at Dunedin; he bowled superbly to take seven for 52 and four for 78 to help Pakistan to an innings victory. A draw at Eden Park in the final Test, where Intikhab took six for 127, secured the series.

Back in the ranks at home against England and obviously upset, he had a point to prove. He confirmed his all-round worth in the 2nd Test at Hyderabad with a brilliant century, striking four sixes and fifteen fours during an innings which demonstrated his great power. He raced to 50 in 45 minutes, and hit England's best bowler in that series, Pat Pocock, out of the attack; in all he batted for four and half hours, and had the presence of mind, when in the nineties, to go into the crowd to ask them to stop running onto the field. He also took seven wickets in the match. Four more wickets in the third at Karachi made him the leading wicket-taker in the series, as well as averaging over fifty with the bat. That winter had brought him 37 Test wickets and over five hundred runs.

He took 72 wickets for Surrey in 1973 and after his best domestic season in 1973/4, in which he took 82 wickets at 20.34 for PIA, he was rightly restored to the captaincy. Pakistan went through the 17-match tour to England (1974) undefeated - a feat not achieved since Don Bradman's famous Australian side of 1948. The Tests were evenly contested but spoiled by the weather. On a batting paradise at the Oval Inti took five wickets, and in the process became the first Pakistani to complete the Test match double of a thousand runs and 100 wickets. This was his 41st Test, and to put this in context, Wasim Akram took four more matches to complete his double. Intikhab lead the side ably throughout and was the leading wicket-taker on tour, with 44 at 22.59.

Against the Westindies that winter Pakistan showed their fighting qualities - Intikhab himself was hit on the head by a bouncer from Andy Roberts but carried on batting - to ensure two evenly contested draws. He was not included in the World Cup squad of 1975, as it was unfashionable to use spinners in one-day cricket then, but he remained in charge of the side for the tour to Sri Lanka in 1975/6 for two unofficial Tests. His five wickets for 58 in the first innings of the 2nd match helped square the series. However, an incident at a cocktail party in Kandy, after which Sarfraz Nawaz was sent home, may ultimately have cost him the captaincy. Even still, with the side developing well under his leadership, it was a surprise that he was deposed again for the hectic winter of 1976/7.

Although eighteen months had elapsed since the last official Test series, it seemed extraordinary that he was not even in the original squad to play New Zealand. He was recalled at the 11th hour and finished the series as the leading wicket-taker, with 15 at 22.06.

When six of the leading players were involved in a pay dispute prior to the tour to Australia and Westindies, Intikhab found himself being offered the captaincy once again by A H Kardar. Yet when the dispute was settled the offer was withdrawn, though at least he retained his place in the squad. However, he was ostracised for not joining Mustaq Mohammad and Co in their stand against the BCCP. Despite this Intikhab remained loyal to the tour, and superficially happy, though undoubtedly hurt and saddened by events.

That he was not wanted, or needed on the field, became apparent when he did not play in any of the Tests in Australia and in only one, the 2nd, in Westindies. Not surprisingly, he retired from international cricket at the end of that tour.

He no longer played domestic cricket but continued to play for Surrey. In his 12 years at the Oval he helped the county to the Championship in 1971, taking 32 wickets after the Pakistani tour, to give him over a hundred in total that season, while his powerful hitting and accurate bowling were well-suited to the one-day game. He played in the 1979 Benson and Hedges final, when he was the most economical bowler, and the Gillette final the following year, when he hit belligerently for 34. Both matches though were lost. He had not played in the World Cup in 1975, but that year returned the remarkable figures of 11-6-5-2 against Glamorgan in a Benson and Hedges match. In his final year at Surrey he was their leading wicket-taker, and he finished with 589 wickets in 232 matches for the county. Inti is remembered at the Oval with great affection for his loyalty and geniality.

Intikhab entered the textile trade in Lahore after retirement, but subsequently became Pakistan's first-choice manager for more than a decade. He struck an excellent partnership with Imran Khan from their first series together in 1982, when Intikhab took a lot of pressure off the new captain by dealing efficiently with the media. Ten years later, his old team-mate at Surrey, Mickey Stewart, was the England manager. However, Inti was still quick to act on behalf of his players, defending Aqib Javed

at Old Trafford. He had backed Ramiz Raja, too, when he led the players from the field in Australia in 1989/90. One might have expected a more conciliatory tone from so mild a man, but his firmness merely confirmed his loyalty to his side and demonstrated the strength of character that served him well throughout an illustrious career, which had its fair share of ups and downs. He was replaced after taking the team to southern Africa in 1994/5, because of the allegations of match-rigging. He felt obliged to get the players to swear on the Koran to their commitment to the team before a Test in Zimbabwe, and he was back in charge for Pakistan's tour to Australia and New Zealand in 1995/6. However, Pakistan's quarter-final exit to India in the World Cup led to him being replaced for the tour to England in 1996, which was unlucky as Pakistan had won their previous two Tests. No doubt he will answer the call again, next time Pakistan is in need.

Intikhab Alam played the game in the best possible spirit. He was described once by John Arlott as "a man of immense honesty, charm and loyalty...who made friends wherever he went" and as "one of the nicest men who ever played cricket" (*Wisden Cricket Monthly*, August 1982); what praise could be more fitting.

Career Details

Born: Hoshiarpur, Punjab, India, 28 December 1941
Role: right-hand, lower middle-order batsman, right-hand leg-break and googly bowler
Clubs: Karachi (1957/8-1970/1), PIA (1960/1-1974/5), Public Works Department (1967/8-1969/70), Surrey (1969-81), Sind (1973/4) and Punjab (1975/6)
First-class record: (1957-81) 14,331 runs (22.14) including 9 centuries, 1,571 wickets (27.67) and 228 catches
Tests: 47
Test Debut: v Australia, Karachi, 1959/60
Test record: 1493 runs (22.28), 125 wickets (35.95) and 20 catches
Best Performances: HS 138 v England, Hyderabad, 1972/3
BB 7-52 v New Zealand, Dunedin, 1972/3
Tours: India; 1960/1
England; 1962, 1963 (Eaglets), 1967, 1971, 1974
Australia; 1964/5, 1972/3; New Zealand 1964/5, 1972/3
Westindies; 1976/7
Overseas Tests; 26
One-day Internationals; 4
Ceylon; 1964
Rest of the World: England 1970; Australia 1971/2
As manager: England 1982, 1987, 1992
Westindies; 1987/8
Australia 1992 (World Cup), 1995/6

Wasim Bari

Wasim Bari is undoubtedly Pakistan's finest wicket-keeper to date, being the first choice behind the stumps for more than fifteen years. When he retired only England's Alan Knott and Australia's Rod Marsh had had more dismissals (since passed by Westindies' Jeff Dujon and Australia's Ian Healy), though he probably had the edge over these standing up to the wicket.

Wasim was the first Test cricketer to be born in the newly formed state of Pakistan. He was born in March 1948 in Karachi where he was brought up and by the time he was 16 was playing first-class cricket for Karachi. Despite being tall for his position at 5ft 9 inches, he was lithe and agile behind the stumps, without unnecessary acrobatics. He was a most reliable catcher, with "soft hands" and excellent timing, who soon became an automatic choice for his country. He played for the Pakistan under-25 side against England in 1966/7 and was selected for the full side for the tour to England in 1967, making his Test debut at Lord's at the age of 19. His great wicket-keeping rival, Alan Knott, who had toured Pakistan with England's under-25s, started his Test career in the same series. Knott was to develop into probably the finest wicket-keeper batsman of modern times, but he always rated Wasim's glove work as unsurpassed.

Wasim Bari was to set several wicket-keeping records. In 1977/8, he made seven dismissals in an innings playing for Pakistan International Airlines against Sind at Lahore, and the following season set a new world Test record for catches in an innings (which has since been equalled), when he held seven of the first eight batsmen against New Zealand at Auckland in 1978/9. Strangely he did not make another dismissal in that game, leaving him one short of his Test best. That was against England at Headingley in 1971, when he equalled the record at the time of eight catches in a Test (since broken). He also made an important fifty in that game.

He could be a very useful batsman and comfortably completed the keepers' double of a thousand runs and 100 dismissals in Tests. However he was a bad starter with the bat and has a very high proportion of ducks (21%) to his name. He usually batted in the lower-middle order, and when he did get off the mark played some important innings. He made his top-score of 85 after going in as night-watchman at No 3 against India, at Lahore in 1978/9, and top-scored once against Australia, at Adelaide in 1972/3, making

72. Coming in at 104 for 6, he doubled the score in partnership with Intikhab Alam. Later that season he also top-scored against England in his home town; he went to the crease after four wickets had fallen for one run and led Pakistan to safety with an innings of 41.

He shared hundred partnerships in two consecutive Tests against Westindies with Wasim Raja, the man he usually shared a room with when on tour. On the first occasion, in the 2nd Test at Karachi in 1974/5, he made 58 of the 128 added for the seventh wicket, and then in Barbados, 1976/7, he helped transform the match with a record tenth wicket partnership for Pakistan of 133 in 110 minutes. Strangely that morning Bari had been involved in a bathing incident and required the assistance of a life-guard; little did he know that later that day he would be rescuing his side from the depths of 158 for 9, a lead of only 172. His spirited innings of 60 not out put Pakistan back in the game and Westindies came close to suffering their first defeat in Bridgetown since 1934/5, their last pair just holding out for a draw (Westindies have since been beaten there, by England in 1993/4 and Australia in 1994/5).

Unfortunately Bari was hit in the face - as he had been by Richard Collinge in New Zealand in 1972/3 - trying to hook Colin Croft in the final Test. His absence from the field dispirited the side, especially when a vital chance off Gordon Greenidge was put down by Majid Khan, who had temporarily taken over behind the stumps, and with it Pakistan saw their slim chance in the series slip away.

The next year the captaincy landed in Wasim Bari's safe hands because of the Packer defections, and he did a remarkable job in holding together a fragmented team. The young side drew all three Tests at home against England, as Bari emphasised to his batsmen the need to sell their wickets dearly. Indeed Mudassar Nazar certainly heeded his instructions, making the slowest-ever Test hundred in the first match at Lahore. However their inexperience showed in England the following summer and they struggled to come to terms with Ian Botham's swing. Although Wasim had conducted himself with great dignity in difficult circumstances, he lost the captaincy when the Packer players returned.

Despite making a record 16 dismissals in the series in India (1979/80) and completing the wicket-keeper's double just two matches before, Bari was replaced by Taslim Arif behind the stumps for the home rubber against Australia later that season, ending a virtually unbroken run of 56 Tests. Arif made a double hundred in the 2nd Test at Faisalabad, the highest score by a 'keeper, and seemed to be established but was forced out by injury when he broke a finger opening the batting against Westindies' pace barrage. Wasim thus returned after a five match absence.

He joined the players' revolt against Javed Miandad's captaincy after the 1981/2 tour to Australia, so missing the series with Sri Lanka that followed it, but was the first choice wicket-keeper for the 1982 tour to England, his fifth Test series here.

Though below par on that tour he still made 29 dismissals in 11 games, and he was soon at his best again for two home series, against Australia and India, as Pakistan enjoyed six wins in the first seven Tests of that winter. He liked the variety of 'keeping to the spinners, able to "read" Abdul Qadir whilst the batsmen were being bamboozled, and to Imran Khan - a man he has always greatly

admired - who was bowling at his fastest. Wasim made 11 dismissals against Australia, including four stumpings off Qadir, and set a national record for a rubber of 17 dismissals, against India, nine of which were catches off his captain, Khan. He made his 200th dismissal (174 catches, 26 stumpings) in the final Test at Karachi, his 73rd and last in Pakistan, when he stumped Ravi Shastri off Qadir.

The following year, after the Prudential World Cup (his third) in the summer of 1983, he completed a short tour of India and was involved in 12 out of 37 dismissals, as well as making 64 in the first Test to take Pakistan to a lead.

Wasim played the last of his 81 Tests on his fifth tour to Australia that winter before slipping out of Test cricket, without the sendoff he deserved, when Anil Dalpat was preferred for the home series with England (1983/4). An impeccable wicket-keeper to the end, Wasim took his 200th Test catch in his final Test, bowling out at the same time as another great wicket-keeper, Australia's Rod Marsh. That was the end of Wasim's first-class career as well, which spanned nearly 20 years; he finished with a respectable batting average of more than 20 and made over 800 dismissals, nearly a fifth of which were stumpings.

Since his retirement he has been working for Pakistan International Airlines.

Career Details

Born: Karachi, Pakistan, 23 March 1948
Role: right-hand, lower middle-order batsman, wicket-keeper
Clubs: Karachi (1964/5-1980/1), PIA (1967/8-1980/ 1), Sind (1973/4)
First-class record: (1964-84) 5,749 runs (21.69) including 2 centuries, 1 wicket (30.00) and 814 dismissals (669 catches, 145 stumpings)
Tests: 81
Test Debut: v England, Lord's, 1967
Test record: 1,366 runs (15.88), 0-2 wickets and 228 dismissals (201 catches, 27 stumpings)
Best Performances: HS 85 v India, Lahore, 1978/9
Took 7 catches in an innings v New Zealand, Auckland 1978/9
Tours: England; 1967, 1971, 1974, 1978, 1982
Australia; 1972/3, 1976/7, 1978/9, 1981/2, 1983/4
New Zealand; 1972/3, 1978/9
Westindies; 1976/7
India; 1979/80, 1983/4.
Overseas Tests; 51
One-day Internationals; 51
World Cups; 1975, 1979, 1983
Ceylon; 1972/3, 1975/6

Without doubt, Pakistan's finest ever wicket-keeper

Javed Burki

Javed Burki was earmarked for captaincy from an early age. He was educated at Oxford University, where he was a Blue from 1958-60, came from an aristocratic family of Lahore land owners, and was just what the Pakistan Board of Control was looking for, a man of high social status to lead the national side.

His family was part of the Khan dynasty, which has a cricketing tradition as rich as that of the Mohammads, who dominated cricket in Karachi and who produced five Test cricketers including two captains. The cricketing credentials of Javed's family are impeccable; it, too, has produced five Test cricketers, including three national captains, and supplied four other first-class players. Javed Burki was the nephew of Baqa Khan Jilani and Jahangir Khan, who both played for India before the Second World War. The former died after an accidental fall from a balcony in 1941, aged just 29, but his brother-in-law, Jahangir, lived to be 78 and married Burki's aunt. They had a son, Majid Khan, who later captained Pakistan. Burki's other aunt gave birth to Imran Khan who also followed in his

footsteps as captain of the national side. His other cousins include Majid's brother Asad, an Oxford blue who also played for Lahore and Punjab University, and Humayun and Javed Zaman, who both played for Lahore.

Javed Burki made his first-class debut for Punjab in 1955/6 at the age of 17, and went up to Oxford in the autumn of 1957, where he excelled in the Blues side for three years (1958-60) and made over 2,000 runs. When he returned to Pakistan after graduating he walked straight into the Test side making his debut at the Brabourne Stadium in Bombay (1960/1). Although unsuccessful in that game he had a most encouraging series with scores of 79 and 48 not out in the next Test at Kanpur, 48 and 42 in the third at Calcutta and 61 in the fifth at Delhi, adding solidity to the middle-order batting. He finished the series with an average of 46.25.

He topped that the following year at home to England, when he averaged 56.66, which was second only to Hanif Mohammad. His reliable and correct batting brought him centuries in the first two Tests, albeit some months apart as England toured India in between. His 138 in the first Test at Lahore included a six and 17 fours and he put on century partnerships with both Saeed Ahmed and

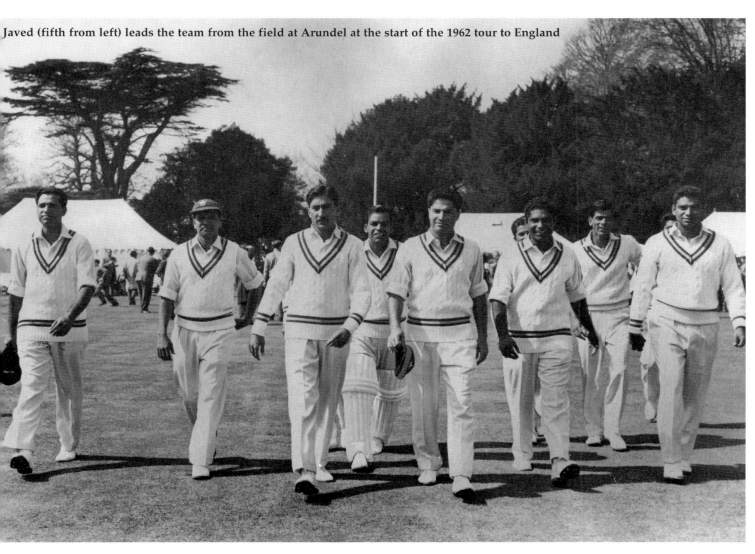

Javed (fifth from left) leads the team from the field at Arundel at the start of the 1962 tour to England

Mustaq Mohammad. At Dacca in the 2nd Test he made 140 with 18 boundaries but on the whole both innings were full of application rather than full of strokes. In the latter he joined Hanif Mohammad in a long, slow stand of 156 for the 3rd wicket in the first innings.

Ironically, as the series was lost, his batting success had paved the way for him to become captain in place of Imtiaz Ahmed at the earliest opportunity.

However he was taking charge of a changing team, with several leading players retired or past their peak. He was also too young at 24, not having the natural authority that the Board assumed would come with his social status. Javed was somewhat reclusive by nature and Hanif Mohammad would probably have been a more prudent choice at this juncture.

Up against a strong side in England in 1962, Pakistan suffered their worst-ever defeat, losing 4-0, and Burki's own form fell away, though he did score a fine hundred at Lord's - the first by a captain for Pakistan. He added 197 with the night-watchman Nasim-ul-Ghani, who also got a century, which established a fifth-wicket record partnership against England. Nasim just pipped his captain to the mark, thus recording the first Test century for Pakistan in England. Javed Burki had set out to play attractive cricket as was shown in the county games, in which he scored well, making over twelve hundred runs in all, but on the whole his captaincy was criticised,

Pakistan played no Test cricket for over two years after that and by the next series (1964/5) Javed Burki had been replaced, despite showing good form in domestic cricket, with scores of 202 not out for Lahore v Universities (1962/3) and his highest score, 227, for Karachi Whites against Khairpur (1963/4). It ensured he retained his place in the side, playing a further ten matches, without ever really recapturing his early success.

He made 62 in the home Test against Australia, and 29 and 47 in the Test at Melbourne, as well as making runs in the state games there and in New Zealand. However he suffered a pair in the Test against New Zealand at Wellington, and he followed this with a stoical 63 at Auckland.

Javed scored a double-hundred against Ceylon in 1966/7 and was selected for the tour to England which followed. Because of his experience in that country he was tried as an opener without success and reverted to the middle-order for the final Test. He was dropped from the side for the reciprocal series with England in 1968/9 but returned for one last appearance against New Zealand in 1969/70.

He was an astute captain of Lahore, and might well have proved a more successful national captain had the opportunity come to him later. He influenced the careers of his cousins Imran Khan and Majid Khan, playing with the latter in a handful of Tests from 1964/5 until Javed's last Test tour in 1967, and captained both at Lahore. Imran has always looked up to Javed, regarding him as his hero.

Javed Burki continued to play first-class cricket until 1975 and remained involved in the game after his retirement, becoming Chairman of the Selectors in 1989. He was the first to pick Waqar Younis at junior level, recognising his potential despite a lack of control in his bowling at that time. He discussed Waqar's development with Imran Khan and the manager, ensuring he was carefully nurtured. Burki became chairman of an *ad hoc* committee at the beginning of 1994, after the previous panel had been sacked following a players' revolt and a change of Prime Minister. While in charge, he put forward some sensible proposals for the restructuring of domestic cricket.

Career Details

Born: Meerut, India, 8 May 1938
Role: right-hand, middle-order batsman, occasional right-hand medium-pace bowler
Clubs: Punjab (1955/6-1956/7), Oxford University (1958-60)
Lahore (1961/2-1970/1), Karachi (1963/4-1967/8), Rawalpindi (1967/8-1972/3, NWFP (1974/5)
First-class record: (1955-75) 9,426 runs (36.39) including 22 centuries (HS 227), 35 wickets (44.40)
Tests: 25
Test Debut: v India, Brabourne Stadium (Bombay), 1960/1
Test record: 1341 runs (30.47), 0-23 and 7 catches
Best Performances: HS 140 v England, at Dacca, 1961/2
Tours: India; 1960/1
England; 1962, 1967
Australia; 1964/5
New Zealand; 1964/5
Overseas Tests; 17
Ceylon; 1964/5

Javed hits out against Surrey

Nasim-ul-Ghani

Nasim-ul-Ghani was a teenage prodigy who had played most of his best cricket for Pakistan by the time he was 21 years old. A sound lower middle-order batsman, he could bowl either medium-pace or slow left-arm spin and tended to favour the latter. His international career was thinly spread over 15 years, and was interspersed with many seasons as a professional in England. He finished with useful all-round figures in Test cricket.

Born in Delhi in May 1941, his childhood was disrupted by Partition and perhaps this was partly why he grew up so quickly. He was from a fine cricketing family; his brothers Anis and Tehzib both played first-class cricket, for Karachi and Commercial Bank respectively.

Nasim made his first-class debut in 1956/7 at the age of 15, bowling 79 overs and taking 3 for 184 for Karachi Blues against the Whites. Half-way through the next season he was selected to tour the Caribbean with Pakistan and became the youngest Test player to that point, when he was chosen to play in the first Test at Bridgetown. He was just 16 years and 248 days old, 104 days younger than the previous record-holder, his compatriot Khalid Hassan, though Mustaq Mohammad was to beat Nasim's record within 15 months. Nasim had a quiet match bowling just 14 overs without taking a wicket and getting 11 and nought with the bat. Unfortunately he got a pair in the next Test but bowled well, taking three wickets in each innings.

However he fractured a finger after bowling just 15 overs in the Third Test in Jamaica, leaving the only two fit bowlers to be mauled by Garry Sobers and Conrad Hunte. He was fit enough to play in the final two Tests and bowled beautifully, taking 15 wickets in all, with figures of 5 for 116 from 41.4 overs in the first innings at Georgetown, and 6 for 67 from 30.5 in Trinidad which was to remain his best in Tests. There he bowled Sobers for the third time in the series and had Jaswick Taylor stumped by Imtiaz Ahmed to secure Pakistan an innings victory with one run to spare. It gave him the excellent return for his first series of 19 wickets at an average of 26.7.

That form continued at home to the Westindies (1958/9), when he took four wickets in the first innings and then bowled with great economy in the second at Karachi. At Dacca he snapped up three wickets for just four runs as Westindies were shot out for 76, and three rather more expensive wickets in the final Test at Lahore.

The next season against Australia he was dropped after two quiet Tests, allowing Intikhab Alam to make his debut. Nasim regained his place

on the tour to India, but had a disastrous series with the ball, taking just three Test wickets before being dropped for the fifth Test at Delhi, thus denying him the opportunity of playing in the city of his birth. However, his batting did show the first signs of its potential when, in the 2nd Test, he made 70 not out at Kanpur.

Against England in 1961/2 he missed the first Test but bowled tidily in the next two, keeping a strong England batting line-up in check. That winter he also produced his best first-class figures six for 24 (12 for 54 in the match) playing for Karachi Whites against East Pakistan. He toured England in 1962 and was again short of wickets in the Tests, taking only three in the five games. However at Lord's he surpassed himself with the bat. Sent in as night-watchman in the 2nd innings, with Pakistan struggling at 77 for 4, the young left-hander shared a fifth-wicket stand of 197 with Javed Burki and just pipped his captain to three figures, thus becoming the first Pakistani to score a Test century in England. It was a bolt out of the blue as, apart from his 70 at Kanpur and an innings of 41 not out in his last Test in Pakistan, he had rarely got to 20, quite often batting at No 11, and indeed had recorded eight ducks in 23 completed innings, which makes his hundred all the more commendable. Although his status as "nightwatchman" can be debated - he was promoted from eight to six and he has batted higher - one can assume that he was the first such batsman to score a Test hundred. On the whole he had a good tour taking 41 wickets, scoring 769 runs and taking 28 catches, including a number at short leg where he was particularly adept.

When Nasim celebrated his 21st birthday on that tour, he had more wickets (42) by that age than any other bowler. That record has since been beaten by the likes of India's Kapil Dev (87) and compatriot Waqar Younis (93) but for Nasim it was no precursor to greater things; his best playing days were already behind him.

He still performed creditably in domestic cricket and bowled a remarkable 75.3 overs in one innings which included 40 maidens, taking six for 94, for Karachi against Pakistan International Airlines in 1962/3. Pakistan's next Tests were not until 1964/5 but he did nothing of significance in the one-off Tests at home and away to Australia or in the three Tests in New Zealand and was dropped when the Kiwis toured Pakistan shortly after.

In 1967 his commitments as a professional playing Lancashire league cricket for Longton, for whom he took fifty wickets at 12.32 that season, precluded his playing a full part in Pakistan's third tour to England. He played in the first two Tests but in only one other tour match. The following year he was to start a long association with Staffordshire, which lasted until 1978.

He played just one more Test when he was called up for the tour to Australia in 1972/3. He was asked to open in the third Test when Saeed Ahmed, who had been unsettled by the pace of Dennis Lillee in the previous match, pulled out complaining of backache. Nasim made a spirited 64, playing some splendid drives but did not bowl in the match. Many believed that his all-round ability should have been better utilised on the tour.

He continued to play first-class cricket for two more years for National Bank and was recalled by Karachi as late as 1981/2 to play in some limited-overs matches, suggesting that the doubt about his true age was unfounded.

He was a fine bowler who flighted the ball, tempting the batsman into the drive or down the pitch and consequently got most of his wickets caught as well as picking up a high proportion of stumpings. His talent never quite fulfilled its potential after its early promise but was not helped by the lack of Test cricket between 1962 and 1967, when his game might have blossomed.

Having previously managed the A team tour to Bangladesh for the SAARD World Cup, Nasim was appointed cricket manager for Pakistan's tour to England in 1996. Despite success in the series and the smooth and harmonious running of the tour off the field, Nasim was replaced at the end of it, much to his disappointment, though remains intrinsically involved as part of a new three-man selection committee.

Career Details

Born: Delhi, India, 14 May 1941
Role: left-hand, middle-order batsman, left-arm medium or slow bowler
Clubs: Karachi (1956/7-1972/3), Universities (1958/ 9), Dacca (1965/6), East Pakistan 1966/7-1967/8), Public Works Department (1966/7-1971/2), Staffordshire (1968-78) and National Bank (1973/4- 1974/5)
First-class record: (1956-73) 4490 runs (28.41) including 7 centuries, 343 wickets (25.15) and 104 catches
Tests: 29
Test Debut: v Westindies, Bridgetown, 1957/8
Test record: 747 runs (16.60), 52 wickets (37.67) and 11 catches
Best Performances: HS 101 v England, Lord's, 1962
BB 6/67 v Westindies, Port of Spain, 1957/8
Tours:
Westindies; 1957/8
India; 1960/1
England; 1962, 1967
Australia; 1964/5, 1972/3
New Zealand; 1964/5
Overseas Tests; 21

Nasim, the 1996 cricket manager, made his Test debut aged 16

Aftab Gul

Aftab Gul was perhaps not amongst the top flight of Test cricketers but his story tells a tale that epitomises some of the difficulties that the country as a whole was facing; conflict with her neighbour India, and civil war between East and West Pakistan that led to the creation of the independent states of Bangladesh and Pakistan. He was student leader at a time when the youth of the world protested at their lot. He was arrested several times and became the first cricketer to play in a first-class match while on bail.

He was born in Ghujar Khan, India, in March 1946, the eve of Partition, and his family was one of many tens of thousands that went through that upheaval.

He made his first-class debut in 1964/5, while studying law at Punjab University. His political involvement was not appreciated by authority and he was arrested during the 1967/8 season for alleged political subversiveness. However such was his influence amongst the left-wing students that, so the story goes, the selectors dare not leave him out of the Test side. In fact he had scored 50 and 55 for the Board of Control XI at Bahawalpur against the MCC and so was selected on merit. However the story grew from a passing comment he made to John Woodcock, the well-known cricket correspondent for *The Times,* who asked him whether he thought he would be playing. His tongue in cheek reply - "I'd better be otherwise there won't be a Test in Lahore," - was taken literally.

In fact there were still frequent disruptions, with minor skirmishes in the crowd sending spectators spilling onto the outfield. The time lost prevented an exciting finale with the match evenly poised. Aftab Gul made 12 and 29 but was not included in the side for the second Test in Dacca. That game was relatively trouble-free, with the crowds being controlled not by the police but by the student leaders of East Pakistan. Aftab returned for the third Test in Karachi, but he did not bat as crowd trouble enforced the abandonment of the match, with England only seven wickets down in the first innings of the match.

Aftab spoke to Mudar Patherya, of *Wisden Cricket Monthly* (June 1990), reflecting on those seemingly troubled times. "It was a great time to be young and alive. We were never short of inspiration. There were leaders like Bobby Kennedy, Martin Luther King [Jnr] and Z A Bhutto around. Besides we were the product of a changing environment. The Beatles and the Prague Spring had their effect. As I say, it was a great time to be alive."

The situation had calmed to some extent the

following season (1969/70) and Aftab played in the third Test against the touring New Zealanders, making 30 and 5. At Lahore he also captained the young Imran Khan who was in his debut season.

Both he and Imran were selected for the tour to England in 1971, and in their first practice session, in the nets at Lord's, the raw pace bowler's first ball almost hit Aftab on the head even though he was batting in the next net! Unfortunately in the Test at Edgbaston he *was* hit on the head with only the third ball of the series, this time though it was from a bouncer bowled by Allan Ward. This blow forced him to retire hurt, but he did resume his innings the next day with Pakistan healthily placed at 469 for 5. He made 28. Aftab had been in excellent form having scored a hundred on the same ground against Warwickshire earlier on the tour, and had made 88 and 106 in the game against Gloucestershire just prior to the first Test. In the Tests though he did not get the big score that his form suggested, each time getting set without managing to go on. Overall on the tour he made 1154 runs at an average of 46.16 which was second only to Zaheer Abbas. In twenty-one completed innings outside the Tests he scored two hundreds and made nine fifties.

However his Test playing days were over. He was selected for the 1974 tour back to England, after scoring over a thousand runs in domestic cricket the previous winter for Punjab, but could not reproduce his form of 1971, making only 193 runs in six matches, and could not force his way into a strong batting line-up for the Tests.

His first-class career was cut short in 1977/8 when he again became embroiled in the country's politics. When General Zia-ul-Haq took power in the military coup in 1977 he threw the deposed Zulfiqar Ali Bhutto into protective custody. Gul challenged the legality of his imprisonment, issuing a habeas corpus, arguing that such an action was applicable only to minors, people of unsound mind or crucial witnesses in an important trial.

Gul told Patherya his story; "I suppose I paid for that. Zia's regime identified me as a troublemaker and made my life hell. I was perpetually shadowed; my passport was confiscated. Finally, I used my connections in Islamabad, managed to get it back, and immediately left to see the 1983 World Cup. I must have been in England for three or four days when I came across flashes in most newspapers that in a military raid on my residence in Lahore, SAM 7s (surface-to-air missiles), bombs and Kalashnikovs had been recovered. And do you know exactly where they said these things were found? Under my bed! As if I was foolish enough to store them there..."

In his absence his family was persecuted and both his father and brother were imprisoned without his mother knowing where, and he had many of his possessions confiscated. Aftab could do nothing but stay in England, unable to work as he did not have a permit, not able to gain political asylum because of the dangerous nature of charges against him, but at least safe against extradition as his life would be at risk if he was forced to return home.

After he had been five and a half years in exile Benazir Bhutto cleared the way for his return by declaring an amnesty, after the death of President Zia-ul-Haq in an air crash in 1988, thus quashing the three concurrent life-sentences lodged against him.

Since then Aftab Gul has been making up for

Aftab keeps on the right side of the law, London 1971

lost time as a lawyer, and is still a member of the People's Party of Pakistan. His career reflects the difficulties of the nation but also its ability to cope in the face of adversity.

Career Details

Born: Gujar Khan, India, 31 March 1946
Role: right-hand, opening batsman, leg-break bowler
Clubs: Punjab University (1964/5-1969/70), Lahore (1964/5-1975/6), Punjab (1972/3-1977/8) and Servis Industries (1976/7)
First-class record: (1964-78) 6129 runs (36.92) including 11 centuries, 14 wickets (33.28) and 11 catches
Tests: 6 (1968/9-1971)
Test Debut: v England, Lahore, 1968/9
Test record: 182 runs (22.75), no wickets for 4 runs, 3 catches
Best Performances: HS 33 v England, Lord's, 1971
Tours: England; 1971, 1974

Mahmood Hussain

Mahmood Hussain played an important part in Pakistan's early Test history. With Fazal Mahmood and Khan Mohammad he gave the side a pace attack to be reckoned with. Though his record is not quite as good as the other two, he was the quickest of the three and probably the quickest for Pakistan until Imran Khan's era.

Like Khan Mohammad, he tended to be prone to injuries and perhaps because of his extra pace, too often he tried to bang the ball in short concentrating on leg-theory, which was physically demanding, sapping his energy. Also he had always been a willing bowler and captains tended to over-bowl him which took its toll on his big frame. However he used his height and could get the ball to lift awkwardly and bowled big inswingers when he pitched the ball up on a full length.

Mahmood first sprung to prominence when he took 16 wickets for Punjab in the Universities Final against Sind in 1949/50. He went on Pakistan's inaugural Test tour to India in 1952/3, and although he missed out on selection for the first Test he made his debut in the 2nd, at the age of 20, bowling 42 overs and taking four for 92 in the match which Pakistan won by an innings. He stayed in the side for the rest of the series, finishing with 12 wickets which was exceeded only by Fazal Mahmood.

He had a poor start to the tour to England in 1954 and had to wait until Khan Mohammad was unavailable to get his chance in the Test side. Once he acclimatised he bowled better and better. In the historic win at the Oval, where Pakistan became the first side to win a Test on its first tour to England, he played his most important innings, hitting 23 at number 11, a score exceeded only by his captain, Kardar. Then in tandem with Fazal Mahmood, he bowled England out for 130 to give Pakistan a narrow lead, taking four for 58 in 21.3 overs. He shared a useful last wicket stand in the 2nd innings, with Wazir Mohammad, of 24 which was the eventual winning margin. He finished the tour with the impressive tally of 72

wickets - only five less than Fazal Mahmood - at an average of 21.30, which included figures of seven for 61 against an England XI at Hastings and four other five-wicket hauls.

He took that form into the home series with India (1954/5), bowling Pakistan into a strong position in the first Test at Dacca with six for 67. Although each missed one Test, the Hussain-Mohammad-Mahmood attack gave Pakistan the edge in a drawn series. Among them they took 51 of the 58 wickets to fall. In a very slow-scoring rubber Mahmood tended to be less frugal than the others but took 14 wickets in all at 26.57.

Due largely to his academic commitments he

played in just one Test in the next three years (though only a handful were played), but a career-best eight for 95 for Karachi Whites against the Greens in 1956/7 helped in his selection for the tour of the Caribbean (1957/8). However, on excellent batting tracks he tended to be expensive, conceding well over a hundred runs in each of the first three innings of the series. He broke down after just five balls in the third Test at Sabina Park (Jamaica) when he pulled a thigh muscle, leaving Fazal Mahmood and Khan Mohammad the thankless task of bowling at Conrad Hunte and Garry Sobers in full flow with precious little support.

He played throughout the return series with Westindies (1958/9), knocking over the tail to speed Pakistan to a narrow win at Dacca in the 2nd Test. He was now coming in to his prime, at 28; a tall, strong man with broad shoulders, he was at his fittest and able to do plenty of bowling. He did a lot of bowling in the series in India, 1960/1, and started by sending down over fifty overs in the only innings of the first Test to take 5-129, after Fazal Mahmood had been injured, and averaged about 40 overs an innings throughout the series. He was the leading bowler with 13 wickets at 38.69 which was a fine effort on the flattest of pitches against a side that averaged over 400 an innings in the series. He also played a crucial innings in the final Test. Coming in with Pakistan 189 for 7 in their second innings, just 12 ahead, he made his highest score in Tests, 35, which took his side just out of reach with time running out. When he was last out, India needed only 74 but there was only time for two overs.

His last few Tests were against another high-scoring side, England, at home and away in 1961-2. He headed the first-class averages on the tour to England with 44 wickets at 23.45, but was over-bowled early on and suffered a groin injury after the third Test at Headingley, which proved to be his last. Fazal Mahmood was called up to replace him.

He continued to play first-class cricket until 1969, when he made his last appearance for the National Tyre and Rubber Company. He remained involved in the administration of the game and was the manager of a difficult tour to England in 1978. Denied the use of the Packer players, there were rumours of other players (Javed Miandad and Haroon Rashid) being signed up as well which did not help the team spirit of an already weakened side. He made his feelings known when the England fast bowler Bob Willis hit the Pakistani tail-ender in the face with a short ball from around the wicket. He described Willis's tactics as "unfair" and was most unhappy, insisting that the umpires should not have allowed him to bowl like that. "Brearley [the England captain] is well aware that the man who was hit is a lower-order batsman and it was a clear infringement of the Playing Conditions." After the Test a list of "non-recognised batsmen" on each side was drawn up.

Mahmood Hussain spent much of his later life in England and was a frequent visitor to Lord's. He died a few miles down the road from the ground at Northwick Park Hospital, Harrow, Middlesex, on Christmas Day 1991 at the age of 59 - one of only eight former Pakistani Test players to have passed away.

Mahmood Hussain's Test figures were only moderate: by way of comparison his statistics are very similar to those of Sikander Bakht, who played for Pakistan from 1977 to 1983, or those of England's Neil Foster or Derek Pringle. However, by the end of the summer of 1996, his 68 Test wickets put him behind only Imran Khan, Wasim Akram, Sarfraz Nawaz, Fazal Mahmood and Waqar Younis amongst Pakistan's seamers and twelfth overall. He played an important role backing up Fazal Mahmood (and to a lesser extent Khan Mohammad) for the first ten years of Pakistan's Test history with his unstinting efforts.

Career Details

Born: Lahore (India), 2 April 1932
Died: Northwick Park, Middlesex, 25 December 1991
Role: right-hand, lower-order batsman, right-hand fast medium bowler
Clubs: Universities (1949/50), West Punjab 1951/2, Karachi (1953/4-1961/2) and East Pakistan (1955/6)
First-class record: (1949-69) 1107 runs (10.74) HS 50, 322 wickets (25.06) and 29 catches
Tests: 27
Test Debut: v India, Lucknow, 1952/3
Test record: 336 runs (10.18), 68 wickets (38.64) and 5 catches
Best Performances: HS 35 v India, Delhi, 1960/1
BB 6-67 v India, Dacca, 1954/5
Tours: India; 1952/3, 1960/1
England; 1954, 1962
Westindies; 1957/8

Asif Iqbal Razvi

Asif Iqbal was a masterful batsman who added a new dimension to improvisation and running between the wickets in one-day cricket. These stood him in good stead in Test cricket too, and he played some brilliant innings especially when the side was in trouble. Critics thought that his high back-lift might hinder his development as a batsman; instead it gave him a natural sense of timing. He was a useful medium-pacer and a marvellously athletic fielder. He led Pakistan and Kent shrewdly, for whom he had a long and distinguished county career.

Asif was born in India in 1943 but unlike other prominent Pakistani players who were born there, generally in the north, and whose families moved on or soon after Partition, Asif came from Hyderabad, in Southern India, and he did not move to Pakistan until 1961. Unfortunately, his father Majid Razvi died when was only six months old, but with the guidance of his four uncles, he was well coached: Rauf was a batsman, Yousaf a bowler, Rahim an all-rounder, while Ghulam Ahmed, was an off-spinner who played 22 Tests for India between 1948/9 and 1958/9, including the first-ever Test against Pakistan.

When he moved to Pakistan, where he joined his brother Dr Shahid Iqbal, Asif had already played two seasons of first-class cricket for Hyderabad, following in his father's footsteps. He had made his debut in the Ranji Trophy in 1959/60, while still at Nizam College, and in 1961, even played against Fazal Mahmood's Pakistan touring side for South Zone.

In 1961/2, his first season in his adopted country, Asif soon caught the eye playing for Karachi. He was selected for the Pakistan Eaglets (a youth side) to tour England in 1963 and finished as the leading wicket-taker with 19 wickets at 14.73. He continued to progress well in three "Tests" against a Commonwealth side, and on tours to Ceylon and Kenya and it was as a bowler that he was initially chosen in the full Test side, sharing the new ball with Majid Khan. They were amongst six new caps at Karachi for the match against Australia in 1964/5. He took two wickets and batted at No 10, making 41, which earned him the job of night-watchman in the second innings. Going in at No 3, he made 36.

He went on the short tour of Australia, playing at Melbourne, and then onto New Zealand where in the first Test at Wellington his brisk medium-pace seamers brought him five wickets for 48. He then saved the day with his batting after Pakistan had collapsed to 64 for 6, by scoring 52 not out including eight boundaries in 81 minutes to secure a draw. Gradually batting was to take over as his strongest suit, especially when charged up by such rearguard actions.

He bowled consistently well in that series, capturing another five wickets in an innings in the next Test at Auckland, and finished with 18 wickets in the series at just 13.77, while conceding under two an over. In the return series at home he continued to make useful runs and take important wickets.

In Pakistan's two-year absence from Test cricket between 1965 and 1967, Asif matured as a player and captained the under-25 national side for the series against the MCC under-25 tourists in early 1967. In a closely contested series that finished nil-all, he saved his side in the second "Test" with a marvellous innings of 117 at Dacca, his maiden first-class hundred. Ever confident, as he went out to bat he said to Maqsood Ahmed, a national coach: "Leave it to me."

When he came to England that summer, he showed that his batting was the equal of anyone in the side. Because he was taking the new ball he still batted down the order, but in the 1st Test at Lord's he helped set a national record for the eighth wicket against all countries, putting on 130 in 191 minutes with Hanif Mohammad to rescue the side from 139 for 7. He made 76 and comfortably out-scored his senior partner, Hanif who marshalled the tail so effectively that Pakistan got within 15 runs of England's 369.

This was just a prelude to greater feats in the third Test at the Oval. With Pakistan 224 behind on the first innings, the side had slumped to 53 for 7, as Ken Higgs cut and swung the ball around to take five wickets. Asif came out to bat with his usual philosophy in mind, of attack being the best form of defence. "You can't go to the crease believing you can't strike the ball", was his motto.

Asif, batting at No 9, was joined by Intikhab Alam, and encouraged him to go for his shots. He knew Intikhab could bat, because the pair had shared a remarkable stand on the tour to Australia, in which they added 100 in 38 minutes against Queensland. They bettered that this time, setting a new world Test record for the ninth wicket of 190 in only 170 minutes. Asif made 146 off 244 balls and played an array of brilliant attacking strokes, hitting two sixes and 21 fours. His heroics did not save the game but at least avoided the embarrassment of the innings defeat, which seemed inevitable at 65 for 8. It certainly worried the England players, who did not know when it might end, and made for a bizarre looking scorecard with only Asif and Alam, who made 51, passing twenty. Asif's innings represented over 57 per cent of the total and he made more than three-quarters of the runs scored while he was at the wicket.

Asif had been spurred on by the somewhat premature announcement near the start of his innings that a 20-over exhibition match was being arranged to compensate the crowd for the early ending of the Test. He said after: "Everyone seemed to accept that it was already over. I certainly didn't. I wanted my team to be spared from taking part in an exhibition. The whole situation made me all the more anxious and determined to succeed."

In a subjective appraisal of famous innings, using indices such as opposition, pitch, match situation and other such variables, cricket writer David Lodge (in *Figures on the Green*) rates Asif's hundred as the best Test innings ever played by a Pakistani and amongst the best for any country. There cannot have been too many better.

He also bowled 46 overs in that game taking five for 80 and his undoubted all-round ability earned him a contract with Kent, starting the following summer (1968). *Wisden* named Asif as one of the Five Cricketers of the Year, and when he got home he was awarded the President's Medal for Pride of Performance.

Asif rightly moved up the order during the series at home to England in 1968/9, making 70 at No 4 in Lahore. Against New Zealand in the last Test match to be played at Dacca in 1969/70, he scored 92 at No 6, where he was to settle in the order.

Back in England as Pakistan's vice-captain in 1971, he flogged a tired attack, making an undefeated 104 out of the last 152, as Pakistan amassed over 600 in the 1st Test at Edgbaston. He was bowling less and less by now, which was a pity as he was a very effective bowler, often getting good players out, bowling very straight as was evident from how he claimed most of his wickets, most of which were clean bowled or caught behind from his leg-cutter.

He struggled with both bat and ball on the tour to Australia in 1972/3, apart from innings of 130 and 62 against a Combined XI outside the Tests, but over in New Zealand he was back to his best. In the 2nd Test at Dunedin, he was involved in another record partnership, this time with Mustaq Mohammad with whom he added 350 for the 4th wicket - Pakistan's record for that wicket in all Tests - in one of the fastest partnerships in Test history. Asif made his highest Test score, 175 in 275 minutes, hitting a six and 18 fours in a dazzling batting display. They both started circumspectly and had only hit three boundaries between them in their first two hours together. However after tea on the first day they were devastating, and the last 150 of their stand took only an hour and ten minutes.

Soon afterwards Asif made another scintillating century, in the first Test against England at Lahore. He played an array of languid, powerful strokes and in particular went after his Kent colleague, Derek Underwood, in style. *Wisden* described his strokes as "almost insolent in a Test match."

For Kent, Asif was the lynchpin of their one-day successes in the early seventies. They won the John Player League in 1972 and 1973, lost in the final of the 1971 Gillette Cup, despite Asif's half-century, which was only ended by a brilliant diving catch by Lancashire's captain Jack Bond, and took the Benson and Hedges in 1973, when Asif won the Gold Award in the final, scoring 59 and taking 4-43 in his eleven overs. Kent also won the championship in 1970, were runners-up in 1968 and 1972, and came fourth in 1971 and 1973.

It is surprising then that he had such a poor series in England in 1974, making only 53 runs in five innings - perhaps he was trying too hard. His form returned to some degree that winter, making a fifty in both Tests against the Westindies. With Pakistan playing little Test cricket, this was merely a quiet spell before a flood of runs in the hectic winter season of 1976/7.

Asif captained Pakistan in the 1975 World Cup, making a fine fifty against Australia but was taken ill after that match and played no further part in the tournament. During the match against the Westindies Bernard Julien, the Trinidadian all-rounder, phoned Asif in hospital shortly after he was out to wish him well and congratulate his Kent colleague on what he presumed would be a Pakistan victory. It must have seemed like a bad joke, as Westindies' final pair put together a thrilling last wicket stand to snatch the game in the very last over. Once he recovered he had a fine season with Kent, averaging just under 50, but was

Asif started his Test career taking the new ball but soon became a brilliant strokemaker with the bat

strangely out of touch the following year in the long hot summer of 1976.

By the winter of 1976/7 the captaincy had passed to Mustaq Mohammad for the home series against New Zealand and the tours to Australia and the Caribbean. At Lahore, in the first of eleven Tests in seven months, Asif started where he had left off against New Zealand, with a big hundred in a record partnership. He made 166 and added 281 for the fifth wicket with Javed Miandad, the highest in all Tests for that wicket by Pakistan. Coming in at 55 for 4, he broke New Zealand's grip on the game by counter-attacking at first and then settled down to ensure a big score.

In Australia, he made another brilliant hundred when Pakistan were on the rack at Adelaide, 188 behind on first innings. Asif finished with 152 not out, an innings full of fluent drives, and with Iqbal Qasim, he put on 87 for the last wicket - another record - of which Qasim made just four. Asif's batting and Iqbal Qasim's bowling had eroded their opponents' confidence to such a degree that Australia declined to chase only 56 in the last 15 (8-ball) overs. Asif played an equally delightful innings in the third Test at the Sydney Cricket Ground, where he made 120 to set up Pakistan's

first win in Australia.

Not surprisingly he was the man that Kerry Packer approached as his agent for World Series Cricket. He had joined the stand against the Board of Control for Cricket in Pakistan (BCCP) over wages before the tour, and was a shrewd businessman who was later involved in setting up and running cricket in the United Arab Emirates, establishing a number of fund-raising one-day competitions in Sharjah. He took some time to find his form of Australia in the Caribbean but needless to say, when Pakistan was in real trouble in the final Test at Guyana he scored his fourth hundred of the winter. With his side struggling at 51 for 4, it could have been worse had Asif been caught at slip when only five. He decided to chance his luck after that and played such a marvellous sequence of shots that Westindies did not know where to bowl at him. He made 69 out of a partnership of 87 with Mustaq Mohammad, and put on 115 with Wasim Raja. Asif's 135 included a six and twenty fours.

That summer with Kent, he captained the side to victory in the final of the Benson and Hedges Cup and to a share of the Championship. He lost the captaincy the following year because of his association with Kerry Packer, but Kent won both the aforementioned competitions again. Over the next two years in World Series Cricket (WSC), Asif proved to be one of the best batsmen, and captained the World XI in the second season, making a hundred against the Westindies.

His commitment to WSC brought an end to his record of 45 consecutive appearances for Pakistan over the previous 13 years, missing two series against England, but he marked his return with a hundred against India at Faisalabad (1978/9), in which he shared a stand of 166 with Zaheer Abbas for the third wicket. When on song his placement and brilliant running between the wickets meant he could out-score anyone. In the third Test when a run chase was on, he was promoted to open and raced to 44, adding 97 in just nine overs in partnership with Javed Miandad to ensure victory.

When the team went on tour to Australasia, he made a hundred in the 2nd Test against New Zealand at Napier, and 134 not out against Australia at Perth. In the last, he showed why he has so many late-wicket partnership records to his name, again because of his placement and running which allowed him to marshal the lower-order so effectively. This time he added 92 with Imran Khan, to which Imran contributed just 15. He was constructing another useful partnership for the last wicket, when the bowler Alan Hurst, ran out the non-striker Sikander Bakht, who was backing up. The normally mild-mannered Asif smashed down the stumps, just as Rodney Hogg had done in the previous Test after a similarly controversial run out. Asif had perhaps provoked the ill-feeling in this series, with some inflammatory remarks on the eve of the 1st Test. He suggested that playing the Australian side, who were without their Packer players, would be "like playing against a load of schoolboys".

That was Mustaq Mohammad's last Test and Asif, despite his lack of diplomacy in Australia, was the clear candidate to take over as captain. He took Pakistan to the semi-final of the World Cup in England in 1979, making fifties against the hosts and the Australians on the way, where his side lost to Westindies.

Surprisingly, he had a disastrous time in his only Test series in charge. He took the side to India in 1979/80, where Pakistan were odds-on favourites to win but he could not motivate his talented, over-confident side, losing 2-0. He found the pressure of captaining in the country of his birth unbearable. He was taking tranquillisers and he lost a lot of weight off his already sleek physique. He had not picked Sarfraz Nawaz for the tour because he did not know how to handle the strong-minded fast bowler, and missed his experience especially when Imran Khan was injured.

He could not face the ignominy of the defeat and stepped down from the captaincy (probably before he was asked to), but surprisingly he also announced his retirement from Test cricket. He was still an excellent player, who had never been left out of the side when available.

The next summer at Kent he played less than half the games as the county adopted a policy of giving their youngsters a chance, yet reinstated him as captain for the following year after a lamentably poor 1980 season. Kent showed an all-round improvement, and Asif enjoyed a successful benefit year.

Since retiring he has been involved in various entrepreneurial activities; he has worked for Abdul Rehman Bukhatir in the United Arab Emirates to establish the Sharjah one-day tournament, proceeds of which go to various nominated players. He was also an expert summariser for BBC TV during Pakistan's 1992 tour of England and appears regularly on Sky Sports.

A sif Iqbal was undoubtedly one of Pakistan's finest cricketers, always playing for the team, and at his best in a crisis, which is reflected by the fact that he has been part of Pakistan's 4th, 5th, 8th and 9th wicket record partnerships in Tests.

He had a distinctive style, shirt-sleeves always buttoned to his steely wrists, and a rather bow-legged, open stance. He was a superb one-day player, with his useful medium-pacers, electric fielding, breathtaking improvisation and impish running between the wickets, helping him to average over fifty with the bat in one-day internationals. His Test career met an unhappy and unnecessarily abrupt end for someone who had always played the game with a smile on his face. He saw out his playing days with Kent for whom he scored nearly 13,000 first-class runs during his career, and was an integral part of their glory years of the seventies.

Asif now lives in England and his sons are showing great promise, playing for Kent's junior teams. His eldest son, Hesham, captained Sevenoaks School in 1993, and averaged over 80 with the bat and has all the makings of becoming a very fine cricketer.

Career Details

Born: Hyderabad, India, 6 June 1943
Role: right-hand middle-order batsman, right-arm medium-pacer
Clubs: Hyderabad (1959/60), Karachi (1961/2-1968/9), PIA (1964/5-1979/80), National Bank (1976/7) and Kent (1968-82)
First-class record: (1959-82) 23,375 runs (37.23) including 45 centuries, 291 wickets (30.15) and 304 catches
Tests: 58
Test Debut: v Australia, Karachi, 1964/5
Test record: 3,308 runs (39.85), 51 wickets (28.03) and 32 catches
Best Performances: HS 175 v New Zealand, Dunedin, 1972/3
BB 5-48 v New Zealand, Wellington, 1964/5
Tours: Australia; 1964/5, 1972/3, 1976/7, 1978/9
England; 1963 (Eaglets), 1967, 1971, 1974
New Zealand; 1964/5, 1972/3, 1978/9
Westindies; 1976/7
India; 1979/80
Overseas Tests; 37
One-day Internationals; 10
World Cups; 1975, 1979
Ceylon (Sri Lanka) ; 1964/5, 1972/3

Abdul Hafeez Kardar

Abdul Hafeez Kardar's importance in establishing Pakistan as a Test playing nation cannot be overestimated. He led them in their first 23 Tests spread over six years, a record period in charge for Pakistan, and easily the most for a country's first captain, which was previously only seven Tests, set by New Zealand's Tom Lowry.

His appointment was the more significant as he had previously played for India, under the name of "Abdul Hafeez." He was the youngest member to be selected for the 1946 tour to England, following fine form for Punjab University and North Zone, which included a career-best 173, and played in three Tests with modest results. However, as he was a Muslim and born in Lahore, he took Pakistani citizenship on Partition in 1947.

He stayed on in England after the India tour to read philosophy at University College, Oxford, playing three times in the Varsity match, and in all taking 124 wickets for the University. He also represented Warwickshire in the County Championship during the university summer holidays and after graduating, playing in 45 matches in all. He also met his match, marrying the daughter of county chairman, Cyril Hastilow.

Kardar's stylish left-handed batting produced steady results, and he picked up some useful wickets with his left-arm spin or medium pace bowling. He was prone in his younger days to dance down the pitch even to the opening bowlers and displayed some original strokes. His captaincy of Pakistan was rather more orthodox but he gave the side, and nation, early confidence and steadiness. He lead with great authority.

He captained a representative side to victory over the MCC touring team in 1951/2 which went a long way towards securing Pakistan Test status. He made 48 in the first match which was drawn, and then in the second with his side slipping at 178 for 5, steadied the ship in a stand of 83 with Anwar Hussain, and saw Pakistan to victory, finishing with 50 not out. Kardar wrote to *The Times* in London presenting his country's case to be included as a full member of the Imperial Cricket Conference. Pakistan was duly elected in July 1952.

As someone who had previously played for India, it was significant that Kardar should lead Pakistan in its inaugural Test that October against his old country. Although the first Test at Delhi was lost by an innings and 70 runs, despite a fighting innings by the captain of 43 not out, Kardar rallied his side to win the next Test at Lucknow by a similar margin, an innings and 43

runs. The five-Test rubber was eventually lost 2-1, but was a creditable result for a country playing in their first Test series. Kardar led astutely and produced steady personal performances throughout the series, his best being an innings of 79 in the fourth Test at Madras. In all first-class matches he finished the tour with 416 runs at 37.81 and with 13 wickets at 23.53.

His earlier experience in England served him well when he led Pakistan on their first tour there in 1954, though initially there was some doubt as to whether he would be able to make the tour because of his commitments to the Pakistan Air Force.

Against all expectations Pakistan drew the series by winning the final Test match at the Oval. Kardar top-scored in the first innings with 36 out of 133, and then got the most out of his bowlers to record the only Test win by a side on their first tour to England.

That winter, however, he was criticised for his leadership in the dull, attritional series against India, the first at home, where old rivalries precluded the risk of losing. He made his highest Test score, 93, in the final match at the National Stadium in Karachi, putting on 155 with Alimuddin in a rare bright partnership, which hinted at what might have been.

He varied his place in the order to accommodate others, but usually batted at five or six, while his bowling was underrated. Kardar led Pakistan to their first series win, against New Zealand in 1955/6, failing with the bat but taking ten wickets at 15 each. The MCC toured in the New Year and he was again in fine form with the ball. He turned in a match-winning performance in the third match at Peshawar, taking six for 40 and five for 26, to follow his knock of 78 in the innings victory in the previous game.

The next season, Pakistan had only one Test - against the Australians, who were on their way home from their tour of England in 1956. He top-scored in the match, leading his side out of trouble at 70 for 5 with a stand of 104 with Wazir Mohammad and on to a significant lead to help beat Australia in the first encounter between the two sides.

He retired after the tour to the Caribbean (1957/8) and although the series was lost, he had the satisfaction of winning his last Test by an innings. He had defied doctor's orders by playing in the third Test despite having a broken finger, making a brave fifty and bowling 37 overs. During the first Test at Bridgetown he used to go to the room shared by Hanif and Wazir Mohammad to listen to the news from Pakistan on their radio while they were out. As Hanif batted heroically playing cricket's longest innings to save the game, Kardar left notes of encouragement for him stuck to the mirror in his room for when he returned each evening. The first read, "You're doing fine, you can save us," and the second the next day, "If you play till tea-time tomorrow the match will be saved," but otherwise he said nothing to him. It was enough to inspire Hanif.

Kardar played his last first-class cricket in 1965/6. He remained very influential in Pakistan's administration, attempting to restructure domestic cricket from its provincial base. It was his idea to bring commercial organisations into the game to ensure financial security through full-time employment with the backers. Unfortunately his scheme backfired as the companies' teams had no parochial following, while the regional associations were diminished. Thus the game developed on too narrow a base around just two centres, Lahore and Karachi.

As President of the Board of Control for Cricket in Pakistan (1972-77), he represented Pakistan at International Cricket Conference meetings. He was ahead of his times, being adamant about changing the constitution, which gave the founder countries England and Australia the right of veto. He considered this undemocratic and he believed a new constitution would allow the annual meetings to be staged outside England rather than always being at Lord's under the chairmanship of the President of the MCC. He also proposed barring the bouncer from the first World Cup in 1975, a measure which has since been introduced for all one-day cricket.

Later he had to preside over several pay disputes, eventually giving in to the demands of the players when six senior cricketers refused to play before the tour to Australia and Westindies in 1976/7. At first, he was not prepared to compromise and he chose a new team and a new captain, Intikhab Alam, but soon had to back down and, in effect, out of cricket's administration in the wake of the Packer schism.

Despite the difficulties he faced in administration, Kardar will be remembered for his role in leading a side that could compete from its very first Test, a factor which helped in establishing Pakistan's national identity as well as its Test status. He had a spell in politics, being a member of the Punjab Provincial Assembly between 1970 and 1977 and was for a short while Minister of Food and Education. Although in politics himself, he resented governmental interference in his sport, believing the game should be run by cricketers.

He would on occasions write his opinions in the newspapers and served as a most able ambassador for his country (to Switzerland, 1991-93), much as he was, figuratively, during his playing days.

While in London in March 1996, he collapsed while watching the World Cup quarter-final match between Pakistan and India. He spent three days in St Mary's Hospital, Paddington, and was well enough to return home to Pakistan. However, he had not fully recovered and died shortly afterwards. He is survived by his three children, one of whom, Shahid, played first-class cricket for Lahore.

Career Details

Born: Lahore, 17 January 1925
Died: Lahore, 21 April 1996
Role: Left-handed, middle-order batsman, left-arm slow/medium bowler, captain.
Clubs: Northern India (1943/4-1945/6), Muslims (1944/5), Services (1953/4-1954/5), Oxford University (1947-49) and Warwickshire (1948-50)
First-class record: [1943-58] 6,815 runs (29.75) including 8 centuries, 344 wickets (24.55) and 108 catches
Tests: India, 3
Pakistan, 23
Test Debut: for India v England, Lord's, 1946
For Pakistan; v India, Delhi, 1952/3
Test record: 847 runs (24.91), 21 wickets (45.42) and 15 catches for Pakistan. [80 runs (16.00) and 1 catch for India]
Tours: with India; England 1946
With Pakistan
India; 1952/3
England; 1954
Westindies; 1957/8
Overseas Tests; 14

Kardar acknowledges the applause of the crowd after
leading Pakistan to victory at the Oval in 1954

Imran Khan, Niazi

Imran Khan is the finest all-round cricketer Pakistan has ever produced and ranks amongst the greatest in the history of the game. His international career spanned 21 years, which at the time of his retirement represented more than half of Pakistan's Test history and is unparalleled amongst fast bowlers from any country. During that period he played in 88 Tests, captaining Pakistan with a fierce patriotism in 48 of those matches and, of course, led the side to victory in the 1992 World Cup, which proved to be his swansong.

He was born in Lahore to a life of privilege, but the most important factor in his outlook was his Pathan heritage, in which he has great pride and has even written a book about his tribal ancestors, *Warrior Race*. That pride is exemplified in the way his own performances were enhanced by the captaincy like no other leader in Test history, averaging more than 50 with the bat and just over 20 with the ball on his way to career totals of 3,807 runs and 362 wickets in Tests. The Pathans are from a small region in Northwest Pakistan near the Khyber Pass, an area measuring some 200 by 100 miles, which has never been conquered. It is their outlook, philosophy and characteristic fighting qualities that have shaped his career. He determined to become the first genuinely fast bowler to come out of Pakistan and in so doing started his own dynasty that has been extended through the likes of Wasim Akram and Waqar Younis.

His family has produced eight cousins who have played first-class cricket. Amongst these are Majid Khan and Javed Burki, quality Test players who both also led Pakistan. The latter was Imran's captain when he made his first-class debut at the age of 16 for Lahore while still at Aitchison College, and Burki was able to nurture his early progress.

Imran's rapid promotion, which saw him jump straight from the under-19 XI into the full Test side is sometimes attributed, at least in part, to his family connections. He was included for the tour to England as a naive 18 year-old reserve seamer who still considered himself to be a batsman. He was rather full of himself and did not like being bossed around by senior members of the team. There was one story that Saeed Ahmed, the senior player on the tour who was sharing a room with Imran, encouraged him to go out partying one night only for him to be reported the next day to the management. Ahmed, who wanted a single room, blamed his poor form on Imran for keeping him awake!

An injury to Sarfraz Nawaz meant that Imran made his debut in the first Test of the series at Edgbaston, in which he was run out for five and did not take a wicket. Without a proper, measured run-up, in unfamiliar conditions and with a shiny new ball, he could not control the swing he was getting from his rather slinging action, spraying the ball all over the place and was promptly dropped from the remaining Tests before he had given the slightest hint of the talent he possessed. After that tour Imran stayed on in England and finished his schooling at Worcester Royal Grammar School. He went up to Oxford University the following autumn (1972) to read politics and economics at Keble College, which is still renowned for its sportsmen. His all-round talent began to flourish there, impressing with his strokeplay at number four, and with his fastish-medium inswingers.

Imran's opportunities in Test cricket, between his debut in 1971 and 1976/7, were limited because of his studies to just one series - against England in 1974. In that series he joined the tour party only after the end of term and not surprisingly struggled to make the step up from university cricket to Test cricket even though his form as captain of Oxford had been superb. This early taste of the leadership hinted at what was to come for his country; he was the leading wicket-taker and run-scorer, making five hundreds including a hundred in each innings against Nottinghamshire, and 170 against Northants, while in the Varsity match he top-scored in the 2nd innings and took ten wickets for 113 in the match.

His part in the inaugural World Cup of 1975 was also limited by the inconvenience of having to sit his finals in the middle of the competition and he had a disastrous second half of the season with Worcester, where the strictures the county put on his all-round ability - batting him down the order and asking him to bowl medium pace line and length - cramped his style. After a fine winter season in which he toured Sri Lanka with Pakistan, he persuaded Norman Gifford, his Worcester captain, to bat him at No 4 and immediately justified the promotion with 143 against Warwickshire. He played one remarkable innings towards the end of the season, in which he scored 166 out of the last 185 against a Northants side including his Pakistan team-mates Sarfraz Nawaz and Mustaq Mohammad. He dominated a partnership with Gifford, making 117 out of the 127 added for the ninth wicket.

Imran averaged over forty with the bat in 1976 and finished as the leading wicket-taker, as well as helping his county reach the Benson and Hedges final, which they lost to Kent. However, although recently capped, at the end of the season he decided to leave Worcester, which he found quaint but dull, and joined Sussex where the wickets suited him better and where he was closer to his graduate friends now in London.

Although Imran had missed thirteen possible Tests while at Oxford, his three years there was time profitably spent as he had matured as a person, growing in confidence and equanimity, which ultimately helped his cricket. He was then considered a batting all-rounder on the county circuit as he always felt he would be. On his return to the Pakistan side though, he was somewhat alarmed to find himself batting as low as No 9, even though his captain Mustaq Mohammad had witnessed his amazing knock a few months before at Northants, and again Imran found it difficult to make the necessary adjustments to his approach to batting.

However it was that winter, 1976/7, that Imran established himself as a fast bowler to be reckoned with. After a satisfactory series at home to New Zealand, he proved a sensation in the two rubbers which followed, in Australia and Westindies. For the first time he was being encouraged to try and bowl fast and after taking five wickets in a lost cause at the Melbourne Cricket Ground (MCG), he inspired Pakistan to a series-levelling win at Sydney with six wickets in each innings (6-102 & 6-63) to give him match figures of 45.7-9-165-12, the best by a Pakistani fast bowler since the days of Fazal Mahmood. He enjoyed the bouncier wickets there, perhaps too much, for he was warned at the SCG for overdoing the bouncer, a tendency at this stage of his career.

His pace and hostility had been comparable with that of Dennis Lillee in that game, though that comparison was scoffed at when Imran first arrived in the Caribbean. He was soon making his point. In tandem with Sarfraz, he nearly bowled Pakistan to a famous victory on the last day of the Barbados Test, which saw Westindies' last pair just hanging on for a draw. He finished the series with a record 25 wickets for Pakistan against the Westindies, which included 6-90 in the last Test in Jamaica, where he bowled with real pace on a quick track.

That summer he joined Sussex, who were captained by Tony Greig who, to Imran's surprise, had asked him to play for the World XI in Australia the following winter in Kerry Packer's cricket "circus." His handsome features were also chosen by the marketing men as one of the faces to promote World Series Cricket. There, the raw edges of his fast bowling talent were smoothed through watching the Westindian quicks and talking with the likes of England's John Snow, who helped him get more side on, and with the South African Mike Procter, who suggested a more vigorous approach to the crease. These adjustments transformed his bowling. He honed his magnificent final leap before his delivery stride to help accommodate the more aggressive run-up and allow him to get sideways, while he continued to work on his mastery of swing bowling. Not tall for a fast bowler at 5 foot 11, but broad-shouldered and athletic, he devised his own fitness regime to sustain bowling at top pace.

His association with WSC precluded his selection for the next series at home to England although he, Mustaq Mohammad and Zaheer Abbas were released by Packer to go and play in the third Test and indeed travelled to Karachi only to be left out of the Test team at the last moment, following general condemnation of their selection from all quarters. This policy of not picking Packer players continued the following summer when Pakistan toured England, so Imran was confined to playing for Sussex, for whom he was the leading run-scorer and wicket-taker, and he helped his county win the Gillette Cup while his country was being well beaten by England.

Thus far Imran had played in only three Tests at home and would have missed the first series with India for seventeen years, in 1978/9, but for a truce between the Board of Control for Cricket in Pakistan and Kerry Packer. He played a major role in Pakistan's first series win over their neighbours as he and Sarfraz Nawaz combined to take 31 of the 49 wickets to fall, while his powerful hitting sped the side to victory in an exciting run-chase at Karachi.

His hectic winter continued, playing WSC, then joining the tour party in New Zealand only to miss the first Test because he had to fly back to Sydney to represent the World XI. On his return to the Pakistan side, he warmed up by taking ten for 39 in the match with Otago and in the second Test at Napier took five wickets in the Kiwis' only innings of a drawn game. Within ten days of that series finishing, Pakistan were involved in a two-match series with Australia.

Up to the winter of 1978/9 Imran had played just 15 Tests in seven years, but in the subsequent 18 months he nearly double that tally as well as competing in the World Cup and a number of WSC "Super Tests." Not surprisingly it began to take its toll, as Imran suffered a sequence of injuries. He broke down during the 2nd Test against India at Delhi, wrenching his hip in mid-over. He played in the next Test at Bombay but could not bowl in the second innings and missed the 4th Test. He came back to take five wickets in Madras, including his 100th in his 26th Test when he bowled Syed Kirmani, and nine in the game at Calcutta where he bowled magnificently to try and salvage some pride from a series that had already been lost.

Later that season injury again kept him out, missing the second Test against Australia, after breaking down during the first at Karachi, and in his absence the opposition made the highest Test score in Pakistan, 617.

Imran always considered a series with the Westindians as the greatest challenge, and this often brought out the best in him. After some disappointing returns with the bat - with just two fifties in 29 Tests and with an average in the low twenties - he celebrated his 28th birthday with a brilliant hundred against an attack consisting of Malcolm Marshall, Colin Croft, Sylvester Clarke and Joel Garner. It took him past 1,000 runs in Tests, thus becoming only the second Pakistani after Intikhab Alam to complete the double. Coming in with Pakistan in trouble at 95 for 5, he virtually doubled the score in partnership with Wasim Raja and then added 168 for the 7th wicket - first with Abdul Qadir, who was forced to retire hurt, and then with Sarfraz Nawaz.

After another highly successful season with Sussex in 1981, in which he helped the county finish runners-up in the Championship just two points from taking their first title, he toured Australia for a three Test series and for the World Series Cup. He took 16 wickets in the Tests at under 20 apiece and when he dismissed Rod Marsh in the third Test at the MCG, became Pakistan's leading wicket-taker, surpassing Fazal Mahmood's 139 victims. Imran also made 70 not out as Pakistan won by an innings to square the series. Dissatisfaction amongst the players with Javed Miandad on that tour provoked a players' revolt which led, ultimately, to the unexpected offer of the captaincy soon after.

Imran was one of those refusing to continue under Miandad's leadership and consequently he missed the first two Tests against Sri Lanka but returned when Javed agreed to stand down for the forthcoming tour of England. Imran did his cause for the soon to be vacant position no harm by producing his best Test match figures, taking 8-58 and then 6-58 to sweep Pakistan to an innings victory. His return of 14-116 is 14th amongst the top analyses in all Tests and the best for Pakistan.

However, despite his form, Imran did not expect to be asked to be captain. At the time it was considered a stopgap measure but Imran kept the post for all but three of his remaining forty-eight Tests and captained with a pride and passion that brought out the best in his own game and thus helped him to lead by example with such conviction for the next ten years.

At first he did not know whether to accept and was advised against it by his friend Iftikhar Ahmed, the well-known Pakistani commentator, who cited Ian Botham's unhappy spell in charge. However at least during Imran's only previous experience of captaincy, his one year in charge at Oxford, his performances had actually been enhanced. Others warned of poor treatment by the press or the Board, as his cousin Majid Khan had found to his cost, but what finally swayed him was the unhappy experiences of the previous year under Miandad, when team morale was almost non-existent and the side seemed full of self-interested parties. He knew he could improve on this situation.

Consider Imran's Test record at this stage. He had proved himself a great bowler without doubt, having taken 158 wickets at 26.56 each with a wicket every 60 balls. Indeed former England captain Mike Brearley considered him the best bowler in the world at the time. With his batting, however, although competent he had underachieved, bringing one hundred and just three fifties in 37 Tests at an average of 25.

The summer of 1982 was billed as the battle of the all-rounders. England had played a three Test series with India just prior to Pakistan's, and Ian Botham had won his duel with Kapil Dev. Imran then comfortably out-performed Botham, being named man-of-the-series, after averaging 53 with the bat and 18 with the ball compared to Botham's 27 with the bat and 26 with the ball. In addition his handling of the side was astute though Brearley, the doyen of captains, suggests that Imran did not know quite when to attack and when to defend. He was over-reliant on himself and Abdul Qadir, and together they bowled nearly two-thirds of Pakistan's overs in the series. He might have allowed more singles to get the lesser batsmen on strike, some of whom had little idea how to play Qadir's leg-spin. On the field he got good advice from Mudassar Nazar, who erred towards caution, and from Miandad who liked to attack but did not rate spinners, while off it Intikhab Alam did most of the talking at first until the novice captain had got used to dealing with the press.

Imran had an invidious decision to make on the eve of his first Test match in charge, when he chose to leave out Majid Khan, who had helped him so much with his own game in his youth. Imran considers it "the toughest and most painful decision" he ever took; since establishing himself, Majid had enjoyed a virtually unbroken run in the side and had been Imran's childhood hero. Majid probably still resents the fact that he was dropped.

Imran started his tenure as captain with some inspired bowling in the first Test at Edgbaston, immediately leading by example. He took seven for 52 and then with his side slipping towards defeat in the 2nd innings at 66 for 5, he rallied the tail with a fine innings of 65 - a watershed innings that made him realise the importance of setting an example with the bat as well. It also gave him the new experience of trying to shield the tail.

Pakistan squared the series with their first win at Lord's and but for some ill-fortune could easily have won at Headingley and thus taken the series. Imran had a fine all-round match there with scores of 67 not out and 46, as well as taking 5-49 and 3-66 to finish with a new record for an away series with England of 21 wickets (since beaten by Waqar Younis in five Tests in 1992). Imran's batting that year had shown a marked transformation. Although still going for his shots, he was now more selective, waiting for the bad ball, and consequently he was soon getting the plaudits for his batting that he had always wanted. *Wisden* chose him as one of the Five Cricketers of the Year for 1982 and speculated that, at the age of 29, he should have a few more years at the top. No one could have imagined that he would still be leading Pakistan nearly ten years later.

The side went straight into a home series in which, under Imran's increasingly confident leadership, Pakistan won every Test in a rubber for the first time, beating Australia 3-0. With the opposition unable to bowl Pakistan out, Imran hardly batted but his bowling was instrumental in the 3rd Test win when he took four wickets in each innings. The series was played in September and October when the pitches were bare and placid and he found it difficult to motivate himself at times to bowl flat out and later in his career he chose not to play at this time of year.

He had no problem with motivation for the series with India that followed, resulting in probably his finest performances as captain and as an all-rounder. Matches against India had produced a history of draws and there was nothing to suggest that the 1982-3 rubber would be any different. Yet Pakistan won the six-Test series emphatically, 3-0. Javed Miandad, Zaheer Abbas and Mudassar Nazar were in brilliant batting form but it was Imran's bowling that was the difference between the two sides. He took 40 wickets at just 13.95 apiece, which is the most wickets by a Pakistani in any series (by ten), comfortably the highest ever taken on the sub-continent, and amongst the most for any series (there have been only six other hauls of 40 or more). Yet the pitches were universally docile and in favour of the batsmen and no one else on either side averaged under 33 with the ball. The calibre of his bowling performances is reflected in the Coopers and Lybrand rating he achieved after the Karachi Test; his score of 916 (out of a thousand) is one of the highest of all time.

Just as he had out-played Ian Botham the previous summer, Imran won his personal duel with Kapil Dev, to confirm that he was now the most complete all-rounder in the game. After a draw in Lahore, Imran took eleven wickets for 79 in Karachi to set up an innings victory, bowling some superb late inswingers or "indippers". During his match-winning return of 8-60 in the 2nd innings, he became the first Pakistani to take 200 Test wickets (in his 45th Test) when he bowled Gundappa Viswanath, in the middle of a very quick spell which saw India collapse from 102 for 1 to 114 for 7. After some stubborn tail-end resistance he came back to finish off the job; his last 25 balls had brought him five wickets for just three runs.

At Faisalabad his all-round contribution was even greater. On a good batting pitch he worked his way through a strong-looking batting line-up to take six for 98. Then with the match in the balance, with Pakistan just behind with five wickets down, Salim Malik and Imran both scored hundreds in a record partnership of 207 to set up a big lead. His 117 - his second Test hundred - took just 192 minutes and 121 balls; he hit five sixes and ten fours and included 21 off an over from Kapil Dev (640461). Not content with that he bowled over thirty overs in the second innings, taking five for 82, to emulate Ian Botham as only the second player to score a hundred and take ten wickets in a Test match.

With Pakistan now 2-0 up Imran made sure of the series with a fourth consecutive five-wicket haul on a benign Hyderabad pitch. After Pakistan had declared at 581 for 3, Imran swept through the Indian middle-order with another devastating spell, bowled at a blistering pace, to take five wickets for 8 runs in 23 balls and secure a lead of 392. Imran considers it to be probably his fastest-ever bowling. India slumped from 44 for 1 to 72 for 7, and eventually succumbed by an innings.

The final two Tests were reduced by rain and crowd disturbances otherwise Imran might have become the first bowler to take fifty wickets in a series. He finished with half the team's 80 wickets in the Tests, as well as scoring 247 runs. He was at his absolute peak as a fast bowler, and growing in stature as a captain and batsman. However the pounding his body had taken bowling on rock-hard surfaces had taken its toll. Imran had felt pain in his left shin on the second day of the Karachi Test but assumed it was just bruising, though could not remember knocking it. Carried along on the adrenaline of his best-ever bowling, he ignored the pain which abated after bowling for a while.

Moreover, on the low-bouncing pitch at Faisalabad the injury was noticeable even when batting as the ball frequently struck him low on the front pad, causing intense pain to his left shin. He consulted a physio who said it was just bruising, yet after his heroics at Hyderabad he could hardly stand on his left leg. A lump developed and he needed a painkilling spray before bowling. It affected his approach to the wicket and though he got through the rest of the series, the damage had been done. As it transpired he had a stress fracture of his shin but it was not correctly diagnosed for over a year and was to take nearly three years for the injury to heal fully.

Further x-rays in April 1983 showed a massive crack in the shin. Imran had not bowled for some months but had kept running to keep fit, which had only aggravated the injury. It was clear he would be unable to bowl in the World Cup but was keen to lead the side, which was beginning to blend as a team, and play for the first time as a batsman only.

The decision was vindicated as Imran was in fine form with the bat. Going in at No 5 he made 56 and 102 (both not out) in the matches against Sri Lanka and 79 not out during a thrilling stand with Zaheer Abbas of 147 in 75 minutes against New Zealand, which ensured qualification for the semi-final. Pakistan then lost to Westindies who in turn lost to India in the final.

Consequently Imran was again criticised in the Karachi press, especially when the captaincy became an issue that winter. Zaheer Abbas took over while Imran was recuperating and played out a dull drawn series in India. The Board of Control for Cricket in Pakistan confirmed that they wanted Imran to take the team to Australia but immediately provoked a dispute by picking a side without consulting him. Imran objected to the inclusion of Hanif Mohammad's son, Shoaib, who had just entered Test cricket with little success in his first two Tests. The press made an issue of this, the Board were divided and the BCCP president, Air Marshall Nur Khan, sacked the selectors. Although Imran eventually got the team he wanted, the matter was to sour the whole tour.

Imran had done some light bowling at the end of the English season for Sussex and off a short run proved very successful. He took six for 6 including a hat-trick against Warwickshire - a game in which he also made 94 and 64 - and in a fine summer with the bat, he averaged 57. The pain, though, returned to his shin and x-rays confirmed that the fracture had opened up again. He took the Pakistan side to

The orthodox strokemaker...

Australia but after further consultation with a specialist in Brisbane, it soon became clear that he would be unable to play for some time. His vice-captain, Abbas, who had been bitterly disappointed not to get the captaincy for the England tour, at first dug his heels in saying that it was not the side he would have chosen and, when he did take over, let it be known that he was only temporarily in charge.

The series started disastrously with an innings defeat in Perth, a result that might have been repeated in Brisbane but for a thunderstorm which washed out the last day and a half. With Imran still unavailable Zaheer was offered the captaincy for the rest of the tour but turned it down, sticking to his affirmation that he was only a caretaker and had not selected the side (though he did not proffer suggestions as to who he would have chosen). He probably saw no prospects of success in the rest of the series and wanted to absolve himself from blame.

After a fine team batting performance in the third Test, Imran was under further pressure to perform when he was fit to take over for the fourth Test. He decided to leave out a bowler, Mohammad Nazir, who had taken just one wicket in the previous three Tests, to accommodate his return. Despite having played in only one first-class match since September, Imran justified the decision with innings of 83 and 72 not out, passing 2000 runs in his 50th Test in the process, to become only the fifth player to do the double "double" after Sir Garry Sobers, Richie Benaud, Ian Botham and Kapil Dev (Sir Richard Hadlee has also joined this quintet since), and the first Pakistani to do so.

The rest of the tour was played out in an unhappy atmosphere. The side missed Imran's bowling and won only one World Series Cup match. He should have gone home to rest but stayed on to try and rally the side - he learned a lot about various team-mates on that tour. When he returned home the press were out to get him. Abbas, who had left the tour early, was leading a campaign of self-promotion in a Karachi newspaper, *Dawn*, while a host of rumours were circulating, including allegations that Imran had used his position to benefit senior players financially to the detriment of the junior players, that he had been unfair in team selection, and to cap it all, later he was named by Qasim Omar, who had just been dropped, as the leader of a drugs ring within the team. Omar made his revelations in *The People,* in the UK, calling Imran a "negative, arrogant, spiteful leader" and wrote the same in a letter to the Board, who banned Omar for seven years.

It was a miserable period for Imran and for the first time he could not let his cricket do the talking. He was thankful to slip out of the limelight at this tumultuous time. With the likelihood that his career was now over

Pakistan's leading wicket-taker

Imran went through a brooding period, confined to his flat in Kensington, West London, with his leg in plaster, following specialist treatment that was, at least, subsidised by the Pakistan government.

He gradually became more philosophical, reflected that the tour to Australia had been a mistake but was now in the past, and soon he was seen increasingly back on the London social scene. With no cricket to report on, the media now moved in to speculate about his various romances and who might become Mrs Imran Khan.

The recovery from injury was a long and slow one. He missed the home series with England in 1983/4, which was won 1-0, and the whole of the next winter's Tests which included a short drawn series at home against India, and a 2-0 victory over New Zealand also at home, a result which was reversed on the return tour shortly after. Eventually the injury healed, but as Imran returned to full fitness, wisely he chose to pace himself rather than going straight back into Test cricket before he was ready. He started by playing Grade cricket in Australia, representing Sydney University, and once fit played for New South Wales, helping them to win the Sheffield Shield and McDonald's Cup. He topped the first-class bowling averages in Australia with 28 wickets at 19.14 each, though it took some time and self-analysis of his action to get the zip back in his bowling.

Sadly Imran's mother, Shaukat Khanum, developed cancer, and he spent much time going to and fro between Sydney and home in Lahore. She died in considerable pain in January 1985, and

witnessing that was the motivation for his unstinting fund-raising towards the end of his cricket career and beyond, to finance Pakistan's first cancer hospital.

The following month he returned to the national side for the World Championship of Cricket, a competition to celebrate Victoria's 150th anniversary, and for Sharjah where he produced his best one-day bowling analysis, six for 14 in 10 overs against India.

After an excellent season with Sussex in 1985, in which he averaged 70 with the bat and 19 with the ball, he made his comeback to the Test arena against Sri Lanka. He had not played in a Test for 21 months and had not bowled in one for 33, missing all but two of the previous 19 matches. He bowled 49 overs on a blameless Faisalabad pitch to take three wickets, and confirmed his recovery with nine wickets in the match at Sialkot and five more in the third despite being hampered with a thigh strain.

Miandad announced after the second Test that he would be standing down at the end of the series to concentrate on his batting and it became clear that Imran would be reinstated as captain. His return brought an excellent period in Pakistan's history though it started with an acrimonious series in Sri Lanka, where the umpiring caused major problems and required a call from President Zia to Imran to prevent the team coming home a Test early. The rubber ended one-all and it was not until the one-day competitions which followed that the games were played in a better atmosphere, incidentally when neutral umpires were used.

For Sussex he again topped the bowling and batting averages in his benefit year (1986). He had planned to finish his cricket career within the next 18 months with the sort of hectic schedule that would have been a fitting finale to a great career. Pakistan had two most important series that winter followed by a tour to England and the World Cup, which was to be staged at home and in India. Each represented a challenge and the chance to carry out unfulfilled ambitions.

The first series, against the Westindies in 1986/7, proved to be a close low-scoring three-match series, which was invigilated by neutral umpires at Imran's insistence. The Pakistan captain played a crucial role; he took 18 wickets at only 11 runs apiece and batted with determination throughout. In the first Test he rescued the side from 37 for 5 with an innings of 61, despite being hit a painful blow on the shoulder first ball, to guide Pakistan to a first innings total of 159. Then in tandem with Abdul Qadir he bowled out Westindies for their lowest-ever total, 53, and defeat by 186 runs to end their winning streak of seven Tests. Imran took four for 30, despite having three stitches in a badly-swollen right index finger after taking a rap on the gloves while batting.

Pakistan were out-played in the next Test at Lahore despite Imran's five for 59, while in the third at Karachi he bowled Pakistan back into the game. He had been struggling with a stomach upset, but recovered to produce an outstanding spell of quick bowling. He took five for 10 in six overs and was twice on a hat-trick. Set 213 to win, Pakistan slumped to 97 for 7 at tea on the last day, but he and Tauseef Ahmed ensured a draw and Imran took the man-of-the-match award on his 34th birthday.

When Imran took the captaincy it was on the understanding that he would have the final say on selection in order to remove the peculiarities of recent years, build up some continuity and team spirit and thus produce a side for the future. Yet while he was away competing in the Perth Challenge in Australia, the team for the tour to India was chosen and announced in his absence. He was livid considering the assurances he had been given and especially as he knew from his previous tours to India that a certain character of player was needed there.

Once there though, he again produced some heartening displays. In the first Test at Madras he came in to bat at 257 for 6 early on the second day and soon was putting together a record partnership for the eighth wicket against India of 112 with Wasim Akram, and then an unbroken stand of 81 for the last wicket with Tauseef Ahmed. He was only on 68 when the ninth wicket fell but he went on the offensive, hitting one of five sixes to reach his hundred and going on to his highest Test score of 135 not out, which also included 14 fours.

Imran struggled with his rhythm when bowling though, as the run-ups were soft and sandy making the footing for his leap uneasy, and in the second Test too he was off-form with the ball. The rest of the series tested Imran's diplomacy and captaincy skills to the full. He called up Younis Ahmed, after a 17-year absence on Miandad's recommendation for his experience against spin, and Iqbal Qasim, the left-armer, as the wickets for the rest of the series were bound to be slow turners.

During the third Test at Jaipur, rain had got under the covers on the rest day. The pitch repairs were inadequate but the Indian authorities pushed for a resumption even though the umpires thought the wicket was unfit. Imran was going to refuse to bat as the playing conditions stated that the pitch should be in a similar condition to that at the end of the previous day's play. However, play got under way on the fourth day when the umpires were overruled by the Indian Board, though the pitch had not fully recovered. President Zia had attended the second day of the match, as part of his "Cricket for Peace" mission, and so there was additional pressure to continue. Luckily, the result was probably not affected, the match ending in a draw.

In the fourth Test Imran continued his fine form with the bat. Pakistan had slipped to 176 for 6 in the first innings when he was joined by Ijaz Faqih who was playing in only his third Test. The pair added 154 for the 7th wicket, Imran making 72 and Faqih 105. Later, the partisan Ahmedabad crowd invaded the pitch when Gavaskar passed 10,000 runs in Tests, holding up play for 20 minutes but that enthusiasm turned to hostility on the fourth afternoon when spectators started pelting the boundary fieldsmen with stones. Imran led the side from the field. Play was again delayed, for 50 minutes, and only resumed after tea when six out-fielders donned helmets!

The final Test was a thriller, and in Imran's opinion the most difficult he has had to captain. A result wicket had been prepared - or left under-prepared to be accurate - to break the deadlock. Pakistan batted badly in the first innings but as the captain told the side before they went out to field, India had not had to bat under pressure before in the series. When the heat was on they collapsed too, from 126 for 4 to 145 all out - a lead of just 29. Second time round, Imran emphasised the need for everyone to sell their wickets dearly and not to worry about the result at this stage; the team responded by fighting all the way down the order to make 249. Then with the tension mounting he kept encouraging his bowlers and tried to remain externally calm when a couple of close decisions went against his side. Victory was achieved by just 16 runs and Pakistan had won their first-ever series in India as the late recruit, Qasim, and Tauseef Ahmed spun the side to victory, thus bringing to an end the 11-Test deadlock between the sides in India.

With that great ambition fulfilled, he came to England with the same sense of purpose, but with England fresh from winning the Ashes in Australia Imran's aspirations were derided by the English media. The tour started in miserable weather conditions and the team struggled to acclimatise. Luckily the first two Tests were largely washed out giving Pakistan the chance to regroup. Javed Miandad and Abdul Qadir, who had both joined the tour late and Imran, who had been unable to bowl in the first Test because of a torn stomach muscle were all beginning to play to their potential. In the third Test at Headingley Imran bowled magnificently. He caused the early damage from which England never really recovered, taking the wickets of Robinson, Athey and Gower as the home team slumped to 31 for 5 and then to 136 all out, to which Pakistan replied with 353 to secure a big lead. Then Imran, varying his pace and types of delivery, ran through the England side to instigate an innings victory. He finished with seven for 40, his 20th five-wicket haul and fifth ten-wicket match in his 68th Test. On the way Ijaz Ahmed, at short leg, took a fine catch to get rid of Jack Richards and bring Imran his 300th Test wicket.

Imran took six first innings wickets at Edgbaston, but a second innings collapse produced a scare with England left to chase a small total. He and Wasim Akram bowled right through the innings to prevent England scoring the 124 needed in 18 overs and at one point it looked like Pakistan might snatch victory as England lost seven wickets in their pursuit of quick runs. Thus the team went into the final Test knowing they needed only a draw to secure the series. The batsmen shut England out of the game as they ran up a massive total, 708, Pakistan's highest in Tests. Imran dominated a partnership of 191 with Miandad which took his side out of reach, as he scored 118 from 200 balls in 252 minutes, which included a six and 11 fours. He averaged 47.75 in the series with the bat and equalled his own record wicket tally, with 21 at 21.66. Once again he comfortably outperformed Botham.

Pakistan were now on the crest of a wave and favourites for the fourth World Cup, which they were soon co-hosting with India at the end of 1987. After playing some excellent cricket in their group matches, turning round games in dramatic style which the team could easily have lost against England and Westindies, Pakistan were defeated in the semi-final by Australia on a day when fate seemed to be against them. Before that game, so the story goes, Imran had kept both the press and the selectors waiting before announcing his side just before the start but injuries before and during the game to key players saw the game slip away. There was great disappointment in Pakistan and Imran, whose 58 had almost seen his side home, was expecting to retire on that unhappy note. He could never have imagined that he would play a starring role in the next World Cup.

Imran was determined to leave the Test scene before his own performances started to decline. He had seen how other top players had been shabbily treated after illustrious careers for Pakistan. Just turned 35, he thought that the time was right to

stop playing. However when Javed Miandad stood down from the captaincy after the unhappy series with England that followed the World Cup, there was increasing pressure for Imran to come straight out of a retirement which he was just beginning to enjoy, going shooting and getting away from it all.

His mailbag swelled to over a hundred letters a day, each pleading with him to carry on. He got constant phone calls, protests were staged outside his house and he even had people threatening to go on hunger-strike. His former team-mates were also keen for him to resume and finally President Zia made a personal request for him to lead the side to the Westindies, appreciating his reasons for retiring but telling him the country needed him - it seems he would not have got any peace had he stayed at home anyway!

The trip to the Caribbean was a risk. Imran was not fully fit to bowl and memories are short when a side loses. Yet it represented a chance to establish Pakistan on a new pinnacle in their history. The tour, though, started badly with all five one-dayers being lost. Pakistan were initially without Qadir, who was suffering from kidney trouble and still in London receiving treatment, Imran and Wasim Akram were not yet fully fit and Tauseef Ahmed had been injured in the first one-dayer and had gone home. Morale was low and Imran was struggling himself, taking to heart jibes that he was past it.

However he kept the team practising, especially against short-pitched bowling and hoped form and confidence would come. In the first Test at Georgetown, Guyana, Imran bowled magnificently to take seven for 80, inducing a collapse from 220 for 4 to 292 all out. Imran had a severe infection in his left big toe and was on antibiotics for the rest of the match but once his batsmen had established a big lead he did not let the opportunity slip. He took four more wickets to finish with a Pakistan record in the Westindies, 11 for 121, and the best performance for any Test in Guyana, to set up a nine wicket win.

The next two Tests were unnervingly tense. Imran went into the first of them, at Port of Spain, Trinidad, carrying a thigh injury but still took nine wickets in the match. After bowling Westindies out for just 174 he was hoping for a big lead but this never materialised. Wasim Akram could bowl only medium pace and Ijaz Faqih was injured so Imran carried the attack, bowling 45 overs which included some of his finest spells as he took the first five wickets before Viv Richards and Jeff Dujon, aided by some umpiring decisions in their favour, took charge. Pakistan made a superb effort to chase 372 for victory, just falling short but securing a draw. The third Test was another nail-biter and the tension boiled over on the last day.

With the benefit of any umpiring doubt remaining with the batsmen the ninth wicket pair edged Westindies to victory with an unbroken partnership of 61. Imran had come within two wickets of securing a third successive away series win and inflicting Westindies' first home defeat in fifteen years. It had been Imran's most exhilarating series and he showed it had been too soon to hang up his boots by taking 23 wickets at 18 apiece.

Imran was still in a quandary over his future. He played in only a handful of Championship games (of his choosing) for Sussex in 1988 though he was a regular in one-day cricket to fulfil the specifications of his contract - one that had become a bit of an embarrassment to the club. Imran turned up late for the Sunday League game with Glamorgan and it was decided mutually that he would not play until the last match of the season, a game he missed anyway through injury. It was an unfitting end to his career with Sussex for whom he had scored 7,216 runs and taken 407 wickets in 131 matches over the previous eleven years. In his last three full seasons at Hove, 1983, 1985 and 1986, he topped both the batting and the bowling averages for the county.

Imran missed the home series with Australia staged shortly after, in protest at the time of year that it was being staged, September and October when the weather is too hot, and was unavailable for the Sharjah and Asia Cup competitions. He returned to the side for the World Series in Australia and Test series in New Zealand, taking over as captain again. However, Pakistan won only two of their eight WSC matches and there was quite a toing and froing of players in the squad as Imran made changes to the side originally selected.

The Test series in New Zealand was marred by controversy over the umpiring after Imran's request for neutrals had again been turned down, and the rubber proved inconclusive mainly because of the weather and the lifeless nature of the pitches. At Auckland, Imran passed 3,000 runs in his 75th Test during his innings of 69 not out, as Pakistan amassed the highest Test score made in New Zealand, 616 for 5 (since beaten by the home side against Sri Lanka).

Much has been made of the story that Imran first saw Waqar Younis on the television when he was recuperating from a virus and picked him straight after. In fact Waqar had already been spotted and Imran was following a tip to watch him. However he did immediately invite him to join the squad in Sharjah and took a special interest in building up Waqar's fitness.

The 1989/90 home series with India returned to the stalemates of earlier contests. At least Imran had secured neutral umpires at long last for what might have been a fraught series, but which instead stayed relatively incident-free. Imran felt that his batting was better than at any time in his career and finished the series with an average of 87.33. He injected some life into the batting in the first Test at Karachi by making his fifth Test hundred, hitting 109 not out in 201 minutes including a six and 17 fours.

Earlier that winter, he had led the side to its first major one-day triumph in the Nehru Cup in India, beating Westindies in a thrilling final, and so with the team exultant, he had great expectations when the side travelled to Australia of securing a first-ever series there, though he had doubts about the side's batting under pressure. Also when Abdul Qadir returned home before the first Test, the inexperience of the cover bowling was exposed. Wasim Akram perhaps took Imran's mantle as the best all-rounder in the world during this series. Imran continued to bat magnificently though admitted to being "so embarrassed" by his bowling. Such an assessment was being harsh on himself, but typically so, for Imran was his own biggest critic - something which he believes was one of the main reasons for his success.

Pakistan made a superb attempt to save the first Test at the MCG, being bowled out with just 22 minutes left to play for 336. Imran had joined Ijaz Ahmed in what looked like being a match-saving partnership until Imran became one of six lbw's in their 2nd innings. The next Test at Adelaide turned into a classic; with Pakistan trailing by 84 on first innings they collapsed to the new ball. Imran, who promoted himself to number five, came in at 7 for 3.

Javed Miandad joined Imran in a partnership of great resolve and determination staying together for nearly three hours, but when Miandad fell Pakistan were still in the mire at 90 for 5, just six runs ahead. Now the captain was joined by Akram and both batted to the best of their ability, Imran playing the dour defensive role, Akram the attacker. Imran said afterwards that Wasim's batting had made him feel like a novice but Imran had played a marvellous hand, ensuring he did not give his wicket away. In all he batted for five minutes over eight hours, hitting ten fours. The pair added 171 - a record for the 6th wicket in the series - and actually got Pakistan into a position from which Imran could set a target, and the game ended with Australia batting out for a draw. Such a long defensive innings was also uncomfortable for him to play as when he was young he fell from a tree and broke his arm which was set in plaster incorrectly, and has meant that he has had to adapt his grip on the bat.

The final Test in Sydney was ruined by the weather, though Imran again made runs, scoring 82 not out, but the chance to square the series disappeared. On the same ground, the SCG, Imran

... or the explosive hitter

not prevent Pakistan taking the match by eight wickets.

A low-scoring game at Faisalabad saw the tourists square the series with a seven wicket win. In the decider at Lahore, Imran bowled for the first time in the rubber and removed Greenidge and Haynes in his opening spell. However Westindies recovered to make 294 on a difficult pitch and in reply Pakistan crashed to 48 for 5. Imran defended diligently but Pakistan still conceded a big lead and although his bowlers responded superbly, with 346 to win too many to chase, Pakistan had to battle it out for a draw. Imran joined the night-watchman Masood Anwar early on the last day with his side 110 for 4. They stayed together for nearly three hours adding just 67. Imran continued his defiance in partnership with Wasim Akram and in all batted 265 minutes and 196 balls for his 58 not out which included just three fours, to earn a worthy draw.

It was another excellent series and once again Pakistan had made a significant challenge to Westindies as the best team in the world. Unlike any other captain Imran had not been beaten in three Test series with them. Also he is the only captain in modern times who has actually enhanced his personal performances with any regularity against the dominant side of the eighties and early nineties. The Westindies have a deliberate policy of trying to reduce the effectiveness of their opponents' captain, hoping his loss of form will make the team suffer vicariously. Some captains, such as Graham Gooch and Dilip Vengsarkar, have managed one good series in charge against the Westindies to earn a share of a rubber but they are the exception to the rule. Although Imran's batting against them overall was slightly below par, this was largely because of the amount of bowling he was required to do, while taking a remarkable 41 wickets at 15 runs each in the first two series. When he hardly bowled in 1990/1 he averaged over fifty with the bat.

This would have been a fitting swan song but he kept himself going in order to continue his fund-raising for the hospital and to play in one last World Cup. The series that preceded the tournament, against Sri Lanka 1991/2, was a big anti-climax, ruined by the weather and was no real preparation for the main event of that winter. Imran declared despite being on 93 not out in the first Test at Sialkot to try and force a result - only the third time a declaration had been made with a player in the nineties. The second Test was almost entirely washed out and in a tight 3rd Test, he did not bowl and made a duck in what proved to be his his final Test innings, but at least he had the consolation of being on the winning side.

Pakistan were highly fancied for the World Cup

ensured two one-day victories over Australia with another fine innings in the first and in the next by bowling a double-wicket maiden in the last over of the match to bring his side a two-run win, but Pakistan were out-played in the finals.

Imran was unavailable for the series with New Zealand as another protest, this time against the tourists for sending what he considered to be a second-rate side, which was vindicated by Pakistan's easy 3-0 win. The series against the Westindies, though, was always going to be much tougher. It went the same way as the previous two against them with Pakistan winning the first Test only for Westindies to bounce back.

After taking the one-day series 3-0, the home side were full of confidence going into the first Test at Karachi. There, a crucial partnership between Shoaib Mohammad and Salim Malik had taken Pakistan within sight of Westindies' first innings score, and then Imran joined the former to add 80 to ensure a telling lead. Imran batted for over five hours for his 73 not out. He did not bowl in the match and in fact was unable to field in the second innings because of bruising to his leg, but this did having won the Nehru Cup and as they had just beaten Westindies and India to take the Wills Trophy a few months before in Sharjah. Yet Imran's team started badly; Waqar Younis was ruled out before the start as was Abdul Qadir. To make matters worse Imran, who along with Miandad was playing in his fifth World Cup, developed a problem with his shoulder, yet had spent weeks training to be at optimum fitness.

He felt sure that his ambitions for the Cup were being tragically removed before a ball had been bowled. He missed the first game and saw his side go down to the Westindies by ten wickets. He returned against Zimbabwe but did not bowl or bat. He missed the game against England and watched helplessly as his team were shot out for 74, only for the rain to save them. Worse was to follow as India beat Pakistan convincingly, with Imran being run out without scoring. Already reduced by injuries, the wheels appeared to have come off for good when, against South Africa, rain intervened at a crucial stage. The new rule regarding stoppages stacked the odds against the side batting second and defeat appeared to be showing Pakistan the exit from the World Cup. Things could not have been worse. Imran looked forlorn.

It is the mark of a true champion to be able to overcome such adversity through sheer will and determination. It was then that Imran gave his famous plea to his team to go out and "fight like cornered tigers." With their backs-to-the-wall the team needed to compete as though their lives depended on it. Controlled wins came against Australia and Sri Lanka and then an emphatic win in their last game against the previously undefeated New Zealanders, meant that the two sides would meet again in the semi-final provided Australia, who were already out of the reckoning, beat Westindies. After an agonising wait they did so.

At last Imran could visualise his dream. He took it upon himself to bat at three, the pivot around which the other batsman could play. It had almost backfired in the semi-final as he got bogged down against New Zealand's medium-pacers and it required a brilliant innings from Inzamam-ul-Haq to see Pakistan through.

Then in the final Imran and Javed Miandad again made slow but sure progress. A crucial moment came when Imran was dropped by his opposite number Gooch running back on the leg-side; Imran saw this is as a sign that the gods were with him and he began to play his strokes. Again Inzamam and Akram gave the innings impetus and after a steady bowling performance, with the odd moment of inspiration from Akram, Pakistan had won. Imran, who was still hampered with his shoulder injury, fittingly took the last wicket.

He gave an emotional speech on receiving the trophy in which he spoke of his personal relief and pleasure at winning the cup as it ensured the future of his fund-raising programme for his cancer hospital project. When Pakistan had, at one point, been bottom of the qualifying table, this programme had almost collapsed. Imran has been criticised for the egotistical and self-centred nature of his words, as he made no mention of the team whose sterling efforts had just helped him win the competition. He has since spoken of his embarrassment at that speech, explaining that it was just the enormous sense of relief that he felt once it was all over as he knew that victory would bring his plans for the hospital to fruition.

The motivation for much of his cricket in the latter years of his career had been to help in his quest to build Pakistan's first cancer hospital in memory of his mother, who had died of the disease in 1985. It became a preoccupation with him and although the cause was a good one, it was an annoyance to several players in the World Cup squad. For once, Imran was aloof and because of his shoulder injury he could not play a full part in practice and it took a few quiet words from Wasim Akram and Salim Malik to correct this oversight.

Imran's deep-rooted desire for success probably inhibited his natural instinct for strokeplay, taking it upon himself to build an innings. It was a gamble that paid off thanks to Inzamam-ul-Haq's excellence in the semi-final and a fine team effort in the final.

Despite the victory he was still fund-raising right up until the hospital was opened nearly three years later. It had become an obsession for him and he fell out with certain senior players after the World Cup. He was at cross purposes with the team about how funds presented to him at a celebratory function on the way home in Singapore should be divided. That Imran was unavailable for the tour to England because of his shoulder injury was probably a good thing for him as the growing amount of dissension in the ranks could have meant that he lost the captaincy.

He announced his retirement once that tour was over and redoubled his fund-raising efforts, contributing much of his personal wealth, even giving away his Mercedes as a lottery prize, to ensure the success of a marvellous, worthy project. Politics also got in the way as he was banned from advertising for donations on television.

Much of Imran Khan's cricket has been driven by stirring ambition and a great pride in his own performance, his team and in his country. He has been outspoken about umpires, strongly advocating neutrals as the panacea to most of cricket's ills, been totally dismissive of Pakistan's domestic cricket, aired his grievances against the International Cricket Conference and its occidental prejudice and, like so many other captains, has been criticised for having favourites. There are those who think he has had too much influence but most back his judgment and good sense, and clearly defined opinions on most cricket issues. In selection he has certainly done his level best to get the team he wanted but that is only understandable as he is the one being judged by his team's performances. He picked the type of player he wanted and backed his judgment to choose those he believed to have the talent. Occasionally a player did not developed as he hoped, every-so-often someone has been overlooked who probably deserved a chance or more opportunities, but nothing as glaring as the omission of David Gower by England under Graham Gooch. The Pakistan Board has all too often been full of non-cricket playing administrators, as it is funded by the government, and he has backed his judgment ahead of theirs.

It is doubtful, though, whether Imran's continued absence from domestic cricket (since 1981) has been good for the country - his protest against the system has seemed somewhat hollow and probably prejudiced his views on the true value of performances in the various domestic competitions, though he has sought the opinions of shrewd cricketing experts on the players to watch. Had he been playing in domestic cricket he could have tested out players for himself and by playing he would have added quality to the cricket played. It is remarkable that he did so well playing only internationals in his own country in the second half of his career. He also played virtually no first-class cricket anywhere after 1987 - apart from a handful of games for Sussex in 1988 - except in Tests or with Pakistan on tour.

It would be churlish though to dwell on this rather than his immense ability as a cricketer and contribution to Pakistan's Test history. A Test career spanning 21 years is not quite unique but it is doubtful whether the game in any era changed as much over a similar period. He was fortunate to play when there were three other great all-rounders in the world in Ian Botham, Kapil Dev and Sir Richard Hadlee. They brought the best out in each other, though Imran usually won the personal duels. Comparison is a dangerous thing, but Botham was perhaps the best batsman, a marvellous match-winner, a devastating swing bowler in his youth and certainly the best all-round fielder of the four. Kapil Dev was a natural hitter and beautiful timer of the ball, who was forced to carry India's pace bowling unstintingly and finished with comfortably the most runs and

wickets of the four through sheer perseverance. Hadlee, who also had to carry the New Zealand attack, perhaps had the edge as a bowler, and was certainly the most refined of them technically but would probably would not have been selected for his batting alone.

Indeed Hadlee rates Imran as the best saying the following, in his book, *Rhythm and Swing,*

"Imran Khan's the all-rounder I most admire and most respect of those I've encountered in my time. I'd undoubtedly tag him the best of his age; the difference between Imran and Botham is summed up in one word - dependability. Imran has been so much more consistent, able to turn on one good performance after another with either bat or ball."

What sets Imran further apart from the others is that he captained his country in more than half his Tests. Whereas Hadlee never had the burdens of captaincy, Kapil had only limited success when in charge and Botham's personal performances declined markedly, Imran's own Test record when he led Pakistan was significantly enhanced. Part of this was because it coincided with his maturing as a Test cricketer, but much of it was the pride with which he led his country and the standards he set himself. Mike Procter is perhaps the all-rounder closest to Imran in style; he too bowled high speed inswingers off a long, bustling run, hit powerfully but from a good basic technique and also captained inspirationally. Unfortunately his skills were only tested seven times at the top level because of South Africa's cricket isolation.

One way of comparing all-rounders is to subtract their bowling average from their batting to give a quotient. Only the great Sir Garfield Sobers, whose figures represent a bench mark and who is widely regarded as the best of all time, gets a bigger score than Imran, with 23 (batting average 57 minus bowling average 34). Imran's score is 15 (37 minus 22), which is very similar to Australia's Keith Miller's, while the differentials for Procter (25 minus 15), Botham (33 minus 28), Hadlee (27 minus 22) and Kapil Dev (30 minus 29) are all much lower.

However if one looks at Imran's figures as a captain (52 with the bat and 20 with the ball), he surpasses all others. His batting from the front has been remarkable and his average compares favourably with those achieved by the world's best batsmen when they captained, such as India's Sunil Gavaskar, Westindies' Clive Lloyd or England's Len Hutton, and betters even Viv Richards and Javed Miandad. Indeed he is amongst Pakistan's top ten batsmen of all time in the Coopers & Lybrand ratings, and heads the bowling.

He has missed a significant number of Tests for

one reason or another; 13 were missed while he was at Oxford, another seven while playing for Kerry Packer, his shin injury kept him out for 17 games and he was not available for two series of three Tests each in protests against the state of the opposition (too weak - v New Zealand, 1990/1) or of the conditions (too hot - v Australia, 1988/9). His attempted retirement cost him another three Tests (v England, 1987/8), and he might have played in the five Test series with England in 1992, when he was mulling over his retirement, though his shoulder injury may have prevented him from playing. Without these absences he might have set unbeatable all-round records; for instance, in the year before the shin injury he took 87 wickets in 13 Tests. He was denied at his peak.

Even without these extra Tests his figures are superb. His part in Pakistan's successes are best illustrated by his figures in the 26 Test wins in which he has played; in those games he took 158 wickets at an average of 14.24, five times taking ten wickets in the match. One must not forget his one-day record as well. He played in 175 one-day internationals, scoring 3709 runs at an average of 33 and took 182 wickets. His batting average is very good for a middle-order player, on a par with India's Mohammad Azharuddin or Australia's Allan Border and, of course, he has led Pakistan to victory in the World Cup, Nehru and a number of Sharjah tournaments.

Imran has been outspoken about many issues and some feel his influence had become too great. Hadlee concurs: "All in all, I'd say he had too much power for the good of cricket." However he needed to be somewhat despotic to get by in Pakistan's administration, but like other such leaders in history he has been enlightened, and his input was always positive, reflecting what he thought was best for Pakistan or world cricket. He was an advisor to the Pakistan Board and its representative at ICC meetings but resigned after speaking out about ball-tampering, which he discussed candidly with his biographer, Ivo Tennant, the revelations of which were sensationalised in the tabloid press in May 1994. Imran wanted to address the issue, which he felt had been left

unsettled. However, he found that he had stirred a hornet's nest which, much to his annoyance, distracted his time and energy away from his cancer hospital. It also reduced the level of donations drastically. He said at the time, "The most important thing now is this project. It has been an obsession for four years and now it's nearing completion, that's all I'm concerned about." Just before the hospital was officially opened on December 28, 1994, Imran went on a whistle-stop tour of 32 cities in Pakistan raising an extra $4 million in just six weeks to take the total raised to over $20 million and ensure the hospital's completion. In its first 18 months after opening, it had treated over 25,000 people, 90 per cent of whom were provided free.

When he resigned from the ICC he reflected, "Cricket is not relevant to my life anymore. I may write occasionally and do the odd interview but its in the past now," though many thought that he would become intrinsically involved in restructuring domestic cricket and perhaps managing the national side.

When Imran retired in 1992 international cricket lost one of its most charismatic and glamourous cricketers and one of the most exciting players in the world to watch, whether he was sprinting in and leaping into his classical bowling action or playing a full array of glorious strokes with the bat.

Imran takes England's last wicket to seal the 1992 World Cup

However, he has continued to grab the headlines in the UK, despite spending more and more time at home in Pakistan, returning to England just for a few weeks in the summer for "the season" (and the odd court case!). His marriage to Jemima Goldsmith, the 21-year-old daughter of an English multi-millionaire, broke a thousand hearts and ended the sort of speculation normally only afforded to royals. He thought previously that it would be too difficult culturally to marry a non-Pakistani but Jemima has endeavoured to embrace Islam and the culture. They already have an heir, Suleiman, who was born in November 1996.

Imran's social work in Pakistan, in particular his desire to see adult literacy improve in his country, manifested itself in his decision to enter politics. He announced in April 1996 that he was launching his own party, Tehrik-e-Insaf (Justice Movement), something he always maintained he would not do, partly because of the risk of assassination. Indeed, on April 14, 1996, there was bomb went off at the hospital, killing eight people, just when Imran had been due to arrive.

Although he is unlikely to gain power in the foreseeable future, Imran, who is still revered, could achieve an enormous amount especially by influencing the other main parties, as he is almost apolitical in his motivation, something certain other politicians are envious of.

Career Details

Born: Lahore, 25 November 1952
Role: right-hand, middle-order batsman, right-hand, fast bowler
Clubs: Lahore (1969/70-1970/1), Worcestershire (1971-6), Oxford University (1973-5), Dawood Club (1975/6), PIA (1975/6-1980/1), Sussex (1977-88) and New South Wales (1984/5)
First-class record: (1969-92) 17,771 runs (36.79) including 30 centuries, 1,287 wickets including 70 five-wicket hauls and 13 ten-wicket matches (22.32) and 117 catches
Tests: 88
Test Debut: 1971, v England
Test record: 3,807 runs (37.69), 362 wickets (22.81) and 28 catches
Best Performances: HS 136 v Australia, Adelaide, 1989/90
BB 8-58 v Sri Lanka, Lahore, 1981/2
Match figures of 14-116 (8-58, 6-58)
All-round 117 and 6-98 & 5-82 v India, Faisalabad, 1982/3
Tours: England; 1971, 1974, 1982, 1987
Australia; 1976/7, 1978/9, 1981/2, 1983/4, 1984/5 (WSC), 1986/7 (Perth Challenge), 1988/9 (WSC), 1989/90, 1991/2
Westindies; 1976/7, 1987/8
New Zealand; 1978/9, 1988/9
India; 1979/80, 1986/7, 1989/90 (Nehru Cup)
Sri Lanka; 1975/6, 1985/6
Overseas Tests; 53
One-day Internationals; 175
World Cups; 1975, 1979, 1983, 1987/8, 1991/2
Sharjah; 1984/5, 1985/6, 1988/9, 1989/90, 1990/1, 1991/2
Rest of the World; England 1987, 1988

A comparison of the four great contemporary all-rounders

	Tests	Runs	Avg	Wkts	Avg
Imran Khan	88	3807	37.69	362	22.81
Kapil Dev	131	5248	31.05	432	29.65
I T Botham	102	5200	33.54	383	28.40
R J Hadlee	86	3124	27.16	431	22.29

The figures below show how Imran Khan performed when playing against Kapil Dev, Richard Hadlee and Ian Botham

Imran Khan v Kapil Dev

		Batting		Bowling	
		Runs	Avg.	Wkts	Avg.
1978/9 in Pakistan	IK -	104	at 52.00	14	at 31.50
	KD -	159	at 31.80	7	at 60.85
1979/80 in India	IK -	154	at 22.00	19	at 19.21
	KD -	278	at 30.88	32	at 17.68
1982/3 in Pakistan	IK -	247	at 61.75	40	at 13.95
	KD -	178	at 22.25	24	at 34.62
1986/7 in India	IK -	324	at 64.80	8	at 49.00
	KD -	182	at 36.40	11	at 39.09
Overall	IK -	725	at 45.31	67	at 19.63
	KD -	638	at 27.74	67	at 27.27

Imran Khan v Richard Hadlee

		Runs	Avg.	Wkts	Avg.
1976/7 in New Zealand	IK -	105	at 35.00	14	at 30.21
	RH -	214	at 53.50	10	at 44.70
1978/9 in New Zealand	IK -	63	at 31.50	10	at 25.50
	RH -	115	at 28.75	18	at 23.00
1988/9 in New Zealand	IK -	140	at 140.0	7	at 28.28
	RH -	53	at 26.50	5	at 33.80
Overall	IK -	308	at 51.33	31	at 28.26
	RH -	382	at 38.20	33	at 31.21

Imran Khan v Ian Botham

		Runs	Avg.	Wkts	Avg.
1982 in England	IK -	212	at 53.00	21	at 18.57
	IB -	163	at 27.16	18	at 26.55
1987 in England	IK -	191	at 47.75	21	at 21.66
	IB -	232	at 33.14	7	at 61.85
Overall	IK -	403	at 50.38	42	at 20.12
	IB -	395	at 31.38	25	at 36.44

Majid Jahangir Khan

Majid Khan was perhaps the most gifted Pakistani player of his generation. He played cricket to its best tradition, with a Corinthian spirit and appreciation of the beauty of the game. It is perhaps for this reason that his figures do not do him justice. Like England's David Gower, he was all style and majesty, seemingly relaxed and icy cool, with entertainment his priority. It was a shame he played in an era of increasing professionalism, with which he had his moments of disillusionment. A most modest, civilised man, he is a strict Muslim, and does not smoke or drink.

Cricket was in his blood; his father Dr Jahangir Khan was a fast-medium bowler for India, playing four Tests in the thirties, who could generate a lot of pace off a short run. An athletic man who liked to entertain with his conjuring tricks, Khan senior became Director of Education for the West Pakistan Government and was also a lecturer in history at Punjab University. He is best remembered for hitting a sparrow in flight when bowling at Thomas Pearce at Lord's (Cambridge University v MCC, 1936), where the bird is still preserved in the museum. Jahangir was also a cricket administrator in Pakistan, who stood down from the selection board when his son was selected, to avoid the slur of nepotism. Majid, like his father before him, was a Cambridge Blue, while his brother Asad and cousins Javed Burki and Imran Khan went to Oxford. His uncle Baqa Jilani (India) and cousins Humayun and Javed Zaman (both Lahore) also played first-class cricket. Majid's son, Bazid, looks set to continue the family tradition, having represented Pakistan at under-15 level.

Majid's potential was obvious from the start. When still at Aitchison College and aged just 15 years and 42 days, he was called up by Lahore B to play against Kaipur Division, and marked the occasion by becoming the youngest player to score a first-class hundred, making 111 not out, and then took six for 67. His father had made a similarly auspicious start by making 108 and taking seven for 42 for Muslims v Hindus in 1928/9. While at Punjab University, Majid once scored 286 not out against Karachi, to win the game after his side had been 5 for 4.

In his early days he was quite sharp as a bowler, and concentrated on this until doubts were raised about the legitimacy of his action, especially when bowling a bouncer. This and a back injury were to change the emphasis in his game, turning to batting and occasional off-spin.

He toured England with the Pakistan Eaglets in 1963, topping the bowling averages, and showing sufficient promise to be selected to make his Test match debut the following year, aged 18 years and 26 days, at Karachi against the Australians. He was in the side to open the bowling with Asif Iqbal, who was also playing in his first game, and was quick enough to bounce out Bill Lawry twice and Brian Booth once. He and Asif batted at eight and ten respectively - how their careers were to change!

Not selected for the short tour to Australia and New Zealand (1964/5), he played at home against New Zealand later that season and showed the first signs of his batting talent, when in the 2nd Test at Lahore, he made 80 and shared in a record sixth wicket stand for Pakistan of 217, with his captain Hanif Mohammad. In the 2nd innings he was promoted to bat at No 5 and top scored with 44.

Pakistan went two years without a Test, though the under-25 side played a series with MCC in 1966/7 in which Majid played, scoring 100, and 57 in the first Test and 95 in the fourth. However, he struggled in the full Tests on the tour to England in 1967, making only 38 runs in six innings, yet had managed nearly a thousand runs on the tour at an average of over 40. He played a magnificent innings against Glamorgan, making 147 not out in 89 minutes. He hit 13 sixes in all - a record in England - including five in an over off Richard Davis, on the ground where Garry Sobers was to go one better the next year. He so impressed the club secretary Wilfred Wooller, who had been a contemporary of his father's at Cambridge, that he persuaded Majid to join the county for the following season.

It was no coincidence that the next three seasons were the best in Glamorgan's history; they finished third in 1968 (up from 14th), won the Championship in 1969 for only the second time in their history, and were runners-up in 1970. Majid played one of his finest innings to clinch the Championship when, on a sharply turning wicket at Cardiff, he scored a dazzling 156 against Worcester, demonstrating marvellous footwork as he tore the attack apart.

He went up to Cambridge in October 1969 to read history at Emmanuel College and scored a double-hundred in his first Varsity match in 1970. He brought the University side one of its more successful periods with his calm and mature leadership in 1971 and 1972. In his last year, Cambridge won the Varsity match for the first time in 14 years, by an innings and 25 runs. In all he made 2554 runs for Cambridge at an average of over 50.

After this his experiences of captaincy were less happy. He took over the leadership of Pakistan

from the popular Intikhab Alam in 1973 in unfortunate circumstances, being appointed in the middle of a successful series just when Alam was playing the best cricket of his life. The team had already sided with "Inti" in the dispute with Saeed Ahmed and Mohammad Ilyas, and so Majid was

the innocent victim of a backlash from the players, who levelled criticism at him from the first and at his aristocratic upbringing which the Board of Control for Cricket in Pakistan so yearned for in their captains. Yet he was spurned by the very same people who had made him captain, just as he

127

was at Glamorgan three years later. Both events soured his erstwhile Corinthian outlook on the game.

In Test cricket he was struggling to establish himself, not because of his ability, but because Pakistan played only nine Tests between 1965/6 and 1969/70. He had averaged over 40 against England in the riot-hit series of 1968/9, but missed the next against New Zealand because of his studies, which also interrupted his availability for Pakistan's series with England in 1971, playing just two matches for them, though he also played against the tourists for Cambridge, making 94.

He made more than 2,000 runs for Cambridge and Glamorgan in 1972 and that winter he began to show that form in international cricket, beginning to establish himself as one of the finest players in the world. Over eight years after his Test debut, and in his 20th international innings, he scored an assured 158 at the Melbourne Cricket Ground, still the highest for Pakistan in Australia, and top-scored again in the 2nd innings, with 47, when his team collapsed. On tour he made 762 runs, with hundreds against Victoria and Queensland. The last named offered him terms for the following season, considering him to be the best overseas batsman to appear in the state since Barry Richards of South Africa. Yet his cricket for Pakistan ebbed between the brilliant and the lackadaisical, and in Sydney he seemed indifferent to proceedings, sometimes sitting down at slip between deliveries.

He was outstanding in New Zealand scoring 79 in both innings of the 1st Test, showing his full range of strokes and perfect placement, sharing 3rd wicket partnerships with Sadiq Mohammad of 171 and then 94. Yet in the final Test, with the pending captaincy in mind, he made a rather sombre 110.

Majid took over for the series at home to England whose captain, Tony Lewis, was the man Majid was replacing at Glamorgan and it was said that Wilf Wooller was in constant communication with them both. Majid moved himself up the order, batting at three, and in the final Test of a drawn rubber, made 99, which in itself is rare in a Test, though on this occasion Mustaq Mohammad and Dennis Amiss both fell one short as well - a unique occurrence.

It marked the end of a superb 12 months for Majid in which he had come from captain at Cambridge, back into the Test side, risen to the captaincy of the national side and of Glamorgan, and scored nearly 4,000 first-class runs in the process. The next twelve months though brought more troughs than peaks, for he lost form and the Test captaincy, which at one time had seemed might be his for an extended period. Unfortunately, Glamorgan's overall decline had also begun, though they did improve their position marginally

in the Championship, from 13th to 11th in his first year in charge. That winter he started brilliantly for Queensland with scores of 107 and 89, against New South Wales, and 100 v Victoria, but failed to reach twenty in the next five games.

Back with Pakistan for the visit to England in 1974, he scored exactly 1,000 runs at an average of 50 on the tour. In the Tests he made 75 at Headingley and 98 at the Oval, where he drove and hooked majestically until playing a crude sweep in search of the boundary that would have brought him a hundred. The innings he will be remembered for on that tour though was the sublime century he made in the first Prudential Trophy match at Trent Bridge, described in _Wisden_ as "an innings of rare brilliance." He reached three figures in only the 28th over off just 88 balls with his 16th four and also hit a six in a thrilling, run-a-minute innings. Despite often batting in murky light, he appeared to have so much time to play his graceful strokes. That summer for Glamorgan, Majid could play in only six matches and the county finished one off the bottom, as it had done last time Pakistan toured.

Majid had been tried as an opener in the last two Tests in England and immediately showed a penchant for the job. He started his prolific association with Sadiq Mohammad at the top of the order with three fifty partnerships and they proved to be Pakistan's most successful opening pairing in Test history. They consistently got Pakistan off to good starts sharing four century partnerships and nine others of fifty or over, and averaged 60.47 in their 26 innings together (in 14 Tests). Only Hobbs and Sutcliffe (England), Rae and Stollmeyer (Westindies), Gooch and Atherton (England), Fingleton and Brown (Australia) and Hobbs and Rhodes (England) averaged more.

Sadiq missed the first Test of the winter against Westindies at Lahore but they both benefited from being reunited for the 2nd Test at Karachi. They put on 94 in the first innings, with Majid dominating the scoring and going on to complete exactly 100. Sadiq made 98 not out in the second innings, though he batted down the order because of injury. A week later in domestic cricket, Majid shared in an opening partnership of 389 with Shafiq Ahmad (166), making 213 for Punjab A v Sind A.

Majid was one of the outstanding batsmen in the inaugural World Cup, with scores of 65, 60 and 84, and took over the captaincy from Asif Iqbal, who was ill in hospital, for the last two games, including the classic encounter with Westindies, when he gambled on bowling Sarfraz Nawaz through, only for the last-wicket pair to add 64 to win the game. He has been criticised too for the imprecision of his field placings in that match.

Majid's time at Glamorgan was drawing to a sad

end. Although the team came ninth in the Championship, a position not bettered until 1990 when they finished 8th, they went out early in both one-day knock-outs, and finished bottom of the John Player Sunday League. Some of the senior players had been unable - or unwilling - to adapt to this type of instant cricket, and in fact Majid was no great fan, but it did not stop him scoring the fastest (televised) fifty in the Sunday League, reaching 50 off just 22 balls against a Northants side including Sarfraz Nawaz and Mustaq Mohammad. He finished with 75 in 27 minutes, hitting five 6s and seven 4s.

Rumblings had started in the committee and dressing rooms. Majid resigned the captaincy, alleging interference from the committee, and then left the club shortly after, bagging a pair in his last home game, while other senior players also resigned when their form was brought under scrutiny. A sensitive man, he was hurt by events at Glamorgan, but found himself embroiled in another quarrel with authority back in Pakistan. He joined the senior players in their pay dispute, and then signed for World Series Cricket, as much because of his general disillusionment as anything else.

He was at his absolute peak that winter, putting his troubles behind him, and making over 1081 runs in 11 Tests, at an average of 54.05. He made a forceful 98 in the 2nd Test against New Zealand at Hyderabad, before coming down the track and being stumped, and put on 136 for the first wicket with Sadiq Mohammad, who had to retire because of cramp. They bettered that in the third Test at Karachi with a stand of 147, which was completely dominated by Majid. Against an attack including three of New Zealand's top four wicket-takers in Tests, Majid scored a brilliant hundred before lunch, becoming only the 4th batsman after Australians Victor Trumper, Charles Macartney and Don Bradman to do so on the first day of a Test, and the first since 1930. He played an array of superb hooks and fluent cover-drives and reached three figures in just 77 balls - the sixth fastest in all Tests in terms of deliveries received, behind only Viv Richards (56 balls), Jack Gregory (67), Roy Fredericks (71), Kapil Dev (74) and Gilbert Jessop (76).

He averaged just under fifty in the drawn series in Australia, his highest amongst consistent scores being the 76 he made at the Melbourne Cricket Ground. Majid infuriated Dennis Lillee as he kept hooking his bouncers nonchalantly from under his bush hat to the boundary. Indeed, at the end of the tour Majid gave Lillee that hat, which the great fast bowler had being trying to knock off his head throughout the series.

This was a precursor to his best series in the Caribbean, in which he was the leading run maker with 530 in the Tests as only he and Wasim Raja coped consistently well with Westindies pace attack. In total Majid made 1243 first-class runs on the combined tour.

Following 88 and 28 in the 1st Test in Barbados, he rescued the side at Port of Spain with Raja after Colin Croft had forced Sadiq Mohammad to retire and threatened to run through the side with some hostile fast bowling. Then, trailing by 136, Majid cleared most of the deficit in an opening partnership of 123 with Sadiq to keep Pakistan in the game, which was eventually lost by six wickets.

In Georgetown, with Pakistan 254 in arrears, Majid played his finest Test innings. He put on 60 with Sadiq, before the left-hander was forced to retire hurt again, but then with Zaheer Abbas took the score to 219 - a national record against Westindies for the first wicket - adding 159 in just two and half hours. Majid carried on to ensure a draw as he hit a brilliant 167, including 25 fours from strokes all round the wicket. More positive batting in the fourth Test back in Trinidad helped set up a winning score. He struck 14 fours and a six in his 92, but in the final Test Majid had a rare failure, where even he seemed unnerved by the extreme pace of Andy Roberts. Majid had to keep wicket in Westindies' 2nd innings, after Wasim Bari had been injured while batting, and finished with four catches but crucially dropped Greenidge early on, which proved costly as the young Bajan and Fredericks put on 182 for the first wicket.

Majid's superb batting over the previous few months made him an ideal target for Kerry Packer's World Series Cricket, though he missed playing for the national side and did not like putting his life on the line against a plethora of fast bowlers in matches that lacked significance. He was out of practice too as he was no longer playing county cricket, and took a while to find his touch.

He was one of the eight "Packerstanis" who were given leave to play against India at home and, after the WSC season, against New Zealand and Australia. He consistently got set against India, without passing fifty, and missed the early part of the New Zealand tour because of injury, but scored an uncharacteristically dour not out hundred on his return to the side at Napier, passing three thousand Test runs in the process, a third of which had been made against New Zealand. He had a bizarre series in Australia; after making just a single in the 1st innings at the MCG, he hit a superb hundred in 220 minutes in the 2nd innings, yet in the last Test at Perth he was out for nought in the first over of each innings to Rodney Hogg.

In the 1979 World Cup Pakistan made a magnificent attempt to chase a big Westindies big total in the semi-final. Majid made 81, adding 166 for the 2nd wicket with Zaheer, but when they were separated Pakistan's chance of reaching the final slipped away.

Majid played on hoping to finish with a flourish in Test cricket but had his worst series, averaging only 20 in six Tests against India (1979/80), eventually regaining some of his touch only after being dropped down the order. Later that season, batting now at number six and seven, he made 89 at Karachi and then 110 not out at Lahore - his only two innings in the three Tests against Australia - where he shared a record 8th wicket stand of 111 with his cousin Imran Khan.

He struggled to find his form playing against the Westindies at home in 1980/1 - the first Tests against them since his halcyon days in 1977 - and by now was past his best, though he still produced the occasional gem such as the 78 (which included an all-run 7) against Australia at the MCG in 1981/2. He joined the rest of the team in their stand against Miandad's captaincy and so played only in the last Test against Sri Lanka, making 63.

His form at the start of the tour to England was modest and the new captain Imran Khan was forced to drop him from the side for the first Test, one of the most difficult decisions he has ever had to make as Majid had been his childhood hero, as well as being a relation. He was happy to be able to recall him for the last Test, which enabled Majid to pass Hanif Mohammad's record aggregate of runs for Pakistan, but being dropped caused a rift between the two cousins. He played the last of his 63 Tests that winter, playing once against India, but finished his career as it had begun, with a duck - a most unfitting end.

By the time Majid played his last first-class match in 1985 he had scored over 27,000 runs at an average of 43, and hit 73 centuries. Since then he has remained involved in the game; he managed the under-19 side's tour to England in 1990 and was appointed Chairman of Selectors at the start of the 1992/3 season, significantly only taking up the post after Imran had retired, and was team manager for the tour to New Zealand in 1993/4. It is ironic that Salim Malik, who had also been at odds with Imran, should have been appointed captain for that tour and that Majid should replace his cousin as Pakistan's ICC representative after Imran's resignation over the ball-tampering controversy. Majid has also been employed by the ICC as a match referee.

He was appointed manager of the Pakistan team for the series against Sri Lanka in 1995/6, but was removed at the end of the series without explanation by Arif Ali Abbasi, the Chief Executive of the PCB. Majid swore never to get involved again, but by the end of the winter had replaced

Abbasi as Chief Executive. Determined to do things his own way, he reconsidered Pakistan's tour preparations for England and postponed the planned use of Ian Chappell, the former Australian captain, as part-time coach. He re-appointed Mustaq Mohammad and called in Haroon Rashid as full-time coaches for the national senior and junior squads respectively.

At his best a glorious player, Majid played the game in the best tradition, but received some shoddy treatment during his career that, perhaps, a more demonstrative, less amiable man might have prevented by kicking up a fuss. He probably played on a couple of years too long at the top, making just one hundred in his last twenty Tests in which he averaged only 27, which damaged a Test record that should have remained comparable with the best players. He wanted to finish on a high note and always felt that he had one good series left in him but unfortunately that never materialised. Still he played many a majestic innings for which he will be remembered.

Career Details

Born: Ludhiana, India, 28 September 1946
Role: right-hand, opening or middle-order batsman, right-hand medium-pace and off-break bowler
Clubs: Lahore (1961/2-1982/3), Punjab (1964/5-1967/8), PIA (1968/9-1980/1), Glamorgan (1968-76), Cambridge University (1970-2), Queensland (1973/4) and Rawalpindi (1984/5)
First-class record: (1961-85) 27,444 runs (43.01) including 73 centuries, 224 wickets (32.12) and 410 catches
Tests: 63
Test Debut: v Australia, Karachi, 1964/5
Test record: 3,931 runs (38.92), 27 wickets (53.92) and 70 catches
Best Performances: HS 167 v Westindies, Georgetown, 1976/7
BB 4-45 v Westindies, Georgetown, 1976/7
Tours: England; 1967, 1971, 1974, 1982;
Australia; 1972/3, 1976/7, 1978/9, 1981/2
Westindies; 1976/7
New Zealand; 1972/3, 1978/9
India; 1979/80.
Overseas Tests; 36
One-day internationals; 23
World Cups; 1975, 1979

Mohsin Hasan Khan

Mohsin Khan was a delightful strokemaker who graced the Pakistan upper order for a decade during which he played in 48 Test matches. A tall, slim right-handed opener, he was stylish and elegant, with a cool, relaxed temperament, and was particularly adept at playing the ball off his legs. He forced his way into the side at a time when Sadiq Mohammad and Majid Khan had been well established as a highly successful opening pair and was soon forming a profitable liaison himself with Mudassar Nazar.

Like many Pakistani players he started his first-class career as a teenager and was not even sixteen when he made his debut for Railways in 1970/1. He came to prominence after a highly successful season with Habib Bank in 1976/7 which included his highest first-class score, 246 against PIA, and he was rewarded with a call-up at the end of that season to reinforce the side in the Caribbean. Despite an attractive fifty in his first game, against the Windward Islands, he could not force his way into the side for the last two Tests.

Mohsin Khan got his chance the following winter because of the Packer defections. He batted all day to make 97 not out for Punjab out of 217 for 9 against the England tourists, before Wasim Raja had to declare at the over-night score. Mohsin had taken a single off the second ball he received but was then marooned on one not out for the next 93 minutes as, with wickets tumbling at the other end, he set out at least to secure his end. He did well in the one-day international that followed and for Sind, making rather more fluent fifties in each game, and he was selected for the final Test match in the city of his birth, Karachi. He made a stylish 44, batting at number three, which was enough to warrant selection for the tour of England the following summer.

He had gained some experience already as the professional for Todmorden in the Lancashire League, and he coped better than most with the conditions. He was the only batsman to score consistently, top scoring in three of the first four innings.

He was unfortunate to lose his place in the side when the Packer players returned (including six batsmen); their release from World Series Cricket for the series with India meant they had to play. Thus Mohsin was trying to force his way into probably Pakistan's strongest ever batting line-up.

Mohsin the matinee idol

However, he went on the tour to New Zealand and Australia (1978/9), playing in the first Test of each rubber, and opened for the first time in a Test against Australia, this being the only unsettled position in the side. He missed the next three series, but following an outstanding domestic season in 1981/2, when he made over a thousand runs for Habib Bank at an average of over sixty, he was called up as a replacement for the tour to Australia, where immediately he showed his ability to handle the pace bowling.

The players' dispute with Javed Miandad kept the door open to him as he returned a Test before the other rebels, cementing his place in the side against Sri Lanka by making 74 in the second Test at Faisalabad, and then 129 in the third at Lahore, a stylish innings including 16 fours.

He was an automatic choice for the 1982 tour to England, after his fine displays over the winter. He had been relatively successful on the last tour to England and had gained further experience in the Lancashire League with Todmorden, and started the tour in absolutely glorious form. He was at his best, scoring over a thousand runs at an average of 73.41. He made 151 against Sussex, putting on 319 for the first wicket with Mudassar Nazar, 165 (retired hurt) against Worcestershire and 203 not out against Leicestershire.

A delightful strokemaker

However his greatest moment came during the second Test, when he scored a magnificent double-hundred, batting for 386 balls and 496 minutes. He hit 23 fours, mainly clips off his legs, or flowing cover-drives, to set up Pakistan's second Test win over England and first at Lord's. In an exciting run-chase in the second innings, with 76 required in 18 overs, he made 39 not out to bring a ten-wicket victory with 29 balls to spare, and kissed the turf after Miandad had made the winning hit.

Mohsin's purple patch continued that winter despite becoming only the third player in a Test to be given out "handled the ball" when he knocked the ball away instinctively as it threatened his stumps in the first Test at Karachi against the Australians. In the second innings he took Pakistan to their third victory over Australia, by nine wickets, in glorious style with a six off the Australian captain Kim Hughes. Scores of 76 in the 2nd Test and 135 in the third gave him an average of over 70 for the series and helped his side to its first clean sweep in a series.

In the next match, against India, he made 94 and 101 not out, to become the first, and as yet only, Pakistani to score a thousand runs in a calendar year, though this was only his ninth Test in 1982. He was averaging over 78, though had been even more prolific in Lahore where he scored 463 of those runs in just four completed innings. He made 91 in the final Test but on the whole his performances were over-shadowed by Mudassar Nazar, Javed Miandad and Zaheer Abbas who were at their most prolific.

In the 1983 World Cup his 70 in the semi-final against the Westindies held the side together but Pakistan's total of 184 was never going to be enough. Surprisingly, Mohsin's record in one-day cricket is not that good for such a fine strokemaker, averaging 26.81 in his 75 matches.

A short lean patch followed, including falling to the first ball of the Jullundar Test against India, 1983/4, but he made a magnificent return to form with 149 at Adelaide, playing handsomely off the back-foot, and sharing a record partnership of 233 for the 2nd wicket with Qasim Omar. His 152 on the first day of the next Test at the Melbourne Cricket Ground was even better, hitting 18 fours and a six, and as usual, he was superb off his legs.

Despite his fine contributions he had become disenchanted on tour, because of the squabbles over the captaincy, and even threatened to retire at the end of the series but had a change of heart and played at home against England. He hit his seventh and final Test hundred (fourth at Lahore) in the third Test, sharing a then record partnership of 173 with Shoaib Mohammad who, ironically, was to replace him twice in the next nine Tests, and then permanently. He passed two thousand Test runs

during that series achieved at an average (of 44) bettered only by Javed Miandad and Zaheer Abbas.

However Mohsin's subsequent form was poor, averaging just over twenty in the next six series and finally he bowed out of Test cricket after a disastrous sequence at home against the Westindies (1986/7), when he failed to reach double figures in five of his last six innings. It was a sad end for a man who had been instrumental in his side's best Test sequence in 1982/3 and who, when on form, was superb to watch. A perfectionist prone to moods, Mohsin was at his best under Imran Khan's leadership in those years.

He returned to the Lancashire Leagues, playing for Walsden, where he was as popular and successful as ever, regularly scoring over a thousand runs a season as well as taking useful wickets. Away from cricket he added his elegant touch to the film world, becoming a star in India's Bollywood.

Career Details

Born: Karachi, 15 March, 1955
Role: right-hand, upper-order or opening batsman
Clubs: Pakistan Railways (1970/1-1971/2), Karachi (1972/3-1974/5), Universities (1973/4), Sind (1974/5-1975/6), Habib Bank (1975/6-1985/6)
First-class record: (1970-88) 11,254 runs (38.94) including 31 centuries (HS 246), 14 wickets (39.00) and 135 catches
Tests: 48
Test Debut: v England, Karachi, 1977/8
Test record: 2,709 runs (37.10), 0-30 and 34 catches
Best Performances: HS 200 v England, Lord's, 1982
Tours: Westindies; 1976/7
England; 1978, 1982
New Zealand; 1978/9, 1984/5
Australia; 1978/9, 1981/2, 1983/4, 1984/5 (WSC)
India; 1979/80, 1983/4
Sri Lanka; 1985/6
Overseas Tests; 24
One-day Internationals; 75
World Cup; 1983
Sharjah; 1983/4, 1984/5, 1985/6, 1986/7

Fazal Mahmood

By his bowling Fazal Mahmood probably did more than any other single player to establish Pakistan's early cricketing credibility. He helped his country to make a better start than any new Test nation, with a sequence of match-winning performances over its first ten years of Test cricket. Fazal played in seven out of eight of Pakistan's Test wins in that period and in those games he took nine five wicket hauls in all, and had four ten-wicket matches; he bowled over 360 overs and took 65 wickets at an average of just 10.69 apiece, while conceding under two runs an over. His influence on the side and its results was enormous as was evident by Pakistan's performances after his retirement, which saw the team win only two games in the next ten years.

A strong, broad-shouldered Pathan, with piercing green eyes, Fazal narrowly missed selection for the Indian tour to England in 1946, following fine performances for Punjab University, where his father was a professor at Islamia College, and for Northern India. Originally a leg-spinner, it was his father who coached him to bowl the leg-cutter that was to become his trademark. His father can be thanked also for his incredible stamina for he insisted on a strict training regime for his son. Between 1940 and 1947 Fazal rose at 4.30 every morning and, rain or shine, he would walk for five miles and then run back.

Fazal was chosen for India's tour to Australia in 1947/8, but on the announcement of Partition decided to play for the new nation. He was the leading bowler on Pakistan's first representative tour to Ceylon [Sri Lanka] in 1949/50, and at home against the same opponents the following season he took 20 wickets in two unofficial matches.

He was a constant thorn against the MCC in 1951/2. He warmed up with five for 58 for the Punjab Cricket Association against them, then in the second representative match, at Karachi, he took six for 40 in 26 overs, to set up a winning position. That win helped Pakistan to gain Test status as it strengthened his country's case for full membership of the Imperial Cricket Conference.

On his return from England with the Pakistan Eaglets he was an automatic selection for Pakistan's first official Test against India in 1952/3, in which he bowled 40 overs taking two wickets including that of the Indian captain Lala Amarnath. In the next, on Lucknow's jute matting wicket, he produced what remained the best Test figures of his career, seven for 42 in the second innings, to give him 12 for 94 in the match from 51.4 overs. It ensured Pakistan's first Test victory,

by an innings, in only their 2nd match. In the fifth, he bowled 64 out of 144 overs in the first innings to take 4-141, and finished the series with 20 wickets at 25.51, as well as scoring 178 runs.

He was vice-captain for the tour to England in 1954 and soon became known as "the Alec Bedser of Pakistan", noted for his accuracy and remarkable stamina. In the first Test, he and Khan Mohammad bowled all the overs between them, reducing a shocked England to 117 for 9 declared. In the final Test, he produced further surprises, taking six wickets in each innings (giving him match figures of 60-27-99-12), to help Pakistan become the only side to have won a Test on their first visit to England. On the tour, Fazal had taken 77 wickets at 17.53, and bowled an average of 33 overs per innings in the Tests. He took 20 wickets in the rubber which remained a record for a series in England until the 1982 tour when Imran Khan took 21. Waqar Younis has since stretched the record by one, in 1992.

In a dour home series against India he took 15 wickets at 22.06, including 5-73 in the last, but his combined efforts with Khan Mohammad and Mahmood Hussain could not break the deadlock. He had relatively little impact on the series against New Zealand in 1955/6, injuring himself in the first Test and so missing the second. On his return in the third Test, he bowled unchanged from one end, supporting Khan Mohammad as New Zealand were bowled out for 70 on a damp matting wicket. He was back at his best with two five-wicket hauls against the MCC in the New Year.

The next season (1956/7) in Australia's solitary Test match in October, Fazal bowled masterfully as the visitors were shot out for 80. He produced Pakistan's best match figures at the time (which were not bettered until Imran Khan took 14 wickets in 1981/2), taking 13 wickets for 113 from 75 overs in the match. Later that season he recorded the best analysis of his career as well, taking nine for 43 for Punjab against Services.

The going was a lot tougher in the Westindies (1957/8), but Fazal was still the leading wicket-taker, with 20 at 38.20. He bowled 62 overs in the first innings of the 1st Test at Bridgetown, Barbados, and over a hundred overs in the 2nd Test at Port of Spain, in which he also made his highest score, 60, but this was just warming him up for the 3rd, where his opening partner, Mahmood Hussain broke down after just five balls, leaving Fazal, always a determined and cheerful man, with the bulk of the bowling duties. He sent down 85.2 overs as Garry Sobers, with 365, and Conrad Hunte, with 260, made hay on a perfect Sabina Park pitch. Although the series by then was lost, he took six for 83 in the innings victory in the final match on the same ground.

Fazal took 65 Test wickets in the seven victories he was part of

His unstinting efforts were rewarded with the captaincy for the reciprocal tour when Abdul Hafeez Kardar stood down at the end of the series. Immediately Fazal made a positive impression by winning the toss and, breaking with convention, putting the opposition in. Then he gained his revenge for his toil in Jamaica by dismissing both Hunte and Sobers for ducks, and finished with four wickets as the Westindies were bowled out for 146, to set Pakistan on her way to winning the match by ten wickets. Another splendid solo effort at Dacca ensured the series, as he took 12-100; this included his best figures as captain, 6-34 in the 1st innings, as Westindies were bowled out for 76. It was his best series as a bowler, taking 21 wickets at an average of only 15.85.

He took five wickets in an innings in both the Tests in which he played against Australia in 1959/60, missing the 2nd because of injury, but could not prevent defeat in the series. Under his leadership divisions began to appear in the side. He ran practices with a policeman's authority, sending players for runs around the field if they dropped catches, but his captaincy on the field was a little vague, and he was accused of favouritism in selection. He lacked Kardar's natural stature and despite a charming personality he could not repair the rift. He was replaced after the "no risks" series against India, even though he still had a most impressive bowling record as captain; 41 wickets at 19.14, compared to 98 wickets at 27.03 as a player.

He played only once against England the following winter, bowling with his usual stamina and accuracy, toiling for 63 overs without reward but conceding only 98 runs. However he was not in the original squad for the 1962 tour to England but was called up as a replacement, when Mahmood Hussain broke down once again. Fazal was past his best, at 35, yet he was used still as both stock and strike bowler. He went straight into the 4th Test and bowled 60 out of the 136 overs in England's only innings and 49 overs in the first innings of his final Test at the Oval - the scene of Pakistan's famous victory eight years before - which ended in a disappointing ten-wicket defeat.

Fazal Mahmood has been somewhat underrated in the history of Test cricket, partly because he played on helpful matting wickets. Although many of his best performances did come on coir or jute on which he was without peer - taking 55 wickets in 10 matches - Fazal's overall record is excellent and he did take 84 wickets in 24 Tests on turf, including his match-winning effort at the Oval in 1954.

He retired from first-class cricket in 1963, and pursued a successful career as a police detective in Lahore, where he became Deputy Inspector General of Police. He married the daughter of Mohammad Saeed, who played first-class cricket for Muslims and Punjab. Saeed captained Pakistan before the side gained Test status and toured Sri Lanka (then Ceylon) with Pakistan alongside Fazal in 1948/9. Fazal's brother-in-law, Yawar Saeed, played for Somerset and Punjab, was later a Test selector, and for the series in England in 1996, was appointed tour manager, a role he had filled previously in New Zealand in 1984/5 .

Career Details

Born: Lahore, 18 February 1927
Role: right-hand, lower-order batsman, right-hand fast-medium bowler
Clubs: Northern India (1943/4-1945/6), Punjab (1951/2-1956/7) and Lahore (1958/9)
First-class record: (1943-64) 2,602 runs (23.02) including 1 century, 460 wickets (23.02), BB 9-43
Tests: 34
Test Debut: v India, Delhi, 1952
Test record: 620 runs (14.09), 139 wickets (24.70) and 11 catches
Best Performances: HS 60 v Westindies, Port-of- Spain, 1957/8
BB 7-42, v India, Lucknow, 1952/3
BB 13-114, v Australia, Karachi, 1956/7
Tours: India; 1952/3, 1960/1.
England; 1954, 1962
Westindies; 1958/9
Overseas Tests; 21
Ceylon; 1948/9

Muhammad Salim Malik

Salim Malik is one of the finest batsman to come out of Pakistan since the seventies. A gifted middle-order strokemaker with lovely timing, and a marvellous array of wristy shots, only Javed Miandad has more runs, more hundreds or a significantly higher batting average for Pakistan than Salim.

Yet in recent years he has experienced extraordinarily mixed fortunes. They began to change when he lost the confidence of his captain Imran Khan during the World Cup and only just survived to be part of the Final winning side. He formed a fine partnership as Javed Miandad's vice-captain on tour to England in 1992, as well as heading the batting averages, yet after some poor one-day form found himself not only overlooked for the captaincy, for which he seemed heir-apparent but was also "rested" from Pakistan's tour to the Caribbean in March 1993. "Rested" is the usual BCCP parlance for something like "spoke out of turn".

There was a rumour that his objection to certain funds going to Imran Khan's cancer appeal from a function after the World Cup could have cost him his place. However this was unsubstantiated conjecture - Imran for his part had had very little contact with the Board since his retirement. Fortune appeared to have gone full circle. General discontent with Wasim Akram's captaincy saw Malik ushered in as Akram's replacement.

Certainly, Salim's continued absence from the team was unjustifiable and he led from the front, averaging over fifty while in charge, but then had his tenure blighted by unproven allegations of attempted match-rigging. He was sacked, lost his place in the side, only to return once more, suggesting that if his form holds he should have at least a couple more years of Test cricket left in him.

Salim's rise was a rapid one. The son of a linen-wear exporter, he started as a leg-spinner for the Victorious Club in Iqbal Park, Lahore. It was there that his batting potential was first spotted by Rabb Nawaz, the club coach, who instilled in him the necessity to play straight and hit the ball in the "V". Salim progressed quickly; he made his first-class debut at the age of 15, and scored a hundred in his second match, for Lahore "A" against Muslim Commercial Bank. He was playing for Pakistan under-19s from the age of 16 and gained an early media following and exposure.

Salim was picked on his potential to tour Australia in 1981/2 with the full Test squad, averaging just under 40 in his three matches, and he stayed on to captain the under-19 side. He was obviously Test calibre but he got his opportunity in the full Test team in fortuitous circumstances because of the team walk-out in objection to Javed Miandad's captaincy, and along with Rashid Khan, Salim Yousuf and Tahir Naqqash made his debut in the first Test against Sri Lanka at Karachi in March 1982. He took his chance; though aged just 18 years and 328 days, he scored a chanceless, five hour hundred in the second innings, to become only the third Pakistani after Khalid Ibadulla and Miandad to reach three figures on his debut.

When the big guns returned for the final Test he was dropped, which seemed rather harsh, but he had done enough to earn his place on the tour to England that summer. His opportunities were scarce and he struggled to come to terms with the conditions.

He showed moments of his undoubted class over the next few series, without the sort of consistency that would have earned him a permanent place. Not selected against Australia (1982/3), he played in all six Tests against India that followed, and was one of four century makers in the innings at Faisalabad, adding a record 207 for the 6th wicket with Imran Khan. With the top-order in such fine form he had only three other innings in that series.

He was out of touch on the 1983/4 tour to India, where he played in the first and third Tests, and he was not originally selected to tour Australia, but was called up as cover for Imran Khan, who was struggling with a shin injury. Salim played in the last three Tests, making 77 at Adelaide, where he put on 186 with Miandad for the 5th wicket - a record against Australia - and scored 54 at the Sydney Cricket Ground.

He established himself in the middle order with a fine series at home against England at the end of that season, in which he averaged 53.66, helping Pakistan to their first rubber over England. He top-scored in the Karachi Test win with 74, and made 116 and 76 at Faisalabad, thus recording his third Test hundred before his 21st birthday to join a very select group comprising George Headley, of the Westindies, and Graeme Pollock, of South Africa, while Sachin Tendulkar has since score four.

In the shortened series with India (1984/5) Salim got his customary hundred at Faisalabad (his third there), where Pakistan amassed 674 for six, and three Tests later against New Zealand passed a thousand runs in only his 21st Test, as he scored his fifth Test century, though still only 21, in just 173 minutes. He put on 168 with Wasim Raja for the sixth wicket to secure a draw, after Pakistan had been only 32 ahead with five wickets down. He averaged 68 in the series, but could not repeat that form against the same opponents on their own wickets.

He captained the under-23 side to Sri Lanka in 1985, making 140 in the unofficial Test at Kandy, but had a moderate series at home and away with the full side. In the 1986/7 home series against Westindies he had the misfortune to have his left arm broken above the wrist by a short delivery from Courtney Walsh. Salim was instigating some sort of recovery, from 37 for 5 to 90, when he was forced to retire hurt. However in the second innings, he courageously came out to bat with his arm in plaster to share an important last wicket stand of 32 with Wasim Akram. He faced the first ball left-handed, and then deciding to adopt his normal stance, survived another 14 balls from Tony Gray and Walsh. His bravery helped inspire a rousing victory.

He was back later that season to play in all five Tests in India. He was still being troubled by stiffness in his wrist and averaged only 22, but the selectors' faith in his ability meant that he kept his place. An exceptional one-day innings between the 2nd and 3rd Tests helped ensure that; in front of over 90,000 spectators at Eden Gardens, and with Pakistan apparently out of the game with 78 required from less than eight overs, Salim played a superb solo hand making 72 of them off only 35 balls with a six and eleven fours. He equalled the fastest ever one-day fifty, the 21-ball fifty scored by Lance Cairns at Melbourne v Australia in 1982/3 (since beaten by Sanath Jayasuriya, who scored a fifty off 17 balls for Sri Lanka against Pakistan in the Singer Cup final at Singapore in April 1996).

Salim toured England in 1987 still needing to prove his ability outside Asia. His moment came with a match-winning innings on a difficult, unfamiliar surface at Headingley. He batted for five and a half hours, falling in the last over of the day for 99, which he put down to nerves after 18 Tests without a Test hundred, but had played what he considers to be his best innings. He did not have to wait long for that elusive three figure score, making 102 in the final Test at the Oval, where he shared a partnership of 234 with Javed to ensure that Pakistan would win its first series in England.

Salim had been known to be impatient but that summer taught him to be more defensive and to wait for the bad ball. He averaged just under fifty in the Tests and just over 50 on the tour, and was named among *Wisden's* Five Cricketers of the Year.

He had a fine World Cup, batting in his preferred position at No 3, with 100 v Sri Lanka, and 65 and 88 in the wins over England, and topped the averages in the notorious Test series with the latter that followed. He was the batsman that Gatting said he had informed about moving a fielder and that umpire Rana felt he had not. There was not total animosity between the two sides as has been made out; for instance Graham Gooch gave Salim his favourite moulded pads at the end of the series.

In a generally low-scoring series in the Westindies (1987/8) Salim produced one fine innings, to give his side a narrow first innings lead in a thrilling drawn Test in Port of Spain, adding a record 94 for the eighth wicket with Salim Yousuf to rescue Pakistan from 68 for seven. He also played a spectacular one-day innings on the same ground, when he scored 85 off 55 balls in a valiant but unavailing effort to chase 315.

He was short of runs the following year, especially at home to Australia (1988/9), though his one big score of the winter, 80 not out, helped Pakistan to the highest total of any Test in New Zealand, 616 for five declared (since beaten by the home team, who made 671/4 against Sri Lanka in 1990/1).

Salim was superb in the Sharjah Cup (1989/90), helping Pakistan to a comfortable win with scores of 74, 68 not out, and 102, and he took that form into the Nehru Cup. In the semi-final against England, in a game reduced to 30 overs, he added 122 with Ramiz Raja in only 77 balls. Despite batting with a runner because of a strained hamstring, Salim made 66 off 41 balls, with three sixes and six fours, and hit 18 off four consecutive balls from Angus Fraser. He was also instrumental in helping Pakistan to chase 274 in the final against Westindies, making 71 from 62 balls, to secure Pakistan's first major one-day trophy.

Within a couple of weeks Pakistan were playing hosts to India in a dull four match series of draws. Salim gave it some sparkle, averaging 72.50, and in the first Test hit a fine hundred - his seventh - in 213 minutes with 13 fours. However he was involved in a slight altercation with Kiran More, the Indian 'keeper, which was unusual for Salim, and both were reported to the Pakistan Board and the team managers.

Salim was absent at the start of the tour to Australia, because of illness, and his absence from the first Test was a crucial loss to the side, who slipped to defeat with just 22 minutes of the game to go. In the 2nd innings at Adelaide he continued the recovery masterminded by Imran and Wasim Akram, making 65 not out in a thrilling drawn Test, but was injured and missed the final match only returning for the last few WSC one-dayers, in which the side was generally out-played.

He top-scored with 87 as his side gained revenge in the Austral-Asia Cup in Sharjah, starting an impressive unbeaten run in one-day cricket that extended through limited-overs series with New Zealand and Westindies.

Salim played one important innings in the 3-0 Test defeat of New Zealand in a generally low-scoring series, making 71 in a partnership of 131 with Shoaib Mohammad, when Pakistan were in trouble, 115 behind on first innings in the third Test at Faisalabad. He was at his best a few weeks later against the Westindies; following one-day scores of 58 and 91 not out he played a match-winning innings in the 1st Test at Karachi. Coming in to join Shoaib at 27 for three on a difficult pitch they were the only two players to reach double figures and put on a record stand of 174 for the 4th wicket against Westindies. He

Malik - not just a flat-track bully

batted for 268 minutes and 208 balls, hitting only eight boundaries in a most determined hundred. In the 2nd Test he made 74 and 71 and finished the leading run-scorer on either side in the series, at an average of 57.

At the time Salim was thought to be a surprising choice as Essex's overseas player for 1991, but they were not disappointed. It was also crucial to his development as an all-round player. Before he went there he had never passed 140 in first-class cricket and in Tests, eight hundreds had brought a top-score of only 119, and he freely admitted that once he got to a hundred he usually slogged. Keith Fletcher, the Essex coach, instilled in him the need to start again once he got to a hundred, and the break-through came with a score of 173 against Kent. He made five more centuries that summer, including a double-hundred against Leicestershire, and only one of them was under 163. He also shared in a 4th wicket record for Essex of 314 with Nasser Hussain against Surrey, after his side had been 9 for 3.

In all he scored just under 2,000 first-class runs at an average of 73, and helped Essex to the Championship. His bowling - slow inswingers or the leg-breaks he had started bowling as a youngster - picked up some useful wickets too, while his catching, usually at 1st slip, and his

ground fielding were assured. "Sal" or "Slim" as he was called at Essex, was a popular figure at Chelmsford, and was offered frequent hospitality around the country by various compatriots.

Salim made a classy hundred in the first Test of the rain-affected series against Sri Lanka, in the build-up to the World Cup. Despite his obvious talent and experience he lost form and the confidence of his captain, Imran, during the competition and ended up batting at seven in the final. There had been a bit of a history of the two clashing; Imran had needled Salim by calling him "the Dean Jones of Pakistan," while Salim and Wasim Akram felt it necessary to point it out to their captain that at times during the World Cup he seemed uninterested in the rest of the team.

Also, in the pre-competition warm-up games Salim was vice-captain, captaining the side regularly as Imran rested his shoulder. However, when Imran missed the opening match of the World Cup with Westindies because of that injury, it was Javed Miandad who took over the captaincy, much to Salim's chagrin. Intikhab Alam explained that Salim was only vice-captain for the warm-up matches in the absence of Miandad, who was still in Pakistan resting his back, but it was the first Salim had heard of it. Not surprisingly he had a disappointing World Cup, making just one fifty, against Sri Lanka, and was not given the encouragement he needed.

Salim formed a better understanding as Javed's vice-captain on the tour to England in 1992, asserting that the team was happier without Imran, who for some time looked as though he might join the tour. Salim came into his own as a Test batsman, imposing himself on the opposition with consistently confident performances. He called the England bowling "a pop-gun attack" and went out to prove it, even on a minefield at Headingley. Ironically Dean Jones had made a similar claim about England's bowling during the 1990/1 Ashes series, after a brilliant one-day hundred, but then hardly scored another run for about a year, and has so slipped out of favour with the Australian selectors that he retired from international cricket at the end of the 1993/4 season. It seemed that Salim's bravado might lead to a similar fate, for he was dropped by Pakistan and released by Essex at the end of the 1993 season.

In the first Test of the 1992 tour at Edgbaston, Salim made the type of big hundred he had been scoring regularly in county cricket the year before. His 165 was full of superbly timed strokes, hitting 19 fours and a six, facing 297 balls in just under five hours at the crease. He put on 322 for the 4th wicket with Javed Miandad, a record for any wicket between the two countries. A fluent fifty at Lord's in the second Test was a crucial knock, ensuring Pakistan a first innings lead, and then at Headingley, where everyone else struggled, he scored 82 and 84, batting for seven and a half hours in the match without being dismissed, a model of technique and temperament, dispelling Imran's notion after the 2nd Test that Salim was "a flat-track bully". The former captain had criticised Salim for the way he got out when set in the first innings at Lord's, saying "under pressure, time and again, he has failed." There are plenty of examples to contradict this theory.

Salim's aggregate of 488 runs in the series was the record for a rubber between the two sides beating the 453 runs made by Denis Compton for England in 1954. Salim finished top of the Test, tour and first-class averages that year, and seemed poised to take over from Javed the mantle as Pakistan's finest batsman and extend a record to compare with any in Pakistan's history.

Yet he struggled to find his form that winter on the short tour to New Zealand and in the one-day tournaments in Australia and, in particular, South Africa where he failed to reach twenty. Consequently he was not selected for the tour to the Westindies, where his experience and ability were sorely missed. Salim suspected Imran's intervention, though this is unlikely to have been anything more than his passive influence in writing often that Salim lacked bottle under pressure and did not practice enough, while singing Wasim Akram's praises. Salim was clearly at odds with the world at Essex in 1993, enjoying less than half the success he had had in his first season there.

Ironically, Salim was the player the Pakistan Board turned to when the majority of the side raised an objection to playing under Wasim Akram's captaincy. His first tour as captain was a great success, not only beating New Zealand 2-1, but getting players such as Saeed Anwar, Basit Ali and Inzamam-ul-Haq to play to their potential. In his second Test in charge, at Wellington, Salim hit his eleventh Test hundred, a marvellous innings of 140, which included 20 boundaries, sharing a stand of 258 for the 5th wicket with Inzamam, and then led the side to another Sharjah victory, over India by 39 runs, in the final of the Austral-Asia Cup.

The side seemed to be on a roll as two crushing Test victories over Sri Lanka at Colombo and Kandy followed in 1994/5. Salim showed some fine form with the bat, particularly in the one-day series, and seemed to be handling the side with skill. The home rubber against Australia was always going to be a lot tougher and Salim rose to the challenge brilliantly, producing the best batting form of his life. In the first Test Salim made 26 and 43 as Pakistan won a classic encounter at Karachi by the narrowest of margins - one wicket. The rest of the series saw Salim fighting a valiant rearguard action to preserve that lead. At Rawalpindi, Pakistan were forced to followed on for only the second time in a home Test, trailing by 261 on first innings. Dropped on 20 by his opposite number, Mark Taylor, Salim never looked like making another mistake. He played Shane Warne with an authority rarely seen before. He shared three consecutive century partnerships - 148 with Saeed Anwar, 109 in only 99 minutes with Aamir Sohail and 133 with Aamir Malik - before a sudden collapse which saw Salim become the third victim of a hat-trick to Test debutant, Damien Fleming. By then the match was safe, Salim having batted for seven hours and 23 minutes for his career-best 237, which included 34 fours.

He was no less impressive in the third and final Test at Lahore. He made 75 in the first innings, sharing a stand of 123 with Inzamam-ul-Haq which was the cornerstone of Pakistan's total of 373, but without Wasim Akram and Waqar Younis at his disposal, Australia replied with 455, and put the home side under pressure by taking the first five wickets for only 107. Salim found an able ally in Aamir Sohail, who came in at No 7 because of a stiff neck. They batted for 215 minutes together adding 196 to secure the match.

Salim was the difference between the two sides in the series. In all he batted for 21 hours in the series, scoring 557 runs at an average of 92.83, eclipsing Graham Yallop's record for Australia-Pakistan Tests in the process. Leading by shining example, it appeared that he would captain Pakistan

Salim celebrates his double-hundred against Australia

for some time to come. However, the tour to South Africa and Zimbabwe proved to be a disaster. It started well with Pakistan winning five of their six one-dayers against South Africa, Sri Lanka and New Zealand, but then dissension ran through the side in the two finals when Salim chose to field first against the common consensus of opinion. Both matches were lost, and the team seemed in no frame of mind for the inaugural Test against South Africa, which was also lost by a wide margin despite another fine innings of 99 from the captain.

By the time the team reached Zimbabwe rumours were abounding about why Salim had chosen to field. The first Test against Zimbabwe was lost by an innings but thanks to eight wickets in the match from Wasim Akram, the series was squared at Bulawayo.

The match-rigging rumours came to a head on the first morning of the third Test, when the story broke in an Australian newspaper that Shane Warne and Tim May alleged that Salim had tried to bribe them to throw the recent game between the two sides in Karachi. Before play the Pakistani players swore on the Koran that they were not involved - Salim was visibly shaking when he went out to bat in the first innings. Despite this backdrop, Pakistan won a notable victory to record the first instance of a touring side coming back to win a three-match series after losing the first game.

Through no fault of his own Salim had lost the confidence of the team. The Pakistan Board sacked and suspended him and it appeared that his playing days were over. He even went to the courts in Islamabad to try and get himself reinstated in the side for the series with Sri Lanka. Eventually when no evidence came to light, Salim came back into contention and was chosen, with delicious irony, to return against the Australians. He arrived in Australia late, making his entrance all the more dramatic. Unfortunately on the first day of the series, Salim split the webbing on his left hand in catching Mark Taylor, which required six stitches, and he was unable to bat in the first innings, and only at eight in the second. Consequently he missed the next Test at Hobart, but returned at Sydney were he made useful scores of 36 and 45 in a winning cause.

The winter season of 1994/5 was a bitter-sweet one for Salim Malik and the rest of 1995 a nightmare. His heroic performances against Australia were clouded by unfounded rumours, which precipitated an end to a highly successful tenure as captain, in which he averaged over fifty with the bat.

Surprisingly, considering his experience in England, Salim looked terribly out of form at the start of the 1996 tour. He had to retire in the match against Warwickshire, complaining of dizziness,

and his batting looked equally shaky going into the Lord's Test as he hadn't passed 37 in first-class cricket on the tour. He was pleased just to be in the side for the first Test and, after failing in the first innings, was happy just to spend time in the middle in the second as Pakistan pushed towards a declaration. His liking for conditions at Headingley brought some confidence back to his batting. He grafted out an important fifty in tricky conditions, which contained only three fours and took 143 balls, during a stand of 130 with Ijaz Ahmed. Again he played with tremendous application at the Oval, where he also has a fine record. He was slow and methodical in compiling his first fifty, ensuring that Pakistan's lead was more than just useful, and then cut loose moving to three figures with assurance. During the innings, he passed 5,000 runs and Zaheer Abbas's aggregate for Pakistan, leaving only Javed Miandad ahead of him. By the end of the Texaco limited-overs series, he was close to passing Miandad's record number of one-day appearances for Pakistan and becoming only the sixth player in the world to reach 6,000 runs.

His batting in the series showed a lot of character, suggesting his career is far from over after the troubles of the previous year. Now that Javed Miandad has retired, Salim's experience should be usefully employed by Pakistan for at least the next couple of years by when he should have passed 100 Test caps.

Career Details

Born: Lahore, 16 April 1963
Role: right-hand, middle-order batsman, right-hand leg-spin bowler
Clubs: Lahore (1978/9-1985/6), Habib Bank (1982/3-1994/5), Essex (1991-93) and Sargodha (1991/2)
First-class record: (1978-95) 14,296 runs (48.13) including 37 centuries and 72 fifties, HS 237, 83 wickets (34.37), BB 5-19, and 143 catches
Tests: 90
Test Debut: 1981/2, v Sri Lanka, Karachi
Test record: 5101 runs (45.14), including 14 hundreds and 25 fifties, 5 wickets (49.40) and 57 catches
Best Performances: HS 165 v England, Edgbaston, 1992
BB 1-3 v Australia, Adelaide, 1983/4
Tours: Australia; 1981/2, 1983/4, 1984/5 (WSC), 1988/9, 1989/90, 1992/3 (WSC), 1995/6
England; 1982, 1987, 1992, 1996
India; 1983/4, 1986/7, 1989/90 (Nehru Cup)
New Zealand 1984/5, 1988/9, 1992/3, 1993/4, 1995/6
Sri Lanka; 1984/5 (under-23), 1985/6, 1994/5
Westindies; 1987/8
South Africa; (1992/3), 1994/5
Zimbabwe; (1992/3), 1994/5
Overseas Tests; 48
One-day Internationals; 229
World Cups; 1987, 1992, 1996
Sharjah; 1983/4, 1984/5, 1985/6, 1986/7, 1988/9, 1989/90, 1990/1, 1991/2, 1993/4, 1994/5, 1995/6
Bangladesh; 1988/9, 1993/4

Javed Miandad Khan

Javed Miandad is quite easily the most prolific batsman in Pakistan's Test history, having scored 8,832 runs from his 124 Tests. He is way ahead of his nearest compatriots, Zaheer Abbas and Salim Malik, who have just over 5,000 runs each, while his 23 centuries also leave Malik (14), Abbas and Hanif Mohammad (each with 12) a long way behind. Only Australia's Allan Border (11,174), India's Sunil Gavaskar (10,122) and England's Graham Gooch (8,900) have scored more Test runs than Javed, but he has made his runs at a better average. He has played in over half of all of his country's Tests and had hardly missed a game in more than seventeen years when he was dropped for the tour to New Zealand in 1993/4, which appeared for a moment to spell the end of his career. Like Imran Khan before him, it took Prime Ministerial persuasion, by Mrs Benazir Bhutto, to get Javed to reconsider his hasty decision to retire, which he announced in protest at his non-selection for Sharjah at the end of that season. His recall for Pakistan's tour to Sri Lanka in August 1994 suggested that he had been welcomed back into the fold. However, he injured his knee playing soccer at a pre-tour training camp and so had to pull out, and he was not selected against Australia or for Pakistan's tour to South Africa and Zimbabwe in 1994/5, but kept hanging on for one last chance at the top level, which eventually came during the 1996 World Cup.

Javed heads a host of records for youth and longevity and for sheer weight of runs. His batting skill should not be underestimated; he has achieved the highest score for Pakistan in the Coopers and Lybrand ratings, while his average rating over his career has often been above the best ratings of the other top batsmen. Viv Richards, during the 1992 World Cup, said that if he had to chose someone to bat for his life, it would be Javed. He might have tempered this by saying as long as he was playing for the same side. For Javed was a fiercely competitive cricketer, who gave little quarter and had a tendency to infuriate opponents. Consequently, Javed's career attracted a fair degree of controversy, which has meant that the plaudits due to him as one of the finest batsmen in Test history and, statistically at least, Pakistan's best-ever, have invariably been clipped.

He is, however, well respected by other players. Westindian opener Des Haynes said of him, "Javed has a lot of flair. I do think he has been unfairly criticised but that is one of the problems of judging people too quickly, which seems to be an unfortunate trait in modern society. It all seems to depend on how people perceive you early on in your career, because that impression tends to stick. To me he is simply a great batsman and a great competitor who just loves to win." (from *The Lion of Barbados* by Rob Steen). Tony Greig once described Miandad as "no angel. He's an irritating little character who keeps baiting people." Yet there is no doubt he is someone you would want on your side - Greig recognised his fighting qualities and recruited him to play under his captaincy at Sussex.

Javed was also an extremely astute captain, rated by many of his compatriots as probably the best that Pakistan has produced. Yet his impact has been masked because he had a remarkable six tenures in office, misrepresenting the quality of the man as a captain. Over the last decade of his career he has been willing, generally, to stand down when Imran Khan was available. Few would have been prepared to take the job on such an *ad hoc* basis, but shows a certain magnanimity of spirit on his behalf. Admittedly, on occasions he probably had little choice, but it was also apparent that Miandad still called a lot of the tactical plays, often moving fielders and running the show to allow Imran to concentrate on his bowling. Many of Pakistan's best results have come when Imran has been in charge with Javed as his field marshal.

Javed has a better record than any other Pakistani captain having won 14 out of 34 matches, and taken six series. He may have benefited at times from being put in charge when Imran Khan has felt the opposition unworthy or the time of year unpleasant, but this has also meant that Miandad has been denied his greatest match-winning all-rounder, whose presence would surely have bettered those figures. Due to fitness or unavailability, Imran Khan has been absent from 21 of those 34 matches, yet Miandad still managed to win nine of them and lose only three.

Javed's early life is often erroneously portrayed, and the impression conveyed is of a street-fighter brought up in the slums of Karachi. He did learn part of his cricket on the backstreets, like most Pakistanis, and some of the sharper practices of that form of cricket remained with him. Although his family was by no means well to do, before Partition his father was an official in charge of sport for fiefdoms around the Kathiawar Peninsula in western India. In 1947, like many others, they lost most of their possessions in their move to Karachi, and the early years in the new state were a struggle for his parents as they tried to bring up seven children, four of whom were to play first-class cricket - Javed's brothers Anwar and Bashir played for Karachi while Sohail represented the Pakistan National Shipping Corporation. Their father became a Karachi cricket official, who was Javed's only ever coach, and Javed was devastated when his father died of a heart attack in 1990.

Under his father's guidance, Javed soon developed into an outstanding player, making his first-class debut at 16 years and five months for Karachi Whites, and the following season made the highest score of his career, 311 against National Bank, batting for ten and a half hours. On the strength of that he was selected for the World Cup squad in 1975, despite being only 17. He played in one game against Sri Lanka, chipping in with 28 not out and taking 2-22 with his briskish leg-spinners.

On the recommendation of Sadiq Mohammad, Tony Greig invited him to play a few games for Sussex II's after the World Cup with a view to his qualification for the following season. A brilliant double-hundred against Hampshire, which left his opponents in awe, ensured he was invited back. He toured Ceylon with Pakistan that winter and on his return to England for the hot, dry summer of 1976, he averaged over seventy in the four Championship matches in which he played, including two hundreds (Sussex made only five in total that season), and impressed with his cheeky running between the wickets and brilliant fielding.

That winter he played in his first Test match, at Lahore against New Zealand, at the age of 19 years and 119 days, and marked the occasion with a hundred, thus becoming only the second Pakistani to do so on debut after Khalid Ibadulla in 1964/5 against Australia. He reached three figures in just two hours and 50 minutes, and went onto 163, which included 21 fours. He was fluent and authoritative, and dominated a partnership of 281 with Asif Iqbal for the fifth wicket - still a record for Pakistan - that rescued the side from 55 for 4. In the third Test, in front of his home crowd, he became the youngest player to score a Test double-hundred (19 years 141 days), batting for 410 minutes and hitting two sixes and 29 fours. He put on 252 for the 4th wicket with his captain Mustaq Mohammad and enjoyed another century partnership with him in the 2nd innings, in which Javed fell just short of completing a hundred in each innings, but his 85 had taken him past 500 runs in his first series at an average of 126. He had also taken several useful wickets with his leg-spin which "Mushy" often used in preference to his own.

Javed was less successful when the side travelled to Australia, though he played a couple of important innings, notably a fifty in the final Test at Sydney where he added 125 in partnership with Asif Iqbal to set up a match winning lead. That Spring, in the Westindies, he lost his place after making 2 and 1 in the first Test in Barbados and was out of touch in the games against the islands.

The Kerry Packer defections suddenly thrust Miandad forward as one of the more senior players and took the opportunity to fully establish himself, beginning a record sequence of 53 consecutive Tests for his country which stretched from 1977 until 1984. He responded to the extra responsibility by averaging 131 in the three home Tests against England (1977/8) with scores of 71, 88 not out and 66 not out. This formed part of his most successful domestic season in which he scored over 1,300 runs at an average of 77. On the return tour in 1978 much was expected of him, but he struggled in the cold, wet conditions, and only returned to form with Sussex after the Tests, averaging over 50 in the Championship and helping his county to the Gillette Cup Final, being man-of-the-match in the semi-final.

With Tony Greig and Imran Khan both at Sussex, it was always likely that Javed would join them in Kerry Packer's World Series Cricket. New arrangements with the Board of Control at home meant that he could still play for Pakistan and that winter, 1978/9, he established himself as a world-class player as he made hundreds in three separate Test series and scored well in WSC. In all, he amassed 837 runs in eight official Tests at an average of over a hundred. He marked the first Test between Pakistan and India for 17 years - and the first to be staged at Faisalabad - with a century, putting on 255 with Zaheer Abbas. In the third Test he made exactly 100 in the first innings and then in the second, saw Pakistan to victory by eight wickets and their first series win against India with a blistering knock of 62 not out. He shared a frantic partnership of 97 in just nine overs with Asif Iqbal, making the winning hit with seven balls to spare.

With four key players still missing because of WSC commitments from the first Test at Christchurch, New Zealand, Javed shouldered the batting responsibilities superbly. Although benefiting from dropped chances early on in both innings, he took full advantage of his let offs, driving and hooking in fine style to top score in both innings with 81 and 160 not out to set his side on the way to victory. At this juncture he achieved the highest-ever Coopers and Lybrand rating for Pakistan, 905.

In Australia, the best and worst of Javed's cricket was evident. He was involved in the first of a number of incidents that spiced his career when the Dr Jekyll in him came out when he ran out tail-ender Rodney Hogg as the batsman wandered from his crease to do some "gardening." Despite Mustaq Mohammad's attempts to recall Hogg, the umpire would not revoke his decision and the injured party demolished his stumps in disgust. Javed's actions were to have their ramifications in the next Test, but Imran Khan thought the whole affair quite amusing, the sort of thing you would expect to see in a typical street match in Pakistan. The Mr Hyde side was evident at Perth where he held the side together with an excellent not out hundred, his sixth in Tests, though he was still only 21.

After the World Cup in 1979 Javed found that Kepler Wessels had established himself at Sussex as the second overseas player, along with Imran Khan. The dour South African opening batsman had been on the club's books for a couple of years but had been away doing his military service. Fast bowler Garth LeRoux had also joined and with the new rules restricting the number of registered overseas players just coming in, Javed was released from his contract. He was not short of offers and was rapidly signed up by Glamorgan.

He went through the 1979/80 series in India without a really big score, but made several useful contributions, finishing with over 400 runs in the series. Defeat in the rubber though meant an inevitable change of captain, but it was a surprise when Javed was chosen ahead of several senior players. It was also a slightly undiplomatic choice as his first opponents were to be Australia, though there were no further furores in that series (1979/80). At 22 years and 260 days, Javed became the third youngest Test captain of all time; only the Nawab of Pataudi of India (21 years and 77 days) and Ian Craig of Australia (22 years and 194 days) were younger, though Waqar Younis has since eclipsed both Craig and Miandad.

Javed became only the third Pakistan captain, after Fazal Mahmood and Mustaq Mohammad, to win his first Test in charge, which was enough to secure victory in a series against Australia for the first time. He marked the second Test with a hundred, to match the one made by his opposite number Greg Chappell, and put on an unbroken 3rd wicket record stand of 223 with Taslim Arif, who made the highest score by a wicket-keeper in Tests, 210 not out. Javed in fact kept for a while towards the end of the final Test, allowing Arif to take a Test wicket and Javed to make a stumping.

Eight months later, Pakistan lost narrowly in a four-match series at home to Westindies which was a creditable result considering the strength of the tourists at that time. On the whole the batting struggled, though Miandad scored fifties in the last three Tests, against a formidable pace attack including Malcolm Marshall, Joel Garner, Colin Croft and Sylvester Clarke.

With a thousand runs at home either side of a successful first season with Glamorgan in 1980, Javed peaked in an historic summer in 1981, in which he was named as one of *Wisden's* Five Cricketers of the Year. He scored more than 2,000 runs at an average of 70, to take his aggregate in the previous two years to nearly 6,000 first-class runs. He beat the 31-year-old county record held by Gilbert Parkhouse by making eight centuries, one of which is widely regarded as one of the great innings of all time. On a difficult Colchester pitch taking spin, and with Glamorgan requiring 325 to win in even time, Miandad made a brilliant not out double-hundred in five-and-a-half hours with 22 fours but was left stranded with his side just 14 runs from a famous victory. No one else could fathom the vagaries of the pitch, the next highest score being 36. As well as his nimble footwork and strokeplay, Javed demonstrated his excellent placement and running between the wickets; he managed to farm the bowling to such good effect, that he scored 43 in nine overs in an eighth wicket partnership with Robin Hobbs before the latter faced his first ball, by which he was dismissed. One of the umpires, Ken Palmer (with whom Javed has had the odd run-in) described it as the best innings he has ever seen.

In Australia 1981/2, his impetuosity got the better of him. With Pakistan struggling to save the first Test, Javed and Dennis Lillee almost came to blows after the Australian fast bowler first deliberately impeded him running between the wickets and then swung a little kick at him. Miandad swung round and threatened to club Lillee over the head with his bat. He said at the time: "I got a terrible surprise when he kicked me. I lifted my bat to ward him off and to tell him that if he hit me I would hit him... He kept saying dirty words to me." Lillee, no blushing violet, claimed he had been provoked by abuse from the batsman. Lillee was fined a token amount by his fellow players; Greg Chappell said after: "If we'd found out Dennis was the instigator we'd have rubbed him out." The umpires felt this insufficient and Lillee went before the Australian Cricket Board, who suspended him for two one-day internationals. A number of former Australian Test players were on Javed's side. Bill O'Reilly, writing in the *Sydney Morning Herald*, wrote: "If the Board is prepared to do its job, Lillee is due a long holiday," while Keith Miller wrote in the *Sydney Daily Telegraph*: "He should be suspended for the rest of the season." Javed, for his part, apologised.

Pakistan were well beaten in the first two Tests but bounced back with their first victory by an innings over Australia in the third Test at the Melbourne Cricket Ground. However, off the field, there was ever-increasing disharmony with Miandad, and dressing room squabbles became more and more frequent. When Javed blamed the series defeat on his senior players his team-mates refused, en masse, to play on under him in the forthcoming series against Sri Lanka unless a new captain was appointed for the summer's tour of England.

Consequently the first two Tests against Sri Lanka were played with an almost entirely different side and despite a comfortable win in the first Test Javed agreed to relinquish the captaincy at the end of the series. The mutineers thus returned for the final Test and the full strength side produced an innings victory. It proved to be Miandad's longest term in office, 13 matches, for he was never again given an extended period in charge.

Imran Khan was appointed, initially as a stopgap measure, for the tour to England. With the loss of the captaincy came a loss of form for Javed though he did make two fine fifties on a tricky pitch at Headingley and scored heavily in the county matches.

Once settled back in the ranks his form soon returned. A hundred in the final Test against Australia at Lahore (1982/3) was the precursor to a run spree against India later that winter in which he made 594 runs at 118.80 in the series, as he, Mudassar Nazar and Zaheer Abbas scored over 2,000 runs among them. Javed, who had scored not out hundreds in the first and third one-dayers, was one of four centurions in Pakistan's ten wicket win in the third Test at Faisalabad, where he shared in a stand of 287 with Zaheer Abbas. In the next Test at Hyderabad he made his highest Test score, 280 not out; only Hanif Mohammad has made a higher score for Pakistan. He shared a partnership of 451 with Mudassar Nazar which equalled the world Test record for any wicket (since beaten) set by Don Bradman and Bill Ponsford for Australia in 1934. In all Javed batted for just over ten hours, hitting 19 fours and a six from 460 balls. He shared century stands with Mudassar in the next two Tests as well, to bring his tally of such partnerships to seven in his last seven Test innings.

In the summer of 1983 he played in the World Cup but missed the semi-final against the Westindies because of 'flu and struggled with injuries for the rest of the season, playing in only four Championship games for Glamorgan. On tour to India that winter he passed 4,000 runs in Test cricket during an innings of 99 in the first Test at Bangalore and made fifties in the other two games. His golden streak ended in Australia, where he had an inconsistent series, though he did make his 11th Test hundred in a record Pakistan score of 624 in the third Test at Adelaide. As that game was drawing to a close, Javed enlivened proceedings with comical impersonations of various bowlers

An orthodox sweep from Javed

including Bob Willis and opponents Rodney Hogg and Dennis Lillee. Javed made a hundred in the state games either side of the Test, to give him three in a row.

Javed missed the 1983/4 series with England that started shortly after because of a back injury that was to become recurrent; it was the first Test he had missed for nearly seven years. His opportunities with Glamorgan that summer were also limited by further restrictions on overseas players as he had to share the duties with Winston Davis, the Westindian fast bowler.

He made little impact in the shortened series with India (1984/5) but was back to his best a month later against New Zealand at home. In the second Test at Hyderabad Javed became only the second Pakistani after Hanif Mohammad, in 1961/2, to score a century in each innings, hitting 104 and 103 not out, and took the side to a seven-wicket victory with a partnership of 212 with Mudassar Nazar. When Zaheer Abbas stood down from the captaincy at the end of the series, there were no other serious contenders to stop Javed returning to the captaincy. His influence was immediately apparent in the selection of the virtually unknown Wasim Akram for the first time, whom he took under his wing. The tour to New Zealand though was not a success, for Pakistan lost 2-0 and there were several dressing room disputes, one of which led to Abdul Qadir being sent home.

Javed led the side in the World Championship of Cricket in Australia that followed, where Pakistan lost in the final to India, and then lost to them again soon after in the Sharjah tournament. Consequently Javed was hounded by criticism in the press and the next season (1985/6) decided, after the 2nd Test with Sri Lanka, to stand down at the end of the series "to concentrate on his batting." This was ironic as he had scored a double-hundred in the first Test at Faisalabad, and been part of another record stand, adding 397 for the third wicket with Qasim Omar. It was Javed's 14th Test century, 11 of which had been made in Pakistan. He and Hanif Mohammad, the Chairman of Selectors, had chosen an old pitch in preference to the livelier re-laid one. You could tell they were both batsmen, because it proved to be one of the most prolific Test pitches, with over 1,000 runs being scored on it for the loss of just 13 wickets.

Imran Khan took over for a most acrimonious tour to Sri Lanka at the end of the season, where the umpiring was plainly biased. In the second Test, Javed got an lbw decision against him that he was clearly not happy with and he almost came to blows with the Sri Lankan players. With the crowd jeering as he returned to the pavilion someone threw a small stone at him, which bounced nearby on the outfield. This enraged Javed who went into the stand to try and find the perpetrator and had to be restrained by his team-mates. That evening the tour was almost called off, until Pakistan's President Zia-ul-Haq advised that the team stay. It had not been a happy series for anyone, though Javed was man-of-the-series in the Asia Cup that followed.

Javed had one of his finest moments in Sharjah soon after; in the Austral-Asia Cup Final against India, who had made 245 in their 50 overs, Javed held the side together with a brilliant hundred, mustering 90 in the last ten overs with some superb placement and running. With one ball left Pakistan still needed four to win, and with all the fielders placed to save the boundary, he hit a full toss from Chetan Sharma clean out of the ground at mid-wicket. Miandad was hailed as a hero and was swamped by spectators bearing gifts of gold and money. By the time he left Sharjah he had been given a Mercedes and about $100,000 worth of other gifts - no doubt the most valuable hit in cricket. Javed rates it as his best innings and it

seems the crowd agreed.

It was Pakistan's first major one-day trophy triumph and the celebrations went on so long that Javed missed the start of the 1986 English season and consequently he was released by Glamorgan. The county finished bottom in the Championship and many felt that Javed should have been reinstated when he turned up at the club in mid-season. However, his former team mates had been annoyed by his early season absence and backed the committee.

That winter against the Westindies, in a low-scoring series in which no one made a hundred, Javed managed the highest score for Pakistan in any of the Tests, with 76 at Faisalabad which went a long way towards ensuring a draw. Then against India, Miandad averaged over 50, including 94 in the first Test before being run out from silly point, but was forced to miss the fourth Test with back problems.

Despite being vice-captain Javed was again late to arrive in England for Pakistan's tour in 1987, partly because he was waiting for the birth of his son but also because he was delayed trying to get a car through customs into Pakistan. When he did arrive he started in magnificent form with a double-hundred against his old club, Sussex, and with scores of 113, 71 not out and 68 in the Texaco Trophy. However it was not until the final match at the Oval that he was at his best in the Tests. For such a good player Javed's Test record in England had been indifferent, but with Pakistan needing only to draw to ensure a first series win in England, Javed played the perfect innings. In all he batted for 617 minutes and 521 balls, hitting a six and 28 fours in his 260, and passed 6,000 Test runs in the process. He added 234 with Salim Malik, and although he became becalmed at one point during his stand of 189 with Imran Khan, he did not give his wicket away, helping Pakistan to amass their highest total in Tests, 708.

Javed had a fine World Cup in 1987/8, making a string of good scores including a hundred against Sri Lanka. However, in the semi-final against Australia, he was forced to keep-wicket from the 19th over onwards after Salim Yousuf had been injured. He did a creditable job, making a stumping, but when he batted he seemed exhausted in the later stages of his innings of 70 and could not lead the charge when the pressure was on.

Next came the notorious series with England. It was held at an inappropriate time just after the World Cup and after that semi-final defeat public interest was low. After some controversial decisions in the first Test, the animosity came to a head at Faisalabad where the umpire and the England captain had their altercation. It has been suggested that Miandad encouraged the umpire, Shakoor Rana, to stick to his guns in demanding an unconditional apology from Gatting. Javed would not be drawn to comment claiming his English was not very good. However when the England manager, Peter Lush, left for Karachi to try and resolve the Rana-Gatting deadlock, Javed hitched a lift with him and spent the next couple of hours making polite conversation with remarkable fluency!

Javed quit at the end of the series despite the prospect of a long period in charge with Imran Khan supposedly retired after the World Cup. However, Imran was persuaded back for the tour to the Caribbean and for the rest of his career took over the reins whenever he was available to play.

In the Westindies in the Spring of 1988 Javed topped the Test and tour averages with some of his finest batting overseas. He followed a hundred in the last one-dayer with a masterly century in the first Test at Bourda, Georgetown, scored in six and three-quarter hours, around which Pakistan built a match-winning score. Another excellent innings saved the day in Port of Spain, where Javed's hundred gave Pakistan a chance of chasing a record score to win, 372. He fell after 427 minutes at the crease in a chanceless innings, but with him went his team's chances as Pakistan's attempt to score 84 off the last 20 overs with three wickets in hand wilted and eventually saw the last pair blocking out for a draw with 31 still required.

Imran Khan refused to play in the home series against Australia in 1988/9, objecting to the time of year at which it was being played, and Javed again took over. He marked his return to the captaincy with a double-hundred, which was slow (636 minutes in all) but was made in great heat and set up his side for an innings victory. He faced 439 balls in all, hitting a six and 29 fours, in an innings of remarkable application on a Karachi pitch offering sharp turn. He followed it with another hundred in the next Test before his innings ended with a rare lbw against him.

Having past 7000 runs in the final Test at Lahore he surged towards the next milestone in New Zealand soon after. Standing down for Imran Khan once again, he hit a hundred at Wellington - his 20th - and recorded his 6th double-hundred in Tests in the next at Auckland, leaving only Don Bradman and England's Wally Hammond with more scores of 200 or more. In all he batted for 558 minute and 465 balls, hitting five sixes and 28 fours. He and Shoaib Mohammad bettered their record partnership of the previous Test (advancing it from 220 to 248). His efforts over the previous 12 months had taken him to the top of the Coopers and Lybrand ratings again (with 903 - just short of his own record), as he made 1,083 runs at an average of over 90.

The next winter, after victories in the Sharjah Champions Trophy and the Nehru Cup, Javed played in his 100th Test for Pakistan during a stalemate series with India. Fittingly, he scored a resolute century to mark the occasion, thus emulating Colin Cowdrey in 1968. Javed became the first player to score a ton in his first and hundredth match, both of which were played at the Gaddafi Stadium in Lahore.

On his fifth Test tour to Australia (1989/90), he had problems with his back and was below his best but played valuable rearguard innings in each Test. Javed took over the captaincy once more against New Zealand the following winter as Imran Khan felt the opposition unworthy, as several senior players had just retired or were unavailable. Miandad had been disinclined at first to take the job on a stopgap basis again. Eventually he agreed and led Pakistan to its first clean sweep though he had a quiet series with the bat himself. He stood down as captain against the Westindies, but his poor form continued and he missed the last Test with a stomach ailment.

Javed's bad run of form continued against Sri Lanka in 1991/2. In marked contrast to the golden period he had enjoyed up to his hundredth Test, in which he scored six hundreds in 12 matches, he had managed only three fifties since then in the same number of Tests.

However he had a fine World Cup (his fifth) in 1992; he did an essential repair job with Imran Khan in the final, while his aping of the Indian wicket-keeper Kiran More in an earlier match, showed he had lost none of his competitiveness. His timing and placement were probably better than at any time in the previous few years. He was one of the most consistent batsmen in the competition and had a lot to do with Pakistan pulling through and finishing strongly, after being on the verge of going out.

With Imran Khan injured and on the point of retiring, Javed took over the captaincy for a record sixth term, though he had to be persuaded to do so by senior players. Pakistan had the youngest national team to tour England, average age 23, and Miandad led the side with avuncular care. For the first time since his first tenure he could feel comfortable in the job, believing it would be his for the rest of his playing days, and it brought the best out of his leadership, making shrewd tactical decisions and precise fielding changes, as well as spurring on his side.

An exchange of views with Ian Botham in the second one-dayer set the press going; he was labelled "cricket's Colonel Gaddafi" by the _Daily Mirror_, but Botham's actions should have been punished. In fact, Botham has great respect for Javed's ability. In his autobiography, he chose him

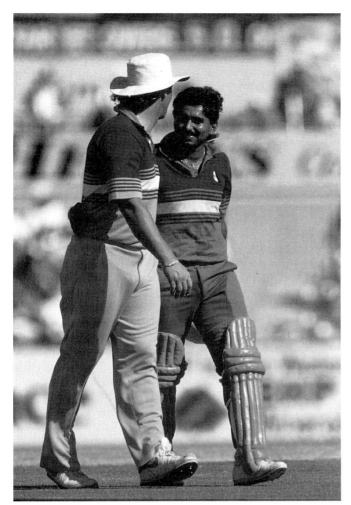

Sharing a lighter moment with old adversary Ian Botham

in his Best of the World side, describing him thus, "He had the qualities of confidence and arrogance all great players possess and they rubbed off on his colleagues. A master improviser, able to conjure runs out of nothing. Pakistan were fortunate to have some great strokeplayers during the period I played against them but he was the best of all."

At Edgbaston, Botham was reminded of those qualities as Javed scored his first Test hundred for two-and-a-half years, his 23rd in total. He put together a partnership of 322 with his vice-captain Salim Malik, a record for any wicket between the two countries. At Old Trafford he fell 12 short of another century, but in an otherwise circumspect innings, showed a masterly array of strokes in one over from Ian Salisbury in which he hit the Sussex leg-spinner for five fours. That Test was marred by the altercation between Aqib Javed and Umpire Roy Palmer. Javed quickly jumped in to defend his young fast bowler, indeed all too readily, showing his old predilection for a confrontation, rather than trying to calm the situation as Imran Khan might have done. Javed was spoken to by the match

referee, Conrad Hunte. However, in the next Test at Headingley where Pakistan had justifiable cause for annoyance with the umpiring, Javed settled his side when tempers were beginning to fray and was commended for his efforts. In the fifth match at the Oval he shared in his 50th three-figure partnership in Tests, adding 111 with Shoaib Mohammad, to establish Pakistan in a strong position in the game that decided the series in their favour.

Javed had a hectic and tumultuous winter in 1992/3, He only played a limited amount of domestic cricket, jetting off to play in the International Hong Kong sixes in the middle of the Wills Cup, before embarking on a worldwide international schedule. He led the side in the World Series matches in Australia which went disastrously, but handled the side shrewdly in a tense one-off Test against New Zealand at Hamilton. He played most responsibly after coming in at 4 for 2, batting for 211 minutes for his 92. Then after a wicketless first 40 minutes on what proved to be the last day, he decided to give Waqar Younis one more over after originally calling up Mustaq Ahmed. The change of plan worked as Younis made the breakthrough to precipitate a remarkable collapse, that brought the side victory by 33 runs.

Despite Pakistan winning two Tests in a rubber with England for the first time and this superb win in New Zealand under his leadership, Miandad was replaced by Wasim Akram for the one-day tournaments in Sharjah and South Africa and for the tour to the Caribbean. Javed was suspicious of Imran Khan's influence as he had recommended his successor, but in truth it was Pakistan's recent one-day record that had cost him the captaincy, as Pakistan had won just three out of 16 matches since the World Cup, and Javed suffered the consequence. His own form had been poor in those games yet he had averaged nearly 60 in Tests during his last term as captain. He was deposed rather unceremoniously and his form in the Westindies continued to decline. In particular, during the 2nd Test, one rash stroke in the last over of the third day - when he tried to hit a second successive six off the penultimate ball - hinted that the end for one of the great batting legends was nigh. He was troubled by injuries and lacked the footwork associated with his pomp.

He played against Zimbabwe at home, and made 70 in the first Test in a generally low-scoring series, but found himself dropped for the tour to New Zealand, despite his record against them. When Akram was deposed after a players' revolt - in similar circumstances to Miandad's demise 12 years earlier - it appeared that Javed might even be reinstated once again as captain. In fact the selectors turned to Salim Malik and there was no

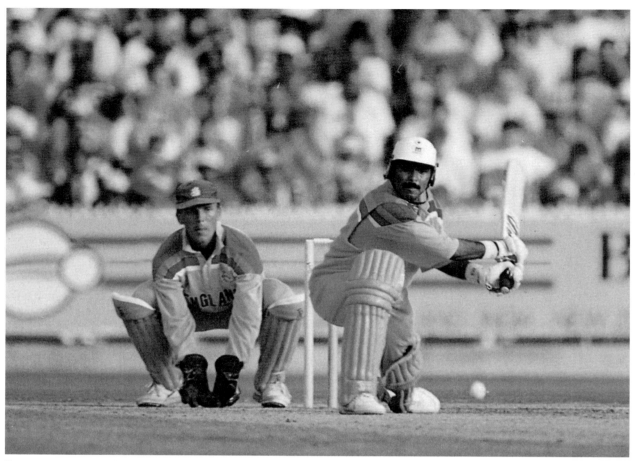

Reverse-sweeping this time, in the World Cup final

recall for Pakistan's most prolific batsman. In Karachi hundreds of children marched through the streets demanding the inclusion of their hero, there were other protests and hunger strikes, while angry fans forced the abandonment of a match between Karachi and Lahore after the umpires and both the captains had been threatened during a pitch invasion.

Left to brood at home while others established themselves in the middle-order on tour, Miandad announced his retirement after being left out of the squad for the Austral-Asia Cup in Sharjah as well, feeling he had been "insulted and humiliated," and complaining "there is a limit to everything and I feel my exclusion from Sharjah is unjust." It took a personal plea from the Prime Minister, Mrs Benazir Bhutto - who, incidentally, was a direct contemporary of Imran Khan's at Oxford University - to persuade him to reconsider. He made himself available for international cricket once more and was selected to tour Sri Lanka for the three-match Test series and one-day tournament there beginning in August 1994, only to injure his knee playing soccer at a pre-tour training camp, which ruled him out.

Fitness remained a problem, but once he proved both his form and fitness, there was no question that he would be allowed his swan song in his sixth (a record) World Cup. It did not prove to be the grand finale he was after, as Javed was left stranded trying to conjure some of the brilliant strokes of his past to get Pakistan out of trouble in their quarter-final against India. He should have batted at number three throughout the tournament, pacing the innings as he and Imran Khan had done during the 1992 triumph. He needed to get in early in one of the opening matches to regain his touch but instead, it looked as though he might have gone on one tournament too long, when really he could have been influential.

At one stage he was hoping to play on until he passed Allan Border's record tally of runs in Test cricket (11,174), but announced his retirement after the World Cup. As it is, he is likely to remain his country's leading run-scorer for many years to come. In retirement, he still has an important role to play in nurturing young talent, and has worked hard as mentor to Basit Ali, who has many of Javed's batting touches.

Javed became less precocious in his later career, and many of the flowing drives seemed to have gone, playing within certain limitations and cutting out some of his riskier strokes. He rarely used the reverse-sweep in his later years (though he favoured the stroke in the World Cup in 1992) - a shot he had inherited from the famous Mohammad brothers. He had problems with his back which affected his flexibility, showing in his fielding as well as his batting. He was still a highly effective player when he retired, if no longer the great improviser and destroyer of bowling he once was in the one-day game. He lost some of the power of his youth and so his batting was less aggressive, becoming more the consummate accumulator with nudges and deflections, relying on his placement.

Javed seems to have been intrinsically involved and blamed for so many of Pakistan's recent run-ins. They reflect his fierce competitive spirit which sometimes "o'er flows the measure" but also they hide a modest man off-the-field, who has a disarming smile and incongruously shrill voice. He is deeply religious, most generous to his friends and a mild-mannered and amusing host.

Leading Pakistani journalist Qamar Ahmed, writing in the London *Evening Standard*, summed him up thus;

"He has been called a street urchin, a street fighter, arrogant. He is none of these...what makes him tough are the fighting qualities of a warrior or marshal leading his army. For those who fail to understand him, he appears to be cocky and rude. For those who know him closely and know his style of play, he is a gift from the gods."

He retires to a fine house in the best part of Lahore. He has married into one of the premier families in Pakistan, the Saigals, and he will be able to watch his sons growing up and learning their cricket at Aitchison College, Imran Khan's old school. There will be those who would rather his sons did not grow up in quite the same mould as their father, but Pakistan would be well served if they can bat half as well as he did. Javed has contributed significantly to Pakistan's rising Test status; between them Javed and Imran Khan led Pakistan to 28 out of their first 50 Test victories. Javed was a shrewd tactician, whose batting was not affected by the extra pressures of the leadership, maintaining a batting average of over fifty throughout his Test career as both captain and player - a fair indication that he is amongst the very best batsmen in the history of the game.

A shrewd tactician, Javed places the field

Career Details

Born: Karachi, 12 June 1957
Role: right-hand, middle-order batsman, right-hand leg-break bowler, occasional wicket-keeper
Clubs: Karachi (1973/4-1975/6), Sind (1973/4-1975/ 6), Sussex (1976-1979), Habib Bank (1976/7-1993/4) and Glamorgan (1980-5)
First-class record: (1973-96) 28,248 runs (53.90) including 80 centuries, 191 wickets (33.48) and 337 catches, 3 stumpings
Tests: 124
Test Debut: v New Zealand, Lahore, 1976/7
Test record: 8,832 runs (52.27), including 23 centuries and 43 fifties, 17 wickets (40.11), 93 catches and 1 stumping
Best Performances: HS 280 not out v India, Hyderabad, 1982/3
Tours: Australia; 1976/7, 1978/79, 1981/2, 1983/4, 1983/4 (WSC), 1986/7 (Perth Challenge), 1989/90, 1992/3 (WSC)
Westindies; 1976/7, 1987/8, 1992/3
New Zealand; 1978/9, 1984/5, 1988/9, 1992/3
England; 1978, 1982, 1987, 1992
India; 1979/80, 1983/4, 1986/7, 1989/90 (Nehru Cup)
Sri Lanka; 1985/6
Overseas Tests; 64
One-day Internationals; 233
World Cups: 1975, 1979, 1983, 1987/8, 1991/2, 1995/6
Sharjah; 1983/4, 1984/5, 1985/6, 1986/7, 1988/9, 1989/90, 1991/2, 1992/3, 1993/4
South Africa; 1992/3 (and Zimbabwe)
Rest of the World: England; 1987, 1991

Hanif Mohammad

Hanif Mohammad was one of the cornerstones on which Pakistan's early Test cricket was built, playing in 55 out of Pakistan's first 57 Tests. He was the most celebrated of the five Mohammad brothers who were to become cricket's most famous family, even eclipsing the Graces. He was a cricketing legend long before he retired from the game, posting record scores and playing many an epic innings. Hanif could play all the shots, but unselfishly denied himself for the sake of the team, dutifully bound to concentrate on defence. He had the same passion for scoring runs, same quickness of movement and eye as Don Bradman, but his country demanded a different approach. He might have become even greater than the player he was, given a freer rein, for his concentration and technique were flawless.

He was born in Junagadh in India in December 1934 where he learned the basics of his game, batting under an electric light on the concrete terrace in front of the family home, first against a tennis ball (shaven to make it swing), then against a cork ball, which would rise fast and steeply. This sharpened Hanif's reactions much in the same way as Bradman had developed his eye-hand co-ordination by hitting a golf ball with a stump against a corrugated fence in his back yard. Hanif's childhood, though, was disrupted by Partition in 1947 and by the death of his father the following year when he was only 13, but he always had perseverance.

Hanif made his first-class debut for Karachi against the Punjab in 1951/2 - after making 305 in a school match for Sind Madarasa School - and got 93 not out. His remarkable efforts against an MCC side that year helped Pakistan's cause in being accepted into the Imperial Cricket Conference, and thus being given full Test status. His innings of 64 set Pakistan on their way to a four wicket win in the 2nd "unofficial" Test at Karachi to confirm that they were ready. He was sent to England for coaching with Alf Gover at his west London cricket school in 1952, to prepare him for Test cricket.

That winter, at the age of 17 and 300 days, played in Pakistan's inaugural Test match against India, opening in the first innings and top-scoring as he made Pakistan's first Test fifty. He also kept wicket in the first three Tests of the five match series with mixed results, before passing over the gloves to Imtiaz Ahmed.

He finished that first series with 287 runs at 35.87, with a top score of 96, made in the third Test at Bombay during which, according to *Wisden*, "he

demonstrated during six hours at the wicket that he possessed the temperament for the big occasion." His skill aroused much interest; he made 917 runs at an average of 65.5 on tour including a hundred in each innings in the opening match against North Zone and 203 against the Bombay Cricket Association, one of only four players to make a double-hundred before their 18th birthday. Another hundred in a charity match took him past 1,000 runs in India.

Hanif did not make a big score in the Tests on the tour to England in 1954, though on difficult pitches in the rain-ruined matches at Lord's and Old Trafford, he top-scored with 20 out of 87, and 32 out of 90 respectively, batting a long time in each, and made 51 at Trent Bridge in between. He topped the series averages for Pakistan albeit with a figure of only 22.65. However, in the other first-class matches he was much more prolific, scoring 1,623 runs in all.

In a dour slow-scoring home series with India, Hanif was in his element. Already the determination not to lose against India at any cost had been established, and the series yielded barely two runs an over. Hanif marked his first Test at Bahawalpur, for whom he played the previous year, with an innings of 142 made in 468 minutes compiled during over 150 overs at the crease, the first of many "thou shall not pass" innings in Tests. At the end of the season the Mohammad brothers dominated the Quaid-e-Azam trophy. Hanif scored 230 not out and Raees 118 not out against Sind; Hanif made 84, Raees 96 and Wazir 120 not out against Railways but the family surpassed itself in the final against Services when each of them scored a hundred to secure Karachi the trophy.

The next season (1955/6), in the third Test v New Zealand, Hanif made a technically excellent hundred on a wet coir-matting pitch at Dacca on which no one else in the match managed fifty.

In Westindies in 1957/8, came Hanif's most famous piece of resistance. In the first Test at Bridgetown, after Westindies had amassed 579 for 9 declared, Pakistan collapsed for just 106 all out against the pace of Roy Gilchrist. Hanif had 2nd top-scored with just 17, and Pakistan were going to have to score 473 just to make Westindies bat again when he and Imtiaz Ahmed started the second innings an hour before tea on the third day. The openers put on 152, Ahmed falling just before the close, at 161 for 1, of which Hanif had made 61.

He batted throughout the fourth day, adding exactly a hundred to his own score and putting on 112 with Alimuddin for the second wicket, to take his side to 339 for 2 at the close. He took his partnership with Saeed Ahmed to 154 on the fifth day, seeing Pakistan past 400, and uniquely, added a fourth consecutive hundred partnership, as he and his oldest brother, Wazir, took Pakistan through to the close taken at 525 for 3, a lead of just 42, with Hanif 270 not out, and on into the sixth and final day.

Abdul Hafeez Kardar, the captain, used to go and listen to the news from home on the radio in Hanif's room while he and Wazir were out, leaving before they had returned from seeing friends. At the end of the fourth day he left a note on the mirror in their room, which simply read, "You're doing fine, you can save us." Then, after another day of staunch resistance, the message read "If you play till tea-time tomorrow the match will be saved." He duly obliged and it was not until shortly after tea, as Hanif tried to steer a single wide of slip off Dennis Atkinson, that he was finally dismissed for 337, edging the ball to the wicket-keeper Gerry Alexander.

It ended the longest-ever first-class innings, which had lasted 970 minutes (16 hours and 10 mins), and included 32 fours, all of which were struck along the ground. Hanif reflected: "I didn't hit one lofted shot - no question of it given our position". Totally drained after his marathon innings, the harsh glare of the sun reflecting off the pitch caused him to shed three layers of skin from under his eyes.

It was on this innings that his reputation was built, already regarded as "the Little Master" at home, it became a universal sobriquet. His own supreme achievement was somewhat eclipsed by Garry Sobers in the rest of the series, who made 365 not out in the third Test at Kingston and followed that with 125 and 109 not out in the fouth at Georgetown, but it was a remarkable effort of concentration, stamina, and courage. Hanif finished with a record aggregate for Pakistan-Westindies series, of 628 runs at an average of just under 70, and shared in eight partnerships of a hundred or more during the rubber.

The following winter, 1958/9, he recorded another famous score when he made 499 for Karachi against Bahawalpur in the semi-final of the Quaid-e-Azam Trophy, batting for 635 minutes and hitting 64 boundaries in a relatively sprightly innings; three years earlier he had taken virtually as long to score 142 against the MCC. It remained, for 36 years, the highest ever first-class score,

superseding the 452 not out Don Bradman scored for New South Wales against Queensland in 1929. However, just as he had done the "impossible" and beaten Bradman, Brian Lara became the first player to pass 500, making 501 not out for Warwickshire against Durham in June 1994.

Hanif made 25 not out in the 40 minutes before the close on the first day, added 230 more in five hours on the next, and was just approaching that elusive, magical 500 towards the end of the third. There is a story behind his dismissal too; with time running out at the end of the day he was run out, trying to keep the strike. He told Rob Steen of *The Independent,* "It was all because of the scoreboard, one of those manual types where the numbers had to be hooked on. It had me on 496 with two balls left on the final day, so when I drove the penultimate ball and extra-cover misfielded, I turned for a second to keep the strike even though the fielder was about to throw. In the end I was two yards out. As I walked back I thought run out, 'so what', but when I saw the boys put 499 against my name I became disturbed. If I'd known my score was 498 instead of 496 I might not have run at all. Still I think God wanted me to make 499." There is a certain irony in that if only he had been a little more patient...! His brother Wazir, the Karachi captain was there to console him, though most players would be happy to get that many runs in a month.

It had made 500 seem the ultimate, impossible score - until Mr Lara changed all that - just as averaging a hundred in Tests suggests perfection. Bradman, too, fell just short of achieving the latter record, but both names will be immortal. Hanif was not sad to pass the mantle as the world's highest scorer to Lara, the Trinidadian left-hander he so admires, saying "I broke the record of Don Bradman after so many years, so records are meant to be broken. I am very pleased at Lara's performance and wish him luck in the future. It is a magnificent achievement to score 501 in first-class cricket. I knew he was capable of it because he broke the world record in Test cricket. I've been watching him for the last three years and he's a magnificent cricketer."

Hanif, who stood 5 ft 5 tall and weighed only 9st in his playing days, also revealed the secret of Lara's success. "It's all in the height. He is very short and many other short Test players have scored lots of runs." The man known as "the Little Master" should know, of course, while their height may have been a help, each of them has impeccable technique, timing and temperament.

Later that season, Hanif made another hundred in the 1st Test of the Westindies' tour of Pakistan, but he injured his knee in the second innings and missed the rest of the series, the only two Tests he missed in his career, though his absence made room for another brother, Mustaq, to join Wazir in the side.

Hanif averaged over sixty against the Australians in 1959/60, including a hundred batting at No 4 in the third Test at Karachi, which was watched in part by Dwight D Eisenhower, the President of the USA, who attended the fourth day. Unfortunately it was one of the slowest day's in Test history, with Pakistan making only 104 for the loss of five wickets.

In his next Test innings, a year later, he made 160 against India at Bombay, sharing a record stand of 246 for the 2nd wicket with Saeed Ahmed, with whom he so often batted well. In another slow-scoring series, Hanif finished with 410 runs at 51.25.

In the 1961/2 season, he scored 1,250 runs (at 59.52), including a hundred in each innings in the 2nd Test against England at Dacca, when he batted for 893 minutes in the match - only Javed Miandad has also scored a hundred in both innings for Pakistan - and Hanif followed it with 67 and 89 in the third at Karachi. It was a surprise then that he had a poor series in England that summer. He was troubled by his old knee injury, was moved around in the order, batting as low as six, and he made just 177 runs in the five Tests without a fifty as Pakistan were well beaten.

It was the one blemish in an otherwise most consistent career, and if his batting needed to regain its resolve, that certainly came with the captaincy. Now permanently in the middle-order, his batting, if anything, became more defensive, something that was mirrored in his leadership. However, once again it must be said that his approach reflected a need in the team, which was rebuilding at that time with young strokemakers such as Mustaq, Asif Iqbal and Majid Khan. Pakistan were underdogs in the sixties and he was not going to give his opponents any easy opportunities. He played each Test, each innings with great pride and patriotism.

He took over the captaincy for the 1964/5 season and in his second match in charge, against Australia at Melbourne, he top-scored in both innings, making 104 and 93, and because Abdul Kadir was injured while batting, he kept wicket throughout the match as well - a commendable feat of concentration and stamina. When the team continued on to New Zealand for a three-match series, which was drawn 0-0, he made a not out hundred in the final Test at Christchurch.

Hanif led the side to a 2-0 win in New Zealand's return tour that followed six weeks later. In Pakistan's first home series for nearly three-and-a-half years, he made his highest Test score at home, rescuing the side from 62 for 4 with a marvellous double-hundred on a tricky, rain-affected wicket at Lahore in the 2nd Test. He shared a partnership of 217 with Majid Khan for the sixth-wicket, his country's highest stand for that wicket in Tests. He batted for 445 minutes and hit 33 fours in his 203 not out, exactly the same score that his son, Shoaib, was to make against India on the same ground 24 years later, a unique father and son achievement.

More than two years elapsed until Pakistan's next series, in England in 1967. Hanif put behind him his poor form on the previous tour, making more runs in the first innings of the series than he did in the entire five Tests in 1962. His innings at Lord's of 187 not out was another defensive masterpiece, made from 556 balls in nine hours and two minutes, with 21 fours. He came to the crease at 4.40pm on the Friday of the Test, and remained unbeaten through to the end of the Pakistan innings at 3.24pm on the following Monday. During that time, he added 130 for the 8th wicket with Asif Iqbal - a record for all Tests for Pakistan and finished with 55 per cent of the total, a rare occurrence. In the 2nd innings Hanif's reluctance to take risks became evident. Set 257 in 210 minutes (or about 70 overs), Pakistan crawled to only 88 for 3 from 62 overs to settle for a draw. It was their best chance of the series, for the last two Tests were lost by wide margins, ending an unbeaten sequence of nine Tests since Hanif took over. He was replaced in controversial circumstances by Saeed Ahmed for the next series at home to England 1968/9.

Although Hanif stayed in the side, he had a poor series, batting as low as No 7, in a rubber that was frequently interrupted by crowd disturbances. He was to play just one more Test, later that year against New Zealand, where he had the pleasure of returning to the top of the order to open the batting with his youngest brother Sadiq, while Mustaq batted at No 4.

By now Hanif was struggling for fitness. All that batting had taken its toll on his slight frame. In the latter part of his career, he had been hindered by a leg injury and recurrent sties around his eyes - a legacy of that innings in Barbados. It was an unfortunate demise for such a great cricketer, whose boyish looks belied a fierce determination. His captaincy has been criticised for its caution and in the end this irked the Board, while he was also too soft on his team-mates. He would rather relax listening to his beloved sitar music than admonish his players. His shrewd cricket brain was not put to best effect. However, his captaincy record is reasonable considering that the side was probably at its weakest under him, winning two, losing two, and drawing seven. As a batsman he redoubled his resolve, averaging 58.73 when captain compared with 41 as a player. Only Bradman, of those who have captained in more than five Tests, averages

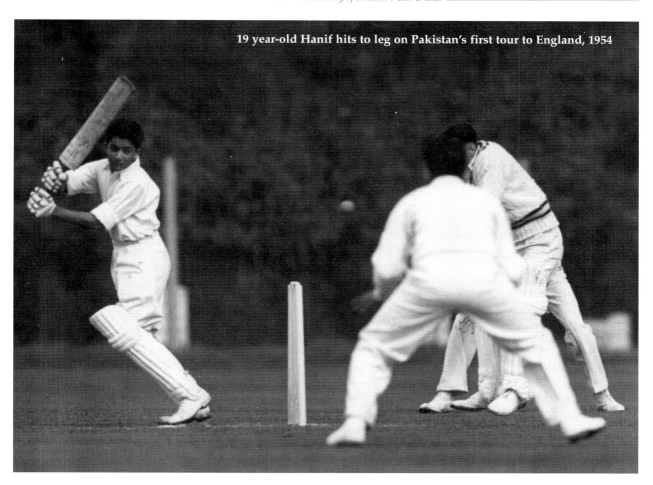

19 year-old Hanif hits to leg on Pakistan's first tour to England, 1954

more. The run-scoring of each is legendary in very different ways. Hanif chose the defensive, dictated by circumstance, for he had all the shots. In one Test, for instance he twice hooked Brian Statham for six, when the England pacer tried to bounce the Little Master. Hanif considered his concentration to be his favourite stroke, and used to pray to keep going when he was batting. He became immune to the slow handclap, though his modest nature prevented him from dwelling on the applause much either. Ian Wooldridge once wrote of him, "The total hours that he has been barracked or slow handclapped around the world may come close to constituting another kind of record."

Since his retirement he has been chairman of selectors, though the selection of his son for the tour to Australia in 1983/4 caused cries of nepotism, and eventually Shoaib had to be left out, while his absence from recent Test sides in the nineties has left Hanif distressed. Shoaib is another stonewaller in Hanif's mould who, surprisingly is just above his father in the Coopers and Lybrand all-time ratings. However Shoaib would never claim to be the better player or Pakistan's best batsman of his generation as Hanif clearly was in the 1950s and 1960s, scoring 12 of his country's

first 32 Test hundreds.

Now past 60, Hanif has recovered from an intestinal operation in 1992 and is back to full health. He continues to edit *Cricket Herald* in Lahore, though has retired from his job as a sports manager for Pakistan International Airlines.

Career Details

Born: Junagadh (India), 21 December 1934
Role: right-hand, opening or middle-order batsman, occasional wicket-keeper
Clubs: Bahawalpur (1953/4), Karachi (1954/5-1968/9) and PIA (1960/1-1975/6)
First-class record: (1951-76) 17,059 runs (52.32) including 55 centuries (HS 499), 53 wickets (28.58), 177 catches and 12 stumpings
Tests: 55
Test Debut: v India, Delhi, 1952/3
Test record: 3,915 runs (43.98) including 12 centuries, 1 wicket for 95 and 40 catches
Best Performances: HS 337, v Westindies, Bridgetown, 1957-8
Tours: India; 1952/3; 1960/1
England; 1954, 1962, 1967
Westindies; 1957/8
Australia; 1964/5
New Zealand; 1964/5
Overseas Tests: 31
Rest of the World; to England 1965, 1966, 1968

Khan Mohammad

Khan Mohammad, in conjunction with Fazal Mahmood and Mahmood Hussain, gave Pakistan a highly creditable trio of seam bowlers who contributed greatly to the young country's early success in the 1950s and helped give it recognition as a Test playing nation. Khan established a record as the quickest to take 50 wickets for Pakistan, just 11 Tests, which stood until the end of 1990 when Waqar Younis eclipsed him.

Born in Lahore on New Year's Day, 1928, he was the son of a timber merchant, Jan Mohammad. Khan and his three brothers, none of whom played much cricket, grew up in troubled times with the Second World War and Partition forming the back drop to their school days. He learned the game at Central Model High School in Lahore alongside another future Test player, Shuja-ud-Din, and with Friends Cricket Club. Khan made his first-class debut for Northern India in 1946/7, playing three matches. After Partition. While studying at Islamia College - a breeding ground for Test cricketers - he played for Punjab University for the next two haphazard seasons, was made 12th man for the unofficial Test against the Westindies in November 1948, but toured Ceylon with a Pakistan representative side later that season. He was very impressive, taking 14 wickets in the two unofficial Tests to top the tour averages.

The newly formed Board of Control for Cricket in Pakistan, recognising his talent, sent him, along with Imtiaz Ahmed and R N Dinshaw, for coaching at Alf Gover's cricket school in London, where his game showed a marked improvement under the guidance of the former England fast bowler. He developed his bowling skills playing in the Lancashire Leagues and he played for the Commonwealth side in England in 1950 and 1951. That year he also played one game for Somerset, against the touring South Africans, and had intended to spend the next three years in England in order to qualify to play county cricket, but those plans were shelved in order to play for Pakistan, when they were elected into the Test playing fraternity.

His bowling in the unofficial Tests against the MCC, 1951/2, advanced Pakistan's cause towards full Test status. He took 5-84 in the first innings of the game at Lahore; *Wisden* reported that "he made the ball fly and attacked the stumps throughout and gave the batsmen an uncomfortable time, especially against the occasional bouncer." Then in the second innings at Karachi he cleaned up the tail to finish with five for 88, to add to his three for 45 in the first innings, and help Pakistan towards a most important victory.

He was an automatic choice in the very first Test team and has the distinction of delivering Pakistan's first ball in Test cricket when he ran in at the Feroz Shah Kotla ground to bowl at India's Vinoo Mankad in October 1952. He also took the new nation's first wicket when he clean bowled Pankaj Roy (see page 6) and followed that shortly after with the wicket of Mankad in a fine opening spell. Unfortunately he was lost to injury - the consistent bane of his career - and did not play again in the series, though stayed with the squad just in case his groin injury healed.

Because of his commitments to Lowerhouse in the Lancashire League, he could not play a full part on the Pakistan tour to England in 1954 but was drafted in for five first-class games. His experience of English conditions was immediately evident. After Pakistan had been shot out for 87 in the first Test at Lord's, Khan and Fazal responded magnificently bowling unchanged throughout until England declared at 117 for 9. Khan bowled Len Hutton, the England captain, for nought first ball with a perfect yorker and proceeded to hit the stumps of Peter May, Bill Edrich, Godfrey Evans and Trevor Bailey - a testimony to his accuracy. He finished with five for 61 in 15 overs, which prompted his club to give him a £200 pay rise. He played in the next Test at Trent Bridge, where he again bowled May, before he had scored, but was unavailable for the last two Tests because of a recurrence of his groin injury and a pay dispute with the Pakistan Board.

He had an excellent home series (Pakistan's first) against India 1954/5 and despite missing the 3rd Test through injury, he finished with the most wickets on either side. His 22 wickets at an average of 15.86 remained the most by a Pakistani in any series until 1976/7 when Imran Khan took 25 wickets in five Tests against the Westindies.

In the first Test at Dacca he took four for 42 from 26.5 overs in the first innings, again bowling all his victims. Then, on his home ground at Bahawalpur, the club he captained, he took five for 74 and two for 50, and completed a most consistent series with four for 79 at Peshawar and five for 73 at Karachi. Among them Mahmood Hussain, Fazal Mahmood and Khan shared 51 of the 58 wickets to fall.

In Pakistan the following season, 1955/6, he produced his finest Test performance. New Zealand had struggled to get him away all series but in the third Test, in humid conditions and on a wet, coir matting pitch laid on grass, he was virtually unplayable. He took six for 21 in 16.2 overs as New Zealand were rolled over for just 70. The Dacca weather had prevented play on the first two days so, with New Zealand 69 for 6 in their second innings, Pakistan ran out of time. Khan had strangled their scoring with figures of 30-19-20-2 which took him to 13 wickets at 16 apiece in Pakistan's first series win.

In the new year he bowled superbly at the touring MCC side. In the second Test at Dacca he took 7-84 and 5-55 to spur Pakistan to an innings victory and in the next game at Peshawar took 5-65, again prompting a win.

In the one-off Test against Australia, as they travelled home after Ashes defeat in England in the summer of 1956, Khan and Fazal Mahmood again combined superbly rendering the tourists virtually strokeless on the matting wicket at Karachi. They bowled through unchanged to dismiss Australia for 80, Khan finishing with four for 43, and in the second innings they again shared all the wickets, Khan supporting Fazal's match-winning effort with three for 69 from over 40 overs. In the process he bowled Keith Miller to take his 50th wicket in only his 11th Test.

He found the going a lot tougher in the Caribbean where he was also hampered by injuries. He did not play until the third Test at Kingston and probably wished he hadn't played there. Mahmood Hussain broke down in the first over and Fazal and Khan had to do the bulk of the bowling, without quite the success of their previous combination. With Garry Sobers compiling his famous 365, then the highest-ever Test score, they conceded the fourth and third most runs in an innings; Khan bowled 54 unrewarded overs for 259, while Fazal sent down 85.2 overs for his two wickets for 247.

Understandably Khan was not fit for the next Test but returned at Port of Spain for what proved to be his final Test match. He had the satisfaction of making his highest Test score in his last Test innings, 26 not out, and helping Pakistan to an innings victory. His eyesight was never very good and later in life he wore distinctive square-framed glasses which were rather on the thick side!

He continued to play first-class cricket in Pakistan until 1961 and played in the Lancashire Leagues for sometime after, and then as a professional in Canada. He remained involved in cricket and took up several coaching assignments in Pakistan, England and Canada. Recently elected an honorary member of the MCC in 1994, he was one of the first coaches at the MCC's indoor school at Lord's, where the author had the pleasure of his guidance.

Khan Mohammad had a short but sweet international career, which was marred only by injury, and so later instilled in his pupils the need for physical fitness. He could bowl at a lively pace, swung the ball and had a very healthy strike-rate, taking a wicket every 58 balls. Indeed he was perhaps the founding father of the swing bowling tradition in Pakistan. His achievements have stood the Test of time; it was 20 years before Imran Khan broke his wicket tally for a series, and over thirty before Waqar Younis took one Test fewer to reach 50 wickets. Of the bowlers who have reached that landmark for Pakistan, only Imran Khan and Waqar Younis have a better average than Khan Mohammad. But for those wearisome days at Kingston he would have pipped them both with an average of under 20.

He bowled full and straight - a particular necessity in those days as the standard of fielding was poor - as Akram and Younis now do, and like his protégés, consequently had a very high percentage of his victims bowled or lbw, 52 per cent, which is amongst the top 20 in Test cricket (nine of his other victims were caught by the wicket-keeper Imtiaz Ahmed).

Khan has served Pakistan as wholeheartedly as a coach as he did as a player in the country's formative years, taking young fast bowlers under his wing. He gave a lot of help and encouragement to Akram in his early days and made some important modifications to the left-arm pace bowler's action, in particular getting him to throw his front arm higher.

Since the early seventies, he has run a travel agency in Ealing, West London, named "Kayem".

Career Details

Born: Lahore (India), 1 January 1928
Role: right-hand, lower-order batsman, right-hand fast medium bowler
Clubs: Northern India (1946/7), Punjab University (1947/8-1948/9), Somerset (1951), Bahawalpur (1953/4), Karachi (1956/7), Lahore (1960/1) and Lancashire League
First-class record: (1946/7-1960/1) 524 runs (11.39) HS 93, 212 wickets (23.29) and 20 catches
Tests: 13
Test Debut: v India, Delhi, 1952/3
Test record: 100 runs (10.00), 54 wickets (23.92) and 4 catches
Best Performances: HS 26 not out v Westindies, Port- of-Spain, 1957/8
BB 6-21 v New Zealand, Dacca, 1955/6
Tours: India; 1952/3, 1954/5
England; 1954
Westindies; 1957/8
Ceylon; 1948/9

Mustaq Mohammad

Mustaq Mohammad was the third of the four famous Mohammad brothers to play Test cricket, was the youngest to do so and proved to be the most talented all-round cricketer amongst them. He represented Pakistan from the late fifties to the late seventies and had he retired just one series later he would have had the distinction of playing Test cricket in four different decades.

His Test batting figures are very similar to those of Hanif though Mustaq was much more inclined to go for his strokes. With all his inherent qualities of timing, technique and temperament he was a powerful, attacking batsman, ready to cut and hook the quicker bowlers, but with the ability to play long defensive innings too. Like his brothers, he was short and stocky and gave the bat a characteristic twirl before settling in his stance. He could hit the ball with great power, but also played with finesse, developing the now popular reverse-sweep. He was perhaps the most aggressively competitive member of his family, belying his jocular, chirpy nature, but indicative too of the team's more ambitious outlook on the cricket field in the seventies as well as the way Pakistan's national identity was changing off it.

Mustaq was the only one of the five Mohammad brothers to develop fully his bowling skills, and could have played in most sides on the strength of his leg-spin and googly bowling alone. Indeed, his best retrospective Coopers and Lybrand rating listed his batting 11th and his bowling 10th in the all-time lists for Pakistan. As captain - in 19 Tests - he lead the side to a number of notable firsts, and managed to develop the team's potential during the most intensive and divisive period in Pakistan's Test cricket history.

He has managed and coached the national side on various occasions since his retirement, and looks set to be intrinsically involved in Pakistan's cricket for the near future. After a short-lived tenure at the start of the 1995/6 season, which might have seen Mustaq turning his back on the game in his country after being replaced, he was re-appointed as full-time coach to the senior side when Majid Khan became the Pakistan Cricket Board's new Chief Executive.

Mustaq was born in Junagadh, Gujarat in India, in November 1943 and although his documents were lost in the family's move at Partition, he was regarded as the youngest player at 13 years and 41 days to play first-class cricket (since beaten). Despite his exceptional youth, he started by scoring 86 and taking five for 28 on his debut for Karachi Whites against Hyderabad in 1956/7 and just over two years later he became the youngest ever Test player at 15 years and 124 days. This early introduction was the beginning of an international career that lasted over 20 years.

That debut appearance was in the last Test of the series with Westindies in 1958/9 at Lahore; he batted at eight - one after his brother Wazir - and bowled a few leg-breaks without much success. His first innings ended when he became the first victim of a Wes Hall hat-trick, lbw for 14, and he did not return to the side until the away series against India in 1960/1, which proved to be the last between the two countries until 1978/9, when Mustaq was captain. Useful knocks of 61 and 41 not out in the third and fourth Tests respectively were the prelude to Mustaq becoming the youngest player to make a Test hundred, at the age of 17 years and 82 days, by scoring 101 in the final Test at Delhi, where he batted for over five hours to rescue Pakistan from a precarious position.

He had a good look at England's bowlers when they toured Pakistan in 1961/2, making 76 in the first Test and averaging 31 in the series, and had his best domestic season for Karachi, with over a thousand runs at an average in the sixties, including 229 not out against East Pakistan two days after his 18th birthday.

On the 1962 tour to England he was the outstanding batsman; he scored over 1,600 runs at 41.4, and topped both the Test and tour averages. After showing some fine form against the counties he was promoted to number three in the order for the fourth Test at Trent Bridge and responded by top-scoring in each innings with 55 and 100 not out, thus becoming the first player to have scored a second Test hundred before his 19th birthday, to help secure Pakistan's only draw of the series. He made 43 and 72 in the next Test, at the Oval, and *Wisden* named him as one of its Five Cricketers of the Year, five years before his older brother, Hanif. Indeed with Hanif out of form in the Tests for one of the only times in his career, Mustaq had taken up the family mantle in style.

Mustaq toured England again the following year with the Pakistani Eaglets and was again in fine touch, averaging 53.9 with the bat and 16.0 with the ball. Against Northamptonshire, he made a hundred which so impressed his opponents that they signed him up for the following season, and in 1964 he started a 14-season association with the county.

Mustaq missed the sequence of Tests in 1964/5 season (Pakistan's only matches between 1962 and 1967) and so he had gone five years without Test cricket when he returned to the side to play against England in 1967, though he appeared in only one of the tourists' matches outside the Tests, because of his commitments to Northants. Although he had scored heavily playing in various Commonwealth and Rest of the World matches during his absence from Test cricket, he was below par with the bat in this rubber. However he took his first Test wickets in this series, topping the bowling averages with nine wickets at just over 17 runs each.

Hanif had given up the captaincy for the riot-hit series at home against England in 1968/9, during which little meaningful cricket was played and the following year he made his final Test match appearance, against New Zealand. Alongside him were both Mustaq and Sadiq, so emulating the Graces and the Hearnes as the only other families to have had three brothers playing in the same match. With Hanif playing in his last Test and Sadiq playing in his first, each was given the opportunity to bowl a couple of overs as the game drew to a close. As Mustaq had also bowled it provided a unique instance of three brothers bowling in a Test. Hanif stood down after that match, and though Mustaq missed the final Test through injury, Sadiq's presence in the side ensured the continuing sequence of Pakistani Test teams containing at least one of the Mohammad brothers. It was to stretch to 100 out of the first 101 Tests.

In the early seventies Mustaq was at his peak. He represented the World XI in two matches against England in 1970, and for Pakistan he scored centuries all around the world, for which he was rewarded with the captaincy in 1976/7.

His succession of hundreds started at Edgbaston, in 1971, where he shared in a record partnership for the second wicket with Zaheer Abbas, making exactly 100 out of their stand of 291, as Pakistan amassed 608 for 7 declared. Again Mustaq played in only three matches outside the Tests because of the prior claims of Northants for whom, the next year, he had his most prolific season with his county, scoring 1,949 runs at an average of 59.06.

He maintained that sort of form through the winter when he played in three Test rubbers, scoring 885 runs at an average of 68. He made a fine hundred at Sydney, which should have been enough to set up Pakistan's first Test win against Australia, but for a batting collapse in the second

innings. After missing the first Test against New Zealand because of injury, he made a dazzling double hundred at Dunedin. He batted for only 383 minutes hitting twenty boundaries all round the ground. Mustaq spent 165 minutes playing himself in over his first fifty, but the subsequent fifties took 100, 64 and 70 minutes respectively. He shared in a spectacular partnership of 350 with Asif Iqbal, put together in just over four-and-a-half hours, to set a fourth wicket record for Pakistan in all Tests. The New Zealand attack had no answer; the last 150 came in just 74 minutes in one of the finest and fastest batting displays in Test history. Then in tandem with Intikhab Alam he bowled Pakistan to an innings victory, taking 5-49, and for the first time he made an impression on the top order. It remains only the second occasion when a player has scored a double hundred and taken five wickets in a Test, following D St E Atkinson for the Westindies in 1954/5. Mustaq scored two more fifties in the final Test to help ensure Pakistan's first series win overseas.

At home against England his purple patch continued, starting the series with 66 and five wickets in the match at Lahore. Then at Hyderabad he made his highest Test score in Pakistan, a masterful innings of 157, where he was involved in another record stand, 145 with Intikhab Alam, Pakistan's highest for the 6th wicket v England. He was one of three batsmen to be out for 99 in the next Test at Karachi, run out trying to complete his hundred, and shared a partnership of 221 for the third wicket with Majid Khan (who also made 99). He finished top of both the batting (327 runs at 81.75) and bowling averages (12 wickets at 24.58) for the series - confirmation of his all-round ability.

His experience of English conditions shone through on the next tour there in 1974. On a drying wicket at Lord's in the second Test, with Derek Underwood bowling in his element, he made a defiant 76 adding 115 with Wasim Raja for the 4th wicket to secure a draw in the match. Then at the Oval he again made 76, putting on 172 in only 202 minutes with Zaheer Abbas, which was then the highest third wicket partnership for Pakistan. Strangely, by the end of the tour he had played more Tests in England than he had in Pakistan, and for the next two seasons he played most of his cricket in England, though in the short, two Test series that winter (1974/5) he scored his fifth Test hundred in ten Tests, making 123 against the Westindies at Lahore, which is still the equal highest Test score against them in Pakistan.

He made a fine fifty in Pakistan's narrow defeat against the same opponents that put them out of the 1975 World Cup, and he had a successful season at Northants afterwards, being the acting captain for the last month of the season. In 1976 he

Mushtaq had all the strokes

took over officially and led them to their best ever season, coming 2nd in the championship, and lifting the county's first major trophy, the Gillette Cup. "Mush" raised his game too, averaging over fifty with the bat, and 27 with the ball.

However a rift developed the following season mainly because Mustaq, who had joined Packer, was not given any guarantees about his future with the club. Also the left-arm spinner Bishan Bedi, India's captain, had been accused of throwing the occasional ball, which riled both Bedi and Mustaq, and Bedi was told he would not be retained for the following season. Mustaq resigned the captaincy a month before the end of the season when his contract had not been clarified. The chairman of the club, Hugh Wright, criticised him for a lack of leadership, even though the team remained behind him, but did at least pay tribute to his batting prowess. It was an unfitting end to his long association with the club, for whom he had scored nearly 16,000 runs and taken 551 wickets in 262 first-class matches.

Disputes were also rife in Pakistani cricket at that time. Mustaq had taken over the captaincy for New Zealand's visit at the end of 1976 but immediately after that series several senior players became involved in a pay and conditions strike with the Board of Control for Cricket in Pakistan, a precursor to some of them joining World Series Cricket. It seemed that he might lose the captaincy, which had been offered by A H Kardar to Intikhab Alam, who had been trying to stay out of the dispute. When Kardar backed down, Mustaq was reinstated and it was he who led the side to Australia and Westindies.

Mustaq started his tenure as captain convincingly against New Zealand, winning the toss in each Test and taking the series 2-0. He made 101 in the 2nd Test at Hyderabad where Sadiq also made a hundred, thus they became only the second pair of brothers after Ian and Greg Chappell to do so in the same innings. Mustaq followed this with 107 and 67 not out in the third Test at Karachi where in the first innings he put on 252 for the fifth wicket with Javed Miandad, who was playing in his first Test series.

Mustaq's sequence of hundreds in seven consecutive series ended in Australia where he was desperately out of form, making only 77 runs in the three matches, but otherwise he lead the side shrewdly, forging an excellent team spirit. Pakistan played positive, attractive cricket and had a big following. Their opponents respected their ability too, passing up a risky opportunity to go for a win in the first Test. Mustaq managed to lift the side after losing the 2nd Test by 348 runs, winning at the Sydney Cricket Ground and so sharing a series in Australia for the first time. Intikhab, though, was

harshly ostracised for not joining the pay row, and Mustaq must be criticised for not burying the hatchet as soon as the matter with the Board had been settled.

In Westindies Pakistan showed their will to fight throughout the series, almost winning the first Test in Barbados, where the home side is virtually invincible. Imran Khan believes Mustaq made a big error there by taking the second new ball at the wrong moment, allowing Clive Lloyd to counter-attack, when Sarfraz Nawaz, whom Mustaq sometimes found difficult to communicate with, and Imran, were happy with the old ball. After defeat in Trinidad and a draw in Guyana, Mustaq produced a match-winning all-round performance to square the series in the 4th Test at Port of Spain. In an otherwise quiet tour for him, he scored a gutsy, resolute hundred made in over six hours - the innings he considers his finest in Test cricket - and followed it with his best Test bowling figures, five for 28. It was the second occasion on which he had scored a hundred and taken five wickets, a feat matched only by Garry Sobers at the time, though Imran Khan and Ian Botham (five times) have done so since. In the 2nd innings Mustaq added another important fifty and collected three middle-order wickets to ensure victory for his team.

By and large though Mustaq was past his peak as a batsman and, as in Australia, he had been unnerved by the pace bowlers and was unable to rally the side for the final Test in Kingston. Indeed when he was caught behind off an Andy Roberts' bouncer, he was less than relieved to hear the late call of no-ball which meant he would have to bat on.

Mustaq relinquished the captaincy the following winter because he was contracted to Kerry Packer, though he flew to Karachi with Imran and Zaheer Abbas when it seemed that they might be able to play in the 3rd Test against England. He was sorely missed on Pakistan's tour to England in 1978, where the weakened side was completely out-played. He was reinstated as captain when cricketing relations with India resumed in 1978/9 after more than 17 years. Victory in the second and third Tests, in which Mustaq made 67 and 78 respectively, broke a deadlock that had lasted for 13 matches, spread over 26 years and gave Pakistan their first series over India.

In New Zealand he returned his best match analysis, nine for 119 (4-60 & 5-59), to set up victory in the first Test at Christchurch. That was enough to secure the series, only Pakistan's second overseas to this point. Mustaq retired from Test cricket in March 1979 after an acrimonious series in Australia, where the general attitude was unsportsmanlike. Asif Iqbal had made unwise remarks about the standard of the Australian team, which lacked its Packer players, before the first Test, which left a cloud of ill-feeling over the series. Rodney Hogg was run out by Miandad as he was inspecting the wicket, and despite Mustaq's efforts to have him recalled, umpire Harvey confirmed his decision. Consequently, Sikander Bakht was run out backing up in the next Test, and the general mood in the Pakistani dressing room was of retaliation at any given opportunity, resulting in an appeal for handled the ball. Mustaq must be held partly responsible for these unsavoury events.

Pakistan won the first Test at the MCG thanks to a remarkable spell by Sarfraz Nawaz, but went into the 2nd at Perth with a defensive attitude, playing an extra batsman when Mustaq should have been pushing home the advantage against a side without many of its experienced players. There he played his hundredth - and final innings - for Pakistan, the first player to reach that landmark. Importantly, Mustaq was unable to bowl and Sikander broke down and with only three front-line bowlers in the side Pakistan lost by seven wickets.

That was only Mustaq's fourth defeat in 19 Tests in charge, and his overall record of eight wins, and only one series lost in six compares favourably with any for Pakistan. He jelled a collection of talented individuals into a powerful, competitive unit, and had the support of his team who had faith in his all-round ability. His captaincy became defensive when his own form suffered, going into the final Tests against Australia in 1976/7 and 1978/9 with ambition set only on drawing those matches, and he seemed resigned to defeat in the final Test in Westindies, where he unwisely brought into question the legitimacy of the bowling actions of Andy Roberts and Joel Garner on the eve of the match.

Mustaq Mohammad was unfortunate not to play more Tests in the sixties, when he scored eight hundreds in unofficial Tests against Commonwealth sides. He was prolific in the early seventies, where his string of hundreds helped Pakistan in an unbeaten sequence of 15 Tests. He was past his prime when asked to take on the Australian, Westindian and WSC pace attacks that he had played so bravely and convincingly in the past. This coincided with his period of captaincy, which is why his average of 33.38 is some way below his average as a player, which was just over 42, rather than an inability to take the strains of the job. His leg-spin bowling was more accurate than most, he could spin the ball prodigiously and should have bowled much more in Tests. Indeed, he is above even Abdul Qadir in the Coopers & Lybrand ratings.

Always a fine performer in county cricket he scored over a thousand runs in a season 12 times for Northants and finished with over 30,000 first-class runs - one of only nine non-English players to have made so many. His all-round achievements have, perhaps, been underestimated; for four seasons in a row (1969-1972), he was peerless in scoring more than 1,500 runs and taking at least 50 wickets in the County Championship.

He has also played Minor Counties cricket with distinction for Northumberland (1980), Staffordshire (1982-3) and Shropshire (1984-5) and helped Old Hill, from the Birmingham League, to the English National Club Championship in 1984 and 1985. When Pakistan tour England, he joins the BBC's Test Match Special commentary team as an expert summariser, where he is known affectionately as "Mushy". He is currently living in Birmingham where he is working for Pakistan International Airlines.

Career Details

Born: Junagadh, Gujarat, India, 22 November 1943
Role: right-hand, middle-order batsman, right-hand leg-break and googly bowler
Clubs: Karachi (1956/7-1967/8), PIA (1960/1-1979/80), Northamptonshire (1964-77), Northumberland (1980), Staffordshire (1982-3) and Shropshire (1984-5)
First-class record: (1956-85) 31,091 runs (42.07) including 72 centuries, 936 wickets (24.34) and 349 catches
Tests: 57
Test Debut: v West Indies, Lahore, 1958/9
Test record: 3,643 runs (39.17), 79 wickets (29.24) and 42 catches
Best Performances: HS 201 v New Zealand, Dunedin, 1972/3
BB 5-28 v Westindies, Port of Spain, 1976/7
Tours: India 1960/1
England; 1962, 1967, 1971, 1974, 1975 (World Cup)
Ceylon; 1972/3
Australia; 1972/3, 1976/7, 1978/9
New Zealand; 1972/3, 1978/9
Westindies; 1976/7
Overseas Tests; 37
One-day Internationals; 10
World Cups; 1975
Commonwealth: India; 1964/5
Rest of the World: England 1966, 1970, 1985; Barbados 1966/7

PREVIOUS PAGE: Asif Iqbal, the great improviser, plays a classical drive
ABOVE: Mudassar Nazar takes on Ian Botham. Only Mudassar and his father, Nazar Mohammad, have carried their bats for Pakistan
OPPOSITE: Sarfraz Nawaz, an early master of reverse swing, bowls to Derek Randall at Karachi

ABOVE: The classical leap that transformed Imran Khan's bowling
OPPOSITE: Javed Miandad, probably Pakistan's greatest batsman

1992 WORLD CUP ACTION
TOP: Akram collides with Chris
Harris of New Zealand as he tries
to make his ground
ABOVE: Wasim Akram with Imran
Khan sporting his cornered tigers
T-shirt, contemplate the next match
RIGHT: Inzamam-ul-Haq on his
way to 60 off only 37 balls in the
semi-final against New Zealand

ABOVE: Wasim Akram appeals against Derek Pringle in the World Cup final
LEFT: Pakistan's two elder statesmen, Imran Khan and Javed Miandad, captained in 82 Test matches between them

OPPOSITE TOP: Moin Khan and Mustaq Ahmed celebrate as Chris Harris of New Zealand is stumped
OPPOSITE BOTTOM: Substitute Wasim Haider congratulates Mustaq Ahmed on another wicket in the 1992 World Cup final

OVERLEAF: PAKISTAN'S FINEST HOUR (Main picture) Wasim Akram and Javed Miandad celebrate Pakistan's World Cup victory; (Top right) Imran Khan parades the World Cup trophy to the MCG; (Bottom right) manager Intikhab Alam joins the rejoicing players on the field

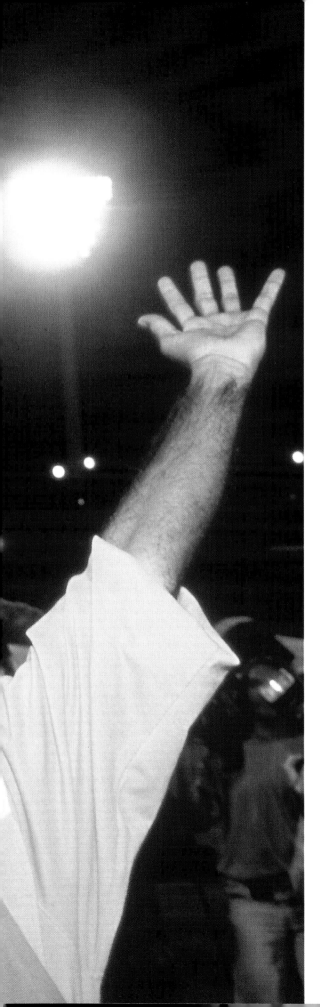

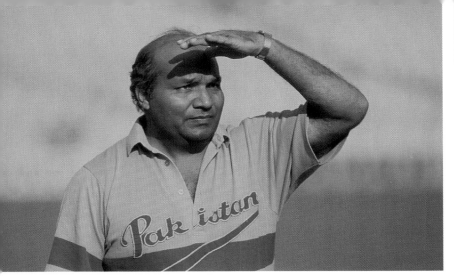

ABOVE: Aamir Sohail pulls a boundary off Devon Malcolm on his way to his double-hundred against England
TOP LEFT: Intikhab Alam, so often Pakistan's manager, has been intrinsically involved with the side since 1959/60
LEFT: Ramiz Raja has an unparalleled one-day record for Pakistan

PREVIOUS PAGE: Pakistan's devastating strike force. (Left) Wasim Akram, the most versatile bowler in the world, celebrates another wicket against England in 1992 and (Right) Waqar Younis, the youngest bowler to 200 Test wickets

Sadiq Mohammad

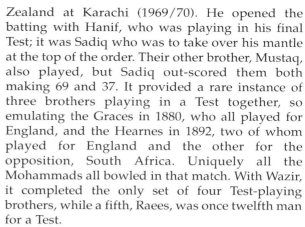

Sadiq is the youngest of the five famous Mohammad brothers whose family always had a player in the side for the first 25 years of Pakistan's Test history. A short and stocky left-handed opening batsman, Sadiq cut and hooked well and played some dazzling, wristy flicks. He was often more pugnacious than other members of his family, but also looser outside the off-stump as left-handers so often are, which perhaps delayed his entry into Test cricket and gave rise later to pronounced fluctuations in form.

Although only 24 when he first appeared for Pakistan he was still older than other members of his family on debut, and some nine years older than Mustaq had been. However he was just 14 years and nine months old when he made his initial first-class appearance in 1959/60, for Fazal Mahmood's XI, and in his early days played alongside his brothers for Karachi.

That it took him nearly ten years to establish himself after his first-class introduction was due, at least in part, to the great pressure he felt in living up to his siblings. He once said, "For a long time I was in the shadow of my famous brothers, Hanif, Mustaq and Wazir. There were, perhaps inevitably, those who were all too ready to say I was a selling plater in a family that produced thoroughbreds,"

However they did help where they could. It was

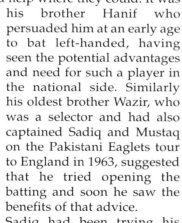

his brother Hanif who persuaded him at an early age to bat left-handed, having seen the potential advantages and need for such a player in the national side. Similarly his oldest brother Wazir, who was a selector and had also captained Sadiq and Mustaq on the Pakistani Eaglets tour to England in 1963, suggested that he tried opening the batting and soon he saw the benefits of that advice.

Sadiq had been trying his luck in the middle-order for Karachi and Pakistan International Airways but really made strides forward

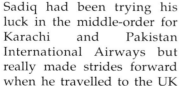

when he travelled to the UK to play for Gloucestershire IIs in 1967, and for Nelson in the Lancashire League the following year. His time in England helped him correct some minor technical flaws, such as his top-hand grip which was too far round on the bat handle.

His progress manifested itself in domestic cricket and brought a Test debut against New

Zealand at Karachi (1969/70). He opened the batting with Hanif, who was playing in his final Test; it was Sadiq who was to take over his mantle at the top of the order. Their other brother, Mustaq, also played, but Sadiq out-scored them both making 69 and 37. It provided a rare instance of three brothers playing in a Test together, so emulating the Graces in 1880, who all played for England, and the Hearnes in 1892, two of whom played for England and the other for the opposition, South Africa. Uniquely all the Mohammads all bowled in that match. With Wazir, it completed the only set of four Test-playing brothers, while a fifth, Raees, was once twelfth man for a Test.

That season in a match between Pakistan International Airlines and Karachi Blues, Hanif (187) and Mustaq (124) each got hundreds for PIA, while it was Mustaq who prevented Sadiq from reaching three figures as well for the Blues, catching him on 96. Their mother, Amir Bi, did not speak to Mustaq for days.

Sadiq, who was in England in 1970 with the Rest of the World side and also played one game for Essex against the touring Jamaicans, had performed well enough to warrant selection for the tour to England the next summer, and in the third Test almost took Pakistan to their first series win over England, making 91 out of 205 on a difficult Headingley pitch, as his side fell just 25 runs short of victory. Remembering that innings still makes the hair stand up on the back of his neck. Sadiq's performances obviously impressed Gloucester, who signed both him and Zaheer Abbas for the following season.

Sadiq's association with Gloucester was a long one, stretching until 1982, by which time he had scored over 11,000 runs for the county at an average of 35 in 193 matches. His leg-breaks, which were seldom seen in Test matches, also brought some useful wickets, especially in his early days there, including five for 37 against Kent in 1973.

For Pakistan he had had a magnificent winter in 1972/3, when he scored 884 Test runs in nine matches. He topped the Test averages on the tour to Australia, scoring 81 at Adelaide and making 137 in the second Test at the Melbourne Cricket Ground, where Hanif had made 104 and 93 the last time the two sides had played there in 1964/5. He fared even better when the team continued to New Zealand, where in the first Test at Wellington he made his highest Test score, 166, which was full of brilliant strokes, and he was again the leading run-scorer in the series, at an average of 73.20.

At home, he made a third Test hundred in as many months, against a third opponent, England, batting for over six hours at Lahore. It included some fine drives as England tried to exploit a

Sadiq - a glorious player when on song

perceived weakness on the off-stump. When he returned to Gloucestershire the following summer he was considered to be the most improved opening batsman in county cricket and was soon awarded his county cap. For the first time in 13 years he was recognised for his own ability - no longer was he introduced to people as the younger brother of Hanif or Mustaq.

However, on the tour to England in 1974, despite over a thousand runs in total, Sadiq had a poor Test series, going through without a fifty. Even so it was a surprise when he was not included in the initial squad for the home series with Westindies. Sadiq, who was playing in Tasmania, got his chance though when he was called up as a replacement for the inexperienced Agha Zahid, who was injured in the first Test and was never to play for Pakistan again. Sadiq batted heroically on his return; he had been hit while fielding at short-leg and was unable to turn his neck, but with Pakistan just three runs ahead and five wickets down in their second innings, he came in at No 7 and batted in pain for 315 minutes, making 98 not out. Wasim Raja, who had his leg in plaster after damaging ankle ligaments, had hobbled in to try and let Sadiq get the hundred he deserved.

In that game he was reunited at the top of the order with Majid Khan. In all they opened together in 14 Tests, and proved to be their country's most successful pair, scoring 1,391 runs in partnership at an average of 60.47, a rate bettered by only a handful of others. They shared four century and nine half-century partnerships in 26 innings (three of which were unbroken).

His best season for Gloucester came in 1976, when he scored 1,759 runs at an average of 47.29, with eight hundreds, including four in a row (108, 163 not out, 150, 109) towards the end of the season, helping lift his side from 16th (in 1975) to third in the championship. The following year Gloucester lost their last game of the season and with it the chance of winning their first Championship since the days of W G Grace a century before. Although Sadiq had a poor season in the three day game he had a good run in the Benson and Hedges Cup, which his side won.

In the next series, at home against New Zealand (1976/77), Sadiq and Mustaq became the second pair of brothers after Greg and Ian Chappell to score hundreds in the same Test, at Hyderabad. Sadiq had to retire half-way through his innings suffering from cramp but came back to complete his hundred. In Australia he missed the first Test after being injured in the State game against Western Australia prior to it, but he hit a fine hundred against a fiery Dennis Lillee at the MCG, as he had done in 1972/3. It was his fifth century in the previous 17 Tests, and there was no hint that his form was waning, yet he was not to score another hundred in his last 18 matches.

In the Westindies he had an indifferent time with the bat. He was forced to retire hurt before he had scored in the first innings at Port of Spain (2nd Test) after being hit on the forearm by Colin Croft but made a defiant 81 in the 2nd innings. In the next, at Georgetown, he was hit again, this time in the face, as he attempted to hook Andy Roberts, and was forced to retire, returning later. Although he again batted bravely in the second innings, making 48, he was never quite the same batsman again. Because of his predilection for the hook he was one of the first to don a helmet when they came into use the following year.

He was dropped for the final match of England's tour in 1977/8, which broke a 89-Test sequence of Pakistan sides including at least one of the Mohammad brothers (Mustaq was missing because of his World Series commitments). Still

without the Packer players on the return tour Sadiq, as the senior batsman, did his best to hold the weakened batting together. His composed 97 at Leeds was the only fifty for Pakistan in the series. When the Packer players became available again he was most unlucky to lose his place after just one match against India (1978/9), though before the first Test he had been hit again on the head by a bouncer from Karson Ghavri.

Following an excellent season in 1979 with Gloucester in which he averaged over 60, and reeled off one superb sequence of consecutive scores (which reads 78-56-156-70-171-103-100), he was recalled for the tour to India, appearing in three of the Tests. He played in one final series at home to the Westindies (1980/1) without much success and for two more seasons with Gloucester, with whom he had a profitable benefit season in 1982.

After that he carried on playing in Pakistan showing he still had some cricket left in him by making over a thousand runs for United Bank in 1982/3, and had one season of minor county cricket, with Cornwall in 1984. He has even dabbled in a spot of umpiring. Sadiq's last first-class game was in 1986 and he finished his career with over 24,000 runs, including 50 centuries. He and/or his brothers played in 106 of Pakistan's first 114 Tests, winning 173 caps among them. Sadiq's nephew Shoaib has subsequently played in 45 Tests, to extend an amazing family line.

Sadiq's own contribution was a significant one; he finished with over 2,500 Test runs including five hundreds made during a glorious period when he was at his peak in the early seventies.

Career Details

Born: Junagadh, India, 3 May 1945
Role: left-hand, opening batsman, leg-spin bowler
Clubs: Karachi (1960/1-1972/3), PIA (1961/2-1966/7), Essex (1970), Gloucestershire (1972-82), Tasmania (1974/5), United Bank (1976/7-84/5) and Cornwall (1984)
First-class record: (1959-86) 24,160 runs (37.51) including 50 centuries, HS 203; 235 wickets (31.81), BB 7/34, and 326 catches
Tests: 41 (1969/70-1980/1)
Test Debut: v New Zealand, Karachi, 1969/70
Test record: 2,579 runs (35.81) including 5 centuries, 0-98 and 28 catches
Best Performances: HS 166 v New Zealand, Wellington, 1972/3
Tours: England; 1963 (Eaglets), 1971, 1974, 1978
Australia; 1972/3, 1976/7
New Zealand; 1972/3
Westindies; 1976/7
India; 1979/80.
Overseas Tests; 25
One-day Internationals; 19
World Cups; 1975 and 1979
Rest of the World: England; 1970, 1985

Shoaib Mohammad

Shoaib Mohammad has had a career of fluctuating fortune. Although only Javed Miandad has a significantly better Test average for Pakistan, Shoaib has been in and out of the side for a decade and never completely lived up to the comparisons with his famous father, Hanif, or suggestions that nepotism was at least a contributory factor in his early Test selection. This is harsh on a man who has served his country diligently, playing within his limitations but filling a vital role for his side, to produce some very impressive performances.

The Mohammad family is perhaps the most important in Pakistan's Test history. Shoaib's uncles Wazir, Mustaq and Sadiq all played Test cricket while a fourth, Raees, was once 12th man for a Test. His cousins Shahid and Asif both played for PIA, for whom Shoaib made his debut a few days before his 16th birthday. He marked the occasion by scoring 113 against Baluchistan at Karachi, where he was born on January 8, 1961. Only Majid Khan and India's Sachin Tendulkar have been younger when they scored their maiden hundreds on first-class debut.

After that, Shoaib's progress was steady rather than spectacular, like his batting. His initial Test selection though was justifiable after two good years in domestic cricket, in which he scored over 1500 runs at an average of 51.8. His captain at PIA, Zaheer Abbas, was in charge of the national side and Shoaib was chosen for the last two Tests against India, making his debut at Jullundar in place of Mudassar Nazar. On his selection, his proud grandmother Amir Bi, who had given birth to four future Test cricketers herself, said, "I can now die happily."

Many felt that Shoaib had almost certainly jumped the queue because his father was chairman of selectors. When Imran Khan returned as captain for the tour to Australia the team had already been selected but he objected to Shoaib's inclusion, feeling he was too inexperienced.

This led to a split in the BCCP and the resignation of the selection committee. Two fractious groups developed, with the press expressing its parochial interest. The Karachi newspapers pointed out that Imran from Lahore was ousting two of "their" players, Zaheer Abbas, as captain, and Shoaib as batsman. The ramifications of this dispute clouded events on the tour to Australia, and as Imran's influence increased, this adversely affected Shoaib's immediate chances. Imran, though, had nothing personal against Shoaib, indeed described him in his book *All Round View* as "an intelligent, hard-working and gutsy cricketer" and later in Shoaib's career insisted on his inclusion.

Shoaib's cause was not helped by indifferent performances in his early Test matches, though he did return to the side on merit for the last Test against England at Lahore at the end of his most prolific domestic season (1983/4) in which he scored over a thousand runs at an average of nearly 50. He made 80 in the second innings, putting on 173 with Mohsin Khan whom he replaced three times in the next nine matches, and eventually on a permanent basis.

On one of those occasions, against New Zealand at Karachi 1984/5, he opened the batting with Mudassar Nazar. In one of those strange sporting coincidences their fathers, Nazar Mohammad and Hanif, had formed Pakistan's first opening pair in Test cricket back in 1952.

Opportunities were limited by the success of Mohsin and Mudassar but after both struggled at home against the Westindies in 1986/7 (as did Shoaib when selected for the one-dayers), he got his chance on the tour to India soon after. He scored a hundred against India's under-25 side in an opening partnership of 287 with Ramiz Raja, and he showed he had all his father's determination and temperament during his dour maiden Test hundred in the first Test at Madras, to complete a father and son set against India, and so emulated the Nazars. This still did not get him an extended run in the side as Pakistan's opener and he missed the last two Tests.

Against England the following summer he got to the crease only twice in the first three Tests, because of the weather, and was dropped for the final Test, though he did average over forty in the county matches.

In the 1987/8 World Cup, he played in just one match, against the Westindies, but batted at No10 and failed to score. He was hit in the face in the third one-dayer against England and consequently missed the first Test. He was fit in time for the next at Faisalabad, but got a duck and was dropped. However Shoaib was one of five specialist openers Pakistan took to Westindies in the spring of 1988, and played his first full series batting at No 3, after making his highest first-class score from there, scoring 208 not out against the Westindies Board XI in Guyana just prior to the first Test. He had a steady series, batting obdurately and staying in

Shoaib has the highest Test average in his family

Tests at an average of 114.5.

He batted for 720 minutes at Wellington, making 163, the sixth-longest innings in Tests, and the longest innings ever in New Zealand. In all he faced 516 balls, hitting 17 fours and a six. It was the slowest 150 (624 minutes) in Test cricket. He added a record 220 for the third-wicket with Javed, which they broke in the next match in Auckland, where they put together a stand of 248 before Shoaib was run out for 112 off 254 balls.

Three Tests later, in a dull draw in Lahore, they were at it again with a partnership of 246 against India (1989/90). Shoaib, batting at No 5, made a relatively spritely double hundred, scored from 335 balls in just over eight hours, though he was almost left stranded on 199. After taking the single that took the scoreboard from 199 to 200, the players started to leave the field but had to return when the scorers confirmed that he still had one to make. He cracked his 19th boundary to make sure that he and Hanif became the first father-and-son combination to score Test double-hundreds (if one excludes Miandad, of course!). If only Hanif had had the same opportunity when the scoreboard failed him on 499.

Shoaib finished the series with an average of 103, but had a torrid time on the faster pitches in Australia, making just 68 runs in five innings. A return home brought a revival of form, and he

line against the quicks, and finished by making 54 and 64 in the third Test at Bridgetown.

The following season against Australia he made 94 at Karachi and 74 in Faisalabad, sharing big partnerships with Javed Miandad of 194 and then 172. This was the prelude to a remarkable sequence, which began on the tour to New Zealand, which brought him 687 in the next six scored another double hundred, this time opening against New Zealand (1990/1) at Karachi, to set up an innings victory, with another marathon knock of over 11 hours. He scored hundreds in the next two matches - 108 not out at Lahore and 142 at Faisalabad - which took him past 2,000 runs after 32 Tests. He had made centuries in five successive Tests against New Zealand, amassing 782 runs in those matches at an average of 156.4. Shoaib has been criticised for making runs only against the lesser opponents, but in a 3-0 win only four other fifties were scored by Pakistan, which illustrates his importance to the side's triumph. Indeed he beat Miandad's record for a series with New Zealand, scoring 507 runs in the three Tests, and he shared the "player of the series" award with Waqar Younis, who also had been in record-breaking form, taking 29 wickets.

Like Mudassar Nazar and Zaheer Abbas before him, he had scored three hundreds in a row in Pakistan and looked like adding a fourth, against the Westindies, when he was dismissed for 86 after nearly eight hours at the crease, the longest innings in a generally low-scoring series. During it, he and Salim Malik set a new record for the fourth wicket against Westindies (174), eclipsing the stand between his father and his uncle Wazir 22 years before.

He did not score well against Sri Lanka the following year, and his defensive style precluded him from the World Cup triumph. Surprisingly, he played little part in the series against England, though at the end of a solid tour he came in for the final Test to strengthen the middle-order, and made a fifty.

He was left out of the tour to the Westindies in 1992/3 - a surprise omission - yet earned a recall against a weak Zimbabwe side when a younger player could have been blooded or a more attacking player utilised. Indeed, after making a typically solid 81 in the first innings on his return, Inzamam-ul-Haq was promoted in the second innings to go for the quick runs needed to precipitate a declaration. In his final innings of the series, his laborious fifty made in 315 minutes perhaps finally persuaded the selectors to pick someone more dashing for the trip to New Zealand, despite his record against them. After an absence of nearly two years, he got a surprise recall to face the Sri Lankans at home in 1995/6. Despite making a solid fifty in the first Test, which was won by an innings, he was dropped after the next match.

With the success of Saeed Anwar and Aamir Sohail there, he will struggle to regain his place at the top of the order. Although he has played in 63 one-day internationals, he is unlikely to play many more, which may leave him out of sight and out of the minds of the selectors. As performances in domestic cricket carry little weight, there is a danger that he may have played his last Test match, though he can always be depended upon to sell his wicket dearly should the selectors want a more defensive player among the middle-order strokemakers.

Shoaib Mohammad's out-and-out ability as a player is difficult to judge. He has marvellous hereditary concentration but his batting average has been swollen by feasts provided by the weaker attacks in Test cricket, on the slow Asian and New Zealand wickets. He has made little impact elsewhere, and does not have the natural talent of his uncles Sadiq and Mustaq, or father Hanif, yet may well finish with better looking statistics than any of them. He has passed the runs and appearances made by Sadiq and could still challenge Mustaq and Hanif, though his international career looked over by the end of the 1996 tour to England. Shoaib's technique is sound, and he watches the ball closely through the customised grill on his helmet, which is fixed much lower than conventionally. Not a flair player but a dependable one who can be relied upon to bat resolutely should he be recalled.

Career Details

Born: Karachi, 8 January 1962
Role: right-hand, opening or middle-order batsman, occasional right-hand off-spin bowler
Clubs: PIA (1976/7-), Karachi (1983/4-)
First-class record: (1976-95) 10161 runs (41.13) including 31 centuries and 45 fifties (HS 208 not out), 19 wickets (47.21), BB 3-14, and 72 catches
Tests: 45
Test Debut: v India, Jullundur 1983/4
Test record: 2,705runs (44.34), including 7 hundreds and 13 fifties, 5 wickets (34.00) and 22 catches
Best Performances: HS 203 not out v India, Lahore, 1989/90, & 203 not out v New Zealand, Karachi, 1990/1
Tours: India; 1983/4, 1986/7, 1989/90 (Nehru Cup)
New Zealand; 1984/5
England; 1987, 1992
Westindies; 1987/8
Australia; 1986/7 (Perth Challenge), 1988/9 (WSC), 1989/90
Overseas Tests: 19
One-day Internationals; 63
World Cup; 1987/8
Sharjah; 1984/5, 1986/7, 1988/9, 1989/90
Bangladesh; 1988/9 (Asia Cup)

Wazir Mohammad

The Mohammad family has provided the back bone of Pakistan's team for much of their Test history. Wazir Mohammad is the oldest of five brothers, four of whom played Test match cricket and the fifth, Raees, was once twelfth man for a Test.

At least one of the Mohammad brothers was playing for Pakistan in 100 out their first 101 Tests spread over 27 years. In most of those (64) two played and on one historic occasion three when Hanif, playing in his last Test match, teamed up with Mustaq and Sadiq, who was playing in his first. Hanif's son Shoaib almost saw the generations over-lapping, beginning his Test career less than three years after Sadiq, the youngest of the five siblings, had ended his.

Among them the four brothers who played Test cricket scored 10,938 runs (at an average of 38.65) in 173 Test matches, hitting 29 centuries. Only Mustaq did much bowling, though uniquely all three brothers who played in the Karachi Test against New Zealand (1969) turned their arms over in that game.

Wazir was born in Junagadh in December 1930 and like Raees learned his cricket in India. He was 17 at the upheaval of Partition; Raees was 15, Hanif 14, Mustaq five and Sadiq just three. Their father died in 1948 and much was left to Wazir to help his mother bring up the young family. Their mother, Amir Bi, was the inspiration though. A keen sportswomen herself who excelled at badminton and table-tennis, she encouraged her sons in their love of cricket. Riaz Ahmed Mansuri, the editor of Pakistan's *The Cricketer* described her as "Cricket's Greatest Mother since Martha Grace." As well as the loss of her husband she had to bear the tragedy of the death of another son and her only daughter when they were in their teens; she had a remarkable will and sense of purpose.

The family settled in Karachi, for whom Wazir played. He was selected in the first match for Pakistan against the touring Marylebone Cricket Club in 1951/2, without success, but played a typically obdurate innings for a Bahawalpur-Karachi XI against them, making 67 in nearly four-and-half hours. He was chosen for Pakistan's first tour to India (1952/3) but despite good form in club matches, averaging just under forty, he played in only one Test, the third at the Brabourne Stadium in Bombay. He had scored a hundred in the previous game against West Zone but could not reproduce that form in the Test.

He toured England in 1954 but had the misfortune to break a finger early on, in the game against

Wazir (left) with younger brother Hanif

Hampshire. When he recovered he showed good form against the counties, indeed he was to finish top of the tour batting averages, and was picked for the last two Tests. He played a crucial innings in the final Test at the Oval; with Pakistan struggling at 82 for 8 he coaxed the best out of the last two batsmen and among them they managed to double the score, Wazir finishing unbeaten on 42 made in 165 minutes. It was just enough for Fazal Mahmood to bowl at and Pakistan won a famous victory.

That winter he played throughout the home series against India without ever being quite at his best. He did make a fine fifty in the third Test and chipped in with the odd twenty or thirty in the rest of the series. His brother Raees very nearly joined Hanif and Wazir in the side for the first Test of that rubber. The captain A H Kardar came to Raees' room on the eve of the Test and told him to get to bed early as he was "going to play in the Test tomorrow morning" but was made 12th man at the last moment. Raees was a fine player too, a steady batsman almost as good as Hanif, according to the rest of the family, and a useful bowler though injury kept him out. Indeed the great Australian all-rounder Keith Miller rated him highly:

"I had the pleasure to bat with this lesser member of this illustrious family when I flew and played in a flood-relief match in Pakistan some years ago and Raees made one of the finest centuries imaginable. Had I been asked to name a potential Test player it most certainly would have been this one member of the family who missed out." (quoted in the 1976 *Wisden*).

Later that season (1955/6) Raees, Hanif and Wazir all scored hundreds in the final of the Quaid-e-Azam tournament against Services XI, emulating the Harvey

Wazir drives past the bowler at the Oval, 1954

brothers - Neil, Clarrie and Ray - who had done so for Victoria.

The next year Wazir was dropped after the second Test against New Zealand despite an important innings of 43 in the previous game at Karachi, where his partnership of 78 for the seventh wicket with Shujauddin took Pakistan to a decisive lead.

He showed some fine form against the MCC touring side a few weeks later; he made 90 not out for Karachi, then top-scored with 86 in Pakistan's innings victory in the 2nd "Test," and again in the 4th with 76 in a narrow defeat.

It ensured Wazir's place in the only Test of 1956/7, against Australia, in which he played a most valuable innings of 67. He shared a partnership of 104 with Kardar which rescued the side from 70 for 5 and did much to set up a win for Pakistan.

He was at his best on the tour to Westindies in 1957/8, in which he and Hanif starred, scoring over a thousand Test runs between them. Wazir finished top of the tour averages, with 70.83, and 850 runs, making more than half of them in the Tests at an average of 55.00 despite a pair in the second Test at Port of Spain.

In the first at Bridgetown, as Pakistan strove to salvage a draw, he was inspired by Hanif's efforts at the other end. Wazir made 35 as the brothers added 121 for the 4th wicket, the fourth century partnership of the innings in a row. In the third Test at Sabina Park it was Wazir who was playing the heroic innings, this time in a lost cause. He made his first Test century (106) lifting Pakistan from 120 for 5 to 286 in partnership with Kardar. He was

denied another in the next Test at Georgetown when he was left stranded on 97 not out when Roy Gilchrist bowled last man Haseeb Ahsan.

In the final Test at Port of Spain Wazir played the innings of his life. Coming in at No 4, his 189 set up an innings victory. He added 169 for the third wicket with Saeed Ahmed, who made 97, and dominated a stand of 154 for the next with Hanif, who scored 54.

The rest of his Test career after that pinnacle was a disappointment. He played in the home series against the Westindies (1958/9) but could not repeat his form of the Caribbean. However he kept the Mohammad dynasty going as Hanif was injured in the first Test and missed the rest of the series. In the third Mustaq made his debut; it was the only Test in which both he and Wazir played.

Wazir appeared in just one more Test - against Australia 1959/60 at Dacca - playing along side Hanif for the 18th time. By the following season Mustaq had won a regular spot in the middle-order and was to share 19 Tests with "the Little Master" before Hanif retired. Mustaq went on to play 26 Tests with the youngest brother Sadiq as well, thus having the unique distinction of playing Test cricket with three brothers.

Wazir's Test career rather petered out. He made just 44 runs in his last seven Test innings which saw his Test average tumble from the respectable mid-30s to 27.62. Wazir captained the Pakistan Eaglets on their tour to England 1963, which was sponsored by Pakistan International Airlines, as the guiding hand to a young team that included both Mustaq and Sadiq.

After his retirement the following year, Wazir stayed in touch with the game and served as a national selector. While Hanif encouraged Sadiq to bat left-handed at an early age, Wazir was able to suggest to Sadiq at the start of his career that the selectors were looking for an opener. Although statistically not as good as his Test playing brothers, Wazir had an important influence on them, and in establishing the Mohammad name in Pakistan's cricket history.

Career Details

Born: Junagadh, India, 22 December 1929
Role: right-hand, middle-order batsman
Clubs: Karachi (1949/50-1963/4), Bahawalpur (1953/4)
First-class record: (1949-64) 4952 runs (40.26) including 11 centuries, no wickets for 41 and 35 catches
Tests: 20
Test debut: v India, Bombay, 1952/3
Test record: 801 runs (27.62), no wickets for 15 runs, and 5 catches
Best Performances: HS 189 v Westindies, Port of Spain, 1957/8
Tours: India; 1952/3
England; 1954, 1963 (Eaglets)
Westindies; 1957/8

Sarfraz Nawaz, Malik

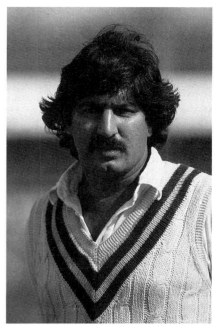

Sarfraz Nawaz was a player never far away from controversy, yet one who served Pakistan wholeheartedly for more than fifteen years. A colourful character, moody but loyal, he was very much underrated, in many ways a great bowler, capable of brilliance, yet he took five wickets in a Test innings on only four occasions, fewer than other bowlers with as many Test wickets (177). His figures though are remarkably similar in some respects to those of Joel Garner, of the Westindies, whose fame is perhaps greater, but who also rarely took five wickets either. Both were too often to be used as stock bowlers in fifty-plus Tests for their respective teams, for they could provide long accurate spells, and both were very economical (under 2.5 runs per over). Garner though had the advantage of playing on hard bouncy pitches most of the time, and having three quick bowlers to back him up. Consequently, he took a lot more wickets (259) and so his average is much healthier (20.97).

However, Sarfraz has played a significant part in establishing Pakistan's own fast bowling heritage. Forced to bowl on placid wickets at home, where the shine would go quickly, he was one of the first to experiment with wetting the shiny side of the ball to make it heavier, and thus make it "reverse-swing" even when it was 70-plus overs old. He became known as "Doctor Swing" and could also nip the ball back sharply off the seam. These tricks of the trade have been passed on to Wasim Akram and Waqar Younis.

Sarfraz was born in Lahore in December 1948, one of the first Test cricketers to be born and bred in the newly formed nation of Pakistan. Six-foot-four tall, with a shock of dark hair, he had a curious stiff-legged and pigeon-toed approach to the wicket, but generated pace from his rock-back at delivery and sharp wrist action. For a long time he bore the brunt of the fast bowling workload and was prone to injury, and occasional whims when he did not fancy bowling. He had his own strong sense of justice which occasionally got him into trouble, both on and off the field, and had no lack of courage in his convictions; early in his career he told the selectors that he should be their captain as he was the best player, in his opinion, and was promptly dropped!

It is not surprising that his first series was a controversial one which ended in similar fashion. The MCC side had been due to tour South Africa in 1968/9 but that was cancelled following objections to the selection of Basil D'Oliveira, a "Cape Coloured" playing for England, so instead they came to Pakistan. Sarfraz was selected for the national side just over a year after making his first-class debut for Lahore. He was the first bowler since the retirement of Fazal Mahmood to have all the makings of a fast bowler. His first Test match played at Karachi was the last in a series of escalating trouble and was abandoned because of student-led protests on the third day. Like Aftab Gul, who also made his debut that series, Sarfraz was a student at Punjab University.

With little opportunity to impress in that match he was not chosen for the following series against New Zealand (1969/70), however Saf's ability to swing the ball had not gone unnoticed. He so impressed Roger Prideaux in the nets that he was invited by him to play a few games at Northamptonshire, whom he captained, and that experience helped in his selection for the 1971 tour to England. However he was injured early on and hardly played, appearing in just three matches in all. He was having problems with his back and his physiotherapist advised against playing full-time county cricket until his back was stronger. So he played instead as a professional for Nelson in the Lancashire League where his all-round form was excellent, with 894 runs and 53 wickets, and for Northants 2nd XI, for whom he averaged 35 with the bat and 15 with the ball in 12 matches.

He was selected to tour Australia (1972/3), where he took 7-76 in the first innings against Queensland (10-102 in the match), but missed the first Test because of injury. He bowled steadily in the 2nd at Melbourne - Jeff Thomson's first Test match - and superbly in the third at Sydney, taking four wickets in each innings to put Pakistan in a winning position, only for the batting to let them down.

The side continued on to New Zealand where Saf had the first of several on-the-field altercations. In the first Test at Wellington Richard Collinge, the Kiwi left-arm seamer, hit Wasim Bari on the head with a bouncer; after a few minutes Bari was able to continue, only for Collinge to bounce him again, after which he retired hurt. This riled Sarfraz and once riled he usually sought retribution. The big man and Salim Altaf retaliated by singling out Bari's opposite number, Ken Wadsworth, sending down up to five bouncers an over. In very windy conditions, Sarfraz bowled with great stamina taking four wickets, but he took only one more wicket in the remaining two Tests.

Although he was unsuccessful at home against England in 1972/3, Sarfraz toured there in 1974, showing considerable improvement since the previous tour and topped the Test bowling averages. Before the tour started he played a handful of county matches for Northamptonshire, for whom he had been the leading wicket-taker the year before in second team cricket. He warmed up for the first Test by taking eight for 27 as Pakistan bowled out Nottinghamshire for 51, and he showed his all-round skill against England at Headingley, where he made a fine fifty, adding 62 for the last wicket on the 2nd morning with Asif Masood who made just four. Then bowling in tandem they made England struggle in conditions favouring the seamers to gain Pakistan a big first innings lead. Sarfraz bowled superbly in the second innings to check England's chances of victory as he took 4-56 in 36 overs and then put Pakistan in contention until rain washed out the chance of an exciting finish.

At the Oval, a bouncer from Sarfraz hit Dennis Amiss, who was on 178, forcing him to retire hurt, and on a frustrating day already curtailed by rain, Sarfraz threw the ball to the ground when spectators, moving behind the bowler's arm in the pavilion, held up play. The next ball was a fast full toss at Keith Fletcher, which he deflected for a single, and he followed it with a head high beamer at Tony Greig, who is 6 foot 7 inches tall! Angry glares were exchanged and it required the umpire, Dickie Bird, to have a quiet word with the bowler to tell him to calm down.

That winter Sarfraz took six wickets in an innings against the Westindies in the first Test at Lahore, before returning to England for the first World Cup (1975), taking 4-44 against the same opposition and won the man-of-the-match award but not the game for Pakistan as Westindies, the eventual winners of the competition, sneaked home by one wicket in a classic match. Sarfraz had completed his ration of 12 overs early on, and with him out of the attack, the last pair managed to add 64.

After the World Cup he was in fine form for Northants, taking over a hundred wickets for them at an average of 20.30 and was awarded his county cap. He followed this in 1976 with 82 wickets, proving to be one of the most dangerous bowlers in the country, as Northants, under Mustaq Mohammad's captaincy, came second in the championship, equalling their best-ever position.

That year they also won the Gillette Cup. In 1980 Northants won the Benson and Hedges Cup; Sarfraz took 3-23 in the Final and was unlucky not to get the Gold Award. They also reached the final of the 1979 Gillette Cup, and of the 1981 Nat West Trophy, and despite losing both it gave Northants one of the best one-day records in the country at that time.

In the 1979 Final, against Somerset, he had the audacity to bounce Joel Garner, who more than returned the compliment. In 1975, he got away with bowling several bouncers at Australia's Jeff Thomson, then the quickest bowler in the world, who took it as a joke, and did not seek revenge. Sarfraz was an able enough batsman though, who reached a thousand runs in his last Test match (1984). There was never a dull moment when Sarfraz was about.

Because of the World Cup (1979), injury and then Pakistan's tour (1982), he played in only 28 matches in his last three years at Northants, where he was known as the "King", and he was not re-engaged after 1982. He also missed out on a benefit year, which contributed to later impecuniosity.

Pakistan toured Sri Lanka early in 1976, but after some fine bowling against the Board XI at Kandy, Sarfraz was sent home because of a mendacious report of the team's misbehaviour at a cocktail party after the game. Originally President Bhutto wanted the whole team to come home, then just the five supposed ring-leaders, but in the end Sarfraz was made the scapegoat as he had been outspoken about the Sri Lankan Board.

In the winter of 1976/7 he bowled consistently well taking 37 wickets in nine Tests spread across three continents, bowling the equivalent of nearly 400 six-ball overs. In three home Tests against New Zealand he took 13 wickets (at 21.76 each), which were mainly front-line batsmen but was injured and could not bowl in the second innings of the final Test. He missed the second Test in Australia too but came back at Sydney to provide an essential foil for Imran Khan at the other end, taking three wickets in each innings to Imran's six, to help Pakistan to their first victory in Australia. In the Caribbean he took 16 wickets, including seven in the first Test in Barbados which Pakistan almost won, though again picked up an injury and missed the next Test.

Another peculiar incident occurred the following winter (1977/8) during the series with England when Sarfraz, who was vice-captain at the time, disappeared after the 1st match of the series, turning up in England with the excuse of wanting to spend Christmas in London. This was not part of a sudden conversion from Islam to Christianity, but part of a pay dispute, in the wake of the Packer affair, which had involved other senior players. He returned for the final Test, but it was no surprise when he joined World Series Cricket the following season.

In England in 1978 he strained his ribs while batting in the first Test at Edgbaston and bowled only half-a-dozen gentle overs in the match. The story goes that at Lord's he did not like the look of the pitch and had the ground attendant file down the studs on his new boots and then presented them to his captain Wasim Bari saying he couldn't play as they were his only pair! When he did return in the 3rd Test at Headingley he bowled beautifully, taking five for 39 from 20 overs, giving Pakistan the new ball hostility they had lacked.

In 1978/9, he had another hectic few months full of bowling - he sent down well over four hundred overs in eight Tests taking 38 wickets - and full of incident, showing Sarfraz at his best and worst. The Packer players were available again for the home series against India and Sarfraz and Imran Khan gave their side the edge with some excellent fast bowling. After 13 consecutive draws between the sides stretching back to the 1950s, Sarfraz took six wickets in the match at Lahore and nine at Karachi to help Pakistan win the series 2-0.

There was a regrettable incident in the third and deciding one-day international at Sahiwal, which threatened the fragile relationship between the sides. He bowled a succession of bouncers which were out of the batsmen's reach, and with no intervention from the umpires, Bishan Bedi, the Indian captain, called his side off in protest, thus conceding the match, which caused further controversy in both countries.

Ironically Sarfraz and Bedi were team-mates at Northants and usually shared a room together. Bishan would get up at the crack of dawn to say his prayers often just as Sarfraz was going to bedi-byes after a night out on the tiles.

Joining the side in New Zealand in the New Year after his World Series commitments, he helped Wasim Bari towards a record number of catches (seven) in an innings, inducing four edges himself. "Caught Bari bowled Sarfraz" was a frequent epithet for batsmen, occurring 28 times in Tests, one less than the Imtiaz Ahmed/Fazal Mahmood combination of the fifties and early sixties.

In Australia, as if to celebrate Pakistan's 100th Test, Sarfraz produced one of the most memorable spells of bowling in Test history. With the home side 305 for 3 on a true Melbourne pitch and requiring only 77 more to win, Sarfraz jagged a delivery back at Allan Border, who played on for 105, to start an incredible spell of seven wickets for one run in 33 balls. He finished with nine in the innings for 86 - at the time the best Test figures recorded in Australia - only being denied all ten by a run out. It gave him eleven wickets in the match.

Yet in the next Test, following two unsporting run outs in the series - one perpetrated by each side - Sarfraz appealed successfully against Andrew Hilditch when the batsman, who was at the

171

bowler's end, helpfully picked the ball up and returned it to him, only to be given out "handled the ball." However, Sarfraz is not solely to blame for this; the team had decided to retaliate at any opportunity after Sikander Bakht had been run out backing-up earlier in the match.

Asif Iqbal took over the captaincy for the series in India (1979/80), but did not know quite how to handle Sarfraz and consequently he was not picked for the tour, on the pretext that he had not been playing domestic cricket, and even when he might have been called up as a replacement Iqbal refused to have him. Pakistan lost and that proved to be the captain's only series in charge.

Sarfraz was not at his best in the next two home series against Australia 1979/80 and the Westindies a year later under the leadership of the new captain Javed Miandad, with whom he did not see eye to eye. In the first of those rubbers he took just two wickets in three Tests but the wickets were lifeless and even Dennis Lillee took only three. Against the Westindies he made a fine fifty in the first Test at Lahore but again the wickets were prepared to suit the spinners, and he did not play again until the final Test. Indeed Iqbal Qasim, the left-arm spinner, opened the bowling in his absence in the third Test at Karachi.

Sarfraz bowled steadily back in Australia (1981/2). He was the spokesman for the rest of the team who were fed up with the leadership of Javed Miandad, who had blamed defeat in Australia on the senior players, and they refused en masse to play on under him against Sri Lanka. Consequently Sarfraz missed that series and only appeared in one Test on his fourth tour to England in 1982 because of injury.

He was much happier under Imran Khan's captaincy. Sarfraz had taken him under his wing when he first came into the side and even helped him with his Punjabi, and they had nicknames for each other; Imran called him "Big" and Sarfraz called Immie "Young." Several captains had distrusted Safs' unorthodox ways, and he had to use Imran Khan as a go-between to express his thoughts to Mustaq Mohammad in the Westindies in 1976/7. Because he was outspoken Sarfraz was thought to be a troublemaker, and Imran had to fight for his inclusion for the 1982/3 home series against India, after missing the Tests against Australia. As it turned out he had his most productive series taking 19 wickets, including seven in the match at Hyderabad, building pressure by containment while Imran bowled flat out at the other end. He helped Pakistan to a most impressive 3-0 victory in the six match series.

In the World Cup that followed he proved consistently difficult to get away and helped Pakistan reach the semi-finals, before again going out to the Westindies.

Without Imran at the helm Sarfraz was ousted for the return series in India (1983/4), again for unfounded, tenuous reasons. The selectors called him to the ground in Karachi to prove his fitness, and after a few laps he was huffing and puffing, and so they declared him unfit to tour, yet he had always got fit by bowling. Pakistan's inexperienced pace attack struggled. Sarfraz launched a tirade against the selectors, saying that he had been excluded because he had refused to agree to play out three draws against India. He was promptly banned for six months and fined Rs10,000 (£500).

With the series going badly in Australia the selectors thought it expedient to swallow their pride and re-called him by the 3rd Test at Adelaide, though by then he had missed the two pitches best suited to him, at Perth and Brisbane. In his final series against England later that winter he was easily the best seamer on either side, taking 14 wickets at 25.64, and also topped the batting averages thanks to his highest Test score, 90, in his final match at Lahore, adding 161 for the ninth-wicket with Zaheer Abbas. He went past a thousand runs in Tests and so became the third Pakistani after Intikhab Alam and Imran Khan to do "the double." A fine striker of the ball, he might have scored a lot more runs if he had not been so stretched as a bowler. He played one more one-day international the following year but with the emergence of the young Wasim Akram he decided to retire to allow Akram every opportunity, though he may have played on for a year or two more.

Just as he had aired his views about pay, captaincy, airfares and the like as a player, after leaving cricket he went into Pakistani politics to express his grievances. As a player he had used his influence to help poor people get jobs, giving their applications to a number of the high ranking officials that always attended Test matches and was concerned to address matters of welfare as a politician. However, when he threatened to uncover government fraud, an assassination attempt was made on him when he was beaten unconscious and left for dead by a gang near his home in Lahore in 1986.

Since then he has had some ups and downs, falling on hard times. He has separated from his film star wife Rani, was charged with unlawfully imprisoning a girl and was banned for drink driving. To add insult to injury, his former county captain Allan Lamb accused him, at the end of Pakistan's 1992 tour, of being the instigator of the alleged ball-tampering practices. The case was brought to trial in November 1993 and ended in a draw with both parties claiming victory. Sarfraz got the statement that he had sought - that he had not cheated - and said afterwards, "It is the

Safraz playing for a world XI in the Westindies

happiest day of my life." In reality it was a Pyrrhic victory for both sides. By writing the article Lamb had, in effect, dashed his chances of playing for England again, while the evidence presented in court stirred further the ball-tampering controversy surrounding Akram and Younis.

Thankfully he was cleared of the charges of "theft and false imprisonment" after the alleged victim Azra Rauf, a classical dancer, declined to give evidence in court. Sarfraz was "ready and willing" to be tried in order to clear his name, but Sarfraz blamed the police for failing to investigate the matter fully in the first place.

Sarfraz was forced to miss out on elections for the Pakistan People's Party as the trial left him unable to hand in his nomination papers. Consequently, he had to shelve his political aspirations temporarily, though he has since been employed as a special adviser for sport by Benazir Bhutto, when she was prime minister.

It is best that Sarfraz is remembered for his on the field achievements and as one of the most interesting characters to have appeared in Test cricket. He was a wholehearted player and it will be interesting to see how far his strong sense of right and wrong will take him as he pursues further his political career.

Career Details

Born: Lahore, 1 December 1948
Role: right-hand, lower middle-order batsman, right-hand fast-medium bowler
Clubs: Lahore (1967/8-1984/5), Punjab University (1968/9-1971/2), Northamptonshire (1969-82), Punjab (1974/5), Railways (1975/6) and United Bank (1975/6)
First-class record: (1967-85) 5,709 runs (19.35) HS 90, 1,005 wickets (24.62) and 162 catches
Tests: 55
Test Debut: v England, Karachi 1968/9
Test record: 1,045 runs (17.71), 177 wickets (32.75) and 26 catches
Best Performances: HS 90 v England, Lahore, 1983/4
BB: 9-86 v Australia, Melbourne, 1979
Tours: England; 1971, 1974, 1978, 1982
Australia; 1972/3, 1976/7, 1978/9, 1981/2, 1983/4
New Zealand; 1972/3, 1978/9
Westindies; 1976/7
Overseas Tests; 28
One-day Internationals; 45
World Cups; 1975, 1979, 1983 (all in England)

Mudassar Nazar

Mudassar Nazar is fourth only to Javed Miandad, Salim Malik and Zaheer Abbas amongst Pakistan's leading run-makers in Test cricket, with over four thousand runs from his 76 Tests - well ahead of the chasing field. Although not blessed with the natural strokemaking talent of the other three, he still scored ten Test centuries, can boast match-winning spells with the ball, and has an excellent record as an all-rounder in one-day internationals. Mudassar, a charming man, made the most of his ability with both bat and ball. It is a surprise that he never played county cricket, but he was greatly admired for his performances in minor county cricket for Cheshire and in the Lancashire League.

Born in Lahore in April 1956, he was the son of the late Nazar Mohammad, who opened the batting with Hanif Mohammad in Pakistan's first ever Test. Nazar Mohammad's own career was curtailed by a serious arm injury that prevented him from playing after that first series but he later

became a National Cricket Coach, supervising the young Mudassar during the early part of his Test career.

Mudassar made his first-class debut at the age of 15 for Lahore, for whom his brother Mubashir also played. After doing well in the inter-provincial under-19 competition he was selected for the national under-19 tour to England in 1974, along with the likes of Javed Miandad and Qasim Omar. He finished the tour top of the averages with 60.80, and with the most runs, 730, including 130 and 155 (both not out) against Sussex 2nd XI.

That winter he made over a thousand first-class runs for United Bank, hitting six hundreds, and gained selection for Pakistan's unofficial visit to Ceylon the following year. It was not long before he made it into the full Test side when, on the tour to Australia in 1976/7 and before he had played a first-class innings on the tour, he was chosen for the first Test at Adelaide to open the batting with Majid Khan because Sadiq Mohammad was injured. He made 13 and 22, but stood down when Sadiq returned for the final two Tests. He toured the Westindies, scoring 137 and 54 against Guyana, but did not make the Test side.

He had the chance to establish himself in 1977/8, because of the Packer defections, and marked his first Test in his home town with the slowest century in first-class cricket, taking 557 minutes to reach three figures. Mudassar was playing to instructions, and when he played some loose strokes just before the lunch interval on the first day he was admonished at the break, and reminded he was playing for his country. Consequently, he batted stoically for the rest of the day, finishing on 52 not out, and on the second his innings even tested the patience of the crowd, who began to celebrate his century when he was still on 99. Some spectators invaded the ground, and when one was violently apprehended by police, fighting broke out. Several policemen were chased across the pitch and sought sanctuary in the England dressing room. After a brief storming of the VIP area, the crowd actually cleared up the debris on the ground, and play proceeded after a loss of just 25 minutes, as the tea interval had been taken when the players left the field.

He celebrated his hundred with three of his 12 fours and in all batted for 575 minutes. Not to be outdone, England's champion stonewaller, Geoff Boycott, was on course to beat the record when he batted, taking twenty minutes longer than Mudassar had to reach his fifty, but he was dismissed shortly after.

Mudassar had added 180 with Haroon Rashid, a record for the third wicket against England, and made rather more fluent fifties in the remaining two Tests.

He had a poor series on the tour to England in 1978, averaging just 17.20 in the Tests, though that put him fourth in the averages, as the Pakistanis were completely out-played. He did score 107 against Hampshire, one of only two hundreds made on the tour, and remained in contention even when the Packer players returned that winter, playing the last two matches against India, in the 1st Test in New Zealand (when four WSC players were absent), and in the last Test in Australia, but without a major score. However, he did show the first signs of his knack of taking important wickets at critical times.

In 1979/80, he made a hundred, reached in 340 minutes, in the 1st Test against India, emulating the achievement of his father 27 years before, who had batted for 515 minutes in scoring Pakistan's first Test century. In so doing they became only the second father and son after David and Dudley Nourse to score centuries against the same country. However in the next four games Mudassar failed to pass 30, Kapil Dev getting him out five times out of seven, and he was dropped for the last Test. He was recalled for the first two Tests against Australia but batted at seven in his only innings, making 29.

He was not selected for the home series against Westindies in 1980/1, but was back for the tour to Australia a year later after showing some excellent form in domestic cricket, which included his highest first-class score of 241, for United Bank against Rawalpindi at Lahore, a game in which he shared an opening stand of 389 with Mansoor Akhtar who got 176. He made the top score for Pakistan in the series, 95, at Melbourne where the tourists made 500 - the second highest total made without a century - to win by an innings. He also bowled particularly well in the triangular one-day tournament, with 12 wickets at 13 apiece.

A players' dispute saw the entire side that had represented Pakistan in the last Test in Australia refuse to go on under Javed Miandad's captaincy, and so he missed the first two Tests against Sri Lanka.

By now he and Mohsin Khan were considered the first-choice openers and they started in fine form on the 1982 tour to England, but Mudassar had the misfortune to get a pair in the first Test at Edgbaston, suffering a poor lbw decision in the 1st innings, and followed that with 20, 65 and nought again in the next two Tests. However he made more of an impact with his bowling. At Lord's, he produced a match-winning spell with the ball. Bowling in imitation of Dennis Lillee, albeit at a fraction of the pace, he became known as "the man with the golden arm" when he took six for 32. With some fine, controlled swing bowling, he knocked out the heart of the batting by taking the first five wickets to fall. It was one of the proudest moments

of his career as it enabled Pakistan to win at Lord's for the first time.

Four more useful wickets at Headingley almost brought his side victory, and his ten wickets in the series cost just 10.40 each. In stark contrast to his poor Test series with the bat, he averaged 165 in the county matches making four hundreds, including 211 not out against Sussex. There he put on 319 for the first wicket with Mohsin, with whom he averaged over eighty for the first wicket against the counties, though they never managed to get Pakistan away to a good start in the Tests.

It was just a matter of time before his appetite for run-scoring came to fruition in internationals, and that winter he was to gorge himself against India. Useful form against Australia was followed by the most prolific scoring for any series by a Pakistani. In six matches, he scored 761 runs at an average of 126.83, with scores of 50, 17, 119, 38, 2 not out, 231, 152 and 152, helping Pakistan to their most impressive series victory over India.

In the 2nd Test at Karachi, he made a hundred batting at No 6 and added 213 for the 5th wicket with Zaheer Abbas, a record against India, to set up an innings victory. He missed out at Faisalabad where four of his team-mates made centuries but made up for it in the 4th at Hyderabad where his double-hundred included a six and 21 fours as he batted for ten hours 27 minutes, facing 444 balls. With Javed Miandad, he added a world record 451 for the third wicket. It also equalled the Test record for any wicket (since beaten) set by Don Bradman and Bill Ponsford for Australia in 1934. It is the only occasion of two double-hundreds in the same innings for Pakistan, and only the fifth instance in all Tests.

In the next Test he became only the second Pakistani to carry his bat in a Test, scoring 152 out of 323 in 495 minutes. Curiously, his father is the other, in the aforementioned century he made in his country's 2nd Test (against India, 1952/3), when he scored an undefeated 124 out of 331 at Lucknow. In so doing he became the first player to be on the field for an entire Test match.

In the final Test, back at Karachi, Mudassar made another big hundred, taking him well past Hanif Mohammad's record of 628 for a rubber (against Westindies in 1957/8), and emulating Zaheer Abbas by scoring three hundreds in a row. It also took him past 2,000 runs in Tests. Among them, Mudassar, Abbas and Javed Miandad had scored over 2,000 runs in the series, each averaging over a hundred - a unique occurrence.

In the return rubber the following season Mudassar was less successful and was moved down the order to accommodate Shoaib Mohammad, despite his fine record when opening with Mohsin Khan. Although re-united at the top

The man with the golden arm

of the order in Australia, Mudassar's lean patch continued, making just one fifty - 84 in the final Test at Sydney - and he featured only once in the home series against England.

Not surprisingly he was back to face India in 1984/5 and made his sixth hundred against them, at Faisalabad, becoming the first player to be dismissed for 199 in a Test when he was caught behind off Yadav. It was another marathon innings; he batted for 552 minutes and faced 408 balls. He put on 141 for the first wicket with Mohsin Khan and 250 for the 2nd with Qasim Omar, the Kenya-born Karachiite, who made a double-hundred.

Mudassar made his eighth Test hundred later that season, against New Zealand, sharing a third-wicket partnership with Miandad of 212, taking the side from 14 for 2 to the brink of victory in Test cricket's 1,000th match. He also opened the bowling in this series, and started with a spell of three wickets for eight runs from 11 overs, and was to finish top of the averages. In New Zealand, he batted throughout the 2nd innings of the Auckland Test, making 89, before being last out, passing 3000 runs in his 51st Test in the process, and finished 2nd in the batting averages to complete a fine all-round series.

At home and away to Sri Lanka, he got a fifty in four Tests in a row, before tailing off in the last two matches, but picked up some more useful wickets. He also enjoyed a brief period of captaincy during the Karachi Test when Javed and Imran were off the field with injuries. He had always given useful advice on the field and might well have been given a period in charge.

The following season (1986/7) Pakistan struggled to find a settled opening pair against the Westindies. Mudassar played in two of the three Tests, but no combination in the Tests or one-day internationals added more than 25 for the first wicket. He was selected for the tour to India that followed, but did not feature in the Tests despite his record against that country.

Mudassar had a happy return against England in 1987, where he had been playing for Burnley in the Lancashire League and for Cheshire with great success in the eighties. In a rain-affected summer he had only four completed innings in the five Tests, but his 124 at Edgbaston - where he got a pair in 1982 - made in just under seven hours, ensured a draw in a game Pakistan came perilously close to losing. He captained in the earlier county games, while Imran was attending to his benefit year arrangements.

He played in only one match in the 1987 World Cup because of injury and his experience and expertise were sorely missed. At the time only four other players had done the double in one-day internationals - indeed his figures were very similar to those of Imran Khan in this form of the game. Mudassar played in the infamous series against England that followed it and set up the innings victory in the first Test with a typically stalwart innings of 120, made in 323 minutes, which proved to be the last of his ten Test hundreds.

He had a difficult tour to the Westindies in 1988. He was concussed when hit on the helmet by a bouncer from Ian Bishop in the first game of the tour and never really regained his confidence. He had an indifferent series too against Australia in 1988/9 though did pass 4,000 Test runs during the second Test, and a poor series in New Zealand, where he played the last of his 76 Test matches, finishing as the fifth most capped player for his country.

He did not pass fifty in his last ten Tests, which dropped his Test average below forty, which is usually considered the benchmark for top batsmen. He worked hard at his game, playing in a style that allowed the middle-order strokemakers to prosper. His overall standing as a player is marred by the fact that most of his runs were scored at home, and against weaker bowling attacks. For instance, he averages 97.5 in ten home Tests against India,

though that is a considerable achievement in its own right. Indeed he averages more than twice as much in home Tests (53.63 in 35 Tests) as abroad (26.14 in 41 matches) and he scored eight of his ten Test hundreds in Pakistan, the others coming at Bangalore and Birmingham. He tended to struggle on faster, bouncier wickets. However this should not diminish the part he played during Pakistan's most successful period in Test cricket during the mid-eighties.

He was a most effective one-day all-rounder, scoring 2,654 runs and taking 111 wickets in 122 internationals, a much admired "pro" in the Lancashire Leagues with Burnley and he helped in Cheshire's resurgence in Minor County cricket, playing for them from 1980 to 1988. Since then he has been a regular in the Rest of the World side that plays in the Scarborough Festival and took the Pakistan side to the Caribbean as manager in 1992/3.

He served the game in the best spirit, always cheerful and prepared to offer advice, while making the most of his own ability. After his playing career, he joined BCCI for a short while, but soon decided he would prefer to be running his own business, and opened a frozen-foods shop in Bolton, Lancashire, near where he lives. He still plays for Bolton Cricket Club, mainly to allow him to watch the development of his 12-year-old son, Danyal, who might just become the third generation of his family to play Test cricket.

Career Details

Born: 6 April 1956
Role: right-hand, opening batsman, right-hand medium-pace bowler
Clubs: Lahore (1971/2-1974/5), Universities (1974/5), Habib Bank (1975/6), PIA (1975/6-1977/8), United Bank (1978/9-87/8)
First-class record: (1971-92) 14,078 runs (43.85) including 42 centuries, 152 wickets (34.34) and 141 catches
Tests: 76
Test Debut: v Australia, Adelaide, 1976/7
Test record: 4,114 runs (38.09), 66 wickets (38.36) and 48 catches
Best Performances: HS 231 v India, Hyderabad, 1982/3
BB 6-32 v England, Lord's, 1982
Tours: Australia; 1976/7, 1978/9, 1981/3, 1983/4, 1984/5 (WSC), 1986/7 (Perth Challenge), 1988/9
England; 1978, 1982, 1987
New Zealand; 1978/9, 1984/5, 1988/9
India; 1979/80, 1983/4
Sri Lanka; 1985/6
Westindies; 1987
Overseas Tests; 41
One-day Internationals; 122
World Cups; 1979, 1983, 1987
Sharjah; 1983/4, 1984/5, 1985/6, 1986/7, 1988/9
For Rest of the World; England 1988, 1989, 1990, 1991, 1992

Abdul Qadir

Abdul Qadir was most successful and the best spin bowler in the world in the eighties. Almost single-handedly he kept the art of leg-spin bowling alive. His successor in the Pakistan side, Mustaq Ahmed, imitates his style and there can be no higher form of respect or flattery, though there were few other role models for him. Qadir, on his day, must rate with the best spinners the game has seen, with each ball meant to tell a story of its own. Admittedly he has performed best on his home wickets, but overseas he has bamboozled batsman too, without always achieving the figures he deserved.

His routine before delivery was as transfixing as the deliveries themselves, for he flicked the ball from one hand to the other, with the non-striker in earshot of the ball fizzing into the palm of his left hand. His jaunty, bouncy run-up had a mystical rhythm to it, deliberately delayed, leaving the batsman in as much trepidation as when a fast bowler reaches the top of his run.

Abdul's success has come despite the humblest of beginnings. The son of a Lahorite muezzin - a mosque official who calls the faithful to prayer - his family was so poor that he often had to wake early to go to the market before school to buy vegetables to sell in his local area, and then return to help out after school as well.

Originally a seamer, Abdul was largely self-taught as a bowler. He could not afford equipment and played in traditional clothes of long baggy shirt and trousers, known as shalwar kameez. He bowled with the aggression of a quick bowler, appealing with fervour, sinking to his knees imploring a decision in his favour from the umpire, and following through as though he meant to field every forward prod himself. He became cricket's cult figure, with players at all levels around the world trying to imitate his mannerisms and idiosyncratic style.

Sunil Gavaskar, the first player to score 10,000 runs in Tests, considers him the best spin bowler he has ever faced, citing his variety as the factor which set him apart from other bowlers. Ian Botham also considered Qadir outstanding, the only spinner worthy of the World XI in his autobiography: "He had exquisite control and wonderful variation, including three or four different types of googly. On a turning pitch an absolute nightmare."

Commentators would put him under the close scrutiny of the camera, trying to pick his various types of googly from his flipper or top-spinner as well as his stock leg-break which might be bowled with either of two slightly different wrist-actions.

He could make good batsmen look foolish, and would often bowl deliveries too good to touch, while his late dip meant he deceived in the air as well as off the pitch.

Coming from nowhere, he was quick to make his mark in first-class cricket, taking six for 67 for the Punjab in his first match (in 1975) and scoring a hundred and taking six for 17 in his next for Lahore C against Bahawalpur. He used to copy Wasim Raja's action and came up to Wasim one day in the nets saying, "I've got it, I've got it." Wasim was curious, "What have you got, the top-spinner, the googly?" The answer came back that he had perfected his imitation of Wasim.

It was not long before the national selectors took an interest in him. Abdul started the 1977/8 season well, playing for Habib Bank; he took seven for 22 against Baluchistan, six for 66 against PIA and then top-scored with 65 not out and took 12 wickets for 115 (including eight for 29 in the first innings) against Universities. With Mustaq Mohammad signed to Packer and Intikhab Alam just retired from international cricket there was a need for a specialist leg-spinner in the Test team and later that season he was selected to play against England. His first Test was in his home town of Lahore but he took just one wicket in a match that was interrupted by rioting. In the 2nd though he hinted at his promise and was described by _Wisden_ as "the most notable discovery of his type for some time". Bowling round the wicket into the rough caused by Bob Willis's follow-through he took six for 44 in 24 overs, including a spell of four for 4 in 16 balls.

Wasim Bari delayed his declaration in the 2nd innings, and England were able to settle comfortably for the draw. In the third, his four wickets in the first innings were all lbw - part of the record six lbw's in the innings. That he got more lbw's in Pakistan has been held against him but whether he has been favoured in his own country or denied overseas is a matter for conjecture; the truth probably lies somewhere between the two.

He was troubled by a shoulder injury on the tour to England in 1978, and in cold, wet conditions made little impression, taking just six wickets at 66 apiece on the tour and failing to make the Test side despite the absence of the Packer players. He did not reappear for Pakistan until the 1979/80 season, once Mustaq Mohammad had retired. In India he took only two wickets in the three Tests in which he played, and did not feature at all in the home series with Australia, in which Iqbal Qasim and Tauseef Ahmed bowled so well.

Fine early season form for Habib Bank, for whom he took seven for 73 in the first innings against Industrial Development Bank of Pakistan and nine for 108 in the match against Railways, ensured a recall the following year, playing in the first two Tests against the Westindies, in which he took eight wickets, before being dropped again. In the 1st Test he was struck a nasty blow on the shoulder from a Colin Croft bouncer and was forced to retire hurt.

Despite taking 87 wickets in domestic cricket in 1981/2 he was not selected to tour Australia, or to appear against the Sri Lankans. He was disillusioned with cricket and was on the verge of giving up to concentrate on business. Imran Khan and Mudassar Nazar encouraged him, advising him to concentrate on his variations, and both said they would push for his selection whoever was captain. When Imran was appointed he had to plead for Abdul's inclusion, but his insistence was fully vindicated when the leg-spinner took easily the most wickets on the tour to England with 57 at 20.82, including 7-44 and 6-78 against Sussex, and 9-51 in the match against Glamorgan. Although he took only ten of those wickets in the Tests (at 40.60), he consistently posed problems that brought pressure and forced error at the other end. He was very unlucky with various umpiring decisions - they could not read him either! He had one impassioned appeal against Ian Botham, who missed a full toss as he tried to sweep, after which he was warned for jumping on the pitch. Derek Randall scored a hundred in the first Test, but admitted later that against Qadir he just hit and hoped and on a slowish, low track got away with it. He made others, particularly Ian Greig and the tail-enders, look embarrassingly inept as they failed to pick the spin.

Imran Khan has been criticised for his over-use of Qadir, but as he was always perplexing to the batsmen and looked like taking a wicket any minute, it was difficult to take him off. Mike Brearley, the former England captain, feels that Imran should have been prepared to give away more singles to allow Abdul to bowl at those batsmen who really had no clue how to play him. At first Imran did not know the precise field to employ when his champion leg-spinner was bowling.

That series was the making of Qadir, giving him the boost in confidence he needed and he was inundated with offers from various English counties. Although he seemed likely to join Kent, he decided to keep his bowling skills a mystery. There was also a possibility that he could have joined Sussex, sharing the overseas duties (and salaries) with Imran Khan, who instigated the proposal, and Garth LeRoux but Sussex were sceptical even though the deal would not have cost them anything extra.

In that one summer Qadir re-kindled the dying art of leg-spin bowling, enthralling the English media and delighting such doyens as Richie Benaud and John Arlott. However when he returned home, he was criticised in the Karachi press, who said his selection was due to Imran's favouritism towards a fellow Lahorite, and his place was again in doubt. Indeed he was actually booed and pelted as he entered the National Stadium in Karachi for the first Test of the series with Australia. However he soon silenced his critics, proving to be the match-winner, as he took 22 wickets in the three Tests - a record for a series with Australia - and was instrumental in Pakistan's 3-0 win. After some indifferent bowling in the first innings following his hostile reception, he took 5-76 in the 2nd innings at Karachi, which included a spell of five for 19, and followed this with four for 76 and seven for 142 at Faisalabad where he bowled over 90 overs. His control was remarkable, spinning the ball both ways, usually from around the wicket, and frustrating batsmen used to using their feet to the spinners. He took some useful wickets against India, in a series surprisingly dominated by the seam bowlers, in particular Imran and Sarfraz Nawaz. This form set him on his way to becoming the first bowler to take a hundred wickets in a domestic season. He twice took nine wickets in an innings, with five for 79 and nine for 82 against Karachi, and nine for 49 and four for 27 against Rawalpindi, which were among the highlights of a superb season.

He showed, too, that attacking spinners could be used in one-day cricket, picking up two man-of-the-match awards in the World Cup in England in 1983, for taking four for 21 and scoring 41 not out against New Zealand, and for his five for 44 against Sri Lanka. Yet, because he was at odds with the Board - and with Imran absent due to injury, he did not tour India the following winter (1983/4), and when he was re-called for Australia, he found himself up against as many as six left-handers in the top eight. This nullified his googly from round the wicket, and he was constantly being swept. However, outside the Tests he maintained his form - he had taken seven wickets in an innings against South Australia - and it was generally thought that he would be the match-winner as he was in the last series against them. With Imran Khan back at the helm for the last two Tests, he took five wickets in an innings in the 4th Test, and did much of his best bowling in the World Series matches. Previously ignored for one-day cricket before the World Cup, he proved once again what an important variation his bowling could bring. In the World Series triangular tournament he took 15 wickets at 18 runs apiece, and he was particularly effective in the five matches against the Westindies, conceding just 2.66 an over.

In the home series against England, Qadir at times bowled superbly. He took eight wickets in the 1st Test at Karachi to help secure Pakistan's first home win against the tourists in 13 Tests. He also made a useful 40 and followed this with his first Test fifty in the next Test at Faisalabad. At Lahore he ensured the series - Pakistan's first over England - by taking ten for 194 in the match, to establish a record of 19 wickets in a home series against England.

The next winter, 1984/5, brought mixed fortunes. He played only in the second of the two Tests against India in which he took his hundredth Test wicket when he had Yadav caught, before the tour was called off because of the assassination of Mrs Indira Gandhi. He then bowled well in tandem with Iqbal Qasim in the 2-0 win at home to New Zealand. He took eight wickets in the second Test at Hyderabad, where the umpiring was severely criticised by the opposition, but he was unable to bowl in the 3rd after being hit on the foot while batting.

In the return series, he was out of form and out of sorts with his captain, Javed Miandad. Qadir made an important fifty in the first Test, helping the bottom half of the order to double the score, but only picked up one wicket in each of the first two Tests. He was sent home for "disciplinary reasons", ostensibly for a half-hearted piece of fielding on the last day of the match against Wellington, as the game was petering into a draw, after which Zaheer Abbas, the acting captain, sent him from the field, though it was at least partly due to his poor form. However, Pakistan suffered in his absence; the final Test was lost when the last wicket added 50, with

Ewan Chatfield making easily his highest Test score. He was also sorely missed in the World Championship of Cricket in Australia, where he had starred the previous winter, and in Sharjah, which were both won by India, for whom novice leg-spinner Laxman Sivaramakrishnan was the pick of the bowlers.

Qadir was rightfully re-instated for home and away series against Sri Lanka, and celebrated Miandad's announcement that he would stand down at the end of the home Tests with a match-winning effort at Karachi, where he took 5-44. It started a sequence of seven home Tests in which he was to take 54 wickets.

The next season (1986/7) Qadir bowled a magnificent spell in the 1st Test against Westindies at Faisalabad. Requiring 240 to win, the tourists crumbled to their lowest Test score, 53, as the leg-spinner mesmerised their batsmen taking six for 16 in 9.3 overs, his tenth five-wicket haul (of which nine had been at home). He added four more wickets in the Westindies' only innings at Lahore, and then despite a broken bone in his left hand, injured while fielding, he took 7-121 from 75.5 overs in the match at Karachi, giving him 18 wickets at 20 in the series.

Abdul played in three of the five Tests in India, taking his 150th wicket in the last of those, but was below his best. He joined the tour of England 50 days late; his whereabouts was a bit of a mystery, though he had stayed at home originally to look after his sick wife, to whom he has been married since he was fifteen. He arrived in time for the 2nd Test at Lord's, going straight into the side because the other spinner Tauseef Ahmed had broken a finger. In another cold wet summer, on moribund pitches, Abdul had taken only one Test wicket, going into the final Test, and there was pressure to drop him. However, on the only pitch of the summer offering some bounce, and with a total of over 700 already secured, he began to flight the ball and bowl with the variety that set him apart from other spinners; he finished with his best Test figures to that date, seizing 7-96 from 44.4 overs. He took three more in the 2nd innings from 53 overs, to give him his first ten wicket haul in Tests but, helped by several dropped catches, England managed to stave off defeat. He was one of the star attractions in the Bicentenary Test match that followed but he bruised his fingers in the first innings fielding off his own bowling and had to leave the field. In the 2nd innings, he had a fascinating duel with Gordon Greenidge in which the great Westindian opener tried to authenticate the reverse-sweep as a cricketing stroke, scoring 27 runs with it during his innings.

That winter in the World Cup, Qadir again proved what a useful one-day bowler he could be,

The art and mystery of Qadir's bowling action

bowling with economy and taking wickets. He also scored 13 of the 14 needed off the last over from Walsh to beat Westindies, including a straight six, much to the delight of the 50,000 spectators at Lahore. Pakistan's run ended in the semi-finals against Australia.

He captained in the one-day matches against England in Miandad's absence, and bowled superbly in the Tests, though the series will, unfortunately, be remembered for the Gatting-Rana incident and other rows rather than for his peerless bowling. At Lahore he returned the best-ever figures for Pakistan, and the best by any leg-spinner (the fifth best in all Tests). It was a shame that there were precious few spectators there to see an epic display, albeit on a pitch offering plenty of turn. He came on after ten overs and bowled through unchanged, taking nine for 56 off 37 overs. David Capel was the only batsman to survive him, but he was one of four more wickets in the 2nd innings and so Qadir became only the fourth bowler to dismiss all eleven players in a Test. He finished with match figures of 13 for 101. The game was marred by umpiring error; Qadir himself had words with the umpire after being given out stumped after making a useful 38.

His seven wickets at Faisalabad have been largely forgotten in the ensuing melee. At Karachi he again bowled his leg-spinners and googlies with such accuracy that in more than a hundred overs in the match he conceded less than two an over,

picking up five wickets in each innings. He also made his highest Test score, helping Pakistan to a useful lead. His 61 included four sixes off John Emburey and six fours, suggesting that more could have been made of his batting in the past. Indeed he was behind only Salim Malik in the batting averages for the rubber. His series figures of thirty wickets (at 14.56) out of the 52 to fall, are the best for Pakistan against England, while only George Lohmann (England) has taken more in any three match series, and that was against a weak inexperienced South African side, in 1895/6.

Qadir was ill with kidney stone trouble before the tour to the Caribbean in the Spring of 1988, perhaps accounting for his later splenetic behaviour, and was initially below par with the ball. He took three important wickets in the first Test, which Pakistan won; took nine wickets in the match against the Under-23 side, and four in each innings in the Port of Spain Test, including his 200th wicket in his 53rd match. He also had to come in for the last over of the match and block out the last five balls from Viv Richards to ensure that Pakistan got a draw and so went to Barbados still one-up. There Abdul's temper boiled over. He was agitated after Jeff Dujon and Winston Benjamin survived close appeals for lbw, and also had a confident shout for a catch from the former turned down during their tense eighth-wicket partnership that was to win the game. He took offence when a spectator, 21 year-old Albert Auguste, made some abusive remark to Qadir, who was fielding on the boundary, and reacted by throwing a punch at the heckler, hitting him on the arm. An out-of-court settlement, in which Abdul agreed to pay Auguste US $1,000, prevented the police from pressing charges.

At home he bowled well against Australia (1988/9), but had an indifferent series in New Zealand. Originally he was not available for the latter, though he was persuaded to change his mind when Imran Khan returned as captain.

Qadir started the tour to Australia in 1989/90, but left before the Tests, after damaging a finger, though he also appeared, again, to be at odds with the world. He played in just one further series, a dull 0-0 draw at home to India, in which he took just six wickets. An Achilles injury kept him out of the World Cup and out of contention for the tour to England in 1992, though many expected him to appear half way through the series. However, had he appeared, the success of Mustaq Ahmed might have precluded his selection.

Although Ahmed has been the first choice leg-spinner for Pakistan recently, his understudy is full of praise for Qadir; "He is the very greatest bowler in the world. He is the complete bowler. He knows everything." Indeed Qadir made a surprise return for Pakistan in the Sharjah tournament in 1993. Haseeb Ahsan, the manager on the 1987 tour to England who had just been reinstated as chairman of selectors, had no hesitation in recalling him after he had produced two match winning-performances in the Wills Cup domestic competition. However, he continued to be plagued by injury, stepping on a ball and hurting his ankle during a practice session, picking up another injury in Sharjah and then, worst of all, went into a coma for three days after being hit on the head while batting in the nets in Lahore.

Abdul Qadir played in 104 one-day internationals in which he took 132 wickets, while conceding just over four runs an over, and proved that it is possible to use spinners effectively in limited-overs cricket.

However he will be remembered as a great attacking leg-spinner in Test cricket, though he had the accuracy also to be a stock bowler. At times his temperament was interpreted as a little suspect and was at his best playing under Imran's guiding hand, while his finances were a constant worry - once he refused to play unless the Pakistan Board paid his mortgage!

Imran Khan has always been a close friend and an admirer of his champion leg-spinner, and Abdul has named his son after his former captain. The young Imran played for Pakistan in the under-15 World Cup side in England in 1996 and bowls leg-spin with many of the mannerisms of his father, which will worry future generations of batsmen.

Very much a family man and a strict Moslem, Abdul Qadir was always happiest living and playing in Pakistan, something that influenced his decision not to play county cricket, first with Kent, and then with Sussex, though this was also to keep his bowling a mystery.

He completed the double of a thousand runs and a hundred wickets in Tests just before what one must assume to be the end of his career (in his 62nd match); he was a capable batsman who could have been a genuine all-rounder. However he chose to concentrate on the infinite variety of his bowling in which he had no equal. He had the look of a sorcerer, and certainly produced some remarkable spells.

Career Details

Born: Lahore, 15 September 1955
Role: right-arm, leg-spin and googly bowler, right-hand lower-order batsman
Clubs: Punjab (1975/6), Lahore (1975/6-1984/5) and Habib Bank (1975/6-1994/5)
First-class record: (1975-95) 3721 runs (18.42) including 2 centuries, 949 wickets (23.29), with 75 five-wicket hauls and 21 ten-wicket matches, BB9-49, 78 catches
Tests: 67
Test Debut: v England, Lahore, 1977/8
Test record: 1,029 runs (15.59), including 3 fifties, 236 wickets (32.80), 15x5w, 5x10m, and 15 catches
Best Performances: HS 61 v England, Karachi, 1987/8
BB 9-56 v England, Lahore 1987/8, 5 ten-wicket matches, 15 five-wicket innings
Tours: England; 1978, 1982, 1987
India; 1979/80, 1986/7, 1989/90 (Nehru Cup)
Australia; 1983/4, 1988/9 (WSC), 1989/90
New Zealand; 1984/5, 1988/9
Sri Lanka; 1985/6
Westindies; 1987/8
Overseas Tests; 27
One-day Internationals; 104
World Cups; 1983, 1987
Sharjah; 1983/4, 1985/6, 1986/7, 1988/9, 1989/90, 1993/4
Bangladesh; 1988/9 (Asia Cup)
Rest of the World; England 1987

Mohammad Iqbal Qasim

Iqbal Qasim is remarkably unsung, especially outside his own country, for someone with such an excellent Test record as a bowler for Pakistan in 50 matches spread over 12 years. In a country known for its right-handed leg-spin bowlers, it is surprising that Iqbal is the one left-arm, finger-spinner to make a mark. He is easily the most capped of his ilk (Nasim-ul-Ghani is next with 29 caps and 52 wickets), and has taken more Test wickets than all the other Pakistani left-arm spinners put together. He is second only to Abdul Qadir in terms of wickets taken amongst Pakistan's slow bowlers.

That he has remained anonymous is partly due to the fact that he was often in Qadir's shadow, but being the second choice spinner also helped him to maintain his impressive figures, playing when the pitch, or the opposition, demanded another slow bowler in addition to Qadir and the batsmen such as Mustaq Mohammad, Javed Miandad and Wasim Raja, who could all bowl useful leg-breaks. This should not detract from his achievements.

Iqbal was born and brought up in Karachi, for whom he played from an early age, making his first-class debut for them in 1971/2. He first caught the selectors' eye by helping National Bank win both the Patron's Trophy and the Quaid-e-Azam in 1975/6 and the following year he was chosen for the tour to Australia. He produced a most noteworthy start to his Test career though, surprisingly, he made his mark initially as a batsman coming in at number eleven; although

scoring only four in the second innings, he helped Asif Iqbal add 87 for the tenth wicket, a national record against Australia. It was the first of several brave innings. Thus, with Australia now chasing 280 to win, he took four wickets including those of Rick McCosker, Greg Chappell and Doug Walters, and bowled with such guile and control that the batsmen blocked out the last fifteen (8-ball) overs, despite needing only 56 more to win.

Only 5 foot 6 tall, he had a natural loop and flight, and in his second game induced four stumpings in the match for Wasim Bari. Yet he was also very accurate and economical, conceding just 2.2 runs an over during his Test career.

He continued on to the Caribbean but played in only two Tests there, as Pakistan were inclined to err on the side of caution and pick an extra batsman. He bowled in tandem with Abdul Qadir for the first time against England in 1977/8, maintaining long periods of pressure, and between them they took 22 of the 34 wickets to fall in the series.

On the tour to England Pakistan had little time to acclimatise and Iqbal had taken only one wicket for 88 by the time of the first Test. His part in the series will be best remembered for an incident while batting. Coming in as night-watchmen in the 2nd innings of the 1st Test, he had already received several short deliveries from England's quickest bowler, Bob Willis when after forty minutes of resistance on the fourth morning, Willis decided to come round the wicket. He immediately bowled another bouncer at the left-hander, which got through his defensive prod and hit him in the face. Luckily he was not badly hurt, but was led from the field, mouth bleeding, and required two stitches in his lip.

This took its ramifications into the next match as the captains drew up lists of those on each side who should be considered "non-recognised batsmen" and therefore not be subjected to bouncers. Iqbal was included as he is a genuine tail-ender even though he could be obdurate with the bat and does feature in record partnerships against four different countries!

That winter Iqbal took only two wickets in three Tests at home against India and although he toured both New Zealand and Australia did not make the Test side. He regained his place for Pakistan's first tour to India for nearly seventeen years, in 1979/80, and played in all six Tests, bowling the most overs and picking up 17 wickets. He put on a record ninth wicket partnership with Wasim Bari, of 60 in the first Test at Bangalore, and two Tests later on a Bombay pitch of variable bounce and offering spin, he took ten for 175 in 72.5 overs in the match, only the second Pakistani player after Sikander Bakht (in the previous Test) to take ten wickets in a Test in India. In the 2nd innings there, India collapsed from 146 for 4 to 160 all-out, as Qasim bowled a magnificent spell, taking five wickets for three runs in 27 balls. He continued to make useful runs, sharing with Wasim Raja an 8th wicket record v India of 84 (since beaten) in the next Test at Kanpur to rescue the side from 132 for 7. Despite his fine efforts India won the series.

Three weeks after that tour Pakistan played Australia at home and in the first Test at Karachi Iqbal produced his best Test match analysis, 11 for 118. He and Tauseef Ahmed shared eight wickets in the first innings and in the second Iqbal, who came on for the fifth over of the innings, bowled virtually

Pakistan's finest left-arm spinner

and made his highest Test score, 56, after going in at No 3 as night watchmen at Karachi. That winter he also recorded his best first-class figures, taking nine for 80 for a Pakistan XI against an International XI at Lahore. However, on a disappointing tour to England that summer, he lost his place after a run of playing in 18 of the previous 19 Tests.

He bowled well at home against Australia (1982/3) in support to Qadir, who was now the first choice spinner, but was dropped for the final Test. For the next couple of years he was in and out of the side, only playing in two of the six Tests at home to India (1982/3), and one in the away series in 1983/4. When he did not tour Australia or feature at home against England (1983/4) or India (1984/5) he must have feared that his international career was over.

At last he was recalled - summoned from Karachi to join the 16-strong squad on the eve of the first Test against New Zealand at Lahore in 1984/5, having missed the previous 13 Tests and played in just four of the last 26. On a grassless pitch, he took eight for 106 in the match to set up victory, and in the 2nd Test at Hyderabad he bowled beautifully in tandem with Qadir, sharing 14 wickets in the match. Qadir was injured while batting in the final Test at Karachi, and Qasim toiled away for 57 overs to pick up four more wickets. He had had a crucial bearing on the series which was won 2-0, with 18 wickets at an average of 22.11. His initial exclusion had been surprising; he was in superb form in domestic first-class cricket and finished the season with 48 wickets at only 12.62 apiece. He toured New Zealand but on the grassier wickets there played only in the first Test at Wellington, even though Abdul Qadir was sent home after the 2nd Test.

There was no place for him in the side for more

unchanged throughout to take 7-49 from 42 overs of immaculate left-arm spin. He was again ably supported by the off-spinner Ahmed, who was playing in his first Test. On a helpful pitch the slow bowlers took 28 of the 33 wickets to fall in the match.

Nine months later he was the leading wicket-taker against the Westindian touring side, with 17 victims at 17.94, including six wickets in the second innings at Faisalabad. At Karachi, he actually opened the bowling, taking four wickets, while four more in the final Test at Multan took him to 50 in Tests in the previous 13 months.

He took a further 25 Test wickets the next season (1981/2) against Australia and Sri Lanka, including 6-141 from 65 overs against the latter at Faisalabad than two years missing another 13 Tests, including home and away series against Sri Lanka and a tour by the Westindies. However Iqbal had another excellent season in 1986/7, taking 75 wickets (at 15.26), which forced a return to the national side. Imran Khan sent for him to join the tour of India, when he realised that, after two Tests, the remaining matches would be prepared to favour India's two left-arm spinners, Maninder Singh and Ravi Shastri. Qasim played a crucial role in the 16-run victory in the final Test, which gave Pakistan their first series in India. On a Bangalore pitch offering him plenty of encouragement, he took nine wickets in the match for 121, while off-spinner Tauseef Ahmed took 9-139.

Strangely Iqbal never played again in a Test under Imran's captaincy, fuelling an age-old debate that he was favouring fellow-Lahorites, but this was probably no more than a coincidence. Iqbal went to England as assistant manager on the 1987 tour, playing in one first-class match, and was back in the Test team on England's infamous trip in 1987/8. Qadir took more than half the wickets in that series for Pakistan, but Iqbal played an important supporting role, taking three wickets in the first Test at Lahore as England could only equal their lowest total against Pakistan, and five wickets in the first innings at Faisalabad, before the Gatting-Rana incident overshadowed everything else in the match.

He did not tour the Westindies at the beginning of 1988, though he remained the most consistent spinner in domestic cricket, again taking 75 wickets (at 16.17) in 1988/9. At home to Australia that season, on an under-prepared pitch at Karachi, he started with a remarkable first innings spell; coming on to bowl in only the fifth over he took four for 14, eventually finishing with 39-24-35-5. He took nine for 84 in the match and was the leading bowler in the series. In the 3rd Test in his home town, which proved to be his last, he defended stoutly to ensure a draw.

Iqbal Qasim was a most consistent performer in Test cricket, yet during his career he had a couple of long absences from the national side. His figures bear comparison with any; he has a slightly better average than either India's Bishan Bedi, perhaps the best modern-day left-arm spinner, or Westindies' off-spinner Lance Gibbs, the most prolific spin bowler in Tests. Iqbal's figures are very similar to those of England's Tony Lock and rather better than those recorded by Phil Edmonds or India's Dilip Doshi. He has a strike-rate only marginally worse than Qadir's - a wicket every 76 balls compared to every 72 deliveries - but has achieved a better average (28 to 32). Yet Iqbal's performances must be viewed in context in which they were played. As mentioned, he had the benefit of playing on pitches at home which invariably encouraged spin, while abroad he was usually included only if two spinners were required. However, his figures at home and abroad are not dissimilar, even if they are boosted by good performances in India. Outside Asia, he took 31 wickets in 11 Tests at 32 each, which are perfectly respectable figures; the disparity with those at home is no more than you would expect from any bowler, who should favour home conditions.

When he did come into the side, he was most dependable; rarely did the batsmen get after him and he often proved to be a match-winner eight times taking five wickets in an innings and twice ten in a match. His lower-order resistance with the bat and fine fielding were a bonus. He was for many years the top-spinner in domestic cricket and went passed a thousand first-class wickets during the 1992/3 season, in which he captained National Bank with intelligence and imagination, leading them to their first major Trophy, the Wills Cup. He was appointed assistant manager for Pakistan's tour to Australasia that season, too, and is likely to remain involved in the administration of the game in his retirement. In 1995, he became only the 27th Pakistani to be awarded honorary membership of the MCC.

Career Details

Born: Karachi, 6 August 1953
Role: left-hand, lower-order batsman, slow left-arm spinner.
Clubs: Karachi (1971/2-1989/90), National Bank (1972/3-1991/2), Sind (1972/3), and Cheshire (1981)
First-class record: (1971-92) 2403 runs (14.38), 998 wickets (20.38), 68 x 5w, 14 x 10w, BB 9-80, and 166 catches
Tests: 50
Test Debut: v Australia, Adelaide, 1976/7
Test record: 549 runs (13.07), 171 wickets (28.11), 8 x 5w, 2 x 10w, and 42 catches
Best Performances: HS 56 v Sri Lanka, Karachi, 1981/2
BB: 7-49 v Australia, 1981/2
Tours: Australia; 1976/7
Westindies; 1976/7
England; 1978, 1982, 1987 (assistant manager)
India; 1979/80, 1983/4, 1986/7
New Zealand; 1984/5
Overseas Test; 21
One-day Internationals; 15
Bangladesh; 1988/9 (Asia Cup)

Ramiz Raja

Ramiz Raja is a most talented strokemaker who has represented Pakistan with distinction since 1983/4. A right-handed opener who can play obdurate defensive innings, his style is more usually that of cavalier opener and perhaps this is why - statistically anyway - he has not fully fulfilled his obvious potential. Originally he could not get into the one-day side because he was thought too slow, but he now has an excellent limited-overs record and is second only to Javed Miandad for Pakistan with over 5,000 runs, at an average of 33 from 171 matches. By the time he played the last of those, he had scored nine hundreds (and 29 fifties) in one-dayers, an achievement surpassed only by Des Haynes (17), Gordon Greenidge (11) and Viv Richards (11) of Westindies.

He has been regarded as one of the best opening batsmen in world cricket yet his return of just two Test hundreds from 55 games is a bit disappointing for someone with so much ability, who was a regular in the side for a decade. The younger brother of Wasim Raja, he shares the family trait of making attractive fifties (21 of them in Tests) without going on to three figures often enough. Whereas with Wasim it was understandable as he was usually batting at six or seven, perhaps with only the tail to partner him, as an opener or No 3 Ramiz should have converted more of those fifties.

Indeed, Ramiz has set a number of unfortunate records for the most innings, runs and time between Test hundreds. He has gone over ten years since his last Test hundred, playing 71 innings in that time in which he made 2,113 runs. Ramiz eclipsed the previous record held by Westindian Gus Logie, of 1,764 runs between centuries, during his second Test in charge of Pakistan in 1995/6.

Cricket is certainly in the blood of Ramiz Raja, who was born in Lyallpur (now Faisalabad) in 1962. His father was Raja Salim Akhtar, who played for Sargodha before going into the civil service, and his other brother Zaeem also played first-class cricket for National Bank alongside Wasim. A cousin, Atif Rauf, recently made his Test debut for Pakistan, against New Zealand at Christchurch in 1993/4.

Ramiz soon progressed through the junior ranks, making his debut for Servis Industries in 1977 when he was only 15, the same age as Wasim's debut. His progress with Lahore City Whites was steady rather than spectacular until 1983/4 when he helped his side to the Patron's Trophy final, and was also in fine form for Allied Bank, making 149 against Habib Bank, on his way to nearly thirteen hundred runs that season. He was selected for the Pakistan under-23 side and made a sparkling 145 against the touring Sri Lankans, and along with Shoaib Mohammad and Anil Dalpat graduated into the full Test side to play England a month later.

He made his debut in the first Test at Karachi. Wasim was also in the side and thus they emulated the Mohammads as the only brothers to have played for Pakistan in the same Test. Ramiz made just a single in each innings batting at number three, was dropped for the second Test, and though he returned for the third, it was without success.

The following season he toured New Zealand but did not make the Test side despite runs against Wellington and in the one-dayers, making 75 at a run a ball at Christchurch. In that game he watched from the non-striker's end as his brother ducked under a couple of bouncers from Richard Hadlee, so he came down and told Wasim to get a single wherever he could and he'd show him what to do. Wasim obliged and Ramiz hooked Hadlee's next bouncer through mid-wicket one bounce for four. The impetuosity of youth!

He continued to make progress in limited-overs cricket, making a dashing 60 to help beat Westindies in the semi-final of the World Championship of Cricket in Australia, taking the man-of-the-match award, and played in Sharjah.

His recall to the Test side came in the last Test at home to Sri Lanka in 1985/6 in place of Zaheer Abbas - the man he was tipped to replace in the long term - and marked the occasion with his first Test fifty. The reciprocal tour to Sri Lanka was full of animosity concerning the umpiring but Ramiz rose above it, making Pakistan's only hundred in the series, as he held the side together with a most determined century, made in 388 minutes from 242 balls and including 17 boundaries. He went on to top the tour and series averages.

The following winter, Ramiz played a painstaking innings against the Westindies, which in hindsight saved the game and the series as Pakistan later struggled on the last day for a draw. He batted for 408 minutes for his 62, and in the process recorded the third slowest fifty in Tests (318 minutes). The series had shown up problems with the opening pair, and in the next rubber, against India, Ramiz was tried as an opener for the first time during the first Test at Madras. In the previous match he and Shoaib Mohammad added 287 for the first wicket against India under-25s, with Ramiz making 167 from only 193 balls, and so he was moved up to open for the second innings of the Test instead of Rizwan-uz-Zaman, who batted at three. Ramiz has batted there consistently since and followed scores of 69 and 29 at Calcutta with a solid innings of 114 from 279 balls in the third Test at Jaipur, after his opening partner Shoaib had gone for nought. He made some very important runs in the low scoring final Test at Bangalore, making the most runs in the match for Pakistan, helping them to a narrow win that secured them the series. He finished the tour with the most runs (381) in the Tests made at an average of over 40, which also earned him his highest (retrospective) Coopers and Lybrand rating.

Ramiz had an unlucky trip to England in 1987, as he dislocated his shoulder while fielding in the game against Northamptonshire prior to the second Test, and did not return until the final Test at the Oval, following his stylish 150 against Hampshire.

Ramiz had an excellent World Cup that winter, averaging just under 50, with scores of 76 against Sri Lanka, 70 against Westindies and 113 against England. In the semi-final he was sent back and run out for one in the first over, which proved a crucial blow to his team's chances.

Non-cricketing events overshadowed the play in the Tests against England that followed, though Ramiz had a reasonable series. In the one-dayers beforehand, the first seeds of animosity were sown when an appeal against Ramiz for "obstructing the field" was upheld as he tried to come back for a second run to complete a deserved hundred off the last ball of the game, the only instance of a player being dismissed in that way in an international. It was his third unusual dismissal that year against England; in the Perth Challenge at the start of the year, he was caught off a no-ball and as he walked off thinking he was out, he was given out, erroneously, run out. The law states that you cannot be run out in such circumstances. In a one-day international at the Oval in the summer, he was run out without facing a ball.

In the Westindies in the Spring of 1988, Ramiz continued his fine one-day form but was below par in the Tests, and he had a third indifferent series in a row the following September, against Australia. Apart from his 69 not out in the opening game, Ramiz was also completely out of form in the World Series in Australia, failing to reach double figures again. He was dropped from the Test side in New Zealand, but he proved in the one-day internationals that perhaps he should have played, with scores of 51, 72 and 101.

Ramiz found form just at the right time in the Nehru Cup. His 77 against India ensured Pakistan a place in the semi-finals, where his 85 not out and partnership of 122 from just 77 balls with Salim Malik against England, took Pakistan to the final. There, in front of a Calcutta crowd of over 70,000, he set his side on its way to a four wicket victory over the Westindies with a brisk 35 off 31 balls.

Consequently, he returned to the Test side against India two weeks later and made three fifties in five innings but again failed to cash in on these beginnings as some of his more prolific compatriots might have done. He arrived late for the tour to Australia following injury, and went straight into the 2nd Test without any match practice and, as a result, struggled. He led the side between the Tests, against Victoria, and was involved in an incident when the umpire, Robin Bailache, informed him that Mustaq Ahmed would not be allowed to bowl again in the innings after being warned twice for running on the pitch in his follow-through. The Pakistanis refused to continue; Intikhab Alam, the manager, came out on to the ground, and the matter was only resolved after half-an-hour when Mustaq was allowed to carry on bowling. This was decided on the strength of Ramiz's contention that he had not been made aware of the final warning.

Once acclimatised in Australia he hit two excellent one-day hundreds in succession against Sri Lanka, opening and batting through the innings on both occasions; in the second he added a World Series Cup record of 202 in 33 overs for the first wicket with Saeed Anwar.

The following season (1990/1), he started the series with New Zealand with an innings of 78 and a partnership of 172 with Shoaib Mohammad, but without a significant score in the rest of the series and following failures in the first Test against Westindies, was dropped. When his replacement Saeed Anwar got a pair on his debut, Ramiz was recalled for the final Test. However on the way to the ground he wrote off his car in an accident with a bus and was unable to open, going in at the fall of the second wicket.

Ramiz came close to reaching that elusive three figure score against Sri Lanka in the first Test at Sialkot but he fell just two runs short when he was caught behind off the left-arm spinner Anurasiri after a fine innings taking four-and-a-half hours, in which he hit 11 fours. He was again well set in the next Test, with 51 not out when rain washed out the rest of the match, and made another fifty in Faisalabad to finish top of the batting averages, with 73.33, for the series.

Ramiz helped Pakistan win four of the five one-dayers against Sri Lanka as well as the Wills Trophy earlier in the season, and Pakistan went to the World Cup amongst the favourites. Ramiz made a hundred in the first game against the Westindies and to that point was the only Pakistani to have made a one-day hundred against them. However he was criticised afterwards for not accelerating sooner as the opposition had romped home by 10 wickets. He missed the games against India and South Africa but he made a third hundred overall in World Cups - to equal Viv Richards record - when he hit 119 not out of the 167 required to beat New Zealand, a remarkable 71% of the runs, and so ensured that Pakistan qualified for the semis. In the final he fell early on but took the catch to clinch the game, and had earlier taken an excellent running catch to dismiss the dangerous Dermot Reeve. Ramiz finished fourth in the batting averages for the competition, with 58.16, behind only Martin Crowe, Peter Kirsten and Javed Miandad.

Ramiz had a solid series in England in 1992, averaging just under forty but again a century eluded him in the Tests. He played a glorious innings in the 2nd Texaco Trophy match, making 86 as he and Aamir Sohail set Pakistan off ahead of the required rate as they chased 303 to win, though eventually the team fell short. He had to fly home briefly before the third Test to have treatment on his back but on his return, at Old Trafford, made 54 and an exciting 88. In the first innings he got a poor decision when he was given out caught behind, despite the half-hearted nature of the appeal. In the next, he was the only batsman other than Salim Malik to come to terms with the vagaries of the Headingley track, making 63 in the second innings, and later in the tour captained in the last of the one-dayers.

He finished the tour with over a thousand runs including his highest first-class score, a stylish innings of 172 against Worcestershire in the first three-day match. He was rewarded with the vice-captaincy for the early tours the following winter to Australia and New Zealand under Javed Miandad. However, after some poor one-day results, both were replaced, by Wasim Akram and Waqar Younis, for the one-day tournaments in Sharjah and South Africa and for the tour to the Caribbean.

It was in Sharjah that Ramiz and Anwar eclipsed their own one-day opening partnership record by

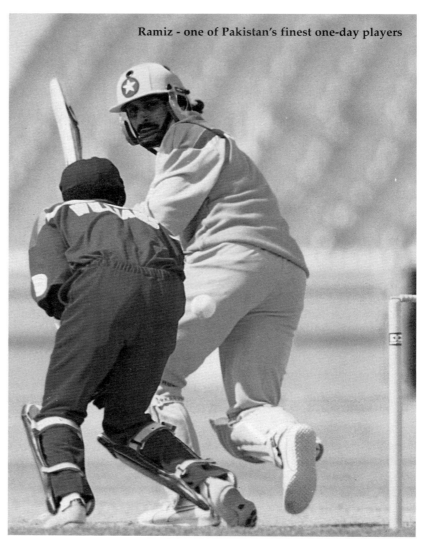

Ramiz - one of Pakistan's finest one-day players

putting on 204 to ensure victory in the Wills Trophy over Sri Lanka, with Ramiz making his eighth one-day hundred at a run a ball, but there after he was out of form. He was unable to emulate the success his brother had enjoyed in the Westindies back in 1977, making just 82 runs in total in the three Tests and finishing the series with a duck. He deserved a chance against the rather tamer attack of Zimbabwe the following winter but was overlooked in favour of Shoaib Mohammad, which seemed a somewhat negative move. In his continued absence, Saeed Anwar established himself as Aamir Sohail's partner after an excellent Sharjah tournament and a good tour to New Zealand.

His international future seemed uncertain when dropped after failing in the Westindies in 1992/3, but a century and 97 not out in trial matches at the end of the 1993/4 season ensured his recall for the tour to Sri Lanka. However, he played only in the one-dayers there and was not selected the following season, despite a career best triple hundred for Allied Bank, made in just under ten hours from 415 balls, which set up an innings victory over Habib Bank. After 10 years in Grade II, Allied reached the final of the Patron's Trophy, beating PIA convincingly by 10 wickets.

When Salim Malik was relieved of the captaincy after allegations of match-rigging, Ramiz got a surprise opportunity to captain his country as a stopgap measure. He had arrived at the pre-season training camp without even packing his pads, thinking he had little chance of a recall, but walked away with the captaincy, as a player with experience who had been outside the squad when the team was squabbling the previous winter. He had a dream start, too. In his first Test for two-and-a-half years, he won the toss, elected to bat and played with a fluency belying his long absence from Test cricket. He looked set to make that elusive third Test century, too, playing elegantly for 78, including 11 boundaries before being quite unexpectedly dismissed to end a fine stand of 132 with Inzamam-ul-Haq, which was the foundation of Pakistan's match-winning total. Ramiz became the first player to start with an innings victory in his first Test in charge.

He continued in fine form in the next Test (hitting 75 and 25 to pass Logie's record!), but was bedevilled with ill-luck, losing first Waqar Younis then Wasim Akram from his bowling attack. He went into the decisive third Test without either of them or a frontline spinner, allowing Sri Lanka to fight back and take the series. Defeat seemed ignominious, though in truth Sri Lanka played to their full potential, while Pakistan were without key players.

Although relieved of the captaincy, at least Ramiz had proved that he was still Test class with the bat, and was selected for the tour to Australia and New Zealand. Though failing in the first Test, Ramiz proved consistent thereafter, hitting scores of 59, 40, 33, 39, 54 and 62, to take him past 500 runs for the winter in seven Tests, even if it did extend his sequence of runs without a Test century, while marching on with his tally of fifties. Against New Zealand, he shared an extraordinary partnership with Aamir Sohail, which was broken 15 minutes before lunch on the first day, with the score on 135. Ramiz should have played an integral part in the 1996 World Cup that followed. After all, he had made three hundreds and averaged over fifty in previous competitions, but he played in only one match, against South Africa, in which he batted down the order at No 8.

Ramiz would have benefited from a spell in county cricket, spending time ironing out flaws in his technique and his tendency to get out when set, like Salim Malik corrected while at Essex. These flaws are indicative of the amount of one-day cricket Pakistan has played in the nineties, while Ramiz has lost his Test place occasionally when the side's one-day form has been indifferent, as was the case after the World Cup in 1992-93. He is one of the few players to score more consistently and average more in one-day cricket than in Tests; only seven players have scored more runs in limited-overs internationals. Yet he is not in the top 30 of the Coopers and Lybrand (Test) ratings, and it is by Test cricket that players are ultimately judged. He tends to work the ball to leg and he has a fallibility outside off-stump which has come from the amount of one-day cricket he plays - look at the number of non-Test tours he has been on. There is a tendency for bowlers to nip the ball into batsmen in one-day cricket and away in Test matches and consequently he is suspect against away-movement.

The overall contribution of Ramiz to Pakistani cricket has been significant in an era when the side has often been at its strongest. While he is hopeful of regaining his Test place, feeling at 34, he still has something to give, he is likely to make an important contribution off the field too. He has been commissioned by Allied Bank, who employ him as their sports manager, to run coaching sessions in England for Asian youngsters. They began in the summer of 1996 and the next best thing for Ramiz to getting his Test place back, would be to unearth a player of Test potential.

Career Details

Born: Lyallpur (Faisalabad), 14 July 1962
Role: right-hand, opening (or middle-order) batsman, very occasional leg-break bowler
Clubs: Servis Industries (1977/8), Punjab (1978/8), Lahore (1978/9-1985/6), Allied Bank (1983/4, 1994/5), PNSC (1987/8-1990/1)
First-class record: (1977-95) 9,178 runs (37.15) including 16 centuries (HS 300), 5 wickets (66.40) and 85 catches
Tests: 55
Test Debut: v England, Karachi, 1983/4
Test record: 2,747 runs (31.94), including 2 hundreds and 21 fifties, and 32 catches
Best Performances: HS 122 v Sri Lanka, Colombo, 1985/6
Tours: New Zealand; 1984/5, 1988/9, 1992/3, 1995/6
Sri Lanka; 1984/5 (under 23's), 1985/6, 1994/5
India; 1986/7, 1989/90 (Nehru Cup)
England; 1987, 1992
Westindies; 1987/8, 1992/3
Australia; 1984/5 (WSC), 1986/7 (Perth Challenge), 1988/9 (WSC), 1989/90, 1991/2, 1992/3 (WSC)
Overseas Tests; 28
One-day Internationals; 171
World Cups; 1987/8, 1991/2, 1995/6
Sharjah; 1984/5, 1985/6, 1986/7, 1988/9, 1989/90, 1991/2, 1992/3
Bangladesh; 1988/9 (Asia Cup)South Africa; 1992/3 (and Zimbabwe)

Wasim Hasan Raja

Wasim Raja was a glorious left-handed strokemaker, who represented Pakistan for a dozen years, during which he played in 57 Test matches. Having captained his country at various junior levels and then his club, National Bank, with aplomb, Wasim would have been a sensible choice in the early eighties to captain the national side in preference to the diffident Zaheer Abbas or the rumbustious Javed Miandad, who had been ousted in a players' revolt.

Wasim's chances were dented though on the tour to England in 1978, when he was vice-captain, as the weakened side without its Packer players was outplayed. He was also prone to let his feelings be known, and spoke out against those who signed for World Series Cricket, feeling they should not play for Pakistan again. Wasim had always remained loyal to his country - indeed was one of the few prepared to carry on under Miandad in Sri Lanka in 1981/2 - and played the game in its true spirit, for love not money. He had his own style and always looked to play his strokes and entertain. As a consequence occasionally he fell foul of the management for not doing things their way. He played the game with a passion and a pride but with enjoyment upper most in his mind.

He was involved in several clashes with the Board of Control for Cricket in Pakistan and he remained on the fringes of a clique of senior players in the Test team. Unlike those, he was often chosen on a match-to-match basis, which put him under unnecessary pressure to succeed. Yet he was performing a difficult role batting in the middle-order and backing up the specialist bowlers.

As a batsman, he was a prodigy at 18, when he captained the national under-19 side. Imran Khan, who had considered his own batting fairly highly at that stage wrote of Wasim (in his book *All Round View*) that "he was in a different class altogether and was already batting with a maturity beyond his years". They used to practice together when they were 14 and 15 and Wasim did not bother to don pads and even widened the wicket to give the bowler a chance, denying Imran his turn to bat until he had got him out. Wasim knew from an early age that he would play Test cricket.

He played his cricket then as now, with a cavalier spirit, going for his shots. Viv Richards thought that his carefree style was more like that of a Westindian, but he was also a determined competitor who had a splendid all-round talent as was evident in 1973/4 when he finished one wicket short of becoming only the second player ever (after Maurice Tate in 1926/7 for the MCC touring

side in India and Ceylon) to do the double in a season outside England, taking 99 wickets at 22.41 and scoring 1010 runs at an average of 32.58; a hundred wickets in a winter season has been achieved only eight times.

Yet in some respects Pakistan never fully utilised this ability. Wasim, like his brother Ramiz, has an unfortunate, misleading record of time between hundreds, reflecting in part the way he played, but also that he usually batted at six or seven, where his cameos were just what was required with the tail at the other end. Had he batted higher he may well have converted more of his eighteen Test fifties into hundreds (of which he made four), while he was unlucky to have a succession of leg-spinners as his captains - Intikhab Alam, Mustaq Mohammad and Javed Miandad - then Abdul Qadir as well, all of whom tended to bowl ahead of him.

Born in Multan in the year of Pakistan's first Test match (1952), Wasim was the eldest of three boys, all of whom played first-class cricket; Ramiz followed Wasim into the Test team while Zaeem played for National Bank. Their father Raja Salim Akhtar also played first-class, captaining Sargodha, before concentrating on his career in the Civil Service, where he rose to the position of Home Secretary. A cousin of Wasim's, Atif Rauf, is another first-class cricketer whose fine form for the Agricultural Development Bank of Pakistan, earned him selection for Pakistan's tour of New Zealand in 1994, at the age of 29.

Wasim made his first-class debut, aged 15, for Lahore, while still at school at Government College, and soon was representing the national youth side. He went on to Punjab University, where he excelled at cricket and academically. He was highly ambitious and that was reflected in his studies, getting a first in his Masters degree in politics.

After some fine performances in domestic cricket and for the under-19 side, Wasim soon came into the Test side. He was called up to join the tour to New Zealand, in 1972/3, when he was flown in as a replacement after Saeed Ahmed and Mohammad Ilyas had been sent home from the Australian leg of the tour for disciplinary reasons. He topped scored with 86 in his first match, against Canterbury, and ensured selection for the first Test with a fine all-round performance against

Northern Districts, taking 3-13 and 6-72 and making 43 not out. He made an attractive forty on his debut, at the age of 20, at Wellington and another in the third at Auckland, but had to sit with his pads on while 350 were added by Mustaq Mohammad and Asif Iqbal in the 2nd at Dunedin. Despite topping the tour bowling averages Wasim had little opportunity to bowl in the Tests with Intikhab Alam bowling at his best and Mustaq Mohammad also in good form. In the final Test New Zealand's last wicket pair, Hastings and Collinge, produced the highest 10th wicket partnership in Test history, taking the score from 251 for 9 to 402, to match exactly Pakistan's first innings score. Wasim was the seventh bowler to be called upon and broke the stand in his second over, and also took all three wickets to fall in the 2nd innings. Being under-bowled became a perennial problem for Wasim. Still, he had contributed well to Pakistan's first series win overseas.

Wasim lost his place after the first Test in the home series against England that followed (1972/3) but after his record-breaking season in 1973/4, when he captained the Under-25s to a convincing victory in Sri Lanka, he was a certainty for the tour to the UK in the summer of 1974. He regained his place in the Test side after making a stylish hundred (including two sixes and 16 fours) against Glamorgan, who offered him a contract for the following season which he declined on Majid Khan's advice. During that innings Zaheer Abbas, after playing a glorious cover drive, had come up to Wasim when he had just come in and said, "Watch me and do as I do. Don't do anything rash." Wasim responded by playing a superb shot of his own and came down the track to say, "Zed, anything you can do I can do better."

He did not expect to be selected for the 2nd Test at Lord's but the manager, Omar Qureshi, took him aside on the eve of the match to break the news that he would be playing. He was surprised by Wasim's lack of nerves when he was told he would be appearing at cricket's headquarters. The next day Pakistan got off to a good start until torrential rain left the pitch almost unplayable against Derek Underwood. The young Wasim, not knowing of the man's great reputation on such wickets, kept carting him to the Mound Stand boundary or driving him straight and his innings was ended only by a spectacular, one-handed catch by Tony Greig in front of the sight-screen at the Nursery End. Wasim alone, after the openers, reached double figures. Again in the 2nd innings only he and Mustaq Mohammad came to terms with the conditions, as they added 125 for the 4th wicket in three and three-quarter hours of masterful batting, a crucial partnership which earned a draw, as once broken the last seven wickets fell for just 32 runs.

Two more useful knocks at the Oval meant that Wasim finished 2nd to Zaheer Abbas in the Test averages and even pipped him to top the tour batting with an average of 54.

Still not fully established, he made an excellent maiden Test hundred against Westindies at Karachi in 1974/5. Pakistan had slipped to 178 for 5 but he masterminded the recovery first with Intikhab Alam, adding 68, and then with Wasim Bari with whom he put on 128, which is still the seventh wicket record for either side in the series. His innings was such a fine one that on completing his hundred the normal posse of spectators that sometimes come onto the field to congratulate a player, became a full-scale invasion. One fan came running up to him but found himself unable to slow up and went sliding into Wasim. The police moved in and play was held up for two and a half hours as they tried to clear the playing area and quell the rioting with tear-gas.

As he waited in the dressing room for a resumption, Wasim was still ecstatic and shaking with excitement. Indeed, he spilt a cup of tea over himself and Asif Iqbal put a further damper on proceedings by jesting that his hundred would not count as the game would have to be abandoned. Still not sure whether Asif was joking, it was one of Wasim's most satisfying moments just to get back on to the pitch and continue the match.

Later in the game he had the misfortune to damage ankle ligaments while bowling as he spun round to appeal - an injury that had to be put in plaster. However pressure was put on him by Hanif Mohammad to bat in the 2nd innings to give his younger brother Sadiq Mohammad, who had a neck injury himself, the chance to complete his hundred. Wasim stood like a flamingo on his one good leg and was able to defend against the quicker bowlers but toppled over when the spinner Lance Gibbs came on, and was bowled. Sadiq was still two runs short but he had not tried to push for the runs to ensure that he complete his hundred.

Despite that injury Wasim finished as the leading wicket-taker and topped the bowling averages in domestic cricket that season, as well as making nearly 1,000 runs. He took that form into the Lancashire Leagues and delighted his new club, Ramsbottom, with his all-round contributions. He also played in that summer's inaugural World Cup, hitting a fine fifty against the Westindies before playing on to Andy Roberts. With the specialist bowlers through their 12-over allocations, he was required to bowl the last over of a thrilling match but could not prevent Westindies making the three runs required.

Wasim toured Sri Lanka that winter and made 71 in the 2nd unofficial Test in 1975/6 - Pakistan's only international cricket that season - but lost his place in the next series, against New Zealand, when in the 1st Test, after watching Javed Miandad and Asif Iqbal add 281, he became the middle victim of a hat-trick. He was selected though for the tour to Australia and Westindies. However, the shortness of the trip to the former meant that Wasim played in only one first-class match but even a brilliant hundred against Queensland, made in just over two hours and including five sixes and 11 fours, was not enough to force a recall. At least it kept him in contention and when Zaheer Abbas was unfit for the first Test in the Caribbean, Wasim came into the side. He was to play the best all-round cricket of his career, finishing top of both the batting and the bowling averages for the Tests.

He top scored in half the Test innings and with all the other batsman apart from Majid Khan struggling to cope with the Westindies newly formed four-pronged pace attack, Wasim played in a sparkling, positive manner. His batting is still remembered with affection in the Caribbean as he remains one of a very select few to have successfully counterattacked against the Westindies. Indeed he hit 14 sixes in the series - a fair indication of the uninhibited nature of his strokeplay.

Surprisingly he had faced just one ball in Tests in two years since his last appearance against the Westindies, but marked his return with another superb not out hundred, which included a six and 12 fours. Coming in with five wickets down for 207, he rallied the lower-order to more than double the total. His mood as he returned to the pavilion was one of defiance, mouthing "you can't drop me now no matter how hard you try."

The story goes that with Wasim nervously excited about his return to Test cricket, he stayed in the bar of the hotel until past two in the morning. The barman kept cajoling him that Pakistan would get beaten easily, while Wasim, gaining courage as the night went on, bet him that he would get a hundred the next day. The barman agreed that if he did, everything would be "on the house" for the rest of his stay in Barbados.

The hospitality obviously suited him because he played an equally important innings second time round. Pakistan had collapsed to 158 for 9, a lead of just 172, when he was joined by the last man Wasim Bari, his usual room-mate on tour. They rescued the side with the highest partnership for the tenth wicket for Pakistan in all Tests. The 133 they added in just 110 minutes meant Westindies were set a challenging target of 306, and came within a wicket of losing a Test in Bridgetown for the first time since 1934-35, as the last pair hung on.

Wasim's prolific form continued in Port of Spain where he again top scored in both innings with 65 and 84. He was the only player able to cope with Colin Croft, who took eight for 29 in the first innings, and Wasim's aggressive three hour knock in the 2nd innings at least gave his side a chance. After surprise failures in Guyana where many of the other Pakistani batsmen found their best form, the side returned to Trinidad where Wasim showed his liking for the Queen's Park Oval pitch once more, top-scoring with 70 in the second innings. He put on 116 with Mustaq Mohammad after Pakistan had slipped to 95 for 5. Then his under-used leg-spin got the breakthrough, after Deryck Murray and Andy Roberts had resisted for two-and-a-half hours on the final day, and his three quick wickets sped the side to a 266-run victory.

He had a long bowl in the final Test, taking the important wickets of Roy Fredericks, Viv Richards and Clive Lloyd, and he made another fifty as he and Asif Iqbal added 115 in a brave attempt to save the game. Despite falling to an injudicious shot in the first innings, holing out to the leg-spin of David Holford, he still attacked and had just added two more sixes to his tally for the series when dismissed again by the spinner, this time caught bat and pad.

He has been criticised on two counts for his batting during this Test match. Firstly for the way he got out, looking to get after the spinner, yet he was batting in quite some discomfort because of a badly swollen top-hand and he considered attack to be the best form of defence. Secondly he was said to be scared of Andy Roberts because when he first came in the second innings, he asked Asif Iqbal - who was batting superbly - to take Roberts, which he was happy to do, which is the essence of what building a partnership is all about.

Wasim's batting was superb in that series, and although he had other fine series, he was now at his peak. Yet in the press conference before the final Test Mustaq Mohammad had been asked how he thought the match would go and he went through the side and failed to mention Wasim's contribution throughout the series. When pressed, his captain put it down to luck! It made Wasim all the more determined to get the sixty runs he needed to give him 500 runs for the series.

Although he could have played for Kerry Packer's "Cricket Circus," he chose to stay loyal to his country. He had a fairly quiet rubber at home against England but with his experience and success on the previous visit he was made vice-captain for the 1978 tour to England. However the tour proved a disaster as the inexperienced side struggled in unfamiliar conditions and inclement weather and this probably scuppered any ambitions he may have had for the captaincy. He also turned down an opportunity to play for Essex, deciding to play Minor Counties cricket for Durham instead.

His reward for staying true to his country was being dropped for the home series against India as soon as the Packer players returned in 1978/9, mainly because of the objections he had raised to the inclusion of the "Packerstanis," who he felt had compromised and contradicted their principles. However he toured New Zealand and returned to the Test side after making a hundred against Wellington and 96 v Young New Zealand. In the first Test at Christchurch he and Mustaq Mohammad went through the Kiwi batting, sharing nine wickets, to win the game by 128 runs, and with it the series as the remaining two Tests were drawn. Wasim played a delightful innings of 74 in 111 minutes at Napier, a bright interlude in a Test Pakistan seemed content to draw. The tour continued on to Australia, where Wasim played in his country's first win there, at Melbourne in Pakistan's 100th Test.

Wasim returned to England the following summer for a season of league cricket and the World Cup, in which he had short but sweet innings against Australia and England. Wasim had just met his wife to be, Anne, and invited her to the latter game at Headingley. Unfortunately, the tickets he had for her were left at the wrong gate and that was almost the end of a beautiful friendship!

Wasim had an excellent series against India (1979/80) and was one of the few batsmen to be consistent. Asif Iqbal put his faith in Wasim, who made sure he responded, whereas many of the other players let the pressure get to them. Wasim's style allowed him to continue to play in his usual relaxed manner, and though occasionally he fell to loose strokes, he scored well throughout the series.

In the 2nd Test he rescued the side from 90 for 4 with a partnership of 130 with Asif Iqbal, and was unlucky to fall just three runs short of his hundred, and again in the second innings top-scored with a more circumspect 61. Despite his fine form he had moved back to number seven (from five) by the fourth Test to accommodate Majid Khan's move down the order. He was called upon to play

Wasim - the free-scoring strokemaker

another cavalier rearguard, marshalling the tail to such good effect that the last three wickets added 117. When the last man, Ehtesham-ud-Din, was out it left Wasim stranded on 94, after 229 minutes in which he had hit a six and ten fours. Roger Binny, who had taken the last wicket, quickly came up to Wasim to apologise for denying him the chance of a much deserved hundred.

The fifth Test at Madras saw Wasim come out to bat in another crisis, this time at 57 for 5 and he responded with another top-score, but could not save the game. At Calcutta, he made his fifth fifty in eight innings and finished the series with 450 runs at an average of 56.25 - the best on either side. With Abdul Qadir out of form and Mustaq Mohammad retired this might have been the series when Wasim's leg-spinners could and should have been fully utilised as well, but he bowled only 23 overs in the six-match series. A three-match series with Australia (1979/80) followed but Wasim had only two completed innings against them, making a fifty at Lahore.

Always at his best against the Westindies (1980/1), Wasim averaged over sixty - almost double the next best - against an attack including Joel Garner, Colin Croft, Malcolm Marshall and Sylvester Clarke. He made 76 at Lahore, was left unbeaten on 38 in Faisalabad, and hit 77 not out at Karachi, each time when Pakistan were in trouble. He passed 2,000 runs in Tests during the final Test in the town of his birth, Multan, and achieved his highest Coopers and Lybrand rating at this juncture, with 752 points, the ninth highest by a Pakistani. Such a rating in 1994 would have put him third behind only Brian Lara of Westindies and virtually level with Sachin Tendulkar of India.

He started the 1981/2 season with 144 against an International XI at Lahore, where he put on 262 with Javed Miandad, and he had a consistent series in Australia with scores of 48, 43, 36 and 50, and bowled 50 overs in support of Iqbal Qasim in the match at the Melbourne Cricket Ground, where Pakistan won by an innings.

He was one of only three players on that tour

who agreed to continue under Javed Miandad's captaincy in Sri Lanka, though he had objected originally, but had an indifferent series. He toured England in 1982, but poor early form meant he was dropped after the first Test at Edgbaston. In that match, however, Imran Khan over-used Abdul Qadir, who bowled 69 overs in the match for his three wickets. In the 2nd innings England's last two wickets added 103 crucial runs and when the captain eventually turned to Wasim, he immediately provided the breakthrough.

At home he remained in contention by playing in the one-dayers against Australia and India and after making a hundred against the latter for the Governor's XI he was recalled for the final Test of a series in which the batsmen had scored heavily, but was run out for ten in his only innings.

He played in his third World Cup in 1983 but was in and out of the side and did not find his best touch. After five years with Durham, he played his minor counties cricket with neighbouring Northumberland, and helped them to be undefeated that season. He was to return to Durham the following year.

After his fine performances on the previous trip to India he was recalled for the 1983/4 tour and again he excelled, averaging 60 and finishing top of the bowling averages. At Jullundar, Wasim made his highest Test score and recorded his best bowling analysis. Again the side was in a precarious position at 169 for 7, but the dashing left-hander took charge in a partnership of 95 with Tahir Naqqash. When Naqqash was dismissed Wasim hit out making 69 out of the last 73 runs before being last out for 125 including two sixes and 17 fours. Under-bowled at first, Wasim took the last four wickets to ensure the man-of-the-match award.

Wasim toured Australia in 1983/4 but had to make way for Salim Malik after two Tests, while Imran's return after injury also blocked his path. When Imran was forced into a further period of convalescence, Wasim was recalled to play against England later that winter, taking his place in the team at Karachi for the first Test alongside his younger brother Ramiz, who was making his debut. Neither scored well in that game but Wasim made his fourth and final Test hundred in the next at Faisalabad. He batted for exactly five hours, hitting two sixes and 14 fours from 210 balls, and raced to three figures with boundaries that whistled to long-off, cover and square leg in an over from Neil Foster.

He was to play just a handful more Tests, but marked his last in Pakistan (in 1984/5) with scores of 51 and 60 not out against New Zealand which assured selection for the tour there, and for the World Championship of cricket that followed in Australia. In excellent form in club cricket, there were plenty of suggestions in the media that he should be recalled to the side for home series with the Westindies in 1986/7, and as the batsmen struggled for runs throughout that rubber, there was an even stronger case for him touring India shortly after because of his experience and record there, which is second to none amongst his compatriots with an average of over fifty there. Strangely Younis Ahmed, who had not played Test cricket for 17 years was chosen as a replacement ahead of him. Omar Qureshi, who was the manager in 1974, was quoted as part of a strong testimony for his inclusion in the Pakistani newspaper, *The Nation*, citing his last innings against India as evidence:

"In Jullundar he played an innings of such stupendous power that it left us breathless. Lala Amarnath who was present said that even Bradman would have been proud to own that innings. He then cut loose. In one over he hit Binny for plenty including a straight six off the back foot that in aviation would have been considered tree-top flying. Straight and low, all the power coming from his wrists. I have seen many great innings from batsmen who are legends. Denis Compton, Keith Miller, Sobers, Kanhai, Richards and our own Majid Khan. Who can say of the future? But I have not seen a better innings and would consider myself a very lucky man if I ever did. He had come into bat in a crisis. None before him had pounded and pummelled the bowling into submission.

"He had built the innings until the foundations were secure. Only then did he go on the rampage. I was told by a senior team-mate of his that he was not a team man. I could not help detecting a certain envy. I dismissed it as pure nonsense. No one can bat in a crisis with the flourish and the courage as Wasim Raja can, can be anything but a team man.

"He is the one player who has been badly done by our cricket establishment. Perhaps there was so much talent that they did not know how to handle it. Perhaps Wasim did not know how to handle it himself."

With his great ability came the sort of self-confidence that can be mistaken for arrogance. Like Imran Khan, he did not like the hierarchy that existed within the team when he first came into the side; once he was told by Salah-ud-Din that the 12th man's duties included putting the great players' socks out to dry. Wasim responded, "you seem so good at it - you do it." There were times when Wasim seemed like a rebel without a cause but this only represented a defiance at the unfair pressure he was put under because of the insecurity of his tenure in the side, which seemed ridiculous as when the going was toughest Wasim could be considered as Pakistan's best batsman.

Instead of being respected for his talent and his experience, he found that whenever he batted his partner seemed to be giving him advice. He remembers even Iqbal Qasim talking him through the finer points of batting! He liked to bat best with Majid Khan, who just got on with his own game.

Wasim went 58 innings between his 3rd and 4th Test hundreds (Ramiz has gone well passed that number since his last century now, beating the record of 64 held by Syed Kirmani of India). However like Allan Border who had a similar sequence at the start of the 1990s, he maintained his Test average, by making 15 fifties including two nineties in between. Surely had he had more opportunity to bat higher up the order, he would have scored more tons, for he was often left stranded with the tail.

Wasim - the leg-spinner; his bowling was under used

His batting ability is best illustrated by his record against the Westindies. In 11 Tests he made 919 runs at an average 57.43, with two hundreds and seven fifties, top-scoring eight times, the best aggregate for Pakistan. Only Greg Chappell of Australia has averaged more (58.77) against the best bowling attack in the world in the last 20 years, and even he was not as consistent as Wasim, as Chappell failed miserably in his last series against them in 1981/2.

In one-day cricket Wasim's athletic fielding, attacking strokeplay and versatile bowling - he quite often opened the bowling with his seamers - made him a useful exponent of this form of the game.

Wasim continued to play first-class cricket until 1987/8 for National Bank and that season he was put in charge of the Pakistan under-19 side for six months, taking them to the inaugural youth World Cup in Australia, where they lost in the final. Under his auspices were the young Inzamam-ul-Haq, Mustaq Ahmed, Aqib Javed and Basit Ali whose talents he has helped nurture but Wasim has received little credit for so doing. They still ring him up if they have a problem with their cricket.

After many happy seasons playing in the Durham League, he decided to take a PGCE teaching degree at Durham University. Unfortunately he suffered a terrible car crash in December 1989, which at one point threatened his

life, and almost as serious, his playing days. He was persuaded by Grenville Holland, who runs Durham University cricket, to try to play again the next summer against medical advice. Although still experiencing some discomfort, his efforts helped Durham win the UAU championship (the 60 over tournament for English universities) by making 57 not out in the final against Exeter University.

He is now teaching geography and physical education at Caterham School, coaching cricket, hockey and rugby. His wife, Anne, whom Wasim met in Durham, is also a fine cricketer, and their sons Ali and Ahmed are showing promise playing junior cricket for Surrey. He is keen to watch them develop, as well as keeping an eye on the continuing career of his brother, Ramiz, and so he has stepped down as captain of the Old Whitgiftians Cricket Club, which plays in the Surrey Championship. Recently elected as an honorary member of the MCC, Wasim is still playing his cricket in the same relaxed, attacking vein.

Career Details

Born: Multan, 3 July 1952
Role: left-hand, middle-order batsman, right-hand leg-spin and googly bowler, occasional medium-pace bowler
Clubs: Lahore (1967/8-1985/6), Sargodha (1969/70), Punjab University (1969/70), Pakistan Universities (1972/3), PIA (1973/4), Punjab (1973/4), National Bank (1974/5-1987/8), Durham (1978-87) and Northumberland (1983).
First-class record: (1967-88) 11,408 runs (35.20) including 17 centuries (HS 165), 558 wickets (29.02) (BB 8-65), and 155 catches
Tests: 57
Test Debut: v New Zealand, Wellington, 1972/3
Test record: 2,821 runs (36.16), including 4 centuries, 51 wickets (35.80) and 20 catches
Best Performances: HS 125 v India, Jullundur, 1982/3
BB 4-50 v India, at Jullundur, 1982/3
Tours: New Zealand; 1972/3, 1978/9, 1984/5
England; 1974, 1978, 1982
Westindies; 1976/7
Australia; 1978/9, 1981/2, 1983/4, 1984/5 (WSC)
India; 1979/80, 1983/4
Overseas Tests; 34
One-day Internationals; 54
World Cups; 1975, 1979, 1983
Sri Lanka; 1973/4, 1975/5

Haroon Rashid, Dar

Haroon Rashid was a marvellous strokemaker, who perhaps never quite fulfilled his potential in Test cricket. He scored three hundreds in his 23 matches but with such competition for batting places in the late seventies, he was not granted the sort of extended run that might have seen him really develop, and was not helped by the inconsistencies of his form and that of the selectors.

Born in Karachi in March 1953, he was one of eight brothers, four of whom played first-class cricket, the others being Mahmood, who played for United Bank, Umar, for Karachi, and Tahir who played for Karachi and Habib Bank, and who set a new world record when he made nine dismissals (eight catches and a stumping) in an innings for the Habib in a Wills Trophy match against Pakistan Automobile Corporation at Gujranwala, 1992/3.

Haroon made his debut for Karachi in 1971/2 but did not really catch the selectors' eye until 1975/6 when he had the best season of his career, making over a thousand runs at an average of 51.70 with four hundreds, including one in the final of the Patron Trophy for National Bank against PIA. He was selected for the short tour to Sri Lanka in the New Year, and made a hundred against the Board XI.

It was enough to win him a place on the full Test tour to Australia and the Westindies in 1976/7. A brilliant fielder, especially at short-leg, he was made twelfth man in the first two Tests against Australia, but a sparkling hundred against Queensland, which included a six and fifteen fours, ensured his maiden Test appearance in the final Test at Sydney. He and Asif Iqbal added 94 for the fifth wicket to help Pakistan set up a match-winning lead and their first victory in Australia. He finished with 57 and was described by *Wisden* as looking like "a batsman of ideal temperament" and "a player of excellent calibre."

He took over the No 3 position for the first two Tests in the Caribbean when Zaheer Abbas was unfit, and had a steady series, playing throughout, again catching the eye where more senior players failed. He made 60 in the third Test at Georgetown and 72 at Kingston, including two magnificent hooks for six off Joel Garner before being brilliantly caught by Gordon Greenidge at second slip off Colin Croft. He held the first innings together when no one else reached 30. He finished second only to Majid Khan in the combined tour averages, scoring 887 runs which included two hundreds, against Barbados and Guyana, at an average of over 40.

With the defection of Mustaq Mohammad, Asif Iqbal, Majid Khan, Zaheer Abbas and Imran Khan to Kerry Packer's World Circus, Haroon suddenly became one of the senior players and he responded by making 337 runs in four Test innings against England in 1977/8. He made a hundred in his first home Test, at Lahore, finishing with 122 which included a six and 17 fours. He dominated a partnership of 180 with Mudassar Nazar, who was compiling the slowest-ever century at the other end. Haroon followed this with an even better hundred at Hyderabad, made in just two hours fifty minutes. He hit ten fours and six sixes - a record for Pakistan - and reached both his 50 and his 100 with blows into the crowd, during an exhilarating century partnership with Javed Miandad. Haroon, tall and powerfully built, played an array of superb strokes, favouring the drive and hit to leg.

Much was expected of him therefore when the side travelled to England in 1978. However he struggled to acclimatise, with the seamers exposing flaws in his technique, and he hardly made a run in the three Tests and fared little better against the counties.

Understandably, when the Packer players returned for the series with India that winter, Haroon's name was not on the team-sheet. He toured New Zealand though, later that winter, regaining his Test place because Asif Iqbal and Zaheer Abbas were tied up with World Series. When they returned in time for the second Test he was again left out, despite useful innings of 40 and 35 at Christchurch, where his drives were again a delight.

The team then travelled to Australia and after scores of 104 and 65 not out against South Australia, he was called up for the second Test when Mustaq Mohammad decided to go into the match with an extra batsman to try and maintain his side's 1-0 lead in the series. Despite a fine innings of 47 from Haroon in the second innings the ploy failed.

He did little of note in the 1979 World Cup but that winter he was a surprise omission from the tour to India, even if he did generally prefer pace to spin. When Asif Iqbal retired at the end of that series, it created a gap. However an experiment to try Haroon as an opener against Australia was not a success and he was dropped after the second Test at Faisalabad.

He missed out on the home series with Westindies but captained United Bank to the Quaid-e-Azam Trophy, though his own form suffered. It required another schism in Pakistani cricket for Haroon to regain his place, when the players who toured Australia in 1981/2 refused to continue under Javed Miandad's captaincy. He took his opportunity superbly, making a marvellous 153 on his return against Sri Lanka at Karachi. He batted for 319 minutes hitting three sixes and 16 fours in his highest first-class score. Yet both he and Salim Malik, who had also made a hundred there, were unjustly dropped from the Third Test to accommodate the return of the rebels to the side.

He again had an indifferent tour to England in 1982, appearing only in the Lord's Test where Pakistan won for the first time. He was restored to the middle-order at home against Australia after making 94 against them for the BCCP Patron's XI and hit a punishing 82 in the first Test and 51 in the second in a 3-0 win in the series. However, he was excluded from the first three Tests against India in the series that followed. Selected again after making a fine hundred for the Governor's XI against the tourists he made a rather incongruous

looking nought on the scorecard, between scores of 231 from Mudassar Nazar and 280 not out by Javed Miandad. Unfortunately this proved to be his last Test innings.

He played on in first-class cricket with Karachi and United Bank for two more seasons before retiring. He remained involved with the game as the cricket manager of United Bank and was the first to spot Waqar Younis. Haroon was the assistant manager and coach of the national under-19 side who toured England in 1990. His ability to spot and nurture talented youngsters was rewarded before the start of the 1996/7 season, when Majid Khan, the new Chief Executive of the Pakistan Cricket Board, appointed him full-time coach to the national junior sides.

Haroon Rashid was a brilliant, powerful strokemaker and his game would have been well-suited to one-day international cricket. However, he played just before the era when such games became commonplace and consequently has only 12 one-day caps to his name, and in which he played just eight completed innings. He was poorly treated by the selectors who discarded this loyal player, in favour of others who had not always been available. A short spell in county cricket may have tightened his technique and given him more experience for despite 14 years of first-class cricket he played in only 149 games, while most of his contemporaries and batting rivals benefited from several seasons in England.

Career Details

Born: Karachi, 15 March 1953
Role: right-hand, middle-order batsman
occasional right-hand bowler
Clubs: Karachi (1971/2-1983/4), National Bank (1972/3-1975/6), PIA (1976/7), and United Bank (1977/8-1984/5)
First-class record: (1971-85) 7500 runs (36.23) including 15 centuries, 8 wickets (31.87) and 126 catches
Tests: 23
Test Debut: v Australia, Sydney, 1976/7
Test record: 1217 runs (34.77) no wickets for 8 runs, and 16 catches
Best Performances: HS 153 v Sri Lanka, Karachi, 1981/2
Tours: Australia; 1976/7, 1978/9
Westindies; 1976/7
England; 1978, 1982
New Zealand; 1978/9
Overseas Tests; 12
One-day Internationals; 12
World Cups; 1979
Sri Lanka; 1975/6

Pervez Sajjad Hassan

Pervez Sajjad is one of the few Pakistani Test cricketers of note whose chief fame came in the sixties when the side was at its weakest. His slow left-armers brought him 59 wickets in 19 Tests at a most impressive average of just 23.89 runs each.

Pervez was born in August 1942 in Lahore; his family had moved from Amristar shortly before, where his brother, Waqar Hassan Mir, had been born in 1932. By the time Pervez had made his first-class debut for Lahore in 1961/2, Waqar had

already finished his Test career, having scored over a thousand runs in his 21 Test matches. The hard-hitting right-hander had been a solid performer in the middle-order in Pakistan's early years, averaging 31.5 with a highest score of 189, made against New Zealand at Lahore in 1955/6.

The potential of the young spinner, Pervez, was soon spotted and he toured England with the Pakistani Eaglets in 1963, but played in only two matches, taking four wickets for 85. After showing some good form that winter and at the start of the 1964/5 season, he was selected for his maiden Test, against Australia at Karachi. It was Pakistan's first Test for more than two years and consequently he was one of six players making their debuts for his

country, the others being openers "Billy" Ibadulla and Abdul Kadir, who also kept-wicket, middle-order batsman Shafqat Rana, and opening bowlers (as they were then) Asif Iqbal and Majid Khan. Pervez bowled tidily but took just one wicket.

The team then travelled to Australasia, and although he did not play in the one-off Test at Melbourne, he had an accomplished first Test series in New Zealand. His 12 wickets at 22.66 runs apiece included a five wicket haul in the second innings at Auckland, where he bowled 25 overs for just 42 runs. He sent panic through the New Zealand dressing room as he took four wickets in ten balls for no runs, reducing the home side from the comfort of 102 for 2 to 102 for 6 as they attempted to chase 220 to win. The match ended with New Zealand batting out for a draw.

New Zealand then travelled to Pakistan and in the first Test at Rawalpindi again they struggled to play Pervez. He took four for 42 in the first innings and then triggered a remarkable collapse in the second, which saw New Zealand slip from 57 for 2 to 59 for 9. The last pair added 20, making slight dents on his figures which in the end read 12 overs 8 maidens 5 runs 4 wickets. It ensured Pakistan's first home win for six years. The opposition played him with great respect for the rest of the series.

It was unfortunate for his development that Pakistan had no Test cricket for the next two years. He toured England in 1967 but did not feature in the Test sides, kept out by Intikhab Alam and Nasim-ul-Ghani despite 34 wickets on the tour, which included seven for 99 against Sussex and six for 21 against Gloucestershire.

Again Pakistan had a long wait - until February 1969 - for their next Test series, which was also against England. Pervez played in only one match, the second Test at Dacca, where he took the wickets of Roger Prideaux, Tom Graveney, Colin Cowdrey and Allan Knott. That season he returned the best match figures of his career, 15 for 112, for Karachi against Khairpur.

He was on the top of his form the following year against New Zealand, taking 22 wickets at an average of 15.63, a record for any series against them that stood until Waqar Younis took 29 in 1990/1. Pervez took the five wickets to fall in the second innings at Karachi, conceding just 33 runs from 24 overs, and in the next, in his home town of Lahore, produced his finest Test performance, seven for 74 in 40 overs. One mid-innings spell brought about a New Zealand collapse that saw them slip from 184 for 4 to 188 for 8. He picked up two more wickets in the 2nd innings to give him the best analysis for any Test at Lahore. He continued to pose problems at Dacca where he bowled 82 overs in the match, taking six for 126.

That form continued throughout the domestic season. He finished with 77 wickets at an average of 16.28, helping PIA to win the Quaid-e-Azam and Ayub Trophies.

He joined Pakistan's 1971 tour to England late because of injury but played in all three Tests, though he was taken ill during the second Test at Lord's and was generally below his best.

He toured Australia in 1972/3 without making the Test side, and when the team continued on to New Zealand, he found that they had at last mastered his bowling to some extent, while his own side was packed with batsman who could all bowl useful spinners and consequently he bowled only 44 overs in the series. A genuine number 11 he had the satisfaction of making his highest Test score, 24, in his final match at Auckland.

He played just one more season of first-class cricket, for Pakistan International Airlines before retiring. He finished with 489 wickets in his career, which included 28 five wicket hauls and six ten wicket matches.

Pervez Sajjad bowled his left-arm spin with great accuracy and cunning, as you might expect from a psychology graduate. His Test average for Pakistan (23.89) is bettered only by fast bowlers, Imran Khan, Wasim Akram and Waqar Younis amongst those with more than twenty wickets, despite playing at a difficult time for the national side. A lack of Test opportunity during his playing days - Pakistan had only 26 Tests from 1962/3 to 1973/4 - prevented him from establishing world renowned Test credentials.

Career Details

Born: Lahore, 30 August 1942
Role: right-hand, lower-order batsman, slow, left-arm bowler
Clubs: Lahore (1961/2-1967/8), PIA (1967/8-1973/4) and Karachi (1968/9)
First-class record: (1961-74) 786 runs (10.48) HS 56 not out, 493 wickets (21.80) and 57 catches
Tests: 19 (1964/5-1972/3)
Test Debut: v Australia 1964/5
Test record: 123 runs (13.66), 59 wickets (23.89) and 9 catches
Best Performances: HS 24 v New Zealand, Auckland, 1972/3
BB 7/74 v New Zealand, Auckland, 1969/70
Tours: Australia; 1964/5, 1972/3
New Zealand; 1964/5, 1972/3
England; 1963 (Eaglets), 1967, 1971
Overseas Tests; 9
Ceylon; 1964/5

Waqar Younis

Waqar Younis is on course to establishing himself as arguably the greatest bowler of all time. Imran Khan predicted so early in Waqar's career and there were not too many jumping up to challenge that opinion. He has achieved so much already in his relatively short 41-Test career, despite persistent problems with his back which have slowed his incredible rate of success recently, where stronger batting line-ups and less conducive wickets failed to hold him in check. Indeed, he thrives on bowling at the best batsmen in the world, rising to the challenge, and in fact has been less successful on the bouncier wickets in Australia. His method owes little to the pitch offering him any favours anyway, as his skill lies in his pace, stamina and remarkable late swing, which is only possible when the ball is pitched up.

He has been hindered by a recurrence of his back injury - a stress fracture of his lower vertebra. Luckily it was diagnosed quickly, and like the great Australian fast bowler Dennis Lillee, who had a similar injury, Waqar came back fitter and stronger after the initial injury. He was getting quicker too, when he was struck down again in 1994/5. It took some time to regain his rhythm but there were times on the 1996 tour to England, when he again reached his peak velocity.

Waqar bowls so full, so straight, and so fast (he was timed regularly at 95 mph during the 1992/3 season) and with such control of his late swing that one cannot envisage him doing badly for long. In some respects, he is still honing the fast bowling art but should he have to cut his pace, it is worth noting that the likes of Imran Khan and Lillee, Malcolm Marshall of Westindies and Richard Hadlee of New Zealand were all at their best in the second half of their international careers.

His bowling skill defies aerodynamics and he has sent scientists back into their labs and wind tunnels to look again at the optimum speed for swinging a cricket ball, which was thought to be around 70 mph. By using "reverse-swing" it has been shown that different aerodynamic forces come into operation above 85 mph.

Waqar's beginnings start in myth, like many a legend. Supposedly he was spotted bowling on television by Imran Khan while he was in hospital recovering from injury, and picked from obscurity on the strength of that brief viewing. In fact, the details have been somewhat warped but still make for a good story. The truth is that he had played first-class cricket already the year before with United Bank, divisional cricket for Multan, and representative cricket with Pakistan under-19s against India. He was picked for the last after taking 6-33 against PNSC for United Bank, but tried to bowl too fast in the first youth Test, losing direction, and was dropped. However, he ensured his recall with another five-wicket haul, against PIA, and he bowled with much greater control on his second chance.

He finished the season with a creditable 24 wickets at 22.75 and by the start of the next, he had filled out considerably and was bowling a yard quicker. Imran Khan had been told to look out for him as a player of promise, and was sufficiently impressed by Waqar's opening spell in the Super Wills Cup, for United Bank v Delhi, for him to leave the comfort of his living room where he was watching on TV, to go down to the ground. Imran invited him to join the training camp for selection for Sharjah, and soon was in no doubt that he wanted him in the squad.

Waqar was born in Vehari, in the Punjab, in November 1971, but his family moved to Sharjah when his father gave up cotton growing to take up a job with a construction company. Despite being only three-and-a-half Waqar stayed at school in Lahore, where he was looked after by his uncle until he was seven. Then, after a brief period at school in Sharjah, his family moved to Abu Dhabi and Waqar was soon sent back to Pakistan to study at one of the top schools, Sadiq in Bahawalpur, where the fine facilities helped him develop his game.

In his first one-day international, in Sharjah, he was watched by everyone from his former school, Sharjah College. He bowled with plenty of pace but got cramp after four overs and had to leave the field. He missed the next game against India, but returned for the second game with Westindies, dismissing both openers, and was reported to be the quickest bowler in the competition, which Pakistan won despite the absence of Imran Khan and Wasim Akram through injury. The team went straight on to win the Nehru Cup, though this time Waqar had to withdraw on the morning of the final against the Westindies as his back had stiffened up after the semi against England.

Consequently he had to have a ten-day rest but he was still selected for his first Test match, which started the day before his 18th birthday, at Karachi. Waqar and Wasim soon had India in trouble at 41 for 4. Waqar's first wicket came when he got the ball to climb off a length, which Sanjay Manjrekar could only glove as it steepled through to the 'keeper. Waqar finished with four for 80, but suffered a recurrence of his back strain and could bowl only two overs in the second innings. Despite it being his debut his absence was considered crucial to the outcome of the match. He missed the next two Tests, needing treatment and then rest, but returned for the fourth, and although bowling within himself still had enough speed and hostility to unsettle most of the batsmen, and hit Sachin Tendulkar on the side of the face with a bouncer.

Waqar struggled on tour in Australia finding it difficult to adjust his length, but it was an important time for him, learning very quickly from Imran Khan and Wasim Akram, the two cricketers he admires most. There was one amusing incident when Waqar dropped one of several catches that had gone down off Akram during the first Test. At the end of the over, Waqar came up to apologise and showed that the ball had slipped through where the little finger on his left hand is missing.

It was Waqar's first experience of Western lifestyle and he was too often tempted by the bright lights of Australia's cities, occasionally falling foul of the management for staying out too late just as Imran Khan had done on his first overseas tour back in 1971. Waqar was not allowed to room with his partner-in-crime Aqib Javed any longer, but was put under the wing of Dr Aslam, as he had been on his first tour to Sharjah.

Waqar was still without much of a reputation but Imran was so convinced of the young bowler's potential that he did his level best to get him more experience by playing county cricket. When Imran's first choice, Sussex, his former county, was rather negative, he approached Surrey who did not take long to be persuaded. After a couple of nets with the Surrey captain Ian Greig and coach Geoff Arnold, they drafted him straight into their Benson and Hedges quarter-final match against Lancashire, in which he dismissed Wasim but finished on the losing side.

That first season at Surrey was crucial. Under Geoff Arnold's watchful eye, he became a match-winner, ousting Tony Gray as the one overseas player allowed by each county in 1991, and was offered an unprecedented five year contract. He had taken 57 wickets at 23.80 in 14 Championship matches. Of these 29 were bowled and eight lbw, while the rest were caught behind the wicket. In all

he took 95 wickets for Surrey that season and was the leading wicket-taker in the Sunday League.

The rough edges to his bowling had been smoothed but the raw pace remained. Waqar returned to Pakistan for the two series there and by the end of the winter he had risen from nowhere to second in the Coopers and Lybrand ratings. Against New Zealand, he simply got better and better; seven wickets in the Test at Karachi were followed by ten in Lahore, including 7-86 in the 2nd innings, which he had bettered within a week by taking 7-76 and 5-54 at Faisalabad. Martin Crowe, New Zealand's captain, admitted even before the series had ended, that he had never faced quality swing bowling of such pace, and said "Waqar is the best bowler I've faced - ever". Although Waqar did not overdo the bouncer, Crowe felt it necessary to affix a grill to his helmet for the first time. "The Burewala Bombshell" finished the series with 29 wickets at just 10.86, and in the one-day internationals that followed took 5-11 and 5-16, as the Kiwi batsmen continued to struggle to come to terms with his late swing.

Westindies were always going to be a tougher prospect, yet Waqar started in similar vein, taking five wickets in the 1st one-dayer, and nine in the first Test match at Karachi (five for 76 and four for 44), to take Pakistan to victory. In the next, at Faisalabad, he took his fiftieth Test wicket in another five-wicket haul (for 46) in what was only his 10th match, thus beating Khan Mohammad's record for Pakistan who took one match longer to reach the landmark. This also gave him his highest C&L rating to date with 910 points which has only been bettered once for Pakistan, by Imran Khan, with 916 out of a maximum of 1000.

The 1990/1 season in Pakistan brought him 70 wickets at 15.97 runs each, including his best in first-class cricket, seven for 64 for United Bank against ADBP at Lahore. It was the prelude to another remarkable summer with Surrey. Waqar took 113 wickets, including 13 five-wicket hauls, at 14.65 which was some five runs less than any other bowler's average that year. It kept his side in contention for the Championship throughout, eventually finishing fifth, and saw Surrey through to the NatWest Final against Hampshire, by turning the semi-final round with an admirable spell against Northants. In all matches for Surrey he took 151 wickets, and as these were predominantly bowled or lbw again, a new word for being yorked - "Waqared" - was coined. *Wisden* wrote of him, "it is doubtful whether anyone has bowled faster or straighter in an English season". Now that the Championship has been reduced to 17 matches, his 113 wickets is unlikely to be bettered in the future.

In the rain affected series with Sri Lanka prior to

the World Cup, Waqar was again the pick of the bowlers, with 16 of the 34 wickets taken by Pakistan. Unfortunately he suffered a recurrence of his back injury, and although it was kept a secret at the time, he was never likely to be fit to appear in the World Cup, and he was soon diagnosed as having a stress fracture in a lower vertebra in his back. He was still only about 80% fit when he came to England for the 1992 tour, and had bowled a mere eleven overs in first-class cricket on the tour when he had to play in the first Test at Edgbaston because Akram was injured, and to help him get match-fit. At Lord's he still seemed to be struggling until suddenly with England well set at 153 for 1, everything clicked. Again the lateness of his swing made batsmen look back in disbelief at their broken wickets, as though beaten by a spinner's turn, as he routed the England middle-order with a 5-wicket burst. Later, with Pakistan struggling at 95 for 8 as they chased 138 to win, he joined Wasim Akram at the crease and they saw the side through to a famous victory, just when the odds seemed to have swung back England's way.

Rain ruined the game at Old Trafford, but at Headingley, after bowling without luck early on (and having a host of lbw shouts turned down), he got his inswinger working and transformed the match with another five wicket spell, which sparked an England collapse from 270 for 1 to 320 all out. He peaked on his "home" ground at The Oval, this time with a devastating new ball blast in the 2nd innings in which he swung the ball both ways at express speed, taking four top-order wickets and in so doing, effectively sealed the series. He finished as the leading wicket-taker on either side, establishing a record for a Pakistani fast bowler against England and aptly shared the man-of-the-series award with Akram.

Waqar took twenty-one wickets at under ten runs a piece in domestic cricket before going on tour where he was in similar form, taking his hundredth Test wicket during a match-winning spell against New Zealand at Hamilton. He took four wickets in the first innings to keep New Zealand's lead in check, but a poor batting display by Pakistan meant that the home side were left needing only 127 to win. New Zealand reached 39 for 3 at the close - all the wickets to Wasim Akram - and the next day after a wicketless first forty minutes, Waqar was just about to be taken off when Miandad decided to give him one more over. Waqar made the breakthrough thanks to a brilliant one-handed catch by Asif Mujtaba at short-leg, off Andrew Jones. It sparked an amazing collapse that saw New Zealand lose their last seven wickets for 28 runs. Wasim and Waqar kept going for well over two hours, demonstrating their remarkable stamina and unflinching will to win.

His 100th wicket came when he "Waqared" Chris Harris with a trademark inswinging yorker during his five wicket blast. It was only his 20th Test, comfortably beating the Pakistan record to the milestone held by Fazal Mahmood who needed 24 Tests to reach a hundred wickets. He joined an elite group of eight Pakistanis who have reached the landmark, including fellow fast bowlers Imran Khan, who took 26 matches, and Akram, 30.

Waqar might have got there sooner but for the weather preventing him bowling at all in the Gujranwala Test against Sri Lanka (1991/2), and limiting him to just one innings on three occasions; at the Sydney Cricket Ground in 1990, the first Test at Edgbaston 1992 (when still not fully fit) and then the third at Old Trafford.

The all-time record of just 16 Tests is held by England's George Lohmann, though he benefited from playing against some very weak South African sides when they were just starting in Test cricket. The only others ahead of Waqar are "Terror" T C B Turner (17 Tests), who played for Australia in the 1880s and 1890s, and Ian Botham (19 Tests) who benefited from the absence of Packer players in the opposition in his early Tests. Both Turner and Botham though took far more overs to reach three figures; Botham requiring 44 balls per wicket, Turner 52.

Waqar made his debut the day before his 18th birthday, picked on his potential and while still very much learning his art. He completed his 100 in just over two years. Lohmann was only 20 when he started his Test career but took nine years to reach 100 wickets. In comparison Kapil Dev took only 470 days between his first and hundredth wicket, during which he played 25 Tests; the Indian all-rounder was also the youngest bowler to the landmark, but Waqar was only 26 days older.

Indeed Waqar made a slow start to his Test career, taking just ten wickets in his first five matches. In his next 15 matches he matched even Lohmann's strike-rate of a wicket every 34 balls, taking five wickets in an innings eleven times, and twice ten in a match. He had become the ultimate match-winner, Pakistan having won eight of those 15 matches and in those wins he took a staggering 69 wickets.

The sensational win in New Zealand contrasted starkly with Pakistan's poor showing in one-day cricket since the World Cup and this prompted the Board of Control to appoint Waqar as vice-captain to Akram soon after, for the tours to Sharjah and South Africa for one-day tournaments and then for the difficult Test series in the Caribbean. It was a gamble but one that appeared to be working as Pakistan won a comfortable victory in Sharjah albeit against only Sri Lanka and Zimbabwe. They got to the final of the triangular competition in

South Africa, but were out-played by the Westindies.

Against the same opponents on their home soil, Pakistan showed the fighting qualities that had been missing in recent limited-overs games, coming back to level the one-day series and so set up the Test rubber which was widely being billed as the decider to determine the best side in the world. However, on the night they arrived in Grenada for the last warm-up match before the Tests, Waqar and the three other main bowlers on tour, Akram, Aqib Javed and Mustaq Ahmed were arrested on the beach and charged with "constructive possession" of marijuana. The charges proved unfounded and were later dropped but it upset the whole team. The start of the first Test was put back by a day, amidst fears that the whole tour might be cancelled.

One will never know what impact this incident had on the series; at first it appeared insignificant as Pakistan bowled out Westindies for only 127 on a poor Port of Spain pitch, after they had been 63 without loss. However, after securing a small lead, Des Haynes and Brian Lara took Westindies out of reach before another collapse to the two W's saw the last eight wickets fall for only 53. Waqar had appeared below his best for most of the tour. Even his four wickets in the 10-wicket defeat at Barbados had come at high cost but in Antigua he found his true form. A five wicket haul in the first innings kept Westindies in check, while a stirring eight over spell in the next cut through the middle-order. Rain washed out the final day, denying Waqar the chance to take ten in the match but left him with 19 wickets in the series at 20 apiece - twice the return of his captain.

The 1993 season was less productive at Surrey - no doubt exhausted by the constant international cricket since the World Cup - though he still managed 62 wickets in 13 matches. Akram injured his hand in the Sharjah triumph at the start of the 1993/4,

No holding back for Waqar

giving Waqar the chance to captain his country in the inaugural Test against Zimbabwe at Karachi. Far from being affected by the added responsibilities, Waqar was inspired. His seven for 91 was his best in Tests and included a burst of four wickets in 15 balls to wrap up the first innings, while in the 2nd, just as Zimbabwe appeared to be holding out for a draw, Waqar bowled Brandes and then trapped Rennie lbw to give him six in the innings and 13 for 135 in the game, all but one of his dismissals being bowled or lbw. Zimbabwe again put up a spirited fight in the next Test at Rawalpindi but another five wickets to Waqar restricted their lead to only nine runs and then with Zimbabwe needing just 105 more to win with nine wickets in hand, the irresistible duo combined to destroy Zimbabwe's hopes as nine wickets fell for 52. Five more at Lahore took Waqar to 27 wickets in only five innings in the series at a mere 13.8 each. The Zimbabwean captain Andy Flower agreed with Akram's assessment, that Waqar had been "the main difference between the two sides". It also took him to the top of the Coopers and Lybrand ratings, equalling his own previous best score of 910, just nine points off the highest-ever total calculated retrospectively for S F Barnes in 1913.

It seems ironic that Waqar was replaced as vice-captain for the tour to New Zealand. There had been general discontent with Akram's captaincy and Waqar led the protest made by ten players who refused to continue under him. Both, thus, were replaced by Salim Malik and Asif Mujtaba. Still, this disappointment did not stop him taking wickets. His six wickets at Auckland took him passed 150 in Tests in only his 27th match, and he took five more at Wellington and seven at Christchurch, including five in an innings for the 17th time. Between them the deposed pair shared 43 wickets in the series.

Waqar's reputation as the greatest match-winner in the world allowed him to renegotiate his contract with Surrey through his agent, Jonathan Barnett, and stood to make £250,000 between 1993 and 1995 as well as having the use of a flat in Chelsea and a luxury car as part of the deal. However, Waqar was unable to play as he was struck down with appendicitis shortly before the start of the Austral-Asia Cup in Sharjah, ruling him out for the first six weeks of the 1994 season. As he was already due to miss the last six weeks to play in Pakistan's series with Sri Lanka, Surrey sought a short-term replacement, Cameron Cuffy.

In 1995, his back injury prevented from playing during a miserable period of Waqar's career, though at least he seemed to be on the road to recovery by the end of the year. Just turned 24, he became the youngest bowler to take 200 Test wickets. Only Clarrie Grimmett the Australian leg-spinner has achieved the feat in fewer matches. But for his back injury, Waqar would surely have shattered that record too. For Waqar's last ten wickets took him five Test matches spread over more than a year.

Unfortunately, his method depends upon him going flat out. It is why, when his rhythm isn't quite right he can be expensive. If he cannot return to his full pace, his future success will depend on whether he can adapt his game. He still has the ability to bowl the unplayable ball and swing the ball like no other, but without the searing pace of his early Tests when he was taking a wicket every 36 balls, he is unlikely to be quite so devastating. It takes a year for any fast bowler to fully recover from serious injury so he may well return to his sensational best.

Waqar's recovery from injury had taken longer than expected, his last six Tests (1995-6) yielding just 12 wickets at relatively high cost. However, at times on the tour to England he produced some of his old magic, delivering the fastest recorded ball of the series at 94 mph to show that he still has frightening pace, and reverse-swinging the old ball to demonstrate that he is still a match-winner.

At Lord's he was just that, taking four wickets in each innings to win the man-of-the-match award. Racing in on the final afternoon, he was back to the Waqar of old, sweeping through England's middle and lower-order just when they seemed likely to survive. He started by bowling Graeme Hick for the second time in the match with an inswinging yorker, a ball which, temporarily at least, ended the batsman's international career. He then had the durable Jack Russell caught behind and yorked Dominic Cork as seven wickets tumbled for 18 runs.

Waqar struggled with the slope and the mat bearing the sponsor's logo at Headingley, both of which upset his approach to the crease. Also, because of the lushness of the outfield, the ball hardly scuffed and even when 120 overs old hardly reverse-swung. Consequently he proved very expensive, even though he did take three wickets in the end.

Not quite the force he was in 1992, but still a force to be reckoned with, Waqar took four wickets in the first innings at the Oval on a flat pitch to help dismiss England for a total well short of expectations. He set Pakistan on their way to a comfortable win and in the series Waqar finished with 16 wickets at 26.92, just behind Mustaq and on a par with his returns in 1992.

He will be back in England in 1997, having signed a lucrative deal with Glamorgan, who are reported to have offered him a six-figure salary in order to secure his services ahead of a number of other interested counties.

Waqar's wicket-taking ability has been incredible. In the modern era he is without peer in terms of strike-rate, having taken his 216 wickets at a rate of one every 39 deliveries. Career figures for some of the best bowlers such as Fred Trueman (every 49 balls), Richard Hadlee (51), Malcolm Marshall (47), Michael Holding (52), Joel Garner (51), Curtly Ambrose (54), Dennis Lillee (52), Kapil Dev (64), Imran Khan (54) and Akram (53) are not even close. Only Lohmann, of those in the hundred club, is ahead of Waqar, with the remarkable strike-rate of a wicket every 34 balls but Waqar was fast catching him up until his back injury struck again. Indeed in seven Tests in 1993 Waqar took 55 wickets at a frequency of one every 29 balls, which is the sort of rate you would not even find in club cricket. The great English bowler S F Barnes (41 deliveries) is the only other bowler to have taken a wicket within every seven overs (42 balls) in Tests. With Wasim Akram, Waqar forms one of the greatest fast bowling partnerships of all time, perhaps unique in terms of their speed and versatility, to compare with the likes of Lillee and Thomson, and Roberts and Holding.

Waqar's remarkable pace and accuracy are illustrated by how he has got batsmen out: of 216 Test victims, 69 have been bowled and 64 have been lbw - an unparalleled percentage among those with over 100 wickets. Of the other 83 dismissals, 35 have been caught by the wicket-keeper.

It is a pleasure to watch him bowl. He has a long, galloping run-up, which bristles with energy and aggression. He shows the batsman a full set of studs as he raises his left leg as he rocks back in his delivery stride, then thunders over the crease, following-through menacingly, leaving him snarling a few yards away from the batsman, letting him know whether or not he thinks he can play.

He is five foot eleven, and 12 stone, with the build of a middle-weight boxer. He has remarkable stamina and natural flexibility, which allows him to be bowled either in long spells to maintain pressure and push home an advantage or, more usually, in short bursts throughout a day, where he can put his heart and soul into every delivery, and can be summoned to provide a breakthrough at any time.

There were allegations of ball-tampering during the 1992 season, but if anything untoward was going on, it was nothing more than all fast bowlers have tried since the game began and was certainly not the reason for his success. His ability to swing the ball at such pace is a joy to watch and is unique.

Imran Khan thinks Waqar is the best in the world, while Martin Crowe rates him as the best bowler he has ever faced, and there are plenty of others who would back both up. He can prove to be expensive as his margin for error when pitching the ball up is so small. Yet even in one-day cricket he looks to attack, which is why he has the best wicket-taking rate of any bowler (1.7 per match) and has taken four wickets in an innings seven times which, if one excludes Akram, is more than all the other Pakistani bowlers put together. The inswinger is his stock delivery but his mastery of the away swinger is improving, producing more catches behind the wicket. His strike-rate far from slowing down increased after he reached 100 Test wickets. He now takes a wicket every six overs and even though his bowling average has just crept above 20, he still has the best average of any current player. Figures can be misleading but Waqar's suggest that he is on his way to becoming the best of all time.

Career Details

Born: Vehari, Pakistan, 16 November 1971
Role: right-hand, lower-order batsman, right-hand fast bowler
Clubs: Multan (1987/8-1990/1), United Bank (1988/9-1994/5), Surrey (1990-3)
First-class record: (1986/7-95) 1239 runs (13.18), HS 55, and 559 wickets (20.24), 50 x 5w, 12 x 10w, BB 7-64, and 30 catches
Tests: 41
Test Debut: v India, Karachi, 1989/90
Test record: 403 runs (9.59), 216 wickets (21.07), 19 x 5, 4 x 10m, and 6 catches
Best Performances: HS 34 v New Zealand, Christchurch, 1995/6
BB 7-76 v New Zealand, Faisalabad,1990/1
Tours: Australia; 1989/90, 1992/3 (WSC), 1995/6
England; 1992, 1996
India; 1989/90 (Nehru Cup)
New Zealand; 1992/3, 1993/4, 1995/6
Westindies; 1992/3
Overseas Tests; 24
One-day Internationals; 128
World Cup; 1995/6
Sharjah; 1989/90, 1992/3, 1993/4, 1994/5, 1995/6
South Africa; 1992/3 (and Zimbabwe)
Bangladesh; 1993/4

Salim Yousuf

S alim Yousuf is only the second Pakistani cricketer to have made a hundred dismissals behind the stumps in Tests and by making over a thousand runs as well, is amongst a very select group of just sixteen players to have completed the wicket-keepers' double. Although not in the same class as a `keeper as Wasim Bari, the first choice for so many years and other to have done the double for Pakistan, he was effective and reliable behind the stumps and a most gutsy batsman in front of them. Salim was a competitive player, sometimes overly so, but he made the most of his ability because of this. Born and brought up in Karachi, Salim made his first-class debut in the 1978/9 season, when selected for Karachi and Sind while still a teenager. He had a fine season in 1981/2 playing for the Industrial Development Bank, finishing as the leading 'keeper with 29 dismissals as well as being well placed in the batting averages. He got his chance at the end of that season because of a players' boycott, when the side who had been touring under Javed Miandad in Australia refused to play on under him. He appeared in the first Test against Sri Lanka in his home town and made a fine impression, taking five catches and making two stumpings in the match, but was injured and missed the rest of the series.

However he had done enough to oust Ashraf Ali (who had toured Australia the previous winter) as Wasim Bari's understudy for the tour to England in 1982. His opportunities though were limited, and he played in just four games.

Bari remained the first choice for the next two years and Salim then had to wait while first Anil Dalpat and then Ashraf Ali, again, were tried ahead of him. Three-and-a-half years after his debut he returned to the side for the last two home Tests against Sri Lanka (1985/6). He finished with 12 dismissals in the series including five catches in the second innings at Karachi and chipped in with some useful runs.

It was a surprise then that he lost his place to Zulqarnain when Pakistan went on to tour Sri Lanka in the New Year. Salim toured too but played in just one game. He really established himself as Pakistan's first choice 'keeper at home to Westindies the following season, when Imran Khan specifically picked known fighters for what was sure to be a tough series.

Yousuf showed that determination in the first Test when Imran promoted him up the order as night-watchman. Coming in at 19 for 2, Yousuf batted well into the next afternoon, adding 94 with Mohsin Khan, to help wipe out the first innings deficit. He batted for 46 overs in making 61. The spirit with which he played rubbed off on the rest of the team; Wasim Akram made his highest Test score as well and Salim Malik, who had had his wrist broken in the first innings, returned to bat at the end of the innings with his arm in plaster. It gave Pakistan a total to bowl at and chance of victory which they took superbly as Abdul Qadir and Imran shot out the Westindies for 53. Consequently Salim was often promoted in the order during the rest of his Test career.

He featured in the Perth challenge and then toured India, which is always a test of character. In the second Test at Calcutta his batting in a crisis again proved crucial. Roger Binny bowled an inspired spell for India, taking 4 for 9 with the new ball, and Pakistan were in danger of having to follow-on. Without Salim's 33, the last seven batsmen would have mustered just five runs among them.

India were still in a strong position though they batted slowly before the declaration. When they took an early wicket on the 4th evening Salim was again promoted and responded with another excellent rearguard, batting 216 minutes for his 43 to help secure a draw. Later in the series he was even tried as an opener but it was back at number nine that he played another vital innings in the fifth Test. With Pakistan 184 for 7, only 155 ahead, he made 41 not out adding 51 for the ninth wicket with Tauseef Ahmed. It gave Pakistan just enough, winning by just 16 runs in one of the tightest finishes in Test cricket.

Salim was the only specialist wicket-keeper on the trip to England in 1987 though Zulqarnain, who was in the country anyway, later joined the squad. He had an excellent tour making 39 dismissals and finished second in the Test batting averages. He did not get in to bat until the third Test where he again did an accomplished job as night-watchman, making 37. Dropped second ball the previous evening he batted through the morning session the next day seeing out a telling spell from Neil Foster.

Unfortunately the bad side of Salim Yousuf was seen in this match. Always an enthusiastic appealer he got carried away in the second innings as Pakistan were surging to victory on the back of a superb spell from Imran Khan. Firstly Salim claimed a catch from Chris Broad which he appeared to take on the half-volley; Broad was doubly unfortunate as the ball in fact hit him on the glove when his hand was off the bat, and thus he should have been given not out anyway.

There are instances where fielders can take a catch and may be uncertain whether or not it was taken cleanly but what followed suggested that it was sharp practice. Salim made good ground to take a tumbling catch down the leg-side off Ian Botham. However as he tumbled over he appeared to lose the ball, scooping it up as it bounced, yet he still claimed the catch. Botham was less than pleased - he was one of the few people in the game who still "walked" when he edged a catch - and made his displeasure with Yousuf known in no uncertain terms, causing umpire Palmer to intervene. Salim's team-mates were rather more muted in their appeal and thankfully he was given not out. Wasim Akram, in his book with Waqar Younis, described it thus; "It was really bad...this wasn't even close." It is poor sportsmanship such as this that can spoil a whole series and mar relations between two sides, setting a precedent which will always be referred to whenever any such controversy might occur again. Imran was quick to move and he too made it quite clear that such behaviour was unacceptable. In mitigation, Salim felt that earlier Bill Athey claimed a catch that was a bump ball.

It was a one-off incident - the sort of practice that might occur in a street match in Karachi but is not de rigueur in a Test match. It did not bear up well under the scrutiny of television and indeed provoked an early demand for the use of a third umpire in the pavilion with a TV monitor.

The best of Salim was seen at Edgbaston. Coming in on a hat-trick, after the dismissal of Salim Malik and Imran Khan, he took on the bowling, helping the last four wickets to add 150. He was denied the chance to make a first Test hundred when the last man, Mohsin Kamal, was run out leaving him stranded on 91, his highest Test score, made in just over three hours from 151 balls and including 14 boundaries. He continued that fine form at the Oval, making 42 to help see Pakistan towards 700. He finished the series with a batting average of 62.33 and was involved in 14 out of 65 dismissals.

That winter Salim had a good World Cup with the bat too, averaging 37.33, consistently making useful runs down the order. His 56 off 49 balls against the Westindies took the side to the brink of victory from whence Abdul Qadir applied the coup de grace. In the semi-final, it proved to be a telling moment when Salim had to go off in the 19th over because of a cut mouth after a ball had deflected off the pad of the batsman, Dean Jones, into his face. Miandad kept tidily in his place but when he batted, appeared quite worn out which stifled his play.

Salim suffered another injury in the first one-dayer of the series with England, when in the first over he had his thumb badly dislocated by a ball from Wasim Akram. He had to leave the field - Gatting refused a specialist substitute - and he was ruled out of the Test series. He was back for the tour to Westindies as first choice but his ill-luck continued when he was injured in the game against a Board XI in Guyana and missed the last limited-overs international. Fortunately, he was fit in time for the first Test and came to the crease with Pakistan just ahead on first innings at 300 for 6 and made a dedicated 62 to ensure a big, and eventually match-winning lead.

In the next at Port of Spain he and Salim Malik rescued the side from 68 for 7 with a record 8th wicket partnership for Pakistan v Westindies of 94, and helped them to a narrow lead. With the Westindies getting away in the 2nd innings, there was a big lbw appeal against Viv Richards, who became embroiled in an argument with the Pakistan players when he was given not out. He ended up threatening Yousuf with his bat and it required umpire Cumberbatch to step in and stop the contest! Not surprisingly the Westindian fast bowlers gave Salim a going over in the rest of the series but he did not flinch. In the second innings he saw Pakistan through to the last over of the match but was out to its first ball, leaving Abdul Qadir an agonising five balls to survive to earn a draw, which he did to everyone's relief.

In the final Test he and Wasim Akram were counter-attacking merrily, adding 67 for eighth wicket, when Salim top-edged a hook off Malcolm Marshall into his face. The ball broke his nose in two places. Although he was unable to keep, he bravely came out to bat in the second innings. At times he was unsteady on his feet because of dizziness and so needed a runner but was able to stay around to put on 52 with Imran Khan.

He finished the series with a batting average of 49, which was bettered only by Miandad. Indeed he got into the world top 20 of the Coopers and Lybrand ratings at the time behind only Miandad and Salim Malik from Pakistan and ahead of Imran Khan, Ramiz Raja and Mudassar Nazar. Not surprisingly Imran rated him as one of the gutsiest players he has ever played with, someone you could depend on in a crisis. He wrote in his book _All Round View_:

"He is not a natural wicket-keeper - something which soon becomes obvious when you study his technique closely - but when under pressure behind the stumps or with the bat he raises his

Salim was a great competitor

game to unlikely levels. As far as I am concerned he would be in my team, even if he had the odd bad match, because I knew he would usually take the important catch, or score a few runs at a crucial moment."

At home to Australia Salim had a useful series behind the stumps, making five stumpings in all, and in the second Test made a fifty in each innings at Faisalabad. Not surprisingly his runs in the first innings averted a pending crisis at 144 for 5, putting on 111 with Ijaz Ahmed. He played in the limited-overs World Series in Australia and then in the fairly dull rubber in New Zealand.

The last two years of his international career were ruined by injuries. He was hurt in the first match of the Nehru Cup in 1989/90 and then again in the first Test of the series with India a few weeks later. Aamer Malik had to take over in the 2nd innings of that game and Salim was ruled out for the rest of the series, his place being taken by Nadeem Abbasi. He was fit again for the tour to Australia and after a typical innings of 38 in the first Test, repeated that score when Imran tried him

at No 3 as a temporary solution to his side's batting problems in the next at Adelaide. Indeed he was employed as an opener a couple of times in the World Series games - an experiment that was successfully repeated in the Sharjah competition that followed. Back at No 8 for the 2nd WSC final, he top-scored for Pakistan in a lost cause with 59.

In his last full series, against New Zealand in 1990/1, he passed a thousand runs during the 2nd Test at Lahore, his 30th, and with the new strike force of Wasim Akram and Waqar Younis in place, he enjoyed his best series behind the stumps with 15 catches, including five in the 2nd innings at Faisalabad. He damaged a finger again in the first Test against the Westindies, ruling him out of contention. Moin Khan made a good impression behind the stumps as his replacement and retained his place, leading to Yousuf's subsequent retirement.

A slight man of average height, Salim was not a natural behind the stumps but proved effective. He was unfortunate with injuries, though some of these were because he did not have classic wicket-

A resilient batsman who completed the Test double

keeping technique and "soft-hands". However he seemed to be a lucky batsman - a case of fortune favouring the brave - often surviving a chance early on before going on to play an important innings. Indeed, at his best he featured amongst Pakistan's top 20 batsmen of all time in the Coopers and Lybrand ratings. Overall he was a most resilient cricketer whose competitive streak enabled him to get the most out of his ability. He had the respect of his team-mates - Akram rates him as one of the bravest batsmen he has seen - who appreciated his tenacity and will to win.

Career Details

Born: 7 December 1959, Karachi
Role: right-hand, lower middle-order batsman, wicket-keeper
Clubs: Karachi (1978/9-1993/4), Sind (1978/9), Industrial Development Bank of Pakistan (1979/80-1981/2), Allied Bank

(1982/3-1984/5).
First-class record: (1978-94) 4553 runs (28.63) including 6 centuries, HS 145 not out, 1 wicket (16.00), 339 dismissals including 298 catches and 41 stumpings
Tests: 32
Test Debut: v Sri Lanka, Karachi, 1981/2
Test record: 1,055 runs (27.05), 104 dismissals, including 91 catches and 13 stumpings
Best Performances: HS 91 not out v England, Headingley, 1987
Tours: Sri Lanka; 1985/6
India; 1986/7
England; 1987
Westindies; 1987/8
New Zealand; 1988/9
Australia; 1989/90
Overseas Tests; 18
One-day Internationals; 86
World Cup; 1987/8
Sharjah; 1985/6, 1986/7, 1988/9, 1989/90

Future greats

Ijaz Ahmed

Despite helping Pakistan win the World Cup final in 1992, Ijaz Ahmed was the only member of that team not to be selected to tour England the following summer. Although he was later called up as a replacement for the one-dayers, it appeared at that stage that his Test future was limited, despite being only 23. However, through his fine performances in domestic cricket for Habib Bank, Ijaz brought himself back into consideration. In the eleven Tests after his return against Australia in 1994, he scored nearly a thousand runs at an average of over 50 and he finished the 1996 series with England behind only Inzamam-ul-Haq in the Coopers and Lybrand ratings for Pakistan, thanks to three centuries overseas in four Tests against Australia, New Zealand and England. He should be reaching his peak as a cricketer, and already has a vast amount of experience under his belt, having played in 30 Tests and well over a hundred (136) one-day internationals, including three World Cups.

Born in Sialkot in September 1968, Ijaz made his first-class debut when he was only 15 during the 1983/4 season. The following year, he demonstrated his enormous potential when he became the youngest cricketer ever to score a first-class double-hundred, 201 not out for PACO against Karachi, and finished the season just short of a thousand runs, which earned him a place on the Pakistan under-23 tour to Sri Lanka.

In 1985/6, Ijaz was the leading run-scorer in domestic cricket, making 1476 runs for Gujranwala and PACO, which included three hundreds in consecutive innings. He was chosen for a pre-season tour to Kenya with Pakistan B and when he started the next season well, hitting a hundred in the Wills Cup semi-final for Habib Bank against ADBP and producing a fine all-round contribution in the final, he was called up to join the Pakistan squad, who were about to embark on a hectic schedule of fixtures. Never shy to introduce talented youngsters, Imran Khan picked him for his international debut in the Champions Trophy in

Sharjah, and for the trip to Australia for the Perth Challenge tournament.

On the tour to India that followed, he won his first Test cap after making 131 against India's under-25 side, but he could not reproduce that form in the first Test at Madras, and played no further part in the series. However, he remained in favour playing in some one-dayers that followed, travelling again to Sharjah and then being picked for the tour to England in 1987.

The start of the tour was blighted by poor weather and Pakistan did not even get in to bat at Lord's, where only just over seven hours play was possible in total. Ijaz made an important fifty in the next match at Headingley, which included some dazzling strokes and helped Pakistan into a lead that was sufficient to secure them an innings victory. In the run feast at the Oval, he made 69 as Pakistan made their highest-ever Test score, 708, to ensure the draw which gave the team their first series win in England.

He was selected for every match in the fourth World Cup (though, in fact, he was still eligible for the youth tournament later that season), making a run-a-ball fifty against England, and throughout the acrimonious series against the same opponents which followed but with limited success. He played in the first two Tests against the Westindies in the Caribbean and contributed a vital innings of 43 at Port of Spain, where he helped Javed Miandad add 113 for the sixth wicket , which took Pakistan within sight of what would have been a famous victory.

Ijaz played throughout the home series against Australia (1988/9) and in the second Test at Faisalabad, he recorded his maiden Test century, made just three days after his twentieth birthday. It could not have come at a more timely moment, for Pakistan were struggling at 25 for four when he came to the crease. He added 119 with Javed Miandad and 111 with Salim Yousuf to get Pakistan out of trouble in a splendid innings, which included two sixes and 17 fours.

He went to two Sharjah events, scoring a hundred against Bangladesh during the second of them, and then onto Australia for the World Series. However, when Imran Khan came back into the side for the Tests in New Zealand, Ijaz was the unlucky one to miss out, making way for the return of the captain.

At the start of the next season, his form in the Nehru Cup was indifferent, but he made amends with 56 from 66 balls in the final against the Westindies, which saw Pakistan on their way to their first major one-day trophy.

It was surprising that he was not required during the home series with India, but he forced his way back into the side in Australia. He marked his return in the first Test at Melbourne by top-scoring in each innings, albeit with only 19 in the first! In the second innings, with Pakistan required to bat for ten hours to save the game, Ijaz played an innings that _Wisden_ described as "wonderfully accomplished." In all, he batted for seven-and-a-half hours for his 121, and it took a brilliant catch in the gully by Geoff Marsh to end it. Unfortunately, his valiant effort came to nought, as Pakistan were dismissed 22 minutes before stumps on the last day, aided by six lbw decisions against his team-mates. His versatility was demonstrated a month later when he scored a run-a-ball hundred in a WSC match against Sri Lanka.

He got only one substantial score against New Zealand in the next home series - his 86 made in just under four hours at Lahore in the second Test - and was dropped for the series against the Westindies that followed.

He stayed in contention by being a regular in the one-day side and went to the World Cup in 1991/2. He was in and out of the side during the tournament as Pakistan tried to hit upon a winning formula, and played in the final. It was a surprise, therefore, when he was not selected for the tour to England, especially as he had the experience of the last tour and had been playing minor counties cricket for Durham the year before.

Despite his disappointment at being dropped by the national team, he led Habib Bank by example in the next home season. He ensured that his side retained the Patron's Trophy by amassing 685 in the final against ADBP, to which Ijaz contributed a classy innings of 94, made from only 97 balls. He finished the season with a batting average of over fifty and took 23 wickets at under 20 runs apiece. His fine form continued in 1993/4, taking the man-of-the-match award in the final of the Wills Cup, helping Habib Bank beat Rawalpindi. Habib also reached the final of the Patron's Trophy, though lost on first innings to ADBP. His brother-in-law, Salim Malik, who had taken over the captaincy of both Habib Bank and Pakistan, could see at first

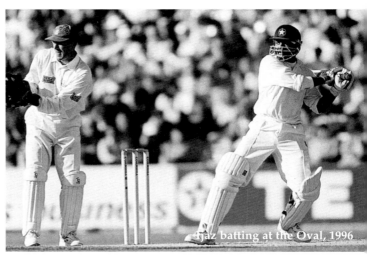

Ijaz batting at the Oval, 1996

hand what good form Ijaz was in.

He was selected to return in the home triangular tournament with Australia and South Africa and, after making scores of 110 and 98 not out at better than a run-a-ball against the latter, he was recalled to the Test arena - still somewhat controversially - for the last Test of the series against Australia at Lahore. In his first Test for four years, he made an accomplished 48 to help put Pakistan into a strong position which ensured a draw and the rubber.

Ijaz played a most significant if unsung role in the team's fightback in the series against Zimbabwe, where Pakistan became the first touring team to come back from one-nil down in a three-match series. Ijaz made a gritty fifty in that first Test defeat, adding 120 with Inzamam-ul-Haq, with whom he was to share the most important stands of the series. They added 70 together in the next Test at Bulawayo, which was comfortably the highest partnership of a low-scoring match, and then at Harare, put on 76 and 116 to set up victory.

That they like batting together was evident again in the second one-dayer. Having watched Saeed Anwar, Asif Mujtaba and Salim Malik all go for ducks, they rescued the side in a superb partnership of 152 in 34 overs.

After his fine contributions to the team, it seemed incongruous that Ijaz should be cast out by the Board after the tour for "selfish and indisciplined play." It had been a troubled tour and it did not help that Salim Malik was at the centre of the controversy, but Ijaz's exclusion from the next series against Sri Lanka (1995/6) seemed petty. That he was missed cannot be doubted. Ironically, his replacement was his exact (unrelated) namesake, Ijaz Ahmed junior, a promising batsman who had topped the domestic batting averages the previous season, but who made no impression in his two Tests.

Ijaz was not even an original selection for the tour to Australia and New Zealand and owed his late call-up to Saeed Anwar's illness. He returned to the side for the second Test at Hobart, only because Salim Malik was injured in the first. Ijaz was left stranded in the first innings on 34 not out, while in the second he got a dubious lbw decision, which left him holding his head in bewilderment. He took his chance at Sydney, batting with great application in making his third hundred against Australia. His stay was the rock on which the innings was built. Coming in at 4 for 1, he shared four consecutive stands of over 50 and in all batted for 444 minutes, before falling with the score on 297 for 7. In all he faced 332 balls for his 137, his highest Test score at that point. Although a watchful innings, he still hit two sixes and 17 fours. It led to an excellent win to salvage some pride at the end of the series and help Pakistan to their first Test victory in Australia for 15 years.

His long-term tenure in the side must now be assured. He hit another century in the one-off Test against New Zealand at Christchurch just eleven days later. Trailing by 78 runs on first innings, Ijaz and Inzamam again changed the course of the match with a stand of 140 for the 2nd wicket. It was another careful yet elegant innings, in which he faced 213 balls and hit two sixes and 13 fours.

Ijaz had an excellent series against England making 344 runs in the three Tests at an average of 68.8 to further enhance his reputation, swell his overall Test average and boost his world rating.

He was in good form leading up to the first Test, the highlight being his 136 not out in a run-chase against Kent. It saw Pakistan to an eight wicket win to make sure the team was on a high going into the match at Lord's. In his first Test in England since 1987, it looked as though Ijaz had forgotten some of the vagaries of the conditions and about the Lord's slope when he was bowled behind his legs virtually offering no stroke to a ball from Dominic Cork . However he showed in the second innings that that dismissal was an aberration. He shared yet another century stand with Inzamam-ul-Haq for the fourth wicket to push home Pakistan's advantage, making 76 with a six and nine fours in just over three hours from 126 balls.

He took that form with him into the Headingley Test where, despite the considerable encouragement given to the bowlers by the swing and seam movement on the first day, he looked totally assured playing a glorious range of strokes. He was determined to be positive, hooking at Andrew Caddick early on, which he top-edged for six, and later climbing into a short delivery from Alan Mullally, which he hit out of the ground over square leg. He also cracked 20 fours as he recorded his third Test hundred - made from only 120 balls - in four matches, each scored in a different country. It was the first for Pakistan at the ground and he went on to record his highest Test score, 141 made

from 201 balls in 279 minutes. His century stand with Salim Malik was the back bone of the innings. He batted with great composure in the second innings - a performance that he rated as better than his hundred - taking four hours over his fifty to shut England out of the game.

At the Oval, he was again involved in the most important stand of the match - 133 for the second wicket with Saeed Anwar - as it drew the sting from the England bowlers. Two consecutive boundaries off Lewis stood out: the first was a nonchalant flick of his legs through square; the second, a glorious pull through mid-wicket as the bowler tried to retaliate. Ijaz played it so early yet the ball speed was recorded at 88 mph.

Ijaz capped a fine summer by being named Pakistan's man-of-the-series in the Texaco one-day series which followed the Tests, hammering scores of 48, 79 and 59.

A shrewd and able all-round cricketer, the absence of Ijaz from the Test side in recent years has been a waste of available talent. His five hundreds in 30 Tests is a fine rate and he is the kind of player around which an innings can be built, because if he gets set he is likely to bat all day. He has a full array of shots himself, cutting and pulling particularly well, but with Pakistan's more exotic strokemakers around him, his solidity at No3 is vital to the side, suggesting he should be set for a fine future.

Career Details

Born: Sialkot, Pakistan, 20 September 1968
Role: right-hand, middle-order batsman, left-arm medium or slow bowler
Clubs: Gujranwala (1983/4-1985/6), PACO (1983/4-1985/6), Habib Bank (1987/8-95/6), Durham (1991)
First-class record: (1983/4-95) 6753 runs (39.72), including 14 centuries, HS 201 out out, and 33 wickets (29.93), 1 x 5w, BB 5-95, and 85 catches
Tests: 30
Test Debut: v India, Madras, 1986/7
Test record: 1723 runs (39.16), including 5 hundreds and 9 fifties, 1 wicket (18.00) and 21 catches
Best Performances: HS 141 v England, Headingley, 1996
BB 1-9
Tours: Australia; 1986/7, 1988/9, 1989/90, 1991/2, 1995/6
England; 1987, 1992, 1996
India; 1986/7, 1989/90 (Nehru Cup)
New Zealand; 1988/9, 1995/6
Westindies; 1987/8
South Africa; 1994/5
Zimbabwe; 1994/5
Sri Lanka; 1984/5 (under-23)
Overseas Tests; 20
One-day Internationals; 136
World Cups; 1987/8, 1991/2, 1995/6
Sharjah; 1986/7, 1988/9, 1989/90, 1990/1, 1991/2, 1994/5, 1995/6
Kenya; 1986/7 (Pakistan B)
Bangladesh; 1988/9, 1993/4

Mustaq Ahmed

Mustaq Ahmed has proved a natural successor to Abdul Qadir as Pakistan's premier leg-spinner, the apprentice replacing the sorcerer on the 1989/90 tour to Australia, where he played in the 2nd Test at Adelaide. It took some time for Mustaq to become a permanent member of the side after that but he was one of the stars of the World Cup in 1992, when he demonstrated how effective a good spinner can be in limited-overs cricket. However, his progress has been checked by a persistent back problem and inconsistent selection. In Test cricket, it took until the winter of 1995/6 to prove himself the match-winner he has always looked like becoming, and continued in that form on the tour to England in 1996.

Born in Sahiwal in June 1970, Mustaq made his first-class debut at the age of 16 for Multan, marking his first appearance in the President's Cup with an innings of 75, which remained his top-score until he started playing county cricket. His father, a cotton-grower around Sahiwal, could not afford to take Mustaq or his three brothers to see Test cricket in Lahore, some three hours drive away, but they had a television which Mustaq watched avidly, studying the action of his hero Abdul Qadir, which he tried to copy down to the last detail.

He proved a worthy imitator for his potential was soon recognised. He was chosen to play for the Punjab Chief Minister's XI against England in December 1987, while still at the Government-run Sahiwal Comprehensive, a school with a fine cricket record. England, who were still haunted by the spectre of Abdul Qadir, who had taken nine for 56 (and 13 wickets in the match) in the first Test of the series which had ended a few days before, must have thought it a bad dream to see another leg-spinner whirling in, in identical manner to Qadir, and then bowling them out. He bowled 36.1 overs and took six for 81 including a spell of five for 28 in 75 balls. With Qadir uncertain for the next Test because of a heel injury, Mustaq, who had played virtually no first-class cricket, was mooted as his likely replacement in the next Test and so only bowled seven overs in the second innings to prevent the England batsmen from getting used to him. As it transpired Qadir was fit and Mustaq was not required, but he was signed up soon after by United Bank, who started him on a salary of Rs5,000 a year and told him to go out and practice his cricket.

Later that season, he represented the Pakistan under-19 side in the McDonald's Bicentennial World Cup, helping his side to the final, where they lost to the hosts, Australia. He bowled consistently well and was comfortably the leading wicket-taker for Pakistan and second only to Wayne Holdsworth of Australia in the tournament bowling averages, his 19 wickets costing 16.21 runs apiece and his overs just 3.71.

He started the next season well and was selected for Pakistan's tour to Australia and New Zealand (1988/9), only to be dropped before its start when Imran Khan returned as captain. He insisted on the inclusion of Abdul Qadir, who had not been available originally but had been persuaded to change his mind as Imran was going to be in charge. Just as the national side were playing their first warm-up matches in Australia, Mustaq dropped a reminder to the selectors by taking six for 42 and eight for 40 for Multan against Peshawar in the Patron's Trophy, and he finished the season with 52 wickets at 22.84. This earned him the call-up for the Sharjah Cup (March 1989), making his one-day international debut against Sri Lanka, and soon after took seven wickets (3-36 & 4-34) in the final Test for Pakistan B against Sri Lanka B at Karachi.

Mustaq was required for a plethora of one-day matches at the start of the following season, bowling effectively in tandem with Qadir in the Sharjah Champions Trophy and in the Nehru Cup, both of which were won by Pakistan. It was a surprise, therefore, when he was not included in the original squad to tour Australia shortly after, for three Tests and the WSC tournament. However, when Qadir returned home just before the first Test ostensibly with a damaged finger, Mustaq was flown in as his replacement. He went straight into the second Test at Adelaide, and bowled tidily enough for someone who had had no time to acclimatise, impressing the likes of Richie Benaud, the cricket commentator and famous Australian leg-spinner. Intikhab Alam, the tour manager, was also able to spend time with him, giving him specialist coaching.

Mustaq's bowling caused an incident in the next match, against Victoria, as he was warned twice for running on the pitch in his follow-through, and then ordered out of the attack when he transgressed again. The match was held up as the players did not accept this verdict, Alam coming onto the field to lead the players from it. The match

to prominence, coming out from under the shadow of Qadir, who was ruled out by an Achilles injury. Mustaq bowled better and better, posing problems throughout, and finished fourth amongst the regular bowlers in the competition bowling averages. He took wickets - indeed only Wasim Akram finished with more than his tally of 16 dismissals - yet he maintained economy, conceding under four runs an over. His bowling was crucial in the victory over Australia, in which he dismissed Dean Jones, Mark Waugh and Allan Border, while in the group match with New Zealand, he checked the runaway start made by Mark Greatbatch, eventually dismissing him and Chris Harris (who was stumped off a wide). He did not concede a boundary and his ten overs only yielded 18 runs, which earned him the man-of-the-match award. In the final, the googly which he delivered to deceive Graeme Hick, trapping him lbw as he tried to cut, was good enough to raise question marks about the batsman's whole technique against spin. He also accounted for Graham Gooch and Dermot Reeve, to finish with figures of three for 41.

He continued to bamboozle batsmen in England during 1992 though his figures, like Qadir's on the previous tour in 1987, did not do him justice or hint at the significant role he played. For instance, his second innings dismissal of Robin Smith, Hick and Allan Lamb in 22 balls was the turning point in the Lord's Test, and surprisingly the three for 32 he took there were for a long time his best Test figures. His eventual tally of 15 wickets (at an average of 31) was a better haul than any of the English bowlers. His accuracy and economy - just 2.6 runs an over - allowed Miandad to rest his strike bowlers Akram and Younis, yet still maintain an attacking threat. Overall on the tour he took 66 wickets, including five in an innings on four occasions and played an integral part in Pakistan picking up a £50,000 jackpot for winning nine of their twelve county matches. He took eight for 124 from 44 overs in the win over Somerset, who were so impressed by his bowling that they offered him a contract for the following season.

Mustaq had a frenetic six months in the winter of 1992/3 with cricket all around the world. He bowled with great control in the one-off Test against New Zealand, sending down 38 overs, but in the WSC matches in Australia, although he retained control, he lost his wicket-taking knack and never really posed the same threat as he had done in the World Cup. This drought continued in Sharjah and South Africa, taking only three wickets in the nine one-day internationals in which he played.

In the Caribbean, his form returned as soon as he had a good long bowl, taking eight wickets (for 129) in the opening match against Jamaica from 54

resumed only when a compromise was struck, based on the contention that the final warning had not be indicated to the acting captain, Ramiz Raja. By coincidence eighteen years before, Alam had been ordered from the attacking for the first time in his career, when captaining the side on the tour to Australia.

Mustaq did not play against New Zealand (1990/1) in the home series dominated by Wasim Akram and Waqar Younis, though he did get two Tests against the Westindies before being dropped for the final match, to accommodate the return of Qadir, who had missed the previous Test with a hip injury. Once again it was Peshawar who paid for his omission shortly after and Multan who benefited, as Mustaq took 14 wickets (for 130) in a match for the second time against them, including a career best nine for 93 in the second innings in the town of his birth.

However, his international opportunities were still limited. Pakistan preferred to choose four quick bowlers in the Test series against Sri Lanka at the end of 1991, though he played in four of the five one-dayers that followed, bowling well enough to cement his place for the World Cup in Australia and New Zealand. It was there that he really came overs. Unfortunately in Grenada he was arrested for "constructive possession of marijuana," along with Wasim Akram, Waqar Younis and Aqib Javed. The charges were unsubstantiated and later dropped. Despite being on bail throughout the match, he took six more wickets against the Westindian under-23 XI, and it was thought that Richie Richardson's decision to bat first in the opening Test at Port of Spain, was because he did not want his side to face Mustaq in the fourth innings of the match. As it transpired, Mustaq was being troubled by a back injury which eventually forced him from the field during Westindies' second innings. Haynes and Lara chose his departure as the moment to begin their assault on the other bowlers and wrested the initiative from Pakistan. Mustaq was forced home for treatment soon after and with him went Pakistan's best chance in the series, for the Westindians have always been fallible against top quality leg-spin.

He was fit in time for the start of the English county season, where he proved to be a match-winner in his own right for Somerset. He finished the season with 85 wickets, behind only Steve Watkin of Glamorgan, who took 92. Three times he took ten wickets in a match and eight times five wickets in an innings in only 16 games. He also made encouraging progress with the bat, averaging nearly 20. In the match against Sussex at Taunton, he produced his best all-round cricket, making a career best score of 90, and then bowling forty overs in each innings to take five for 84 and seven for 91. He was most popular with team-mates and spectators alike, leading _Wisden_ to write: "it was his huge and obvious enthusiasm for the team which so endeared him to the supporters." Even when luck wasn't going his way he remained sanguine with an air of insouciant youthfulness about his cricket.

That Mustaq was not yet fulfilling his potential at Test level was not helped by the fact that his club, United Bank, did not always play him in their side. The experience he was gaining from county cricket, therefore, was invaluable. His performances in 1993 were largely unsung and he was unlucky not to have been named among _Wisden's_ Five Cricketers of the Year. He was somewhat overshadowed by Shane Warne for Australia, who was receiving such plaudits and achieving such prodigious turn, but who finished the summer with ten less wickets and at greater cost.

That winter he bowled well in tandem with Waqar Younis in the inaugural Test against Zimbabwe, but was dropped to make way for the return of Wasim Akram, who had been injured, for the next match on a seamer's pitch at Rawalpindi. Recalled for the final Test, which was impaired by

the weather, he was hardly used as Wasim and Waqar bowled nearly eighty percent of the overs. He toured New Zealand but, after taking three important first innings wickets in the first Test win at Auckland, he was forced to return home with a recurrence of his back problem.

He had recovered in time for his second season with Somerset, though this was cut short by his selection for Pakistan's tour to Sri Lanka, which began in August 1994. However, in his nine matches for his county he still managed to take 45 wickets. As a fine farewell, he bowled splendidly against Worcestershire, sending down more than sixty overs in the match to take 12 for 160, to ensure victory. On tour, he was required to bowl only thirty overs in two Tests as Pakistan defeated Sri Lanka easily, but he still played his part by picking up three top wickets in the first innings at Colombo and three more to wrap up the tail, and the match, at Kandy.

He dismissed four more top order players in the first Test against Australia at Karachi, but he will always be remembered for the part he played with the bat in that match, adding 57 for the last wicket with Inzamam-ul-Haq to record a nail-biting one-wicket win. It was the highest last-wicket partnership to win a Test. Unfortunately, he could not repeat his heroics in the next Test at Rawalpindi, getting a pair and bowling poorly as Australia's batsmen began to master him. He got much of his control back in the final Test at Lahore, where he shouldered the bowling responsibilities well in the absence of Wasim and Waqar, to register his best Test figures, four for 121 from 45.1 overs.

Struggling for form and fitness, he was absent from the tour party to southern Africa and suffered a loss of confidence. The 1995 season with Somerset proved vital. Given the opportunity to do plenty of bowling and make slight adjustments to his bowling action, he had his best county season. He played in every Championship game bar one, taking 92 wickets, 58 of them coming in the seven games which Somerset won. How well he bowled was not reflected in his average, which appears high at just under 30 , but one must remember that Somerset were riddled with injuries to key bowlers such as Andy Caddick and Andre van Troost, each of whom played in only six matches. Often he got little quality support from the other end. Just as Shane Warne stole some of his limelight in 1993, Anil Kumble's heroics for title-aspirants, Northamptonshire, again grabbed most of the headlines. Mustaq bowled more overs than anyone else (952) and was second only to Kumble's 105 wickets.

Mustaq, who had taken his tally in two-and-a-half seasons with Somerset to 225 wickets, missed the pre-season training camp in Pakistan because of his county commitments, but it was a surprise that he played no part in the series with Sri Lanka. The home side paid the consequence slipping to their first home series defeat for 15 years. Again, he was overlooked for the first Test of the series in Australia, at Brisbane, where Shane Warne took 13 wickets to help his team to an innings victory. Who knows what might have been had Mustaq played, for in the next two Tests he proved that at last he had become a world class match-winner.

At Hobart, Mustaq took his first five-wicket haul (for 115) in Tests as he accounted for Australia's strong middle-order, bamboozling the less experienced Greg Blewett with his googly in the process. He bowled with even more control in the second innings to pick up four more wickets for 83 from 38 overs. In a classic Test at Sydney, the home team knew they had to respect him but that only played into his hands. Again he took five wickets as Australia were bowled out for 257, to ensure Pakistan a telling lead of 42. His dismissal of Mark Taylor early on the last day - lured down the pitch to be stumped - set Pakistan on their way to victory as seven wickets tumbled for 51. He bettered his figures of the previous Test, taking 5-95 & 4-91, and was named man-of-the-match as his side salvaged

some pride at the end of the series with their first win Down Under since 1981/2.

Mustaq's jovial demeanour epitomised the much improved relations between the two sides, while his control and attacking variety made him a threat at all times. He lost nothing in comparison with Warne, generally regarded as the best leg-spinner bowler in the world and top of the Coopers and Lybrand ratings. It would have been a nice touch if Warne (19 wickets at 10.42) and Mustaq (18 wickets at 21.33) had shared the man-of-the-series award, as they bowled with equal skill and gave equal delight to fans of wrist-spin.

Mustaq's form lifted the spirits of the whole side. In the one-off Test against New Zealand at Christchurch, Mustaq improved upon his Test best for the third match in a row. Three wickets in the first innings were the prelude to a mesmerising piece of bowling in the second, triggering a collapse from 50 without loss to 75 for 5. Only Roger Twose, the former Warwickshire batsman, played him with any comfort. Though favouring his googlies and top-spinners, Mustaq reminded everyone how far he can turn a leg-break by bowling Dipak Patel round his legs. He finished with seven for 56 from 34.4 overs, to take his tally from his three Tests that winter to 28.

With his control and confidence now at an all-time high, Mustaq proved vital to Pakistan's success in England in 1996, a fact reflected in his man-of-the-series award. As in 1992, he was asked to perform a stock bowling role to allow Wasim Akram to rotate his faster bowlers. He averaged nearly 40 overs an innings and at least this time he was rewarded with better returns for all his hard work in the series. In the second innings at Lord's and the Oval, he was instrumental in bringing Pakistan victory just when England looked capable of holding out for a draw.

Both times Mike Atherton and Alec Stewart had resisted Wasim and Waqar with great skill. At Lord's, Mustaq's decision to bowl round the wicket in the manner of Shane Warne, proved decisive. Despite conceding less than two runs an over, after 59 overs of toil in the match, his efforts had brought just one wicket. Then, as soon as he changed his angle of attack, he turned a delivery out of the rough, finding the edge to have Atherton caught at slip. In his next over, Stewart gloved a ball to silly point as it ballooned off his pad, and was unfortunate to see Hick being given the benefit of the doubt off a similar chance a few balls later. But by now the match situation was completely transformed. England had been coasting along at 171 for 1 when he struck, opening the door for Waqar to castle Hick and then knock over the tail in a dramatic collapse which brought seven wickets for 18 runs. Waqar stole his thunder, finishing with eight wickets in the Test and the match award, but it was Mustaq who had taken four of the five frontline wickets to fall on the last day which turned the game.

At the Oval, he came into his own. Despite a big first innings deficit of 195, England should have been able to bat out for a draw on the last day as they had all their wickets in tact. Again, once the breakthrough was made, one could sense Lord's repeating itself. This time Mustaq took the first five wickets to fall, bowling with such control and variety that none of the batsman after the openers looked settled. It was a remarkable unchanged spell of 37 overs, in which he took 6-78, to take his tally since his return to the side to 45 in only six matches.

By the end of the series he had risen to sixth in the world rankings, with a total of 779, just behind his captain Wasim with a rating far in excess of anything attained by Abdul Qadir and close to catching Warne.

Mustaq had to undergo an operation on a knee injury when he returned home, but if he can sustain his form, he will establish himself as one of Pakistan's greatest-ever match-winning bowlers.

Somerset fans will be surprised that Mustaq Ahmed has taken so long to reproduce his county form at Test level and fulfil the promise he had shown in 1992. On the 1996 tour, he took ten wickets (for 108) in the match against his former employers to prompt them into action about offering him a new contract, which will keep him at Somerset until 1998.

With his back better, his action grooved and his confidence high he is sure to feature strongly in the years to come and continue Pakistan's line of delightful leg-spinners. Mustaq bowls a little slower than Warne or Qadir, and so draws more batsmen down the pitch. Brian Lara rates Mustaq more highly than the Australian, because of his extra variety, and not surprisingly, so does his captain, Wasim Akram. Mustaq favours the googly, of which he has three different types, and top-spinner, though does not as yet have as big a turning leg-break as other two. He does not yet have quite the variety of his mentor Qadir, who has helped him greatly in his development at various national squad training camps, and who he still considers "the very greatest bowler in the world." He still has many of Qadir's mannerisms, from making the ball hum in the palm of his hand before he starts to run in, to the passion which he puts into his appeals. Short and stocky, he is closer in build, though, to Mustaq Mohammad and just as he was, is a fine close to the wicket catcher.

Mustaq and Warne talked a lot during the 1995/6 series, conspiring the downfall of batsmen.

Mustaq has been working on another delivery since, one which spirals into the batsman, and hurries on off the pitch. He has found, too, that by running in straighter, like Warne, it has become easier to give his leg-break more of a rip.

Worryingly for batsmen around the world, Mustaq is still improving. He could become exceptionally good, perhaps Pakistan's best-ever spinner.

Career Details

Born: Sahiwal, 28 June 1970
Role: right-hand, lower-order batsman, right-hand leg-spin and googly bowler
Clubs: Multan (1986/7-1990/1) United Bank (1987/8-1995/6), Somerset (1993-5)
First-class record: (1986-95) 1809 runs (15.20), HS 90, 6 fifties, 495 wickets (26.18) BB 9-93, 32 x 5wi, 8 x 10wm, and 63 catches
Tests: 24
Test Debut: v Australia, Adelaide, 1989/90
Test record: 246 runs (8.93), 89 wickets (29.29), 5 x 5wi, 1 x 10wm and 9 catches
Best Performances: HS 27 v Australia, Lahore, 1994/5
BB 7-56 v New Zealand, Christchurch, 1995/6
Tours: Australia; 1989/90, 1991/2, 1992/3 (WSC), 1995/6
England; 1992, 1996
New Zealand; (1991/2), 1992/3, 1993/4, 1995/6
Westindies; 1992/3
Overseas Test; 17
One-day Internationals; 102
World Cups; 1991/92, 1995/6
Sharjah; 1988/9, 1989/90,1990/1, 1991/2, 1992/3, 1993/4,1994/5, 1995/6
India; 1989/90
South Africa; 1992/3
Zimbabwe; 1992/3

Basit Ali

Basit Ali made as bright a start to his international career as any batsman for Pakistan since Javed Miandad. After just over a year with the national side, he was averaging in the mid-forties in both Test and one-day international cricket. He was taken under the wing of Miandad and obviously adopted several of his mentor's batting mannerisms. Although probably not blessed with quite the same natural talent, Basit has many of the more precocious strokes associated with Miandad in his youth - improvising, deflecting, driving wristily, difficult to bowl at when set. He even uses the same make of bat and dons a similar white helmet when he goes to the wicket. He is a brave competitor, too, and has showed the application necessary to make big scores consistently at the highest level. He was on stand by for the 1996 tour to England, suggesting he is still in contention, but with Pakistan's plethora of young batsmen, he needs to re-establish himself soon if he is to have the sort of international career he once promised.

Born in Karachi in 1970, he was playing first-class cricket for the city of his birth by the time he was fifteen, gaining selection after scoring 170 in a Grade II match for Pakistan Education Board. He finished the season with a top score of 98 for Karachi against Lahore in the PACO Cup. The following season, he made over 500 first-class runs but at a modest average of 25.

He was chosen as an opening batsman for the Youth World Cup in Australia at the beginning of 1988. Although he had obvious ability, he was not that highly rated then as he was thought to be older than the seventeen he claimed. However, he performed well enough helping Pakistan reach the final against Australia, at the Adelaide Oval, in which he made 23. A year later he captained the under-19 side against India, making 189 at Gujranwala.

He made great strides forward in 1988/89, when he scored over five hundred runs in seven games and finished seventh in the national batting averages. He was selected to open for the Northwest Frontier Province Governor's XI against the touring Australians, and he starred in Karachi's Patron's Trophy triumph, scoring 135 and 84 in the final against Rawalpindi. In the off-season, he was signed up by the Pakistan Automobile Corporation (PACO) and began playing for Karachi Blues which, combined with a restructuring of the Quaid-e-Azam Trophy, gave him much more opportunity of playing first-class cricket. His nineteen matches produced 1,479 runs, including a hundred in each innings twice, 106 and 127 for Karachi Blues against Multan, and 128 and 157 for PACO v Agricultural Development Bank of Pakistan.

This earned him a tour to Zimbabwe with Pakistan B at the start of the following season, and he marked the third "Test" at Harare with a stylish hundred, which set the side on its way to an innings victory. On his return to Pakistan, his first-class opportunities were limited. PACO had been relegated after finishing last the year before, and so he left their employ for United Bank, who he helped to reach the final of the Patron's Trophy.

While his contemporaries in the under-19 World Cup squad, Inzamam-ul-Haq, Aqib Javed and Mustaq Ahmed, were having a ball at the real thing in 1992, "Cinderella" Ali was left at home. Basit must have felt that his international career was still along way off, but he had a good season at home, averaging nearly fifty, and contributed towards Karachi Whites' success in winning the Quaid-e-Azam Trophy.

He topped that the following year, scoring 845 runs at an average of over fifty, including four centuries. His sparkling 145 in the final of the Quaid-e-Azam Trophy against Sargodha propelled him into the national side for the tour to the Caribbean. While many of the established players had been drained by a surfeit of one-day internationals, Basit approached every innings with the required application. By leaving out Salim Malik and Shoaib Mohammad, Pakistan were dangerously short of experience, but this oversight did at least give Basit the chance to establish himself.

He was the find of the tour and batted with a maturity beyond his twenty-two years. Undefeated innings of 51 and 84 in the opening game against Jamaica booked his place in the middle-order for the entire one-day and Test series. He top-scored in the last two one-day internationals, with 60 and 57, helping Pakistan to level the series, but made an inauspicious start to his Test career, falling lbw to Ian Bishop for a duck in the first innings at Port of Spain. He rallied the side in the second, top-scoring with 37.

In the next Test at Bridgetown he was again the pick of the batsmen. He played what *Wisden* described as "the most heroic innings played for Pakistan in the series." Coming in at 79 for 4, he batted superbly, hitting 11 fours and a six in a stay of 224 minutes but was left stranded on 92 not out (made out of the last 142), as the last four batsmen could manage just one run among them. It was an innings good enough to impress Garry Sobers, who commented at the time that Basit looked a born Test cricketer. He again batted impeccably under pressure in the second innings, making 37. He carried on the good work in the final Test at St John's, Antigua, making a fine fifty and the quality of his stand of 88 with Inzamam-ul-Haq there seemed to augur well for the future of the middle-order batting.

During the tour he had demonstrated a full range of powerful, crisp strokes, as well as fine placement as he worked, nudged or deflected good deliveries into the gaps for ones and twos, much as Miandad had always done. He played valiantly throughout with a poise and certainty that was not evident from some of the other players, to finish top of both the Test and tour averages.

That he is a high class player, there is no doubt. In the final of the Champions Trophy in Sharjah, he scored a brilliant hundred from only 67 balls. His last fifty came from just 25 deliveries and he pasted the bowling of Curtly Ambrose as it has never been pasted before. In all he hit five sixes in his 127 not out (from 79 deliveries) and added 172 for the fourth wicket with Salim Malik.

As the adrenaline settled after an innings of that velocity, Zimbabwe were not the ideal opponents to play next in Test cricket. Against their lesser challenge he was steady but did nothing spectacular, making scores of 36, 13, 25, 40 and 29.

His true form returned against New Zealand, where he averaged 57 for the series. He just missed out on a first Test century at Wellington, where he made 85 and added 197 for the third wicket with Saeed Anwar to set up the big score that led to an innings victory. He followed it in the 2nd Test with 103 and 67 at Christchurch, where he looked the best player on either side. After a mid-innings collapse which left Pakistan 206 for 5, he took the attack to the bowlers, blazing

to 98 not out at the close of play on the first day, with Pakistan 334 for 7. In his haste to complete his hundred that evening he had been dropped on 97, cracking a square cut, but went to a well-deserved century the next morning. In the second innings he held the batting together, making 67 out of the last 102, before being run out as he tried to farm the bowling.

He went on the short tour to Sri Lanka,

contributing an important fifty towards an emphatic victory in the final Test at Kandy, but after failing in both innings in the first Test at home to Australia, he was dropped in favour of the experienced Aamir Malik. Good form in the one-day tournament, which saw him share an unbroken stand of 148 with Ijaz Ahmed against South Africa and top-score for Pakistan in the final against Australia with 63, ensured a recall for the final Test. He could not reproduce that form, getting a duck in the first innings and just two in the second when he opened in place of the injured Aamir Sohail.

With no particular form in one-day cricket in the Mandela Trophy, Basit did not make the Test side for the inaugural Test against South Africa or the first Test against Zimbabwe. When he was recalled for the second Test at Bulawayo, he had the misfortune to record his third duck in five Test innings and was dropped for the final match of the series.

With two internationals still to play, Basit and Rashid Latif left the tour early. They had been uncomfortable with the atmosphere in the dressing room on the tour, following allegations of match rigging, and both announced their retirements from international cricket. Javed Burki, the chairman of the *ad hoc* committee in charge of cricket in Pakistan at the time, was furious at the walk out and both were banned from first-class cricket also.

However three months later, after discussions with the newly-formed Pakistan Cricket Board, Basit and Latif reconsidered their positions. With their differences reconciled and in a spirit of compromise, as the PCB attempted to wipe the slate clean after an unhappy period in Pakistan's cricket history, they were reinstated. Basit was the first to be re-selected, returning for the third Test against Sri Lanka, and then going on tour to Australia and New Zealand. He appeared in excellent form in Australia, scoring a hundred in each innings (137 and 101 not out) in a state game against South Australia, but failed in the Tests. His five Tests that winter brought a mere 101 runs and he lost his place in the World Cup squad to make way for the return of Javed Miandad. Although not selected for the 1996 tour to England, at least the selectors let him know he was still in the running by making him the reserve batsman for the tour.

For Basit, 1995 was an annus horribilis, failing miserably with the bat and, for a while, he was left feeling disenchanted with Pakistan cricket. There is no doubt that he is a talented player, but one who has lost confidence recently. He showed an excellent temperament in his early matches and has a tight technique and the ability to play all the shots even against the best bowlers. He uses his feet well to the spinners and is adept at picking up quick singles. His success in New Zealand in 1993/4 meant that Javed Miandad was hardly missed. His ground fielding is excellent as he demonstrated in that series by twice running out Andrew Jones in the Test at Christchurch with direct hits.

Basit needs to reset his sights if he is to have a productive international future. He has a very good one-day record, averaging 35 which is high for a middle-order player, and could get back in the side through this form of the game. However, Pakistan has many talented batsmen and there is always a danger that the selectors may feel he has had his chance. After 11 Tests he was averaging over 43 and seemed on the verge of establishing himself among Pakistan's finest, but he has had a disastrous run since. He is good enough to regain his place.

Career Details

Born: Karachi, 13 December 1970
Role: right-hand, middle-order batsman, occasional right-hand bowler
Clubs: Karachi (1985/6, 1991/2), Karachi Blues (1989/90), PACO (1989/90), United Bank (1990/1-1994/5), Karachi Whites (1991/2-93/4)
First-class record: (1984-95) 6116 runs (39.45) including 16 hundreds, HS 157, 6 wickets (66.50) and 52 catches
Tests: 19
Test Debut: v Westindies, Port of Spain, 1992/3
Test record: 858 runs (26.81), including 1 hundred and 5 fifties, and 6 catches
Best Performances: HS 103 v New Zealand, Christchurch, 1993/4
Tours: Westindies; 1992/3
New Zealand; 1993/4, 1995/6
Sri Lanka: 1994/5
South Africa: 1994/5
Zimbabwe: 1991/2 (Pakistan B),1994/5
Australia: 1995/6
Overseas Test; 13
One-day Internationals; 47
World Cups; 1987 (under-19s)
Sharjah; 1992/3, 1993/4, 1994/5

Saeed Anwar

Saeed Anwar, with Aamir Sohail, have established themselves as Pakistan's first choice opening pair over the last couple of years. A pugnacious left-handed batsman, Saeed has recovered from the worst possible start in Test cricket, recording a pair on his debut, to make 1400 runs in his next 16 Tests at an average of over 48. Everyone knew he could bat by the brilliance of his strokeplay in one-day internationals, but he has managed to temper his game enough to be successful at Test level.

Saeed was born in Karachi in September 1968 and made his first-class debut as an 18-year-old during the 1986/7 season for Karachi. He scored over 700 runs in his first season, including 150 against National Bank.

A graduate in computer science, he was encouraged to make cricket his full-time profession at the start of the 1988/9 season when he made a hundred for the NWFP Governor's XI against the touring Australians at Peshawar, and was chosen to go to Australia for the World Series, making his one-day international debut against the Westindies at Perth. At the end of that season, he represented Pakistan B in the home series against Sri Lanka B, and he contributed well in three of the four unofficial Tests, with scores of 82, 56 and 39.

He made a splendid start the following season, with three hundreds for Karachi Whites, including a double (221) against Multan at Peshawar and 150 against the Indians at Rawalpindi, which earned him a call-up for the one-dayers. He was to finish the domestic season with over a thousand runs at an average of 67.62, including five hundreds.

He was called into the full Pakistan squad to tour Australia. Although, Imran Khan was tempted to unleash this talented player in the Tests, he could not quite force his way into the side. Originally a middle-order batsman, the lack of opportunities there encouraged him to try opening. He showed his liking for taking on the new ball bowlers in the World Series Cup that followed, really catching the eye with some superb if audacious shots. One stroke in particular stands out: against Australia at Sydney, he came down the track and hoisted Terry Alderman onto the roof of the Ladies Stand at mid-wicket. In the previous match, he had shared a dazzling opening stand of 202 (a record for WSC matches) in 132 minutes with Ramiz Raja, making 126 from only 99 balls, six of which he struck into the crowd, as well as hitting eight fours.

Perhaps he should have been brought into the Test side to face New Zealand at home in 1990/1, as he made scores of 101, 67 and 35 at a run-a-ball in the one-dayers that followed. Instead, he made his Test debut against the might of the Westindies in the second Test at Faisalabad, which proved to be a cheerless experience. By the end of the second day of the match, he had already recorded a pair, and he had lasted just five balls in total. However, like Graham Gooch before him, who also got a duck in each innings on his debut against the Australians in 1975, he was not unduly disheartened, drawing solace from the notoriety if that is possible, and proved his character by persevering.

He toured Sri Lanka with Pakistan A in 1991/2, but missed out on selection for the World Cup, despite his fast-scoring style, and did not make the tour to England that followed.

He was given few opportunities on the short tour to Australasia (1992/3), but continued to be picked regularly for one-day internationals. Indeed, Ramiz and Saeed bettered their opening stand against Sri Lanka, putting on 204 in only 34 overs for the first wicket in the final of the Wills Trophy in Sharjah (1992/3), as the dashing left-hander raced to 110 off 105 deliveries. He was injured early on in the one-day tournament that followed in South Africa and played only in the first match, ruling him out of contention for the tour to the Caribbean.

Saeed's international future seemed to be uncertain, but then came the Champions Trophy in Sharjah in 1993/4. He scored three run-a-ball hundreds in a row, to equal the achievement of Zaheer Abbas against India in 1982/3, making the highest score for Pakistan in one-day internationals (since beaten) in the process by hitting 131 against the Westindies, an innings which included three sixes and twelve fours. Although there was a danger that this might have labelled him permanently as a one-day player, the sheer quality of his batting meant that his claims for a place in the Test team could not be ignored much longer.

Again, a chance was missed to blood him at home in the series against Zimbabwe, but he was chosen for the tour to New Zealand and ensured a recall to the Test side after a three-year absence by making two hundreds in the warm-up matches. In only his fifth Test innings, in the second Test at Wellington, he scored a brilliant century, hitting exactly one hundred out of his 169 in boundaries, which set up an innings victory. In the next, at

Saeed plays another dazzling stroke

massive 301-run victory. With Aamir Sohail, he also established a highly effective opening pairing in the series, sharing stands of 65, 128 and 94.

Their fine form together continued against Australia in a tense series at home. Saeed top-scored in each innings at Karachi, making 85 and 77, knocks described by *Wisden* as "wonderfully expressive hands." Pakistan edged home in the most dramatic fashion by one wicket. In the next, at Rawalpindi, he scored a resolute 75 to help ensure a draw. Sortly after on the same ground, he made a glorious unbeaten hundred in a one-day game to see Pakistan past Australia's score of 250 with 11 overs to spare.

Saeed was a bit out-of-form on the tour to South Africa and Zimbabwe and he lost his place for the second Test against the latter. However, in the first one-dayer after the Tests, he was back to his best, making another century, but could only watch from the other end, as an injured Wasim Akram, batting at number 11, hit the penultimate ball of the match back to the bowler, Whittall, with the scores tied. It was Saeed's eighth limited-overs international hundred, a number only Ramiz Raja (with nine) has exceeded for Pakistan, while only Australia's Graham Marsh (9), and Westindians Viv Richards (11), Gordon

Christchurch, he survived two early chances to make 69, as he put on 125 for the first wicket with Aamir Sohail.

In the first Test of the tour to Sri Lanka in August 1994, he fell just short of scoring a hundred in each innings, a feat that only Hanif Mohammad and Javed Miandad have achieved for Pakistan, as he made 94 and 136 to lay the foundations for a

Greenidge (11) and Des Haynes (17) also have more. He is the sort of player who could pass all of them.

He got the chance to captain the side when Moin Khan was laid low with chickenpox during the Pepsi Asia Cup tournament in Sharjah. Unfortunately it was Saeed who was taken ill in the next home series. Having scored three fifties in as many innings against Sri Lanka, he was struck down on the eve of the third Test and was unable to play. He was diagnosed as having typhoid fever, which prevented him from touring Australia and New Zealand, where his commanding presence at the top of the order was sorely missed.

Back for the World Cup, Saeed was Pakistan's outstanding player, making fifties against Holland, England and New Zealand and in the quarter-final against India, he made 48 from only 32 balls in his own inimitable style, before the middle-order lost their way. He finished the tournament fourth in the averages, with 82.25.

His calibre as a Test match opener to rank with any in the world was demonstrated in the series against England in 1996. He was his team's leading scorer making 362 runs at an average of over 60 in the Tests, and amassed 1224 runs on tour in only ten games. He always played in such a positive manner that it often disconcerted the bowlers. He was in brilliant form leading up to the first Test, cracking three centuries in six completed first-class innings, including 219 not out against Glamorgan, and although he had played against England in only one limited-overs game before, he helped set the tone for the whole series in the first innings at Lord's by making a rapid 74. One of the features of his knock was the he kept clipping England's two left-arm seamers, Brown and Mullally, off straight and through mid-wicket like a southpaw Viv Richards. In the second, he made 88 in a vital opening stand of 136, in which he cajoled the best from his young opening partner, Shadab Kabir, who was on Test debut and had been moved up the order because of an injury to Aamir Sohail.

At the Oval, Saeed recorded his third and highest Test score, hammering 176 from only 264 balls including 26 fours. England had made a below par score of 326 on a good pitch and came out fired up to make some early inroads into the Pakistan batting. Instead, Saeed and Aamir Sohail totally removed the sting from the bowling, making a mockery of the tactic to bowl to their strengths square of the wicket on the off-side. Saeed, in particular, kept peppering the boundary behind point. By the close on the second day, England were demoralised, knowing their chance of squaring the series had gone, as Pakistan raced passed 200 for the loss of only one wicket. He extended his stand with Ijaz to 133 and then added 95 in quick time with Inzamam, before falling as he attempted to pull Cork for another boundary, to end an exhilarating innings of just over six hours.

During the Texaco one-day series, Saeed and Aamir Sohail became only the third pair of openers to pass 2,000 runs together (average 38.81) in that form of cricket to emulate Greenidge and Haynes for Westindies and Marsh and Boon for Australia.

Saeed is a glorious strokemaker in one-day cricket, who has the ability to score at a run-a-ball. He has a record to match or even better anyone's in world cricket. He has a very good record of converting almost ever other fifty into a hundred and his eight centuries have come at a rate of one for every ten games he has played, which is unparalleled. Formerly considered a one-day specialist, he has put the disappointments of his first Test behind him to become a most reliable batsman at Test level, going for his shots a little more selectively to average over 40, the mark of a very good player. The real test is still to come against the world's strongest sides, but he has already been successful against the likes of the Westindies and Australia in one-dayers, suggesting he should fare well in the longer game. Imran Khan rates only Sachin Tendulkar and Brian Lara ahead of him for natural ability, and Imran is normally a fairly shrewd judge of such matters.

Saeed has developed a highly profitable pairing with Aamir Sohail at the top of the order, even if it must be a little bit nerve-racking for the number three as they both go for their strokes from the start. They are the most exciting opening pair in the world, yet still have managed to average around 45 together as an opening pair over 20 innings. As both should be at their peaks as players over the next few years, they should continue to serve Pakistan well.

Career Details

Born: Karachi, 6 September 1968
Role: left-hand, opening batsman, occasional slow left-armer
Clubs: Karachi (1986/7-), ADBP
First-class record: (1986/7-95) 5244 runs (42.63), including 15 centuries, HS 221, 9 wickets (43.66) and 42 catches
Tests: 17
Test Debut: v Westindies, Faisalabad, 1990/1
Test record: 1400 runs (45.16), including 3 hundreds and 10 fifties, 0 wickets, 9 catches
Best Performances: HS 176 v England, the Oval, 1996
Tours: Australia; 1989/90, 1992/3 (WSC)
England; 1996
New Zealand; 1993/4
South Africa; 1994/5
Zimbabwe; 1990/1 (Pakistan B), 1994/5
Sri Lanka; 1990/1 (Pakistan A), 1993/4
Overseas Tests; 10
World Cups; 1996
One-day Internationals; 98
Sharjah; 1991/2, 1992/3, 1993/4, 1994/5, 1995/6
Bangladesh; 1993/4

Inzamam-ul-Haq

Inzamam-ul-Haq has threatened to set the cricket world alight at times, most notably in the World Cup where his superb strokeplay transformed Pakistan's position in the semi-final and final. Pakistan has had many talented youngsters who have not made the most of their ability, but Inzamam looks set to become the equal of the batting stars of previous eras. After 33 Tests he was already established as Pakistan's first choice batsman, riding high in the Coopers and Lybrand ratings and in the averages, and looks set to be predominant into the next century.

He was selected on the strength of the way he played so comfortably and confidently forward to Waqar Younis during a net at a pre-season training camp, and made an instant impact when he was drafted straight into Pakistan's one-day side. It took him a little longer to realise his potential in Tests, though he is now showing he is a batsman of real Test calibre, who is on the verge of becoming a great player.

Imran Khan had heard some good reports about Inzamam but as soon as he saw the apparent ease with which he faced the pace of Younis in practice, he decided there and then that he wanted him in his side. "Every other batsman, including the regular Test batsmen, were beaten three times out of six balls but he played a couple off shots of his hip which went out of the ground. I only ever saw Viv Richards play like that."

In fact it was a surprise that it had taken so long for him to win full international honours. Born in Multan in March 1970, Inzamam was one of six children. His brother Intizar had already played for Multan when Inzamam made his first-class debut for the city of his birth at the age of 15 during the 1985/6 season and the following year he helped Multan win their group in the BCCP President's Cup, scoring 131 against Hyderabad, and then made 94 not out in the Group League against Pakistan National Shipping Corporation. However, as he was playing outside the two main centres of Karachi and Lahore, his opportunities for first-class cricket were limited.

This was especially so the next season as Pakistan were co-hosting the World Cup. Consequently the first-class programme was drastically cut, and Inzamam's team were knocked out of the BCCP Patron's Trophy early on, at the pre-quarter-finals stage by Karachi Blues, despite another hundred from the young right-hander. He was selected for the McDonald's Bicentennial Youth World Cup and played a prominent part in Pakistan reaching the final, heading the team's batting averages for the

competition. He played in every game and top-scored with 37 in the final, though he could not prevent Pakistan slipping to defeat against the hosts, Australia, by five wickets.

It was obvious he would have to move to one of the big commercial clubs if he was to progress and so he joined United Bank for the 1988/9 season. Generally, he had a quiet time, though hinted at his true potential by making his highest first-class score, 201 not out, for United Bank against PNSC at Karachi. This was a precursor to his most prolific and consistent season in 1989/90, when he finished just five runs away from beating the domestic record of 1649 runs set by Saadat Ali for House Building Finance Corporation in 1983/4, as well as taking some useful wickets with his left-arm spinners. Indeed, he helped Multan beat Faisalabad almost single-handedly by making 139 not out - one of his six hundreds that year - as well as taking five for 93. He followed this with another productive season, making over a thousand runs once again, at an even better average (63.52), to give him a record aggregate for two back-to-back seasons.

Consequently, Inzamam was chosen for the tour to Sri Lanka with Pakistan A during the off-season, but it was at the pre-season training camp in 1991/2 that he really made his lasting impression. Imran Khan was amazed by his ability and felt that as long as he was captain Inzamam would play. Inzamam was selected for his one-day international debut against the Westindies, striking 20 and 60 against them, and then ensured his selection for the World Cup by making 48, 60, 101 and 117 against Sri Lanka. The first of those hundreds was made in front of his home crowd at Multan and came off only 121 balls, dominating a stand of 149 for the first wicket with Ramiz Raja. The next, at Rawalpindi, was even more destructive, coming off just 104 balls and including 13 fours. He added 204 for the 2nd wicket with Salim Malik as Pakistan amassed 271 in only 40 overs.

Imran Khan revelled in this new found star in his side, declaring Inzamam as the player to watch and as "one of the most talented cricketers" he had seen. Perhaps this aggrandisement put undue pressure on Inzamam, for his contributions early in the World Cup on the unfamiliar wickets were disappointing and there was a danger that he might be dropped. He seemed to be playing with a deference to the importance of the competition, rather than his natural, free-flowing game. He showed a glimpse of his ability with 48 against South Africa, before his innings ended in the most spectacular of fashions with Jonty Rhodes hurling himself at the stumps to execute a run out, the start of an unfortunate sequence of such dismissals for Inzamam, who was to be run out nine times in his next thirty one-day innings.

Perhaps Inzamam most typified Imran's call to arms, "to fight like cornered tigers." Certainly Pakistan appeared to have nowhere to go when the tall, right-hander strode to the crease in the semi-final, a game he was going to withdraw from on the morning of the match because of an upset stomach. He was persuaded by Wasim Akram to play, who told him that the team needed him and to put his faith in his own ability. After a slow start against accurate New Zealand bowling, the game seemed beyond Pakistan with 123 still required in 15 overs. Yet Inzamam played with a carefree brilliance, striking the ball to all parts with great force as he raced to his fifty off a mere 31 balls. He had added 87 in ten overs with Javed Miandad when he was eventually run out for 60 (off 37 balls), which included a six and seven fours. His innings had transformed the game and rightfully he received the man-of-the-match award.

Imran Khan reminded the media of what he had said, that Inzamam "was one of the most talented players...with one of the coolest temperaments," which he showed again in the final. It was Inzamam who played the cavalier innings after Khan and Miandad had laid the careful foundations, mixing force with finesse to make 42 in 35 balls, as 52 came in the last six overs in partnership with Akram.

Inzamam was the player to watch when Pakistan came to England in the summer of 1992, yet despite some sparkling form outside the Tests, he never really lived up to expectations. He played some fine innings on the tour but generally against lesser opponents. He hit a dazzling hundred in a one-day match against Sussex, smashing five sixes in his 157 not out from 148 balls and another run-a-ball hundred against the England Amateur XI. He showed the full range of his strokeplay with a marvellous unbeaten double-hundred against Oxford and Cambridge, hitting four sixes and 21 fours in a stay of only 203 minutes, but it was not until after the final Test that he scored a fifty in a first-class match against county opposition. His tour average of over fifty flattered to deceive. In the Tests he had a miserable time and was dropped for the final match. Only in the last one-dayer did he show his true ability at international level, making 75.

Perhaps Miandad made a mistake in the first Test at Edgbaston. With the game always likely to be inconclusive after the first two days had been washed out, he declared just after Inzamam had

come to the crease on his debut. An hour's batting then, with Miandad at the other end encouraging him to go for his strokes, could have set him up for the series. Instead he finished with 8 not out, and Alec Stewart, Robin Smith and Graeme Hick were the ones allowed the batting practice on an easy-paced pitch. His lack of basic experience was all too evident in the second Test at Lord's, when he came out to bat, as usual, without a helmet and was immediately bounced out. He got an earful from his vice-captain when he returned to the pavilion.

Pakistan's schedule for the 1992/3 season was a hectic one, touring New Zealand and Australia, Sharjah, South Africa and the Westindies. Indeed he managed only two first-class games in Pakistan, hitting 178 for United Bank against PNSC in one of them. In the one-off Test against New Zealand at Hamilton, he played a vital 2nd innings knock which turned the game Pakistan's way. Coming in at 25 for 4, Pakistan were still nine runs in arrears when the next wicket fell. However, with Rashid Latif in support, he rebuilt the innings with an accomplished knock of 75, which gave Akram and Younis just enough runs to bowl at to secure a famous victory.

Inzamam hit a powerful 90 against Zimbabwe in Sharjah to set Pakistan's one-day record, which had been poor since the World Cup, back on the right path, but unfortunately he broke a finger during the triangular tournament in South Africa and missed all but the first two games. However, once in the Caribbean he started in fine form with a hundred against Jamaica and 84 against the Board XI at Georgetown, while a superb innings of 90 not out got Pakistan back into the one-day series and broke a bad run of results against the Westindies. Collectively, Pakistan were a disappointment in the Tests, though Inzamam produced one of the highlights of the series for his team by making his first Test hundred, at St John's, Antigua. He and Basit Ali shared a stand of 88 and then in partnership with Nadeem Khan, who was making his Test debut, he ensured that Pakistan avoided the follow on with a ninth wicket stand of 96. At first Inzamam rebuilt the innings with some excellent, controlled batting, and then he began to dominate the bowling, eventually hitting 11 fours and a six. He enjoyed one slice of luck when badly dropped by Winston Benjamin at long-leg but overall was totally in command, batting for over five hours for his 123, made from 226 balls.

Following the disappointing defeat to the Westindies in the Champions Trophy final in Sharjah, Inzamam had an indifferent series against Zimbabwe. Playing Test cricket for the first time in his own country, he made just one fifty in the three Tests, though returned to form in the one-dayers with undefeated innings of 44 and 80 to ensure a clean sweep in the series. In the first Test in New Zealand, he top scored with 43 when Pakistan were struggling at 93 for 6 in the first innings and saw his side through to a five wicket win in the 2nd innings when they again looked precarious. At Wellington, he made his highest Test score as he and Salim Malik shared a stand of 258 for the 5th wicket as Pakistan raced along at four runs an over to set up an innings victory. Inzamam cruised to a largely untroubled 135 not out, hitting 19 boundaries.

He helped Pakistan take the Austral-Asia Cup in Sharjah, going through unbeaten to the final, in which they defeated India by 39 runs. It was in the semi-final, against New Zealand, that he and Aamir Sohail shared in a new record stand for any wicket in a one-day international, as the pair took the bowling apart with a partnership of 263 for the 2nd wicket, thus beating the previous record set by Allan Border and Dean Jones for Australia against Sri Lanka in 1984/5. Inzamam finished on 137 not out - Pakistan's highest one-day score - scored from only 129 balls and including 15 fours, and in the process passed 2,000 runs in his 59th one-day international.

Inzamam by now had developed a harder edge to his cricket and during the winter season of 1994/5 produced a string of good scores, often when the pressure was on. Pakistan overwhelmed Sri Lanka in their short away series, winning the first Test by 301 runs and the third by an innings (the second was cancelled because of civil unrest). Inzamam was the pick of the batsmen, following his 81 at Colombo with a not out 100 at Kandy, after his side had slipped to 158 for 5.

Pakistan returned home to play a gripping series with Australia. In the first Test, the big right-hander rescued his side from what seemed certain to be their first ever loss at Karachi. Chasing 314 to win, Pakistan had slumped to 179 for 6 when Inzamam strode to the crease. He soon lost Akram, but gave his team some hope in stand of 52 with Rashid Latif. However, when the ninth wicket fell with 56 still required defeat seemed inevitable. Yet he found a worthy ally in Mustaq Ahmed and the pair proceeded to make history by recording the highest ever last-wicket partnership to win a Test, beating the 48 that South Africa's last pair, Nourse and Sherwell, made to beat England at Johannesburg in 1905-6. The denouement was excruciating as Ian Healy, the Australian wicket-keeper, fumbled a half-chance for a stumping, only to see the ball run away for four leg-byes to give Pakistan a one-wicket victory - only the seventh such result in Tests. Pakistan had never before made more than 230 to win a Test in the final innings.

Inzamam, who finished with 58 not out in 155 tense minutes, was the hero of the hour. Despite failing in the second Test (including being the

middle victim of a hat-trick), he was moved up the order to try and solve Pakistan's problems at No 3, and responded with a solid innings of 66 at Lahore, where he added 123 for the third wicket with Salim Malik.

Pakistan's form in South Africa was poor and the visitors slipped to a resounding defeat by 324 runs in the inaugural Test between the two sides at the Wanderers, Johannesburg. Inzamam was the only player to do himself credit in the second innings. He made a gritty yet stylish 95 from 179 balls, after coming in when three wickets had fallen with only five runs on the board.

The same was true in the first Test against Zimbabwe in Harare, which was lost by an innings and 64 runs. Inzamam top-scored in each innings, making 71 and 65, despite carrying a painful shoulder injury, which prevented him from batting until No 8 first time round.

His fine form continued throughout the series, finishing with 367 runs at an average of 73.40, as he led Pakistan's fine comeback as their man-of-the-series. His innings of 47 helped give Pakistan a telling lead in the second Test at Bulawayo, which was won by eight wickets. Then, back at Harare, he played the two decisive innings of the series. In a low-scoring game, in which only one other batsman made a fifty, he scored nearly 40 per cent of his side's runs in the match to ensure that

Inzamam hits out during the 1992 World Cup

Pakistan became only the third side in Test history to win a three-match series after losing the first Test, and the first to do so away from home.

In the first innings, Inzamam recorded his fourth Test century, which included 12 fours and two sixes, scored from 168 balls. After adding 76 with Ijaz Ahmed, he completely dominated the scoring as he raced from fifty to a hundred in only 66 balls, while the last five batsmen mustered just six runs among them, until being last out caught at long-off. He was promoted to No 3 again in the second innings, showing he was up to the task by making 83, though once he was dismissed the side fell away badly, losing their last four wickets for as many runs. Still, Inzamam had ensured that Pakistan set a target that was beyond Zimbabwe.

His string of solid performances was reflected in his new standing in the Coopers and Lybrand world ratings, in which he was second only to Jimmy Adams of the Westindies.

Inzamam marked Pakistan's return to Peshawar after 41 years with a responsible innings of 95 against Sri Lanka, made in nearly six hours and including 12 fours. It was the sixth time in seven innings that he had top-scored for Pakistan and his fine effort helped set up a convincing victory.

Unfortunately his form fell away in the rest of the series, as Pakistan suffered a rare home defeat.

Wasim Akram looked to bat Inzamam higher, usually at four, in the Tests in Australasia and he proved fairly consistent. His most important knock was at Sydney where, with the match in the balance, he made a patient fifty to push home Pakistan's advantage. Then at Christchurch against New Zealand, with Pakistan trailing by 78 on first innings, he joined Ijaz Ahmed in a record second wicket stand of 140 to build a match winning total. Inzamam made 82, including 13 fours from 141 balls, before edging Dion Nash to slip.

One sensed that a destructive innings was just around the corner in the 1996 World Cup. He hit a powerful unbeaten fifty against England, but his old problem of being run out when well set reared its ugly head again against South Africa and New Zealand. The stage was set in the quarter-final against India, but he got a good ball from Prasad to nip his innings in the bud.

A new slimmer-looking version of Inzamam - he had lost over a stone - came to England determined to put the disappointments of his first tour in 1992, when so much was expected, behind him. He struck 169 in an unbroken stand of 362 with Saeed

Anwar in the opening first-class match against Glamorgan and he demonstrated how much his game has developed in recent years in the first innings of the Test series. He showed excellent footwork and a classic range of strokes to enlighten a full house at Lord's with a batting display that has been described as reminiscent of Wally Hammond. His shots had power and timing as well as quite some panache, dropping virtually to one knee as he dispatched his booming drives through the covers. It helped establish Pakistan's ascendancy in the series, as he and Saeed Anwar added 130 for the third wicket. He went on to record his highest Test score - 148 made from 219 balls and including 19 fours and the six over long-on off Graeme Hick which took him to three figures.

Despite a slight leg strain in the second innings, he helped take the game beyond England as he added 118 with Ijaz Ahmed to send his side towards a lead of over 400. He was beginning to unleash some great shots, which had brought 20 in 28 balls since reaching his fifty, when unfortunately he fell to Cork, just when he looked set to emulate Hanif Mohammad and Javed Miandad as the only Pakistanis to make a hundred in each innings of a Test. His efforts had taken his world rating to a new high score of 878, a tally only Miandad has exceeded. He had a rare failure in the first innings at Headingley but played with great authority in the second, to extinguish England's brief hopes, making 65 in 83 balls. He made a useful 35 at the Oval to help take Pakistan past England's total for the loss of only two wickets, and finished among five players to average over 60 for the series. At the end of the tour, he had to have an operation on a troublesome knee, which ruled him out of Pakistan's first engagement of the winter, two Tests at home against Zimbabwe.

Inzamam is already amongst Pakistan's top 15 highest run-scorers after 33 Tests. He seems certain to go much higher, possibly to challenge Miandad's tally for his country.

Only twenty-six but already with plenty of experience, Inzamam looks set to establish himself as one of Pakistan's finest batsmen. He averages over forty in both Test and one-day cricket, is an excellent slip fielder - a problem area when Akram and Younis first combined - who is averaging more than a catch a match in Tests, is an ambidextrous fielder and useful part-time slow left-armer. Yet he has been criticised for not being hungry enough (and being overweight!). He sometimes seems a bit dreamy in the Carl Hooper mould. Geoff Boycott, recognising the talent in each, would like to shake the two of them out of that apparent slumber, and has spoken to both about their batting. Imran, too, is frustrated by him getting out when set.

Inzamam-ul-Haq's development epitomises what is good and bad about Pakistani cricket. He was picked relatively early on, but had to move away from Multan to get established, while his overall lack of good first-class experience meant a slightly stumbling start to his international career. With the plethora of one-days games that Pakistan played during his first two years in international cricket, Inzamam's technique was suffering, picking up a tendency to play across the line as he looked to work the ball to leg. He was lbw in such a manner five times in a row during the winter Tests of 1992/3. This was exaggerated by a rather slouching stance which took his head too far across to the off-side, resulting in him being off-balance, while his eyes were not absolutely level. The poor standard of domestic cricket in Pakistan left other basic skills unlearned. For instance, he was run out ten times in his first forty completed innings in limited-overs cricket (four times in the 1992 World cup alone) and has run out a few of his team-mates as well.

Tall at 6'2", he is a very powerful striker of the ball who seems to have plenty of time to play his full array of strokes. A natural front-foot driver, not unlike Graeme Hick, he has proved through his hundred in Antigua and runs in South Africa and Australia, that he has the technique to deal with short-pitched fast bowling too. He is very well established now and his ability is well respected within an ever-improving Pakistan batting line-up. He has hinted at touches of genius, yet has also been very consistent, resulting in his high placing in the Coopers and Lybrand ratings. He still has a tendency to get out when set, but seems on course to becoming one of the best batsmen in Pakistan's Test history.

Career Details

Born: Multan, 3 March 1970
Role: right-hand, middle-order batsman, slow left-arm bowler
Clubs: Multan (1985/6-1993/4), United Bank (1988/9-1994/5)
First-class record: (1985-95) 7208 runs (51.85) including 20 centuries, HS 201 not out, 37 wickets (33.97), BB 5-80, and 87 catches
Tests: 33
Test Debut: v England, Edgbaston, 1992
Test record: 2367 runs (47.34) including 5 centuries and 16 fifties, 34 catches
Best Performances: HS 148 v England, Lord's 1996
Tours: New Zealand; (1991/2), 1992/3, 1993/4, 1995/6
Sri Lanka; 1990/1 (Pakistan A), 1994/5
Westindies; 1992/3
Australia; 1987/8 (under-19 World Cup), 1991/2, 1992/3 (WSC), 1995/6
England; 1992, 1996
South Africa: 1992/3, 1994/5
Zimbabwe: 1992/3, 1994/5
Overseas Test; 24
One-day Internationals; 111
World Cups; 1991/2, 1995/6
Sharjah; 1991/2, 1992/3, 1993/4, 1994/5, 1995/6

Aqib Javed

Aqib Javed is from the new breed of international cricketer, whose chief fame so far has come from limited-overs cricket. By the end of the 1996 World Cup, Aqib had already played in 126 such matches; only a handful of Pakistanis have played in more. Yet despite becoming the second youngest Test cricketer of all time, when he made his debut aged just 16 years 189 days against New Zealand in 1988/9, he has never fully established himself in the Test side. He played for Pakistan a year before Waqar Younis and it seemed he would become the permanent third prong to Akram and Younis but this has not fully materialised. He played an integral part in Pakistan's World Cup victory, being the steadiest bowler throughout the competition and was widely tipped to star in the summer of 1992. However, since then he has attracted a fair degree of controversy, off and on the field, and has also suffered from injury and loss of form, and consequently he played in only one Test match in the two years after the tour to England in 1992. He missed out on selection for the next tour to the UK in 1996, though he was at least made the reserve bowler, but at present his Test future looks unsure, despite his dozens of one-day internationals, which must keep him in contention.

Born in Sheikhupura in August 1972, Aqib was playing first-class cricket virtually before he was wearing long trousers. He is regarded as the youngest-ever first-class cricketer, making his debut for Lahore Division in the 1984/5 season, at the age of 12 years and 76 days. He played little other first-class cricket in the next few years, while being educated at the Government School in the town of his birth. He represented Pakistan in the inaugural Youth (under-19) World Cup in Australia in 1987/8, though he was still only 15, but missed out on the final - something that he was able to atone for six years later in the senior side, when he played alongside Inzamam-ul-Haq and Mustaq Ahmed, who had played in the youth final as well.

Aqib Javed got his chance when Javed Miandad stood down from the captaincy in favour of Imran Khan for the tour to Australia and New Zealand in 1988/9. Imran, as is his want, insisted on changes being made to the side originally selected and plucked Aqib from obscurity - he was not even playing for a first-class side at the time, as Lahore Division had been relegated to Grade II - but Aqib had so impressed Imran in a net session that the captain backed his judgment to spot talent, and

immediately entrusted his young protege with the new ball in the World Series Cup matches in Australia. In New Zealand, Aqib was selected in the XII for the first Test at Dunedin, which was abandoned without a ball being bowled because of torrential rain, but made his Test debut in the next at Wellington, becoming the second youngest Test cricketer after Mustaq Mohammad in 1958/9. On a plumb batting pitch he went wicketless, conceding 103 runs from his 34 overs, and tended to over-use the bouncer. He was dropped for the next Test, which was another high scoring draw, but had impressed enough for _Wisden_ to write that he "looked like developing into a very useful fast bowler."

Aqib helped Pakistan to beat India in the final of the Champions Trophy in Sharjah, and despite playing in only the last of the five qualifying matches in the Nehru Cup, he was the pick of the bowlers when he was drafted in for the final, when Waqar Younis was injured, conceding just 25 runs in his ten overs against Westindies. Yet he was not chosen for any of the home Tests against India, when Younis was preferred, only featuring in the one-day matches that followed. By now he was playing for the Pakistan Automobile Corporation, which employed him as a department manager, but PACO finished last in the Quaid-e-Azam Trophy and so they, too, were relegated.

He was chosen for the tour to Australia where his main rival for a Test place, Waqar, also became a close friend. Indeed the team management felt it necessary to stop them sharing hotel rooms on tour as they were invariably tempted out by the bright lights of Australia's unfamiliar and exciting cities. Aqib played in the first Test at Melbourne when Pakistan fielded four quick bowlers for the first time, but lost with just 22 minutes to go when Aqib was lbw to Alderman for nought - his fifth Test duck in a row! Although Aqib had returned the better figures at the Melbourne Cricket Ground, the extra pace of Younis was preferred for the next two Tests when Pakistan played only three seamers.

The following winter, Aqib played throughout the home series with New Zealand, but lost his place when Imran Khan returned to the side for the series with the Westindies. It was imperative that Aqib's lack of first-class cricket experience was addressed and Imran Khan went out of his way to get Aqib a county contract for the 1991 season in

England. He helped secure a contract with Hampshire, for whom Aqib took 53 first-class wickets at 31 apiece - including a career-best six for 91 against Nottinghamshire - in 18 matches, which compares quite favourably with the return of Akram for Lancashire that year (56 wickets in 14 matches) and Younis in his first season in county cricket, the year before, when he took 57 wickets in 14 games for Surrey. Aqib helped Hampshire take the NatWest Trophy for the first time, and that winning habit continued through the winter.

In the Wills Trophy final against India in Sharjah, Aqib had perhaps his finest hour. Coming on for the tenth over, with India going well as they chased 263 to win, he immediately had Najvot Sidhu caught behind and then, in his third over, initiated a dramatic collapse by taking only the seventh hat-trick in over a thousand limited-overs internationals. With the third, fourth and fifth balls of the over he trapped Ravi Shastri, Mohammad Azharuddin and Sachin Tendulkar, all lbw. He returned later to take three more wickets, to give him the best-ever figures in an international one-dayer, seven for 37, surpassing the 7-51 achieved by Winston Davis for Westindies against Australia in the 1983 Prudential World Cup. This ensured his place in the Test side for the home series against Sri Lanka. He caused a mid-innings collapse in the first Test at Sialkot with three wickets in 18 balls and bowled well through the rest of the curtailed series, and in the five one-dayers that followed.

With Younis out of the World Cup because of his back injury and Imran Khan suffering with a shoulder problem and unable to bowl at his best, Aqib's form was vital. He bowled consistently well, particularly in the defeat of Australia, and finished the tournament amongst the leading wicket-takers with eleven, as well as being economical, conceding just 3.86 per over. He invariably swung the white ball away from the right-handers and had the presence of mind to deliver a superb, slower off-break to bowl Mark Greatbatch in the semi-final against New Zealand, as the big left-hander looked to attack from the start as usual. Indeed, Aqib had demonstrated what a good temperament he has in the previous match, against the same opponents, when Greatbatch again flailed at everything. Aqib was hit for a six and two fours in his opening over but maintained his composure and only conceded 20 runs in his remaining nine overs. In the final itself, he was Pakistan's most economical bowler and took the important wickets of Alec Stewart and the dangerous Neil Fairbrother, to finish with two for 27, as well as taking a fine catch at deep square to account for Graham Gooch off Mustaq Ahmed.

It was this sang-froid that led Imran Khan to write, in *The Daily Telegraph* before the 1992 series

in England, that he felt that "the key to the series is Aqib. He has the best temperament I have seen in any cricketer. The bigger the match the better he bowls. In all the crucial World Cup matches he bowled beautifully." Aqib, to some extent, carried the attack early on when Akram and Younis were both injured and when both were fully fit he played an important supporting role to them.

He fell foul of the match referee, Conrad Hunte, during the third Test at Old Trafford, and was fined half his match fee (about £300), so becoming the first player to be thus censured. Aqib was warned for intimidatory bowling by the umpire, Roy Palmer, after bowling several short balls at the England No 11, Devon Malcolm, which infuriated Aqib as he believed he was being warned for over-use of the bouncer, of which he had bowled only one in the over. Aqib was incensed and mistook the way the umpire returned his sweater to him as rude as it caught in the umpire's coat and required a sharp tug to extricate it. A melee ensued. This was unfortunate as Aqib was in the middle of recording his best Test figures, four for 100, and unnecessary as the first full length ball that he bowled was too good for Malcolm. Aqib has been castigated for his behaviour here, but it must be remembered that he was still only 19 at the time; the vastly experienced Courtney Walsh was criticised for adopting the same tactics at Malcolm during the first Test of the Westindies-England series 1993/4 in Jamaica. The Old Trafford Test was petering towards a draw, as England had just avoided the follow-on. The incident stemmed in part from frustration and in part from a misunderstanding of the law - something that is understandable from a player of his age and experience. It is significant that the law has since been changed to make it unequivocal for both umpires and players, and thus easier to implement.

In the next Test, at Headingley, Aqib was hampered by injury going into the match and could not bowl in the second innings. He picked up the important wickets of Gooch and Gower in the final Test, at the Oval, but this took him to only nine wickets in the series, which does not fully reflect his contribution. He deserved more for the support role he provided Akram and Younis.

Controversy stayed with Aqib when six months later he became the first player to be banned by a referee for his behaviour on the field, for obscene abuse of an umpire, during a one-day international in New Zealand. Again the situation arose after Aqib had been no-balled for bowling a short delivery which bounced above shoulder height and so invalidated the gloved catch taken at slip. The umpire, Aldridge, reported him to the match referee, Peter Burge, who suspended Aqib from the next match after a 75-minute hearing, which was attended by the non-striker, Martin Crowe, and the nearest fielder to the altercation, Ramiz Raja. Aqib returned for the one-off Test at Hamilton. He was below par in the WSC matches in Australia, and so in and out of the side as Pakistan tried to find a winning combination, which was not found until the team had gone to Sharjah under a new captain, Wasim Akram.

Another triangular, limited-overs competition followed in South Africa, as the team worked their way to the Caribbean for a three-Test series. The constant demands of international cricket had taken their toll on Aqib's body and he broke down with a back problem during the game against the Board President's XI. He was forced to return home soon after when this was diagnosed as stress fractures in the lower vertebrae, but not before being involved in another unfortunate incident, which literally added insult to injury. He was one of four players - Akram, Younis and Ahmed being the others - who were arrested in Grenada for "constructive possession" of marijuana. These charges were unfounded and later dropped, but it was a miserable end to a nightmare tour for him. Indeed, since the highs of the World Cup only 12 months before, the following year had been a most difficult one.

Aqib did not feature against Zimbabwe or tour New Zealand during the 1993/4 season and his exclusion, along with that of Javed Miandad and Ramiz Raja, was blamed on the captain, Wasim Akram, who was soon to be ousted in a players' revolt. Although Akram was replaced, by Salim Malik, Aqib was not reinstated and in his absence, Ata-ur-Rehman looked like he had stolen some ground on Aqib as Pakistan's third seamer. Aqib was recalled to the squad for the Austral-Asia Cup in Sharjah but he was not required for Pakistan's Test series in Sri Lanka in August 1994, where two other young seamers, Ashfaq Ahmed and Kabir Khan were tried.

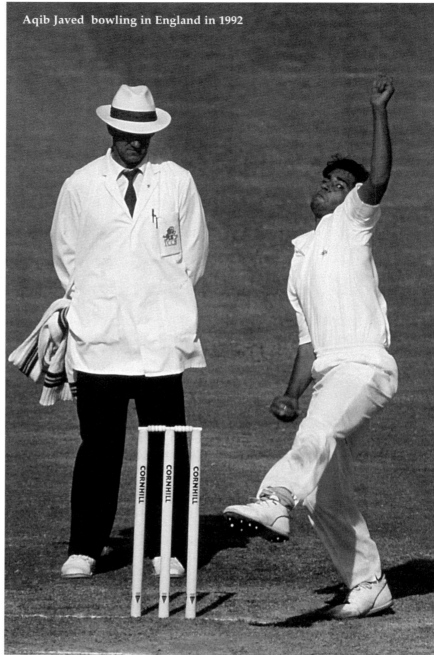

Aqib Javed bowling in England in 1992

Overlooked for the first two Tests of the home series against Australia, he was recalled to the side after a 22-month absence to spearhead the attack, as both Wasim Akram (sinus trouble) and Waqar Younis (hamstring) were unfit. He bowled steadily enough on a bland pitch, sending down 31 overs for 75 runs but without taking a wicket.

In the inaugural Test against South Africa at Johannesburg, he was again required to take the new ball in Waqar's absence and took five wickets in the match in a losing cause. Against Zimbabwe, he was the pick of the bowlers in the first Test at Harare, where again Pakistan were disappointing.

He took two of the four wickets to fall, before being injured, and maintained some semblance of control as the home side ran up a huge total. He had the misfortune to drop a caught-and-bowled chance when Grant Flower had made only 35 of his mammoth 201 not out.

He missed the next Test but returned to record his best Test figures in the decisive third Test. He took four for 64 to restrict Zimbabwe's first innings lead to just 12, and in the second, took two for 26 from 17.4 overs as the Pakistan seamers combined well to bowl Zimbabwe out for just 139. Victory, by 99 runs, represented a remarkable turn around in the series, which was won 2-1.

Aqib was the pick of Pakistan's bowlers at home against Sri Lanka, and he even made his highest Test score in the first Test, 28 not out, and finished the series batting as high as number eight. Having taken three wickets in the first innings of the next match at Faisalabad, and with Wasim Akram injured, Aqib responded superbly to take his first five-wicket haul in his 20th Test. In the series decider at Sialkot, he again had to shoulder the bowling responsibilities of a very inexperienced attack, lacking both Wasim and Waqar. He bowled skillfully, taking five wickets in the match, including his 50th in Tests, to complete his best series (16 wickets at 19.56).

He toured Australia but was injured in the match against Victoria and could play no part in the Test series. This was a great shame as his potential was just coming to fruition. It also meant that Pakistan were once again denied the chance to field the four bowlers, Wasim, Waqar, Mustaq and Aqib, who combined so effectively in 1992. They have not played together since the one Test against New Zealand in January 1993.

He was fit in time for the World Cup, and bowled steadily throughout, but it was a blow to him when not selected for the tour to England, suggesting he is considered primarily a one-day player. This is unlucky as his recent Test performances have been improving.

Much the same height and weight as Imran, at 5ft 11in and twelve and a half stone, though without quite his physical presence, Aqib has a long run-up and good high action, but perhaps has been striving for pace that is not there, and this probably has led to his back problems. It was not until Imran was older that he began to bowl really fast, so there is still plenty of potential in Aqib, at 23, if he is prepared to do the physical work.

Aqib has played more Tests and one-day internationals than he has first-class matches. This lack of overall first-class experience early in his career was evident on a number of occasions.

During the 1992 World Cup he was struck on the forehead as the ball was returned to him when he was not watching, and on another occasion at the Oval (in 1992) in a Texaco one-day international, he came racing in from the boundary to attack the ball but was completely confounded when the sliced hit bounced in front of him, causing the ball to spin violently past him. Some of his reactions to umpire's decisions that have got him into trouble have also highlighted this yet he remains a very mature cricketer for his age, with a cool temperament under pressure. It is understandable that someone who is forced to grow up quickly by being thrust into the international limelight at an early age, should show some signs of adolescent rebellion at some point in his early career. Aqib's returns from his first 21 Tests, spread over more than seven years, are only modest. However, he still has potential to develop while his vast experience in one-day cricket should keep him in the reckoning for some time to come.

Career Details

Born: Sheikhupura, 5 August 1972
Role: right-hand, lower-order batsman, right-hand fast-medium bowler
Clubs: Lahore Division (1984/5-1986/7), PACO (1989/90), Hampshire (1991)
First-class record: (1984-95) 199 runs (5.10) HS 32 not out, 161 wickets (34.60), BB 6-77, and 8 catches
Tests: 21
Test Debut: v New Zealand, Wellington, 1988/89
Test record: 100 runs (5.26), 54 wickets (33.07) and 2 catches
Best Performances: HS 28 not out v Sri Lanka, Peshawar 1995/6
BB 5-84 v Sri Lanka, Faisalabad 1995/6
Tours: New Zealand; 1988/9, 1992/3, 1993/4
Australia; 1989/90, 1991/2, 1992/3 (WSC)
India; 1989/90 (Nehru Cup)
England; 1992
Westindies; 1992/3
South Africa: 1992/3, 1994/5
Zimbabwe; 1992/3, 1994/5
Overseas Test; 11
One-day Internationals; 126
World Cups; 1987 (under-19's), 1991/2, 1995/6
Sharjah; 1988/9, 1989/90, 1990/1, 1992/3, 1993/4, 1994/5, 1995/6

Moin Khan

Moin Khan came to prominence during the 1992 World Cup tournament, in which he played in every match, and though subsequently he enjoyed a period as Pakistan's first choice wicket-keeper, the progress of Rashid Latif, a more orthodox batsman and cleaner gloveman, has limited Moin's opportunities. However, when he has come into the side he has performed creditably, scoring two Test hundreds in five matches (1994-5) in his own idiosyncratic style, and adding a record third when given another unexpected chance at Headingley on the 1996 tour to England. He played in the last two Tests, which just nudged him ahead of Latif in terms of caps won. He may now enjoy an extended run as since that first century, Moin has averaged nearly fifty in Test cricket with the bat - a remarkable effort.

Born in Rawalpindi in 1971, Moin is one of the few Pakistani Test players to have grown up outside the two main centres, Lahore and Karachi. However, like many of the others, he established himself only once he moved to the latter. A vibrant, competitive player, he was soon spotted, making his first-class debut when he was just 15 for Karachi Whites.

He finished the 1989/90 season on a high, by making a hundred in the final of the BCCP Patron's Trophy, to help Karachi Whites to a one wicket win over Karachi Blues, and was chosen to captain the under-19 side on their tour to England in the summer of 1990. He had a fine tour, making an undefeated hundred in the second Test, and was rewarded with a place on the tour with Pakistan B to Zimbabwe in 1990/1.

His rapid rise continued as later that season, he was called up to face the Westindies, firstly in a one-day international and then in the Test series, as a replacement for the long-serving Salim Yousuf, who twice damaged a finger forcing him to withdraw from the side. Coming in for the final limited-overs game at Multan, Moin shared a crucial sixth wicket stand of 58 with Imran Khan, and when Yousuf was injured again during the first Test, Moin was given his chance at Test level in the next match at Faisalabad. He rose to the challenge, making useful contributions in each innings with the bat, hitting 24 and 32. He helped Salim Malik add 47 in the first innings and then 89 in the second after going in as night-watchman.

He toured Sri Lanka with the A Team in the summer of 1991 and he was considered as the first choice wicket-keeper when the side competed for the Wills Trophy in Sharjah. The Test series at home

to Sri Lanka was largely ruined by the weather, but in a tense third Test, Moin made some useful runs to ensure Pakistan a three-wicket win.

Moin was very much one of Imran's "cornered tigers" in the World Cup, and when the side's backs were really against the wall, in the semi-final against New Zealand, he clubbed 20 off 11 balls, including a mighty six over long-on, to help secure Pakistan a place in the final.

Moin toured England in 1992 but, although he had been steady through the summer, he was replaced by Latif for the final Test to give the batting depth.

Not required on the short tour to Australia and New Zealand, he went to the Westindies (1992/3) as the reserve 'keeper, and when Latif was hampered by a back injury, he was drafted in for the first two Tests. Unfortunately for Moin, Latif was fit again for the final Test at Antigua, so he was denied the opportunity to keep to his older brother, Nadeem, the 23-year-old National Bank slow left-arm bowler, who was making his Test debut in that match.

Left on the sidelines the next season, Moin made a triumphant return to the side when called up against Australia at Lahore for the final Test of the 1994/5 series. He exceeded all expectations as he scored only the second first-class hundred of his career, making 115 not out. His previous 11 Tests had yielded a top score of just 32 and an average of only 13. It was unlucky that that innings kept him in the side for only one further Test, the inaugural match against South Africa at Johannesburg, after which Rashid Latif, who was also vice-captain on the tour resumed. However, Latif had his differences with Salim Malik and returned home early from the tour, going into temporary retirement.

Moin played out the rest of the domestic season and helped Karachi Blues beat Lahore City by an innings and 180 runs in the final of the Quaid-e-Azam. He was one of four players to score a hundred for Karachi as they amassed 802 for 8 declared, and then he had the pleasure of keeping to Nadeem, while his brother took five wickets in each innings (5-135 and 5-96) to seal victory.

With Latif absent, it allowed Moin to not only return to the international side but to do so temporarily as captain in place of Malik, who was suspended. Moin took over for a tournament in Sharjah as a stopgap measure. Unfortunately, Moin was struck down by chickenpox before the end of the tournament and Pakistan did not even qualify for the final. Imran Khan was once appointed as a temporary measure and went on to captain his country 48 times in Tests. However, when the squad was chosen for the series against Sri Lanka, Ramiz Raja was appointed as the new captain, as a man of experience who had been outside the team when the match-rigging allegations surfaced. Moin stayed in the side, though, and proved to be Pakistan's best batsman in a disappointing series, in which the team suffered a rare home defeat.

With his array of improvised strokes, Moin averaged 68.5 over the three matches and made important contributions in every innings. He followed his fifty in the first Test with 30 and 50 (from 90 balls) in the second at Faisalabad, giving his side hope of making the 252 runs they needed to win, but with little support from the other end, Pakistan fell 42 runs short. In the series decider at Sialkot, he made a useful 26 in the first innings, to edge Pakistan close to Sri Lanka's total. Then, in the second innings, having been set 357 to win, he came to the crease at 15 for 5, facing a lost cause. However, he saw Pakistan to a respectable total as he marshalled the tail to such good effect that he scored 70 per cent of the remaining runs off the bat. He delayed the inevitable with a last wicket stand of 65 - the highest of the innings - with Aamir Nazir. The partnership enabled him to record his second, and highest, Test century, facing only 165 balls for his 117 not out, which included two sixes and 13 fours.

Unfortunately, his keeping became untidy in Australia and he missed several chances. With Pakistan's out-cricket being of a generally poor standard, he lost his place to Rashid Latif for the third Test and one-off match against New Zealand.

Once again, Rashid Latif was preferred to Moin at the start of the tour to England, but he was called up on the morning of the second Test at Headingley when Latif reported injured.

He took his chance with astonishing skill, blasting a hundred which made the England bowling look decidedly ragged at a crucial stage in the match. Coming in at 266 for 6, the game was in the balance. Moin survived a difficult chance to long leg when he had only eight, and for the next four hours he made the fielding side pay. He became the first Pakistan wicket-keeper to make a century against England and only the second to score three Test tons, matching the record of Imtiaz Ahmed in the 1950s and 60s. In all he faced 191 balls, hitting ten fours and a straight six off Dominic Cork, England's premier strike bowler. In their very contrasting styles, Moin and Asif Mujtaba added 112 for the seventh wicket, a record against England. The pair again combined well in the

Moin celebrates his third Test century, Headingley, 1996

second to ensure the game petered out into a draw.

Moin finished the series top of the batting with an average of 79, to stake another convincing claim to the role on a permanent basis.

Moin has worked hard on his pugnacious right-handed batting, which has been a revelation in recent Tests. If he could just get a bit more consistency into his wicket-keeping, he could become a permanent fixture in the side. His ability to invent shots has been more than useful in one-day cricket - indeed, he once hit Ian Bishop of the Westindies for 22 off the last four balls of the last over of an innings - and he he sure to vie for Pakistan's number one slot for some time.

Career Details

Born: Rawalpindi, 23 September 1971
Role: right-hand, lower middle-order batsman, wicket-keeper
Clubs: Karachi (1986/7-), PIA (1991/2-1995/6)
First-class record: (1986/7-95) 2807 runs (28.35), 5 hundreds, HS 129, 220 catches and 23 stumpings
Tests: 20
Test Debut: v Westindies, Faisalabad, 1990/1
Test record: 782 runs (30.07), including 3 hundreds and 2 fifties, 46 catches and 4 stumpings
Best Performances: HS 117 not out v Sri Lanka, Sialkot, 1995/6
Tours: Australia; 1991/2, 1995/6
England; 1992, 1996
New Zealand; 1991/2, 1995/6
Westindies; 1992/3
South Africa; 1994/5
Zimbabwe; 1990/1 (Pakistan B), 1994/5
Sri Lanka; 1990/1 (Pakistan A)
Overseas Tests; 11
World Cups; 1991/2, 1995/6
One-day Internationals; 42
Sharjah; 1991/2, 1994/5, 1995/6
Bangladesh; 1993/4

Rashid Latif

Rashid Latif has been Pakistan's first choice wicket-keeper since ousting Moin Khan for the final Test of the 1992 tour to England. As well as being an accomplished 'keeper, it was his stylish batting that initially won him selection over Moin. Rashid has the potential to become one of Pakistan's longest serving glove men, who could develop into a wicket-keeper batsman in the mould of Jeff Dujon, of the Westindies. Rashid has outstanding credentials: he has the best dismissal-per-Test ratio (3.47) among Pakistan's 'keepers and also tops the list for fewest byes conceded (five per Test).

Born in Karachi in October 1968, Rashid made his debut for Karachi Whites as a teenager in 1986/7, playing in three matches in which he made 12 dismissals. A product of Karachi University, he caught the eye playing for the Combined Universities against Sri Lanka B and was signed up soon after by United Bank. Two good seasons for his new employers, which included a total of 15 dismissals in the semi-final and final of the Patron's Trophy triumph in 1990/1, brought him to the attention of the national selectors. He was chosen to go to Sharjah to gain experience, though he did not play, and was picked as Moin Khan's understudy for the tour to England in 1992. An enthusiastic tourist, who had appeared several times in the first four Tests as a substitute fieldsman, Rashid was a surprise inclusion for the final Test at the Oval, the series decider. He soon got on the score sheet, catching his opposite number, Alec Stewart, before lunch, but it was as a batsman that he really caught the eye. Spurred on by a £5 wager with former England opener, Geoff Boycott, who said he had to make 35 to be considered a proper batsman, a determined Latif strode to the crease wearing a baggy green Pakistani cap, even though Devon Malcolm was bowling with pace.

He batted with an old-fashioned style, striking the ball elegantly and with natural timing, despite it being only his fifth first-class innings of the tour. He won his bet with Boycott, saluting to the commentary box when he reached his mark, and went on to fifty from only 87 balls, including six fours. It helped take Pakistan's lead from 85 to 173, and that proved to be almost enough for an innings victory.

It secured him his place as the team's first choice wicket-keeper that winter. He made two significant scores in the one-off Test against New Zealand, making 32 not out and 33, to help Pakistan win a low-scoring game at Hamilton, after which he was required to play in a plethora of one-day internationals across the globe. He returned to Australia to compete in the World Series Cup, then went onto Sharjah for the Wills Trophy, to South Africa for the Total international series, Zimbabwe for a one-off match and then to the Caribbean for a series of five more one-dayers.

Not surprisingly, the constant cricket took its toll and a back injury kept Rashid out of the first two Tests against the Westindies, returning to the side only for the final match in Antigua.

He was fully fit in time for the next home series against Zimbabwe and performed creditably in each match. He hit 68 not out in the first Test - his highest Test score - played at Karachi's Defence Stadium, important knocks of 33 and 61 in the next, a low-scoring game at Rawalpindi, and claimed five catches in Zimbabwe's only innings at Lahore. He followed that by taking nine catches - a Pakistani record - in the next Test against New Zealand at Auckland, and sealed victory with a six over mid-wicket.

The following season, he played a telling part in the one-wicket win over Australia in the first Test at Rawalpindi, adding 52 for the eighth wicket with Inzamam-ul-Haq, when Pakistan's cause already seemed lost. Unfortunately, injury ruled him out of the third Test.

He missed the inaugural Test against South Africa, too, and although vice-captain on the tour, Rashid clashed over tactics with the captain, Salim Malik. Also, with the backdrop of match-rigging allegations, he became disenchanted with the atmosphere in the team dressing room and, with Basit Ali, decided to leave the second leg of the tour (to Zimbabwe) early. Both players announced

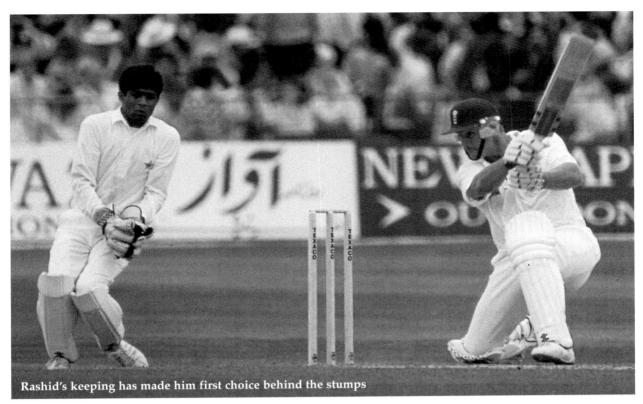
Rashid's keeping has made him first choice behind the stumps

their retirement from international cricket, but were subsequently banned from all first-class cricket in Pakistan and it appeared that two promising careers had come to a premature end.

Thankfully, with various changes at the top, Rashid and the Pakistan Cricket Board settled their differences, though his place in the side was blocked by the fine form of Moin Khan.

He toured Australia as the reserve 'keeper but when Moin lost form behind the stumps, Rashid was recalled for the final Test at Sydney. He kept with aplomb, making eight dismissals in all, including a sharp stumping to get rid of Steve Waugh in the first innings, and an easier one in the second to take the crucial wicket of Mark Taylor. He took five more catches and made a stumping in the one-off Test against the Kiwis to again establish himself as Pakistan's No 1 behind the timbers.

Rashid played an important innings of 45 in the first Test of the series at Lord's, adding 50 for the last wicket with Ata-ur-Rehman to tip the balance of the game Pakistan's way. However, he hurt his back in the county game against Durham and had to pull out of the side for the second Test because of the injury. Once again he saw his replacement Moin Khan come in and make a hundred, which will make it difficult for Rashid to exact an immediate return.

Rashid invariably seems to make telling contributions when he plays, though he has often been hampered by injuries since making his Test debut, which have restricted his number of appearances. His batting is a source of untapped potential and he needs to turn more of his twenties and thirties into big scores if he is to ensure his place among Pakistan's finest wicket-keeper-batsmen and keep off the challenge of Moin Khan.

Career Details

Born: Karachi, 14 October 1968
Role: right-hand, lower middle-order batsman, wicket-keeper
Clubs: Karachi (1986/7-1991/2), United Bank (1991/2-95/6)
First-class record: (1986/7-95) 1734 runs (24.77), 3 wickets (25.33), 164 catches and 29 stumpings
Tests: 19
Test Debut: v England, the Oval, 1992
Test record: 623 runs (24.92), including 3 fifties, 58 catches and 8 stumpings
Best Performances: HS 68 not out v Zimbabwe, Karachi, 1993/4
Tours: England; 1992, 1996
New Zealand; 1992/3, 1995/6
Australia; 1992/3 (WSC), 1995/6
South Africa; 1992/3, 1994/5
Zimbabwe; 1992/3, 1994/5
Westindies; 1992/3
Sri Lanka; 1994/5
Overseas Tests; 15
World Cup; 1995/6
One-day Internationals; 84
Sharjah; 1992/3, 1993/4, 1994/5, 1995/6
Bangladesh; 1993/4

Aamir Sohail

Aamir Sohail is a dashing left-handed opening batsman, who established himself during the 1992 World Cup triumph and is very much one of Imran Khan's "cornered tigers." Initially he seemed to approach every innings in the same way, whether in a Test or one-day international, always looking to play his shots. He averages roughly the same in both forms of the game, and has developed a highly effective pairing with Saeed Anwar at the top of the order. Aamir has tightened his technique and tempered his approach slightly in Test cricket, but needs to convert more of his fifties - of which he had made 13 in his first 32 Tests - into hundreds. As he settles into his role as vice-captain, perhaps the big scores will start to come. He is certainly highly regarded; the great Hanif Mohammad would choose Aamir above all others to open the batting with him in an all-time Pakistan side.

In a country which so readily promotes talented youth, Aamir took some time to come into the international reckoning. Born in Lahore in 1966, he made his first-class debut when just turned 17, for Lahore City Blues against Quetta in the Patron's Trophy (1983/4). However, he did not make his Test debut until 1992, though he had been playing for Pakistan's various junior representative sides for some time. In 1986/7, fine all-round performances in domestic cricket earned him a tour to Zimbabwe with Pakistan B at the end of that season, in which he had scored 839 runs and taken 37 wickets with his slow left-armers in 12 matches. This included taking four for 118 and a career-best seven for 53 against Habib Bank, as well as scoring 45 and 77 to secure Lahore a one-wicket win. Not surprisingly Habib signed him up for the start of the next season, which proved a shrewd move as he averaged over 50 for his new employers, hitting four hundreds, and helping the bank win the Patron's Trophy for the first time in ten years, which took him to the fringes of the Test team.

Sohail's career stood still for the next three years; his batting returns were consistent, scoring nearly two thousand runs at an average of 40 in domestic cricket over that period, but were not eye-catching enough to warrant a run in the national side. However, he remained in contention, earning selection for the Sharjah Cup in December 1990, and on his debut against Sri Lanka helped rescue the side after a disastrous start, making 32 before being run out.

Good form on the Pakistan A tour to Sri Lanka, which included a hundred in the final "Test,"

helped him make the side for the next Sharjah tournament for the Wills Trophy, but only as a late replacement after a number of injuries. Having just flown in, he went straight into the match with India, playing a fine innings of 91 which ensured the victory which took Pakistan into the final, which they duly won. He was dropped after two one-day failures at home against Westindies, and despite scoring 71 and a brilliant 102 from only 106 balls for the Punjab Governor's XI against the touring Sri Lankans, he did not play in the limited-overs internationals against them.

Originally not in the squad for the World Cup, Aamir got a surprise call-up when Pakistan suffered several injuries. With only one established opener in the side in Ramiz Raja, Aamir went straight into the side and soon justified his selection with a fine hundred against Zimbabwe, scored from 136 balls and including 12 fours. He rode his luck to benefit from four dropped chances after he had passed fifty, and he also took two wickets with his rather round-arm spinners. He top-scored with 62 in a losing cause against India, and played a vital innings against Australia which kept Pakistan in the World Cup. Caught off a Reid no-ball before he had scored, he went onto 76 and took the man-of-the-match award. His form tailed off after that, though he continued to bowl some tidy spells and set an example in the field - an area of his game which had previously been a weak point. Overall he proved to be a vital cog in

Pakistan's World Cup campaign.

Aamir had a highly successful tour to England, averaging over fifty in the five Tests and scoring over eleven hundred runs in all first-class matches. Having played in fifteen one-day internationals already, Aamir made his Test debut at Edgbaston, and although he was not out until the third morning, only two balls had been possible on the first two days, from which he scored three runs. In the next Test, at Lord's, Sohail was the leading scorer for Pakistan in a tight, low-scoring match, making 73 and 39, holding the batting together in both innings. He was unfortunate in the first innings that the rain came at lunch on the second day when he was well set, having made 63 in the pre-lunch session, for he fell immediately on the resumption of play on the third morning.

In only his third Test in the next match at Old Trafford, he scored a superb double-hundred, which included 32 fours. It was an innings full of fine shots, particularly his strokes through the covers and square of the wicket. It was also scored at a startling rate as when he was out for 205 at 378 for 3, there were still 20 minutes to go before the close of play on the first day. It was one of the fastest Test double-hundreds of all time, made from only 284 balls in all, and was the most runs scored by one batsman in a single day since Garry Sobers made 208 of his famous 365 against Pakistan in 1957/8. He shared century partnerships for each of the first three wickets; the tone was set during his opening stand of 115 with Ramiz Raja before lunch, which was particularly entertaining as both decided to attack the bowling on an unusually fast pitch.

In the final Test at the Oval, Aamir made 49 in the first innings and he had the satisfaction of making the winning hit in the second to secure a ten-wicket win and with it the series. In his debut series, he finished with 413 runs which passed the previous record for a rubber against England, though not the total achieved by Salim Malik in the series, who made 488 runs in the five Tests.

Despite the quality of his innings at Old Trafford, Ray Illingworth said at the time that, because of the way Aamir played, he was the sort of player who might not get another Test hundred. For a while that prediction seemed prophetic. Aamir never found his form on the tour to New Zealand recording a pair in the one-off Test at Hamilton, and had a terrible time in the World Series Cup matches in Australia, failing to reach double-figures in all but one of his six innings. Dropped for the Wills Trophy in Sharjah and the triangular tournament in South Africa, he returned home only to discover that he had been banned for the rest of the season and fined Rs10,000 (about £200) by the Pakistan Board for his misconduct during the Wills Patron's Trophy Grade II final at Lahore the previous October.

However, when Inzamam-ul-Haq broke a finger in South Africa, Aamir received a reprieve and was summoned to join the tour. He top-scored with fifties in two of his three games, and took the man-of-the-match award in the final, which was enough to book his place for the tour to the Caribbean.

There, after a string of useful scores and wickets in the one-dayers in which he cut and pulled the quick bowlers with aplomb, he made a fine fifty in the first Test at Port of Spain. He played in the next at Bridgetown despite being incapacitated by groin and hamstring injuries which affected his mobility, and which forced him home soon after, missing the final Test.

Sohail returned to the side for the inaugural home rubber with Zimbabwe (1993/4), but after a fluent fifty in the first Test, he had an indifferent series. On the tour to New Zealand, he topped scored in the first Test at Auckland, seeing his side to the verge of victory with an accomplished innings of 78, and made 60 out of a dashing opening stand of 125 with Saeed Anwar in the third at Christchurch.

Following on from some good scores in the one-dayers against New Zealand, Aamir smashed a glorious hundred against the same opponents in the semi-final of the Austral-Asia Cup in Sharjah. He and Inzamam-ul-Haq set a new record for any wicket in one-day cricket, adding 263 for the 2nd wicket to eclipse the previous record of 224 for the third wicket set by Allan Border and Dean Jones, for Australia against Sri Lanka in 1984/5. His 134 came from 146 balls, with 12 fours, and he continued in fine form in the final against India, making 69 which won him the man-of-the-match award and set Pakistan up for victory.

Aamir had a most accomplished winter season in 1994/5. In the shortened series against Sri Lanka, he made 41 and 65 at Colombo, and 94 at Kandy as Pakistan overwhelmed their opponents. Each time he and Saeed Anwar got Pakistan off to a fine start, sharing opening stands of 65, 128 and 94. That form continued at home against Australia. He followed scores of 36 and 34 in the epic first Test, with 80 and 72 at Rawalpindi. He held the batting together in the first innings, hitting a six and thirteen fours, and in the second, helped Salim Malik rescue the side, returning to the crease after retiring to have four stitches in a lip, to add 109 with his captain.

Aamir was again in the wars in the third Test. He was forced to bat down the order in the second innings because of a strained neck, which required him to wear a brace, a consequence of being hit on the head by Craig McDermott in the first innings. Coming in at No 7, with Pakistan just 25 runs ahead with only five wickets in hands, he and Malik put together a record stand for their side against Australia, adding 196 for the sixth wicket to remove the threat of defeat and so secure the series. Aamir finished with 105, including 17 fours. It laid to rest the prediction that he might never score

another hundred though, ironically, it was not scored from the top of the order. He finished the series with 328 runs at an average of 54.67,

He had a modest tour to Southern Africa, averaging in the mid-twenties in the four Tests (one against South Africa and three in Zimbabwe), but

240

he did bat spectacularly well at Bulawayo, caning 46 off 26 balls, including 22 off an over from David Brain, to make sure Pakistan beat Zimbabwe inside three days. He had used up his best form in the one-day quadrangular series for the Mandela Trophy which preceded the Tests, making a string of useful scores including a hundred against Sri Lanka.

He was below par in the next home series against Sri Lanka, making only 101 runs in the three Tests, but came back to form in the first Test against Australia at Brisbane, top-scoring in each innings. Facing a massive first innings deficit, Aamir played with cavalier abandon, flailing the quicker bowling all round the ground. He notched fifty, including nine fours, in an hour from only 56 balls and though he slowed down as he approached three figures, he continued to play some thrilling strokes. That elusive second century from the top of the order was not to be. McGrath, from round the wicket, speared in a perfect yorker to leave Aamir agonisingly short on 99. A religious man, Aamir took his fate philosophically, seeing it as "the will of God."

Aamir continued to take the attack to the bowlers in the next Test at Hobart, though his first innings effort there was cut short by a debatable umpiring decision and in the second he had to retire hurt with a painful knee, returning later to complete his fifty.

That Aamir only seems to know how to play one way was evident against New Zealand. On the first day of the match, he set about the bowling with some typically bold strokes. He looked on course to becoming only the second Pakistani after Majid Khan to score a hundred before lunch, when he was out hit wicket for 88 off a mere 96 deliveries. With Ramiz Raja he had added 135 in 15 minutes short of a session.

In the World Cup, he hammered a pugnacious hundred against South Africa, 42 against England and 50 against New Zealand as Pakistan cruised through to the quarter-finals. At Bangalore, Aamir and Saeed Anwar gave Pakistan a thrilling start in response to India's 287, taking 84 off the first ten overs. However, Aamir's impetuosity got the better of him at a crucial stage. Playing a captain's innings in Akram's absence, he flailed his way to fifty and then clubbed Prasad through the covers for a rousing boundary. He exchanged words with the bowler, who had the last laugh knocking out Aamir's off-stump next ball as he tried to repeat the stroke.

His form on the tour to England was patchy and he had the misfortune to injure his wrist in the first Test at Lord's attempting a catch. It prevented him from batting in the second innings and ruled him out of the next Test. Back for the decider at the

Oval, his batting with Saeed Anwar on the second afternoon stole the initiative as Pakistan raced past 100. Aamir fell for 46 off only 76 balls, seven of which he hit for four, passing 2000 Test runs in the process. It was a tour which promised much for Aamir, as the team's vice-captain, but he knows he must remain consistent to ward off the challenge of a number of young batsmen and keep intact one of Pakistan's most prolific opening pairings, both in Test and one-day cricket, with Saeed Anwar.

Aamir has made some necessary adjustments to his technique and no longer shuffles across the crease. There is a danger, though, that the amount of one-day cricket he is playing could ultimately hinder his achievement at Test level.

Aamir's style makes him one of the most exciting opening batsman in the world and he has certainly got his side off to some flying starts. He delights in dispatching anything slightly loose, but sometimes pays for his aggression. He has only made one hundred from the top of the order and the magnificence of that innings suggests that that is an underachievement. The other came when restrained by injury, batting at No 7, and so playing within his limitations.

A calm, modest man off the field, he plays his cricket with a passion which occasionally boils over. He has such talent that if he were to slightly temper his attacking approach he might reap the benefits.

Career Details

Born: Lahore, 14 September 1966
Role: left-hand, opening batsman, slow left-arm bowler
Clubs: Lahore (1983/4-86/7), Habib Bank (1987/8-95/6), Sargodha (1990/1)
First-class record: (1984-95) 8392 runs (38.67) including 17 centuries, HS 205, 111 wickets (35.35), BB 7-53, and 112 catches
Tests: 32
Test Debut: v England, Edgbaston, 1992
Test record: 2037 runs (35.73), including 2 hundreds and 13 fifties, 17 wickets (39.76), and 31 catches
Best Performances: HS 205 v England, Old Trafford, 1992
BB 4-54 v Sri Lanka, Peshawar, 1995/6
Tours: Sri Lanka: 1991/2 (Pakistan A), 1994/5
England 1992, 1996
New Zealand; 1992/3, 1993/4, 1995/6
Westindies; 1992/3
Australia; 1991/2, 1992/3 (WSC), 1995/6
South Africa: 1992/3, 1994/5
Zimbabwe: 1986/7 (Pakistan B),1992/3, 1994/5
Overseas Test; 23
One-day Internationals; 101
World Cups; 1991/2, 1995/6
Sharjah; 1991/2, 1992/3, 1993/4, 1994/5, 1995/6

Obituary

Of all the 137 players who have represented Pakistan between 1952 and 1996 only eight have passed away. A H Kardar and Mahmood Hussain are featured earlier, others include **Miran Bux** who became the second oldest Test debutant, aged 47 years and 284 days, when he was called to play in the third Test against India in Lahore in 1954/5. His best days were perhaps behind him - he had taken 10-82 against the Commonwealth XI in 1949/50 - but bowled his off-spinners tidily enough on his debut, sending down 48 overs and taking two for 82. The next Test was his last. Mahmood Hussain played in both of these matches. Miran died in Dhok Rata, Rawalpindi, 8th February 1991, at the age of 84.

Another who sadly is no longer with us is **Gul Mahomed** who, in fact, played against Hussain on the latter's debut, against India in 1952. A Muslim, he was later to play for his new country, Pakistan, in one Test against Australia in 1956/7 and made the winning hit. He will be best remembered for his part in the world record partnership of 577, of which he made 319 in 8 hours 53 minutes. He died in Lahore, where he was born, on 8 May 1992. Others include **Mufasir-ul-Haq**, a left-handed seamer who played in one Test in New Zealand in 1964/5, who died just before his fortieth birthday in 1983, and **Amir Elahi**, another who played for India prior to Partition, before adopting Pakistan for whom he played throughout the first Test series against India in 1952/3, when he was aged 44. Surprisingly he had been asked to open in the second innings of his only Test for India, but it was batting at number 11 that he surpassed himself against them with an innings of 47 and a last-wicket stand of 104 with Zulfiqar Ahmed in the 4th Test of that first series. A joyous character, he was the first Pakistani Test cricketer to go to the great cricket ground in the sky. He died in Multan on 28 December 1980 at the age of 82.

Wallis Mathias, a tourist to England in 1962, died of a brain haemorrhage on 1 September 1994, at the age of 59. He had been suffering from a chest infection. Mathias was a fine middle-order batsman and an excellent close catcher, who played in 21 Tests for Pakistan. He became the first non-Muslim to play for his country when he made his Test debut at Dacca in November 1955, against New Zealand. Born in Karachi on 4 February, 1935, his first-class career stretched from 1953 to 1976. After that, he managed his old club, National Bank, was a Test selector and was the assistant manager on the under-19 tour to Sri Lanka.

Nazar Mohammad died on 12 July 1996 in Lahore, aged 75. Nazar was a solid opening batsman and reliable close fielder, who helped Pakistan in their quest for Test status by making 140 for Punjab against the MCC in 1951/2, and 66 in the first unofficial Test against the same opponents.

Duly elected to the ICC, Nazar was chosen to face Pakistan's first ball in Test cricket, against India the following season. Then 31, he opened the batting with the 17-year-old Hanif Mohammad. Both Nazar and Hanif, and their respective sons, Mudassar and Shoaib, were to score centuries for Pakistan.

Indeed Nazar's hundred came in the very next match at Lucknow. Not only was it the first for Pakistan, but he carried his bat as well for 124 not out, helping his side to record an innings victory. He also became the first man to be on the field for every minute of a Test match. Scores of 55 and 47 in the final match at Calcutta helped him top the series averages with 39.57.

Unfortunately, a serious arm injury prevented him from playing first-class cricket again after that season. He continued in cricket, becoming a National coach and keeping an eye on his son's development. In 1982/3 he saw Mudassar emulate his achievement of 30 years before, by carrying his bat against India.

TEST SCORECARDS

1952/3 - 1996

INDIA vs PAKISTAN
at Delhi starting on 16/10/1952
India won by an innings and 70 runs

INDIA

M.H.Mankad	b Khan Mohammad	11
Pankaj Roy	b Khan Mohammad	7
V.S.Hazare	b Amir Elahi	76
V.L.Manjrekar	c Nazar Mohammad b Amir Elahi	23
L.Amarnath *	c Khan Mohammad b Fazal Mahmood	9
P.R.Umrigar	lbw b Kardar	25
Gul Mahomed	c Hanif Mohammad b Amir Elahi	24
H.R.Adhikari	not out	81
G.S.Ramchand	c Imtiaz Ahmed b Fazal Mahmood	13
P.Sen +	c Nazar Mohammad b Kardar	25
Ghulam Ahmed	b Amir Elahi	50
	Extras (b 28)	28
	TOTAL	372

PAKISTAN

Nazar Mohammad	run out	27	b Mankad		7
Hanif Mohammad +	c Ramchand b Mankad	51	b Amarnath		1
Israr Ali	b Mankad	1	lbw b Mankad		9
Imtiaz Ahmed	lbw b Mankad	0	lbw b Ghulam Ahmed		41
Maqsood Ahmed	c Roy b Mankad	15	c Adhikari b Mankad		5
A.H.Kardar *	c Roy b Mankad	4	not out		43
Anwar Hussain	c & b Mankad	4	lbw b Ghulam Ahmed		4
Waqar Hassan	lbw b Mankad	8	c Gul Mahomed b Ghulam Ahmed		5
Fazal Mahmood	not out	21	c & b Ghulam Ahmed		27
Khan Mohammad	c Ramchand b Mankad	0	st Sen b Mankad		5
Amir Elahi	c Gul Mahomed b Ghulam Ahmed	9	c Ramchand b Mankad		0
	Extras (b 9,lb 1)	10	(b 5)		5
	TOTAL	150			152

PAKISTAN	O	M	R	W		O	M	R	W
Khan Mohammad	20	5	52	2					
Maqsood Ahmed	6	1	13	0					
Fazal Mahmood	40	13	92	2					
Amir Elahi	39.4	4	134	4					
Kardar	34	12	53	2					

INDIA	O	M	R	W		O	M	R	W
Ramchand	14	7	24	0		6	1	21	0
Amarnath	13	9	10	0		5	2	12	1
Mankad	47	27	52	8		24.2	3	79	5
Ghulam Ahmed	22.3	6	51	1		23	7	35	4
Hazare	6	5	3	0					
Gul Mahomed	2	2	0	0					

FALL OF WICKETS	1st	2nd	3rd	4th	5th	6th	7th	8th	9th	10th
IND	19	26	65	76	110	180	195	229	263	372
PAK	64	65	65	97	102	111	112	129	129	150
PAK	2	17	42	48	73	79	87	121	152	152

INDIA vs PAKISTAN
at Lucknow starting on 23/11/1952
Pakistan won by an innings and 43 runs

INDIA

Pankaj Roy	lbw b Fazal Mahmood	30	c Imtiaz Ahmed b Mahmood Hussain		2
D.K.Gaekwad	b Maqsood Ahmed	6	c Nazar Mohammad b Fazal Mahmood		32
Gul Mahomed	lbw b Maqsood Ahmed	0	(6) b Fazal Mahmood		2
V.L.Manjrekar	b Fazal Mahmood	3	lbw b Fazal Mahmood		3
G.Kishenchand	lbw b Fazal Mahmood	0	(3) c N.Mohammad b Fazal Mahmood		20
P.R.Umrigar	b Mahmood Hussain	15	(5) lbw b Fazal Mahmood		32
L.Amarnath *	c Zulfiqar Ahmed b Mahmood Hussain	10	not out		61
P.G.Joshi +	b Mahmood Hussain	9	(9) b Amir Elahi		15
H.G.Gaekwad	b Fazal Mahmood	14	(8) b Fazal Mahmood		8
S.Nyalchand	not out	6	(11) lbw b Fazal Mahmood		1
Ghulam Ahmed	c Hanif Mohammad b Fazal Mahmood	8	(10) c sub b Amir Elahi		0
	Extras (b 5)	5	(b 5,nb 1)		6
	TOTAL	106			182

PAKISTAN

Nazar Mohammad	not out	124
Hanif Mohammad +	c Umrigar b Ghulam Ahmed	34
Waqar Hassan	lbw b Amarnath	23
Imtiaz Ahmed	lbw b Amarnath	0
Maqsood Ahmed	lbw b Nyalchand	41
A.H.Kardar *	c Ghulam Ahmed b Nyalchand	16
Anwar Hussain	b Nyalchand	5
Fazal Mahmood	c Joshi b Gul Mahomed	29
Zulfiqar Ahmed	lbw b Ghulam Ahmed	34
Mahmood Hussain	b Ghulam Ahmed	13
Amir Elahi	b Gul Mahomed	4
	Extras (b 4,lb 3,nb 1)	8
	TOTAL	331

PAKISTAN	O	M	R	W		O	M	R	W
Mahmood Hussain	23	7	35	3		19	5	57	1
Kardar	3	2	2	0		13	5	15	0
Fazal Mahmood	24.1	8	52	5		27.3	11	42	7
Maqsood Ahmed	5	1	12	2		5	0	25	0
Amir Elahi						7	1	20	2
Zulfiqar Ahmed						5	1	17	0

INDIA	O	M	R	W		O	M	R	W
Amarnath	40	18	74	2					
Umrigar	1	0	1	0					
Nyalchand	64	33	97	3					
Gaekwad H.G.	37	21	47	0					
Ghulam Ahmed	45	19	83	3					
Gul Mahomed	7.3	2	21	2					

FALL OF WICKETS	1st	2nd	3rd	4th	5th	6th	7th	8th	9th	10th
IND	17	17	20	22	55	65	68	85	93	106
PAK	63	118	120	167	194	201	239	302	318	331
IND	4	27	43	73	77	103	115	170	170	182

* Captain
+ Wicket-keeper
Scores supplied by Gordon Vince, Lightwater, Surrey

INDIA vs PAKISTAN
at Bombay on 13/11/1952
India won by 10 wickets

PAKISTAN

Nazar Mohammad	b Amarnath	4	c Umrigar b Dani		0
Hanif Mohammad +	b Mankad	15	c sub b Mankad		96
A.H.Kardar *	c Dani b Amarnath	20	(5) lbw b Mankad		3
Imtiaz Ahmed	b Amarnath	0	c Adhikari b Gupte		28
Maqsood Ahmed	c Umrigar b Amarnath	6	(6) c Hazare b Mankad		9
Wazir Mohammad	c & b Mankad	8	(7) lbw b Mankad		4
Waqar Hassan	st Rajinderanth b Mankad	81	(3) c Hazare b Mankad		65
Fazal Mahmood	c Amarnath b Mankad	33	st Rajinderanth b Gupte		0
Israr Ali	b Gupte	10	st Rajinderanth b Gupt		5
Mahmood Hussain	st Rajinderanth b Gupte	2	not out		21
Amir Elahi	not out	0	run out		1
	Extras (b 5,lb 2)	7	(b 4,lb 6)		10
	TOTAL	186			242

INDIA

M.H.Mankad	c Nazar Mohammad b Kardar	41	not out		35
M.L.Apte	c Imtiaz Ahmed b M.Hussain	30	not out		10
R.S.Modi	b M.Hussain	32			
V.S.Hazare	not out	146			
P.R.Umrigar	b M.Hussain	102			
H.R.Adhikari	not out	31			
L.Amarnath *					
H.T.Dani					
Rajinderanth +					
S.P.Gupte					
Ghulam Ahmed					
	Extras (b 1,lb 4)	5			0
	TOTAL (for 4 wkts dec)	387	(for 0 wkts)		45

INDIA	O	M	R	W		O	M	R	W
Amarnath	21	10	40	4		18	9	25	0
Dani	4	2	10	0		6	3	9	1
Hazare	7	1	21	0		6	2	13	0
Mankad	25	11	52	3		65	31	72	5
Ghulam Ahmed	7	1	14	0		21	8	36	0
Gupte	9	1	42	2		33.2	10	77	3

PAKISTAN	O	M	R	W		O	M	R	W
Mahmood Hussain	35	5	121	3		6	2	21	0
Fazal Mahmood	39	10	111	0		7.2	2	22	0
Maqsood Ahmed	7	2	20	0					
Kardar	14	2	54	1		2	1	2	0
Amir Elahi	14	0	65	0					
Israr Ali	3	1	11	0					

FALL OF WICKETS	1st	2nd	3rd	4th	5th	6th	7th	8th	9th	10th
PAK	10	40	40	44	56	60	143	174	182	186
IND	55	103	122	305						
PAK	1	166	171	183	201	215	215	215	232	242
IND										

INDIA vs PAKISTAN
at Madras on 28/11/1952
Match drawn

PAKISTAN

Nazar Mohammad	run out	13
Hanif Mohammad	lbw b Divecha	22
Waqar Hassan	st Maka b Mankad	49
Imtiaz Ahmed +	c Maka b Divecha	6
A.H.Kardar *	b Ramchand	79
Maqsood Ahmed	c sub b Mankad	1
Anwar Hussain	run out	17
Fazal Mahmood	c Maka b Phadkar	30
Zulfiqar Ahmed	not out	63
Mahmood Hussain	b Phadkar	0
Amir Elahi	b Amarnath	47
	Extras (b 9,lb 7,nb 1)	17
	TOTAL	344

INDIA

M.H.Mankad	b F.Mahmood	7
M.L.Apte	c Maqsood Ahmed b Kardar	42
V.S.Hazare	c Zulfiqar Ahmed b M.Hussain	1
C.D.Gopinath	c Nazar Mohammad b M.Hussain	0
P.R.Umrigar	c Nazar Mohammad b F.Mahmood	62
L.Amarnath *	c Imtiaz Ahmed b Kardar	14
D.G.Phadkar	not out	18
G.S.Ramchand	not out	25
R.V.Divecha		
E.S.Maka +		
S.P.Gupte		
	Extras (b 4,nb 2)	6
	TOTAL (for 6 wkts)	175

INDIA	O	M	R	W		O	M	R	W
Phadkar	19	3	61	2					
Divecha	19	4	36	2					
Ramchand	20	3	66	1					
Amarnath	6.5	3	9	1					
Mankad	35	3	113	2					
Gupte	5	2	14	0					
Hazare	6	0	28	0					

PAKISTAN	O	M	R	W		O	M	R	W
Mahmood Hussain	22	4	70	2					
Fazal Mahmood	27	11	52	2					
Maqsood Ahmed	4	1	10	0					
Kardar	21	7	37	2					

FALL OF WICKETS	1st	2nd	3rd	4th	5th	6th	7th	8th	9th	10th
PAK	26	46	73	111	115	195	195	240	240	344
IND	21	28	30	104	132	134				

INDIA vs PAKISTAN
at Calcutta on 12/12/1952
Match drawn

PAKISTAN

Nazar Mohammad	c Amarnath b Ghulam Ahmed	55	lbw b Mankad	47
Hanif Mohammad	c Ramchand b Phadkar	56	b Ramchand	12
Waqar Hassan	lbw b Phadkar	29	b Ramchand	97
Imtiaz Ahmed +	c Gaekwad b Phadkar	57	b Mankad	13
A.H.Kardar *	b Phadkar	7	c Ramchand b Ghulam Ahmed	1
Maqsood Ahmed	c Manjrekar b Amarnath	17	c Shodhan b Ghulam Ahmed	8
Anwar Hussain	lbw b Phadkar	9	c Mankad b Ghulam Ahmed	3
Fazal Mahmood	c Mankad b Ramchand	5	not out	28
Zulfiqar Ahmed	not out	6	not out	5
Mahmood Hussain	st Sen b Ramchand	5		
Amir Elahi	c Sen b Ramchand	4		
	Extras (b 3,lb 3,nb 1)	7	(b 14,lb 6,nb 2)	22
	TOTAL	257	(for 7 wkts dec)	236

INDIA

Pankaj Roy	c Zulfiqar Ahmed b Amir Elahi	29	not out	8
D.K.Gaekwad	b Mahmood Hussain	21	not out	20
M.H.Mankad	lbw b Fazal Mahmood	35		
V.L.Manjrekar	c Fazal Mahmood b Mahmood Hussain	29		
P.R.Umrigar	c Kardar b Fazal Mahmood	22		
D.G.Phadkar	c Imtiaz Ahmed b Kardar	57		
L.Amarnath *	c Maqsood Ahmed b Fazal Mahmood	11		
R.H.Shodhan	c Imtiaz Ahmed b Fazal Mahmood	110		
G.S.Ramchand	b Mahmood Hussain	25		
P.Sen +	b Anwar Hussain	13		
Ghulam Ahmed	not out	20		
	Extras (b 7,lb 16,nb 2)	25		0
	TOTAL	397	(for 0 wkts)	28

INDIA

	O	M	R	W		O	M	R	W
Phadkar	32	10	72	5		21	8	30	0
Ramchand	13	6	20	3		16	3	43	2
Amarnath	21	7	31	1		3	2	1	0
Mankad	28	7	78	0		41	18	68	2
Ghulam Ahmed	22	6	49	1		33	11	56	3
Shodhan						2	1	6	0
Roy						2	1	4	0
Manjrekar						2	0	6	0

PAKISTAN

	O	M	R	W		O	M	R	W
Mahmood Hussain	46	11	114	3					
Fazal Mahmood	64	19	141	4					
Maqsood Ahmed	8	2	20	0					
Amir Elahi	6	0	29	1					
Kardar	15	3	43	1					
Anwar Hussain	5	1	25	1		1	0	4	0
Nazar Mohammad						2	1	4	0
Hanif Mohammad						2	0	10	0
Waqar Hassan						1	0	10	0

FALL OF WICKETS

	1st	2nd	3rd	4th	5th	6th	7th	8th	9th	10th
PAK	94	128	169	185	215	233	240	242	253	257
IND	37	87	99	135	157	179	265	319	357	397
PAK	18	96	126	131	141	152	216			
IND										

ENGLAND vs PAKISTAN
at Lord's on 10/06/1954
Match drawn

PAKISTAN

Hanif Mohammad	b Tattersall	20	lbw b Laker	39
Alimuddin	c Edrich b Wardle	19	b Bailey	0
Waqar Hassan	c Compton b Wardle	9	c Statham b Compton	53
Maqsood Ahmed	st Evans b Wardle	0	not out	29
Imtiaz Ahmed +	b Laker	12		
A.H.Kardar *	b Statham	2		
Fazal Mahmood	b Wardle	5		
Khalid Wazir	b Wardle	3		
Khan Mohammad	b Statham	0		
Zulfiqar Ahmed	b Statham	11		
Shujauddin	not out	0		
	Extras (b 4,lb 1,nb 1)	6		0
	TOTAL	87	(for 3 wkts)	121

ENGLAND

L.Hutton *	b Khan Mohammad	0
R.T.Simpson	lbw b Fazal Mahmood	40
P.B.H.May	b Khan Mohammad	27
D.C.S.Compton	b Fazal Mahmood	0
W.J.Edrich	b Khan Mohammad	4
J.H.Wardle	c Maqsood Ahmed b Fazal Mahmood	3
T.G.Evans +	b Khan Mohammad	25
T.E.Bailey	b Khan Mohammad	3
J.C.Laker	not out	13
J.B.Statham	b Fazal Mahmood	0
R.Tattersall		
	Extras (b 2)	2
	TOTAL (for 9 wkts dec)	117

ENGLAND

	O	M	R	W		O	M	R	W
Statham	13	6	18	4		5	2	17	0
Bailey	3	2	1	0		6	2	13	1
Wardle	30.5	22	33	4		8	6	6	0
Tattersall	15	8	12	1		10	1	27	0
Laker	22	12	17	1		10.2	5	22	1
Compton						13	2	36	1

PAKISTAN

	O	M	R	W		O	M	R	W
Fazal Mahmood	16	2	54	4					
Khan Mohammad	15	3	61	5					

FALL OF WICKETS

	1st	2nd	3rd	4th	5th	6th	7th	8th	9th	10th
PAK	24	42	43	57	67	67	71	71	87	87
ENG	9	55	59	72	75	79	85	110	117	
PAK	0	71	121							

ENGLAND vs PAKISTAN
at Trent Bridge on 01/07/1954
England won by an innings and 129 runs

PAKISTAN

Hanif Mohammad	lbw b Appleyard	19	c Evans b Bedser	51
Alimuddin	b Statham	4	b Statham	18
Waqar Hassan	b Appleyard	7	c Evans b Statham	7
Maqsood Ahmed	c Evans b Appleyard	6	c Statham b Appleyard	69
Imtiaz Ahmed +	b Appleyard	11	lbw b Wardle	33
A.H.Kardar *	c Compton b Bedser	28	c Graveney b Wardle	4
Fazal Mahmood	c Sheppard b Bedser	14	b Statham	36
M.E.Z.Ghazali	b Statham	18	c Statham b Bedser	14
Mohammad Aslam	b Wardle	16	c Sheppard b Appleyard	18
Khalid Hassan	c May b Appleyard	10	(11) not out	7
Khan Mohammad	not out	13	(10) c Compton b Wardle	8
	Extras (b 9,lb 1,nb 1)	11	(b 4,lb 3)	7
	TOTAL	157		272

ENGLAND

Rev.D.S.Sheppard *	c Imtiaz Ahmed b Khan Mohammad	37
R.T.Simpson	b Khalid Hassan	101
P.B.H.May	b Khan Mohammad	0
D.C.S.Compton	b Khalid Hassan	278
T.W.Graveney	c Maqsood Ahmed b Kardar	84
T.E.Bailey	not out	36
T.G.Evans +	b Khan Mohammad	4
J.H.Wardle	not out	14
A.V.Bedser		
J.B.Statham		
R.Appleyard		
	Extras (b 2,lb 1,nb 1)	4
	TOTAL (for 6 wkts dec)	558

ENGLAND

	O	M	R	W		O	M	R	W
Bedser	21	8	30	2		30	11	83	2
Statham	18	3	38	2		20	3	66	3
Appleyard	17	5	51	5		30.4	8	72	2
Bailey	3	0	18	0					
Wardle	6	3	9	1		32	17	44	3

PAKISTAN

	O	M	R	W		O	M	R	W
Fazal Mahmood	47	7	148	0					
Khan Mohammad	40	3	155	3					
Kardar	28	4	110	1					
Khalid Hassan	21	1	116	2					
Maqsood Ahmed	3	0	25	0					

FALL OF WICKETS

	1st	2nd	3rd	4th	5th	6th	7th	8th	9th	10th
PAK	26	37	43	50	55	86	111	121	138	157
ENG	98	102	185	339	531	536				
PAK	69	70	95	164	168	189	216	242	254	272

ENGLAND vs PAKISTAN
at Old Trafford on 22/07/1954
Match drawn

ENGLAND

Rev.D.S.Sheppard *	b Fazal Mahmood	13
T.E.Bailey	run out	42
P.B.H.May	c Imtiaz Ahmed b Shujauddin	14
D.C.S.Compton	c Imtiaz Ahmed b Shujauddin	93
T.W.Graveney	st Imtiaz Ahmed b Shujauddin	65
J.M.Parks	b Fazal Mahmood	15
T.G.Evans +	c Hanif Mohammad b Fazal Mahmood	31
J.H.Wardle	c Waqar Hassan b Fazal Mahmood	54
A.V.Bedser	not out	22
J.E.McConnon	not out	5
J.B.Statham		
	Extras (b 1,lb 4)	5
	TOTAL (for 8 wkts dec)	359

PAKISTAN

Hanif Mohammad	c Wardle b McConnon	32	c Sheppard b Wardle	1
Imtiaz Ahmed +	c McConnon b Wardle	13		
Waqar Hassan	c & b McConnon	11		
Maqsood Ahmed	c Wardle b McConnon	4		
A.H.Kardar *	b Wardle	9	(4) not out	0
M.E.Z.Ghazali	c Sheppard b Wardle	0	(5) c Wardle b Bedser	0
Wazir Mohammad	c McConnon b Bedser	5	(3) c Parks b Bedser	7
Fazal Mahmood	c Compton b Bedser	9		
Khalid Wazir	c McConnon b Wardle	2	(6) not out	9
Shujauddin	not out	0	(2) c Graveney b Bedser	1
Mahmood Hussain	b Bedser	0		
	Extras (b 4,nb 1)	5	(b 2,lb 4,nb 1)	7
	TOTAL	90	(for 4 wkts)	25

PAKISTAN

	O	M	R	W		O	M	R	W
Fazal Mahmood	42	14	107	4					
Mahmood Hussain	27	5	88	0					
Shujauddin	48	12	127	3					
Ghazali	8	1	18	0					
Maqsood Ahmed	4	0	14	0					

ENGLAND

	O	M	R	W		O	M	R	W
Statham	4	0	11	0					
Bedser	15.5	4	36	3		8	5	9	3
Wardle	24	16	19	4		7	2	9	1
McConnon	13	5	19	3					

FALL OF WICKETS

	ENG	PAK	PAK		ENG	PAK	PAK
1st	20	26	1	6th	242	69	
2nd	57	58	8	7th	293	80	
3rd	97	63	10	8th	348	87	
4th	190	66	10	9th	89		
5th	217	66		10th	90		

ENGLAND vs PAKISTAN
at The Oval on 12/08/1954
Pakistan won by 24 runs

PAKISTAN

Hanif Mohammad	lbw b Statham	0	c Graveney b Wardle	19
Alimuddin	b Tyson	10	(7) lbw b Wardle	0
Waqar Hassan	b Loader	7	run out	9
Maqsood Ahmed	b Tyson	0	c Wardle b McConnon	4
Imtiaz Ahmed +	c Evans b Tyson	23	c Wardle b Tyson	12
A.H.Kardar *	c Evans b Statham	36	c & b Wardle	17
Wazir Mohammad	run out	0	(8) not out	42
Fazal Mahmood	c Evans b Loader	0	(9) b Wardle	6
Shujauddin	not out	16	(2) c May b Wardle	12
Zulfiqar Ahmed	c Compton b Loader	16	c May b Wardle	34
Mahmood Hussain	b Tyson	23	c Statham b Wardle	6
	Extras (nb 2)	2	(b 3)	3
	TOTAL	133		164

ENGLAND

L.Hutton *	c Imtiaz Ahmed b Fazal Mahmood	14	c Imtiaz Ahmed b Fazal Mahmood	5
R.T.Simpson	c Kardar b Mahmood Hussain	2	c & b Zulfiqar Ahmed	27
P.B.H.May	c Kardar b Fazal Mahmood	26	c Kardar b Fazal Mahmood	53
D.C.S.Compton	c Imtiaz Ahmed b Fazal Mahmood	53	c Imtiaz Ahmed b Fazal Mahmood	29
T.W.Graveney	c Hanif Mohammad b Fazal Mahmood	1	(6) lbw b Shujauddin	0
T.G.Evans +	c Maqsood Ahmed b Mahmood Hussain	0	(5) b Fazal Mahmood	3
J.H.Wardle	c Imtiaz Ahmed b Fazal Mahmood	8	c Shujauddin b Fazal Mahmood	9
F.H.Tyson	c Imtiaz Ahmed b Fazal Mahmood	3	c Imtiaz Ahmed b Fazal Mahmood	3
J.E.McConnon	c Fazal Mahmood b Mahmood Hussain	11	(10) run out	2
J.B.Statham	c Shujauddin b Mahmood Hussain	1	(11) not out	2
P.J.Loader	not out	8	(9) c Waqar Hassan b Mahmood Hussain	5
	Extras (lb 1,w 1,nb 1)	3	(lb 2,nb 3)	5
	TOTAL	130		143

ENGLAND	O	M	R	W		O	M	R	W
Statham	11	5	26	2		18	7	37	0
Tyson	13.4	3	35	4		9	2	22	1
Loader	18	5	35	3		16	6	26	0
McConnon	9	2	35	0		14	5	20	1
Wardle						35	16	56	7

PAKISTAN	O	M	R	W		O	M	R	W
Fazal Mahmood	30	16	53	6		30	11	46	6
Mahmood Hussain	21.3	6	58	4		14	4	32	1
Zulfiqar Ahmed	5	2	8	0		14	2	35	1
Shujauddin	3	0	8	0		10	1	25	1

FALL OF WICKETS	PAK	ENG	PAK	ENG		PAK	ENG	PAK	ENG
1st	0	6	19	15	6th	51	92	73	121
2nd	10	26	38	66	7th	51	106	76	131
3rd	10	56	43	109	8th	77	115	82	138
4th	26	63	54	115	9th	106	116	140	138
5th	51	69	63	116	10th	133	130	164	143

PAKISTAN vs INDIA
at Dacca on 01/01/1955
Match drawn

PAKISTAN

Hanif Mohammad	c Tamhane b Ghulam Ahmed	41	c Umrigar b Phadkar	14
Alimuddin	c Phadkar b Ghulam Ahmed	7	c sub b Gupte	51
Waqar Hassan	c & b Ghulam Ahmed	52	st Tamhane b Gupte	51
Maqsood Ahmed	c Tamhane b Ghulam Ahmed	11	c Mantri b Gupte	16
Wazir Mohammad	c Phadkar b Gupte	23	(8) not out	0
Imtiaz Ahmed +	b Phadkar	54	(5) c Umrigar b Gupte	5
A.H.Kardar *	b Ramchand	29	(6) c Mantri b Phadkar	3
Shujauddin	st Tamhane b Mankad	25	(7) run out	1
Fazal Mahmood	c Tamhane b Ramchand	0	not out	15
Mahmood Hussain	b Ghulam Ahmed	9	c Punjabi b Gupte	0
Khan Mohammad	not out	4	run out	0
	Extras (lb 2)	2	(lb 2)	2
	TOTAL	257		158

INDIA

Pankaj Roy	b Mahmood Hussain	0	not out	67
P.H.Punjabi	b Khan Mohammad	26	lbw b Khan Mohammad	3
M.K.Mantri	b Mahmood Hussain	0	c Imtiaz Ahmed b Khan Mohammad	2
V.L.Manjrekar	b Mahmood Hussain	18	not out	74
P.R.Umrigar	c Kardar b Mahmood Hussain	32		
G.S.Ramchand	c Imtiaz Ahmed b Mahmood Hussain	37		
D.G.Phadkar	c Imtiaz Ahmed b Mahmood Hussain	11		
M.H.Mankad *	c Imtiaz Ahmed b Mahmood Hussain	2		
N.S.Tamhane +	b Khan Mohammad	5		
Ghulam Ahmed	b Mahmood Hussain	2		
S.P.Gupte	not out	0		
	Extras (b 7,lb 5,nb 2)	14	(b 1)	1
	TOTAL	148	(for 2 wkts)	147

INDIA	O	M	R	W		O	M	R	W
Phadkar	18	11	24	1		28.2	11	57	2
Ramchand	15	7	19	2		19	10	30	0
Gupte	46	14	79	1		6	0	18	5
Ghulam Ahmed	45	8	109	5					
Mankad	12.2	3	24	1		18	6	34	0
Umrigar						15	8	17	0

PAKISTAN	O	M	R	W		O	M	R	W
Fazal Mahmood	25	19	18	0		23	11	34	0
Mahmood Hussain	27	6	67	6		7	2	21	0
Khan Mohammad	26.5	12	42	4		12	5	18	2
Shujauddin	4	2	7	0		14	6	25	0
Maqsood Ahmed						3	1	4	0
Kardar						12	3	17	0
Hanif Mohammad						5	1	15	0
Alimuddin						5	0	12	0
Imtiaz Ahmed						1	1	0	0

FALL OF WICKETS	PAK	IND	PAK	IND		PAK	IND	PAK	IND
1st	21	17	24	15	6th	207	129	140	
2nd	74	19	116	17	7th	227	131	140	
3rd	88	45	122		8th	227	143	148	
4th	125	56	137		9th	240	145	156	
5th	157	115	139		10th	257	148	158	

PAKISTAN vs INDIA
at Bahawalpur on 15/01/1955
Match drawn

INDIA

Pankaj Roy	b Fazal Mahmood	0	c Kardar b Khan Mohammad	78
P.H.Punjabi	b Khan Mohammad	18	c M.Ahmed b Mahmood Hussain	33
M.H.Mankad *	c Imtiaz Ahmed b Fazal Mahmood	6	c Imtiaz Ahmed b Fazal Mahmood	1
V.L.Manjrekar	c Mahmood Hussain b Khan Mohammad	50	c Imtiaz Ahmed b Fazal Mahmood	59
P.R.Umrigar	b Khan Mohammad	20		
G.S.Ramchand	b Mahmood Hussain	53		
C.V.Gadkari	lbw b Khan Mohammad	2	(6) not out	4
C.D.Gopinath	c Waqar Hassan b Fazal Mahmood	0	(5) c M.Ahmed b Khan Mohammad	8
N.S.Tamhane +	not out	54	(7) not out	12
S.P.Gupte	b Khan Mohammad	15		
Ghulam Ahmed	b Fazal Mahmood	8		
	Extras (lb 4,nb 5)	9	(b 12,lb 1,nb 1)	14
	TOTAL	235	(for 5 wkts)	209

PAKISTAN

Hanif Mohammad	c Gadkari b Umrigar	142
Alimuddin	b Ghulam Ahmed	64
Waqar Hassan	c Gupte b Umrigar	48
Maqsood Ahmed	c Gadkari b Umrigar	10
Imtiaz Ahmed +	st Tamhane b Gupte	3
A.H.Kardar *	c Punjabi b Umrigar	13
Fazal Mahmood	b Umrigar	9
Mahmood Hussain	c Gadkari b Umrigar	0
Shujauddin	run out	7
Wazir Mohammad	not out	4
Khan Mohammad	not out	1
	Extras (b 6,lb 5)	11
	TOTAL (for 9 wkts dec)	312

PAKISTAN	O	M	R	W		O	M	R	W
Fazal Mahmood	52.5	23	86	4		28	6	58	2
Mahmood Hussain	25	6	56	1		17	3	47	1
Khan Mohammad	33	7	74	5		22	6	50	2
Shujauddin	9	4	10	0		8	6	2	0
Maqsood Ahmed						7	3	19	0
Kardar						7	0	19	0

INDIA	O	M	R	W		O	M	R	W
Ramchand	13	5	26	0					
Umrigar	58	25	74	6					
Gupte	17	8	49	1					
Ghulam Ahmed	36	4	63	1					
Mankad	40	19	89	0					

FALL OF WICKETS	IND	PAK	IND		IND	PAK	IND
1st	0	127	58	6th	100	286	
2nd	16	220	62	7th	107	286	
3rd	61	226	185	8th	189	301	
4th	93	229	189	9th	205	307	
5th	95	250	193	10th	235		

PAKISTAN vs INDIA
at Lahore on 29/01/1955
Match drawn

PAKISTAN

Hanif Mohammad	c Tamhane b Gupte	12	(6) not out	0
Alimuddin	run out	38	b Mankad	58
Waqar Hassan	c Mankad b Gupte	9	c Tamhane b Mankad	12
Maqsood Ahmed	st Tamhane b Gupte	99	c Punjabi b Mankad	15
A.H.Kardar *	c Ramchand b Mankad	44		
Wazir Mohammad	lbw b Mankad	55		
Imtiaz Ahmed +	run out	55	(5) c Tamhane b Gupte	9
Shujauddin	c Mankad b Ghulam Ahmed	3	(1) c sub b Gupte	40
Fazal Mahmood	st Tamhane b Gupte	12		
Mahmood Hussain	b Gupte	0		
Miran Bux	not out	1		
	Extras	0	(b 2)	2
	TOTAL	328	(for 5 wkts dec)	136

INDIA

Pankaj Roy	b Mahmood Hussain	23	c Imtiaz Ahmed b Kardar	23
P.H.Punjabi	b Miran Bux	27	c Maqsood Ahmed b Kardar	1
C.V.Gadkari	b Fazal Mahmood	13	not out	27
V.L.Manjrekar	b Miran Bux	0	not out	22
P.R.Umrigar	c Hanif Mohammad b Mahmood Hussain	78		
G.S.Ramchand	c Maqsood Ahmed b Fazal Mahmood	12		
C.D.Gopinath	c Fazal Mahmood b Shujauddin	41		
M.H.Mankad *	c Imtiaz Ahmed b Mahmood Hussain	33		
N.S.Tamhane +	c Imtiaz Ahmed b Mahmood Hussain	0		
Ghulam Ahmed	c Imtiaz Ahmed b Fazal Mahmood	0		
S.P.Gupte	not out	0		
	Extras (b 12,lb 10,nb 2)	24	(nb 1)	1
	TOTAL	251	(for 2 wkts)	74

INDIA	O	M	R	W		O	M	R	W
Umrigar	14	4	23	0					
Ramchand	10	5	12	0		6	1	20	0
Ghulam Ahmed	46	11	95	1		14	2	47	0
Gupte	73.5	32	133	5		36.3	22	34	2
Mankad	44	25	65	2		28	17	33	3

PAKISTAN	O	M	R	W		O	M	R	W
Mahmood Hussain	26.1	6	70	4		1	0	1	0
Fazal Mahmood	47	24	62	3		1	0	2	0
Miran Bux	48	20	82	2					
Shujauddin	7	1	13	1		6	1	20	0
Maqsood Ahmed						4	2	4	0
Kardar						12	3	20	2
Alimuddin						3	0	12	0
Hanif Mohammad						3	0	9	0
Wazir Mohammad						2	0	5	0

FALL OF WICKETS	PAK	IND	PAK	IND		PAK	IND	PAK	IND
1st	32	52	83	3	6th	286	179		
2nd	55	56	109	40	7th	302	243		
3rd	62	58	112		8th	327	243		
4th	198	91	135		9th	327	251		
5th	202	117	136		10th	328	251		

PAKISTAN vs INDIA
at Peshawar on 13/02/1955
Match drawn

PAKISTAN

Hanif Mohammad	c Phadkar b Gupte	13	c & b Mankad	21
Alimuddin	b Ramchand	0	lbw b Ghulam Ahmed	4
Waqar Hassan	c & b Gupte	43	lbw b Gupte	16
Maqsood Ahmed	c Punjabi b Phadkar	31	(5) c & b Mankad	44
Imtiaz Ahmed +	b Phadkar	0	(6) c Punjabi b Mankad	69
Wazir Mohammad	hit wicket b Mankad	34	(4) b Mankad	0
A.H.Kardar *	b Gupte	11	b Phadkar	0
Shujauddin	c Tamhane b Gupte	37	run out	11
Khan Mohammad	c Mankad b Ghulam Ahmed	4	c sub b Mankad	3
Mahmood Hussain	not out	5	st Tamhane b Phadkar	2
Miran Bux	lbw b Gupte	0	not out	0
	Extras (b 5,lb 4,nb 1)	10	(b 8,lb 4)	12
	TOTAL	**188**		**182**

INDIA

Pankaj Roy	run out	16	not out	13
P.H.Punjabi	b Khan Mohammad	16	b Hanif Mohammad	6
P.R.Umrigar	run out	108	not out	3
V.L.Manjrekar	run out	32		
C.V.Gadkari	c Maqsood Ahmed b Mahmood Hussain	15		
G.S.Ramchand	c Shujauddin b Khan Mohammad	18		
M.H.Mankad *	not out	3		
N.S.Tamhane +	run out	0		
D.G.Phadkar	b Khan Mohammad	13		
S.P.Gupte	c Waqar Hassan b Mahmood Hussain	2		
Ghulam Ahmed	b Khan Mohammad	8		
	Extras (b 5,lb 4,w 1,nb 4)	14	(nb 1)	1
	TOTAL	**245**	**(for 1 wkt)**	**23**

INDIA

	O	M	R	W		O	M	R	W
Phadkar	24	14	19	2		18	2	42	2
Ramchand	7	2	13	1		2	1	3	0
Gupte	41.3	22	63	5		35	16	52	1
Mankad	61	34	71	1		54	26	64	5
Ghulam Ahmed	13	7	12	1		13	9	9	1

PAKISTAN

	O	M	R	W		O	M	R	W
Khan Mohammad	36	14	79	4		4	0	10	0
Mahmood Hussain	38	11	78	2		2	1	2	0
Miran Bux	8	2	30	0		2	0	3	0
Kardar	19	6	34	0		1	1	0	0
Maqsood Ahmed	7	3	10	0		6	2	6	0
Hanif Mohammad						4	3	1	1

FALL OF WICKETS

	PAK	IND	PAK	IND		PAK	IND	PAK	IND
1st	2	30	10	19	6th	111	218	156	
2nd	31	44	50		7th	171	219	176	
3rd	81	135	68		8th	176	232	177	
4th	81	182	85		9th	188	235	182	
5th	96	210	153		10th	188	245	182	

PAKISTAN vs INDIA
at Karachi on 26/02/1955
Match drawn

PAKISTAN

Hanif Mohammad	c Tamhane b Phadkar	2	(3) c Tamhane b Umrigar	28
Alimuddin	c Tamhane b Ramchand	7	not out	103
Waqar Hassan	c Umrigar b Ramchand	12	(7) not out	1
Maqsood Ahmed	c Tamhane b Ramchand	22	c Bhandari b Umrigar	2
Imtiaz Ahmed +	c Ramchand b Patel	37	run out	1
Wazir Mohammad	c Phadkar b Patel	23		
A.H.Kardar *	c Tamhane b Ramchand	14	(6) st Tamhane b Gupte	93
Shujauddin	c Mankad b Ramchand	0	(1) b Ramchand	8
Fazal Mahmood	lbw b Patel	3		
Khan Mohammad	not out	15		
Mahmood Hussain	c Phadkar b Ramchand	14		
	Extras (b 10,nb 3)	13	(b 1,lb 3,nb 1)	5
	TOTAL	**162**	**(for 5 wkts dec)**	**241**

INDIA

Pankaj Roy	c Kardar b Khan Mohammad	37	lbw b Maqsood Ahmed	16
P.H.Punjabi	lbw b Khan Mohammad	12	c Imtiaz Ahmed b Fazal Mahmood	22
P.R.Umrigar	b Fazal Mahmood	16	not out	14
V.L.Manjrekar	c Kardar b Khan Mohammad	14		
M.H.Mankad *	c Maqsood Ahmed b Fazal Mahmood	6		
G.S.Ramchand	c Hanif Mohammad b Fazal Mahmood	15	(4) not out	12
N.S.Tamhane +	b Fazal Mahmood	9		
P.Bhandari	b Khan Mohammad	19		
D.G.Phadkar	not out	6		
J.M.Patel	lbw b Khan Mohammad	0		
S.P.Gupte	c Shujauddin b Fazal Mahmood	1		
	Extras (lb 7,nb 3)	10	(b 1,lb 1,nb 3)	5
	TOTAL	**145**	**(for 2 wkts)**	**69**

INDIA

	O	M	R	W		O	M	R	W
Phadkar	10	6	7	1		34	6	95	0
Ramchand	28	10	49	6		11	4	27	1
Patel	33	12	49	3		7	1	23	0
Gupte	15	4	24	0		6	0	24	1
Mankad	5	0	16	0		1	0	3	0
Umrigar	5	3	4	0		27	6	64	2

PAKISTAN

	O	M	R	W		O	M	R	W
Khan Mohammad	28	5	73	5		7	5	4	0
Mahmood Hussain	7	0	14	0		3	0	16	0
Fazal Mahmood	28.3	7	48	5		11	4	21	1
Hanif Mohammad						6	1	18	0
Maqsood Ahmed						5	2	5	1

FALL OF WICKETS

	PAK	IND	PAK	IND		PAK	IND	PAK	IND
1st	2	22	25	34	6th	119	110		
2nd	19	45	69	49	7th	119	131		
3rd	37	68	77		8th	122	144		
4th	66	89	81		9th	135	144		
5th	88	95	236		10th	162	145		

PAKISTAN vs NEW ZEALAND
at Karachi on 13/10/1955
Pakistan won by an innings and 1 run

NEW ZEALAND

J.G.Leggat	c Imtiaz Ahmed b Fazal Mahmood	16	lbw b Zulfiqar Ahmed	39
B.Sutcliffe	c Kardar b Zulfiqar Ahmed	15	b Shujauddin	17
M.B.Poore	st Imtiaz Ahmed b Zulfiqar Ahmed	43	b Shujauddin	0
J.R.Reid	c Khan Mohammad b Kardar	10	(5) c Waqar Hassan b Zulfiqar Ahmed	11
P.G.Z.Harris	c Wazir Mohammad b Kardar	7	(6) run out	21
S.N.McGregor	c Alimuddin b Shujauddin	10	(4) lbw b Shujauddin	0
H.B.Cave *	b Kardar	0	c sub b Zulfiqar Ahmed	21
J.C.Alabaster	c sub b Zulfiqar Ahmed	14	b Zulfiqar Ahmed	8
A.R.MacGibbon	b Zulfiqar Ahmed	33	c Hanif Mohammad b Zulfiqar Ahmed	0
A.M.Moir	c Khan Mohammad b Zulfiqar Ahmed	10	c Alimuddin b Zulfiqar Ahmed	2
T.G.McMahon +	not out	0	not out	0
	Extras (b 4,lb 2)	6	(b 1,lb 4)	5
	TOTAL	**164**		**124**

PAKISTAN

Hanif Mohammad	c McGregor b Cave	5
Alimuddin	c MacGibbon b Moir	28
Waqar Hassan	c McMahon b Cave	17
Maqsood Ahmed	b MacGibbon	2
Imtiaz Ahmed +	c McMahon b MacGibbon	64
A.H.Kardar *	run out	22
Wazir Mohammad	c & b Cave	43
Shujauddin	b MacGibbon	47
Zulfiqar Ahmed	b MacGibbon	10
Fazal Mahmood	not out	34
Khan Mohammad	run out	5
	Extras (b 4,lb 1,nb 7)	12
	TOTAL	**289**

PAKISTAN

	O	M	R	W		O	M	R	W
Fazal Mahmood	31	12	46	1		13	3	33	0
Khan Mohammad	23	9	27	0					
Zulfiqar Ahmed	37.2	19	37	5		46.3	21	42	6
Kardar	31	10	35	3		27	15	22	0
Shujauddin	11	7	13	1		22	12	22	3

NEW ZEALAND

	O	M	R	W		O	M	R	W
MacGibbon	37.1	8	98	4					
Cave	24	6	56	3					
Reid	30	17	34	0					
Moir	37	9	87	1					
Poore	2	0	2	0					

FALL OF WICKETS

	NZ	PAK	NZ			NZ	PAK	NZ
1st	18	5	27	6th	95	144	109
2nd	50	25	27	7th	114	222	118
3rd	71	32	27	8th	129	240	120
4th	95	74	42	9th	163	251	122
5th	95	140	79	10th	164	289	124

PAKISTAN vs NEW ZEALAND
at Lahore on 26/10/1955
Pakistan won by 4 wickets

NEW ZEALAND

B.Sutcliffe	c Waqar Hassan b Khan Mohammad	4	lbw b Shujauddin	25
M.B.Poore	c Alimuddin b Khan Mohammad	6	c Imtiaz Ahmed b Zulfiqar Ahmed	9
P.G.Z.Harris	run out	28	b Shujauddin	11
S.N.McGregor	lbw b Kardar	14	b Kardar	86
J.R.Reid	c Maqsood Ahmed b Khan Mohammad	5	b Kardar	43
N.S.Harford	c Maqsood Ahmed b Khan Mohammad	93	(7) c Khan Mohammad b Zulfiqar Ahmed	64
A.R.MacGibbon	lbw b Zulfiqar Ahmed	61	(6) c Wazir Mohammad b Kardar	40
E.C.Petrie +	b Kardar	0	c Hanif Mohammad b Kardar	7
H.B.Cave *	c & b Zulfiqar Ahmed	14	c Alimuddin b Zulfiqar Ahmed	17
A.M.Moir	b Mahmood Hussain	8	not out	11
J.A.Hayes	not out	0	lbw b Zulfiqar Ahmed	0
	Extras (b 4,lb 10,nb 4)	18	(b 6,lb 5,nb 4)	15
	TOTAL	**348**		**328**

PAKISTAN

Hanif Mohammad	hit wicket b Hayes	10	lbw b Reid	33
Alimuddin	c Sutcliffe b MacGibbon	4	c MacGibbon b Reid	37
Shujauddin	b Moir	29	(7) not out	14
Waqar Hassan	c Petrie b MacGibbon	189	(5) c MacGibbon b Hayes	17
Wazir Mohammad	lbw b Moir	0	(8) not out	2
A.H.Kardar *	b Moir	2	c Reid b Hayes	11
Khan Mohammad	run out	10		
Imtiaz Ahmed +	b Moir	209	(3) c Cave b Reid	0
Maqsood Ahmed	c Cave b Reid	33	(4) c McGregor b Reid	8
Zulfiqar Ahmed	not out	21		
Mahmood Hussain	c MacGibbon b Sutcliffe	32		
	Extras (b 3,lb 7,nb 12)	22	(b 2,lb 4,nb 2)	8
	TOTAL	**561**	**(for 6 wkts)**	**117**

PAKISTAN

	O	M	R	W		O	M	R	W
Khan Mohammad	34	10	78	4		18	6	26	1
Mahmood Hussain	31.5	4	67	1		21	6	47	0
Shujauddin	43	11	84	0		38	12	79	2
Zulfiqar Ahmed	35	13	71	2		43.2	10	114	4
Maqsood Ahmed	3	1	4	0					
Kardar	14	5	26	2		38	15	47	3

NEW ZEALAND

	O	M	R	W		O	M	R	W
Hayes	37	12	107	1		8.5	2	25	2
MacGibbon	40	7	135	2		5	0	20	0
Reid	35	13	82	1		8	2	38	4
Cave	30	6	84	0		5	0	26	0
Moir	39	13	114	4					
Poore	3	0	13	0					
Sutcliffe	1.3	0	4	1					

FALL OF WICKETS

	NZ	PAK	NZ	PAK		NZ	PAK	NZ	PAK
1st	8	11	34	45	6th	267	111	237	115
2nd	13	23	43	49	7th	267	419	252	
3rd	48	84	60	80	8th	333	482	293	
4th	76	84	148	93	9th	348	517	324	
5th	226	87	224	107	10th	348	561	328	

PAKISTAN vs NEW ZEALAND
at Dacca on 07/11/1955
Match drawn

NEW ZEALAND

J.G.Leggat	b Khan Mohammad	1	c Agha Saadat Ali b Fazal Mahmood	1
B.Sutcliffe	b Fazal Mahmood	3	c Imtiaz Ahmed b Khan Mohammad	17
M.B.Poore	b Fazal Mahmood	0	c Agha Saadat Ali b Kardar	18
S.N.McGregor	b Khan Mohammad	7	c Imtiaz Ahmed b Zulfiqar Ahmed	4
J.R.Reid	c Imtiaz Ahmed b Khan Mohammad	9	b Kardar	12
N.S.Harford	c Imtiaz Ahmed b Fazal Mahmood	0	c Hanif Mohammad b Khan Mohammad	1
J.W.Guy	st Imtiaz Ahmed b Zulfiqar Ahmed	11	not out	8
A.R.MacGibbon	not out	29	not out	7
E.C.Petrie +	lbw b Khan Mohammad	6		
H.B.Cave *	c Agha Saadat Ali b Khan Mohammad	0		
A.M.Moir	c Shujauddin b Khan Mohammad	0		
Extras	(lb 4)	4	(lb 1)	1
TOTAL		70	(for 6 wkts)	69

PAKISTAN

Alimuddin	b Reid	5
Hanif Mohammad	c Reid b Cave	103
Waqar Hassan	lbw b Reid	8
Shujauddin	c Guy b Cave	3
Imtiaz Ahmed +	b Cave	11
A.H.Kardar *	b MacGibbon	14
W.Mathias	not out	41
Agha Saadat Ali	not out	8
Fazal Mahmood		
Zulfiqar Ahmed		
Khan Mohammad		
Extras	(lb 1,nb 1)	2
TOTAL	(for 6 wkts dec)	195

PAKISTAN

	O	M	R	W		O	M	R	W
Fazal Mahmood	20	7	34	3		6	3	12	1
Khan Mohammad	16.2	6	21	6		30	19	20	2
Zulfiqar Ahmed	3	1	11	1		16	8	13	1
Kardar						28	17	21	2
Shujauddin						9	8	1	0
Hanif Mohammad						1	0	1	0

NEW ZEALAND

	O	M	R	W		O	M	R	W
MacGibbon	20	4	64	1					
Cave	20	4	45	3					
Reid	30	10	67	2					
Moir	6	1	17	0					

FALL OF WICKETS

	NZ	PAK	NZ		NZ	PAK	NZ
1st	1	22	12	6th	26	182	56
2nd	4	30	32	7th	54		
3rd	9	37	32	8th	64		
4th	15	55	51	9th	68		
5th	20	86	52	10th	70		

PAKISTAN vs AUSTRALIA
at Karachi on 11/10/1956
Pakistan won by 9 wickets

AUSTRALIA

C.C.McDonald	c Imtiaz Ahmed b Fazal Mahmood	17	b Fazal Mahmood	3
J.W.Burke	c Mathias b Fazal Mahmood	4	c Mathias b Fazal Mahmood	10
R.N.Harvey	lbw b Fazal Mahmood	2	b Fazal Mahmood	4
I.D.Craig	c Imtiaz Ahmed b Fazal Mahmood	0	lbw b Fazal Mahmood	18
K.R.Miller	c Wazir Mohammad b Fazal Mahmood	21	b Khan Mohammad	11
R.G.Archer	c Imtiaz Ahmed b Fazal Mahmood	10	c Fazal Mahmood b Khan Mohammad	27
R.Benaud	c Waqar Hassan b Fazal Mahmood	4	b Fazal Mahmood	56
A.K.Davidson	c Kardar b Khan Mohammad	3	c Imtiaz Ahmed b Khan Mohammad	37
R.R.Lindwall	c Mathias b Khan Mohammad	2	lbw b Fazal Mahmood	0
I.W.Johnson	not out	13	b Fazal Mahmood	0
G.R.A.Langley +	c Waqar Hassan b Khan Mohammad	1	not out	13
Extras	(lb 2,nb 1)	3	(lb 2,nb 6)	8
TOTAL		80		187

PAKISTAN

Hanif Mohammad	c Langley b Miller	0	c Harvey b Davidson	5
Alimuddin	c Lindwall b Archer	10	not out	34
Gul Mahomed	b Davidson	12	not out	27
Imtiaz Ahmed +	c McDonald b Benaud	15		
Waqar Hassan	c Langley b Miller	6		
Wazir Mohammad	c & b Johnson	67		
A.H.Kardar *	lbw b Johnson	69		
W.Mathias	b Johnson	0		
Fazal Mahmood	not out	10		
Zulfiqar Ahmed	c Langley b Lindwall	0		
Khan Mohammad	b Johnson	3		
Extras	(b 5,lb 2)	7	(lb 1,nb 2)	3
TOTAL		199	(for 1 wkt)	69

PAKISTAN

	O	M	R	W		O	M	R	W
Fazal Mahmood	27	11	34	6		48	17	80	7
Khan Mohammad	26.1	9	43	4		40.5	13	69	3
Zulfiqar Ahmed						9	1	18	0
Kardar						12	5	12	0

AUSTRALIA

	O	M	R	W		O	M	R	W
Lindwall	27	8	42	1		16	8	22	0
Miller	17	5	40	2		12	4	18	0
Archer	4	0	18	1		3.5	3	1	0
Davidson	6	4	6	1		9	5	9	1
Benaud	17	5	36	1					
Johnson	20.3	3	50	5		7.5	2	16	0

FALL OF WICKETS

	AUS	PAK	AUS	PAK		AUS	PAK	AUS	PAK
1st	19	3	6	7	6th	52	174	111	
2nd	23	15	10		7th	56	174	141	
3rd	24	25	23		8th	65	189	141	
4th	43	35	46		9th	76	190	143	
5th	48	70	47		10th	80	199	187	

WEST INDIES vs PAKISTAN
at Bridgetown on 17/01/1958
Match drawn

WEST INDIES

C.C.Hunte	c Imtiaz Ahmed b Fazal Mahmood	142	not out	11
R.B.Kanhai	c Mathias b Mahmood Hussain	27	not out	17
G.St A.Sobers	c Mathias b Mahmood Hussain	52		
E.de C.Weekes	c Imtiaz Ahmed b Mahmood Hussain	197		
C.L.Walcott	c Mathias b Kardar	43		
O.G.Smith	c Mathias b Alimuddin	78		
D.St E.Atkinson	b Mahmood Hussain	4		
E.St E.Atkinson	b Fazal Mahmood	0		
F.C.M.Alexander *+	b Mahmood Hussain	9		
A.L.Valentine	not out	5		
R.Gilchrist				
Extras	(b 9,lb 4,w 3,nb 6)	22		0
TOTAL	(for 9 wkts dec)	579	(for 0 wkts)	28

PAKISTAN

Hanif Mohammad	b Atkinson E.St E.	17	c Alexander b Atkinson D.St E.	337
Imtiaz Ahmed +	lbw b Gilchrist	20	lbw b Gilchrist	91
Alimuddin	c Weekes b Gilchrist	3	c Alexander b Sobers	37
Saeed Ahmed	st Alexander b Smith	13	c Alexander b Smith	65
Wazir Mohammad	lbw b Valentine	4	c Alexander b Atkinson E.St E.	35
W.Mathias	c Alexander b Smith	17	lbw b Atkinson E.St E.	17
A.H.Kardar *	c Atkinson D.St E. b Smith	4	not out	23
Fazal Mahmood	b Gilchrist	4	b Valentine	19
Nasim-ul-Ghani	run out	11	b Valentine	0
Mahmood Hussain	b Gilchrist	3	not out	0
Haseeb Ahsan	not out	1		
Extras	(b 4,lb 5)	9	(b 19,lb 7,nb 7)	33
TOTAL		106	(for 8 wkts dec)	657

PAKISTAN

	O	M	R	W		O	M	R	W
Fazal Mahmood	62	21	145	3		2	1	3	0
Mahmood Hussain	41.2	4	153	4					
Kardar	32	4	107	1		3	1	13	0
Haseeb Ahsan	21	0	84	0					
Nasim-ul-Ghani	14	1	51	0					
Alimuddin	2	0	17	1					
Hanif Mohammad						3	1	10	0
Saeed Ahmed						2	2	0	0
Wazir Mohammad						1	0	2	0

WEST INDIES

	O	M	R	W		O	M	R	W
Gilchrist	15	4	32	4		41	5	121	1
Atkinson E.St E.	8	0	27	1		49	5	136	2
Smith	13	4	23	3		61	30	93	1
Valentine	6.2	1	15	1		39	8	109	2
Atkinson D.St E.						62	35	61	1
Sobers						57	25	94	1
Walcott						10	5	10	0

FALL OF WICKETS

	WI	PAK	PAK	WI		WI	PAK	PAK	WI
1st	122	35	152		6th	551	84	626	
2nd	209	39	264		7th	556	91	649	
3rd	266	44	418		8th	570	93	649	
4th	356	53	539		9th	579	96		
5th	541	81	598		10th		106		

WEST INDIES vs PAKISTAN
at Port of Spain on 05/02/1958
West Indies won by 120 runs

WEST INDIES

C.C.Hunte	c Imtiaz Ahmed b Fazal Mahmood	8	c Kardar b Nasim-ul-Ghani	37
E.D.A.St J.McMorris	b Kardar	13	lbw b Fazal Mahmood	16
G.St A.Sobers	b Nasim-ul-Ghani	52	(6) lbw b Fazal Mahmood	80
E.de C.Weekes	run out	78	(5) b Nasim-ul-Ghani	24
R.B.Kanhai	c Mathias b Mahmood Hussain	96	(3) c Mathias b Mahmood Hussain	5
O.G.Smith	c Kardar b Mahmood Hussain	41	(7) c Waqar Hassan b Fazal Mahmood	51
F.C.M.Alexander *+	c Imtiaz Ahmed b Nasim-ul-Ghani	26	(4) run out	57
I.S.Madray	lbw b Fazal Mahmood	1	lbw b Mahmood Hussain	0
L.R.Gibbs	c Kardar b Nasim-ul-Ghani	2	b Nasim-ul-Ghani	22
R.Gilchrist	run out	0	b Fazal Mahmood	7
D.T.Dewdney	not out	0	not out	5
Extras	(b 5,lb 2,nb 1)	8	(b 4,lb 2,nb 2)	8
TOTAL		325		312

PAKISTAN

Hanif Mohammad	c Gibbs b Smith	30	c Sobers b Gilchrist	81
Alimuddin	b Gilchrist	9	b Gilchrist	0
Imtiaz Ahmed +	lbw b Smith	39	(4) b Sobers	18
Saeed Ahmed	lbw b Smith	11	(3) c Alexander b Sobers	64
W.Mathias	b Dewdney	73	(6) c Weekes b Dewdney	10
Nasim-ul-Ghani	c Alexander b Gilchrist	0	(11) b Gibbs	0
Wazir Mohammad	c Weekes b Gilchrist	0	(5) b Gilchrist	0
Waqar Hassan	c Weekes b Gibbs	17	(7) st Alexander b Gibbs	28
A.H.Kardar *	st Alexander b Smith	4	b Gibbs	24
Fazal Mahmood	c Madray b Sobers	60	(8) b Gilchrist	0
Mahmood Hussain	not out	19	(10) not out	1
Extras	(b 13,lb 5,nb 2)	20	(b 1,lb 5,nb 3)	9
TOTAL		282		235

PAKISTAN

	O	M	R	W		O	M	R	W
Mahmood Hussain	36	6	128	2		37	4	132	2
Fazal Mahmood	50	24	76	2		51	21	89	4
Kardar	32	13	71	1		9	2	19	0
Nasim-ul-Ghani	13.1	3	42	3		33.2	11	64	3

WEST INDIES

	O	M	R	W		O	M	R	W
Gilchrist	21	4	67	3		19	5	61	4
Dewdney	17	3	50	1		18	8	29	1
Smith	25	7	71	4		19	7	31	0
Sobers	5.3	1	14	1		22	8	41	2
Madray	6	0	22	0		13	5	32	0
Gibbs	12	2	38	1		13.5	6	32	3

FALL OF WICKETS

	WI	PAK	WI	PAK		WI	PAK	WI	PAK
1st	11	21	38	1	6th	302	116	255	180
2nd	51	66	51	131	7th	307	150	277	180
3rd	129	90	71	159	8th	325	155	277	222
4th	177	91	105	161	9th	325	226	288	235
5th	276	104	206	180	10th	325	282	312	235

WEST INDIES vs PAKISTAN

at Kingston on 26/02/1958
West Indies won by an innings and 174 runs

PAKISTAN

Hanif Mohammad	c Alexander b Gilchrist	3	b Gilchrist	13
Imtiaz Ahmed +	c Alexander b Gilchrist	122	lbw b Dewdney	0
Saeed Ahmed	c Weekes b Smith	52	c Gilchrist b Gibbs	44
W.Mathias	b Dewdney	77	c Alexander b Atkinson	19
Alimuddin	c Alexander b Atkinson	15	b Gibbs	30
A.H.Kardar *	c Sobers b Atkinson	15	(7) lbw b Dewdney	57
Wazir Mohammad	c Walcott b Dewdney	2	(6) lbw b Atkinson	106
Fazal Mahmood	c Alexander b Atkinson	6	c Alexander b Atkinson	0
Nasim-ul-Ghani	b Atkinson	5	absent hurt/ill	
Mahmood Hussain	b Atkinson	20	absent hurt/ill	
Khan Mohammad	not out	3	(9) not out	0
	Extras (lb 5,nb 3)	8	(b 16,lb 3)	19
	TOTAL	**328**		**288**

WEST INDIES

C.C.Hunte	run out	260
R.B.Kanhai	c Imtiaz Ahmed b Fazal Mahmood	25
G.St A.Sobers	not out	365
E.de C.Weekes	c Hanif Mohammad b Fazal Mahmood	39
C.L.Walcott	not out	88
O.G.Smith		
F.C.M.Alexander *+		
L.R.Gibbs		
E.St E.Atkinson		
R.Gilchrist		
D.T.Dewdney		
	Extras (b 2,lb 7,w 4)	13
	TOTAL (for 3 wkts dec)	**790**

WEST INDIES	O	M	R	W		O	M	R	W
Gilchrist	25	3	106	2		12	3	65	1
Dewdney	26	4	88	2		19.3	2	51	2
Atkinson	21	7	42	5		18	6	36	3
Gibbs	7	0	32	0		21	6	46	2
Smith	18	3	39	1		8	2	20	0
Sobers	5	1	13	0		15	4	41	0
Weekes						3	1	10	0

PAKISTAN	O	M	R	W		O	M	R	W
Mahmood Hussain	0.5	0	2	0					
Fazal Mahmood	85.2	20	247	2					
Khan Mohammad	54	5	259	0					
Nasim-ul-Ghani	15	3	39	0					
Kardar	37	2	141	0					
Mathias	4	0	20	0					
Alimuddin	4	0	34	0					
Hanif Mohammad	2	0	11	0					
Saeed Ahmed	6	0	24	0					

FALL OF WICKETS	PAK	WI	PAK			PAK	WI	PAK
1st	4	87	8		6th	291		286
2nd	122	533	20		7th	299		286
3rd	223	602	57		8th	301		288
4th	249		105		9th	317		
5th	287		120		10th	328		

WEST INDIES vs PAKISTAN

at Georgetown on 13/03/1958
West Indies won by 8 wickets

PAKISTAN

Alimuddin	b Smith	30	lbw b Smith	41
Imtiaz Ahmed +	c Walcott b Smith	32	b Gibbs	7
Saeed Ahmed	b Gibbs	150	run out	12
Hanif Mohammad	b Gilchrist	79	c Madray b Gilchrist	14
Wazir Mohammad	lbw b Gilchrist	7	not out	97
W.Mathias	b Gilchrist	16	lbw b Gibbs	18
A.H.Kardar *	b Smith	26	c Smith b Gibbs	56
Fazal Mahmood	c Gibbs b Gilchrist	39	c Alexander b Gibbs	31
S.F.Rehman	b Gibbs	8	run out	2
Nasim-ul-Ghani	b Dewdney	13	c & b Gibbs	22
Haseeb Ahsan	not out	0	b Gilchrist	0
	Extras (b 2,lb 2,w 2,nb 2)	8	(b 8,lb 4,w 1,nb 5)	18
	TOTAL	**408**		**318**

WEST INDIES

C.C.Hunte	b Fazal Mahmood	5	b Rehman	114
G.St A.Sobers	b Nasim-ul-Ghani	125	(3) not out	109
C.L.Walcott	run out	145		
E.de C.Weekes	c Rehman b Nasim-ul-Ghani	41	not out	16
O.G.Smith	c sub b Haseeb Ahsan	27		
R.B.Kanhai	st Imtiaz Ahmed b Nasim-ul-Ghani	24	(2) c Mathias b Haseeb Ahsan	62
F.C.M.Alexander *+	c Mathias b Haseeb Ahsan	2		
I.S.Madray	c Fazal Mahmood b Nasim-ul-Ghani	2		
L.R.Gibbs	run out	11		
R.Gilchrist	c Alimuddin b Nasim-ul-Ghani	12		
D.T.Dewdney	not out	0		
	Extras (b 4,lb 9,w 1,nb 2)	16	(b 12,lb 1,w 2,nb 1)	16
	TOTAL	**410**	**(for 2 wkts)**	**317**

WEST INDIES	O	M	R	W		O	M	R	W
Gilchrist	28	3	102	4		19.1	3	66	2
Dewdney	16.1	1	79	1		11	3	30	0
Gibbs	30	12	56	2		42	12	80	5
Sobers	16	2	47	0		17	6	32	0
Smith	25	2	74	3		44	12	80	1
Madray	10	0	42	0		6	1	12	0

PAKISTAN	O	M	R	W		O	M	R	W
Fazal Mahmood	25	5	74	1		4	2	12	0
Kardar	6	1	24	0		2	0	10	0
Nasim-ul-Ghani	41.4	11	116	5		28	4	76	0
Haseeb Ahsan	44	10	124	2		41	7	151	1
Rehman	17	1	56	0		17	2	43	1
Wazir Mohammad						1	0	8	0
Saeed Ahmed						0.1	0	1	0

FALL OF WICKETS	PAK	WI	PAK	WI		PAK	WI	PAK	WI
1st	60	11	22	125	6th	337	370	224	
2nd	69	280	44	260	7th	349	384	263	
3rd	205	297	62		8th	365	389	265	
4th	221	336	102		9th	408	410	304	
5th	249	361	130		10th	408	410	318	

WEST INDIES vs PAKISTAN

at Port of Spain on 26/03/1958
Pakistan won by an innings and 1 run

WEST INDIES

C.C.Hunte	c Hanif Mohammad b Fazal Mahmood	0	c Fazal Mahmood b Nasim-ul-Ghani	45
R.B.Kanhai	c Imtiaz Ahmed b Khan Mohammad	0	b Haseeb Ahsan	43
G.St A.Sobers	c Kardar b Fazal Mahmood	14	b Nasim-ul-Ghani	27
E.de C.Weekes	c Imtiaz Ahmed b Khan Mohammad	51	b Haseeb Ahsan	9
C.L.Walcott	st Imtiaz Ahmed b Fazal Mahmood	47	c Wazir Mohammad b Nasim-ul-Ghani	62
O.G.Smith	lbw b Fazal Mahmood	86	st Imtiaz Ahmed b Nasim-ul-Ghani	0
F.C.M.Alexander *+	b Fazal Mahmood	38	b Nasim-ul-Ghani	1
E.St E.Atkinson	c Hanif Mohammad b Fazal Mahmood	0	b Fazal Mahmood	19
L.R.Gibbs	lbw b Fazal Mahmood	14	c Mathias b Fazal Mahmood	2
J.Taylor	not out	4	st Imtiaz Ahmed b Nasim-ul-Ghani	0
R.Gilchrist	c Kardar b Nasim-ul-Ghani	9	not out	2
	Extras (b 5)	5	(b 12,lb 4,nb 1)	17
	TOTAL	**268**		**227**

PAKISTAN

Imtiaz Ahmed +	b Taylor	15
Alimuddin	b Gibbs	21
Saeed Ahmed	c Alexander b Taylor	97
Wazir Mohammad	b Gibbs	189
Hanif Mohammad	b Taylor	54
W.Mathias	b Atkinson	4
A.H.Kardar *	c Walcott b Gibbs	44
Fazal Mahmood	b Taylor	0
Nasim-ul-Ghani	c Alexander b Gibbs	15
Khan Mohammad	not out	26
Haseeb Ahsan	b Taylor	2
	Extras (b 14,lb 10,w 1,nb 4)	29
	TOTAL	**496**

PAKISTAN	O	M	R	W		O	M	R	W
Fazal Mahmood	32	10	83	6		9	1	35	2
Khan Mohammad	25	8	79	2		2	0	19	0
Nasim-ul-Ghani	22.1	6	53	2		30.5	9	67	6
Haseeb Ahsan	14	2	48	0		24	3	89	2

WEST INDIES	O	M	R	W		O	M	R	W
Gilchrist	7	2	16	0					
Taylor	36.5	6	109	5					
Atkinson	31	3	66	1					
Smith	23	4	63	0					
Gibbs	41	9	108	4					
Sobers	34	6	95	0					
Walcott	2	0	6	0					
Weekes	3	1	4	0					

FALL OF WICKETS	WI	PAK	WI			WI	PAK	WI
1st	0	22	71		6th	219	407	162
2nd	2	69	115		7th	219	408	219
3rd	48	238	130		8th	249	463	223
4th	78	392	140		9th	254	478	225
5th	141	407	141		10th	268	496	227

PAKISTAN vs WEST INDIES

at Karachi on 20/02/1959
Pakistan won by 10 wickets

WEST INDIES

C.C.Hunte	c Imtiaz Ahmed b Fazal Mahmood	0	lbw b Fazal Mahmood	21
J.K.Holt	lbw b Nasim-ul-Ghani	29	c Ijaz Butt b Fazal Mahmood	2
R.B.Kanhai	c Hanif Mohammad b Nasim-ul-Ghani	33	c Imtiaz Ahmed b Mahmood Hussain	12
G.St A.Sobers	lbw b Fazal Mahmood	0	(6) lbw b Fazal Mahmood	14
O.G.Smith	st Imtiaz Ahmed b Nasim-ul-Ghani	0	lbw b Mahmood Hussain	11
B.F.Butcher	not out	45	(4) c Imtiaz Ahmed b Nasim-ul-Ghani	61
J.S.Solomon	c Hanif Mohammad b D'Souza	14	run out	66
F.C.M.Alexander *+	b D'Souza	0	lbw b Shujauddin	16
L.R.Gibbs	b Nasim-ul-Ghani	5	b Shujauddin	21
W.W.Hall	b Fazal Mahmood	7	st Imtiaz Ahmed b Shujauddin	4
J.Taylor	b Fazal Mahmood	0	not out	0
	Extras (b 3,nb 10)	13	(lb 7,nb 10)	17
	TOTAL	**146**		**245**

PAKISTAN

Hanif Mohammad	c Alexander b Smith	103	retired hurt/ill	5
Ijaz Butt	c Alexander b Hall	14	not out	41
Saeed Ahmed	run out	78	not out	33
Imtiaz Ahmed +	lbw b Smith	31		
Wazir Mohammad	st Alexander b Gibbs	23		
W.Mathias	b Hall	16		
Fazal Mahmood *	c Alexander b Hall	0		
Shujauddin	run out	1		
Nasim-ul-Ghani	b Gibbs	11		
Mahmood Hussain	b Gibbs	1		
A.D'Souza	not out	3		
	Extras (b 9,lb 3,w 1,nb 10)	23	(nb 9)	9
	TOTAL	**304**	**(for 0 wkts)**	**88**

PAKISTAN	O	M	R	W		O	M	R	W
Fazal Mahmood	22	9	35	4		36	9	89	3
Mahmood Hussain	8	3	13	0		26	10	59	2
D'Souza	14	0	50	2		13	5	28	0
Nasim-ul-Ghani	16	5	35	4		25	16	34	1
Shujauddin						13	7	18	3

WEST INDIES	O	M	R	W		O	M	R	W
Hall	30	7	57	3		8	1	35	0
Taylor	21	7	43	0		6	2	15	0
Gibbs	38.2	13	92	3		7	4	8	0
Sobers	40	24	45	0		9	5	12	0
Smith	27	14	36	2		3	2	9	0
Solomon	4	1	8	0					
Holt						1	1	0	0

FALL OF WICKETS	WI	PAK	WI	PAK		WI	PAK	WI	PAK
1st	0	33	12		6th	104	287	140	
2nd	62	211	34		7th	104	289	189	
3rd	64	214	55		8th	117	290	233	
4th	65	263	84		9th	145	291	241	
5th	69	284	109		10th	146	304	245	

PAKISTAN vs WEST INDIES
at Dacca on 06/03/1959
Pakistan won by 41 runs

PAKISTAN

Ijaz Butt	b Hall	2	b Ramadhin	21
Alimuddin	c & b Hall	6	c Smith b Atkinson	0
Saeed Ahmed	c Alexander b Hall	6	lbw b Ramadhin	22
Imtiaz Ahmed +	b Ramadhin	3	c Smith b Atkinson	4
Wazir Mohammad	b Hall	1	c Alexander b Atkinson	4
W.Mathias	c Atkinson b Gibbs	64	b Atkinson	45
Shujauddin	b Atkinson	26	b Hall	17
Fazal Mahmood *	c Alexander b Ramadhin	12	(9) not out	7
Nasim-ul-Ghani	run out	7	(8) b Hall	0
Mahmood Hussain	b Ramadhin	4	b Hall	2
Haseeb Ahsan	not out	4	b Hall	0
	Extras (b 5,lb 2,nb 3)	10	(b 9,lb 4,w 1,nb 8)	22
	TOTAL	**145**		**144**

WEST INDIES

J.K.Holt	b M.Hussain	4	c Imtiaz Ahmed b Fazal Mahmood	5
R.B.Kanhai	c Wazir Mohammad b Fazal Mahmood	4	(3) lbw b Fazal Mahmood	8
G.St A.Sobers	lbw b Fazal Mahmood	29	(5) c Fazal Mahmood b M.Hussain	45
F.C.M.Alexander *+	st Imtiaz Ahmed b Nasim-ul-Ghani	4	(2) c Imtiaz Ahmed b Fazal Mahmood	18
B.F.Butcher	c Shujauddin b Fazal Mahmood	11	(4) b Fazal Mahmood	8
O.G.Smith	c Nasim-ul-Ghani b Fazal Mahmood	0	b Fazal Mahmood	39
J.S.Solomon	c Imtiaz Ahmed b Nasim-ul-Ghani	0	c M.Hussain b Fazal Mahmood	8
E.St E.Atkinson	c Mathias b Fazal Mahmood	0	(9) lbw b M.Hussain	20
L.R.Gibbs	st Imtiaz Ahmed b Nasim-ul-Ghani	0	(8) b M.Hussain	0
W.W.Hall	c Mathias b Fazal Mahmood	0	lbw b M.Hussain	6
S.Ramadhin	not out	0	not out	4
	Extras (b 5,lb 3,nb 6)	14	(lb 5,nb 6)	11
	TOTAL	**76**		**172**

WEST INDIES	O	M	R	W		O	M	R	W
Hall	13	5	28	4		16.5	2	49	4
Atkinson	10	2	22	1		22	9	44	4
Ramadhin	23.3	6	45	3		15	9	10	2
Gibbs	21	8	33	1		6	0	17	0
Sobers	8	4	7	0		3	2	4	0

PAKISTAN	O	M	R	W		O	M	R	W
Fazal Mahmood	18.3	9	34	6		27	10	66	6
Mahmood Hussain	10	1	21	1		19.5	1	48	4
Nasim-ul-Ghani	7	5	4	3		8	2	34	0
Haseeb Ahsan	1	0	3	0					
Shujauddin						6	2	13	0

FALL OF WICKETS	PAK	WI	PAK	WI		PAK	WI	PAK	WI
1st	6	4	2	12	6th	108	71	130	134
2nd	15	19	33	31	7th	126	72	130	141
3rd	18	56	40	35	8th	130	74	131	150
4th	22	65	54	48	9th	139	74	139	159
5th	22	68	71	113	10th	145	76	144	172

PAKISTAN vs AUSTRALIA
at Dacca on 13/11/1959
Australia won by 8 wickets

PAKISTAN

Hanif Mohammad	b Mackay	66	b Benaud	19
Ijaz Butt	c Grout b Davidson	0	b Mackay	20
Saeed Ahmed	c Harvey b Davidson	37	b Mackay	15
W.Mathias	c & b Benaud	4	lbw b Mackay	1
D.Sharpe	run out	56	lbw b Mackay	35
Wazir Mohammad	c Meckiff b Benaud	0	lbw b Benaud	5
Imtiaz Ahmed +	b Davidson	13	b Mackay	4
Israr Ali	st Grout b Benaud	7	(9) b Benaud	1
Shujauddin	not out	2	(8) not out	16
Fazal Mahmood *	c & b Mackay	1	c & b Mackay	4
Nasim-ul-Ghani	b Davidson	5	c McDonald b Benaud	0
	Extras (b 5,lb 1,nb 3)	9	(b 7,lb 5,nb 2)	14
	TOTAL	**200**		**134**

AUSTRALIA

C.C.McDonald	lbw b Fazal Mahmood	19	not out	44
L.E.Favell	b Israr Ali	0	c & b Israr Ali	4
R.N.Harvey	b Fazal Mahmood	96	b Fazal Mahmood	30
N.C.O'Neill	b Nasim-ul-Ghani	2	not out	26
P.J.P.Burge	c Imtiaz Ahmed b Nasim-ul-Ghani	0		
R.Benaud *	lbw b Nasim-ul-Ghani	16		
K.D.Mackay	b Fazal Mahmood	7		
A.K.Davidson	lbw b Israr Ali	4		
A.T.W.Grout +	not out	66		
R.R.Lindwall	lbw b Fazal Mahmood	4		
I.Meckiff	b Fazal Mahmood	2		
	Extras (lb 9)	9	(b 3,lb 3,nb 2)	8
	TOTAL	**225**	(for 2 wkts)	**112**

AUSTRALIA	O	M	R	W		O	M	R	W
Davidson	23.5	7	42	4		11	3	23	0
Meckiff	10	2	33	0		3	1	8	0
Lindwall	15	1	31	0		2	0	5	0
Benaud	38	10	69	4		39.3	26	42	4
Mackay	19	12	16	1		45	27	42	6

PAKISTAN	O	M	R	W		O	M	R	W
Fazal Mahmood	35.5	11	71	5		20.1	4	52	1
Israr Ali	23	5	85	2		9	0	20	1
Nasim-ul-Ghani	17	4	51	3		10	2	16	0
Shujauddin	3	0	9	0		8	4	12	0
Saeed Ahmed						1	0	4	0

FALL OF WICKETS	PAK	AUS	PAK	AUS		PAK	AUS	PAK	AUS
1st	3	0	32	12	6th	170	134	94	
2nd	75	51	57	65	7th	184	143	117	
3rd	82	53	62		8th	191	151	128	
4th	145	53	68		9th	193	189	133	
5th	146	112	81		10th	200	225	134	

PAKISTAN vs WEST INDIES
at Lahore on 26/03/1959
West Indies won by an innings and 156 runs

WEST INDIES

F.C.M.Alexander *+	lbw b Fazal Mahmood	21
M.R.Bynoe	c Mahmood Hussain b Fazal Mahmood	1
R.B.Kanhai	c & b Shujauddin	217
G.St A.Sobers	b Nasim-ul-Ghani	72
O.G.Smith	c Waqar Hassan b Saeed Ahmed	31
B.F.Butcher	run out	8
J.S.Solomon	c Mathias b Mahmood Hussain	56
E.St E.Atkinson	c Mathias b Nasim-ul-Ghani	20
L.R.Gibbs	c Saeed Ahmed b Nasim-ul-Ghani	18
S.Ramadhin	not out	4
W.W.Hall	b Shujauddin	0
	Extras (b 7,lb 8,nb 6)	21
	TOTAL	**469**

PAKISTAN

Ijaz Butt	not out	47	c Gibbs b Atkinson	2
Imtiaz Ahmed +	run out	40	c Gibbs b Atkinson	1
Saeed Ahmed	c Gibbs b Smith	27	c Kanhai b Atkinson	33
Waqar Hassan	b Gibbs	41	c Alexander b Gibbs	28
W.Mathias	b Hall	14	c Alexander b Ramadhin	9
Shujauddin	b Hall	1	(7) c & b Ramadhin	0
Wazir Mohammad	run out	11	(6) c Alexander b Ramadhin	0
Mushtaq Mohammad	lbw b Hall	14	b Ramadhin	4
Fazal Mahmood *	c Sobers b Hall	0	b Gibbs	14
Nasim-ul-Ghani	b Hall	0	not out	6
Mahmood Hussain	c Sobers b Atkinson	0	c Bynoe b Gibbs	1
	Extras (b 1,lb 3,nb 10)	14	(b 2,lb 2,nb 2)	6
	TOTAL	**209**		**104**

PAKISTAN	O	M	R	W		O	M	R	W
Fazal Mahmood	40	10	109	2					
Mahmood Hussain	28	4	99	1					
Nasim-ul-Ghani	30	6	106	3					
Shujauddin	34.3	7	81	2					
Mushtaq	6	0	34	0					
Saeed Ahmed	11	1	19	1					

WEST INDIES	O	M	R	W		O	M	R	W
Hall	24	2	87	5		9	1	31	0
Atkinson	14.2	1	40	1		12	8	15	3
Ramadhin	22	9	41	0		10	4	25	4
Smith	7	3	11	1		2	1	4	0
Gibbs	12	5	16	1		9.5	3	14	3
Sobers						6	1	9	0

FALL OF WICKETS	WI	PAK	PAK			WI	PAK	PAK	
1st	11	70	4		6th	407	180	73	
2nd	38	75	5		7th	426	208	78	
3rd	200	98	55		8th	463	208	97	
4th	290	105	72		9th	464	208	97	
5th	307	160	73		10th	469	209	104	

PAKISTAN vs AUSTRALIA
at Lahore on 21/11/1959
Australia won by 7 wickets

PAKISTAN

Hanif Mohammad	c Grout b Meckiff	49	(5) b Kline	18
Imtiaz Ahmed *+	b Davidson	18	c O'Neill b Kline	54
Saeed Ahmed	c Grout b Meckiff	17	st Grout b Kline	166
Alimuddin	b Meckiff	8	(1) b Kline	7
D.Sharpe	c Grout b Kline	12	(6) st Grout b Kline	1
Waqar Hassan	c Grout b Davidson	12	(7) b Kline	4
Shujauddin	b Benaud	17	(4) lbw b O'Neill	45
Israr Ali	lbw b Benaud	0	(10) not out	0
Nasim-ul-Ghani	c Stevens b Davidson	6	(8) b Benaud	15
Mohammad Munaf	c Grout b Davidson	5	(9) c Davidson b Kline	19
Haseeb Ahsan	not out	0	c Grout b Benaud	4
	Extras (b 1,lb 1)	2	(b 31,lb 2)	33
	TOTAL	**146**		**366**

AUSTRALIA

C.C.McDonald	c Imtiaz Ahmed b Haseeb Ahsan	42		
G.B.Stevens	c Imtiaz Ahmed b Mohammad Munaf	9	c Alimuddin b Mohammad Munaf	8
R.N.Harvey	lbw b Mohammad Munaf	43	b Mohammad Munaf	37
N.C.O'Neill	st Imtiaz Ahmed b Shujauddin	134	not out	43
L.E.Favell	c Israr Ali	32	(1) b Israr Ali	4
A.T.W.Grout +	lbw b Nasim-ul-Ghani	12		
R.Benaud *	b Haseeb Ahsan	29	(5) not out	21
A.K.Davidson	c Imtiaz Ahmed b Israr Ali	47		
K.D.Mackay	c Imtiaz Ahmed b Haseeb Ahsan	26		
L.F.Kline	not out 0			
I.Meckiff				
	Extras (b 5,lb 5,nb 7)	17	(b 6,lb 4)	10
	TOTAL (for 9 wkts dec)	**391**	(for 3 wkts)	**123**

AUSTRALIA	O	M	R	W		O	M	R	W
Davidson	19	2	48	4		35	9	56	0
Meckiff	19	7	45	3		22	4	44	0
Benaud	16	6	36	2		54.4	22	92	2
Kline	12	6	15	1		44	21	75	7
O'Neill						13	5	37	1
Mackay						6	1	21	0
Harvey						5	2	8	0

PAKISTAN	O	M	R	W		O	M	R	W
Mohammad Munaf	31	8	100	2		10	2	38	2
Israr Ali	13	5	29	2		5	1	20	1
Nasim-ul-Ghani	21	3	72	1		3.3	0	18	0
Shujauddin	20	2	58	1		3	0	16	0
Haseeb Ahsan	33.3	3	115	3		4	0	21	0

FALL OF WICKETS	PAK	AUS	PAK	AUS		PAK	AUS	PAK	AUS
1st	39	27	45	13	6th	120	310	324	
2nd	56	83	87	15	7th	121	311	325	
3rd	92	114	256	77	8th	126	391	362	
4th	109	213	312		9th	142	391	362	
5th	115	247	319		10th	146		366	

PAKISTAN vs AUSTRALIA
at Karachi on 04/12/1959
Match drawn

PAKISTAN

Hanif Mohammad	lbw b Lindwall	51	(4) not out		101
Imtiaz Ahmed +	b Davidson	18	c Harvey b Davidson		9
Saeed Ahmed	c Harvey b Lindwall	91	c Harvey b Davidson		8
Shujauddin	c O'Neill b Benaud	5	(6) c Favell b Mackay		4
D.Sharpe	c Burge b Benaud	4	c Mackay b Lindwall		26
Ijaz Butt	c Grout b Benaud	58	(1) run out		8
W.Mathias	c Favell b Mackay	43	c Davidson b Benaud		13
Intikhab Alam	run out	0	c Burge b Mackay		6
Fazal Mahmood *	c Harvey b Benaud	7	c Benaud b Davidson		11
Mohammad Munaf	not out	4	not out		4
Munir Malik	st Grout b Benaud				
	Extras (lb 3,nb 3)	6	(lb 2,nb 2)		4
	TOTAL	287	(for 8 wkts dec)		194

AUSTRALIA

C.C.McDonald	b Intikhab Alam	19	lbw b Munir Malik		30
G.B.Stevens	c Mathias b Fazal Mahmood	13	c Imtiaz Ahmed b Intikhab Alam		28
A.T.W.Grout +	c & b Intikhab Alam	20			
K.D.Mackay	c Ijaz Butt b Fazal Mahmood	40			
R.N.Harvey	c Imtiaz Ahmed b Fazal Mahmood	54	(3) not out		13
N.C.O'Neill	b Munir Malik	6	(4) not out		7
L.E.Favell	c Sharpe b Fazal Mahmood	10			
P.J.P.Burge	c Sharpe b Mohammad Munaf	12			
R.Benaud *	c Imtiaz Ahmed b Munir Malik	18			
A.K.Davidson	not out	39			
R.R.Lindwall	c Imtiaz Ahmed b Fazal Mahmood	23			
	Extras (lb 1,nb 2)	3	(lb 3,nb 2)		5
	TOTAL	257	(for 2 wkts)		83

AUSTRALIA

	O	M	R	W		O	M	R	W
Davidson	26	5	59	1		34	8	70	3
Lindwall	25	6	72	2		17	10	14	
Benaud	49.5	17	93	5		26	13	48	1
Mackay	27	8	53	1		32.4	11	58	2
O'Neill	4	1	4	0					

PAKISTAN

	O	M	R	W		O	M	R	W
Fazal Mahmood	30.2	12	74	5		10	5	16	0
Mohammad Munaf	8	0	42	1		3	0	10	0
Intikhab Alam	19	4	49	2		6	1	13	1
Munir Malik	22	5	76	2		9	1	24	1
Shujauddin	3	0	13	0		2	1	9	0
Saeed Ahmed						3	0	6	0

FALL OF WICKETS

	PAK	AUS	PAK	AUS		PAK	AUS	PAK	AUS
1st	36	29	11	54	6th	265	145	124	
2nd	124	33	25	76	7th	267	174	159	
3rd	143	82	25		8th	276	184	179	
4th	149	106	78		9th	287	207		
5th	181	122	91		10th	287	257		

INDIA vs PAKISTAN
at Bombay on 02/12/1960
Match drawn

PAKISTAN

Hanif Mohammad	run out	160	c Umrigar b Desai		0
Imtiaz Ahmed +	b Desai	19	c Roy b Nadkarni		69
Saeed Ahmed	st Joshi b Gupte	121	c & b Gupte		41
Mushtaq Mohammad	lbw b Gupte	6	lbw b Nadkarni		19
W.Mathias	c Nadkarni b Desai	0	not out		6
Javed Burki	lbw b Gupte	7	not out		13
Nasim-ul-Ghani	c Joshi b Desai	4			
Fazal Mahmood *	c Joshi b Gupte	1			
Mahmood Hussain	c Desai b Nadkarni	23			
Mohammad Farooq	not out	2			
Haseeb Ahsan	c Contractor b Nadkarni	0			
	Extras (b 6,lb 1)	7	(b 16,lb 1,nb 1)		18
	TOTAL	350	(for 4 wkts)		166

INDIA

Pankaj Roy	c Mahmood Hussain b Mohammad Farooq	23	
N.J.Contractor *	c Javed Burki b Mohammad Farooq	62	
A.A.Baig	c Hanif Mohammad b Mohammad Farooq	1	
V.L.Manjrekar	b Mahmood Hussain	73	
P.R.Umrigar	c sub b Mahmood Hussain	33	
C.G.Borde	lbw b Mahmood Hussain	41	
R.G.Nadkarni	c Javed Burki b Mahmood Hussain	34	
R.F.Surti	c Nasim-ul-Ghani b Mohammad Farooq	11	
P.G.Joshi +	not out	52	
R.B.Desai	b Mahmood Hussain	85	
S.P.Gupte			
	Extras (b 14,lb 11,nb 9)	34	
	TOTAL (for 9 wkts dec)	449	

INDIA

	O	M	R	W		O	M	R	W
Desai	36	6	116	3		8	2	27	1
Surti	9	0	37	0		8	1	21	0
Umrigar	17	2	46	0					
Nadkarni	37.4	14	75	2		15	10	9	2
Gupte	31	15	43	4		25	10	46	1
Borde	6	1	26	0		16	4	25	0
Contractor	1	1	0	0		7	2	16	0
Roy						1	0	4	0

PAKISTAN

	O	M	R	W		O	M	R	W
Mahmood Hussain	51.4	10	129	5					
Fazal Mahmood	6	2	5	0					
Mohammad Farooq	46	7	139	4					
Nasim-ul-Ghani	41	19	74	0					
Haseeb Ahsan	31	10	68	0					
Mushtaq	1	1	0	0					

FALL OF WICKETS

	PAK	IND	PAK		PAK	IND	PAK
1st	55	56	0	6th	319	289	
2nd	301	58	80	7th	321	296	
3rd	302	121	142	8th	331	300	
4th	303	206	147	9th	349	449	
5th	318	207		10th	350		

INDIA vs PAKISTAN
at Kanpur on 16/12/1960
Match drawn

PAKISTAN

Hanif Mohammad	c Contractor b Umrigar	5	c Jaisimha b Muddiah		19
Imtiaz Ahmed +	b Gupte	20	c Contractor b Muddiah		16
Saeed Ahmed	c Tamhane b Desai	32	b Gupte		4
Javed Burki	run out	79	not out		48
W.Mathias	lbw b Desai	37	not out		46
Alimuddin	c Nadkarni b Umrigar	24			
Mushtaq Mohammad	c Umrigar b Muddiah	13			
Nasim-ul-Ghani	not out	70			
Fazal Mahmood *	lbw b Umrigar	16			
Mahmood Hussain	c Borde b Umrigar	7			
Haseeb Ahsan	c Tamhane b Gupte	13			
	Extras (b 13,lb 6)	19	(b 2,lb 5)		7
	TOTAL	335	(for 3 wkts)		140

INDIA

N.J.Contractor *	b Haseeb Ahsan	47	
M.L.Jaisimha	run out	99	
A.A.Baig	b Haseeb Ahsan	13	
V.L.Manjrekar	c Nasim-ul-Ghani b Fazal Mahmood	52	
P.R.Umrigar	c Javed Burki b Mahmood Hussain	115	
C.G.Borde	c Fazal Mahmood b Nasim-ul-Ghani	0	
R.G.Nadkarni	b Haseeb Ahsan	16	
R.B.Desai	b Haseeb Ahsan	14	
N.S.Tamhane +	c Mathias b Haseeb Ahsan	3	
V.M.Muddiah	b Mahmood Hussain	11	
S.P.Gupte	not out	1	
	Extras (b 20,lb 1,nb 12)	33	
	TOTAL	404	

INDIA

	O	M	R	W		O	M	R	W
Desai	30	6	54	2		4	1	3	0
Umrigar	55	23	71	4		3	0	10	0
Gupte	42.4	14	84	2		17	6	29	1
Muddiah	22	6	62	1		18	7	40	2
Nadkarni	32	24	23	0		7	4	6	0
Borde	6	2	16	0		10	0	36	0
Contractor	1	0	6	0					
Jaisimha						3	0	5	0
Manjrekar						1	0	2	0
Baig						1	0	2	0

PAKISTAN

	O	M	R	W		O	M	R	W
Mahmood Hussain	44.5	1	101	2					
Fazal Mahmood	36	14	37	1					
Nasim-ul-Ghani	55	17	109	1					
Haseeb Ahsan	56	15	121	5					
Mushtaq	2	1	3	0					

FALL OF WICKETS

	PAK	IND	PAK		PAK	IND	PAK
1st	21	71	31	6th	214	294	
2nd	29	92	42	7th	240	334	
3rd	93	182	42	8th	293	342	
4th	174	258		9th	305	403	
5th	177	263		10th	335	404	

INDIA vs PAKISTAN
at Calcutta on 30/12/1960
Match drawn

PAKISTAN

Hanif Mohammad	c Baig b Desai	56	not out		63
Imtiaz Ahmed +	b Surenranath	9	b Desai		9
Saeed Ahmed	c Nadkarni b Surenranath	41	lbw b Surenranath		13
Javed Burki	lbw b Borde	48	run out		42
W.Mathias	c Umrigar b Desai	8			
Mushtaq Mohammad	c Jaisimha b Borde	61			
Nasim-ul-Ghani	b Surenranath	0			
Intikhab Alam	c Tamhane b Surenranath	56	(5) not out		11
Fazal Mahmood *	lbw b Borde	8			
Mahmood Hussain	b Borde	4			
Haseeb Ahsan	not out	1			
	Extras (b 6,lb 3)	9	(b 3,lb 5)		8
	TOTAL	301	(for 3 wkts dec)		146

INDIA

N.J.Contractor *	b Intikhab Alam	25	c Fazal Mahmood b Haseeb Ahsan		12
M.L.Jaisimha	c Mathias b Mahmood Hussain	28	c Mathias b Intikhab Alam		26
A.A.Baig	b Intikhab Alam	19	b Haseeb Ahsan		1
P.R.Umrigar	c Imtiaz Ahmed b Mahmood Hussain	1	(5) b Intikhab Alam		4
V.L.Manjrekar	b Fazal Mahmood	29	(4) not out		45
C.G.Borde	c Imtiaz Ahmed b Fazal Mahmood	44	not out		23
R.G.Nadkarni	c Imtiaz Ahmed b Fazal Mahmood	1			
R.B.Desai	b Haseeb Ahsan	14			
N.S.Tamhane +	c Intikhab Alam b Fazal Mahmood	0			
Surenranath	not out	5			
S.P.Gupte	b Fazal Mahmood	0			
	Extras (b 10,lb 3,nb 1)	14	(b 3,lb 9,nb 4)		16
	TOTAL	180	(for 4 wkts)		127

INDIA

	O	M	R	W		O	M	R	W
Desai	35	3	118	2		16	4	37	1
Surenranath	46	19	93	4		18	2	51	1
Umrigar	6	2	15	0		7	2	14	0
Gupte	18	5	41	0		1	1	0	0
Borde	16.2	7	21	4					
Nadkarni	6	5	4	0		7	0	36	0

PAKISTAN

	O	M	R	W		O	M	R	W
Mahmood Hussain	31	12	56	2		8	3	9	0
Fazal Mahmood	25.3	12	26	5		12	5	19	0
Intikhab Alam	24	11	35	2		15	2	33	2
Nasim-ul-Ghani	12	5	32	0		2	1	5	0
Haseeb Ahsan	7	1	17	1		14	6	25	2
Saeed Ahmed						1	0	2	0
Mushtaq						3	1	9	0
Hanif Mohammad						1	0	6	0
Javed Burki						1	0	3	0

FALL OF WICKETS

	PAK	IND	PAK	IND		PAK	IND	PAK	IND
1st	12	59	15	47	6th	186	147		
2nd	84	83	34	47	7th	274	174		
3rd	135	83	116	48	8th	296	175		
4th	164	85		65	9th	296	180		
5th	185	145			10th	301	180		

INDIA vs PAKISTAN
at Madras on 13/01/1961
Match drawn

PAKISTAN

Hanif Mohammad	c Kunderan b Surenranath	62		
Imtiaz Ahmed +	b Desai	135	not out	20
Saeed Ahmed	c Kunderan b Desai	103	(1) not out	38
Javed Burki	c Contractor b Borde	19		
W.Mathias	lbw b Umrigar	49		
Mushtaq Mohammad	not out	41		
Nasim-ul-Ghani	c Kunderan b Umrigar	5		
Intikhab Alam	c Kunderan b Desai	13		
Fazal Mahmood *	lbw b Desai	4		
Mahmood Hussain				
Haseeb Ahsan				
Extras	(b 12,lb 3,nb 2)	17	(nb 1)	1
TOTAL	(for 8 wkts dec)	448	(for 0 wkts)	59

INDIA

M.L.Jaisimha	c Intikhab Alam b Mahmood Hussain	32
N.J.Contractor *	c Intikhab Alam b Haseeb Ahsan	81
D.K.Gaekwad	c & b Haseeb Ahsan	9
V.L.Manjrekar	b Haseeb Ahsan	30
P.R.Umrigar	b Haseeb Ahsan	117
C.G.Borde	not out	177
A.G.Milkha Singh	c Fazal Mahmood b Haseeb Ahsan	18
B.K.Kunderan +	b Haseeb Ahsan	12
R.B.Desai	st Imtiaz Ahmed b Nasim-ul-Ghani	18
Surenranath	st Imtiaz Ahmed b Nasim-ul-Ghani	6
B.P.Gupte	not out	17
Extras	(b 10,lb 7,nb 5)	22
TOTAL	(for 9 wkts dec)	539

INDIA

	O	M	R	W		O	M	R	W
Desai	28.5	0	66	4		3	0	14	0
Surenranath	38	10	99	1		3	2	8	0
Gupte	30	9	97	0		5	0	19	0
Umrigar	53	24	64	2					
Borde	33	4	105	1					
Jaisimha						3	0	8	0
Manjrekar						2	0	6	0
Contractor						1	0	1	0
Milkha Singh						1	0	2	0

PAKISTAN

	O	M	R	W		O	M	R	W
Mahmood Hussain	37	12	86	1					
Fazal Mahmood	43	22	66	0					
Haseeb Ahsan	84	19	202	6					
Intikhab Alam	17	5	40	0					
Nasim-ul-Ghani	46	12	123	2					

FALL OF WICKETS	PAK	IND	PAK			PAK	IND	PAK
1st	162	84			6th	420	396	
2nd	252	102			7th	444	416	
3rd	322	146			8th	448	447	
4th	338	164			9th	476		
5th	408	341			10th			

INDIA vs PAKISTAN
at Delhi on 08/02/1961
Match drawn

INDIA

M.L.Jaisimha	b Mohammad Farooq	27	not out	14
N.J.Contractor *	c & b Intikhab Alam	92		
R.F.Surti	c Imtiaz Ahmed b Fazal Mahmood	64		
V.L.Manjrekar	c Mathias b Haseeb Ahsan	18		
P.R.Umrigar	b Fazal Mahmood	112		
C.G.Borde	c Imtiaz Ahmed b Mohammad Farooq	45		
A.G.Milkha Singh	b Mahmood Hussain	35		
R.G.Nadkarni	b Fazal Mahmood	21		
B.K.Kunderan +	not out	12	(2) not out	1
R.B.Desai	b Mahmood Hussain	3		
V.V.Kumar	b Mahmood Hussain	6		
Extras	(b 6,lb 13,nb 9)	28	(nb 1)	1
TOTAL		463	(for 0 wkts)	16

PAKISTAN

Hanif Mohammad	c Milkha Singh b Desai	1	b Desai	44
Imtiaz Ahmed +	b Kumar	25	lbw b Nadkarni	53
Saeed Ahmed	c Umrigar b Nadkarni	36	c sub b Nadkarni	31
Javed Burki	c Manjrekar b Desai	61	c & b Kumar	8
W.Mathias	c Nadkarni b Kumar	10	c Borde b Nadkarni	2
Mushtaq Mohammad	c Kumar b Desai	101	lbw b Desai	22
Intikhab Alam	b Desai	0	b Kumar	10
Fazal Mahmood *	c Nadkarni b Kumar	13	lbw b Desai	18
Mahmood Hussain	lbw b Kumar	20	b Nadkarni	35
Haseeb Ahsan	b Kumar	5	b Desai	6
Mohammad Farooq	not out	0	not out	14
Extras	(b 8,lb 1,w 1,nb 4)	14	(b 2,lb 5)	7
TOTAL		286		250

PAKISTAN

	O	M	R	W		O	M	R	W
Mahmood Hussain	40	9	115	3		1	0	7	0
Fazal Mahmood	38	8	86	3					
Mohammad Farooq	29	2	101	2		1	0	8	0
Haseeb Ahsan	17	5	57	1					
Intikhab Alam	34	6	76	1					

INDIA

	O	M	R	W		O	M	R	W
Desai	28	5	102	4		27	3	88	4
Surti	11	1	38	0		7	0	34	0
Nadkarni	34	24	24	1		52.4	38	43	4
Kumar	37.5	21	64	5		36	17	68	2
Borde	10	3	30	0		2	0	2	0
Umrigar	5	1	14	0		3	2	8	0

FALL OF WICKETS	IND	PAK	PAK	IND		IND	PAK	PAK	IND
1st	43	10	83		6th	401	229	165	
2nd	150	60	107		7th	439	254	189	
3rd	201	78	126		8th	441	265	196	
4th	324	89	131		9th	453	281	212	
5th	338	225	142		10th	463	286	250	

PAKISTAN vs ENGLAND
at Lahore on 21/10/1961
England won by 5 wickets

PAKISTAN

Hanif Mohammad	b White	19	c Murray b Brown	17
Imtiaz Ahmed *+	c Murray b White	4	b Dexter	12
Saeed Ahmed	c Murray b Barber	74	c Murray b Brown	0
Javed Burki	c Murray b Allen	138	c Allen b Barber	15
Mushtaq Mohammad	run out	76	c Pullar b Allen	23
W.Mathias	c Smith b Barber	3	lbw b Allen	32
Intikhab Alam	b Barber	24	b Barber	17
Mohammad Munaf	b Allen	7	c Dexter b Brown	12
Mahmood Hussain	b White	14	b Allen	7
Afaq Hussain	not out	10	not out	35
Haseeb Ahsan	not out	7	c Smith b Barber	14
Extras	(b 4,lb 3,nb 4)	11	(b 9,lb 2,nb 5)	16
TOTAL	(for 9 wkts dec)	387		200

ENGLAND

P.E.Richardson	c Afaq Hussain b Mohammad Munaf	4	c Imtiaz Ahmed b Intikhab Alam	48
G.Pullar	c Mahmood Hussain b Mohammad Munaf	0	b Mohammad Munaf	0
K.F.Barrington	run out	139	lbw b Mahmood Hussain	6
M.J.K.Smith	run out	99	c Afaq Hussain b Haseeb Ahsan	34
E.R.Dexter *	hit wicket b Afaq Hussain	20	not out	66
W.E.Russell	b Intikhab Alam	34	b Intikhab Alam	0
R.W.Barber	st Imtiaz Ahmed b Haseeb Ahsan	6	not out	39
J.T.Murray +	b Mohammad Munaf	4		
D.A.Allen	lbw b Mohammad Munaf	40		
D.W.White	b Saeed Ahmed	0		
A.Brown	not out	3		
Extras	(b 21,lb 1,nb 9)	31	(b 10,lb 4,nb 2)	16
TOTAL		380	(for 5 wkts)	209

ENGLAND

	O	M	R	W		O	M	R	W
White	22	3	65	3		12	2	42	0
Brown	15.5	3	44	0		14	4	27	3
Dexter	7	1	26	0		7	2	10	1
Barber	40	4	124	3		20.5	6	54	3
Allen	33	14	67	2		22	13	51	3
Russell	19	9	25	0					
Barrington	6	0	25	0					

PAKISTAN

	O	M	R	W		O	M	R	W
Mahmood Hussain	25	8	35	0		12	3	30	1
Mohammad Munaf	31.1	15	42	4		15	1	54	1
Intikhab Alam	48	6	118	1		16	3	37	2
Afaq Hussain	23	6	40	1		5	0	21	0
Haseeb Ahsan	36	7	95	1		9	0	42	1
Saeed Ahmed	11	3	19	1		2	0	9	0

FALL OF WICKETS	PAK	ENG	PAK	ENG		PAK	ENG	PAK	ENG
1st	17	2	33	1	6th	324	306	113	
2nd	24	21	33	17	7th	327	322	138	
3rd	162	213	33	86	8th	365	361	146	
4th	315	275	69	108	9th	369	362	148	
5th	324	294	93	108	10th	380	200		

PAKISTAN vs ENGLAND
at Dacca on 19/01/1962
Match drawn

PAKISTAN

Hanif Mohammad	c Lock b Allen	111	b Allen	104
Alimuddin	c Smith b Lock	7	c Dexter b Richardson	50
Saeed Ahmed	b Knight	69	c Parfitt b Lock	13
Javed Burki	c & b Lock	140	c Knight b Lock	0
Intikhab Alam	c Barrington b Lock	18	(9) b Lock	5
Mushtaq Mohammad	b Allen	26	(5) c & b Allen	6
Imtiaz Ahmed *+	b Lock	0	(6) hit wicket b Allen	0
Nasim-ul-Ghani	not out	15	c Richardson b Allen	12
Shujauddin	(7) b Lock	0		
Mohammad Munaf	b Allen	12		
A.D'Souza	not out	7		
Extras	(b 4,lb 3)	7	(b 5,lb 1,nb 1)	7
TOTAL	(for 7 wkts dec)	393		216

ENGLAND

G.Pullar	c & b D'Souza	165	not out	8
R.W.Barber	lbw b Nasim-ul-Ghani	86		
K.F.Barrington	b D'Souza	84		
M.J.K.Smith	lbw b D'Souza	10		
E.R.Dexter *	b Mohammad Munaf	12		
P.E.Richardson	c D'Souza b Nasim-ul-Ghani	19	(2) not out	21
P.H.Parfitt	c & b Shujauddin	9		
B.R.Knight	b D'Souza	10		
D.A.Allen	b Shujauddin	0		
G.Millman +	not out	3		
G.A.R.Lock	c Hanif Mohammad b Shujauddin	4		
Extras	(b 16,lb 15,nb 6)	37	(b 2,lb 6,nb 1)	9
TOTAL		439	(for 0 wkts)	38

ENGLAND

	O	M	R	W		O	M	R	W
Knight	29	13	52	1		14	6	19	0
Dexter	28	12	34	0		5	4	1	0
Lock	73	24	155	4		42	23	70	4
Allen	40.3	13	94	2		23.1	11	30	5
Barrington	11	1	39	0		21	13	17	0
Barber	11	8	12	0					
Parfitt						8	3	14	0
Richardson						12	5	28	1
Pullar						9	3	30	0

PAKISTAN

	O	M	R	W		O	M	R	W
Mohammad Munaf	30	5	55	1					
D'Souza	46	13	94	4					
Shujauddin	34	10	73	3		3	3	0	0
Nasim-ul-Ghani	50	19	119	2		5	0	16	0
Intikhab Alam	9	0	43	0		4	2	2	0
Saeed Ahmed	12	3	18	0		2	1	3	0
Javed Burki						2	1	3	0
Hanif Mohammad						2	0	8	0

FALL OF WICKETS	PAK	ENG	PAK	ENG		PAK	ENG	PAK	ENG
1st	14	198	122		6th	365	414	159	
2nd	127	345	137		7th	393	418	184	
3rd	283	358	137		8th	422	191		
4th	344	373	158		9th	432	201		
5th	361	386	158		10th	439	216		

PAKISTAN vs ENGLAND

at Karachi on 02/02/1962
Match drawn

PAKISTAN

Hanif Mohammad	c Dexter b Lock	67	c Dexter b Knight	89
Imtiaz Ahmed *+	b White	0	(5) c Smith b Dexter	86
Saeed Ahmed	c Millman b Knight	16	c & b Barber	19
Javed Burki	c Millman b Dexter	3	c Millman b Dexter	44
Mushtaq Mohammad	lbw b Knight	14	(6) b Lock	41
Alimuddin	c Lock b Knight	109	(2) c Parfitt b Barber	53
Shujauddin	c Parfitt b Allen	15	c Lock b Barber	5
Nasim-ul-Ghani	b Barber	3	not out	41
Fazal Mahmood	b Knight	12	b Dexter	0
A.D'Souza	b Dexter	3	not out	10
Haseeb Ahsan	not out	4		
Extras	(b 2,lb 1,nb 4)	7	(b 8,lb 2,nb 6)	16
TOTAL		253	(for 8 wkts)	404

ENGLAND

P.E.Richardson	c Alimuddin b Nasim-ul-Ghani	26
G.Pullar	c Alimuddin b Nasim-ul-Ghani	60
E.R.Dexter *	c Saeed Ahmed b D'Souza	205
M.J.K.Smith	c Imtiaz Ahmed b Nasim-ul-Ghani	56
P.H.Parfitt	c Saeed Ahmed b D'Souza	111
R.W.Barber	st Imtiaz Ahmed b Haseeb Ahsan	23
B.R.Knight	c Imtiaz Ahmed b D'Souza	6
D.A.Allen	c Nasim-ul-Ghani b Haseeb Ahsan	0
G.Millman +	not out	0
G.A.R.Lock	b D'Souza	0
D.W.White	Extras (b 7,lb 11,nb 1)	19
	TOTAL	507

ENGLAND

	O	M	R	W		O	M	R	W
Knight	19	4	66	4		17	3	43	1
White	2.4	0	12	1					
Dexter	18.2	4	48	2		32	9	86	3
Allen	27	14	51	1		35	19	42	0
Barber	14	1	44	1		41	7	117	3
Lock	14	8	25	1		37	16	86	1
Parfitt						3	2	4	0
Richardson						2	1	10	0

PAKISTAN

	O	M	R	W		O	M	R	W
Fazal Mahmood	63	23	98	0					
D'Souza	57.5	16	112	5					
Nasim-ul-Ghani	45	10	125	3					
Haseeb Ahsan	36	7	68	2					
Shujauddin	27	5	63	0					
Saeed Ahmed	3	0	12	0					
Mushtaq	2	0	10	0					

FALL OF WICKETS

	PAK	ENG	PAK			PAK	ENG	PAK	
1st	2	77	91		6th	183	497	337	
2nd	25	107	129		7th	196	502	373	
3rd	36	250	211		8th	245	503	383	
4th	56	438	227		9th	248	507		
5th	148	493	256		10th	253	507		

ENGLAND vs PAKISTAN

at Edgbaston on 31/05/1962
England won by an innings and 24 runs

ENGLAND

G.Pullar	b D'Souza	22
M.C.Cowdrey	c Imtiaz Ahmed b Intikhab Alam	159
E.R.Dexter *	c Javed Burki b Intikhab Alam	72
T.W.Graveney	c Ijaz Butt b Mahmood Hussain	97
K.F.Barrington	lbw b Mahmood Hussain	9
P.H.Parfitt	not out	101
D.A.Allen	not out	79
G.Millman +		
G.A.R.Lock		
F.S.Trueman		
J.B.Statham		
Extras	(lb 5)	5
TOTAL	(for 5 wkts dec)	544

PAKISTAN

Hanif Mohammad	c Millman b Allen	47	c Cowdrey b Allen	31
Ijaz Butt	c Lock b Statham	10	c Trueman b Allen	33
Saeed Ahmed	c Graveney b Trueman	5	(5) c Trueman b Allen	65
Mushtaq Mohammad	c Cowdrey b Lock	63	c Millman b Allen	8
Javed Burki *	c Barrington b Allen	13	(6) b Statham	9
Imtiaz Ahmed +	b Trueman	39	(3) c Graveney b Lock	46
W.Mathias	b Statham	21	b Statham	4
Nasim-ul-Ghani	b Statham	0	c Parfitt b Trueman	35
Intikhab Alam	b Lock	16	c Cowdrey b Lock	0
Mahmood Hussain	b Statham	0	c Graveney b Trueman	22
A.D'Souza	not out	23	not out	9
Extras	(b 8,lb 1)	9	(b 1,lb 1)	2
TOTAL		246		274

PAKISTAN

	O	M	R	W		O	M	R	W
Mahmood Hussain	43	14	130	2					
D'Souza	46	9	161	1					
Intikhab Alam	25	2	117	2					
Nasim-ul-Ghani	30	7	109	0					
Saeed Ahmed	2	0	22	0					

ENGLAND

	O	M	R	W		O	M	R	W
Statham	21	9	54	4		19	6	32	2
Trueman	13	3	59	2		24	5	70	2
Dexter	12	6	23	0		7	2	16	0
Allen	32	16	62	2		36	16	73	3
Lock	19	8	37	2		36	14	80	3
Parfitt	2	1	2	0					
Barrington	2	2	0	0					
Cowdrey						1	0	1	0

FALL OF WICKETS

	ENG	PAK	PAK			ENG	PAK	PAK	
1st	31	11	60		6th	202	199		
2nd	197	30	77		7th	206	207		
3rd	304	108	119		8th	206	207		
4th	330	144	127		9th	206	257		
5th	391	146	187		10th	246	274		

ENGLAND vs PAKISTAN

at Lord's on 21/06/1962
England won by 9 wickets

PAKISTAN

Hanif Mohammad	c Cowdrey b Trueman	13	lbw b Coldwell	24
Imtiaz Ahmed +	b Coldwell	1	(7) c Trueman b Coldwell	33
Saeed Ahmed	b Dexter	10	b Coldwell	20
Javed Burki *	c Dexter b Trueman	5	(5) lbw b Coldwell	101
Mushtaq Mohammad	c Cowdrey b Trueman	7	(4) c Millman b Trueman	1
Alimuddin	b Coldwell	9	(2) c Graveney b Allen	10
W.Mathias	b Trueman	15	(8) c Graveney b Trueman	1
Nasim-ul-Ghani	b Millman b Trueman	17	(6) c Graveney b Coldwell	101
Mahmood Hussain	c Cowdrey b Coldwell	1	b Coldwell	20
A.D'Souza	not out	6	not out	12
Mohammad Farooq	c Stewart b Trueman	13	b Trueman	1
Extras	(b 1,lb 2)	3	(b 6,lb 4,w 4)	14
TOTAL		100		355

ENGLAND

M.J.Stewart	c Imtiaz Ahmed b D'Souza	39	not out	34
M.C.Cowdrey	c D'Souza b Mohammad Farooq	41	c Imtiaz Ahmed b D'Souz	20
E.R.Dexter *	c Imtiaz Ahmed b Mohammad Farooq	65	not out	32
T.W.Graveney	b D'Souza	153		
K.F.Barrington	c Imtiaz Ahmed b Mohammad Farooq	0		
D.A.Allen	lbw b Mohammad Farooq	2		
P.H.Parfitt	b Mahmood Hussain	16		
G.Millman +	c Hanif Mohammad b Mahmood Hussain	7		
G.A.R.Lock	c Mathias b Saeed Ahmed	7		
F.S.Trueman	lbw b Saeed Ahmed	29		
L.J.Coldwell	not out	0		
Extras	(b 1,lb 5,nb 5)	11		0
TOTAL		370	(for 1 wkt)	86

ENGLAND

	O	M	R	W		O	M	R	W
Trueman	17.4	6	31	6		33.3	6	85	3
Coldwell	14	2	25	3		41	13	85	6
Dexter	12	3	41	1		15	4	44	0
Allen						15	6	41	1
Lock						14	1	78	0
Barrington						1	0	8	0

PAKISTAN

	O	M	R	W		O	M	R	W
Mahmood Hussain	40	9	106	2					
Mohammad Farooq	19	4	70	4		7	1	37	0
D'Souza	35.4	3	147	2		7	0	29	1
Nasim-ul-Ghani	2	0	15	0					
Saeed Ahmed	5	1	21	2		2	0	12	0
Mushtaq						1	0	8	0

FALL OF WICKETS

	PAK	ENG	PAK	ENG		PAK	ENG	PAK	ENG
1st	2	59	36	36	6th	51	221	299	
2nd	23	137	36		7th	77	247	300	
3rd	25	168	57		8th	78	290	333	
4th	31	168	77		9th	78	366	354	
5th	36	184	274		10th	100	370	355	

ENGLAND vs PAKISTAN

at Headingley on 05/07/1962
England won by an innings and 117 runs

ENGLAND

M.J.Stewart	lbw b Munir Malik	86
M.C.Cowdrey *	c Saeed Ahmed b Mahmood Hussain	7
E.R.Dexter	b Mahmood Hussain	20
T.W.Graveney	c Ijaz Butt b Munir Malik	37
K.F.Barrington	c Mushtaq b Mohammad Farooq	1
P.H.Parfitt	c & b Nasim-ul-Ghani	119
F.J.Titmus	c & b Munir Malik	2
J.T.Murray +	c & b Nasim-ul-Ghani	29
D.A.Allen	c Ijaz Butt b Munir Malik	62
F.S.Trueman	lbw b Munir Malik	20
J.B.Statham	not out	26
Extras	(b 6,lb 9,w 1,nb 3)	19
TOTAL		428

PAKISTAN

Alimuddin	c Barrington b Titmus	50	c Titmus b Allen	60
Ijaz Butt +	b Trueman	1	b Trueman	6
Saeed Ahmed	c Trueman b Statham	16	(5) c Cowdrey b Statham	54
Mushtaq Mohammad	c Murray b Dexter	27	c Trueman b Allen	8
Hanif Mohammad	b Statham	9	(6) c Barrington b Allen	4
Javed Burki *	b Trueman	1	(7) c Murray b Statham	21
Nasim-ul-Ghani	c Graveney b Titmus	5	(3) lbw b Statham	19
Mahmood Hussain	not out	0	c & b Dexter	0
Munir Malik	b Dexter	3	b Statham	4
Javed Akhtar	b Dexter	2	not out	2
Mohammad Farooq	c Statham b Dexter	8	c Statham b Trueman	0
Extras	(b 8,nb 1)	9	(lb 2)	2
TOTAL		131		180

PAKISTAN

	O	M	R	W		O	M	R	W
Mohammad Farooq	28	8	74	1					
Mahmood Hussain	25	5	87	2					
Munir Malik	49	11	128	5					
Javed Akhtar	16	5	52	0					
Nasim-ul-Ghani	14	2	68	2					

ENGLAND

	O	M	R	W		O	M	R	W
Trueman	23	6	55	2		10.4	3	33	2
Statham	20	9	40	2		20	3	50	4
Dexter	9.1	3	10	4		8	1	24	1
Allen	9	6	14	0		24	11	47	3
Titmus	4	1	3	2		11	2	20	0
Barrington						1	0	4	0

FALL OF WICKETS

	ENG	PAK	PAK			ENG	PAK	PAK	
1st	7	13	10		6th	180	118	163	
2nd	43	51	40		7th	247	118	178	
3rd	108	72	57		8th	346	121	179	
4th	117	88	130		9th	377	123	179	
5th	177	118	136		10th	428	131	180	

ENGLAND vs PAKISTAN
at Trent Bridge on 26/07/1962
Match drawn

ENGLAND

G.Pullar	lbw b Munir Malik	5			
Rev.D.S.Sheppard	c Imtiaz Ahmed b Intikhab Alam	83			
E.R.Dexter *	c Javed Burki b Fazal Mahmood	85			
T.W.Graveney	c Intikhab Alam b Fazal Mahmood	114			
P.H.Parfitt	not out	101			
B.R.Knight	c Saeed Ahmed b Fazal Mahmood	14			
F.J.Titmus	not out	11			
J.T.Murray +					
F.S.Trueman					
G.A.R.Lock					
J.B.Statham					
	Extras (lb 13,nb 2)	15			
	TOTAL (for 5 wkts dec)	428			

PAKISTAN

Hanif Mohammad	c Titmus b Trueman	0	c & b Trueman	3
Shahid Mahmood	c Graveney b Trueman	16	(7) c Statham b Dexter	9
Mushtaq Mohammad	c Lock b Knight	55	not out	100
Javed Burki *	c Murray b Knight	19	c sub b Titmus	28
Saeed Ahmed	c Murray b Statham	43	c Trueman b Lock	64
Imtiaz Ahmed +	lbw b Statham	15	lbw b Statham	1
Alimuddin	b Trueman	0	(2) c Murray b Statham	11
Nasim-ul-Ghani	c Murray b Knight	41	not out	0
Intikhab Alam	c Murray b Statham	14		
Fazal Mahmood	lbw b Knight	2		
Munir Malik	not out	0		
	Extras (b 2,lb 10,nb 2)	14		0
	TOTAL	219	(for 6 wkts)	216

PAKISTAN	O	M	R	W		O	M	R	W
Fazal Mahmood	60	15	130	3					
Munir Malik	34	4	130	1					
Nasim-ul-Ghani	20.2	1	76	0					
Intikhab Alam	14	3	49	1					
Shahid Mahmood	6	1	23	0					
Saeed Ahmed	2	0	5	0					

ENGLAND	O	M	R	W		O	M	R	W
Trueman	24	3	71	4		19	5	35	1
Statham	18.1	5	55	2		22	8	47	2
Knight	17	1	38	4		21	6	48	0
Lock	14	5	19	0		15	4	27	1
Titmus	13	2	22	0		16	7	29	1
Dexter						7	0	25	1
Parfitt						1	0	5	0

FALL OF WICKETS	ENG	PAK	PAK			ENG	PAK	PAK
1st	11	0	4		6th	120	216	
2nd	172	39	22		7th	171		
3rd	185	95	78		8th	213		
4th	369	98	185		9th	217		
5th	388	120	187		10th	219		

ENGLAND vs PAKISTAN
at The Oval on 16/08/1962
England won by 10 wickets

ENGLAND

Rev.D.S.Sheppard	c Fazal Mahmood b Nasim-ul-Ghani	57	not out	9
M.C.Cowdrey	c Hanif Mohammad b Fazal Mahmood	182		
E.R.Dexter *	b Fazal Mahmood	172		
K.F.Barrington	not out	50		
P.H.Parfitt	c Imtiaz Ahmed b D'Souza	3		
B.R.Knight	b D'Souza	3		
R.Illingworth	not out	2		
J.T.Murray +			(2) not out	14
D.A.Allen				
L.J.Coldwell				
J.D.F.Larter				
	Extras (b 4,lb 5,nb 2)	11	(b 4)	4
	TOTAL (for 5 wkts dec)	480	(for 0 wkts)	27

PAKISTAN

Ijaz Butt	c Cowdrey b Larter	10	run out	6
Imtiaz Ahmed +	c Murray b Knight	49	c Cowdrey b Larter	98
Mushtaq Mohammad	lbw b Larter	43	b Illingworth	72
Javed Burki *	b Larter	3	(6) c Parfitt b Knight	42
Saeed Ahmed	c Parfitt b Allen	21	c Knight b Allen	4
Hanif Mohammad	b Larter	46	(4) c Dexter b Larter	0
W.Mathias	c Murray b Larter	0	run out	48
A.D'Souza	c Parfitt b Coldwell	1	(10) not out	2
Nasim-ul-Ghani	c Murray b Coldwell	5	(8) b Coldwell	24
Intikhab Alam	not out	3	(9) b Larter	12
Fazal Mahmood	b Coldwell	0	b Larter	5
	Extras (nb 2)	2	(b 4,lb 5,nb 1)	10
	TOTAL	183		323

PAKISTAN	O	M	R	W		O	M	R	W
Fazal Mahmood	49	9	192	2		4	1	10	0
D'Souza	42	9	116	2		3	1	8	0
Intikhab Alam	38	5	109	0					
Javed Burki	1	0	12	0		1	0	2	0
Nasim-ul-Ghani	9	1	39	1					
Saeed Ahmed	1	0	1	0					
Mushtaq						0.3	0	3	0

ENGLAND	O	M	R	W		O	M	R	W
Coldwell	28	11	53	3		23	4	60	1
Larter	25	4	57	5		21.1	0	88	4
Allen	22	9	33	1		27	14	52	1
Knight	9	5	11	1		11	3	33	1
Illingworth	13	5	27	0		21	9	54	1
Dexter						6	1	16	0
Barrington						2	0	10	0

FALL OF WICKETS	ENG	PAK	PAK	ENG		ENG	PAK	PAK	ENG
1st	117	11	34		6th	168	250		
2nd	365	93	171		7th	175	294		
3rd	441	102	171		8th	179	316		
4th	444	115	180		9th	183	316		
5th	452	165	186		10th	183	323		

PAKISTAN vs AUSTRALIA
at Karachi on 24/10/1964
Match drawn

PAKISTAN

Khalid Ibadulla	c Grout b McKenzie	166	c Redpath b McKenzie	3
Abdul Kadir +	run out	95	hit wicket b Veivers	26
Saeed Ahmed	c Redpath b Martin	7	(4) c sub b Martin	35
Javed Burki	hit wicket b McKenzie	8	(5) c Grout b Cowper	62
Hanif Mohammad *	c & b McKenzie	2	(6) c McKenzie b Booth	40
Shafqat Rana	c Grout b McKenzie	0	(7) lbw b McKenzie	24
Nasim-ul-Ghani	c Redpath b Hawke	15	(8) c Grout b Veivers	22
Majid Khan	lbw b Martin	0		
Intikhab Alam	c Grout b McKenzie	53	not out	21
Asif Iqbal	c Booth b McKenzie	41	(3) c & b Simpson	36
Pervez Sajjad	not out	3		
	Extras (b 9,lb 12,nb 3)	24	(b 1,lb 6,nb 3)	10
	TOTAL	414	(for 8 wkts dec)	279

AUSTRALIA

W.M.Lawry	hit wicket b Majid Khan	7	c Ibadulla b Majid Khan	22
R.B.Simpson *	c Pervez Sajjad b Saeed Ahmed	153	c Ibadulla b Nasim-ul-Ghani	115
I.R.Redpath	lbw b Intikhab Alam	19	not out	40
P.J.P.Burge	c Majid Khan b Pervez Sajjad	54	not out	28
B.C.Booth	c Asif Iqbal b Majid Khan	15		
R.M.Cowper	b Asif Iqbal	16		
T.R.Veivers	st Abdul Kadir b Saeed Ahmed	25		
J.W.Martin	b Asif Iqbal	26		
A.T.W.Grout +	c Asif Iqbal b Saeed Ahmed	0		
G.D.McKenzie	lbw b Intikhab Alam	2		
N.J.N.Hawke	not out	8		
	Extras (b 12,lb 8,nb 7)	27	(lb 14,nb 8)	22
	TOTAL	352	(for 2 wkts)	227

AUSTRALIA	O	M	R	W		O	M	R	W
McKenzie	30	9	69	6		25	5	62	2
Hawke	20	2	84	1		6	2	20	0
Martin	36	11	106	2		17	4	42	1
Veivers	16	5	33	0		30	16	44	2
Simpson	30	8	69	0		20	5	47	1
Booth	5	2	15	0		13	4	18	1
Redpath	1	0	14	0					
Cowper						11	3	36	1

PAKISTAN	O	M	R	W		O	M	R	W
Majid Khan	30	9	55	2		16	3	42	1
Asif Iqbal	23.5	5	68	2		12	4	28	0
Pervez Sajjad	22	5	52	1		8	2	17	0
Intikhab Alam	28	5	83	2		16	3	48	0
Nasim-ul-Ghani	4	0	17	0		12	3	24	1
Saeed Ahmed	19	5	41	3		13	6	28	0
Ibadulla	7	3	9	0		2	0	14	0
Javed Burki						2	1	3	0
Shafqat Rana						1	0	1	0

FALL OF WICKETS	PAK	AUS	PAK	AUS		PAK	AUS	PAK	AUS
1st	249	10	13	54	6th	301	315	224	
2nd	266	78	65	173	7th	302	315	236	
3rd	284	194	81		8th	334	315	236	
4th	296	228	118		9th	383	320		
5th	296	257	202		10th	414	352		

AUSTRALIA vs PAKISTAN
at Melbourne on 04/12/1964
Match drawn

PAKISTAN

Abdul Kadir +	c Chappell b McKenzie	0	(7) c Jarman b Hawke	35
Mohammad Ilyas	run out	6	lbw b McKenzie	3
Saeed Ahmed	c Chappell b Hawke	80	c Chappell b McKenzie	24
Javed Burki	c Simpson b McKenzie	29	b Hawke	47
Hanif Mohammad *	c McKenzie b Sincock	104	st Jarman b Veivers	93
Nasim-ul-Ghani	b McKenzie	27	b Sincock	10
Asif Iqbal	c McKenzie b Hawke	1	(8) c Jarman b Hawke	15
Intikhab Alam	c Shepherd b Hawke	13	(9) c Simpson b Hawke	61
Afaq Hussain	not out	8	(10) not out	13
Arif Butt	c Chappell b Sincock	7	(1) c Jarman b McKenzie	12
Farooq Hamid	b Sincock	0	b McKenzie	3
	Extras (b 4,lb 4,w 3,nb 1)	12	(b 5,lb 2,w 2,nb 1)	10
	TOTAL	287		326

AUSTRALIA

R.B.Simpson *	b Arif Butt	47	c Hanif Mohammad b Arif Butt	1
W.M.Lawry	c Hanif Mohammad b Arif Butt	41	run out	19
I.M.Chappell	c Hanif Mohammad b Farooq Hamid	11		
B.K.Shepherd	c sub b Asif Iqbal	55	(3) not out	43
B.C.Booth	c Hanif Mohammad b Arif Butt	57		
R.M.Cowper	c Intikhab Alam b Saeed Ahmed	83		
T.R.Veivers	c Hanif Mohammad b Arif Butt	88	(4) not out	16
B.N.Jarman +	b Asif Iqbal	33		
D.J.Sincock	b Arif Butt	7		
G.D.McKenzie	b Arif Butt	1		
N.J.N.Hawke	not out	1		
	Extras (b 6,lb 3,w 1,nb 14)	24	(b 2,lb 4,w 2,nb 1)	9
	TOTAL	448	(for 2 wkts)	88

AUSTRALIA	O	M	R	W		O	M	R	W
McKenzie	22	5	66	3		24.4	1	74	4
Hawke	21	1	69	3		21	2	72	4
Sincock	17.6	0	67	3		28	5	102	1
Simpson	9	1	21	0					
Chappell	15	2	49	0		11	2	31	0
Veivers	3	2	3	0		12	4	37	1

PAKISTAN	O	M	R	W		O	M	R	W
Farooq Hamid	19	1	82	1		4	0	25	0
Asif Iqbal	19	1	90	2		2	0	25	0
Arif Butt	21.3	1	89	6		5.5	0	29	1
Afaq Hussain	9	1	45	0					
Intikhab Alam	10	0	51	0					
Saeed Ahmed	10	0	31	1					
Nasim-ul-Ghani	4	0	36	0					

FALL OF WICKETS	PAK	AUS	PAK	AUS		PAK	AUS	PAK	AUS
1st	0	81	6	12	6th	226	372	198	
2nd	18	105	37	55	7th	255	418	229	
3rd	112	105	46		8th	275	434	267	
4th	127	200	130		9th	287	446	323	
5th	225	233	152		10th	287	448		

NEW ZEALAND vs PAKISTAN
at Wellington on 22/01/1965
Match drawn

NEW ZEALAND

Batsman	1st innings		2nd innings	
S.G.Gedye	b Asif Iqbal	1	b Arif Butt	26
G.T.Dowling	c Javed Burki b Pervez Sajjad	29	b Arif Butt	19
B.W.Sinclair	c Nasim-ul-Ghani b Saeed Ahmed	65	c Saeed Ahmed b Pervez Sajjad	17
B.E.Congdon	c Naushad Ali b Asif Iqbal	42	b Asif Iqbal	30
J.R.Reid *	b Arif Butt	97	c Saeed Ahmed b Pervez Sajjad	14
S.N.McGregor	lbw b Asif Iqbal	11	not out	37
B.W.Yuile	b Asif Iqbal	4	(8) run out	7
A.E.Dick +	b Arif Butt	1		
R.C.Motz	b Asif Iqbal	0	(7) b Arif Butt	13
R.O.Collinge	not out	0		
F.J.Cameron	lbw b Arif Butt	0		
Extras	(b 2,lb 14)	16	(b 12,lb 3,nb 1)	16
TOTAL		266	(for 7 wkts dec)	179

PAKISTAN

Batsman	1st innings		2nd innings	
Naushad Ali +	run out	11	c & b Motz	3
Mohammad Ilyas	b Collinge	13	c Reid b Motz	4
Saeed Ahmed	c Congdon b Motz	11	c Yuile b Collinge	4
Javed Burki	b Motz	0	c Dick b Collinge	0
Hanif Mohammad *	b Collinge	5	b Collinge	25
Abdul Kadir	c & b Motz	46	b Motz	0
Nasim-ul-Ghani	c Cameron	16	c Dowling b Reid	23
Asif Iqbal	c Sinclair b Yuile	30	not out	52
Intikhab Alam	b Motz	28	not out	13
Arif Butt	b Yuile	20		
Pervez Sajjad	not out	1		
Extras	(b 2,lb 4)	6	(b 8,lb 6,w 1,nb 1)	16
TOTAL		187	(for 7 wkts)	140

PAKISTAN	O	M	R	W		O	M	R	W
Arif Butt	22.2	10	46	3		29	10	62	3
Asif Iqbal	25	11	48	5		20.4	6	33	1
Pervez Sajjad	24	7	48	1		25	5	61	2
Intikhab Alam	17	6	35	0		5	1	7	0
Saeed Ahmed	16	7	40	1		1	1	0	0
Nasim-ul-Ghani	3	1	5	0					
Mohammad Ilyas	7	1	28	0					

NEW ZEALAND	O	M	R	W		O	M	R	W
Collinge	17	6	51	2		13	3	43	3
Cameron	19	11	33	1		8	5	10	0
Motz	20	9	45	4		15	6	34	3
Yuile	26	16	28	2		8	2	21	0
Reid	13	6	24	0		8	3	16	1

FALL OF WICKETS	NZ	PAK	NZ	PAK		NZ	PAK	NZ	PAK
1st	1	26	35	3	6th	261	64	156	64
2nd	82	26	62	8	7th	266	114	179	104
3rd	114	26	83	10	8th	266	144		
4th	223	41	102	17	9th	266	179		
5th	261	47	140	19	10th	266	187		

NEW ZEALAND vs PAKISTAN
at Auckland on 29/01/1965
Match drawn

PAKISTAN

Batsman	1st innings		2nd innings	
Naushad Ali +	b Yuile	14	c Yuile b Reid	8
Abdul Kadir	c & b Yuile	12	b Collinge	58
Saeed Ahmed	c Dick b Yuile	17	c Dick b Cameron	16
Javed Burki	c sub b Cameron	63	c Congdon b Collinge	15
Nasim-ul-Ghani	c Dowling b Yuile	2	lbw b Cameron	14
Hanif Mohammad *	b Collinge	27	c Congdon b Collinge	27
Mohammad Ilyas	lbw b Cameron	10	lbw b Reid	36
Asif Iqbal	c Morgan b Collinge	3	b Cameron	0
Intikhab Alam	lbw b Cameron	45	c Morgan b Cameron	7
Arif Butt	b Cameron	20	c Dick b Cameron	0
Pervez Sajjad	not out	2	not out	0
Extras	(b 5,lb 4,nb 2)	11	(b 9,lb 8,nb 9)	26
TOTAL		226		207

NEW ZEALAND

Batsman	1st innings		2nd innings	
G.T.Dowling	lbw b Asif Iqbal	0	c Asif Iqbal b Nasim-ul-Ghani	62
B.E.Congdon	b Asif Iqbal	9	c Intikhab Alam b Pervez Sajjad	42
R.W.Morgan	b Pervez Sajjad	66	b Asif Iqbal	5
J.R.Reid *	run out	52	b Pervez Sajjad	11
S.N.McGregor	c Hanif Mohammad b Saeed Ahmed	1	c Saeed Ahmed b Pervez Sajjad	0
P.G.Z.Harris	c Hanif Mohammad b Asif Iqbal	1	b Pervez Sajjad	0
B.W.Yuile	b Asif Iqbal	0	(8) not out	30
A.E.Dick +	b Saeed Ahmed	19	(9) not out	3
R.C.Motz	c Naushad Ali b Asif Iqbal	31	(7) c Intikhab Alam b Pervez Sajjad	0
R.O.Collinge	b Arif Butt	13		
F.J.Cameron	not out	5		
Extras	(b 7,lb 8,nb 2)	17	(b 6,lb 2,nb 5)	13
TOTAL		214	(for 7 wkts)	166

NEW ZEALAND	O	M	R	W		O	M	R	W
Collinge	28	8	57	2		22.1	9	41	3
Motz	12	4	15	0		6	1	15	0
Cameron	26	11	36	4		23	11	34	5
Yuile	54	38	43	4		30	15	39	0
Reid	20	14	26	0		19	7	52	2
Harris	7	2	14	0					
Morgan	7	3	24	0					

PAKISTAN	O	M	R	W		O	M	R	W
Arif Butt	17.4	4	43	1		1	0	19	0
Asif Iqbal	27	6	52	5		18	4	40	1
Intikhab Alam	29	10	52	0		15	7	17	0
Pervez Sajjad	15	4	35	1		25	7	42	5
Saeed Ahmed	10	4	15	2		9	3	14	0
Mohammad Ilyas						2	0	12	0
Nasim-ul-Ghani						5	2	9	1

FALL OF WICKETS	PAK	NZ	PAK	NZ		PAK	NZ	PAK	NZ
1st	19	9	25	68	6th	151	127	197	102
2nd	44	25	51	82	7th	156	148	200	150
3rd	70	101	75	102	8th	159	195	207	
4th	99	113	95	102	9th	211	195	207	
5th	129	125	139	102	10th	226	214	207	

NEW ZEALAND vs PAKISTAN
at Christchurch on 12/02/1965
Match drawn

PAKISTAN

Batsman	1st innings		2nd innings	
Khalid Ibadulla	c Ward b Cameron	28	b Collinge	9
Naushad Ali +	c Truscott b Motz	12	c Collinge b Yuile	20
Javed Burki	b Collinge	4	(4) b Collinge	12
Saeed Ahmed	c Ward b Cameron	1	lbw b Reid	87
Hanif Mohammad *	c & b Collinge	10	not out	100
Mohammad Ilyas	st Ward b Yuile	88	b Yuile	13
Nasim-ul-Ghani	b Motz	5	c Collinge	12
Asif Iqbal	c Motz b Yuile	3	c Bartlett b Cameron	20
Intikhab Alam	c Sinclair b Yuile	27	c Reid b Yuile	15
Pervez Sajjad	b Motz	9	not out	0
Mufasir-ul-Haq	not out	8		
Extras	(lb 4,nb 7)	11	(b 9,lb 6,w 1,nb 5)	21
TOTAL		206	(for 8 wkts dec)	309

NEW ZEALAND

Batsman	1st innings		2nd innings	
B.E.Congdon	b Mufasir-ul-Haq	21	c Hanif Mohammad b Asif Iqbal	8
P.B.Truscott	lbw b Asif Iqbal	3	c & b Asif Iqbal	26
B.W.Sinclair	c Naushad Ali b Intikhab Alam	46	(3) not out	7
R.W.Morgan	c Nasim-ul-Ghani b Mufasir-ul-Haq	19	(3) c & b Mufasir-ul-Haq	97
J.R.Reid *	b Asif Iqbal	27	(4) c Mohammad Ilyas b Intikhab Alam	28
B.W.Yuile	c Hanif Mohammad b Nasim-ul-Ghani	7	(5) c Mohammad Ilyas b Pervez Sajjad	42
G.A.Bartlett	b Pervez Sajjad	1	not out	4
R.C.Motz	c Naushad Ali b Pervez Sajjad	21		
J.T.Ward +	c Naushad Ali b Asif Iqbal	2		
R.O.Collinge	c Hanif Mohammad b Asif Iqbal	32		
F.J.Cameron	not out	8		
Extras	(b 3,lb 3,w 1,nb 8)	15	(b 7,nb 4)	11
TOTAL		202	(for 5 wkts)	223

NEW ZEALAND	O	M	R	W		O	M	R	W
Bartlett	18	6	47	0		14.3	2	46	0
Collinge	12	3	23	2		17	3	50	3
Cameron	24	15	29	2		14	2	61	1
Motz	18	4	48	3		17	7	43	0
Yuile	11	3	48	3		20	9	64	3
Reid						11	5	24	1

PAKISTAN	O	M	R	W		O	M	R	W
Asif Iqbal	25.5	9	46	4		16	6	29	2
Mufasir-ul-Haq	29	11	50	2		8	1	34	1
Ibadulla	9	5	17	0		3	0	12	0
Pervez Sajjad	21	6	53	2		21	8	33	1
Intikhab Alam	7	1	17	1		21	6	60	1
Nasim-ul-Ghani	4	3	3	1		3	1	5	0
Saeed Ahmed	3	2	1	0		8	1	25	0
Mohammad Ilyas						3	0	14	0

FALL OF WICKETS	PAK	NZ	PAK	NZ		PAK	NZ	PAK	NZ
1st	36	7	27	18	6th	78	112	222	
2nd	41	34	58	41	7th	81	129	254	
3rd	42	76	97	98	8th	132	137	300	
4th	62	81	159	179	9th	160	178		
5th	66	83	199	219	10th	206	202		

PAKISTAN vs NEW ZEALAND
at Rawalpindi on 27/03/1965
Pakistan won by an innings and 64 runs

NEW ZEALAND

Batsman	1st innings		2nd innings	
G.T.Dowling	b Mohammad Farooq	5	b Majid Khan	0
T.W.Jarvis	c Naushad Ali b Asif Iqbal	4	c Majid Khan b Salahuddin	17
B.W.Sinclair	b Mohammad Farooq	22	c Salahuddin b Pervez Sajjad	21
J.R.Reid *	b Salahuddin	4	(6) c Asif Iqbal b Mohammad Farooq	0
R.W.Morgan	c Mohammad Farooq b Salahuddin	0	(4) b Pervez Sajjad	6
B.Sutcliffe	b Pervez Sajjad	7	(8) b Pervez Sajjad	0
B.R.Taylor	b Pervez Sajjad	76	(9) not out	7
A.E.Dick +	b Pervez Sajjad	4	(7) b Mohammad Farooq	0
V.Pollard	lbw b Pervez Sajjad	15	(10) c Hanif Mohammad b Pervez Sajjad	0
B.W.Yuile	not out	11	run out	1
R.O.Collinge	c Mohammad Ilyas b Intikhab Alam	15	c Asif Iqbal b Mohammad Farooq	8
Extras	(b 1,lb 7,nb 8)	16	(b 6,lb 10,nb 3)	19
TOTAL		175		79

PAKISTAN

Mohammad Ilyas	c Pollard b Reid	56
Naushad Ali +	b Reid	2
Saeed Ahmed	b Taylor	68
Javed Burki	b Collinge	6
Asif Iqbal	b Taylor	51
Hanif Mohammad *	b Pollard	16
Majid Khan	b Collinge	11
Salahuddin	not out	34
Intikhab Alam	c Yuile b Reid	1
Pervez Sajjad	c Dick b Taylor	18
Mohammad Farooq	c Dowling b Morgan	47
Extras	(b 5,lb 3)	8
TOTAL		318

PAKISTAN	O	M	R	W		O	M	R	W
Asif Iqbal	4	1	7	1		4	3	4	0
Majid Khan	4	2	11	0		5	2	9	1
Mohammad Farooq	16	3	57	2		12	3	25	3
Salahuddin	15	5	36	2		11	5	16	1
Pervez Sajjad	16	5	42	4		12	8	5	4
Intikhab Alam	1.5	0	6	1		3	2	1	0

NEW ZEALAND	O	M	R	W		O	M	R	W
Collinge	21	9	36	2					
Taylor	15	3	38	3					
Pollard	22	6	80	1					
Reid	34	18	80	3					
Yuile	16	5	42	0					
Morgan	8.3	1	34	1					

FALL OF WICKETS	NZ	PAK	NZ		NZ	PAK	NZ
1st	5	13	3	6th	91	215	59
2nd	24	127	42	7th	91	217	59
3rd	34	135	57	8th	143	220	59
4th	39	145	58	9th	148	253	59
5th	39	177	59	10th	175	318	79

PAKISTAN vs NEW ZEALAND
at Lahore on 02/04/1965
Match drawn

PAKISTAN

Mohammad Ilyas	c Dick b Cameron	17	c sub b Taylor		4
Naushad Ali +	c Collinge b Cameron	9	b Cameron		29
Saeed Ahmed	b Pollard	23	(8) c & b Sutcliffe		4
Salahuddin	c Dick b Taylor	23	(3) b Cameron		25
Javed Burki	c Dick b Cameron	10	(4) c Reid b Sinclair		14
Hanif Mohammad *	not out	20			
Majid Khan	c Reid b Taylor	80	(5) c Reid b Sutcliffe		44
Asif Iqbal	lbw b Cameron	4	(6) c Sutcliffe b Pollard		43
Intikhab Alam	not out	10	(7) not out		5
Pervez Sajjad	(9) st sub b Sinclair	16			
Mohammad Farooq	(10) not out	0			
Extras	(b 2,lb 3,nb 1)	6	(b 6,lb 3,nb 1)		10
TOTAL	(for 7 wkts dec)	385	(for 8 wkts dec)		194

NEW ZEALAND

G.T.Dowling	c Naushad Ali b Mohammad Farooq	83	
T.W.Jarvis	b Salahuddin	55	
B.W.Sinclair	c Hanif Mohammad b Intikhab Alam	130	
J.R.Reid *	lbw b Majid Khan	88	
R.W.Morgan	c Majid Khan b Mohammad Farooq	50	
B.Sutcliffe	b Asif Iqbal	23	
B.R.Taylor	not out	25	
V.Pollard	not out	8	
A.E.Dick +			
F.J.Cameron			
R.O.Collinge			
Extras	(b 5,lb 8,nb 7)	20	
TOTAL	(for 6 wkts dec)	482	

NEW ZEALAND	O	M	R	W	O	M	R	W
Collinge	27	6	85	0	11	4	11	0
Cameron	44	12	90	4	11	5	15	2
Reid	9	3	21	0				
Pollard	42	20	76	1	19	6	41	1
Morgan	17	8	46	0	8	1	32	0
Taylor	28	9	61	2	7	3	15	1
Sinclair					10	3	32	2
Sutcliffe					11	4	38	2

PAKISTAN	O	M	R	W	O	M	R	W
Asif Iqbal	33	12	85	1				
Majid Khan	24	3	57	1				
Mohammad Farooq	41	12	71	2				
Pervez Sajjad	43	18	72	0				
Salahuddin	33	8	76	1				
Intikhab Alam	33	5	92	1				
Saeed Ahmed	1	0	1	0				
Mohammad Ilyas	1	0	8	0				

FALL OF WICKETS	PAK	NZ	PAK			PAK	NZ	PAK
1st	14	136	5		6th	338	469	169
2nd	45	164	61		7th	362		173
3rd	49	342	74		8th			194
4th	62	391	99		9th			
5th	121	439	169		10th			

PAKISTAN vs NEW ZEALAND
at Karachi on 09/04/1965
Pakistan won by 8 wickets

NEW ZEALAND

T.W.Jarvis	lbw b Salahuddin	27	b Asif Iqbal		0
A.E.Dick +	c Naushad Ali b Asif Iqbal	33	b Majid Khan		2
B.W.Sinclair	c Majid Khan b Mohammad Farooq	24	lbw b Mohammad Farooq		14
J.R.Reid *	b Asif Iqbal	128	c Majid Khan b Salahuddin		76
R.W.Morgan	lbw b Saeed Ahmed	13	c Salahuddin b Pervez Sajjad		25
B.E.Congdon	c sub b Intikhab Alam	17	(8) b Intikhab Alam		57
B.R.Taylor	c Pervez Sajjad b Intikhab Alam	6	c Hanif Mohammad b Intikhab Alam		3
V.Pollard	b Mohammad Farooq	1	(9) b Salahuddin		4
R.C.Motz	b Intikhab Alam	0	(10) lbw b Intikhab Alam		2
B.Sutcliffe	not out	13	(6) c Majid Khan b Intikhab Alam		18
F.J.Cameron	c Naushad Ali b Asif Iqbal	9	not out		10
Extras	(lb 2,nb 12)	14	(b 1,lb 3,nb 8)		12
TOTAL		285			223

PAKISTAN

Mohammad Ilyas	lbw b Motz	20	st Dick b Reid		126
Naushad Ali +	c Taylor b Motz	9	c sub b Pollard		39
Saeed Ahmed	b Cameron	172	not out		19
Javed Burki	c Morgan b Pollard	29	not out		4
Hanif Mohammad *	b Reid	1			
Majid Khan	run out	12			
Salahuddin	not out	11			
Asif Iqbal	lbw b Cameron	4			
Intikhab Alam	c Dick b Congdon	3			
Pervez Sajjad	not out	8			
Mohammad Farooq					
Extras	(b 17,lb 12,nb 9)	38	(b 8,lb 2,w 1,nb 3)		14
TOTAL	(for 8 wkts dec)	307	(for 2 wkts)		202

PAKISTAN	O	M	R	W	O	M	R	W
Asif Iqbal	11	3	35	3	14	7	29	1
Majid Khan	20	1	63	0	8	0	30	1
Mohammad Farooq	21	5	59	2	17	5	41	1
Salahuddin	6	4	3	1	26	5	56	2
Pervez Sajjad	11	4	29	0	8	3	16	1
Intikhab Alam	24	6	53	3	26.4	10	39	4
Saeed Ahmed	10	3	29	1				

NEW ZEALAND	O	M	R	W	O	M	R	W
Motz	22	11	35	2				
Cameron	28	7	70	2	11	3	29	0
Pollard	27	13	41	1	18	3	52	1
Taylor	15	2	54	0	14	3	43	0
Morgan	13	2	31	0	7	2	31	0
Reid	10	5	28	1	1	0	6	1
Congdon	6	3	10	1	9	2	27	0

FALL OF WICKETS	NZ	PAK	NZ	PAK		NZ	PAK	NZ	PAK
1st	50	21	0	121	6th	220	286	133	
2nd	76	84	10	198	7th	226	290	151	
3rd	123	198	45		8th	233	297	157	
4th	167	201	93		9th	268		160	
5th	206	248	129		10th	285		223	

ENGLAND vs PAKISTAN
at Lord's on 27/07/1967
Match drawn

ENGLAND

C.Milburn	c Wasim Bari b Asif Iqbal	3	c Asif Iqbal b Majid Khan		32
W.E.Russell	b Intikhab Alam	43	b Majid Khan		12
K.F.Barrington	c Wasim Bari b Asif Iqbal	148	b Intikhab Alam		14
T.W.Graveney	b Salim Altaf	81	c Ibadulla b Asif Iqbal		30
B.L.D'Oliveira	c Intikhab Alam b Mushtaq	59	not out		81
D.B.Close *	c sub b Salim Altaf	4	st Wasim Bari b Nasim-ul-Ghani		36
J.T.Murray	b Salim Altaf	0	c & b Nasim-ul-Ghani		0
R.Illingworth	b Asif Iqbal	4	c & b Nasim-ul-Ghani		9
K.Higgs	lbw b Mushtaq	14	c Hanif Mohammad b Intikhab Alam		1
J.A.Snow	b Mushtaq	0	c Hanif Mohammad b Mushtaq		7
R.N.S.Hobbs	not out	1	not out		1
Extras	(lb 5,nb 7)	12	(b 12,lb 5,nb 1)		18
TOTAL		369	(for 9 wkts dec)		241

PAKISTAN

Khalid Ibadulla	b Higgs	8	c Close b Illingworth		32
Javed Burki	lbw b Higgs	31	c & b Barrington		13
Mushtaq Mohammad	c Murray b Higgs	4	(4) not out		30
Hanif Mohammad *	not out	187			
Majid Khan	c & b Hobbs	5	(3) c Close b Barrington		5
Nasim-ul-Ghani	c D'Oliveira b Snow	4			
Saeed Ahmed	c Graveney b Snow	6	(5) not out		6
Intikhab Alam	lbw b Illingworth	17			
Asif Iqbal	c Barrington b Illingworth	76			
Wasim Bari +	c Close b Barrington	13			
Salim Altaf	c Milburn b Snow	2			
Extras	(b 1,lb 2)	3	(b 1,lb 1)		2
TOTAL		354	(for 3 wkts)		88

PAKISTAN	O	M	R	W	O	M	R	W
Salim Altaf	33	6	74	3	0.3	0	4	0
Asif Iqbal	28	10	76	3	21	5	50	1
Ibadulla	3	0	5	0				
Majid Khan	11	2	28	0	10	1	32	0
Nasim-ul-Ghani	12	1	36	0	13	3	32	3
Intikhab Alam	29	3	86	1	30	7	70	2
Mushtaq	11.3	3	23	3	16	4	35	1
Saeed Ahmed	11	3	29	0				

ENGLAND	O	M	R	W	O	M	R	W
Snow	45.1	11	120	3	4	2	6	0
Higgs	39	12	81	3	6	3	6	0
D'Oliveira	15	7	17	0				
Illingworth	31	14	48	2	15	11	10	1
Hobbs	35	16	46	1	16	9	28	0
Barrington	11	1	29	1	13	2	23	2
Close	6	3	10	0	8	5	13	0

FALL OF WICKETS	ENG	PAK	ENG	PAK		ENG	PAK	PAK	PAK
1st	5	19	33	27	6th	287	99	201	
2nd	82	25	48	39	7th	292	139	215	
3rd	283	67	76	77	8th	352	269	220	
4th	283	76	95		9th	354	310	239	
5th	287	91	199		10th	369	354		

ENGLAND vs PAKISTAN
at Trent Bridge on 10/08/1967
England won by 10 wickets

PAKISTAN

Khalid Ibadulla	c Knott b Higgs	2	c Knott b Close		5
Javed Burki	lbw b Arnold	1	c Knott b Higgs		3
Saeed Ahmed	c Knott b Arnold	44	c Arnold b Underwood		68
Mushtaq Mohammad	b Higgs	29	(6) lbw b Underwood		0
Hanif Mohammad *	c Titmus b Underwood	16	c Knott b Higgs		4
Majid Khan	lbw b D'Oliveira	17	(7) c Close b Underwood		5
Asif Iqbal	b Higgs	18	(8) c sub b Titmus		1
Nasim-ul-Ghani	run out	11	(4) c Close b Titmus		6
Intikhab Alam	c Knott b Arnold	0	c Knott b Underwood		16
Wasim Bari +	b Higgs	0	c Barrington b Underwood		3
Niaz Ahmed	not out	0	not out		1
Extras	(lb 1,nb 1)	2	(lb 1,nb 1)		2
TOTAL		140			114

ENGLAND

G.Boycott	b Asif Iqbal	15	not out		1
M.C.Cowdrey	c Majid Khan b Nasim-ul-Ghani	14	not out		2
K.F.Barrington	not out	109			
T.W.Graveney	c Niaz Ahmed b Ibadulla	28			
B.L.D'Oliveira	run out	7			
D.B.Close *	c Wasim Bari b Niaz Ahmed	41			
F.J.Titmus	lbw b Asif Iqbal	13			
A.P.E.Knott +	c Hanif Mohammad b Mushtaq	0			
G.G.Arnold	lbw b Niaz Ahmed	14			
K.Higgs	not out	0			
D.L.Underwood					
Extras	(b 3,lb 3,w 1,nb 4)	11			0
TOTAL	(for 8 wkts dec)	252	(for 0 wkts)		3

ENGLAND	O	M	R	W	O	M	R	W
Arnold	17	5	35	3	5	3	5	0
Higgs	19	12	35	4	6	1	8	2
D'Oliveira	18	9	27	1				
Close	3	0	12	0	4	1	11	1
Titmus	7	3	12	0	23	11	36	2
Underwood	5	2	17	1	26	8	52	5

PAKISTAN	O	M	R	W	O	M	R	W
Asif Iqbal	39	10	72	2				
Niaz Ahmed	37	10	72	2				
Nasim-ul-Ghani	8	2	20	1				
Saeed Ahmed	2	2	0	0	1	1	0	0
Intikhab Alam	7	2	19	0				
Ibadulla	32	13	42	1	1.1	0	3	0
Mushtaq	9.3	3	16	1				

FALL OF WICKETS	PAK	ENG	PAK	ENG		PAK	ENG	PAK	ENG
1st	3	21	4		6th	116	213	89	
2nd	21	31	35		7th	140	214	93	
3rd	65	75	60		8th	140	251	99	
4th	82	92	71		9th	140		113	
5th	104	187	76		10th	140		114	

ENGLAND vs PAKISTAN
at The Oval on 24/08/1967
England won by 8 wickets

PAKISTAN

Hanif Mohammad *	b Higgs	3	(5) c Knott b Higgs	18
Mohammad Ilyas	b Arnold	2	c Cowdrey b Higgs	1
Saeed Ahmed	b Arnold	38	c Knott b Higgs	0
Majid Khan	c Knott b Arnold	6	b Higgs	0
Mushtaq Mohammad	lbw b Higgs	66	(7) c D'Oliveira b Underwood	17
Javed Burki	c D'Oliveira b Titmus	27	(8) b Underwood	7
Ghulam Abbas	c Underwood b Titmus	12	(6) c Knott b Higgs	0
Asif Iqbal	c Close b Arnold	26	(9) st Knott b Close	146
Intikhab Alam	b Higgs	20	(10) b Titmus	51
Wasim Bari +	c Knott b Arnold	1	(1) b Titmus	12
Salim Altaf	not out	7	not out	0
	Extras (b 5,lb 2,nb 1)	8	(b 1,lb 1,nb 1)	3
	TOTAL	**216**		**255**

ENGLAND

M.C.Cowdrey	c Mushtaq b Majid Khan	16	c Intikhab Alam b Asif Iqbal	9
D.B.Close *	c Wasim Bari b Asif Iqbal	6	b Asif Iqbal	8
K.F.Barrington	c Wasim Bari b Salim Altaf	142	not out	13
T.W.Graveney	c Majid Khan b Intikhab Alam	77		
D.L.Amiss	c Saeed Ahmed b Asif Iqbal	26	(4) not out	3
B.L.D'Oliveira	c Mushtaq b Asif Iqbal	3		
F.J.Titmus	c sub b Mushtaq	65		
A.P.E.Knott +	c Mohammad Ilyas b Mushtaq	28		
G.G.Arnold	c Majid Khan b Mushtaq	59		
K.Higgs	b Mushtaq	7		
D.L.Underwood	not out	2		
	Extras (lb 4,nb 5)	9	(nb 1)	1
	TOTAL	**440**	(for 2 wkts)	**34**

ENGLAND

	O	M	R	W		O	M	R	W
Arnold	29	9	58	5		17	5	49	0
Higgs	29	10	61	3		20	7	58	5
D'Oliveira	17	6	41	0					
Close	5	1	15	0		1	0	4	1
Titmus	13	6	21	2		29.1	8	64	2
Underwood	9	5	12	0		26	12	48	2
Barrington						8	2	29	0

PAKISTAN

	O	M	R	W		O	M	R	W
Salim Altaf	40	14	94	1		2	1	8	0
Asif Iqbal	42	19	66	3		4	1	14	2
Majid Khan	10	0	29	1					
Mushtaq	26.4	7	80	4					
Saeed Ahmed	21	5	69	0		2	0	7	0
Intikhab Alam	28	3	93	1					
Hanif Mohammad						0.2	0	4	0

FALL OF WICKETS

	PAK	ENG	PAK	ENG		PAK	ENG	PAK	ENG
1st	3	16	1	17	6th	155	276	41	
2nd	5	35	5	20	7th	182	323	53	
3rd	17	176	5		8th	188	416	65	
4th	74	270	26		9th	194	437	255	
5th	138	276	26		10th	216	440	255	

PAKISTAN vs ENGLAND
at Lahore on 21/02/1969
Match drawn

ENGLAND

J.H.Edrich	c Asif Masood b Intikhab Alam	54	c Majid Khan b Asif Masood	8
R.M.Prideaux	c Shafqat Rana b Asif Masood	9	b Majid Khan	5
M.C.Cowdrey *	c Wasim Bari b Majid Khan	100	c Wasim Bari b Asif Masood	12
T.W.Graveney	c Asif Iqbal b Intikhab Alam	13	run out	12
K.W.R.Fletcher	c Intikhab Alam b Saeed Ahmed	20	b Majid Khan	83
B.L.D'Oliveira	c Mohammad Ilyas b Intikhab Alam	26	c Mushtaq b Saeed Ahmed	5
A.P.E.Knott +	lbw b Saeed Ahmed	52	b Asif Masood	30
D.L.Underwood	c Intikhab Alam b Saeed Ahmed	0	c Aftab Gul b Mushtaq	6
D.J.Brown	b Saeed Ahmed	7	not out	44
P.I.Pocock	b Intikhab Alam	12	b Saeed Ahmed	1
R.M.H.Cottam	not out	4		
	Extras (b 4,lb 2,nb 3)	9	(b 6,lb 9,nb 4)	1
	TOTAL	**306**	(for 9 wkts dec)	**225**

PAKISTAN

Mohammad Ilyas	lbw b Brown	0	c Fletcher b Brown	1
Aftab Gul	c D'Oliveira b Brown	12	c Pocock b Underwood	2
Saeed Ahmed *	c Knott b D'Oliveira	18	b Cottam	39
Asif Iqbal	c D'Oliveira b Cottam	70	c & b Cottam	0
Mushtaq Mohammad	c Fletcher b Cottam	4	not out	34
Hanif Mohammad	b Brown	7	(7) not out	23
Majid Khan	c Pocock b Underwood	18	(6) c Pocock b Brown	68
Shafqat Rana	c Knott b Cottam	30		
Intikhab Alam	c D'Oliveira b Pocock	12		
Wasim Bari +	not out	14		
Asif Masood	b Cottam	11		
	Extras (b 8,lb 4,nb 1)	13	(b 3,lb 5,nb 1)	9
	TOTAL	**209**	(for 5 wkts)	**203**

PAKISTAN

	O	M	R	W		O	M	R	W
Asif Masood	21	5	59	1		25	4	68	3
Asif Iqbal	4	2	11	0					
Majid Khan	18	8	25	1		20	5	41	2
Intikhab Alam	40.1	8	117	4		15	5	29	0
Saeed Ahmed	20	5	64	4		15.5	3	44	2
Mushtaq	14	6	15	0		9	1	24	1
Shafqat Rana	2	0	6	0					

ENGLAND

	O	M	R	W		O	M	R	W
Brown	14	0	43	3		15	4	47	2
Cottam	22.2	5	50	4		13	1	35	2
D'Oliveira	8	2	28	1					
Underwood	16	4	36	1		19	8	29	1
Pocock	10	3	39	1		16	4	41	0
Fletcher						8	2	31	0
Graveney						6	0	11	0
Prideaux						2	2	0	0

FALL OF WICKETS

	ENG	PAK	ENG	PAK		ENG	PAK	ENG	PAK
1st	41	0	8	6	6th	246	119	136	
2nd	92	32	25	71	7th	257	145	151	
3rd	113	32	41	71	8th	287	176	201	
4th	182	52	46	71	9th	294	187	225	
5th	219	72	68	156	10th	306	209		

PAKISTAN vs ENGLAND
at Dacca on 28/02/1969
Match drawn

PAKISTAN

Mohammad Ilyas	c Knott b Snow	20	c Snow b Cottam	21
Salahuddin	c Brown b Snow	6	lbw b Underwood	5
Saeed Ahmed *	b Brown	19	(5) c Knott b Underwood	33
Asif Iqbal	b Brown	44	(3) b Underwood	16
Mushtaq Mohammad	c Cottam b Snow	52	(4) c D'Oliveira b Underwood	31
Majid Khan	c Knott b Brown	27	not out	49
Hanif Mohammad	b Snow	8	lbw b Underwood	8
Intikhab Alam	lbw b Underwood	25	not out	19
Wasim Bari +	c Knott b Cottam	14		
Niaz Ahmed	not out	16		
Pervez Sajjad	b Cottam	2		
	Extras (b 4,lb 4,nb 5)	13	(lb 5,nb 8)	13
	TOTAL	**246**	(for 6 wkts dec)	**195**

ENGLAND

J.H.Edrich	c Mushtaq b Intikhab Alam	24	not out	12
R.M.Prideaux	c Hanif Mohammad b Pervez Sajjad	4	not out	18
T.W.Graveney	b Pervez Sajjad	46		
K.W.R.Fletcher	c Hanif Mohammad b Saeed Ahmed	16		
M.C.Cowdrey *	lbw b Pervez Sajjad	7		
B.L.D'Oliveira	not out	114		
A.P.E.Knott +	c & b Pervez Sajjad	2		
D.J.Brown	c Hanif Mohammad b Saeed Ahmed	4		
J.A.Snow	c Majid Khan b Niaz Ahmed	9		
D.L.Underwood	c Mohammad Ilyas b Mushtaq	22		
R.M.H.Cottam	c Hanif Mohammad b Saeed Ahmed	4		
	Extras (b 14,lb 8)	22	(b 2,nb 1)	3
	TOTAL	**274**	(for 0 wkts)	**33**

ENGLAND

	O	M	R	W		O	M	R	W
Snow	25	5	70	4		12	7	15	0
Brown	23	8	51	3		6	1	18	0
Underwood	27	13	45	1		44	15	94	5
Cottam	27.1	6	52	2		30	17	43	0
D'Oliveira	8	1	15	0		9	2	12	0

PAKISTAN

	O	M	R	W		O	M	R	W
Niaz Ahmed	10	4	20	1		2	0	2	0
Majid Khan	11	4	15	0					
Pervez Sajjad	37	8	75	4		3	2	1	0
Saeed Ahmed	37.4	15	59	3		3	2	4	0
Intikhab Alam	26	7	65	1		4	0	19	0
Mushtaq	11	3	18	1					
Asif Iqbal						4	2	2	0
Hanif Mohammad						3	2	1	0
Mohammad Ilyas						1	0	1	0

FALL OF WICKETS

	PAK	ENG	PAK	ENG		PAK	ENG	PAK	ENG
1st	16	17	8		6th	184	117	147	
2nd	39	61	48		7th	186	130		
3rd	55	96	50		8th	211	170		
4th	123	100	97		9th	237	236		
5th	168	113	129		10th	246	274		

PAKISTAN vs ENGLAND
at Karachi on 06/03/1969
Match drawn

ENGLAND

C.Milburn	c Wasim Bari b Asif Masood	139
J.H.Edrich	c Saeed Ahmed b Intikhab Alam	32
T.W.Graveney	c Asif Iqbal b Intikhab Alam	105
M.C.Cowdrey *	c Hanif Mohammad b Intikhab Alam	14
K.W.R.Fletcher	b Mushtaq	38
B.L.D'Oliveira	c Aftab Gul b Mushtaq	16
A.P.E.Knott +	not out	96
J.A.Snow	b Asif Masood	9
D.J.Brown	not out	25
D.L.Underwood		
R.N.S.Hobbs		
	Extras (b 5,lb 12,nb 11)	28
	TOTAL (for 7 wkts)	**502**

PAKISTAN

Aftab Gul
Hanif Mohammad
Mushtaq Mohammad
Asif Iqbal
Saeed Ahmed *
Majid Khan
Shafqat Rana
Intikhab Alam
Wasim Bari +
Asif Masood
Sarfraz Nawaz

	Extras	
	TOTAL	

PAKISTAN

	O	M	R	W		O	M	R	W
Asif Masood	28	2	94	2					
Majid Khan	20	5	51	0					
Sarfraz Nawaz	34	6	78	0					
Intikhab Alam	48	4	129	3					
Saeed Ahmed	22	5	53	0					
Mushtaq	23.1	5	69	2					

ENGLAND

	O	M	R	W		O	M	R	W

FALL OF WICKETS

	ENG			ENG
1st	78	6th	374
2nd	234	7th	427
3rd	286	8th	
4th	309	9th	
5th	360	10th	

PAKISTAN vs NEW ZEALAND
at Karachi on 24/10/1969
Match drawn

PAKISTAN

Batsman	Dismissal	R	Dismissal	R
Hanif Mohammad	c Yuile b Howarth	22	lbw b Yuile	35
Sadiq Mohammad	b Howarth	69	run out	37
Younis Ahmed	c Dowling b Howarth	8	(5) c Dowling b Cunis	62
Mushtaq Mohammad	b Yuile	14	c Murray b Howarth	19
Zaheer Abbas	c Murray b Yuile	12	(6) c Burgess b Hadlee	27
Asif Iqbal	st Wadsworth b Howarth	22	(3) c Hastings b Yuile	0
Intikhab Alam *	c Congdon b Howarth	0	(8) c Yuile b Cunis	47
Wasim Bari +	c Murray b Hadlee	15	(7) c Congdon b Howarth	19
Mohammad Nazir	not out	29	not out	17
Pervez Sajjad	b Hadlee	0		
Asif Masood	c Howarth b Hadlee	17		
Extras	(b 2,lb 10)	12	(b 13,lb 7)	20
TOTAL		220	(for 8 wkts dec)	283

NEW ZEALAND

Batsman	Dismissal	R	Dismissal	R
G.T.Dowling *	b Mohammad Nazir	40	lbw b Pervez Sajjad	3
B.A.G.Murray	c Hanif Mohammad b Mohammad Nazir	50	c Asif Iqbal b Pervez Sajjad	6
B.E.Congdon	c Sadiq Mohammad b Pervez Sajjad	20	c Sadiq Mohammad b Pervez Sajjad	2
B.F.Hastings	b Mohammad Nazir	22	b Pervez Sajjad	9
M.G.Burgess	b Mohammad Nazir	21	c Asif Iqbal b Pervez Sajjad	45
V.Pollard	b Mohammad Nazir	2	not out	28
B.W.Yuile	not out	47	not out	5
K.J.Wadsworth +	st Wasim Bari b Pervez Sajjad	0		
D.R.Hadlee	lbw b Mushtaq	56		
R.S.Cunis	b Mohammad Nazir	5		
H.J.Howarth	b Mohammad Nazir	0		
Extras	(b 6,lb 3,nb 2)	11	(b 12,lb 2)	14
TOTAL		274	(for 5 wkts)	112

NEW ZEALAND	O	M	R	W		O	M	R	W
Hadlee	17.2	5	27	3		16	5	31	1
Cunis	11	5	18	0		15.4	4	38	2
Congdon	8	5	14	0					
Howarth	33	10	80	5		31	13	60	2
Pollard	15	5	34	0		31	11	50	0
Yuile	13	3	35	2		35	13	70	2
Burgess						6	1	14	0

PAKISTAN	O	M	R	W		O	M	R	W
Asif Masood	3	0	18	0		2	1	7	0
Asif Iqbal	3	0	12	0		2	0	2	0
Intikhab Alam	13	3	51	0		5	1	18	0
Mohammad Nazir	30.1	3	99	7		14	5	15	0
Pervez Sajjad	31	7	71	2		24	12	33	5
Mushtaq	5	0	12	1		12	5	20	0
Sadiq Mohammad						2	0	2	0
Hanif Mohammad						2	1	1	0

FALL OF WICKETS	PAK	NZ	PAK	NZ		PAK	NZ	PAK	NZ
1st	55	92	75	9	6th	142	163	195	
2nd	78	99	75	10	7th	153	164	244	
3rd	111	125	83	11	8th	191	264	283	
4th	121	139	133	44	9th	191	273		
5th	135	144	183	92	10th	220	274		

PAKISTAN vs NEW ZEALAND
at Lahore on 30/10/1969
New Zealand won by 5 wickets

PAKISTAN

Batsman	Dismissal	R	Dismissal	R
Sadiq Mohammad	b Congdon	16	c & b Howarth	17
Salahuddin	c Wadsworth b Taylor	2	b Taylor	11
Younis Ahmed	b Hadlee	0	(5) c Murray b Pollard	19
Mushtaq Mohammad	c Wadsworth b Pollard	25	c Yuile b Howarth	1
Shafqat Rana	c Murray b Congdon	4	(6) c Hastings b Hadlee	95
Asif Iqbal	c Murray b Pollard	20	(3) c Congdon b Yuile	22
Intikhab Alam *	c Dowling b Howarth	6	b Pollard	11
Wasim Bari +	c Burgess b Pollard	7	c Murray b Hadlee	11
Salim Altaf	c Hastings b Howarth	1	lbw b Hadlee	0
Mohammad Nazir 4	c Wadsworth b Howarth	12	not out	0
Pervez Sajjad	not out	6	lbw b Taylor	2
Extras	(b 9,lb 6)	15	(b 4,lb 9,nb 2)	15
TOTAL		114		208

NEW ZEALAND

Batsman	Dismissal	R	Dismissal	R
G.T.Dowling *	b Salim Altaf	10	c Salahuddin b Pervez Sajjad	9
B.A.G.Murray	c Shafqat Rana b Pervez Sajjad	90	c Asif Iqbal b Pervez Sajjad	8
B.E.Congdon	lbw b Pervez Sajjad	22	c Shafqat Rana b Mohammad Nazir	5
B.F.Hastings	not out	80	c Mushtaq b Mohammad Nazir	16
M.G.Burgess	c Mushtaq b Pervez Sajjad	0	not out	29
V.Pollard	c Wasim Bari b Pervez Sajjad	11	st Wasim Bari b Mohammad Nazir	0
B.W.Yuile	c Asif Iqbal b Pervez Sajjad	2	not out	4
D.R.Hadlee	c & b Pervez Sajjad	0		
B.R.Taylor	b Pervez Sajjad	0		
K.J.Wadsworth +	b Salim Altaf	13		
H.J.Howarth	b Salim Altaf	4		
Extras	(b 1,lb 6,nb 2)	9	(b 4,lb 5,nb 2)	11
TOTAL		241	(for 5 wkts)	82

NEW ZEALAND	O	M	R	W		O	M	R	W
Hadlee	7	3	10	1		17	4	27	3
Taylor	9	3	12	1		19.5	7	27	2
Congdon	10	4	15	2		8	4	17	0
Howarth	21.4	13	35	3		26	7	63	2
Pollard	20	7	27	3		20	7	32	2
Yuile						14	6	16	1
Burgess						1	0	11	0

PAKISTAN	O	M	R	W		O	M	R	W
Salim Altaf	17	3	33	3		4	0	12	0
Asif Iqbal	4	0	6	0		2	1	2	0
Pervez Sajjad	40	15	74	7		14	6	38	2
Mohammad Nazir	36	15	54	0		12.3	4	19	3
Mushtaq	8	1	34	0					
Intikhab Alam	10	2	31	0					

FALL OF WICKETS	PAK	NZ	PAK	NZ		PAK	NZ	PAK	NZ
1st	8	20	30	19	6th	83	186	116	
2nd	13	61	48	28	7th	87	188	194	
3rd	33	162	56	29	8th	90	188	194	
4th	39	162	66	66	9th	100	230	205	
5th	70	184	85	78	10th	114	241	208	

PAKISTAN vs NEW ZEALAND
at Dacca on 08/11/1969
Match drawn

NEW ZEALAND

Batsman	Dismissal	R	Dismissal	R
B.A.G.Murray	b Asif Iqbal	7	c Asif Iqbal b Intikhab Alam	2
G.M.Turner	c Shafqat Rana b Pervez Sajjad	110	c Intikhab Alam b Pervez Sajjad	26
G.T.Dowling *	c Asif Iqbal b Intikhab Alam	15	b Wasim Bari b Intikhab Alam	2
B.E.Congdon	c Pervez Sajjad b Intikhab Alam	6	b Pervez Sajjad	0
B.F.Hastings	b Intikhab Alam	22	b Pervez Sajjad	3
M.G.Burgess	c Wasim Bari b Pervez Sajjad	59	not out	119
V.Pollard	c Shafqat Rana b Intikhab Alam	2	b Intikhab Alam	11
D.R.Hadlee	c Javed Burki b Intikhab Alam	16	lbw b Intikhab Alam	0
K.J.Wadsworth +	c Wasim Bari b Salim Altaf	7	c Aftab Gul b Pervez Sajjad	0
R.S.Cunis	lbw b Salim Altaf	0	b Shafqat Rana	23
H.J.Howarth	not out	0	c Wasim Bari b Intikhab Alam	2
Extras	(b 14,lb 11,nb 4)	29	(b 2,lb 8,nb 2)	12
TOTAL		273		200

PAKISTAN

Batsman	Dismissal	R	Dismissal	R
Aftab Gul	c & b Howarth	30	b Cunis	5
Sadiq Mohammad	c Turner b Pollard	21	b Cunis	3
Javed Burki	c Turner b Howarth	22	not out	17
Shafqat Rana	run out	65	(5) c Dowling b Cunis	3
Aftab Baloch	lbw b Pollard	25		
Asif Iqbal	c Wadsworth b Howarth	92	(4) b Cunis	16
Intikhab Alam *	b Howarth	20	(6) not out	3
Wasim Bari +	not out	6		
Salim Altaf				
Mohammad Nazir				
Pervez Sajjad				
Extras	(b 6,lb 3)	9	(b 1,lb 3)	4
TOTAL (for 7 wkts dec)		290	(for 4 wkts)	51

PAKISTAN	O	M	R	W		O	M	R	W
Salim Altaf	19.3	6	27	2		11	4	18	0
Asif Iqbal	13	4	22	1		7	2	8	0
Pervez Sajjad	48	20	66	2		34	11	60	4
Intikhab Alam	56	26	91	5		39.4	13	91	5
Mohammad Nazir	30	15	38	0		3	1	3	0
Sadiq Mohammad						2	1	4	0
Aftab Baloch						2	0	2	0
Shafqat Rana						3	1	2	1

NEW ZEALAND	O	M	R	W		O	M	R	W
Hadlee	17	2	41	0		7	0	17	0
Cunis	23	5	65	0		7	0	21	4
Congdon	14	2	41	0					
Howarth	33.1	8	85	4					
Pollard	14	2	49	2		1	0	9	0

FALL OF WICKETS	NZ	PAK	NZ	PAK		NZ	PAK	NZ	PAK
1st	13	53	12	7	6th	241	277	92	
2nd	67	55	14	12	7th	251	290	92	
3rd	99	81	17	40	8th	271		101	
4th	147	150	25	46	9th	272		197	
5th	226	201	70		10th	273		200	

ENGLAND vs PAKISTAN
at Edgbaston on 03/06/1971
Match drawn

PAKISTAN

Aftab Gul	b D'Oliveira	28
Sadiq Mohammad	c & b Lever	17
Zaheer Abbas	c Luckhurst b Illingworth	274
Mushtaq Mohammad	c Cowdrey b Illingworth	100
Majid Khan	c Lever b Illingworth	35
Asif Iqbal	not out	104
Intikhab Alam *	c Underwood b D'Oliveira	9
Imran Khan	run out	5
Wasim Bari +	not out	4
Asif Masood		
Pervez Sajjad		
Extras	(b 6,lb 14,nb 12)	32
TOTAL (for 7 wkts dec)		608

ENGLAND

Batsman	Dismissal	R	Dismissal	R
J.H.Edrich	c Zaheer Abbas b Asif Masood	0	c Wasim Bari b Asif Masood	15
B.W.Luckhurst	c Sadiq Mohammad b Pervez Sajjad	35	not out	108
M.C.Cowdrey	b Asif Masood	16	b Asif Masood	34
D.L.Amiss	b Asif Masood	4	c Pervez Sajjad b Asif Masood	22
B.L.D'Oliveira	c Mushtaq b Intikhab Alam	73	c Mushtaq b Asif Iqbal	22
R.Illingworth *	b Intikhab Alam	1	c Wasim Bari b Asif Masood	1
A.P.E.Knott +	b Asif Masood	116	not out	4
P.Lever	c Pervez Sajjad b Asif Masood	47		
K.Shuttleworth	c Imran Khan b Pervez Sajjad	21		
D.L.Underwood	not out	9		
Alan Ward	c Mushtaq b Pervez Sajjad	0		
Extras	(b 16,lb 6,w 3,nb 6)	31	(b 4,lb 5,w 6,nb 8)	23
TOTAL		353	(for 5 wkts)	229

ENGLAND	O	M	R	W		O	M	R	W
Ward	29	3	115	0					
Lever	38	7	126	1					
Shuttleworth	23	2	83	0					
D'Oliveira	38	17	78	2					
Underwood	41	13	102	0					
Illingworth	26	5	72	3					

PAKISTAN	O	M	R	W		O	M	R	W
Asif Masood	34	6	111	5		23.5	7	49	4
Imran Khan	23	9	36	0		5	0	19	0
Majid Khan	4	1	8	0					
Intikhab Alam	31	13	82	2		20	8	52	0
Pervez Sajjad	15.5	6	46	3		14	4	27	0
Mushtaq	13	3	39	0		8	2	23	0
Asif Iqbal						20	6	36	1

FALL OF WICKETS	PAK	ENG	ENG		PAK	ENG	ENG
1st	68	0	34	6th	567	148	
2nd	359	29	114	7th	581	307	
3rd	441	46	169	8th		324	
4th	456	112	218	9th		351	
5th	469	127	221	10th		353	

ENGLAND vs PAKISTAN
at Lord's on 17/06/1971
Match drawn

ENGLAND

G.Boycott	not out	121			
B.W.Luckhurst	c Wasim Bari b Salim Altaf	46	(1) not out	53	
J.H.Edrich	c Asif Masood b Pervez Sajjad	37			
D.L.Amiss	not out	19			
R.A.Hutton			(2) not out	58	
B.L.D'Oliveira					
R.Illingworth *					
A.P.E.Knott +					
P.Lever					
N.Gifford					
J.S.E.Price					
	Extras (b 6,lb 2,w 5,nb 5)	18	(b 1,lb 1,nb 4)	6	
	TOTAL (for 2 wkts dec)	241	(for 0 wkts)	117	

PAKISTAN

Aftab Gul	c Knott b Hutton	33
Sadiq Mohammad	c Knott b D'Oliveira	28
Zaheer Abbas	c Hutton b Lever	40
Mushtaq Mohammad	c Amiss b Hutton	2
Asif Iqbal	c Knott b Gifford	9
Majid Khan	c Edrich b Price	9
Intikhab Alam *	c Gifford b Lever	18
Wasim Bari +	c Knott b Price	0
Salim Altaf	not out	0
Asif Masood	b Price	0
Pervez Sajjad	absent hurt/ill	
	Extras (lb 5,w 1,nb 3)	9
	TOTAL	148

PAKISTAN	O	M	R	W		O	M	R	W
Asif Masood	21	3	60	0		3	1	3	0
Salim Altaf	19	5	42	1		5	2	11	0
Asif Iqbal	13	2	24	0		4	1	11	0
Majid Khan	4	0	16	0		6	2	7	0
Intikhab Alam	20	2	64	0		9	1	26	0
Pervez Sajjad	6	2	17	1					
Mushtaq						11	3	31	0
Sadiq Mohammad						5	1	17	0
Aftab Gul						1	0	4	0
Zaheer Abbas						1	0	1	0

ENGLAND	O	M	R	W		O	M	R	W
Price	11.4	5	29	3					
Lever	16	3	38	2					
Gifford	12	6	13	1					
Illingworth	7	6	1	0					
Hutton	16	5	36	2					
D'Oliveira	10	5	22	1					

FALL OF WICKETS	ENG	PAK	ENG				ENG	PAK	ENG
1st	124	57				6th		146	
2nd	205	66				7th		148	
3rd		97				8th		148	
4th		117				9th		148	
5th		119				10th			

ENGLAND vs PAKISTAN
at Headingley on 08/07/1971
England won by 25 runs

ENGLAND

G.Boycott	c Wasim Bari b Intikhab Alam	112	c Mushtaq b Asif Masood	13	
B.W.Luckhurst	c Wasim Bari b Salim Altaf	0	c Wasim Bari b Asif Masood	0	
J.H.Edrich	c Wasim Bari b Asif Masood	2	c Mushtaq b Intikhab Alam	33	
D.L.Amiss	c Wasim Bari b Pervez Sajjad	23	c & b Saeed Ahmed	56	
B.L.D'Oliveira	b Intikhab Alam	74	c Wasim Bari b Salim Altaf	72	
A.P.E.Knott +	b Asif Masood	10	c Zaheer Abbas b Intikhab Alam	7	
R.Illingworth *	b Asif Iqbal	20	c Wasim Bari b Salim Altaf	45	
R.A.Hutton	c Sadiq Mohammad b Asif Iqbal	28	c Zaheer Abbas b Intikhab Alam	4	
R.N.S.Hobbs	c Wasim Bari b Asif Iqbal	6	b Salim Altaf	0	
P.Lever	c Salim Altaf b Intikhab Alam	19	b Salim Altaf	8	
N.Gifford	not out	3	not out	2	
	Extras (b 5,lb 5,nb 9)	19	(b 6,lb 11,w 2,nb 5)	24	
	TOTAL	316		264	

PAKISTAN

Aftab Gul	b Gifford	27	c Hobbs b Illingworth	18	
Sadiq Mohammad	c Knott b Gifford	28	c & b D'Oliveira	91	
Zaheer Abbas	c Edrich b Lever	72	c Luckhurst b Illingworth	0	
Mushtaq Mohammad	c Knott b Hutton	57	c Edrich b Illingworth	5	
Saeed Ahmed	c Knott b D'Oliveira	22	c D'Oliveira b Gifford	5	
Asif Iqbal	c Hutton b D'Oliveira	14	st Knott b Gifford	33	
Intikhab Alam *	c Hobbs b D'Oliveira	17	c Hutton b D'Oliveira	4	
Wasim Bari +	c Edrich b Gifford	63	c Knott b Lever	10	
Salim Altaf	c Knott b Hutton	22	not out	8	
Asif Masood	c & b Hutton	0	c Knott b Lever	1	
Pervez Sajjad	not out	9	lbw b Lever	0	
	Extras (b 6,lb 11,w 1,nb 1)	19	(b 17,lb 9,w 1,nb 3)	30	
	TOTAL	350		205	

PAKISTAN	O	M	R	W		O	M	R	W
Asif Masood	18	2	75	2		20	7	46	2
Salim Altaf	20.1	4	46	1		14.3	9	11	4
Asif Iqbal	13	2	37	3					
Pervez Sajjad	20	2	65	1		16	3	46	0
Intikhab Alam	27.1	12	51	3		36	10	91	3
Saeed Ahmed	4	0	13	0		15	4	30	1
Mushtaq	3	1	10	0		6	1	16	0

ENGLAND	O	M	R	W		O	M	R	W
Lever	31	9	65	1		3.3	1	10	3
Hutton	41	8	72	3		6	0	18	0
Gifford	53.4	26	69	3		34	14	51	2
Illingworth	28	14	31	0		26	11	58	3
Hobbs	20	5	48	0		4	0	22	0
D'Oliveira	36	18	46	3		11	4	16	2

FALL OF WICKETS	ENG	PAK	ENG	PAK			ENG	PAK	ENG	PAK
1st	4	54	0	25		6th	234	249	248	184
2nd	10	69	21	25		7th	283	256	252	187
3rd	74	198	112	54		8th	286	313	252	203
4th	209	198	120	65		9th	294	313	262	205
5th	234	223	142	160		10th	316	350	264	205

AUSTRALIA vs PAKISTAN
at Adelaide on 22/12/1972
Australia won by an innings and 114 runs

PAKISTAN

Sadiq Mohammad	c Chappell G.S. b Massie	11	c & b Mallett	81	
Talat Ali	retired hurt/ill	7	(11) c Edwards b Mallett	0	
Zaheer Abbas	c Marsh b Lillee	7	c Marsh b O'Keefe	0	
Majid Khan	c Sheahan b Massie	11	c Chappell I.M. b Mallett	11	
Mushtaq Mohammad	c Chappell G.S. b Lillee	3	lbw b Mallett	32	
Saeed Ahmed	c Marsh b Massie	36	(2) lbw b Mallett	39	
Asif Iqbal	c Marsh b Massie	16	(6) c Chappell G.S. b Lillee	0	
Intikhab Alam *	c Edwards b Lillee	64	(7) c Chappell G.S. b Lillee	30	
Wasim Bari +	c Redpath b Mallett	72	(8) c O'Keefe b Mallett	0	
Salim Altaf	not out	17	(9) not out	9	
Asif Masood	c Marsh b Mallett	0	(10) c Marsh b Mallett	1	
	Extras (b 4,lb 3,w 4,nb 2)	13	(b 3,lb 4,w 1,nb 3)	11	
	TOTAL	257		214	

AUSTRALIA

A.P.Sheahan	b Asif Masood	44
I.R.Redpath	c Wasim Bari b Asif Masood	2
I.M.Chappell *	c Asif Iqbal b Majid Khan	196
G.S.Chappell	lbw b Salim Altaf	28
R.Edwards	lbw b Asif Masood	89
J.Benaud	lbw b Salim Altaf	24
R.W.Marsh +	b Mushtaq	118
K.J.O'Keefe	b Mushtaq	40
A.A.Mallett	c sub b Majid Khan	0
D.K.Lillee	c Saeed Ahmed b Mushtaq	14
R.A.L.Massie	not out	12
	Extras (b 2,lb 12,nb 4)	18
	TOTAL	585

AUSTRALIA	O	M	R	W		O	M	R	W
Lillee	20.3	7	49	4		15	3	53	1
Massie	24	3	70	4		9	3	26	0
Chappell G.S.	11	2	29	0		4	0	21	0
Mallett	12	3	52	1		23.6	6	59	8
O'Keefe	8	1	44	0		14	1	44	1

PAKISTAN	O	M	R	W		O	M	R	W
Asif Masood	19	1	110	3					
Salim Altaf	25	1	83	2					
Asif Iqbal	14	0	76	0					
Intikhab Alam	18	2	115	0					
Saeed Ahmed	3	0	28	0					
Majid Khan	20	1	88	2					
Mushtaq	11.2	0	67	3					

FALL OF WICKETS	PAK	AUS	PAK			PAK	AUS	PAK
1st	30	3	88		6th	104	413	182
2nd	30	103	89		7th	208	533	182
3rd	33	158	111		8th	255	534	211
4th	74	330	162		9th	257	566	214
5th	95	390	162		10th	585	214	

AUSTRALIA vs PAKISTAN
at Melbourne on 29/12/1972
Australia won by 92 runs

AUSTRALIA

I.R.Redpath	c Saeed Ahmed b Intikhab Alam	135	c Wasim Bari b Salim Altaf	6	
A.P.Sheahan	run out	23	c Sarfraz Nawaz b Asif Masood	127	
I.M.Chappell *	c Wasim Bari b Sarfraz Nawaz	66	(4) st Wasim Bari b Majid Khan	9	
G.S.Chappell	not out	116	(5) run out	62	
J.Benaud	c Sarfraz Nawaz b Intikhab Alam	13	(3) c Wasim Bari b Salim Altaf	142	
R.W.Marsh +	c Wasim Bari b Sarfraz Nawaz	74	c Asif Iqbal b Asif Masood	3	
K.J.O'Keefe	b Sarfraz Nawaz	24			
A.A.Mallett	c Wasim Bari b Sarfraz Nawaz	8			
M.H.N.Walker	run out	11			
J.R.Thomson	not out	19			
D.K.Lillee	c Mushtaq b Intikhab Alam	2			
	Extras (b 1,lb 6,nb 7)	14	(lb 3,nb 9)	12	
	TOTAL	441	(for 5 wkts dec)	425	

PAKISTAN

Sadiq Mohammad	lbw b Lillee	137	c Marsh b Walker	5	
Saeed Ahmed	c Chappell G.S. b Walker	50	c Mallett b Lillee	6	
Zaheer Abbas	run out	51	run out	25	
Majid Khan	c Marsh b Walker	158	c Marsh b Lillee	47	
Mushtaq Mohammad	c Marsh b O'Keefe	60	run out	13	
Asif Iqbal	c Lillee b Mallett	7	c Redpath b Walker	37	
Intikhab Alam *	c Sheahan b Mallett	68	c Chappell I.M. b Mallett	48	
Wasim Bari +	b Mallett	7	b Walker	0	
Salim Altaf	not out	13	b O'Keefe	10	
Sarfraz Nawaz	not out	0	run out	8	
Asif Masood			not out	1	
	Extras (b 12,lb 7,w 1,nb 3)	23		0	
	TOTAL (for 8 wkts dec)	574		200	

PAKISTAN	O	M	R	W		O	M	R	W
Asif Masood	17	0	97	0		12	0	100	2
Salim Altaf	9	0	49	0		14	0	50	2
Sarfraz Nawaz	22.5	4	100	2		22	2	99	2
Intikhab Alam	16	0	101	2		15.6	3	70	1
Majid Khan	21	2	80	0		17	1	61	1
Mushtaq						7	0	33	0

AUSTRALIA	O	M	R	W		O	M	R	W
Lillee	16.6	1	90	1		11	1	59	2
Thomson	17	1	100	0		2	0	10	0
Walker	24	1	112	2		14	3	39	3
Mallett	38	4	124	3		17.5	3	56	1
O'Keefe	23	1	94	1		9	4	10	1
Chappell I.M.	5	0	21	0		3	0	16	0
Redpath	1	0	10	0					
Chappell G.S.						1	0	10	0

FALL OF WICKETS	AUS	PAK	AUS	PAK			AUS	PAK	AUS	PAK
1st	60	128	18	11		6th	519	375	138	
2nd	183	323	251	15		7th	541	391	138	
3rd	273	395	288	80		8th	572	392	161	
4th	295	416	298	83		9th		418	181	
5th	441	429	305	128		10th		425	200	

AUSTRALIA vs PAKISTAN
at Sydney on 06/01/1973
Australia won by 52 runs

AUSTRALIA

K.R.Stackpole	c Wasim Bari b Sarfraz Nawaz	28		c Intikhab Alam b Salim Altaf	9
I.R.Redpath	run out	79		c Nasim-ul-Ghani b Sarfraz Nawaz	18
I.M.Chappell *	lbw b Sarfraz Nawaz	43		c Wasim Bari b Sarfraz Nawaz	27
G.S.Chappell	b Majid Khan	30		(6) lbw b Sarfraz Nawaz	6
R.Edwards	c Wasim Bari b Salim Altaf	69		(4) lbw b Salim Altaf	3
K.D.Walters	b Asif Iqbal	19		(5) lbw b Salim Altaf	6
R.W.Marsh +	c Wasim Bari b Salim Altaf	15		c Zaheer Abbas b Salim Altaf	0
M.H.N.Walker	c Majid Khan b Sarfraz Nawaz	5		c Mushtaq b Sarfraz Nawaz	16
J.R.Watkins	not out	3		c Zaheer Abbas b Intikhab Alam	36
D.K.Lillee	b Sarfraz Nawaz	2		(11) not out	0
R.A.L.Massie	b Salim Altaf	2		(10) c Sadiq Mohammad b Mushtaq	42
	Extras (b 18,lb 8,w 4,nb 9)	39		(b 10,lb 3,nb 8)	21
	TOTAL	334			184

PAKISTAN

Sadiq Mohammad	c Chappell G.S. b Lillee	30		c Edwards b Massie	6
Nasim-ul-Ghani	c Redpath b Chappell G.S.	64		b Lillee	5
Zaheer Abbas	c Marsh b Massie	14		c Redpath b Lillee	47
Majid Khan	b Massie	0		lbw b Walker	12
Mushtaq Mohammad	c Walker b Chappell G.S.	121		c Marsh b Lillee	15
Asif Iqbal	c Marsh b Chappell G.S.	65		c Marsh b Walker	5
Intikhab Alam *	c Marsh b Massie	9		c Watkins b Walker	8
Wasim Bari +	b Chappell G.S.	1		c Edwards b Walker	0
Salim Altaf	c Marsh b Walker	12		c Massie b Walker	0
Sarfraz Nawaz	b Chappell G.S.	12		c Redpath b Walker	1
Asif Masood	not out	1		not out	3
	Extras (b 12,lb 10,w 6,nb 3)	31		(lb 2,w 1,nb 1)	4
	TOTAL	360			106

PAKISTAN

	O	M	R	W		O	M	R	W
Asif Masood	18	1	81	0		3	0	15	0
Salim Altaf	21.5	3	71	3		20	5	60	4
Sarfraz Nawaz	19	3	53	4		21	7	56	4
Majid Khan	18	1	66	1					
Intikhab Alam	2	0	13	0		4	2	9	1
Asif Iqbal	2	0	11	1		2	0	10	0
Mushtaq						3.1	0	13	1

AUSTRALIA

	O	M	R	W		O	M	R	W
Lillee	10	2	34	1		23	5	68	3
Massie	28	6	123	3		7	4	19	1
Walker	16	2	65	1		16	8	15	6
Chappell G.S.	18.6	5	61	5					
Walters	9	3	25	0					
Watkins	6	1	21	0					
Chappell I.M.	1	1	0	0					

FALL OF WICKETS

	AUS	PAK	AUS	PAK		AUS	PAK	AUS	PAK
1st	56	56	29	7	6th	315	279	73	93
2nd	138	79	31	11	7th	324	280	94	95
3rd	196	83	34	52	8th	327	336	101	95
4th	220	131	44	83	9th	329	349	184	103
5th	271	270	70	88	10th	334	360	184	106

NEW ZEALAND vs PAKISTAN
at Dunedin on 07/02/1973
Pakistan won by an innings and 166 runs

PAKISTAN

Sadiq Mohammad	b Hadlee	61
Zaheer Abbas	c Wadsworth b Hadlee	15
Majid Khan	c & b Taylor	26
Mushtaq Mohammad	c Wadsworth b Congdon	201
Asif Iqbal	c Hastings b Taylor	175
Wasim Raja	not out	8
Intikhab Alam *	c Pollard b Howarth	3
Wasim Bari +	not out	2
Salim Altaf		
Sarfraz Nawaz		
Pervez Sajjad		
	Extras (lb 13,nb 3)	16
	TOTAL (for 6 wkts dec)	507

NEW ZEALAND

G.M.Turner	c Mushtaq b Intikhab Alam	37		c Mushtaq b Intikhab Alam	24
T.W.Jarvis	c Mushtaq b Sarfraz Nawaz	7		c Wasim Bari b Mushtaq	39
B.E.Congdon *	c Wasim Bari b Intikhab Alam	35		c Majid Khan b Mushtaq	7
B.F.Hastings	c Sarfraz Nawaz b Intikhab Alam	4		b Mushtaq	9
M.G.Burgess	b Intikhab Alam	10		c Pervez Sajjad b Intikhab Alam	4
V.Pollard	c Sarfraz Nawaz b Intikhab Alam	3		b Intikhab Alam	61
B.R.Taylor	c Sarfraz Nawaz b Intikhab Alam	0		(8) run out	3
K.J.Wadsworth +	b Mushtaq	45		(7) c Majid Khan b Intikhab Alam	17
D.R.Hadlee	st Wasim Bari b Intikhab Alam	1		c Majid Khan b Mushtaq	0
D.R.O'Sullivan	c Wasim Raja b Mushtaq	4		b Mushtaq	1
H.J.Howarth	not out	4		not out	7
	Extras (b 1,lb 2,nb 3)	6		(b 5,lb 7,nb 1)	13
	TOTAL	156			185

NEW ZEALAND

	O	M	R	W		O	M	R	W
Hadlee	24	3	100	2					
Taylor	22	3	91	2					
Congdon	17	1	72	1					
Howarth	29	6	83	1					
Pollard	13	2	64	0					
O'Sullivan	18	2	81	0					

PAKISTAN

	O	M	R	W		O	M	R	W
Salim Altaf	5	0	23	0		4	2	11	0
Sarfraz Nawaz	5	0	20	1		4	0	16	0
Intikhab Alam	21	3	52	7		18.4	2	78	4
Pervez Sajjad	17	5	40	0		3	0	10	0
Mushtaq	3.5	1	15	2		18	2	49	5
Wasim Raja						2	0	8	0

FALL OF WICKETS

	PAK	NZ	NZ		PAK	NZ	NZ
1st	23	15	48	6th	504	99	127
2nd	81	73	57	7th		104	150
3rd	126	84	78	8th		116	159
4th	476	87	87	9th		139	169
5th	500	99	91	10th		156	185

NEW ZEALAND vs PAKISTAN
at Wellington on 02/02/1973
Match drawn

PAKISTAN

Sadiq Mohammad	c sub b Hadlee	166		c Congdon b Howarth	68
Talat Ali	c Turner b Collinge	6		lbw b Taylor	2
Zaheer Abbas	c Hadlee b Taylor	5		c Wadsworth b Collinge	8
Majid Khan	c Congdon b Taylor	79		c Burgess b Howarth	79
Asif Iqbal	c & b Hadlee	39		c Hastings b Howarth	23
Wasim Raja	c Congdon b Taylor	10		c sub b Howarth	41
Intikhab Alam *	run out	16		not out	53
Wasim Bari +	retired hurt/ill	13			
Salim Altaf	c Howarth b Taylor	14		(8) not out	6
Sarfraz Nawaz	c Wadsworth b Collinge	0			
Pervez Sajjad	not out	1			
	Extras (b 1,lb 5,nb 5)	11		(b 4,lb 2,nb 4)	10
	TOTAL	357		(for 6 wkts dec)	290

NEW ZEALAND

G.M.Turner	c Intikhab Alam b Sarfraz Nawaz	43		not out	49
T.W.Jarvis	c Majid Khan b Sarfraz Nawaz	0		c Majid Khan b Salim Altaf	0
B.E.Congdon *	run out	19		c & b Salim Altaf	0
B.F.Hastings	c Majid Khan b Sarfraz Nawaz	72		c Wasim Bari b Salim Altaf	0
M.G.Burgess	c & b Intikhab Alam	79		not out	21
B.R.Taylor	c Zaheer Abbas b Majid Khan	5			
K.J.Wadsworth +	c Asif Iqbal b Sarfraz Nawaz	28			
R.J.Hadlee	c Asif Iqbal b Salim Altaf	46			
H.J.Howarth	not out	3			
R.O.Collinge	b Salim Altaf	0			
J.M.Parker	absent hurt/ill				
	Extras (b 9,lb 9,nb 12)	30		(lb 1,w 1,nb 6)	8
	TOTAL	325		(for 3 wkts)	78

NEW ZEALAND

	O	M	R	W		O	M	R	W
Hadlee	18	0	84	2		7	0	28	0
Collinge	20	1	63	2		13	1	50	1
Taylor	24.4	1	110	4		11	2	63	1
Howarth	25	6	73	0		31	7	99	4
Congdon	3	0	16	0		9	0	40	0

PAKISTAN

	O	M	R	W		O	M	R	W
Salim Altaf	16.4	3	70	2		6	1	15	3
Sarfraz Nawaz	29	5	126	4		5	1	15	0
Asif Iqbal	2	1	6	0					
Intikhab Alam	13	1	55	1		3	0	11	0
Pervez Sajjad	5	0	19	0		4	1	5	0
Majid Khan	9	2	19	1					
Wasim Raja						4	0	10	0
Sadiq Mohammad						3	0	13	0
Talat Ali						1	0	1	0

FALL OF WICKETS

	PAK	NZ	PAK	NZ		PAK	NZ	PAK	NZ
1st	20	4	20	1	6th	308	261	255	
2nd	26	55	35	1	7th	334	302		
3rd	197	88	129	11	8th	342	325		
4th	271	216	177		9th	357	325		
5th	308	221	202		10th				

NEW ZEALAND vs PAKISTAN
at Auckland on 16/02/1973
Match drawn

PAKISTAN

Sadiq Mohammad	c Wadsworth b Collinge	33		c Hadlee b Taylor	38
Zaheer Abbas	c Turner b Taylor	10		c Turner b Taylor	0
Majid Khan	c Wadsworth b Taylor	110		c Wadsworth b Howarth	33
Mushtaq Mohammad	c Hastings b Congdon	61		b Howarth	52
Asif Iqbal	b Taylor	34		(6) lbw b Congdon	39
Wasim Raja	c Wadsworth b Collinge	1		(7) b Collinge	49
Intikhab Alam *	c Wadsworth b Taylor	34		(8) b Howarth	2
Wasim Bari +	c & b Howarth	30		(9) lbw b Hadlee	27
Salim Altaf	not out	53		(5) lbw b Congdon	11
Sarfraz Nawaz	c Taylor b Collinge	2		c Taylor b Collinge	4
Pervez Sajjad	lbw b Congdon	24		not out	8
	Extras (b 1,lb 3,nb 6)	10		(b 3,lb 3,nb 2)	8
	TOTAL	402			271

NEW ZEALAND

R.E.Redmond	c Mushtaq b Pervez Sajjad	107		c Intikhab Alam b Wasim Raja	56
G.M.Turner	c Sarfraz Nawaz b Intikhab Alam	58		b Wasim Raja	24
B.E.Congdon *	b Intikhab Alam	24		not out	6
B.F.Hastings	c Sarfraz Nawaz b Intikhab Alam	110		(5) not out	4
M.G.Burgess	b Intikhab Alam	2		(4) c Mushtaq b Wasim Raja	1
T.W.Jarvis	lbw b Intikhab Alam	0			
K.J.Wadsworth +	c Sadiq Mohammad b Intikhab Alam	6			
B.R.Taylor	c Majid Khan b Pervez Sajjad	2			
D.R.Hadlee	b Intikhab Alam	0			
H.J.Howarth	c Majid Khan b Mushtaq	8			
R.O.Collinge	not out	68			
	Extras (b 8,lb 6,nb 3)	17		(b 1)	1
	TOTAL	402		(for 3 wkts)	92

NEW ZEALAND

	O	M	R	W		O	M	R	W
Collinge	24	2	72	2		7	2	19	2
Hadlee	18	3	100	0		5.7	0	35	1
Taylor	32	9	86	4		19	5	66	2
Howarth	32	5	86	2		31	11	99	3
Congdon	11.5	0	48	2		16	3	44	2

PAKISTAN

	O	M	R	W		O	M	R	W
Salim Altaf	20	1	58	0		4	0	17	0
Sarfraz Nawaz	16	1	85	0		4	0	13	0
Intikhab Alam	30	4	127	6					
Majid Khan	3	0	30	0		3	0	11	0
Pervez Sajjad	15	3	50	2					
Mushtaq	5	0	26	1					
Wasim Raja	1.6	0	9	1		8	2	32	3
Sadiq Mohammad						5	1	18	0

FALL OF WICKETS

	PAK	NZ	PAK	NZ		PAK	NZ	PAK	NZ
1st	43	159	4	80	6th	267	225	203	
2nd	43	180	61	81	7th	295	235	206	
3rd	147	203	71	87	8th	342	236	238	
4th	233	205	116		9th	354	251	242	
5th	238	205	159		10th	402	402	271	

PAKISTAN vs ENGLAND
at Lahore on 02/03/1973
Match drawn

ENGLAND

M.H.Denness	lbw b Salim Altaf	50	c Wasim Bari b Intikhab Alam	68
D.L.Amiss	b Salim Altaf	112	c Mushtaq b Intikhab Alam	16
G.R.J.Roope	c Wasim Bari b Pervez Sajjad	15	st Wasim Bari b Intikhab Alam	0
A.R.Lewis *	b Wasim Raja	29	b Salim Altaf	74
K.W.R.Fletcher	c Wasim Bari b Pervez Sajjad	55	c Majid Khan b Intikhab Alam	12
A.W.Greig	c Majid Khan b Sarfraz Nawaz	41	c Talat Ali b Mushtaq	72
A.P.E.Knott +	c Wasim Bari b Mushtaq	29	c Majid Khan b Mushtaq	34
C.M.Old	b Pervez Sajjad	0	not out	17
G.G.Arnold	c Sarfraz Nawaz b Mushtaq	0	not out	3
D.L.Underwood	not out	0		
P.I.Pocock	c Talat Ali b Mushtaq	5		
	Extras (lb 11,nb 3)	14	(b 6,lb 3,nb 1)	10
	TOTAL	355	(for 7 wkts dec)	306

PAKISTAN

Sadiq Mohammad	c Roope b Greig	119	c Roope b Greig	9
Talat Ali	c Greig b Arnold	35	c & b Pocock	57
Majid Khan *	run out	32	c & b Greig	43
Mushtaq Mohammad	b Underwood	66	not out	5
Asif Iqbal	c Denness b Arnold	102		
Intikhab Alam	b Underwood	3		
Wasim Raja	c Roope b Greig	23	(5) not out	6
Salim Altaf	not out	11		
Wasim Bari +	b Underwood	7		
Sarfraz Nawaz	b Greig	8		
Pervez Sajjad	lbw b Greig	4		
	Extras (b 1,lb 6,nb 5)	12	(lb 4)	4
	TOTAL	422	(for 3 wkts)	124

PAKISTAN

	O	M	R	W		O	M	R	W
Salim Altaf	28	3	80	2		11	2	24	1
Sarfraz Nawaz	31	14	51	1		17	7	41	0
Wasim Raja	21	0	69	1		14	7	36	0
Pervez Sajjad	23	9	58	3		23	9	37	0
Intikhab Alam	32	14	62	0		35	10	80	4
Mushtaq	8.3	1	21	3		16	2	66	2
Majid Khan						3	1	12	0

ENGLAND

	O	M	R	W		O	M	R	W
Arnold	43	10	95	2		4	1	12	0
Old	27	2	98	0					
Underwood	35	15	58	3		13	5	38	0
Pocock	24	6	73	0		15	3	42	1
Greig	29.2	5	86	4		6	0	28	2

FALL OF WICKETS

	ENG	PAK	ENG	PAK		ENG	PAK	ENG	PAK
1st	105	99	63	9	6th	333	383	282	
2nd	147	155	63	102	7th	333	391	287	
3rd	201	222	108	114	8th	334	404		
4th	219	294	154		9th	345	413		
5th	286	310	203		10th	355	422		

PAKISTAN vs ENGLAND
at Karachi on 24/03/1973
Match drawn

PAKISTAN

Sadiq Mohammad	c Denness b Gifford	89	(6) b Gifford	1
Talat Ali	c Amiss b Gifford	33	b Gifford	39
Majid Khan *	c Amiss b Pocock	99	(1) b Gifford	23
Mushtaq Mohammad	run out	99	(5) c Denness b Birkenshaw	0
Asif Iqbal	c & b Pocock	6	(4) c Fletcher b Gifford	36
Intikhab Alam	c & b Birkenshaw	61	(7) c Greig b Birkenshaw	0
Zaheer Abbas	not out	22	(3) c Knott b Gifford	4
Wasim Bari +	not out	17	c Denness b Birkenshaw	41
Salim Altaf	c Knott b Birkenshaw	13		
Sarfraz Nawaz	not out	33		
Asif Masood	c Gifford b Birkenshaw	0		
	Extras (lb 4,lb 9,nb 6)	19	(lb 4,nb 5)	9
	TOTAL (for 6 wkts dec)	445		199

ENGLAND

B.Wood	c Sarfraz Nawaz b Asif Masood	3	c Asif Masood b Salim Altaf	5
D.L.Amiss	c Sarfraz Nawaz b Intikhab Alam	99	not out	21
K.W.R.Fletcher	c Talat Ali b Intikhab Alam	54	not out	1
M.H.Denness	lbw b Asif Masood	47		
A.R.Lewis *	c Asif Iqbal b Intikhab Alam	88		
P.I.Pocock	c Sarfraz Nawaz b Mushtaq	4		
A.W.Greig	b Majid Khan	48		
A.P.E.Knott +	b Majid Khan	2		
J.Birkenshaw	c Majid Khan b Mushtaq	21		
G.G.Arnold	c Mushtaq b Intikhab Alam	2		
N.Gifford	not out	4		
	Extras (b 3,lb 3,nb 8)	14	(nb 3)	3
	TOTAL	386	(for 1 wkt)	30

ENGLAND

	O	M	R	W		O	M	R	W
Arnold	19	2	69	0		15	2	52	0
Greig	20	1	76	0		10	2	26	0
Pocock	38	7	93	2					
Gifford	46	12	99	2		29	9	55	5
Birkenshaw	31	5	89	1		18.3	5	57	5

PAKISTAN

	O	M	R	W		O	M	R	W
Salim Altaf	15	3	38	0		5	1	16	1
Asif Masood	21	4	41	2		4	1	11	0
Intikhab Alam	39	8	105	4					
Sarfraz Nawaz	25	3	64	0		1	1	0	0
Mushtaq	34.3	9	73	2					
Majid Khan	22	5	51	2					

FALL OF WICKETS

	PAK	ENG	PAK	ENG		PAK	ENG	PAK	ENG
1st	79	13	39	27	6th	413	334	106	
2nd	176	143	51		7th	370	108		
3rd	297	182	105		8th	373	129		
4th	307	220	106		9th	381	198		
5th	389	323	106		10th	386	199		

PAKISTAN vs ENGLAND
at Hyderabad on 16/03/1973
Match drawn

ENGLAND

M.H.Denness	b Salim Altaf	8	c Mushtaq b Salim Altaf	0
D.L.Amiss	st Wasim Bari b Mushtaq	158	c Sadiq Mohammad b Intikhab Alam	0
K.W.R.Fletcher	c Zaheer Abbas b Intikhab Alam	78	c Asif Iqbal b Intikhab Alam	21
A.R.Lewis *	c Wasim Bari b Mushtaq	7	c Pervez Sajjad b Intikhab Alam	21
G.R.J.Roope	st Wasim Bari b Intikhab Alam	27	b Mushtaq	18
A.W.Greig	b Mushtaq	36	c Wasim Bari b Asif Iqbal	64
A.P.E.Knott +	c Mohammad Nazir b Mushtaq	71	not out	63
G.G.Arnold	c Wasim Bari b Intikhab Alam	8	not out	19
N.Gifford	b Intikhab Alam	24		
D.L.Underwood	not out	20		
P.I.Pocock	b Pervez Sajjad	33		
	Extras (b 2,lb 11,nb 4)	17	(b 1,lb 5,nb 6)	12
	TOTAL	487	(for 6 wkts)	218

PAKISTAN

Sadiq Mohammad	c Knott b Pocock	30
Talat Ali	c Fletcher b Gifford	22
Majid Khan *	c Knott b Pocock	17
Mushtaq Mohammad	lbw b Gifford	157
Zaheer Abbas	c Roope b Pocock	24
Asif Iqbal	c Roope b Pocock	68
Intikhab Alam	b Arnold	138
Salim Altaf	c Gifford b Pocock	2
Wasim Bari +	c Pocock b Gifford	48
Mohammad Nazir	not out	22
Pervez Sajjad	not out	10
	Extras (b 14,lb 10,nb 7)	31
	TOTAL (for 9 wkts dec)	569

PAKISTAN

	O	M	R	W		O	M	R	W
Salim Altaf	29	10	63	1		10	1	40	1
Asif Iqbal	11	5	31	0		1	0	3	1
Intikhab Alam	65	17	137	4		19	5	44	3
Mohammad Nazir	36	9	84	0		16	3	41	0
Pervez Sajjad	21.2	5	56	1		11	5	11	0
Mushtaq	35	10	93	4		20	5	42	1
Sadiq Mohammad	3	1	6	0		3	0	14	0
Majid Khan						2	0	4	0
Talat Ali						2	1	6	0
Zaheer Abbas						1	0	1	0

ENGLAND

	O	M	R	W
Arnold	24	2	78	1
Greig	13	2	39	0
Pocock	52	9	169	5
Gifford	52	16	111	3
Underwood	48	15	119	0
Fletcher	3	0	22	0

FALL OF WICKETS

	ENG	PAK	ENG		ENG	PAK	ENG
1st	22	53	0	6th	343	437	189
2nd	190	66	0	7th	364	449	
3rd	250	77	36	8th	428	514	
4th	259	139	52	9th	432	553	
5th	319	292	77	10th	487		

ENGLAND vs PAKISTAN
at Headingley on 25/07/1974
Match drawn

PAKISTAN

Sadiq Mohammad	c Lloyd b Hendrick	28	c Greig b Old	12
Shafiq Ahmed	b Old	7	c Greig b Arnold	18
Majid Khan	c & b Greig	75	c Knott b Arnold	4
Mushtaq Mohammad	c Fletcher b Underwood	6	c Greig b Hendrick	43
Zaheer Abbas	c Knott b Hendrick	48	c Greig b Hendrick	19
Asif Iqbal	c Knott b Arnold	14	b Old	8
Intikhab Alam *	c Knott b Arnold	3	lbw b Old	10
Imran Khan	c Greig b Old	23	c Greig b Hendrick	31
Wasim Bari +	c Denness b Old	2	b Hendrick	3
Sarfraz Nawaz	b Arnold	53	c Fletcher b Arnold	2
Asif Masood	not out	4	not out	2
	Extras (lb 5,w 2,nb 15)	22	(lb 14,w 1,nb 12)	27
	TOTAL	285		179

ENGLAND

D.L.Amiss	c Sadiq Mohammad b Sarfraz Nawaz	13	lbw b Sarfraz Nawaz	8
D.Lloyd	c Sadiq Mohammad b Asif Masood	48	c Wasim Bari b Sarfraz Nawaz	9
J.H.Edrich	c Asif Iqbal b Asif Masood	9	c Sadiq Mohammad b Imran Khan	70
M.H.Denness *	b Asif Masood	9	c Sarfraz Nawaz b Intikhab Alam	44
K.W.R.Fletcher	lbw b Sarfraz Nawaz	11	not out	67
A.W.Greig	c Wasim Bari b Imran Khan	37	c Majid Khan b Sarfraz Nawaz	12
A.P.E.Knott +	c Wasim Bari b Asif Iqbal	35	c Majid Khan b Sarfraz Nawaz	5
C.M.Old	c Asif Masood b Imran Khan	0	not out	10
G.G.Arnold	c Intikhab Alam b Sarfraz Nawaz	0		
D.L.Underwood	run out	9		
M.Hendrick	not out	1		
	Extras (b 1,lb 3,w 4,nb 2)	10	(b 4,lb 3,w 1,nb 5)	13
	TOTAL	183	(for 6 wkts)	238

ENGLAND

	O	M	R	W		O	M	R	W
Arnold	31.5	8	67	3		23.1	11	36	3
Old	21	4	65	3		17	0	54	3
Hendrick	26	4	91	2		18	6	39	3
Underwood	12	6	26	1		1	1	0	0
Greig	11	4	14	1		9	3	23	1

PAKISTAN

	O	M	R	W		O	M	R	W
Asif Masood	16	3	50	3		19	2	63	0
Sarfraz Nawaz	22	4	51	3		36	14	56	4
Imran Khan	21	1	55	2		29	7	55	1
Mushtaq	1	1	0	0		4	1	8	0
Intikhab Alam	6	2	14	0		14	4	25	1
Asif Iqbal	6	3	3	1		5	1	18	0

FALL OF WICKETS

	PAK	ENG	PAK	ENG		PAK	ENG	PAK	ENG
1st	12	25	24	17	6th	189	172	115	213
2nd	60	69	35	22	7th	198	172	154	
3rd	70	79	38	94	8th	209	172	168	
4th	170	84	83	174	9th	223	182	177	
5th	182	100	97	198	10th	285	183	179	

ENGLAND vs PAKISTAN
at Lord's on 08/08/1974
Match drawn

PAKISTAN

Sadiq Mohammad	lbw b Hendrick	40	lbw b Arnold		43
Majid Khan	c Old b Greig	48	lbw b Underwood		19
Zaheer Abbas	c Hendrick b Underwood	1	c Greig b Underwood		1
Mushtaq Mohammad	c Greig b Underwood	0	c Denness b Greig		76
Wasim Raja	c Greig b Underwood	24	c Lloyd b Underwood		53
Asif Iqbal	c Amiss b Underwood	2	c Greig b Underwood		0
Intikhab Alam *	b Underwood	5	(8) b Underwood		0
Imran Khan	c Hendrick b Greig	4	(7) c Lloyd b Underwood		0
Wasim Bari +	lbw b Greig	4	(10) lbw b Underwood		1
Sarfraz Nawaz	not out	0	(9) c Lloyd b Underwood		1
Asif Masood	not out	17			
Extras	(nb 2)	2	(lb 8,nb 7)		15
TOTAL	(9 wkts dec)	130			226

ENGLAND

D.L.Amiss	c Sadiq Mohammad b Asif Masood	2	not out		14
D.Lloyd	c Zaheer Abbas b Sarfraz Nawaz	23	not out		12
J.H.Edrich	c Sadiq Mohammad b Intikhab Alam	40			
M.H.Denness *	b Imran Khan	20			
K.W.R.Fletcher	lbw b Imran Khan	8			
A.W.Greig	run out	9			
A.P.E.Knott +	c Wasim Bari b Asif Masood	83			
C.M.Old	c Wasim Bari b Mushtaq	41			
G.G.Arnold	c Wasim Bari b Asif Masood	10			
D.L.Underwood	not out	12			
M.Hendrick	c Imran Khan b Intikhab Alam	6			
Extras	(lb 14,w 1,nb 1)	16	(nb 1)		1
TOTAL		270	(for 0 wkts)		27

ENGLAND

	O	M	R	W		O	M	R	W
Arnold	8	1	32	0		15	3	37	1
Old	5	0	17	0		14	1	39	0
Hendrick	9	2	36	1		15	4	29	0
Underwood	14	8	20	5		34.5	17	51	8
Greig	8.5	4	23	3		19	6	55	1

PAKISTAN

	O	M	R	W		O	M	R	W
Asif Masood	25	10	47	3		4	0	9	0
Sarfraz Nawaz	22	8	42	1		3	0	7	0
Intikhab Alam	26	4	80	2		1	1	0	0
Wasim Raja	2	0	8	0					
Mushtaq	7	3	16	1					
Imran Khan	18	2	48	2					
Asif Iqbal	5	0	13	0					
Majid Khan						2	0	10	0

FALL OF WICKETS

	PAK	ENG	PAK	ENG		PAK	ENG	PAK	ENG
1st	71	2	55		6th	111	118	200	
2nd	91	52	61		7th	116	187	200	
3rd	91	90	77		8th	130	231	206	
4th	91	94	192		9th	130	254	208	
5th	103	100	192		10th	270	226		

ENGLAND vs PAKISTAN
at The Oval on 22/08/1974
Match drawn

PAKISTAN

Sadiq Mohammad	c Old b Willis	21	c & b Arnold		4
Majid Khan	b Underwood	98	c Denness b Old		18
Zaheer Abbas	b Underwood	240	c Knott b Arnold		15
Mushtaq Mohammad	b Arnold	76	b Underwood		8
Asif Iqbal	c & b Greig	29			
Wasim Raja	c Denness b Greig	28	(5) not out		30
Imran Khan	c Knott b Willis	24	(6) not out		10
Intikhab Alam *	not out	32			
Sarfraz Nawaz	not out	14			
Wasim Bari +					
Asif Masood					
Extras	(b 6,lb 18,nb 14)	38	(b 5,nb 4)		9
TOTAL	(for 7 wkts dec)	600	(for 4 wkts)		94

ENGLAND

D.L.Amiss	c Majid Khan b Intikhab Alam	183	
D.Lloyd	c Sadiq Mohammad b Sarfraz Nawaz	4	
D.L.Underwood	lbw b Wasim Raja	43	
J.H.Edrich	c Wasim Bari b Intikhab Alam	25	
M.H.Denness *	c Imran Khan b Asif Masood	18	
K.W.R.Fletcher	run out	122	
A.W.Greig	b Intikhab Alam	32	
A.P.E.Knott +	b Intikhab Alam	9	
C.M.Old	lbw b Intikhab Alam	65	
G.G.Arnold	c Wasim Bari b Mushtaq	2	
R.G.D.Willis	not out	1	
Extras	(b 8,lb 13,nb 20)	41	
TOTAL		545	

ENGLAND

	O	M	R	W		O	M	R	W
Arnold	37	5	106	1		6	0	22	2
Willis	28	3	102	2		7	1	27	0
Old	29.3	3	143	0		2	0	6	1
Underwood	44	14	106	2		8	2	15	1
Greig	25	5	92	2		7	1	15	0
Lloyd	2	0	13	0					

PAKISTAN

	O	M	R	W		O	M	R	W
Asif Masood	40	13	66	1					
Sarfraz Nawaz	38	8	103	1					
Intikhab Alam	51.4	14	116	5					
Imran Khan	44	16	100	0					
Mushtaq	29	12	51	1					
Wasim Raja	23	6	68	1					

FALL OF WICKETS

	PAK	ENG	PAK			PAK	ENG	PAK	
1st	66	14	8		6th	550	401		
2nd	166	143	33		7th	550	531		
3rd	338	209	41		8th		539		
4th	431	244	68		9th		539		
5th	503	383			10th		545		

PAKISTAN vs WEST INDIES
at Lahore on 15/02/1975
Match drawn

PAKISTAN

Majid Khan	c Murray b Roberts	2	b Roberts		17
Agha Zahid	c Gibbs b Roberts	14	lbw b Roberts		1
Zaheer Abbas	c Murray b Roberts	18	lbw b Holder		33
Mushtaq Mohammad	c Murray b Gibbs	27	b Holder		123
Asif Iqbal	c Lloyd b Roberts	25	b Roberts		52
Wasim Raja	c Fredericks b Boyce	13	b Holder		35
Aftab Baloch	c Holder b Boyce	12	not out		60
Intikhab Alam *	b Gibbs	29	c Gibbs b Roberts		19
Wasim Bari +	lbw b Boyce	8	not out		1
Sarfraz Nawaz	c Richards b Roberts	1			
Asif Masood	not out	30			
Extras	(b 1,lb 3,nb 16)	20	(b 4,lb 5,nb 23)		32
TOTAL		199	(for 7 wkts dec)		373

WEST INDIES

R.C.Fredericks	lbw b Sarfraz Nawaz	44	lbw b Sarfraz Nawaz		14
L.Baichan	c Majid Khan b Sarfraz Nawaz	20	not out		105
A.I.Kallicharran	not out	92	c Wasim Bari b Intikhab Alam		44
I.V.A.Richards	b Asif Masood	7	lbw b Intikhab Alam		0
C.H.Lloyd *	b Sarfraz Nawaz	8	c Wasim Bari b Asif Masood		83
D.L.Murray +	run out	10	not out		1
B.D.Julien	b Sarfraz Nawaz	2			
K.D.Boyce	lbw b Sarfraz Nawaz	13			
V.A.Holder	lbw b Intikhab Alam	4			
A.M.E.Roberts	lbw b Sarfraz Nawaz	0			
L.R.Gibbs	lbw b Asif Masood	0			
Extras	(b 6,lb 5,nb 3)	14	(b 1,lb 4,nb 6)		11
TOTAL		214	(for 4 wkts)		258

WEST INDIES

	O	M	R	W		O	M	R	W
Roberts	23	5	66	5		26	4	121	4
Julien	2	1	4	0		15	4	53	0
Holder	13	4	33	0		19.6	5	69	3
Boyce	15	1	55	3		14	4	47	0
Gibbs	6.4	0	21	2		20	4	51	0

PAKISTAN

	O	M	R	W		O	M	R	W
Asif Masood	19.5	0	63	2		17	2	70	1
Sarfraz Nawaz	27	1	89	6		20	3	71	1
Asif Iqbal	2	0	16	0					
Wasim Raja	4	1	15	0		4	0	10	0
Intikhab Alam	9	2	17	1		18	3	61	2
Mushtaq						6	0	20	0
Aftab Baloch						4	0	15	0

FALL OF WICKETS

	PAK	WI	PAK	WI		PAK	WI	PAK	WI
1st	2	66	8	30	6th	117	156	330	
2nd	35	83	53	89	7th	130	199	370	
3rd	40	92	58	89	8th	140	212		
4th	92	105	137	253	9th	142	213		
5th	98	141	214		10th	199	214		

PAKISTAN vs WEST INDIES
at Karachi on 01/03/1975
Match drawn

PAKISTAN

Majid Khan	c Baichan b Gibbs	100	(2) run out		18
Sadiq Mohammad	c Murray b Roberts	27	(7) not out		98
Zaheer Abbas	c Murray b Gibbs	18	(1) c Fredericks b Roberts		2
Mushtaq Mohammad	c Murray b Holder	5	(3) c Kallicharran b Boyce		1
Asif Iqbal	c Boyce b Holder	3	(4) c Holder b Julien		77
Wasim Raja	not out	107	(11) b Gibbs		1
Intikhab Alam *	c Fredericks b Julien	34	(5) c Richards b Fredericks		6
Wasim Bari +	c Baichan b Roberts	58	(6) run out		0
Sarfraz Nawaz	b Gibbs	0	(8) run out		15
Asif Masood	not out	5	(9) c Julien b Gibbs		0
Liaqat Ali			(10) c & b Richards		12
Extras	(b 1,lb 16,nb 32)	49	(b 6,lb 6,nb 14)		26
TOTAL	(for 8 wkts dec)	406			256

WEST INDIES

R.C.Fredericks	c Liaqat Ali b Intikhab Alam	77	not out		0
L.Baichan	c Wasim Bari b Intikhab Alam	36	not out		0
A.I.Kallicharran	c Zaheer Abbas b Sarfraz Nawaz	115			
I.V.A.Richards	lbw b Mushtaq	10			
C.H.Lloyd *	c Sadiq Mohammad b Asif Masood	73			
D.L.Murray +	c Majid Khan b Intikhab Alam	19			
B.D.Julien	b Asif Masood	101			
K.D.Boyce	run out	2			
V.A.Holder	lbw b Liaqat Ali	29			
A.M.E.Roberts	run out	6			
L.R.Gibbs	not out	4			
Extras	(b 1,lb 2,nb 18)	21	(nb 1)		1
TOTAL		493	(for 0 wkts)		1

WEST INDIES

	O	M	R	W		O	M	R	W
Roberts	25	3	81	2		16	0	54	1
Julien	11	0	51	1		16	7	37	1
Holder	19	2	66	2		6	3	19	0
Boyce	12	1	60	0		3	0	15	1
Fredericks	1	0	10	0		12	3	39	1
Gibbs	26	4	89	3		37.1	19	49	2
Richards						9	2	17	1

PAKISTAN

	O	M	R	W		O	M	R	W
Asif Masood	15.2	2	76	2					
Sarfraz Nawaz	21	1	106	1					
Liaqat Ali	19	1	90	1					
Intikhab Alam	28	1	122	3					
Mushtaq	15	4	56	1					
Wasim Raja	4.7	0	22	0					
Zaheer Abbas						1	1	0	0

FALL OF WICKETS

	PAK	WI	PAK	WI		PAK	WI	PAK	WI
1st	94	95	2		6th	246	391	148	
2nd	144	136	11		7th	374	399	212	
3rd	167	151	61		8th	393	449	213	
4th	170	290	88		9th	474	253		
5th	178	336	90		10th	493	256		

PAKISTAN vs NEW ZEALAND
at Lahore on 09/10/1976
Pakistan won by 6 wickets

PAKISTAN

Majid Khan	c Lees b Hadlee	23	c Turner b Collinge	21
Sadiq Mohammad	c Burgess b Hadlee	5	c Parker b Howarth	38
Zaheer Abbas	b Burgess	15	c Morrison b Petherick	0
Mushtaq Mohammad *	b Hadlee	4	(5) c Morrison b Petherick	5
Javed Miandad	c Hadlee b Petherick	163	(4) not out	25
Asif Iqbal	b Hadlee	166	not out	1
Wasim Raja	c & b Petherick	0		
Intikhab Alam	c Howarth b Petherick	0		
Imran Khan	c Burgess b Hadlee	29		
Sarfraz Nawaz	lbw b O'Sullivan	4		
Wasim Bari +	not out	2		
	Extras (b 1,lb 2,nb 3)	6		0
	TOTAL	**417**	**(for 4 wkts)**	**105**

NEW ZEALAND

J.F.M.Morrison *	c Wasim Bari b Sarfraz Nawaz	3	c Zaheer Abbas b Sarfraz Nawaz	0
G.M.Turner	c Wasim Raja b Sarfraz Nawaz	8	b Imran Khan	1
G.P.Howarth	c & b Intikhab Alam	38	c Sadiq Mohammad b Sarfraz Nawaz	0
J.M.Parker	c Wasim Bari b Imran Khan	9	lbw b Imran Khan	22
M.G.Burgess	b Imran Khan	17	b Intikhab Alam	111
R.W.Anderson	c Mushtaq b Intikhab Alam	14	c Majid Khan b Mushtaq	92
W.K.Lees +	st Wasim Bari b Intikhab Alam	8	c Mushtaq b Imran Khan	42
R.J.Hadlee	c Wasim Raja b Mushtaq	27	c Majid Khan b Javed Miandad	42
D.R.O'Sullivan	c Javed Miandad b Mushtaq	8	(11) not out	23
R.O.Collinge	c Wasim Bari b Intikhab Alam	8	(9) b Imran Khan	0
P.J.Petherick	not out	1	(10) c Mushtaq b Sarfraz Nawaz	1
	Extras (b 1,lb 4,nb 11)	16	(b 4,lb 11,nb 11)	26
	TOTAL	**157**		**360**

NEW ZEALAND	O	M	R	W		O	M	R	W
Collinge	14	0	81	0		6	0	30	1
Hadlee	19	0	121	5		5	0	36	0
Burgess	4	1	20	1					
O'Sullivan	25.5	3	86	1					
Petherick	18	1	103	3		4.7	2	26	2
Howarth						3	0	13	1

PAKISTAN	O	M	R	W		O	M	R	W
Sarfraz Nawaz	13	5	33	2		18	1	69	3
Imran Khan	15	1	57	2		21	4	59	4
Asif Iqbal	2	0	10	0					
Intikhab Alam	16.4	6	35	4		26	4	85	1
Mushtaq	3	0	6	2		13	2	56	1
Wasim Raja						7	1	31	0
Javed Miandad						7.4	1	34	1

FALL OF WICKETS	PAK	NZ	NZ	PAK		PAK	NZ	NZ	PAK
1st	23	9	1	49	6th	336	105	245	
2nd	33	26	1	74	7th	336	106	306	
3rd	44	64	1	74	8th	408	146	306	
4th	55	72	62	96	9th	413	149	315	
5th	336	99	245		10th	417	157	360	

PAKISTAN vs NEW ZEALAND
at Karachi on 30/10/1976
Match drawn

PAKISTAN

Sadiq Mohammad	c Burgess b Hadlee	34	c Lees b Collinge	31
Majid Khan	c Burgess b Collinge	112	run out	50
Zaheer Abbas	b O'Sullivan	3	c Lees b O'Sullivan	16
Javed Miandad	c Hadlee b Collinge	206	(5) st Lees b O'Sullivan	85
Mushtaq Mohammad *	c Lees b Hadlee	107	(6) not out	67
Asif Iqbal	c Lees b Hadlee	12	(4) st Lees b Roberts	30
Imran Khan	c O'Sullivan b Hadlee	59	not out	4
Intikhab Alam	lbw b O'Sullivan	4		
Sarfraz Nawaz	lbw b Cairns	15		
Shahid Israr +	not out	7		
Sikander Bakht				
	Extras (b 3,lb 5,nb 2)	10	(lb 4,nb 3)	7
	TOTAL (for 9 wkts dec)	**565**	**(for 5 wkts dec)**	**290**

NEW ZEALAND

N.M.Parker	c Shahid Israr b Sarfraz Nawaz	2	c Imran Khan b Intikhab Alam	40
J.F.M.Morrison	b Sarfraz Nawaz	4	c Mushtaq b Sikander Bakht	31
J.M.Parker	c Majid Khan b Imran Khan	24	c Sadiq Mohammad b Javed Miandad	16
A.D.G.Roberts	b Imran Khan	39	b Sikander Bakht	45
M.G.Burgess	c Javed Miandad b Sarfraz Nawaz	44	c Majid Khan b Javed Miandad	1
R.W.Anderson	lbw b Imran Khan	8	lbw b Imran Khan	30
W.K.Lees +	b Sikander Bakht	152	c Asif Iqbal b Imran Khan	46
R.J.Hadlee	c Shahid Israr b Intikhab Alam	87	not out	30
B.L.Cairns	not out	52	not out	9
D.R.O'Sullivan	c Mushtaq b Intikhab Alam	1		
R.O.Collinge	b Intikhab Alam	3		
	Extras (b 12,lb 7,nb 33)	52	(b 4,lb 5,nb 5)	14
	TOTAL	**468**	**(for 7 wkts)**	**262**

NEW ZEALAND	O	M	R	W		O	M	R	W
Collinge	21	1	141	2		12	0	88	1
Hadlee	20.2	1	138	4		12	0	75	0
Cairns	28	2	142	1					
O'Sullivan	35	6	131	2		17	0	96	2
Morrison	1	0	3	0		2	0	6	0
Roberts						4.4	2	18	1

PAKISTAN	O	M	R	W		O	M	R	W
Sarfraz Nawaz	20	1	84	3					
Imran Khan	24.6	4	107	3		21.6	4	104	2
Sikander Bakht	16	3	68	1		8	2	38	2
Intikhab Alam	20.7	5	76	3		17	5	42	1
Mushtaq	6	2	30	0		6	2	9	0
Javed Miandad	10	3	34	0		17	4	45	2
Majid Khan	5	2	17	0		9	4	6	0
Sadiq Mohammad	1	1	0	0		1	0	4	0

FALL OF WICKETS	PAK	NZ	PAK	NZ		PAK	NZ	PAK	NZ
1st	147	5	76	43	6th	524	195		200
2nd	151	10	88	90	7th	525	381		241
3rd	161	78	117	91	8th	548	433		
4th	413	93	137	93	9th	565	434		
5th	427	104	275	140	10th		468		

PAKISTAN vs NEW ZEALAND
at Hyderabad on 23/10/1976
Pakistan won by 10 wickets

PAKISTAN

Sadiq Mohammad	not out	103		
Majid Khan	st Lees b O'Sullivan	98		
Zaheer Abbas	lbw b Roberts	11		
Javed Miandad	c sub b Cairns	25		
Mushtaq Mohammad *	run out	101		
Asif Iqbal	st Lees b Petherick	73		
Imran Khan	c Turner b O'Sullivan	13		
Intikhab Alam	lbw b Hadlee	4		
Sarfraz Nawaz	c Turner b Petherick	10	(1) not out	4
Wasim Bari +	not out	13	(2) not out	0
Farrukh Zaman				
	Extras (b 17,lb 3,nb 2)	22		0
	TOTAL (for 8 wkts dec)	**473**	**(for 0 wkts)**	**4**

NEW ZEALAND

G.M.Turner *	c Wasim Bari b Imran Khan	49	b Sarfraz Nawaz	2
G.P.Howarth	b Sarfraz Nawaz	0	c Javed Miandad b Mushtaq	23
J.M.Parker	c Javed Miandad b Imran Khan	7	c Mushtaq b Javed Miandad	82
A.D.G.Roberts	c Wasim Bari b Sarfraz Nawaz	8	b Javed Miandad	33
M.G.Burgess	c Wasim Bari b Imran Khan	33	c sub b Intikhab Alam	21
R.W.Anderson	b Intikhab Alam	30	c Zaheer Abbas b Intikhab Alam	4
W.K.Lees +	lbw b Intikhab Alam	15	c sub b Javed Miandad	29
B.L.Cairns	c Majid Khan b Javed Miandad	18	lbw b Intikhab Alam	3
R.J.Hadlee	not out	28	c Wasim Bari b Intikhab Alam	0
D.R.O'Sullivan	b Javed Miandad	4	b Sarfraz Nawaz	23
P.J.Petherick	b Sarfraz Nawaz	0	not out	12
	Extras (b 13,lb 8,nb 6)	27	(b 15,lb 2,nb 5)	22
	TOTAL	**219**		**254**

NEW ZEALAND	O	M	R	W		O	M	R	W
Hadlee	19	1	77	1					
Cairns	26	7	101	1					
Roberts	8	1	23	1					
Petherick	36	5	158	2					
O'Sullivan	39	10	92	2					
Lees						0.5	0	4	0

PAKISTAN	O	M	R	W		O	M	R	W
Sarfraz Nawaz	17.6	4	53	3		10.4	1	45	2
Imran Khan	15	4	41	3		16	1	53	0
Intikhab Alam	20	7	51	2		20	7	44	4
Farrukh Zaman	6	1	8	0		4	1	7	0
Javed Miandad	8	1	20	2		19	2	74	3
Mushtaq	7	2	19	0		9	4	9	1
Majid Khan						2	2	0	0

FALL OF WICKETS	PAK	NZ	NZ	PAK		PAK	NZ	NZ	PAK
1st	164	5	5		6th	410	161	190	
2nd	176	27	70		7th	415	178	193	
3rd	220	38	147		8th	427	200	193	
4th	384	101	158		9th		208	226	
5th	387	111	172		10th		219	254	

AUSTRALIA vs PAKISTAN
at Adelaide on 24/12/1976
Match drawn

PAKISTAN

Majid Khan	c McCosker b Thomson	15	lbw b Lillee	47
Mudassar Nazar	c Marsh b Gilmour	13	c Marsh b O'Keefe	22
Zaheer Abbas	c Walters b O'Keefe	85	c Davis b Lillee	101
Mushtaq Mohammad *	c McCosker b Thomson	18	c Marsh b Lillee	37
Javed Miandad	b O'Keefe	15	b Gilmour	54
Asif Iqbal	c Marsh b O'Keefe	0	not out	152
Imran Khan	b Chappell	48	b O'Keefe	5
Salim Altaf	c Davis b Chappell	16	c Turner b Lillee	21
Wasim Bari +	run out	21	lbw b Lillee	0
Sarfraz Nawaz	c Marsh b Lillee	29	c Lillee b O'Keefe	0
Iqbal Qasim	not out	1	run out	4
	Extras (lb 6,nb 5)	11	(b 14,lb 1,nb 8)	23
	TOTAL	**272**		**466**

AUSTRALIA

I.C.Davis	c Mushtaq b Javed Miandad	105	b Sarfraz Nawaz	0
A.Turner	c Zaheer Abbas b Imran Khan	33	c Sarfraz Nawaz b Javed Miandad	48
R.B.McCosker	b Mushtaq	65	c Wasim Bari b Iqbal Qasim	42
G.S.Chappell *	c Zaheer Abbas b Javed Miandad	52	c Mushtaq b Iqbal Qasim	70
K.D.Walters	c Javed Miandad b Sarfraz Nawaz	107	c Wasim Bari b Iqbal Qasim	51
G.J.Cosier	c Asif Iqbal b Javed Miandad	33	(7) not out	25
R.W.Marsh +	b Mushtaq	36	(8) not out	13
G.J.Gilmour	c Iqbal Qasim b Mushtaq	3	(6) b Iqbal Qasim	5
K.J.O'Keefe	not out	3		
D.K.Lillee	c Majid Khan b Mushtaq	0		
J.R.Thomson	absent hurt/ill			
	Extras (lb 4,nb 13)	17	(b 1,lb 3,nb 3)	7
	TOTAL	**454**	**(for 6 wkts)**	**261**

AUSTRALIA	O	M	R	W		O	M	R	W
Lillee	19	1	104	1		47.7	10	163	5
Thomson	8.5	2	34	2					
Gilmour	14.2	1	55	1		14	1	67	1
Walters	3	0	12	0		2	1	5	0
O'Keefe	19	5	42	3		53	12	166	3
Chappell	7	2	14	2		11	3	31	0
Cosier						5	1	11	0

PAKISTAN	O	M	R	W		O	M	R	W
Sarfraz Nawaz	24	3	75	1		8	1	24	1
Salim Altaf	15	0	71	0					
Imran Khan	22	2	92	1		5	0	25	0
Iqbal Qasim	14	0	56	0		30	6	84	4
Javed Miandad	25	3	85	3		21	6	71	0
Mushtaq	19.4	2	58	4		9	1	50	0

FALL OF WICKETS	PAK	AUS	PAK	AUS		PAK	AUS	PAK	AUS
1st	19	63	58	0	6th	157	445	298	228
2nd	56	188	92	92	7th	220	451	368	
3rd	98	244	182	100	8th	221	451	378	
4th	140	278	236	201	9th	271	454	379	
5th	152	366	293	219	10th	272		466	

AUSTRALIA vs PAKISTAN
at Melbourne on 01/01/1977
Australia won by 348 runs

AUSTRALIA

I.C.Davis	c Imran Khan b Asif Iqbal	56	c Asif Iqbal b Iqbal Qasim	88
A.Turner	b Asif Iqbal	82	lbw b Imran Khan	5
R.B.McCosker	lbw b Asif Iqbal	0	st Wasim Bari b Iqbal Qasim	105
G.S.Chappell *	c Wasim Bari b Iqbal Qasim	121	c Majid Khan b Imran Khan	67
K.D.Walters	st Wasim Bari b Iqbal Qasim	42	b Imran Khan	0
G.J.Cosier	c Asif Masood b Majid Khan	168	b Imran Khan	8
R.W.Marsh +	lbw b Iqbal Qasim	2	st Wasim Bari b Iqbal Qasim	13
G.J.Gilmour	st Wasim Bari b Iqbal Qasim	0	not out	7
K.J.O'Keefe	not out	28		
D.K.Lillee	(9) b Imran Khan	6		
M.H.N.Walker				
	Extras (b 3,lb 7,w 1,nb 7)	18	(b 2,lb 11,nb 3)	16
	TOTAL (for 8 wkts dec)	517	(for 8 wkts dec)	315

PAKISTAN

Majid Khan	c Marsh b Lillee	76	b Lillee	35
Sadiq Mohammad	c McCosker b O'Keefe	105	c Walters b Gilmour	0
Zaheer Abbas	b Gilmour	90	lbw b Walker	58
Mushtaq Mohammad *	lbw b Lillee	9	c Chappell b Lillee	4
Javed Miandad	lbw b Lillee	5	c Turner b O'Keefe	10
Asif Iqbal	c sub b Gilmour	35	lbw b Lillee	6
Imran Khan	c Marsh b Lillee	5	c & b O'Keefe	28
Salim Altaf	c Chappell b Lillee	0	b O'Keefe	0
Wasim Bari +	lbw b Lillee	0	c Walker b O'Keefe	2
Iqbal Qasim	run out	1	c Marsh b Lillee	1
Asif Masood	not out	0	not out	0
	Extras (lb 2,nb 5)	7	(b 1,lb 6)	7
	TOTAL	333		151

PAKISTAN

	O	M	R	W		O	M	R	W
Imran Khan	22	0	115	0		25.5	2	122	5
Salim Altaf	17	2	117	0		6	1	28	0
Asif Masood	13	1	79	0					
Asif Iqbal	16	3	52	3					
Javed Miandad	2	0	15	0					
Iqbal Qasim	21	5	111	4		25	2	119	3
Majid Khan	1.6	0	10	1		2	0	12	0
Mushtaq						3	0	18	0

AUSTRALIA

	O	M	R	W		O	M	R	W
Lillee	23	4	82	6		14	1	53	4
Gilmour	16.1	2	78	2		3	0	19	1
Walker	22	1	93	0		9	2	34	1
O'Keefe	21	4	63	1		18.1	5	38	4
Cosier	2	0	10	0					

FALL OF WICKETS

	AUS	PAK	AUS	PAK		AUS	PAK	AUS	PAK
1st	134	113	6	4	6th	400	303	301	124
2nd	134	241	182	86	7th	400	303	301	128
3rd	151	270	223	99	8th	517	303	315	136
4th	227	285	226	104	9th			332	145
5th	398	292	244	120	10th			333	151

WEST INDIES vs PAKISTAN
at Bridgetown on 18/02/1977
Match drawn

PAKISTAN

Majid Khan	b Garner	88	c Garner b Croft	28
Sadiq Mohammad	c Croft b Garner	37	c Garner b Croft	9
Haroon Rashid	c Kallicharran b Foster	33	b Roberts	39
Mushtaq Mohammad *	c Murray b Croft	0	c Murray b Roberts	6
Asif Iqbal	c Murray b Croft	36	b Croft	0
Javed Miandad	lbw b Garner	2	c Greenidge b Croft	1
Wasim Raja	not out	117	c Garner b Foster	71
Imran Khan	c Garner b Roberts	20	c Fredericks b Garner	1
Salim Altaf	lbw b Garner	19	b Garner	2
Sarfraz Nawaz	c Kallicharran b Foster	38	c Murray b Roberts	6
Wasim Bari +	lbw b Croft	10	not out	60
	Extras (b 5,lb 6,w 1,nb 23)	35	(b 29,lb 11,nb 28)	68
	TOTAL	435		291

WEST INDIES

R.C.Fredericks	c & b Sarfraz Nawaz	24	b Sarfraz Nawaz	52
C.G.Greenidge	c Majid Khan b Imran Khan	47	c Wasim Raja b Sarfraz Nawaz	2
I.V.A.Richards	c Salim Altaf b Sarfraz Nawaz	32	c Sadiq Mohammad b Sarfraz Nawaz	92
A.I.Kallicharran	c Sarfraz Nawaz b Imran Khan	17	c Wasim Bari b Salim Altaf	9
C.H.Lloyd *	c Sadiq Mohammad b Salim Altaf	157	c Wasim Bari b Imran Khan	11
M.L.C.Foster	b Sarfraz Nawaz	15	b Sarfraz Nawaz	4
D.L.Murray +	c Mushtaq b Imran Khan	52	c Wasim Bari b Salim Altaf	20
J.Garner	b Javed Miandad	43	b Salim Altaf	0
A.M.E.Roberts	c Wasim Bari b Salim Altaf	4	not out	9
C.E.H.Croft	not out	1	(11) not out	5
V.A.Holder	absent hurt/ill		(10) b Imran Khan	6
	Extras (b 2,lb 6,nb 21)	29	(b 1,lb 8,w 1,nb 31)	41
	TOTAL	421	(for 9 wkts)	251

WEST INDIES

	O	M	R	W		O	M	R	W
Roberts	30	3	124	1		25	5	66	3
Croft	31.4	6	85	3		15	3	47	4
Holder	4	0	13	0					
Garner	37	7	130	4		17	4	60	2
Foster	27	13	41	2		8	2	34	1
Richards	3	1	3	0		2	0	16	0
Fredericks	1	0	4	0					

PAKISTAN

	O	M	R	W		O	M	R	W
Imran Khan	28	3	147	3		32	16	58	2
Sarfraz Nawaz	29	3	125	3		34	10	79	4
Salim Altaf	21	3	70	2		21	7	33	3
Javed Miandad	10.4	3	22	1		11	4	31	0
Mushtaq	5	0	27	0					
Majid Khan	1	0	1	0		1	0	1	0
Asif Iqbal						1	0	8	0

FALL OF WICKETS

	PAK	WI	PAK	WI		PAK	WI	PAK	WI
1st	72	59	29	12	6th	233	334	113	206
2nd	148	91	68	142	7th	271	404	126	210
3rd	149	120	102	166	8th	335	418	146	217
4th	186	134	103	179	9th	408	421	158	237
5th	207	183	108	185	10th	435		291	

AUSTRALIA vs PAKISTAN
at Sydney on 14/01/1977
Pakistan won by 8 wickets

AUSTRALIA

I.C.Davis	b Sarfraz Nawaz	20	c Haroon Rashid b Imran Khan	25
A.Turner	c Wasim Bari b Sarfraz Nawaz	0	c Majid Khan b Sarfraz Nawaz	11
R.B.McCosker	c Mushtaq b Imran Khan	8	c Wasim Bari b Imran Khan	8
G.S.Chappell *	c Zaheer Abbas b Imran Khan	28	c Wasim Bari b Sarfraz Nawaz	5
K.D.Walters	c Wasim Bari b Imran Khan	2	c Wasim Bari b Imran Khan	38
G.J.Cosier	c Wasim Bari b Imran Khan	50	c Wasim Bari b Sarfraz Nawaz	4
R.W.Marsh +	c & b Imran Khan	14	run out	41
G.J.Gilmour	c Javed Miandad b Sarfraz Nawaz	32	c Zaheer Abbas b Imran Khan	0
K.J.O'Keefe	c Asif Iqbal b Imran Khan	1	c Haroon Rashid b Imran Khan	7
D.K.Lillee	lbw b Javed Miandad	14	c Zaheer Abbas b Imran Khan	27
M.H.N.Walker	not out	34	not out	3
	Extras (b 5,nb 3)	8	(b 7,nb 4)	11
	TOTAL	211		180

PAKISTAN

Majid Khan	c Marsh b Walker	48	not out	26
Sadiq Mohammad	c Cosier b Walker	25	c Marsh b Lillee	0
Zaheer Abbas	c Turner b Lillee	5	c Walters b Lillee	4
Mushtaq Mohammad *	c Turner b Lillee	9	not out	0
Haroon Rashid	c Marsh b Gilmour	57		
Asif Iqbal	b Gilmour	120		
Javed Miandad	c Walters b Walker	64		
Imran Khan	c Turner b Gilmour	0		
Sarfraz Nawaz	c Turner b Walker	13		
Wasim Bari +	c Walters b Lillee	5		
Iqbal Qasim	not out	0		
	Extras (b 6,lb 6,nb 2)	14	(b 1,nb 1)	2
	TOTAL	360	(for 2 wkts)	32

PAKISTAN

	O	M	R	W		O	M	R	W
Sarfraz Nawaz	16	4	42	3		15	3	77	3
Imran Khan	26	6	102	6		19.7	3	63	6
Asif Iqbal	15	5	53	0					
Mushtaq	2	1	2	0					
Iqbal Qasim	4	3	2	0		2	1	2	0
Javed Miandad	1.2	0	2	1		5	0	27	0

AUSTRALIA

	O	M	R	W		O	M	R	W
Lillee	22.3	0	114	3		4	0	24	2
Gilmour	16	1	81	3					
Walker	29	4	112	4		3.2	1	6	0
Walters	4	1	7	0					
O'Keefe	11	2	32	0					

FALL OF WICKETS

	AUS	PAK	AUS	PAK		AUS	PAK	AUS	PAK
1st	3	42	32	1	6th	125	320	99	
2nd	26	51	41	22	7th	138	322	99	
3rd	28	77	51		8th	146	339	115	
4th	38	111	61		9th	159	360	177	
5th	100	205	75		10th	211	360	180	

WEST INDIES vs PAKISTAN
at Port of Spain on 04/03/1977
West Indies won by 6 wickets

PAKISTAN

Majid Khan	lbw b Garner	47	c Kallicharran b Jumadeen	54
Sadiq Mohammad	c & b Croft	17	c Kallicharran b Garner	81
Haroon Rashid	b Lloyd b Croft	4	lbw b Fredericks	7
Mushtaq Mohammad *	c Fredericks b Croft	9	c Greenidge b Roberts	21
Asif Iqbal	c Murray b Croft	0	b Garner	12
Wasim Raja	b Croft	65	c Garner b Croft	84
Imran Khan	c Fredericks b Jumadeen	1	(8) c Murray b Roberts	35
Intikhab Alam	b Croft	0	(9) b Garner	12
Wasim Bari +	c Murray b Croft	21	(10) c Fredericks b Roberts	2
Salim Altaf	b Croft	1	(11) not out	4
Iqbal Qasim	not out	0	(7) b Roberts	4
	Extras (b 3,lb 3,nb 9)	15	(b 13,lb 4,nb 11)	28
	TOTAL	180		340

WEST INDIES

R.C.Fredericks	c Sadiq Mohammad b Mushtaq	120	c Asif Iqbal b Wasim Raja	57
C.G.Greenidge	b Salim Altaf	5	c Wasim Bari b Imran Khan	70
I.V.A.Richards	b Salim Altaf	4	b Imran Khan	30
A.I.Kallicharran	c Wasim Bari b Intikhab Alam	37	not out	11
I.T.Shillingford	lbw b Mushtaq	39	c Wasim Bari b Imran Khan	2
C.H.Lloyd *	c Haroon Rashid b Intikhab Alam	22	not out	23
D.L.Murray +	b Mushtaq	10		
J.Garner	lbw b Imran Khan	36		
A.M.E.Roberts	b Mushtaq	4		
C.E.H.Croft	not out	23		
R.R.Jumadeen	lbw b Imran Khan	0		
	Extras (b 5,lb 11)	16	(b 1,lb 11,w 1)	13
	TOTAL	316	(for 4 wkts)	206

WEST INDIES

	O	M	R	W		O	M	R	W
Roberts	17	2	34	0		26	4	85	4
Croft	18.5	7	29	8		25	3	66	1
Garner	16	1	47	1		20.1	6	48	3
Jumadeen	16	3	55	1		35	13	72	1
Fredericks						6	2	14	1
Richards						12	4	27	0

PAKISTAN

	O	M	R	W		O	M	R	W
Imran Khan	21	5	50	2		24	8	59	3
Salim Altaf	18	3	44	2		21	3	58	0
Intikhab Alam	29	6	90	2		2	1	6	0
Majid Khan	8	3	9	0					
Iqbal Qasim	10	2	26	0		13	6	30	0
Mushtaq	20	7	50	4		9	1	27	0
Wasim Raja	10	1	31	0		5	1	13	1

FALL OF WICKETS

	PAK	WI	PAK	WI		PAK	WI	PAK	WI
1st	10	18	123	97	6th	150	243	315	
2nd	21	22	155	159	7th	154	258	315	
3rd	21	102	167	166	8th	159	270	334	
4th	103	183	181	170	9th	161	316	340	
5th	112	216	223		10th	180	316	340	

WEST INDIES vs PAKISTAN
at Georgetown on 18/03/1977
Match drawn

PAKISTAN

Batsman	Dismissal	R	Dismissal 2	R2
Majid Khan	c Murray b Roberts	23	c Greenidge b Roberts	167
Sadiq Mohammad	c Murray b Garner	12	lbw b Croft	48
Zaheer Abbas	b Garner	0	c Fredericks b Croft	80
Haroon Rashid	c Murray b Croft	32	(5) c & b Garner	60
Mushtaq Mohammad *	c Murray b Julien	41	(4) b Roberts	19
Asif Iqbal	c & b Croft	15	(7) lbw b Garner	35
Wasim Raja	c & b Croft	5	(8) b Garner	0
Imran Khan	c Shillingford b Roberts	47	(9) lbw b Roberts	35
Sarfraz Nawaz	c Kallicharran b Garner	6	(10) c Kallicharran b Fredericks	25
Wasim Bari +	c Murray b Garner	1	(11) not out	25
Salim Altaf	not out	0	(6) lbw b Garner	6
Extras	(lb 5,nb 7)	12	(b 13,lb 7,w 1,nb 19)	40
TOTAL		**194**		**540**

WEST INDIES

Batsman	Dismissal	R	Dismissal 2	R2
R.C.Fredericks	c Majid Khan b Sarfraz Nawaz	5	not out	52
C.G.Greenidge	b Majid Khan	91	c Haroon Rashid b Imran Khan	96
I.V.A.Richards	lbw b Imran Khan	50		
A.I.Kallicharran	lbw b Imran Khan	72		
I.T.Shillingford	c Haroon Rashid b Sarfraz Nawaz	120		
B.D.Julien	b Salim Altaf	5		
D.L.Murray +	c Zaheer Abbas b Majid Khan	42		
J.Garner	b Majid Khan	4		
C.H.Lloyd *	c Imran Khan b Majid Khan	14		
A.M.E.Roberts	not out	20		
C.E.H.Croft	b Mushtaq	6		
Extras	(b 1,lb 9,w 3,nb 6)	19	(lb 5,nb 1)	6
TOTAL		**448**	**(for 1 wkt)**	**154**

WEST INDIES	O	M	R	W	O	M	R	W
Roberts	16.3	3	49	2	45	6	174	3
Croft	15	3	60	3	35	7	119	2
Garner	16	4	48	4	39	8	100	4
Julien	9	2	25	1	28	3	63	0
Richards					5	0	11	0
Fredericks					11.3	2	33	1

PAKISTAN	O	M	R	W	O	M	R	W
Imran Khan	31	6	119	2	12.5	0	79	1
Sarfraz Nawaz	45	16	105	2	9	0	58	0
Salim Altaf	29	6	71	1				
Asif Iqbal	4	1	15	0				
Mushtaq	29.3	7	74	1				
Majid Khan	24	9	45	4	3	0	11	0

FALL OF WICKETS	PAK	WI	PAK	WI		PAK	WI	PAK	WI
1st	36	11	219	154	6th	133	378	417	
2nd	40	94	304		7th	143	390	417	
3rd	46	193	311		8th	174	422	471	
4th	96	244	381		9th	188	422	491	
5th	125	255	404		10th	194	448	540	

WEST INDIES vs PAKISTAN
at Port of Spain on 01/04/1977
Pakistan won by 266 runs

PAKISTAN

Batsman	Dismissal	R	Dismissal 2	R2
Majid Khan	c Murray b Croft	92	c Murray b Croft	16
Sadiq Mohammad	c Lloyd b Roberts	0	b Inshan Ali	24
Zaheer Abbas	b Roberts	14	lbw b Garner	9
Haroon Rashid	c Kallicharran b Inshan Ali	11	lbw b Garner	11
Mushtaq Mohammad *	c Greenidge b Richards	121	c Fredericks b Roberts	56
Asif Iqbal	c Inshan Ali b Roberts	11	c & b Inshan Ali	10
Wasim Raja	c & b Inshan Ali	28	b Garner	70
Imran Khan	c Greenidge b Inshan Ali	1	c & b Croft	30
Sarfraz Nawaz	c Richards b Croft	29	c Lloyd b Croft	51
Wasim Bari +	not out	5	not out	2
Iqbal Qasim	b Richards	2		
Extras	(b 4,lb 8,nb 15)	27	(b 8,lb 11,nb 3)	22
TOTAL		**341**	**(for 9 wkts dec)**	**301**

WEST INDIES

Batsman	Dismissal	R	Dismissal 2	R2
R.C.Fredericks	b Imran Khan	41	c Majid Khan b Iqbal Qasim	17
C.G.Greenidge	b Iqbal Qasim	32	c Majid Khan b Sarfraz Nawaz	11
I.V.A.Richards	b Imran Khan	4	st Wasim Bari b Mushtaq	33
A.I.Kallicharran	c Sarfraz Nawaz b Mushtaq	11	c Asif Iqbal b Mushtaq	45
I.T.Shillingford	st Wasim Bari b Mushtaq	15	c Iqbal Qasim b Mushtaq	23
J.Garner	c Iqbal Qasim b Mushtaq	0	(8) b Sarfraz Nawaz	0
C.H.Lloyd *	lbw b Imran Khan	22	(6) b Sarfraz Nawaz	17
D.L.Murray +	lbw b Imran Khan	0	(7) c Sadiq Mohammad b Wasim Raja	30
A.M.E.Roberts	c Iqbal Qasim b Mushtaq	6	c Majid Khan b Wasim Raja	35
Inshan Ali	c Iqbal Qasim b Mushtaq	4	c Sadiq Mohammad b Wasim Raja	0
C.E.H.Croft	not out	0	not out	0
Extras	(b 11,lb 2,nb 6)	19	(b 7,lb 1,nb 3)	11
TOTAL		**154**		**222**

WEST INDIES	O	M	R	W	O	M	R	W
Roberts	25	2	82	3	20	2	56	1
Croft	21	4	56	2	22.5	6	79	3
Garner	24	6	55	0	23	4	71	3
Inshan Ali	32	9	86	3	20	2	73	2
Richards	18.3	6	34	2				
Fredericks	1	0	1	0				

PAKISTAN	O	M	R	W	O	M	R	W
Imran Khan	21	6	64	4	21	5	46	0
Sarfraz Nawaz	10	4	17	0	19.1	10	21	3
Iqbal Qasim	13	6	26	1	20	6	50	1
Mushtaq	10.5	3	28	5	31	9	69	3
Wasim Raja	1	1	0	0	3.5	1	22	3
Majid Khan					10	8	3	0

FALL OF WICKETS	PAK	WI	PAK	WI		PAK	WI	PAK	WI
1st	1	73	25	24	6th	246	122	211	154
2nd	19	77	46	42	7th	252	125	213	154
3rd	51	82	58	82	8th	320	144	286	196
4th	159	106	74	126	9th	331	154	301	196
5th	191	106	95	148	10th	341			154	222

WEST INDIES vs PAKISTAN
at Kingston on 15/04/1977
West Indies won by 140 runs

WEST INDIES

Batsman	Dismissal	R	Dismissal 2	R2
R.C.Fredericks	c & b Imran Khan	6	c Majid Khan b Wasim Raja	83
C.G.Greenidge	c Wasim Bari b Sikander Bakht	100	c Majid Khan b Sikander Bakht	82
I.V.A.Richards	c Wasim Bari b Imran Khan	5	b Wasim Raja	7
C.H.Lloyd *	c Zaheer Abbas b Imran Khan	22	c Asif Iqbal b Wasim Raja	48
A.I.Kallicharran	c Wasim Bari b Imran Khan	34	c Majid Khan b Sikander Bakht	22
C.L.King	c Wasim Bari b Sikander Bakht	41	c Majid Khan b Sikander Bakht	3
D.L.Murray +	c Sikander Bakht b Imran Khan	31	c Wasim Bari b Imran Khan	33
D.A.J.Holford	c Majid Khan b Imran Khan	2	c Wasim Bari b Sarfraz Nawaz	37
J.Garner	c Mushtaq b Sarfraz Nawaz	9	c Sadiq Mohammad b Imran Khan	0
A.M.E.Roberts	b Sarfraz Nawaz	7	c Wasim Bari b Sarfraz Nawaz	2
C.E.H.Croft	not out	6	not out	12
Extras	(lb 9,nb 8)	17	(b 13,lb 7,nb 10)	30
TOTAL		**280**		**359**

PAKISTAN

Batsman	Dismissal	R	Dismissal 2	R2
Majid Khan	c Richards b Croft	11	c Fredericks b Croft	4
Sadiq Mohammad	b Roberts	3	c Greenidge b Croft	14
Zaheer Abbas	lbw b Roberts	28	c Richards b Croft	0
Haroon Rashid	c Greenidge b Croft	72	c Greenidge b Garner	31
Mushtaq Mohammad *	c Lloyd b Garner	24	b Garner	17
Asif Iqbal	c Kallicharran b Holford	5	st Murray b Holford	135
Wasim Raja	c King b Holford	13	c Fredericks b Holford	64
Imran Khan	c & b Croft	23	c Lloyd b Holford	22
Sarfraz Nawaz	c Holford b Croft	8	b Garner	9
Wasim Bari +	retired hurt/ill	0	run out	0
Sikander Bakht	not out	1	not out	0
Extras	(lb 1,nb 9)	10	(b 3,nb 2)	5
TOTAL		**198**		**301**

PAKISTAN	O	M	R	W	O	M	R	W
Imran Khan	18	2	90	6	27.2	3	78	2
Sarfraz Nawaz	24.3	5	81	2	27	6	93	2
Sikander Bakht	12	0	71	2	16	3	55	3
Asif Iqbal	4	1	6	0				
Mushtaq	7	2	15	0	11	3	38	0
Wasim Raja					21	5	65	3

WEST INDIES	O	M	R	W	O	M	R	W
Roberts	14	4	36	2	18	6	57	0
Croft	13.3	1	49	4	20	5	86	3
Garner	9	1	57	1	18.2	0	72	3
Holford	16	3	40	2	18	3	69	3
King	4	2	6	0	3	0	12	0

FALL OF WICKETS	WI	PAK	WI	PAK		WI	PAK	WI	PAK
1st	6	11	182	5	6th	229	140	269	253
2nd	22	26	182	9	7th	252	174	335	289
3rd	56	47	193	32	8th	254	190	343	296
4th	146	106	252	51	9th	268	198	345	301
5th	200	122	260	138	10th	280		359	301

PAKISTAN vs ENGLAND
at Lahore on 14/12/1977
Match drawn

PAKISTAN

Batsman	Dismissal	R	Dismissal 2	R2
Mudassar Nazar	c & b Miller	114	c Taylor b Willis	26
Sadiq Mohammad	lbw b Miller	18	b Lever	1
Shafiq Ahmed	c Rose b Old	0	lbw b Willis	7
Haroon Rashid	c & b Lever	122	not out	45
Javed Miandad	c Taylor b Lever	71	not out	19
Wasim Raja	st Taylor b Cope	24		
Abdul Qadir	lbw b Cope	11		
Wasim Bari *+	c Cope b Miller	17		
Sarfraz Nawaz	b Cope	0		
Iqbal Qasim	not out	8		
Liaqat Ali	not out	0		
Extras	(b 1,lb 4,nb 17)	22	(nb 8)	8
TOTAL (for 9 wkts dec)		**407**	**(for 3 wkts)**	**106**

ENGLAND

G.Boycott	b Iqbal Qasim	63
J.M.Brearley *	run out	23
B.C.Rose	lbw b Sarfraz Nawaz	1
D.W.Randall	c Iqbal Qasim b Liaqat Ali	19
G.R.J.Roope	b Iqbal Qasim	19
G.Miller	not out	98
C.M.Old	c Mudassar Nazar b Iqbal Qasim	2
R.W.Taylor +	b Sarfraz Nawaz	32
G.A.Cope	lbw b Sarfraz Nawaz	0
J.K.Lever	c Wasim Bari b Sarfraz Nawaz	0
R.G.D.Willis	c Iqbal Qasim b Abdul Qadir	14
Extras	(b 2,lb 8,nb 7)	17
TOTAL		**288**

ENGLAND	O	M	R	W	O	M	R	W
Willis	17	3	67	0	7	0	34	2
Lever	16	1	47	2	3	0	13	1
Old	21	7	63	1	4	0	18	0
Miller	37	10	102	3	10	4	24	0
Cope	39	6	102	3	3	0	7	0
Boycott	3	0	4	0				
Randall					1	0	2	0

PAKISTAN	O	M	R	W	O	M	R	W
Sarfraz Nawaz	34	11	68	4				
Liaqat Ali	27	11	43	1				
Abdul Qadir	32.7	7	82	1				
Iqbal Qasim	32	12	57	3				
Wasim Raja	10	2	21	0				

FALL OF WICKETS	PAK	ENG	PAK		PAK	ENG	PAK
1st	48	53	15	6th	378	162	
2nd	49	55	40	7th	387	251	
3rd	229	96	45	8th	387	251	
4th	329	127		9th	403	253	
5th	356	148		10th		288	

PAKISTAN vs ENGLAND
at Hyderabad on 02/01/1978
Match drawn

PAKISTAN

Mudassar Nazar	c Edmonds b Cope	27	c Taylor b Willis	66
Sadiq Mohammad	c Taylor b Willis	9	c Edmonds b Cope	22
Shafiq Ahmed	c Miller b Edmonds	13	(6) not out	27
Haroon Rashid	c & b Edmonds	108	c Brearley b Cope	35
Javed Miandad	not out	88	not out	61
Wasim Raja	c Brearley b Edmonds	0	(3) c Edmonds b Willis	24
Abdul Qadir	c Brearley b Cope	4		
Wasim Bari *+	run out	10		
Iqbal Qasim	c Roope b Willis	0		
Liaqat Ali	c Edmonds b Lever	0		
Sikander Bakht	run out	3		
Extras	(b 4,lb 7,nb 2)	13	(b 13,lb 11)	24
TOTAL		275	(for 4 wkts dec)	259

ENGLAND

G.Boycott	run out	79	not out	100
J.M.Brearley *	c Wasim Bari b Iqbal Qasim	17	c sub b Wasim Raja	74
B.C.Rose	b Abdul Qadir	27		
D.W.Randall	c & b Abdul Qadir	7		
G.R.J.Roope	c & b Abdul Qadir	1		
G.Miller	c Wasim Bari b Iqbal Qasim	5		
R.W.Taylor +	b Abdul Qadir	0		
P.H.Edmonds	c Wasim Bari b Abdul Qadir	4		
G.A.Cope	c Sadiq Mohammd b Wasim Raja	22		
J.K.Lever	b Abdul Qadir	4	(3) not out	0
R.G.D.Willis	not out	8		
Extras	(b 10,lb 6,w 1)	17	(b 4,lb 7,nb 1)	12
TOTAL		191	(for 1 wkt)	186

ENGLAND	O	M	R	W		O	M	R	W
Willis	16	2	40	2		11	2	26	2
Lever	16.6	7	41	1		20	2	62	0
Edmonds	24	2	75	3		30	6	95	0
Cope	14	6	49	2		24	9	42	2
Miller	9	0	57	0		2	0	8	0
Roope						1	0	2	0

PAKISTAN	O	M	R	W		O	M	R	W
Sikander Bakht	16	4	35	0		10	3	22	0
Liaqat Ali	6	0	18	0		4	1	14	0
Iqbal Qasim	34	11	54	2		24.4	6	42	0
Javed Miandad	5	0	21	0		4	0	10	0
Abdul Qadir	24	8	44	6		27	5	72	0
Wasim Raja	1.6	0	2	1		12	5	14	1

FALL OF WICKETS	PAK	ENG	PAK	ENG		PAK	ENG	PAK	ENG
1st	14	40	55	185	6th	222	142		
2nd	40	123	116		7th	247	146		
3rd	101	137	117		8th	248	152		
4th	213	139	189		9th	249	157		
5th	213	142			10th	275	191		

PAKISTAN vs ENGLAND
at Karachi on 18/01/1978
Match drawn

ENGLAND

G.Boycott *	b Iqbal Qasim	31	c Javed Miandad b Sikander Bakht	56
B.C.Rose	c Javed Miandad b Sarfraz Nawaz	10	c Haroon Rashid b Abdul Qadir	18
D.W.Randall	lbw b Iqbal Qasim	23	b Sikander Bakht	55
G.R.J.Roope	lbw b Sikander Bakht	56	not out	33
M.W.Gatting	lbw b Abdul Qadir	5	lbw b Iqbal Qasim	6
G.Miller	c Mudassar Nazar b Wasim Raja	11	c Wasim Bari b Iqbal Qasim	3
R.W.Taylor +	lbw b Abdul Qadir	36	not out	18
P.H.Edmonds	lbw b Abdul Qadir	6		
G.A.Cope	b Iqbal Qasim	18		
J.K.Lever	not out	33		
R.G.D.Willis	lbw b Abdul Qadir	5		
Extras	(b 3,lb 21,nb 8)	32	(b 9,lb 6,w 3,nb 15)	33
TOTAL		266	(for 5 wkts)	222

PAKISTAN

Mudassar Nazar	c sub b Edmonds	76	
Shafiq Ahmed	c sub b Willis	10	
Mohsin Khan	c Willis b Cope	44	
Haroon Rashid	c Taylor b Edmonds	27	
Javed Miandad	c Roope b Edmonds	23	
Wasim Raja	c Gatting b Edmonds	47	
Abdul Qadir	c Roope b Edmonds	21	
Wasim Bari *+	lbw b Miller	6	
Sarfraz Nawaz	c Gatting b Edmonds	0	
Iqbal Qasim	b Edmonds	8	
Sikander Bakht	not out	7	
Extras	(b 2,lb 3,nb 7)	12	
TOTAL		281	

PAKISTAN	O	M	R	W		O	M	R	W
Sarfraz Nawaz	15	6	27	1		28	7	57	0
Sikander Bakht	15	4	39	1		17	4	40	2
Iqbal Qasim	40	20	56	3		29	11	51	2
Abdul Qadir	40.1	9	81	4		8	2	26	1
Wasim Raja	13	3	31	1					
Mudassar Nazar						1	0	1	0
Javed Miandad						2	0	5	0
Shafiq Ahmed						1	0	1	0
Wasim Bari						1	0	2	0
Haroon Rashid						1	0	3	0
Mohsin Khan						1	0	3	0

ENGLAND	O	M	R	W		O	M	R	W
Willis	8	1	23	1					
Lever	12	4	32	0					
Edmonds	33	7	66	7					
Cope	28	8	77	1					
Miller	14	0	71	1					

FALL OF WICKETS	ENG	PAK	ENG			ENG	PAK	ENG
1st	17	33	35		6th	189	243	
2nd	69	121	125		7th	197	263	
3rd	72	167	148		8th	203	263	
4th	85	170	162		9th	232	269	
5th	107	230	171		10th	266	281	

ENGLAND vs PAKISTAN
at Edgbaston on 01/06/1978
England won by an innings and 57 runs

PAKISTAN

Mudassar Nazar	c & b Botham	14	b Edmonds	30
Sadiq Mohammad	c Radley b Old	23	b Old	79
Mohsin Khan	b Willis	35	(4) c Old b Miller	38
Javed Miandad	c Taylor b Old	15	(5) c Brearley b Edmonds	39
Haroon Rashid	c Roope b Willis	3	(6) b Willis	4
Wasim Raja	c Taylor b Old	17	(7) b Edmonds	9
Sarfraz Nawaz	not out	32	(8) not out	6
Wasim Bari *+	b Old	0	(9) c Miller b Edmonds	3
Iqbal Qasim	c Taylor b Old	0	(3) retired hurt/ill	5
Sikander Bakht	c Roope b Old	0	c Roope b Miller	2
Liaqat Ali	c Brearley b Old	9	b Willis	3
Extras	(lb 3,nb 13)	16	(b 4,lb 4,w 1,nb 4)	13
TOTAL		164		231

ENGLAND

J.M.Brearley *	run out	38
B.Wood	lbw b Sikander Bakht	14
C.T.Radley	lbw b Sikander Bakht	106
D.I.Gower	c Javed Miandad b Sikander Bakht	58
G.R.J.Roope	b Sikander Bakht	32
G.Miller	c Wasim Bari b Mudassar Nazar	48
I.T.Botham	c Iqbal Qasim b Liaqat Ali	100
C.M.Old	c Mudassar Nazar b Iqbal Qasim	5
P.H.Edmonds	not out	4
R.W.Taylor +		
R.G.D.Willis		
Extras	(lb 26,w 5,nb 16)	47
TOTAL	(for 8 wkts dec)	452

ENGLAND	O	M	R	W		O	M	R	W
Willis	16	2	42	2		23.4	3	70	2
Old	22.4	6	50	7		25	12	38	1
Botham	15	4	52	1		17	3	47	0
Wood	3	2	2	0					
Edmonds	4	2	2	0		26	10	44	4
Miller						12	4	19	2

PAKISTAN	O	M	R	W		O	M	R	W
Sarfraz Nawaz	6	1	12	0					
Liaqat Ali	42	9	114	1					
Mudassar Nazar	27	7	59	1					
Iqbal Qasim	14	2	56	1					
Sikander Bakht	45	13	132	4					
Wasim Raja	10	1	32	0					

FALL OF WICKETS	PAK	ENG	PAK			PAK	ENG	PAK
1st	20	36	94		6th	125	399	220
2nd	56	101	123		7th	125	448	224
3rd	91	190	176		8th	126	452	227
4th	94	275	193		9th	126		231
5th	103	276	214		10th	164		

ENGLAND vs PAKISTAN
at Lord's on 15/06/1978
England won by an innings and 120 runs

ENGLAND

J.M.Brearley *	lbw b Liaqat Ali	2
G.A.Gooch	lbw b Wasim Raja	54
C.T.Radley	c Mohsin Khan b Liaqat Ali	8
D.I.Gower	b Iqbal Qasim	56
G.R.J.Roope	c Mohsin Khan b Iqbal Qasim	69
G.Miller	c Javed Miandad b Iqbal Qasim	0
I.T.Botham	b Liaqat Ali	108
R.W.Taylor +	c Mudassar Nazar b Sikander Bakht	10
C.M.Old	c Mohsin Khan b Sikander Bakht	0
P.H.Edmonds	not out	36
R.G.D.Willis	b Mudassar Nazar	18
Extras	(lb 2,nb 1)	3
TOTAL		364

PAKISTAN

Sadiq Mohammad	c Botham b Willis	11	c Taylor b Willis	0
Mudassar Nazar	c Edmonds b Willis	1	c Taylor b Botham	10
Mohsin Khan	c Willis b Edmonds	31	c Roope b Willis	46
Haroon Rashid	b Old	15	(5) b Botham	4
Javed Miandad	c Taylor b Willis	0	(6) c Gooch b Botham	22
Wasim Raja	b Edmonds	28	(7) c & b Botham	1
Talat Ali	c Radley b Edmonds	2	(4) c Roope b Botham	40
Wasim Bari *+	c Brearley b Willis	0	c Taylor b Botham	2
Iqbal Qasim	b Willis	0	(10) b Botham	0
Sikander Bakht	c Brearley b Edmonds	4	(9) c Roope b Botham	1
Liaqat Ali	not out	4	not out	0
Extras	(nb 9)	9	(b 1,lb 3,w 5,nb 4)	13
TOTAL		105		139

PAKISTAN	O	M	R	W		O	M	R	W
Sikander Bakht	27	3	115	2					
Liaqat Ali	18	1	80	3					
Mudassar Nazar	4.2	0	16	1					
Iqbal Qasim	30	5	101	3					
Wasim Raja	12	3	49	1					

ENGLAND	O	M	R	W		O	M	R	W
Willis	13	1	47	5		10	2	26	2
Old	10	3	26	1		15	4	36	0
Botham	5	2	17	0		20.5	8	34	8
Edmonds	8	6	6	4		12	4	21	0
Miller						9	3	9	0

FALL OF WICKETS	ENG	PAK	PAK			ENG	PAK	PAK
1st	5	11	1		6th	252	96	119
2nd	19	22	45		7th	290	97	121
3rd	120	40	100		8th	290	97	130
4th	120	41	108		9th	324	105	130
5th	134	84	114		10th	364	105	139

ENGLAND vs PAKISTAN
at Headingley on 29/06/1978
Match drawn

PAKISTAN

Sadiq Mohammad	c Brearley b Botham	97
Mudassar Nazar	c Botham b Old	31
Mohsin Khan	lbw b Willis	41
Talat Ali	c Gooch b Willis	0
Haroon Rashid	c Brearley b Botham	7
Javed Miandad	b Old	1
Wasim Raja	lbw b Botham	0
Sarfraz Nawaz	c Taylor b Botham	4
Sikander Bakht	b Old	4
Wasim Bari *+	not out	7
Iqbal Qasim	lbw b Old	0
	Extras (lb 8,nb 1)	9
	TOTAL	**201**

ENGLAND

J.M.Brearley *	c Wasim Bari b Sarfraz Nawaz	0
G.A.Gooch	lbw b Sarfraz Nawaz	20
C.T.Radley	b Sikander Bakht	7
D.I.Gower	lbw b Sarfraz Nawaz	39
G.R.J.Roope	c Sadiq Mohammad b Javed Miandad	11
G.Miller	not out	18
R.W.Taylor +	c Wasim Bari b Sarfraz Nawaz	2
I.T.Botham	lbw b Sarfraz Nawaz	4
P.H.Edmonds	not out	1
C.M.Old		
R.G.D.Willis		
	Extras (b 1,lb 5,w 1,nb 10)	17
	TOTAL (for 7 wkts)	**119**

ENGLAND	O	M	R	W		O	M	R	W
Willis	26	8	48	2					
Old	41.4	22	41	4					
Botham	18	2	59	4					
Edmonds	11	2	22	0					
Miller	9	3	22	0					

PAKISTAN	O	M	R	W		O	M	R	W
Sarfraz Nawaz	20	6	39	5					
Sikander Bakht	15	4	26	1					
Mudassar Nazar	5	2	12	0					
Iqbal Qasim	11	8	11	0					
Javed Miandad	3	0	14	1					

FALL OF WICKETS	PAK	ENG				PAK	ENG
1st	75	0			6th	183	110
2nd	147	24			7th	189	116
3rd	147	51			8th	190	
4th	169	77			9th	201	
5th	182	102			10th	201	

PAKISTAN vs INDIA
at Faisalabad on 16/10/1978
Match drawn

PAKISTAN

Majid Khan	b Bedi	47	c Chauhan b Prasanna	34
Sadiq Mohammad	c & b Bedi	41	c Gavaskar b Kapil Dev	16
Zaheer Abbas	c Viswanath b Prasanna	176	c Chauhan b Gavaskar	96
Mushtaq Mohammad *	c Gavaskar b Chandrasekhar	5		
Javed Miandad	not out	154	not out	6
Asif Iqbal	c Chauhan b Bedi	0	(4) b Amarnath S.	104
Imran Khan	c Vengsarkar b Chandrasekhar	32		
Wasim Bari +	b Chandrasekhar	3		
Sarfraz Nawaz	lbw b Chandrasekhar	18		
Sikander Bakht	not out	16		
Iqbal Qasim				
	Extras (lb 5,nb 6)	11	(b 2,lb 3,nb 3)	8
	TOTAL (for 8 wkts dec)	**503**	(for 4 wkts dec)	**264**

INDIA

S.M.Gavaskar	b Iqbal Qasim	89	not out	8
C.P.S.Chauhan	c Wasim Bari b Sarfraz Nawaz	46	not out	30
S.Amarnath	c Javed Miandad b Mushtaq	35		
G.R.Viswanath	b Mushtaq	145		
D.B.Vengsarkar	c Wasim Bari b Imran Khan	83		
M.Amarnath	c Wasim Bari b Sarfraz Nawaz	4		
S.M.H.Kirmani +	c Iqbal Qasim b Mushtaq	1		
Kapil Dev	c sub b Mushtaq	8		
E.A.S.Prasanna	not out	10		
B.S.Bedi *	run out	1		
B.S.Chandrasekhar				
	Extras (b 3,lb 3,nb 34)	40	(b 1,lb 1,nb 3)	5
	TOTAL (for 9 wkts dec)	**462**	(for 0 wkts)	**43**

INDIA	O	M	R	W		O	M	R	W
Kapil Dev	16	2	71	0		12	3	25	1
Amarnath M.	7	0	44	0		10	1	43	0
Prasanna	42	11	123	1		14	4	34	1
Bedi	49	9	124	3		12	4	40	0
Chandrasekhar	38	6	130	4		12	1	49	0
Chauhan						5	0	26	0
Gavaskar						5	0	34	1
Amarnath S.						1.5	0	5	1

PAKISTAN	O	M	R	W		O	M	R	W
Imran Khan	34.5	7	111	1		6	2	15	0
Sarfraz Nawaz	37	6	105	2		2	1	3	0
Sikander Bakht	24	1	86	0					
Mushtaq	27	10	55	4		4	4	0	0
Iqbal Qasim	20	3	65	1		3	1	4	0
Javed Miandad						4	0	16	0
Sadiq Mohammad									

FALL OF WICKETS	PAK	IND	PAK	IND		PAK	IND	PAK	IND
1st	84	97	54		6th	445	425		
2nd	99	147	60		7th	452	445		
3rd	110	248	226		8th	476	447		
4th	365	414	264		9th		462		
5th	378	421			10th				

PAKISTAN vs INDIA
at Lahore on 27/10/1978
Pakistan won by 8 wickets

INDIA

S.M.Gavaskar	c Majid Khan b Salim Altaf	5	c Sarfraz Nawaz b Mushtaq	97
C.P.S.Chauhan	b Imran Khan	10	c Wasim Bari b Javed Miandad	93
S.Amarnath	c Asif Iqbal b Imran Khan	8	c Mudassar Nazar b Mushtaq	60
G.R.Viswanath	b Sarfraz Nawaz	20	b Mudassar Nazar	83
D.B.Vengsarkar	c Wasim Bari b Imran Khan	76	(6) c Wasim Bari b Mudassar Nazar	17
M.Amarnath	hit wicket b Sarfraz Nawaz	20	(7) c Iqbal Qasim b Sarfraz Nawaz	7
S.M.H.Kirmani +	lbw b Mudassar Nazar	12	(8) not out	39
Kapil Dev	lbw b Sarfraz Nawaz	15	(5) c Majid Khan b Imran Khan	43
E.A.S.Prasanna	not out	1	c Mushtaq b Imran Khan	4
B.S.Bedi *	lbw b Sarfraz Nawaz	4	b Sarfraz Nawaz	1
B.S.Chandrasekhar	b Imran Khan	0	b Imran Khan	4
	Extras (b 17,lb 4,nb 7)	28	(b 8,lb 4,nb 5)	17
	TOTAL	**199**		**465**

PAKISTAN

Majid Khan	c Kirmani b Bedi	45	c & b Amarnath M.	38
Mudassar Nazar	c Gavaskar b Kapil Dev	12	b Kapil Dev	29
Wasim Bari +	c Kirmani b Bedi	85		
Zaheer Abbas	not out	235	(3) not out	34
Asif Iqbal	b Chandrasekhar	29	(4) not out	21
Javed Miandad	b Amarnath M.	35		
Mushtaq Mohammad *	run out	67		
Imran Khan	not out	9		
Sarfraz Nawaz				
Iqbal Qasim				
Salim Altaf				
	Extras (b 12,lb 8,w 1,nb 1)	22	(lb 6)	6
	TOTAL (for 6 wkts dec)	**539**	(for 2 wkts)	**128**

PAKISTAN	O	M	R	W		O	M	R	W
Imran Khan	18.5	2	54	4		42.3	12	110	3
Salim Altaf	13	3	34	1		16	6	36	0
Sarfraz Nawaz	16	4	46	4		38	7	112	2
Mushtaq	6	0	32	0		30	6	106	2
Mudassar Nazar	3	2	5	1		4	1	4	2
Iqbal Qasim						33	12	68	0
Javed Miandad						5	1	7	1
Majid Khan						2	0	5	0

INDIA	O	M	R	W		O	M	R	W
Kapil Dev	28	1	98	1		10	1	53	1
Gavaskar	4	1	10	0					
Bedi	34	6	130	2		4	0	23	0
Chandrasekhar	21	2	109	1					
Amarnath M.	21	1	76	1		6	0	39	1
Prasanna	25	2	94	0					
Viswanath						0.4	0	7	0

FALL OF WICKETS	IND	PAK	IND	PAK		IND	PAK	IND	PAK
1st	15	19	192	57	6th	186	502	407	
2nd	19	144	202	89	7th	192		415	
3rd	48	161	301		8th	194		437	
4th	49	216	371		9th	198		438	
5th	151	356	406		10th	199		465	

PAKISTAN vs INDIA
at Karachi on 14/11/1978
Pakistan won by 8 wickets

INDIA

S.M.Gavaskar	c Sarfraz Nawaz b Imran Khan	111	c Wasim Bari b Sarfraz Nawaz	137
C.P.S.Chauhan	c Iqbal Qasim b Sarfraz Nawaz	33	c Wasim Bari b Sarfraz Nawaz	0
S.Amarnath	c Mushtaq b Iqbal Qasim	30	(6) run out	14
G.R.Viswanath	b Imran Khan	0	(5) c Wasim Bari b Sarfraz Nawaz	1
D.B.Vengsarkar	c Majid Khan b Sikander Bakht	11	(7) c Wasim Bari b Sikander Bakht	1
M.Amarnath	lbw b Sarfraz Nawaz	14	(3) b Imran Khan	53
S.M.H.Kirmani +	c Mushtaq b Sikander Bakht	14	(4) c Iqbal Qasim b Imran Khan	4
K.D.Ghavri	c Majid Khan b Sarfraz Nawaz	42	c Javed Miandad b Imran Khan	35
Kapil Dev	lbw b Sarfraz Nawaz	59	c Mushtaq b Sarfraz Nawaz	34
B.S.Bedi *	c Majid Khan b Imran Khan	4	not out	0
B.S.Chandrasekhar		0	b Sarfraz Nawaz	0
	Extras (b 10,lb 6,w 1,nb 9)	26	(b 9,lb 4,w 1,nb 7)	21
	TOTAL	**344**		**300**

PAKISTAN

Majid Khan	b Kapil Dev	44	c Chauhan b Kapil Dev	14
Mudassar Nazar	c Chauhan b Chandrasekhar	57		
Wasim Bari +	c Kirmani b Ghavri	3		
Zaheer Abbas	c Viswanath b Bedi	42		
Asif Iqbal	lbw b Chandrasekhar	1	(2) c Kirmani b Amarnath M.	44
Javed Miandad	c Kirmani b Kapil Dev	100	(3) not out	62
Mushtaq Mohammad *	c sub b Ghavri	78	(4) not out	31
Imran Khan	b Chandrasekhar	32		
Sarfraz Nawaz	c sub b Kapil Dev	28		
Iqbal Qasim	not out	29		
Sikander Bakht	not out	22		
	Extras (b 5,lb 20,w 1,nb 19)	45	(b 3,lb 9,nb 1)	13
	TOTAL (for 9 wkts dec)	**481**	(for 2 wkts)	**164**

PAKISTAN	O	M	R	W		O	M	R	W
Imran Khan	32	12	75	3		28	7	76	3
Sarfraz Nawaz	31.2	4	89	4		24	5	70	5
Sikander Bakht	22	6	76	2		10	2	42	1
Iqbal Qasim	23	6	67	1		7	1	27	0
Mudassar Nazar	4	2	5	0		2	0	13	0
Mushtaq	3	0	6	0		9	0	36	0
Javed Miandad						2	0	15	0

INDIA	O	M	R	W		O	M	R	W
Kapil Dev	42	4	132	3		9	0	47	1
Ghavri	24	5	66	2		6	0	36	0
Amarnath M.	14	2	39	0		5.5	0	35	1
Chandrasekhar	25	4	97	3					
Bedi	35	5	99	1		4	0	33	0
Chauhan	1	0	3	0					

FALL OF WICKETS	IND	PAK	IND	PAK		IND	PAK	IND	PAK
1st	58	84	5	21	6th	219	341	173	
2nd	131	104	122	118	7th	253	374	246	
3rd	132	153	143		8th	337	408	297	
4th	179	155	147		9th	344	447	299	
5th	217	187	170		10th	344		300	

NEW ZEALAND vs PAKISTAN
at Christchurch on 02/02/1979
Pakistan won by 128 runs

PAKISTAN

Mudassar Nazar	c Edgar b Bracewel	7	retired hurt/ill		4
Talat Ali	c Wright b Hadlee	40	c Coney b Hadlee		61
Mohsin Khan	lbw b Hadlee	12	lbw b Coney		7
Javed Miandad	b Hadlee	81	not out		160
Haroon Rashid	c Howarth b Hadlee	40	b Cairns		35
Wasim Raja	c Boock b Cairns	12	c Hadlee b Coney		17
Mushtaq Mohammad *	lbw b Hadlee	10	c Burgess b Hadlee		12
Sarfraz Nawaz	not out	31	b Hadlee		4
Wasim Bari +	b Cairns	9			
Anwar Khan	c Lees b Boock	12	(9) not out		3
Sikander Bakht	c Edgar b Boock	0			
Extras	(b 5,lb 8,nb 4)	17	(b 1,lb 19)		20
TOTAL		271	(for 6 wkts dec)		323

NEW ZEALAND

B.A.Edgar	c Wasim Bari b Sikander Bakht	129	c Sarfraz Nawaz b Sikander Bakht		16
J.G.Wright	c Wasim Bari b Sikander Bakht	27	b Mushtaq		21
G.P.Howarth	c Wasim Raja b Mushtaq	19	(4) b Mushtaq		0
M.G.Burgess *	c Javed Miandad b Sikander Bakht	16	(5) c Sarfraz Nawaz b Wasim Raja		6
J.M.Parker	c Wasim Bari b Sarfraz Nawaz	2	(6) lbw b Mushtaq		33
J.V.Coney	c Javed Miandad b Mushtaq	6	(3) c Mohsin Khan b Wasim Raja		36
W.K.Lees +	c & b Mushtaq	8	c Wasim Bari b Wasim Raja		19
R.J.Hadlee	c Wasim Bari b Wasim Raja	42	c Sikander Bakht b Wasim Raja		4
B.L.Cairns	lbw b Mushtaq	11	not out		23
S.L.Boock	b Wasim Raja	1	(11) c Mohsin Khan b Mushtaq		0
B.P.Bracewell	not out	0	(10) st Wasim Bari b Mushtaq		5
Extras	(b 8,lb 9,nb 12)	29	(b 4,lb 6,nb 3)		13
TOTAL		290			176

NEW ZEALAND	O	M	R	W		O	M	R	W
Hadlee	25	2	62	5		26	4	83	3
Bracewel	12	1	50	1		7	0	53	0
Coney	7	3	10	0		12	1	33	2
Cairns	31	5	96	2		23	7	46	1
Boock	14.6	5	22	2		19	4	70	0
Howarth	3	1	14	0		6	0	18	0

PAKISTAN	O	M	R	W		O	M	R	W
Sarfraz Nawaz	24	7	67	1		8	3	22	0
Sikander Bakht	21	4	88	3		6	0	14	1
Mushtaq	25	4	60	4		22	5	59	5
Anwar Khan	4	0	12	0					
Wasim Raja	10.4	5	18	2		20	3	68	4
Mudassar Nazar	4	1	16	0					

FALL OF WICKETS	PAK	NZ	PAK	NZ		PAK	NZ	PAK	NZ
1st	19	63	24	33	6th	198	290	316	136
2nd	48	96	128	62	7th	242	254		142
3rd	75	147	209	62	8th	255	288		152
4th	135	151	273	77	9th	271	289		176
5th	183	176	298	98	10th	271	290		176

NEW ZEALAND vs PAKISTAN
at Auckland on 23/02/1979
Match drawn

NEW ZEALAND

J.G.Wright	c Wasim Bari b Sikander Bakht	32	b Sarfraz Nawaz		10
B.A.Edgar	c Wasim Bari b Imran Khan	1	b Imran Khan		0
G.P.Howarth	c Wasim Bari b Sarfraz Nawaz	5	c Wasim Raja b Sikander Bakht		38
J.F.Reid	c Wasim Bari b Imran Khan	4	(5) c Majid Khan b Mushtaq		19
M.G.Burgess *	c Sarfraz Nawaz b Sikander Bakht	3	(4) c Asif Iqbal b Sarfraz Nawaz		71
J.V.Coney	c Wasim Bari b Sarfraz Nawaz	82	c Mushtaq b Imran Khan		49
W.K.Lees +	c Wasim Bari b Sarfraz Nawaz	25	not out		45
B.L.Cairns	c Wasim Bari b Asif Iqbal	17	b Sarfraz Nawaz		4
R.J.Hadlee	not out	53	c Talat Ali b Sarfraz Nawaz		5
G.B.Troup	c Mushtaq q Sikander Bakht	7			
S.L.Boock	c Javed Miandad b Imran Khan	2			
Extras	(b 5,lb 3,w 1,nb 20)	29	(b 8,lb 13,w 1,nb 18)		40
TOTAL		254	(for 8 wkts dec)		281

PAKISTAN

Majid Khan	b Cairns	10			
Talat Ali	c Lees b Hadlee	1	(1) not out		8
Zaheer Abbas	c Lees b Troup	135			
Javed Miandad	lbw b Cairns	30	(2) not out		0
Asif Iqbal	c Coney b Cairns	35			
Mushtaq Mohammad *	lbw b Hadlee	48			
Wasim Raja	c Coney b Troup	19			
Imran Khan	c Lees b Hadlee	33			
Sarfraz Nawaz	c Howarth b Hadlee	5			
Wasim Bari +	not out	25			
Sikander Bakht	c Cairns b Hadlee	6			
Extras	(b 4,lb 7,nb 1)	12			0
TOTAL		359	(for 0 wkts)		8

PAKISTAN	O	M	R	W		O	M	R	W
Imran Khan	17.7	2	77	3		32	9	72	2
Sarfraz Nawaz	15	3	56	3		28.2	9	61	4
Asif Iqbal	7	1	24	1		2	0	5	0
Sikander Bakht	16	4	68	3		18	2	64	1
Mushtaq						11	2	39	1

NEW ZEALAND	O	M	R	W		O	M	R	W
Hadlee	27	3	104	5		0.6	0	8	0
Troup	22	5	70	2					
Cairns	28	5	94	3					
Coney	19	4	51	0					
Boock	6	0	28	0					
Howarth	1	1	0	0					

FALL OF WICKETS	NZ	PAK	NZ	PAK		NZ	PAK	NZ	PAK
1st	11	5	1		6th	109	273	261	
2nd	31	22	52		7th	166	321	275	
3rd	32	118	85		8th	209	322	281	
4th	50	195	121		9th	251	345		
5th	60	231	205		10th	254	359		

NEW ZEALAND vs PAKISTAN
at Napier on 16/02/1979
Match drawn

PAKISTAN

Majid Khan	c Lees b Cairns	29	not out		119
Talat Ali	b Hadlee	4	b Hadlee		13
Zaheer Abbas	c Parker b Cairns	2	c & b Boock		40
Javed Miandad	run out	26			
Asif Iqbal	b Cairns	104			
Mushtaq Mohammad *	c Lees b Hadlee	24	(4) c Cairns b Boock		28
Wasim Raja	lbw b Hadlee	74			
Imran Khan	c Lees b Hadlee	3	(5) not out		27
Sarfraz Nawaz	c Edgar b Coney	31			
Wasim Bari +	not out	37			
Sikander Bakht	lbw b Troup	19			
Extras	(b 2,lb 3,nb 2)	7	(b 2,lb 1,w 4)		7
TOTAL		360	(for 3 wkts dec)		234

NEW ZEALAND

B.A.Edgar	c Mushtaq b Imran Khan	3
J.G.Wright	c Javed Miandad b Sikander Bakht	88
G.P.Howarth	b Sikander Bakht	114
J.M.Parker	lbw b Sikander Bakht	3
M.G.Burgess *	c Javed Miandad b Imran Khan	40
J.V.Coney	lbw b Sikander Bakht	69
S.L.Boock	b Imran Khan	4
W.K.Lees +	b Imran Khan	8
R.J.Hadlee	c Sikander Bakht b Imran Khan	11
B.L.Cairns	c Zaheer Abbas b Mushtaq	13
G.B.Troup	not out	3
Extras	(b 10,lb 14,nb 22)	46
TOTAL		402

NEW ZEALAND	O	M	R	W		O	M	R	W
Hadlee	25	3	101	4		14	1	56	1
Cairns	19	1	86	3		11	2	23	0
Troup	22.5	2	86	1		16	3	25	0
Boock	12	3	41	0		30	6	77	2
Coney	25	9	38	1		10	2	21	0
Howarth	1	0	1	0		5	1	25	0

PAKISTAN	O	M	R	W		O	M	R	W
Imran Khan	33	6	106	5					
Sarfraz Nawaz	26	5	90	0					
Sikander Bakht	17	2	67	4					
Mushtaq	17.3	0	70	1					
Wasim Raja	3	1	10	0					
Majid Khan	5	1	13	0					

FALL OF WICKETS	PAK	NZ	PAK			PAK	NZ	PAK
1st	19	24	27		6th	221	301	
2nd	23	219	110		7th	228	318	
3rd	42	230	188		8th	283	351	
4th	128	241			9th	313	388	
5th	180	292			10th	360	402	

AUSTRALIA vs PAKISTAN
at Melbourne on 10/03/1979
Pakistan won by 71 runs

PAKISTAN

Majid Khan	c Wright b Hogg	1	b Border		108
Mohsin Khan	c Hilditch b Hogg	14	c & b Hogg		14
Zaheer Abbas	b Hogg	11	c Wright b Border		59
Javed Miandad	b Hogg	19	c Wright b Border		16
Asif Iqbal	c Wright b Clark	9	lbw b Hogg		44
Mushtaq Mohammad *	c Wright b Hurst	36	c sub b Sleep		28
Wasim Raja	b Hurst	13	c Wright b Hurst		28
Imran Khan	c Wright b Hurst	33	c Clark b Hurst		28
Sarfraz Nawaz	c Wright b Sleep	35	lbw b Hurst		1
Wasim Bari +	run out	0	not out		8
Sikander Bakht	not out	5			
Extras	(b 2,lb 7,w 1,nb 10)	20	(b 4,lb 6,nb 9)		19
TOTAL		196	(for 9 wkts dec)		353

AUSTRALIA

G.M.Wood	not out	5	(6) c Wasim Bari b Sarfraz Nawaz		0
A.M.J.Hilditch	c Javed Miandad b Imran Khan	3	b Sarfraz Nawaz		62
A.R.Border	b Imran Khan	20	b Sarfraz Nawaz		105
G.N.Yallop *	b Imran Khan	25	run out		8
K.J.Hughes	run out	19	c Mohsin Khan b Sarfraz Nawaz		84
D.F.Whatmore	lbw b Sarfraz Nawaz	43	(1) b Sarfraz Nawaz		15
P.R.Sleep	c Wasim Bari b Imran Khan	10	b Sarfraz Nawaz		0
K.J.Wright +	c Imran Khan b Wasim Raja	9	not out		1
W.M.Clark	c Mushtaq b Wasim Raja	9	b Sarfraz Nawaz		0
R.M.Hogg	run out	9	lbw b Sarfraz Nawaz		0
A.G.Hurst	c & b Sarfraz Nawaz	0	c Wasim Bari b Sarfraz Nawaz		0
Extras	(b 1,lb 5,w 2,nb 8)	16	(b 13,lb 13,nb 9)		35
TOTAL		168			310

AUSTRALIA	O	M	R	W		O	M	R	W
Hogg	17	4	49	4		19	2	75	3
Hurst	20	4	55	3		19.5	1	115	3
Clark	17	4	56	1		21	6	47	0
Sleep	7.7	2	16	1		8	0	62	1
Border						14	5	35	2

PAKISTAN	O	M	R	W		O	M	R	W
Imran Khan	18	8	26	4		27	9	73	0
Sarfraz Nawaz	21.6	6	39	2		35.4	7	86	9
Sikander Bakht	10	1	29	0		7	0	29	0
Mushtaq	7	0	35	0		11	0	42	0
Wasim Raja	5	0	23	2		3	0	11	0
Majid Khan						9	1	34	0

FALL OF WICKETS	PAK	AUS	PAK	AUS		PAK	AUS	PAK	AUS
1st	2	11	30	49	6th	99	140	299	306
2nd	22	53	165	109	7th	122	152	330	308
3rd	28	63	204	128	8th	173	167	332	309
4th	40	97	209	305	9th	177	167	353	310
5th	83	109	261	305	10th	196	168		310

AUSTRALIA vs PAKISTAN
at Perth on 24/03/1979
Australia won by 7 wickets

PAKISTAN

Batsman	Dismissal	Runs	Dismissal 2	Runs 2
Majid Khan	c Hilditch b Hogg	0	c sub b Hogg	0
Mudassar Nazar	c Wright b Hurst	5	c Hilditch b Hurst	25
Zaheer Abbas	c Wright b Hurst	29	c Wright b Hogg	18
Javed Miandad	not out	129	c Wright b Hurst	19
Haroon Rashid	c Border b Hurst	4	c Yardley b Dymock	47
Asif Iqbal	run out	35	not out	134
Mushtaq Mohammad *	run out	23	lbw b Yardley	1
Imran Khan	c Wright b Dymock	14	c Wright b Hurst	15
Sarfraz Nawaz	c Wright b Hurst	27	c Yardley b Hurst	3
Wasim Bari +	c Hilditch b Dymock	0	c Whatmore b Hurst	0
Sikander Bakht	b Dymock	0	run out	0
Extras	(lb 3,w 3,nb 5)	11	(b 3,lb 8,nb 12)	23
TOTAL		277		285

AUSTRALIA

Batsman	Dismissal	Runs	Dismissal 2	Runs 2
W.M.Darling	lbw b Mudassar Nazar	75	run out	79
A.M.J.Hilditch	c Zaheer Abbas b Imran Khan	41	handled the ball	29
A.R.Border	c Majid Khan b Javed Miandad	85	not out	66
K.J.Hughes *	lbw b Sikander Bakht	9		
J.K.Moss	c Wasim Bari b Mudassar Nazar	22	not out	38
D.F.Whatmore	c Asif Iqbal b Imran Khan	15		
K.J.Wright +	c Wasim Bari b Mudassar Nazar	16		
B.Yardley	b Sarfraz Nawaz	19	(4) run out	1
G.Dymock	not out	5		
R.M.Hogg	b Imran Khan	3		
A.G.Hurst	c Wasim Bari b Sarfraz Nawaz	16		
Extras	(b 3,lb 4,w 1,nb 13)	21	(lb 13,nb 10)	23
TOTAL		327	(for 3 wkts)	236

AUSTRALIA	O	M	R	W		O	M	R	W
Hogg	19	2	88	1		20	5	45	2
Hurst	23	6	61	4		24.7	2	94	5
Dymock	21.6	3	65	3		23	5	72	1
Yardley	14	2	52	0		14	3	42	1
Border						4	0	9	0

PAKISTAN	O	M	R	W		O	M	R	W
Imran Khan	32	5	105	3		17	1	81	0
Sarfraz Nawaz	35.1	7	112	2		19	1	85	0
Sikander Bakht	10.5	1	33	1					
Mudassar Nazar	16	2	48	3		10.1	2	35	0
Javed Miandad	2	0	8	1		2	0	12	0

FALL OF WICKETS	PAK	AUS	PAK	AUS		PAK	AUS	PAK	AUS
1st	0	96	0	87	6th	176	273	153	
2nd	27	143	35	153	7th	224	297	245	
3rd	41	161	68	155	8th	276	301	263	
4th	49	219	86		9th	277	304	263	
5th	90	246	152		10th	277	327	285	

INDIA vs PAKISTAN
at Bangalore on 21/11/1979
Match drawn

PAKISTAN

Batsman	Dismissal	Runs	Dismissal 2	Runs 2
Majid Khan	c Kirmani b Ghavri	1	st Kirmani b Doshi	19
Mudassar Nazar	c Doshi b Yadav	126	c Kapil Dev b Yadav	17
Zaheer Abbas	st Kirmani b Doshi	40	not out	31
Javed Miandad	lbw b Doshi	76	not out	30
Wasim Raja	lbw b Kapil Dev	36		
Asif Iqbal *	c & b Doshi	55		
Imran Khan	c Viswanath b Yadav	6		
Wasim Bari +	not out	49		
Abdul Qadir	lbw b Kapil Dev	8		
Iqbal Qasim	run out	20		
Ehteshamuddin				
Extras	(b 1,lb 6,nb 7)	14	(b 4,nb 7)	11
TOTAL	(for 9 wkts dec)	431	(for 2 wkts)	108

INDIA

Batsman	Dismissal	Runs
S.M.Gavaskar *	c Javed Miandad b Abdul Qadir	88
C.P.S.Chauhan	c Majid Khan b Imran Khan	13
G.R.Viswanath	c Wasim Bari b Ehteshamuddin	73
D.B.Vengsarkar	b Imran Khan	33
Yashpal Sharma	c Javed Miandad b Majid Khan	62
R.M.H.Binny	c Ehteshamuddin b Imran Khan	46
S.M.H.Kirmani +	c Iqbal Qasim b Ehteshamuddin	37
Kapil Dev	b Majid Khan	38
K.D.Ghavri	b Majid Khan	2
N.S.Yadav	not out	1
D.R.Doshi	b Imran Khan	0
Extras	(b 13,lb 10)	23
TOTAL		416

INDIA	O	M	R	W		O	M	R	W
Kapil Dev	24	4	67	2		4	2	6	0
Ghavri	24	3	83	1		8	3	30	0
Binny	10	1	49	0		3	2	1	0
Doshi	52.3	20	102	3		12	3	26	1
Yadav	39	5	116	2		11	2	20	1
Viswanath						3	1	6	0
Gavaskar						1	0	8	0

PAKISTAN	O	M	R	W		O	M	R	W
Imran Khan	28.4	12	53	4					
Ehteshamuddin	18	2	52	2					
Iqbal Qasim	41	17	75	0					
Majid Khan	28	9	55	3					
Abdul Qadir	35	8	114	1					
Wasim Raja	8	2	30	0					
Mudassar Nazar	6	1	14	0					

FALL OF WICKETS	PAK	IND	PAK			PAK	IND	PAK
1st	5	17	41		6th	345	347	
2nd	62	122	41		7th	348	410	
3rd	196	164			8th	371	414	
4th	256	266			9th	431	415	
5th	334	307			10th		416	

INDIA vs PAKISTAN
at Delhi on 04/12/1979
Match drawn

PAKISTAN

Batsman	Dismissal	Runs	Dismissal 2	Runs 2
Majid Khan	b Kapil Dev	0	c Kirmani b Binny	40
Mudassar Nazar	c Chauhan b Kapil Dev	18	c Kirmani b Kapil Dev	12
Zaheer Abbas	b Kapil Dev	3	c Kirmani b Binny	50
Javed Miandad	lbw b Ghavri	34	run out	0
Wasim Raja	lbw b Kapil Dev	97	c Kapil Dev b Doshi	61
Asif Iqbal *	c Vengsarkar b Ghavri	64	c Kirmani b Kapil Dev	38
Imran Khan	lbw b Binny	30	c Chauhan b Doshi	2
Wasim Bari +	b Kapil Dev	9	b Ghavri	5
Abdul Qadir	b Binny	9	c Vengsarkar b Kapil Dev	11
Iqbal Qasim	run out	2	not out	5
Sikander Bakht	not out	1	lbw b Kapil Dev	6
Extras	(lb 2,nb 4)	6	(b 6,lb 4,nb 2)	12
TOTAL		273		242

INDIA

Batsman	Dismissal	Runs	Dismissal 2	Runs 2
S.M.Gavaskar *	c Wasim Bari b Sikander Bakht	31	c Wasim Bari b Sikander Bakht	21
C.P.S.Chauhan	c Wasim Bari b Sikander Bakht	11	lbw b Sikander Bakht	40
D.B.Vengsarkar	c Javed Miandad b Sikander Bakht	1	not out	146
G.R.Viswanath	run out	4	b Iqbal Qasim	34
Yashpal Sharma	not out	28	c & b Sikander Bakht	60
R.M.Binny	lbw b Sikander Bakht	1	(7) c Abdul Qadir b Asif Iqbal	10
S.M.H.Kirmani +	b Sikander Bakht	5	(8) not out	11
Kapil Dev	lbw b Sikander Bakht	15	(6) lbw b Mudassar Nazar	21
K.D.Ghavri	lbw b Sikander Bakht	0		
N.S.Yadav	c Abdul Qadir b Sikander Bakht	4		
D.R.Doshi	c Javed Miandad b Asif Iqbal	10		
Extras	(b 2,lb 5,nb 9)	16	(b 2,lb 5,w 1,nb 13)	21
TOTAL		126	(for 6 wkts)	364

INDIA	O	M	R	W		O	M	R	W
Kapil Dev	23.5	8	58	5		22.5	6	63	4
Ghavri	21	4	58	2		17	4	59	1
Binny	10	3	32	2		17	3	56	2
Doshi	17	3	51	0		19	6	31	2
Yadav	20	2	68	0		5	0	21	0

PAKISTAN	O	M	R	W		O	M	R	W
Imran Khan	7.3	4	11	0		1	0	2	0
Sikander Bakht	21	3	69	8		38	7	121	3
Asif Iqbal	6.2	4	3	1		20	7	46	1
Majid Khan	1	0	12	0		4	2	8	0
Iqbal Qasim	3	0	7	0		30	5	87	1
Mudassar Nazar	3	0	8	0		25	8	61	1
Abdul Qadir						11	3	16	0
Wasim Raja						2	1	2	0

FALL OF WICKETS	PAK	IND	PAK	IND		PAK	IND	PAK	IND
1st	3	19	39	37	6th	224	70	209	343
2nd	13	35	68	92	7th	250	87	210	
3rd	36	46	68	154	8th	270	87	230	
4th	90	52	143	276	9th	271	94	232	
5th	220	56	201	308	10th	273	126	242	

INDIA vs PAKISTAN
at Bombay on 16/12/1979
India won by 131 runs

INDIA

Batsman	Dismissal	Runs	Dismissal 2	Runs 2
S.M.Gavaskar *	c Abdul Qadir b Sikander Bakht	4	c Zaheer Abbas b Iqbal Qasim	48
C.P.S.Chauhan	c Wasim Bari b Imran Khan	5	b Mudassar Nazar	0
D.B.Vengsarkar	c Majid Khan b Iqbal Qasim	58	c Wasim Bari b Sikander Bakht	45
G.R.Viswanath	c & b Iqbal Qasim	47	lbw b Abdul Qadir	9
Yashpal Sharma	b Iqbal Qasim	3	c Majid Khan b Iqbal Qasim	16
R.M.H.Binny	c Wasim Bari b Iqbal Qasim	0	(9) c & b Sikander Bakht	0
S.M.H.Kirmani +	c Asif Iqbal b Sikander Bakht	41	(6) c Asif Iqbal b Iqbal Qasim	15
Kapil Dev	c Wasim Raja b Sikander Bakht	69	(7) c Wasim Bari b Iqbal Qasim	3
K.D.Ghavri	c Asif Iqbal b Sikander Bakht	36	(8) c Wasim Bari b Iqbal Qasim	1
N.S.Yadav	not out	29	st Wasim Bari b Iqbal Qasim	1
D.R.Doshi	c Wasim Bari b Sikander Bakht	9	not out	1
Extras	(b 10,lb 10,w 2,nb 11)	33	(b 9,lb 7,nb 5)	21
TOTAL		334		160

PAKISTAN

Batsman	Dismissal	Runs	Dismissal 2	Runs 2
Majid Khan	c Kirmani b Binny	5	lbw b Ghavri	7
Mudassar Nazar	c Gavaskar b Doshi	25	b Ghavri	13
Zaheer Abbas	b Binny	2	b Kapil Dev	11
Javed Miandad	lbw b Binny	16	lbw b Doshi	64
Wasim Raja	c Viswanath b Doshi	24	c Vengsarkar b Ghavri	4
Asif Iqbal *	c & b Yadav	14	c Viswanath b Doshi	26
Imran Khan	c Gavaskar b Doshi	15	c Gavaskar b Ghavri	1
Wasim Bari +	b Yadav	23	lbw b Doshi	3
Abdul Qadir	not out	29	c Binny b Yadav	15
Iqbal Qasim	c Kirmani b Yadav	0	c Vengsarkar b Yadav	6
Sikander Bakht	lbw b Kapil Dev	3	not out	1
Extras	(b 1,lb 2,nb 14)	17	(b 2,lb 11,nb 8)	21
TOTAL		173		190

PAKISTAN	O	M	R	W		O	M	R	W
Imran Khan	15	7	35	1					
Sikander Bakht	22.1	5	55	5		17	6	30	2
Iqbal Qasim	44	15	135	4		28.5	14	40	6
Majid Khan	23	8	52	0		4	1	14	0
Abdul Qadir	3	1	16	0		11	5	27	1
Mudassar Nazar	5	0	7	0		8	3	18	1
Asif Iqbal	2	1	1	0					
Wasim Raja						1	0	10	0

INDIA	O	M	R	W		O	M	R	W
Kapil Dev	14.3	4	23	1		6	1	26	1
Ghavri	7	2	17	0		18	4	63	4
Binny	12	1	53	3		2	1	2	0
Doshi	27	8	52	3		19	4	42	3
Yadav	8	4	11	3		6.4	0	36	2

FALL OF WICKETS	IND	PAK	IND	PAK		IND	PAK	IND	PAK
1st	13	11	5	16	6th	154	105	154	145
2nd	31	15	78	32	7th	249	117	156	161
3rd	111	53	97	41	8th	250	146	157	178
4th	129	57	132	48	9th	310	146	157	189
5th	129	83	146	84	10th	334	173	160	190

INDIA vs PAKISTAN
at Kanpur on 25/12/1979
Match drawn

INDIA

Batsman	1st innings	R	2nd innings	R
S.M.Gavaskar *	b Sikander Bakht	2	c Mudassar Nazar b Ehteshamuddin	81
C.P.S.Chauhan	c Zaheer Abbas b Sikander Bakht	6	c Sadiq Mohammad b Wasim Raja	61
D.B.Vengsarkar	c Wasim Bari b Sikander Bakht	0	not out	16
G.R.Viswanath	c Mudassar Nazar b Ehteshamuddin	2	not out	17
Yashpal Sharma	c Wasim Bari b Ehteshamuddin	16		
R.M.H.Binny	b Sikander Bakht	29		
S.M.H.Kirmani +	b Ehteshamuddin	0		
Kapil Dev	c Mudassar Nazar b Sikander Bakht	2		
K.D.Ghavri	not out	45		
N.S.Yadav	c Majid Khan b Ehteshamuddin	25		
D.R.Doshi	c Wasim Bari b Ehteshamuddin	20		
Extras	(b 1,lb 1,nb 13)	15	(b 4,lb 1,nb 13)	18
TOTAL		162	(for 2 wkts)	193

PAKISTAN

Batsman		R
Mudassar Nazar	c Kirmani b Kapil Dev	6
Sadiq Mohammad	c Kirmani b Ghavri	47
Zaheer Abbas	c Gavaskar b Kapil Dev	5
Javed Miandad	lbw b Kapil Dev	8
Majid Khan	lbw b Kapil Dev	19
Asif Iqbal *	c Viswanath b Doshi	11
Wasim Raja	not out	94
Wasim Bari +	b Binny	0
Iqbal Qasim	b Kapil Dev	32
Sikander Bakht	c Kirmani b Kapil Dev	4
Ehteshamuddin	b Binny	2
Extras	(lb 11,nb 10)	21
TOTAL		249

PAKISTAN

	O	M	R	W	O	M	R	W
Sikander Bakht	24	9	56	5	23.2	5	63	0
Ehteshamuddin	26.4	11	47	5	26	9	40	1
Mudassar Nazar	10	0	22	0	3	1	19	0
Asif Iqbal	8	3	22	0				
Iqbal Qasim					16	7	28	0
Wasim Raja					9	2	25	1

INDIA

	O	M	R	W	O	M	R	W
Kapil Dev	28	5	63	6				
Ghavri	21	5	42	1				
Binny	18.5	2	76	2				
Doshi	17	8	26	1				
Yadav	5	1	21	0				

FALL OF WICKETS

	IND	PAK	IND			IND	PAK	IND
1st	4	12	125		6th	67	131	
2nd	4	35	168		7th	69	132	
3rd	11	63			8th	69	214	
4th	17	92			9th	117	226	
5th	58	108			10th	162	249	

INDIA vs PAKISTAN
at Calcutta on 29/01/1980
Match drawn

INDIA

Batsman	1st innings	R	2nd innings	R
S.M.Gavaskar	c Iqbal Qasim b Imran Khan	44	(6) c Javed Miandad b Imran Khan	15
C.P.S.Chauhan	lbw b Ehteshamuddin	18	(1) b Ehteshamuddin	21
R.M.H.Binny	lbw b Imran Khan	15	(2) c Wasim Raja b Imran Khan	0
G.R.Viswanath *	b Ehteshamuddin	6	b Imran Khan	13
S.M.Patil	b Imran Khan	62	run out	31
Yashpal Sharma	c Wasim Bari b Imran Khan	62	(7) b Ehteshamuddin	21
Kapil Dev	st Wasim Bari b Iqbal Qasim	16	(8) b Iqbal Qasim	30
S.M.H.Kirmani +	c Iqbal Qasim b Ehteshamuddin	37	(3) c Sadiq Mohammad b Imran Khan	0
K.D.Ghavri	run out	16	not out	37
N.S.Yadav	not out	18	c & b Iqbal Qasim	3
D.R.Doshi	b Ehteshamuddin	3	c Asif Iqbal b Imran Khan	6
Extras	(b 3,lb 9,nb 15)	27	(b 9,lb 3,nb 16)	28
TOTAL		331		205

PAKISTAN

Batsman	1st innings	R	2nd innings	R
Taslim Arif	c Chauhan b Kapil Dev	90	c & b Binny	46
Sadiq Mohammad	lbw b Kapil Dev	5	b Ghavri	8
Majid Khan	c Kirmani b Binny	54	b Doshi	11
Javed Miandad	lbw b Ghavri	50	c & b Doshi	46
Wasim Raja	not out	50	run out	12
Asif Iqbal *	not out	5	run out	15
Imran Khan			not out	19
Wasim Bari +			not out	0
Iqbal Qasim				
Sikander Bakht				
Ehteshamuddin				
Extras	(b 1,lb 8,nb 9)	18	(b 12,lb 8,nb 2)	22
TOTAL	(for 4 wkts dec)	272	(for 6 wkts)	179

PAKISTAN

	O	M	R	W	O	M	R	W
Imran Khan	33	5	67	4	23.5	3	63	5
Sikander Bakht	22	5	87	0	6	2	18	0
Ehteshamuddin	35	7	87	4	19	5	44	2
Iqbal Qasim	17	3	53	1	21	5	50	2
Majid Khan	2	0	10	0				
Wasim Raja					1	0	2	0

INDIA

	O	M	R	W	O	M	R	W
Kapil Dev	26	4	65	2	20	7	49	0
Ghavri	21.5	3	77	1	11	2	32	1
Doshi	25	12	38	0	20	5	46	2
Binny	17	3	35	1	8	2	20	1
Yadav	10	0	39	0	4	3	10	0

FALL OF WICKETS

	IND	PAK	IND	PAK		IND	PAK	IND	PAK
1st	48	20	7	24	6th	218		92	162
2nd	72	112	10	58	7th	252		135	
3rd	91	185	33	86	8th	292		162	
4th	99	258	48	111	9th	307		172	
5th		187	88	154	10th	331		205	

INDIA vs PAKISTAN
at Madras on 15/01/1980
India won by 10 wickets

PAKISTAN

Batsman	1st innings	R	2nd innings	R
Mudassar Nazar	c Kirmani b Kapil Dev	6	c Vengsarkar b Kapil Dev	8
Sadiq Mohammad	c Kirmani b Kapil Dev	46	c Binny b Kapil Dev	0
Majid Khan	run out	56	c Patil b Ghavri	11
Zaheer Abbas	c Kirmani b Kapil Dev	0	c Chauhan b Kapil Dev	15
Javed Miandad	c Vengsarkar b Kapil Dev	45	c Kirmani b Doshi	52
Asif Iqbal *	c Kirmani b Ghavri	34	c Kirmani b Kapil Dev	5
Wasim Raja	c Kapil Dev b Doshi	15	c Viswanath b Doshi	57
Imran Khan	run out	34	c Doshi b Kapil Dev	29
Wasim Bari +	c Binny b Ghavri	13	lbw b Kapil Dev	15
Iqbal Qasim	not out	3	not out	19
Sikander Bakht	c Vengsarkar b Ghavri	1	b Kapil Dev	2
Extras	(lb 3,nb 16)	19	(lb 3,nb 17)	20
TOTAL		272		233

INDIA

Batsman	1st innings	R	2nd innings	R
S.M.Gavaskar *	c Iqbal Qasim b Imran Khan	166	not out	29
C.P.S.Chauhan	c Iqbal Qasim b Mudassar Nazar	5	not out	46
D.B.Vengsarkar	c Javed Miandad b Imran Khan	17		
G.R.Viswanath	c Mudassar Nazar b Iqbal Qasim	16		
S.M.Patil	c Javed Miandad b Sikander Bakht	15		
Yashpal Sharma	b Iqbal Qasim	46		
S.M.H.Kirmani +	b Imran Khan	2		
Kapil Dev	lbw b Imran Khan	84		
R.M.H.Binny	not out	42		
K.D.Ghavri	b Iqbal Qasim	1		
D.R.Doshi	c Javed Miandad b Imran Khan	9		
Extras	(b 1,lb 2,nb 24)	27	(nb 3)	3
TOTAL		430	(for 0 wkts)	78

INDIA

	O	M	R	W	O	M	R	W
Kapil Dev	19	5	90	4	23.4	7	56	7
Ghavri	18.4	3	73	3	14	0	82	1
Binny	10	1	42	0	13	2	33	0
Doshi	26	6	48	1	16	3	42	2

PAKISTAN

	O	M	R	W	O	M	R	W
Imran Khan	38.2	6	114	5	5	1	20	0
Sikander Bakht	32	5	105	1	6	0	37	0
Mudassar Nazar	16	3	54	1	2	0	21	0
Iqbal Qasim	37	13	81	3	4	1	12	0
Wasim Raja	2	0	19	0				
Majid Khan	9	1	30	0				
Sadiq Mohammad					1	0	4	0

FALL OF WICKETS

	PAK	IND	PAK	IND		PAK	IND	PAK	IND
1st	33	30	1		6th	215	279	147	
2nd	79	88	17		7th	225	339	171	
3rd	80	135	33		8th	266	412	197	
4th	151	160	36		9th	268	413	229	
5th	187	265	58		10th	272	430	233	

PAKISTAN vs AUSTRALIA
at Karachi on 27/02/1980
Pakistan won by 7 wickets

AUSTRALIA

Batsman	1st innings	R	2nd innings	R
B.M.Laird	lbw b Imran Khan	6	c Javed Miandad b Iqbal Qasim	23
G.N.Yallop	c Taslim Arif b Tauseef Ahmed	12	c Majid Khan b Iqbal Qasim	16
K.J.Hughes	c Majid Khan b Tauseef Ahmed	85	st Taslim Arif b Tauseef Ahmed	8
G.S.Chappell *	st Taslim Arif b Iqbal Qasim	20	c Taslim Arif b Tauseef Ahmed	13
D.W.Hookes	c Majid Khan b Iqbal Qasim	0	lbw b Iqbal Qasim	0
A.R.Border	lbw b Iqbal Qasim	30	not out	58
R.W.Marsh +	c Haroon Rashid b Tauseef Ahmed	13	c Mudassar Nazar b Iqbal Qasim	1
G.R.Beard	b Imran Khan	9	b Iqbal Qasim	4
R.J.Bright	c Majid Khan b Iqbal Qasim	15	c Majid Khan b Iqbal Qasim	0
D.K.Lillee	not out	12	lbw b Iqbal Qasim	5
G.Dymock	c Wasim Raja b Tauseef Ahmed	3	b Tauseef Ahmed	0
Extras	(b 8,lb 9,nb 3)	20	(b 4,lb 5,w 1,nb 2)	12
TOTAL		225		140

PAKISTAN

Batsman	1st innings	R	2nd innings	R
Taslim Arif +	c Marsh b Bright	58	b Bright	8
Haroon Rashid	b Bright	6	b Bright	10
Zaheer Abbas	c Lillee b Bright	8	not out	18
Javed Miandad *	c Border b Chappell	40	b Bright	21
Wasim Raja	c sub b Chappell	0	not out	12
Majid Khan	c Border b Bright	89		
Mudassar Nazar	c Border b Bright	29		
Imran Khan	c Border b Chappell	9		
Sarfraz Nawaz	c Chappell b Bright	17		
Iqbal Qasim	not out	14		
Tauseef Ahmed	b Bright	0		
Extras	(lb 12,nb 10)	22	(lb 3,nb 4)	7
TOTAL		292	(for 3 wkts)	76

PAKISTAN

	O	M	R	W	O	M	R	W
Imran Khan	16	4	28	2				
Sarfraz Nawaz	13	4	20	0	7	2	7	0
Mudassar Nazar	2	0	6	0	2	0	4	0
Iqbal Qasim	30	12	69	4	42	22	49	7
Tauseef Ahmed	30.2	9	64	4	34	11	62	3
Majid Khan	2	0	13	0	1	1	0	0
Wasim Raja	2	0	5	0	4	1	6	0

AUSTRALIA

	O	M	R	W	O	M	R	W
Lillee	28	4	76	0	11	2	22	0
Dymock	5	2	5	0	2	0	9	0
Bright	46.5	17	87	7	11	5	24	3
Beard	17	8	39	0	1.1	0	14	0
Chappell	20	3	49	3				
Yallop	2	0	14	0				

FALL OF WICKETS

	AUS	PAK	AUS	PAK		AUS	PAK	AUS	PAK
1st	8	34	38	17	6th	177	210	90	
2nd	39	44	51	26	7th	181	238	106	
3rd	93	120	55	60	8th	199	266	108	
4th	93	121	89		9th	216	292	139	
5th	161	134	89		10th	225	292	140	

PAKISTAN vs AUSTRALIA
at Faisalabad on 06/03/1980
Match drawn

AUSTRALIA

J.M.Wiener	b Ehteshamuddin	5
B.M.Laird	c Taslim Arif b Sarfraz Nawaz	0
K.J.Hughes	c Ehteshamuddin b Tauseef Ahmed	88
G.S.Chappell *	lbw b Sarfraz Nawaz	235
G.N.Yallop	b Wasim Raja	172
A.R.Border	run out	4
R.W.Marsh +	lbw b Tauseef Ahmed	71
G.R.Beard	c Sarfraz Nawaz b Tauseef Ahmed	13
R.J.Bright	b Wasim Raja	5
D.K.Lillee	lbw b Wasim Raja	0
G.Dymock	not out	0
Extras	(b 11,lb 10,nb 3)	24
TOTAL		617

PAKISTAN

Taslim Arif +	not out	210
Haroon Rashid	lbw b Dymock	21
Zaheer Abbas	run out	19
Javed Miandad *	not out	106
Mudassar Nazar		
Majid Khan		
Wasim Raja		
Sarfraz Nawaz		
Ehteshamuddin		
Tauseef Ahmed		
Iqbal Qasim		
Extras	(b 7,lb 4,nb 15)	26
TOTAL	(for 2 wkts)	382

PAKISTAN

	O	M	R	W		O	M	R	W
Sarfraz Nawaz	49	13	119	2					
Ehteshamuddin	18	2	59	1					
Iqbal Qasim	56	11	156	0					
Tauseef Ahmed	33	3	77	3					
Wasim Raja	30	6	100	3					
Majid Khan	22	2	66	0					
Javed Miandad	3	0	16	0					

AUSTRALIA

	O	M	R	W		O	M	R	W
Lillee	21	4	91	0					
Dymock	20	5	49	1					
Bright	33	9	71	0					
Border	3	2	3	0					
Beard	15	4	30	0					
Hughes	8	1	19	0					
Laird	2	1	3	0					
Chappell	6	3	5	0					
Wiener	5	1	19	0					
Marsh	10	1	51	0					
Yallop	3	0	15	0					

FALL OF WICKETS

	AUS	PAK			AUS	PAK
1st	1	87	6th		561	
2nd	21	159	7th		585	
3rd	200		8th		592	
4th	417		9th		612	
5th	434		10th		617	

PAKISTAN vs AUSTRALIA
at Lahore on 18/03/1980
Match drawn

AUSTRALIA

J.M.Wiener	lbw b Iqbal Qasim	93	c Mudassar Nazar b Imran Khan	4
B.M.Laird	b Tauseef Ahmed	17	c Taslim Arif b Tauseef Ahmed	63
K.J.Hughes	b Iqbal Qasim	1	c Iqbal Qasim b Imran Khan	0
G.S.Chappell *	lbw b Imran Khan	56	b Iqbal Qasim	57
G.N.Yallop	lbw b Iqbal Qasim	3	c & b Wasim Raja	34
A.R.Border	not out	150	st Javed Miandad b Azhar Khan	153
R.W.Marsh +	b Iqbal Qasim	8	run out	13
G.R.Beard	lbw b Imran Khan	39	c sub b Taslim Arif	49
R.J.Bright	not out	26	not out	10
D.K.Lillee	not out	1		
G.Dymock				
Extras	(b 4,lb 6,nb 4)	14	(lb 4,nb 3)	7
TOTAL	(for 7 wkts dec)	407	(for 8 wkts)	391

PAKISTAN

Mudassar Nazar	c Yallop b Lillee	59
Taslim Arif +	c Marsh b Bright	31
Iqbal Qasim	c Marsh b Lillee	5
Azmat Rana	c Chappell b Beard	49
Javed Miandad *	c Marsh b Bright	14
Wasim Raja	c Border b Lillee	55
Majid Khan	not out	110
Azhar Khan	b Bright	14
Imran Khan	c Chappell b Bright	56
Sarfraz Nawaz	st Marsh b Bright	5
Tauseef Ahmed		
Extras	(lb 4,w 1,nb 17)	22
TOTAL	(for 9 wkts dec)	420

PAKISTAN

	O	M	R	W		O	M	R	W
Imran Khan	28	7	86	2		12	3	30	2
Sarfraz Nawaz	28	6	67	0		14	5	42	0
Mudassar Nazar	6	1	16	0		2	0	20	0
Iqbal Qasim	39	10	90	4		34	8	111	1
Tauseef Ahmed	21	3	81	1		26	3	72	1
Wasim Raja	14	3	45	0		9	1	42	1
Azhar Khan	2	1	1	0		1	0	1	1
Javed Miandad	2	0	5	0		4	0	14	0
Majid Khan	2	0	2	0		9	3	24	0
Taslim Arif						5	0	28	1

AUSTRALIA

	O	M	R	W		O	M	R	W
Lillee	42	9	114	3					
Dymock	24	6	66	0					
Bright	56	14	172	5					
Beard	10	5	26	1					
Chappell	8	3	20	0					

FALL OF WICKETS

	AUS	PAK	AUS			AUS	PAK	AUS
1st	50	37	4	6th		218	270	223
2nd	53	53	7	7th		298	299	357
3rd	136	133	115	8th			410	390
4th	153	161	149	9th			420	
5th	204	177	192	10th				

PAKISTAN vs WEST INDIES
at Lahore on 24/11/1980
Match drawn

PAKISTAN

Sadiq Mohammad +	c Murray b Marshall	19	lbw b Croft	28
Taslim Arif	c Murray b Garner	32	retired hurt/ill	8
Mansoor Akhtar	c Murray b Croft	13	b Clarke	0
Javed Miandad *	c Richards b Croft	6	run out	30
Majid Khan	c Bacchus b Garner	4	not out	62
Wasim Raja	c Kallicharran b Richards	76	lbw b Clarke	3
Imran Khan	lbw b Marshall	123	c Marshall b Richards	9
Abdul Qadir	retired hurt/ill	18	c Haynes b Richards	1
Sarfraz Nawaz	c Richards b Croft	55	c Garner b Haynes	4
Iqbal Qasim	b Marshall	3		
Mohammad Nazir	not out	1		
Extras	(b 1,lb 4,w 1,nb 13)	19	(b 2,lb 2,nb 7)	11
TOTAL		369	(for 7 wkts)	156

WEST INDIES

D.L.Haynes	c Iqbal Qasim b Mohammad Nazir	40
S.F.A.F.Bacchus	lbw b Imran Khan	0
I.V.A.Richards	b Mohammad Nazir	75
A.I.Kallicharran	c Sadiq Mohammad b Abdul Qadir	11
C.H.Lloyd *	c Javed Miandad b Iqbal Qasim	22
H.A.Gomes	b Wasim Raja	43
D.A.Murray +	c Majid Khan b Abdul Qadir	50
M.D.Marshall	b Sarfraz Nawaz	9
J.Garner	c Taslim Arif b Abdul Qadir	15
C.E.H.Croft	not out	7
S.T.Clarke	st Taslim Arif b Abdul Qadir	15
Extras	(b 3,lb 6,nb 1)	10
TOTAL		297

WEST INDIES

	O	M	R	W		O	M	R	W
Clarke	23	3	69	0		12	2	26	2
Croft	28	4	91	3		20	7	37	1
Marshall	21.5	5	88	3		15	4	30	0
Garner	27	6	71	2		9	3	17	0
Richards	7	0	31	1		11	4	20	2
Gomes						4	1	9	0
Kallicharran						1	0	4	0
Haynes						1	0	2	1

PAKISTAN

	O	M	R	W		O	M	R	W
Imran Khan	16	2	39	1					
Sarfraz Nawaz	13	3	40	1					
Abdul Qadir	40.4	4	131	4					
Iqbal Qasim	12	4	18	1					
Wasim Raja	10	3	21	1					
Mohammad Nazir	17	5	38	2					

FALL OF WICKETS

	PAK	WI	PAK			PAK	WI	PAK
1st	31	1	15	6th		188	225	133
2nd	65	118	57	7th		356	255	156
3rd	67	119	101	8th		368	275	
4th	72	143	112	9th		369	276	
5th	95	158	125	10th			297	

PAKISTAN vs WEST INDIES
at Faisalabad on 08/12/1980
West Indies won by 156 runs

WEST INDIES

D.L.Haynes	lbw b Iqbal Qasim	15	lbw b Abdul Qadir	12
S.F.A.F.Bacchus	c Sikander Bakht b Abdul Qadir	45	b Iqbal Qasim	17
I.V.A.Richards	b Mohammad Nazir	72	(4) c sub b Iqbal Qasim	67
A.I.Kallicharran	lbw b Abdul Qadir	8	(6) lbw b Mohammad Nazir	27
C.H.Lloyd *	c Mansoor Akhtar b Mohammad Nazir	20	(4) lbw b Iqbal Qasim	37
H.A.Gomes	c Iqbal Qasim b Mohammad Nazir	8	(7) c Mansoor Akhtar b Iqbal Qasim	1
D.A.Murray +	c Majid Khan b Abdul Qadir	31	(8) b Mohammad Nazir	19
M.D.Marshall	b Mohammad Nazir	0	(9) c Javed Miandad b Mohammad Nazir	1
R.Nanan	lbw b Mohammad Nazir	1	(10) c Wasim Raja b Iqbal Qasim	8
C.E.H.Croft	c Taslim Arif b Iqbal Qasim	2	(3) lbw b Iqbal Qasim	1
S.T.Clarke	not out	8	not out	35
Extras	(b 12,lb 5,nb 1)	18	(b 9,lb 7,nb 1)	17
TOTAL		235		242

PAKISTAN

Taslim Arif +	lbw b Clarke	0	c Richards b Croft	18
Mansoor Akhtar	c Lloyd b Marshall	16	c Nanan b Marshall	7
Zaheer Abbas	b Clarke	2	lbw b Marshall	33
Javed Miandad *	c & b Clarke	50	(5) c Lloyd b Croft	22
Majid Khan	c Murray b Marshall	26	(6) b Clarke	3
Wasim Raja	st Murray b Nanan	21	(7) not out	38
Imran Khan	c Richards b Croft	29	(9) c Richards b Nanan	0
Abdul Qadir	b Nanan	4	b Croft	0
Iqbal Qasim	b Croft	0	(10) c Richards b Nanan	5
Sikander Bakht	c Lloyd b Richards	6	(4) c Lloyd b Marshall	1
Mohammad Nazir	not out	2	c Nanan b Marshall	0
Extras	(b 4,lb 7,nb 9)	20	(b 4,lb 4,nb 10)	18
TOTAL		176		145

PAKISTAN

	O	M	R	W		O	M	R	W
Imran Khan	10	0	36	0		3	0	6	0
Sikander Bakht	7	2	22	0		4	0	9	0
Iqbal Qasim	19	3	54	2		32.2	5	89	6
Abdul Qadir	15.3	1	48	3		17	4	45	1
Mohammad Nazir	22	7	44	5		33	13	76	3
Wasim Raja	4	0	13	0					

WEST INDIES

	O	M	R	W		O	M	R	W
Clarke	13	2	28	3		12	3	36	1
Croft	16	4	35	2		13	0	29	3
Marshall	9	1	39	2		9.4	0	25	4
Nanan	20	1	54	2		16	6	37	2
Richards	0.2	0	0	1					

FALL OF WICKETS

	WI	PAK	WI	PAK			WI	PAK	WI	PAK
1st	39	0	22	14	6th		187	132	171	122
2nd	99	2	47	43	7th		187	149	186	122
3rd	127	32	129	60	8th		207	150	189	124
4th	150	73	150	71	9th		223	167	198	132
5th	176	122	153	77	10th		235	176	242	145

271

PAKISTAN vs WEST INDIES
at Karachi on 22/12/1980
Match drawn

PAKISTAN

Shafiq Ahmed	lbw b Clarke	0	lbw b Garner	17
Sadiq Mohammad	lbw b Croft	0	c Bacchus b Clarke	36
Zaheer Abbas	not out	13	(5) lbw b Croft	1
Javed Miandad *	c Lloyd b Clarke	60	c Haynes b Clarke	5
Majid Khan	c Bacchus b Croft	0	(3) c Murray b Croft	18
Wasim Raja	c Bacchus b Croft	2	not out	77
Imran Khan	lbw b Garner	21	c Murray b Marshall	12
Ijaz Faqih	b Marshall	0	c Murray b Marshall	8
Wasim Bari +	c Murray b Clarke	23	b Garner	3
Iqbal Qasim	c Richards b Clarke	0	b Croft	2
Mohammad Nazir	b Garner	0	not out	2
Extras	(lb 1,w 1,nb 7)	9	(b 4,lb 3,nb 16)	23
TOTAL		128	(for 9 wkts)	204

WEST INDIES

D.L.Haynes	lbw b Iqbal Qasim	1
S.F.A.F.Bacchus	b Imran Khan	16
I.V.A.Richards	c Zaheer Abbas b Iqbal Qasim	18
A.I.Kallicharran	b Imran Khan	4
C.H.Lloyd *	c Javed Miandad b Imran Khan	1
D.A.Murray +	c Javed Miandad b Iqbal Qasim	42
H.A.Gomes	c Javed Miandad b Mohammad Nazir	61
M.D.Marshall	b Mohammad Nazir	0
S.T.Clarke	b Iqbal Qasim	17
J.Garner	lbw b Imran Khan	1
C.E.H.Croft	not out	3
Extras	(lb 1,w 4)	5
TOTAL		169

WEST INDIES	O	M	R	W		O	M	R	W
Clarke	15	7	27	4		11	3	14	2
Croft	14	5	27	4		23	6	50	3
Garner	18.1	8	27	2		19	4	39	2
Marshall	14	0	38	1		17	1	54	2
Richards						8	2	10	0
Gomes						6	0	14	0

PAKISTAN	O	M	R	W		O	M	R	W
Imran Khan	29	5	66	4					
Iqbal Qasim	34.1	11	48	4					
Mohammad Nazir	9	2	21	2					
Ijaz Faqih	4	1	9	0					
Wasim Raja	1	0	8	0					
Majid Khan	8	3	12	0					

FALL OF WICKETS	PAK	WI	PAK			PAK	WI	PAK
1st	0	19	30		6th	57	143	122
2nd	0	21	76		7th	111	143	146
3rd	5	43	78		8th	112	160	150
4th	14	43	82		9th	112	161	178
5th	53	44	85		10th	128	169	

AUSTRALIA vs PAKISTAN
at Perth on 13/11/1981
Australia won by 286 runs

AUSTRALIA

B.M.Laird	c Wasim Bari b Imran Khan	27	c Wasim Bari b Imran Khan	85
G.M.Wood	lbw b Sikander Bakht	33	b Iqbal Qasim	49
G.S.Chappell *	lbw b Imran Khan	22	b Imran Khan	6
K.J.Hughes	b Sarfraz Nawaz	14	c Majid Khan b Imran Khan	106
G.N.Yallop	c & b Iqbal Qasim	20	c Imran Khan b Sikander Bakht	38
A.R.Border	c Wasim Bari b Sarfraz Nawaz	3	c Mudassar Nazar b Sikander Bakht	37
R.W.Marsh +	c Iqbal Qasim b Sikander Bakht	16	c Mansoor Akhtar b Wasim Raja	47
B.Yardley	c Wasim Bari b Imran Khan	9	st Wasim Bari b Iqbal Qasim	22
D.K.Lillee	c Wasim Bari b Wasim Raja	16	not out	4
J.R.Thomson	b Imran Khan	2	not out	5
T.M.Alderman	not out	0		
Extras	(lb 5,w 1,nb 12)	18	(b 1,lb 9,w 1,nb 14)	25
TOTAL		180	(for 8 wkts dec)	424

PAKISTAN

Mudassar Nazar	c Marsh b Lillee	0	lbw b Alderman	5
Rizwan-uz-Zaman	lbw b Alderman	0	c Marsh b Alderman	8
Mansoor Akhtar	c Marsh b Alderman	6	c Hughes b Thomson	36
Javed Miandad *	c Hughes b Alderman	6	b Yardley	79
Majid Khan	c Marsh b Lillee	3	c Marsh b Yardley	0
Wasim Raja	c Thomson b Lillee	4	c Hughes b Yardley	48
Imran Khan	c Yardley b Lillee	4	c Alderman b Yardley	31
Sarfraz Nawaz	c Marsh b Alderman	26	c & b Yardley	9
Wasim Bari +	c Marsh b Lillee	1	c Border b Yardley	20
Iqbal Qasim	c Alderman b Thomson	5	c Alderman b Lillee	4
Sikander Bakht	not out	3	not out	0
Extras	(nb 4)	4	(lb 1,nb 15)	16
TOTAL		62		256

PAKISTAN	O	M	R	W		O	M	R	W
Imran Khan	31.4	8	66	4		39	12	90	3
Sarfraz Nawaz	27	10	43	2		27	5	88	0
Sikander Bakht	21	4	47	2		23	3	79	2
Iqbal Qasim	3	1	6	1		26	4	81	2
Wasim Raja	1	1	0	1		20	3	58	1
Javed Miandad						1	0	2	0
Mudassar Nazar						2	1	1	0

AUSTRALIA	O	M	R	W		O	M	R	W
Lillee	9	3	18	5		20	3	78	1
Alderman	10.2	2	36	4		16	4	43	2
Thomson	2	1	4	1		12	4	35	1
Yardley						25.5	5	84	6

FALL OF WICKETS	AUS	PAK	AUS	PAK			AUS	PAK	AUS	PAK
1st	45	1	92	8		6th	136	25	360	198
2nd	81	1	105	27		7th	154	25	412	229
3rd	89	14	192	96		8th	165	26	416	236
4th	113	17	262	99		9th	180	57		254
5th	119	21	327	174		10th	180	62		256

PAKISTAN vs WEST INDIES
at Multan on 30/12/1980
Match drawn

WEST INDIES

D.L.Haynes	b Imran Khan	5	st Wasim Bari b Iqbal Qasim	31
S.F.A.F.Bacchus	lbw b Imran Khan	2	c Zaheer Abbas b Iqbal Qasim	39
I.V.A.Richards	not out	120	c Sadiq Mohammad b Mohammad Nazir	12
A.I.Kallicharran	lbw b Imran Khan	18	not out	12
H.A.Gomes	lbw b Iqbal Qasim	32		
C.H.Lloyd *	run out	9	(7) not out	17
D.A.Murray +	c Wasim Bari b Iqbal Qasim	0	(6) lbw b Mohammad Nazir	0
S.T.Clarke	c Javed Miandad b Imran Khan	28		
M.D.Marshall	c Javed Miandad b Mohammad Nazir	3		
J.Garner	c Mohammad Nazir b Imran Khan	2		
C.E.H.Croft	lbw b Sarfraz Nawaz	3	(5) lbw b Mohammad Nazir	1
Extras	(b 15,lb 6,w 3,nb 3)	27	(lb 3,w 1)	4
TOTAL		249	(for 5 wkts)	116

PAKISTAN

Shafiq Ahmed	c Garner b Clarke	0
Sadiq Mohammad	b Clarke	3
Majid Khan	c Richards b Garner	41
Javed Miandad *	c Haynes b Croft	57
Wasim Bari +	run out	8
Zaheer Abbas	c Murray b Marshall	8
Wasim Raja	not out	29
Imran Khan	c Haynes b Croft	10
Sarfraz Nawaz	b Garner	1
Iqbal Qasim	c Richards b Garner	1
Mohammad Nazir	lbw b Garner	0
Extras	(nb 8)	8
TOTAL		166

PAKISTAN	O	M	R	W		O	M	R	W
Imran Khan	22	6	62	5		10	0	27	0
Sarfraz Nawaz	15.2	6	24	1		5	1	15	0
Iqbal Qasim	28	9	61	2		12	2	35	2
Mohammad Nazir	26	8	69	1		15	3	35	3
Wasim Raja	2	0	6	0					

WEST INDIES	O	M	R	W		O	M	R	W
Clarke	12	1	42	2					
Croft	16	3	33	2					
Garner	17.2	4	38	4					
Marshall	12	1	45	1					

FALL OF WICKETS	WI	PAK	WI			WI	PAK	WI
1st	9	2	57		6th	153	137	
2nd	22	4	84		7th	198	163	
3rd	58	104	84		8th	201	164	
4th	134	104	85		9th	208	166	
5th	146	120	85		10th	249	166	

AUSTRALIA vs PAKISTAN
at Brisbane on 27/11/1981
Australia won by 10 wickets

PAKISTAN

Mudassar Nazar	c Marsh b Lillee	36	c Laird b Lillee	33
Mohsin Khan	c Border b Chappell	11	c Marsh b Lillee	43
Majid Khan	c Chappell b Lillee	29	c Chappell b Yardley	15
Javed Miandad *	b Lillee	20	lbw b Lillee	38
Zaheer Abbas	b Lillee	80	lbw b Yardley	0
Wasim Raja	c Laird b Lillee	43	b Lillee	36
Imran Khan	c Marsh b Alderman	0	c Wellham b Yardley	3
Ijaz Faqih	b Yardley	34	c Chappell b Thomson	21
Sarfraz Nawaz	c Border b Alderman	4	c Alderman b Yardley	13
Wasim Bari +	c Marsh b Thomson	7	not out	4
Sikander Bakht	not out	1	b Thomson	2
Extras	(b 12,lb 1,w 1,nb 12)	26	(b 2,lb 3,w 1,nb 9)	15
TOTAL		291		223

AUSTRALIA

B.M.Laird	c Zaheer Abbas b Ijaz Faqih	44	not out	3
G.M.Wood	c Mudassar Nazar b Wasim Raja	72	not out	0
G.S.Chappell *	c Zaheer Abbas b Sikander Bakht	201		
A.R.Border	b Imran Khan	36		
K.J.Hughes	b Imran Khan	28		
D.M.Wellham	b Imran Khan	36		
R.W.Marsh +	c Zaheer Abbas b Imran Khan	27		
B.Yardley	b Sarfraz Nawaz	2		
D.K.Lillee	b Sarfraz Nawaz	14		
J.R.Thomson	not out	22		
T.M.Alderman	not out	5		
Extras	(b 1,lb 5,w 2,nb 17)	25		0
TOTAL (for 9 wkts dec)		512	(for 0 wkts)	3

AUSTRALIA	O	M	R	W		O	M	R	W
Lillee	20	3	81	5		19	4	51	4
Alderman	25	6	74	2		15	3	37	0
Thomson	15	2	52	1		15	3	43	2
Chappell	3	1	6	1					
Yardley	15	1	51	1		24	4	77	4
Border	1	0	1	0					

PAKISTAN	O	M	R	W		O	M	R	W
Imran Khan	40	6	92	4		1.2	1	2	0
Sarfraz Nawaz	35	4	121	2					
Sikander Bakht	24	2	81	1		1	0	1	0
Ijaz Faqih	22	1	76	1					
Wasim Raja	17	0	68	1					
Mudassar Nazar	2	0	10	0					
Javed Miandad	3	0	18	0					
Majid Khan	9	1	21	0					

FALL OF WICKETS	PAK	AUS	PAK	AUS			PAK	AUS	PAK	AUS
1st	40	109	72			6th	237	448	178	
2nd	60	149	90			7th	245	469	189	
3rd	105	219	115			8th	263	470	216	
4th	111	298	115			9th	285	492	219	
5th	236	429	177			10th	291		223	

AUSTRALIA vs PAKISTAN
at Melbourne on 11/12/1981
Pakistan won by an innings and 82 runs

PAKISTAN

Mudassar Nazar	c Lillee b Yardley	95
Mohsin Khan	c Thomson b Yardley	17
Majid Khan	c Wood b Yardley	74
Javed Miandad *	lbw b Yardley	62
Zaheer Abbas	c & b Yardley	90
Wasim Raja	c Laird b Yardley	50
Imran Khan	not out	70
Sarfraz Nawaz	c Yardley b Chappell	0
Wasim Bari +	b Yardley	8
Iqbal Qasim	not out	16
Sikander Bakht		
	Extras (b 1,lb 5,nb 12)	18
	TOTAL (for 8 wkts dec)	500

AUSTRALIA

B.M.Laird	lbw b Iqbal Qasim	35	c Sarfraz Nawaz b Iqbal Qasim	52
G.M.Wood	c Mohsin Khan b Sarfraz Nawaz	100	c Wasim Bari b Sarfraz Nawaz	1
G.S.Chappell *	c Wasim Bari b Wasim Raja	22	c Javed Miandad b Sarfraz Nawaz	0
A.R.Border	run out	7	run out	1
K.J.Hughes	c & b Iqbal Qasim	34	c Majid Khan b Iqbal Qasim	11
D.M.Wellham	c Mudassar Nazar b Sarfraz Nawaz	26	b Sarfraz Nawaz	13
R.W.Marsh +	c Mudassar Nazar b Imran Khan	31	c Mohsin Khan b Iqbal Qasim	21
B.Yardley	b Iqbal Qasim	20	b Imran Khan	0
D.K.Lillee	lbw b Imran Khan	1	c Wasim Bari b Iqbal Qasim	4
J.R.Thomson	not out	3	b Imran Khan	17
T.M.Alderman	lbw b Imran Khan	1	not out	4
	Extras (b 4,lb 6,nb 3)	13	(b 1)	1
	TOTAL	293		125

AUSTRALIA

	O	M	R	W		O	M	R	W
Lillee	36.3	9	104	0					
Alderman	27	8	62	0					
Thomson	25	2	85	0					
Yardley	66	16	187	7					
Border	4	1	16	0					
Chappell	9	2	17	1					
Hughes	3	1	2	0					
Laird	1	0	9	0					

PAKISTAN

	O	M	R	W		O	M	R	W
Imran Khan	24.1	7	41	3		14.1	5	21	2
Sarfraz Nawaz	14	3	43	2		15	10	11	3
Wasim Raja	37	7	73	1		13	2	34	0
Iqbal Qasim	55	17	104	3		24	11	44	4
Sikander Bakht	2	0	9	0					
Majid Khan	2	0	10	0		4	1	5	0
Javed Miandad						2	0	9	0

FALL OF WICKETS

	PAK	AUS	AUS			PAK	AUS	AUS
1st	40	75	1	6th	443	235	78
2nd	181	118	9	7th	444	286	79
3rd	201	127	13	8th	456	288	92
4th	329	173	29	9th		289	121
5th	363	232	77	10th		293	125

PAKISTAN vs SRI LANKA
at Karachi on 05/03/1982
Pakistan won by 204 runs

PAKISTAN

Mansoor Akhtar	c Goonatillake b de Mel	6	c Mendis b De Silva D.S.	23
Rizwan-uz-Zaman	c Goonatillake b Ratnayeke	42	c Goonatillake b de Mel	10
Salim Malik	b De Silva D.S.	12	(4) not out	100
Javed Miandad *	c Goonatillake b de Mel	4	(5) st Goonatillake b De Silva D.S.	92
Wasim Raja	c Dias b de Mel	31	(6) not out	12
Haroon Rashid	run out	153		
Salim Yousuf +	st Goonatillake b De Silva D.S.	4		
Tahir Naqqash	c Mendis b De Silva D.S.	57		
Iqbal Qasim	lbw b De Silva D.S.	1	(3) c sub b De Silva D.S.	56
Rashid Khan	c Madugalle b de Silva G.R.A.	59		
Tauseef Ahmed	not out	5		
	Extras (lb 9,w 4,nb 9)	22	(b 5,lb 1,w 1,nb 1)	8
	TOTAL	396	(for 4 wkts dec)	301

SRI LANKA

B.Warnapura *	lbw b Tahir Naqqash	13	b Tahir Naqqash	0
S.Wettimuny	c Mansoor Akhtar b Rashid Khan	71	c Salim Yousuf b Rashid Khan	14
R.L.Dias	lbw b Iqbal Qasim	53	lbw b Tahir Naqqash	19
R.S.Madugalle	c Salim Yousuf b Rashid Khan	29	c Tauseef Ahmed b Iqbal Qasim	18
J.R.Ratnayeke	c Rizwan-uz-Zaman b Iqbal Qasim	24	(10) c Salim Malik b Wasim Raja	0
L.R.D.Mendis	c Rashid Khan b Tahir Naqqash	54	(5) c Salim Yousuf b Rashid Khan	15
A.Ranatunga	st Salim Yousuf b Tauseef Ahmed	13	(6) c Salim Yousuf b Tauseef Ahmed	33
D.S.De Silva	b Tauseef Ahmed	26	(7) st Salim Yousuf b Iqbal Qasim	12
H.M.Goonatillake +	c Salim Yousuf b Tahir Naqqash	14	c Haroon Rashid b Wasim Raja	13
A.L.F.de Mel	run out	9	(8) c Javed Miandad b Iqbal Qasim	2
G.R.A.de Silva	not out	10	not out	0
	Extras (b 1,lb 12,w 3,nb 12)	28	(b 9,lb 11,w 1,nb 2)	23
	TOTAL	344		149

SRI LANKA

	O	M	R	W		O	M	R	W
de Mel	28	2	124	3		23.2	3	100	1
Ratnayeke	16	6	49	1		5.4	2	20	0
De Silva D.S.	38	8	102	4		26	3	99	3
de Silva G.R.A.	17.2	2	69	1		35	5	74	0
Warnapura	2	0	9	0					
Wettimuny	2	0	21	0					

PAKISTAN

	O	M	R	W		O	M	R	W
Tahir Naqqash	32	11	83	3		9	1	34	2
Rashid Khan	26	7	53	2		8	3	25	1
Iqbal Qasim	28	7	88	2		15.1	8	27	4
Tauseef Ahmed	21.4	6	64	2		12	1	39	1
Wasim Raja	5	1	28	0		3	2	1	2

FALL OF WICKETS

	PAK	SRI	PAK	SRI		PAK	SRI	PAK	SRI
1st	6	24	16	1	6th	126	242		121
2nd	46	120	53	27	7th	230	285		125
3rd	53	152	107	41	8th	232	308		139
4th	72	199	269	68	9th	359	322		149
5th	113	221		91	10th	396	344		149

PAKISTAN vs SRI LANKA
at Faisalabad on 14/03/1982
Match drawn

SRI LANKA

S.Wettimuny	b Wasim Raja	157	c Ashraf Ali b Tahir Naqqash	13
H.M.Goonatillake +	c Salim Malik b Iqbal Qasim	27	b Iqbal Qasim	56
R.L.Dias	c Salim Malik b Tahir Naqqash	98	c Mohsin Khan b Tahir Naqqash	7
R.S.Madugalle	not out	91	lbw b Iqbal Qasim	12
L.R.D.Mendis *	b Iqbal Qasim	16	run out	0
A.Ranatunga	b Iqbal Qasim	0	c Ashraf Ali b Tauseef Ahmed	2
A.N.Ranasinghe	c Javed Miandad b Iqbal Qasim	6	c Javed Miandad b Tauseef Ahmed	5
A.L.F.de Mel	c Salim Malik b Iqbal Qasim	4	(9) not out	25
D.S.De Silva	b Rizwan-uz-Zaman	25	(8) st Ashraf Ali b Tauseef Ahmed	8
L.W.Kaluperuma	b Rizwan-uz-Zaman	0	not out	11
G.R.A.de Silva	lbw b Rizwan-uz-Zaman	5		
	Extras (lb 11,w 2,nb 12)	25	(lb 9,w 1,nb 5)	15
	TOTAL	454	(for 8 wkts dec)	154

PAKISTAN

Rizwan-uz-Zaman	b de Silva G.R.A.	36	b de Mel	16
Mohsin Khan	c Wettimuny b de Mel	12	c de Mel b De Silva D.S.	74
Salim Malik	b de Mel	23	lbw b de Mel	4
Javed Miandad *	c Ranatunga b De Silva D.S.	18	c Madugalle b De Silva D.S.	36
Wasim Raja	c Madugalle b De Silva D.S.	22	c Wettimuny b De Silva D.S.	0
Haroon Rashid	c de Mel b De Silva D.S.	25	b De Silva D.S.	0
Ashraf Ali +	b Ranasinghe	58	not out	29
Tahir Naqqash	c de Mel b De Silva b G.R.A.	1	c sub b De Silva D.S.	13
Iqbal Qasim	run out	5		
Rashid Khan	not out	43	(9) not out	3
Tauseef Ahmed	c Madugalle b De Silva D.S.	18		
	Extras (lb 1,nb 8)	9	(b 3,lb 7,nb 1)	11
	TOTAL	270	(for 7 wkts)	186

PAKISTAN

	O	M	R	W		O	M	R	W
Tahir Naqqash	26	4	108	0		13	3	53	2
Rashid Khan	13	3	52	0		1	0	4	0
Iqbal Qasim	65	18	141	6		30	9	51	2
Tauseef Ahmed	12	3	35	0		14	4	18	3
Wasim Raja	26	6	66	1					
Javed Miandad	1	0	1	0					
Rizwan-uz-Zaman	12	3	26	3		5	2	13	0

SRI LANKA

	O	M	R	W		O	M	R	W
de Mel	23	4	73	2		17	2	71	2
Ranasinghe	7	1	23	1		5	0	17	0
De Silva D.S.	32	3	103	4		18	2	59	5
de Silva G.R.A.	24	10	38	2		19	4	28	0
Kaluperuma	6	0	24	0					

FALL OF WICKETS

	SRI	PAK	SRI	PAK		SRI	PAK	SRI	PAK
1st	77	19	19	24	6th	355	154	104	137
2nd	294	54	44	40	7th	385	156	114	174
3rd	304	83	82	132	8th	446	185	114	
4th	341	116	82	132	9th	448	222		
5th	341	124	86	132	10th	454	270		

PAKISTAN vs SRI LANKA
at Lahore on 22/03/1982
Pakistan won by an innings and 102 runs

SRI LANKA

B.Warnapura *	c Mohsin Khan b Imran Khan	7	c Javed Miandad b Tauseef Ahmed	26
S.Wettimuny	c Iqbal Qasim b Imran Khan	20	c Majid Khan b Imran Khan	41
R.S.A.Jayasekera	b Imran Khan	0	(6) b Imran Khan	2
R.L.Dias	c Tauseef Ahmed b Imran Khan	109	(3) c Wasim Raja b Tauseef Ahmed	9
R.S.Madugalle	c Ashraf Ali b Imran Khan	0	(4) b Tauseef Ahmed	5
L.R.D.Mendis	c & b Tauseef Ahmed	26	(5) c Mudassar Nazar b Tauseef Ahmed	5
D.S.De Silva	b Imran Khan	7	not out	36
A.L.F.de Mel	st Ashraf Ali b Iqbal Qasim	34	lbw b Imran Khan	0
H.M.Goonatillake +	b Imran Khan	15	c & b Imran Khan	21
J.R.Ratnayeke	not out	1	b Imran Khan	0
R.G.C.E.Wijesuriya	b Imran Khan	0	b Imran Khan	3
	Extras (lb 11,w 6,nb 4)	21	(b 4,lb 2,w 1,nb 3)	10
	TOTAL	240		158

PAKISTAN

Mudassar Nazar	c Madugalle b De Silva	37
Mohsin Khan	b Ratnayeke	129
Majid Khan	c sub b Ratnayeke	63
Javed Miandad *	c Goonatillake b de Mel	26
Zaheer Abbas	b Ratnayeke	134
Wasim Raja	c Goonatillake b de Mel	1
Imran Khan	c Mendis b de Mel	39
Ashraf Ali +	not out	45
Tahir Naqqash	not out	1
Iqbal Qasim		
Tauseef Ahmed		
	Extras (b 5,lb 5,w 5,nb 10)	25
	TOTAL (for 7 wkts dec)	500

PAKISTAN

	O	M	R	W		O	M	R	W
Imran Khan	29.3	8	58	8		22.5	3	58	6
Tahir Naqqash	10	0	54	0		6	0	22	0
Iqbal Qasim	12	4	21	1		1	0	1	0
Mudassar Nazar	8	1	23	0					
Tauseef Ahmed	12	1	50	1		25	7	58	4
Wasim Raja	5	1	13	0		6	4	9	0
Majid Khan						1	1	0	0

SRI LANKA

	O	M	R	W		O	M	R	W
de Mel	28	3	120	3					
Ratnayeke	28	3	121	3					
De Silva	39	4	129	1					
Wijesuriya	24	2	105	0					

FALL OF WICKETS

	SRI	PAK	SRI			SRI	PAK	SRI
1st	17	79	56	6th	171	406	95
2nd	17	230	78	7th	209	494	96
3rd	79	247	84	8th	231		142
4th	83	297	90	9th	239		142
5th	141	306	93	10th	240		158

ENGLAND vs PAKISTAN
at Edgbaston on 29/07/1982
England won by 113 runs

ENGLAND

D.W.Randall	b Imran Khan	17	b Imran Khan		105
C.J.Tavare	c Javed Miandad b Abdul Qadir	54	c Mohsin Khan b Imran Khan		17
A.J.Lamb	c Wasim Bari b Sikander Bakht	6	lbw b Tahir Naqqash		5
D.I.Gower	c Wasim Bari b Imran Khan	74	c Mudassar Nazar b Tahir Naqqash		13
I.T.Botham	b Imran Khan	2	(6) lbw b Tahir Naqqash		0
M.W.Gatting	b Tahir Naqqash	17	(5) c Wasim Bari b Tahir Naqqash		5
G.Miller	b Imran Khan	47	b Tahir Naqqash		5
I.A.Greig	c sub b Imran Khan	14	b Abdul Qadir		7
E.E.Hemmings	lbw b Imran Khan	2	c Mansoor Akhtar b Abdul Qadir		19
R.W.Taylor +	lbw b Imran Khan	1	c Abdul Qadir b Wasim Raja		54
R.G.D.Willis *	not out	28	not out		28
	Extras (b 4,lb 10,w 6,nb 18)	38	(b 10,lb 11,w 7,nb 5)		33
	TOTAL	272			291

PAKISTAN

Mudassar Nazar	lbw b Botham	0	lbw b Botham		0
Mohsin Khan	c Willis b Botham	26	b Hemmings		35
Tahir Naqqash	c Taylor b Greig	12	(9) c & b Hemmings		39
Mansoor Akhtar	c Miller b Hemmings	58	(4) run out		0
Javed Miandad	c Willis b Hemmings	30	(5) c Taylor b Willis		10
Zaheer Abbas	lbw b Greig	40	(5) c Taylor b Willis		4
Wasim Raja	c Tavare b Willis	26	(6) c Gower b Willis		16
Imran Khan *	c Taylor b Willis	22	(7) b Miller		65
Wasim Bari +	not out	16	(8) c Taylor b Botham		12
Abdul Qadir	lbw b Greig	7	c Randall b Miller		9
Sikander Bakht	c Hemmings b Greig	1	not out		1
	Extras (b 5,lb 2,w 1,nb 5)	13	(lb 3,nb 5)		8
	TOTAL	251			199

PAKISTAN

	O	M	R	W		O	M	R	W
Imran Khan	25.3	11	52	7		32	5	84	2
Tahir Naqqash	15	4	46	1		18	7	40	5
Sikander Bakht	18	5	58	1		13	5	34	0
Mudassar Nazar	5	2	8	0					
Abdul Qadir	29	7	70	1		40	10	100	2
Wasim Raja						2.3	2	0	1

ENGLAND

	O	M	R	W		O	M	R	W
Botham	24	1	86	2		21	7	70	4
Greig	14.2	3	53	4		4	1	19	0
Willis	15	3	42	2		14	2	49	2
Hemmings	24	5	56	2		10	4	27	1
Miller	2	1	1	0		7.4	1	26	2

FALL OF WICKETS

	ENG	PAK	ENG	PAK		ENG	PAK	ENG	PAK
1st	29	0	62	0	6th	228	198	146	77
2nd	37	29	98	0	7th	263	217	170	98
3rd	164	53	127	38	8th	265	227	188	151
4th	172	110	137	54	9th	271	248	212	178
5th	179	164	137	66	10th	272	251	291	199

ENGLAND vs PAKISTAN
at Lord's on 12/08/1982
Pakistan won by 10 wickets

PAKISTAN

Mohsin Khan	c Tavare b Jackman	200	not out		39
Mudassar Nazar	c Taylor b Jackman	20			
Mansoor Akhtar	c Lamb b Botham	57			
Javed Miandad	run out	6	(2) not out		26
Zaheer Abbas	b Jackman	75			
Haroon Rashid	lbw b Botham	1			
Imran Khan *	c Taylor b Botham	12			
Tahir Naqqash	c Gatting b Jackman	2			
Wasim Bari +	not out	24			
Abdul Qadir	not out	18			
Sarfraz Nawaz					
	Extras (b 3,lb 8,nb 2)	13	(b 1,lb 10,w 1)		12
	TOTAL (for 8 wkts dec)	428	(for 0 wkts)		77

ENGLAND

D.W.Randall	b Sarfraz Nawaz	29	b Mudassar Nazar		9
C.J.Tavare	b Sarfraz Nawaz	8	c Javed Miandad b Imran Khan		82
A.J.Lamb	c Haroon Rashid b Tahir Naqqash	33	lbw b Mudassar Nazar		0
D.I.Gower *	c Mansoor Akhtar b Imran Khan	29	c Wasim Bari b Mudassar Nazar		0
I.T.Botham	c Mohsin Khan b Abdul Qadir	31	c Sarfraz Nawaz b Mudassar Nazar		69
M.W.Gatting	not out	32	c Wasim Bari b Mudassar Nazar		7
D.R.Pringle	c Haroon Rashid b Abdul Qadir	5	c Javed Miandad b Abdul Qadir		14
I.A.Greig	lbw b Abdul Qadir	3	lbw b Mudassar Nazar		2
E.E.Hemmings	b Sarfraz Nawaz	6	c Wasim Bari b Imran Khan		14
R.W.Taylor +	lbw b Abdul Qadir	5	not out		24
R.D.Jackman	lbw b Imran Khan	17	c Haroon Rashid b Abdul Qadir		17
	Extras (b 11,lb 12,w 13,nb 10)	46	(b 10,lb 19,w 5,nb 4)		38
	TOTAL	227			276

ENGLAND

	O	M	R	W		O	M	R	W
Botham	44	8	148	3		7	0	30	0
Jackman	36	5	110	4		4	0	22	0
Pringle	26	9	62	0					
Greig	13	2	42	0					
Hemmings	20	3	53	0		2.1	0	13	0

PAKISTAN

	O	M	R	W		O	M	R	W
Imran Khan	23	4	55	2		42	13	84	2
Sarfraz Nawaz	23	4	56	3		14	5	22	0
Tahir Naqqash	12	4	25	1		7	5	6	0
Abdul Qadir	24	9	39	4		37.5	15	94	2
Mudassar Nazar	4	1	6	0		19	7	32	6

FALL OF WICKETS

	PAK	ENG	ENG	PAK		PAK	ENG	ENG	PAK
1st	53	16	9		6th	380	187	171	
2nd	197	69	9		7th	382	197	180	
3rd	208	89	9		8th	401	217	224	
4th	361	157	121		9th		226	235	
5th	364	173	132		10th		227	276	

ENGLAND vs PAKISTAN
at Headingley on 26/08/1982
England won by 3 wickets

PAKISTAN

Mohsin Khan	c Taylor b Botham	10	c Taylor b Willis		0
Mudassar Nazar	b Botham	65	c Botham b Willis		0
Mansoor Akhtar	c Gatting b Willis	0	lbw b Botham		39
Javed Miandad	c Fowler b Willis	54	c Taylor b Botham		52
Zaheer Abbas	c Taylor b Jackman	8	lbw b Botham		4
Majid Khan	lbw b Jackman	21	c Gower b Botham		10
Imran Khan *	not out	67	c Randall b Botham		46
Wasim Bari +	b Jackman	23	c Taylor b Willis		7
Abdul Qadir	c Willis b Botham	5	b Jackman		17
Sikander Bakht	c Tavare b Willis	7	c Gatting b Marks		7
Ehteshamuddin	not out	0	not out		0
	Extras (b 1,lb 7,w 4,nb 3)	15	(lb 6,w 4,nb 7)		17
	TOTAL	275			199

ENGLAND

C.J.Tavare	c sub b Imran Khan	22	c Majid Khan b Imran Khan		33
G.Fowler	b Ehteshamuddin	9	c Wasim Bari b Mudassar Nazar		86
M.W.Gatting	lbw b Imran Khan	25	lbw b Imran Khan		25
A.J.Lamb	c Mohsin Khan b Imran Khan	0	c Wasim Bari b Mudassar Nazar		4
D.I.Gower	c sub b Sikander Bakht	74	c Wasim Bari b Mudassar Nazar		7
I.T.Botham	c sub b Sikander Bakht	57	c Wasim Bari b Mudassar Nazar		4
D.W.Randall	run out	8	lbw b Imran Khan		0
V.J.Marks	b Abdul Qadir	7	not out		12
R.W.Taylor +	c Javed Miandad b Imran Khan	18	not out		6
R.D.Jackman	c Mohsin Khan b Imran Khan	11			
R.G.D.Willis *	not out	1			
	Extras (b 4,lb 10,w 2,nb 8)	24	(b 19,lb 16,w 1,nb 6)		42
	TOTAL	256	(for 7 wkts)		219

ENGLAND

	O	M	R	W		O	M	R	W
Willis	26	6	76	3		19	3	55	3
Botham	24.5	9	70	4		30	8	74	5
Jackman	37	14	74	3		28	11	41	1
Marks	5	0	23	0		2	1	8	1
Gatting	8	2	17	0		2	1	4	0

PAKISTAN

	O	M	R	W		O	M	R	W
Imran Khan	25.2	7	49	5		30.2	8	66	3
Ehteshamuddin	14	4	46	1					
Sikander Bakht	24	5	47	2		20	4	40	0
Abdul Qadir	22	5	87	1		8	2	16	0
Mudassar Nazar	4	1	3	0		22	7	55	4

FALL OF WICKETS

	PAK	ENG	PAK	ENG		PAK	ENG	PAK	ENG
1st	16	15	0	103	6th	168	159	115	189
2nd	19	67	3	168	7th	207	170	128	199
3rd	119	69	81	172	8th	224	209	169	
4th	128	77	85	187	9th	274	255	199	
5th	160	146	108	189	10th	275	256	199	

PAKISTAN vs AUSTRALIA
at Karachi on 22/09/1982
Pakistan won by 9 wickets

AUSTRALIA

G.M.Wood	c Wasim Bari b Imran Khan	0	c sub b Abdul Qadir		17
B.M.Laird	run out	32	c Mansoor Akhtar b Imran Khan		3
J.Dyson	b Iqbal Qasim	87	b Abdul Qadir		6
K.J.Hughes *	c Wasim Bari b Iqbal Qasim	54	(5) c Wasim Bari b Abdul Qadir		14
A.R.Border	not out	55	(4) c sub b Abdul Qadir		8
G.M.Ritchie	c Haroon Rashid b Abdul Qadir	4	b Iqbal Qasim		17
R.W.Marsh +	b Tahir Naqqash	19	lbw b Imran Khan		32
B.Yardley	c Javed Miandad b Tahir Naqqash	0	lbw b Abdul Qadir		0
R.J.Bright	c Haroon Rashid b Tahir Naqqash	2	not out		32
G.F.Lawson	c Wasim Bari b Tahir Naqqash	0	run out		11
J.R.Thomson	st Wasim Bari b Iqbal Qasim	14	c Wasim Bari b Iqbal Qasim		18
	Extras (b 4,lb 10,w 1,nb 2)	17	(b 2,lb 19)		21
	TOTAL	284			179

PAKISTAN

Mohsin Khan	handled the ball	58	not out		14
Mansoor Akhtar	c Bright b Thomson	32	(3) not out		26
Haroon Rashid	c Laird b Yardley	82			
Javed Miandad	b Lawson	32			
Zaheer Abbas	c Marsh b Lawson	91			
Mudassar Nazar	not out	52	(2) c Border b Thomson		5
Imran Khan *	c Yardley b Bright	1			
Tahir Naqqash	st Marsh b Bright	15			
Wasim Bari +	b Bright	0			
Abdul Qadir	run out	29			
Iqbal Qasim	not out	2			
	Extras (b 4,lb 8,w 1,nb 12)	25	(nb 2)		2
	TOTAL (for 9 wkts dec)	419	(for 1 wkt)		47

PAKISTAN

	O	M	R	W		O	M	R	W
Imran Khan	23	3	38	1		12	5	17	2
Tahir Naqqash	16	3	61	4		7	3	17	0
Mudassar Nazar	13	0	33	0					
Abdul Qadir	21.4	1	80	2		26	7	76	5
Iqbal Qasim	26	10	55	2		21.5	6	48	2

AUSTRALIA

	O	M	R	W		O	M	R	W
Thomson	29	5	103	1		3	1	16	1
Lawson	39	10	93	2					
Bright	36	8	96	3		5	0	14	0
Yardley	23	2	98	1		3	1	9	0
Border	1	0	4	0					
Hughes						0.1	0	6	0

FALL OF WICKETS

	AUS	PAK	AUS	PAK		AUS	PAK	AUS	PAK
1st	0	43	10	5	6th	249	329	72	
2nd	71	168	29		7th	249	351	73	
3rd	169	188	32		8th	255	353	137	
4th	202	277	45		9th	267	419	161	
5th	211	328	72		10th	284		179	

PAKISTAN vs AUSTRALIA

at Faisalabad on 30/09/1982
Pakistan won by an innings and 3 runs

PAKISTAN

Mohsin Khan	c Marsh b Lawson	76
Mudassar Nazar	c Hughes b Border	79
Mansoor Akhtar	c Marsh b Lawson	111
Javed Miandad	c Laird b Lawson	6
Zaheer Abbas	b Sleep	126
Haroon Rashid	c Laird b Lawson	51
Imran Khan *	not out	24
Tahir Naqqash	not out	15
Wasim Bari +		
Abdul Qadir		
Iqbal Qasim		
	Extras (b 4,lb 1,nb 8)	13
	TOTAL (for 6 wkts dec)	501

AUSTRALIA

B.M.Laird	lbw b Abdul Qadir	8	c Mudassar Nazar b Abdul Qadir	60
G.M.Wood	c Wasim Bari b Mudassar Nazar	49	(7) c Wasim Bari b Iqbal Qasim	22
J.Dyson	c Mudassar Nazar b Iqbal Qasim	23	(2) c Iqbal Qasim b Abdul Qadir	43
A.R.Border	c Javed Miandad b Imran Khan	9	(3) c Haroon Rashid b Abdul Qadir	31
K.J.Hughes *	c Imran Khan b Abdul Qadir	11	(4) lbw b Abdul Qadir	7
G.M.Ritchie	run out	34	(5) not out	106
P.R.Sleep	lbw b Imran Khan	0	(6) c Mohsin Khan b Abdul Qadir	29
R.W.Marsh +	b Abdul Qadir	0	run out	8
R.J.Bright	c Haroon Rashid b Abdul Qadir	0	c sub b Iqbal Qasim	0
G.F.Lawson	c Zaheer Abbas b Iqbal Qasim	14	lbw b Abdul Qadir	0
J.R.Thomson	not out	1	st Wasim Bari b Abdul Qadir	11
	Extras (b 8,lb 6,w 2,nb 3)	19	(lb 7,w 1,nb 5)	13
	TOTAL	168		330

AUSTRALIA	O	M	R	W		O	M	R	W
Thomson	23	5	79	0					
Lawson	33	6	97	4					
Sleep	36	3	158	1					
Bright	41	5	107	0					
Border	11	3	47	1					

PAKISTAN	O	M	R	W		O	M	R	W
Imran Khan	14	6	16	2		10	5	20	0
Tahir Naqqash	15	4	21	0		9	1	25	0
Abdul Qadir	42	14	76	4		50.5	12	142	7
Iqbal Qasim	24.5	11	28	2		46	18	97	2
Mudassar Nazar	7	2	8	1		9	3	26	0
Zaheer Abbas						3	0	5	0
Javed Miandad						1	0	2	0

FALL OF WICKETS	PAK	AUS	AUS			PAK	AUS	AUS	
1st	123	20	73		6th	482	123	290	
2nd	181	82	125		7th		124	309	
3rd	201	96	133		8th		124	309	
4th	356	113	162		9th		167	310	
5th	428	123	218		10th		168	330	

PAKISTAN vs AUSTRALIA

at Lahore on 14/10/1982
Pakistan won by 9 wickets

AUSTRALIA

G.M.Wood	c Javed Miandad b Abdul Qadir	85	c Mudassar Nazar b Jalaluddin	30
B.M.Laird	lbw b Abdul Qadir	28	lbw b Tahir Naqqash	6
J.Dyson	b Jalaluddin	10	lbw b Tahir Naqqash	51
A.R.Border	lbw b Imran Khan	9	st Wasim Bari b Abdul Qadir	6
K.J.Hughes *	b Tahir Naqqash	29	st Wasim Bari b Abdul Qadir	39
G.M.Ritchie	lbw b Imran Khan	26	lbw b Imran Khan	18
R.W.Marsh +	c sub b Imran Khan	1	c Mudassar Nazar b Jalaluddin	12
B.Yardley	c Haroon Rashid b Jalaluddin	40	b Imran Khan	21
G.F.Lawson	not out	57	c sub b Imran Khan	9
J.R.Thomson	lbw b Jalaluddin	0	not out	5
T.M.Alderman	b Imran Khan	7	c Zaheer Abbas b Imran Khan	0
	Extras (b 1,lb 13,w 5,nb 5)	24	(b 4,lb 5,nb 8)	17
	TOTAL	316		214

PAKISTAN

Mohsin Khan	b Border	135	lbw b Lawson	14
Mudassar Nazar	lbw b Lawson	23	not out	39
Abdul Qadir	c Laird b Yardley	1		
Mansoor Akhtar	lbw b Lawson	12	(3) not out	2
Javed Miandad	c Hughes b Alderman	138		
Zaheer Abbas	c Yardley b Alderman	52		
Haroon Rashid	c Ritchie b Thomson	15		
Imran Khan *	not out	39		
Tahir Naqqash	not out	7		
Wasim Bari +				
Jalaluddin				
	Extras (b 3,lb 13,w 2,nb 27)	45	(b 4,lb 5)	9
	TOTAL (for 7 wkts dec)	467	(for 1 wkt)	64

PAKISTAN	O	M	R	W		O	M	R	W
Imran Khan	24.2	10	45	4		20	6	35	4
Tahir Naqqash	18	4	65	1		16	3	39	2
Mudassar Nazar	6	1	17	0		2	0	5	0
Jalaluddin	19	4	77	3		16	8	15	2
Abdul Qadir	37	7	86	2		35	7	102	2
Zaheer Abbas	2	0	2	0		1	0	1	0

AUSTRALIA	O	M	R	W		O	M	R	W
Thomson	19	1	73	1		5	0	24	0
Lawson	35	4	91	2		7	1	21	1
Alderman	34	4	144	2		3	0	10	0
Yardley	27	6	102	1					
Border	4	1	12	1					

FALL OF WICKETS	AUS	PAK	AUS	PAK		AUS	PAK	AUS	PAK
1st	85	92	21	55	6th	202	402	170	
2nd	120	93	55		7th	203	442	189	
3rd	140	119	64		8th	264		203	
4th	140	269	138		9th	264		214	
5th	197	392	157		10th	316		214	

PAKISTAN vs INDIA

at Lahore on 10/12/1982
Match drawn

PAKISTAN

Mohsin Khan	c Amarnath b Madan Lal	94	not out	101
Mudassar Nazar	c Gavaskar b Kapil Dev	50	c Arun Lal b Doshi	17
Mansoor Akhtar	c Gavaskar b Kapil Dev	3	not out	14
Javed Miandad	c Gavaskar b Madan Lal	17		
Zaheer Abbas	b Doshi	215		
Salim Malik	b Madan Lal	6		
Imran Khan *	c Madan Lal b Doshi	45		
Wasim Bari +	c Arun Lal b Doshi	12		
Tahir Naqqash	st Kirmani b Doshi	20		
Sarfraz Nawaz	c Amarnath b Doshi	18		
Jalaluddin	not out	1		
	Extras (lb 3,nb 1)	4	(lb 3)	3
	TOTAL	485	(for 1 wkt)	135

INDIA

S.M.Gavaskar *	c Wasim Bari b Sarfraz Nawaz	83
Arun Lal	c Mudassar Nazar b Imran Khan	51
D.B.Vengsarkar	c Mudassar Nazar b Imran Khan	3
G.R.Viswanath	c Wasim Bari b Imran Khan	1
M.Amarnath	not out	109
S.M.Patil	run out	68
Kapil Dev	c Wasim Bari b Sarfraz Nawaz	9
R.J.Shastri	lbw b Jalaluddin	7
S.M.H.Kirmani +	c Wasim Bari b Jalaluddin	10
Madan Lal	c Salim Malik b Sarfraz Nawaz	7
D.R.Doshi	b Sarfraz Nawaz	0
	Extras (b 2,lb 11,nb 18)	31
	TOTAL	379

INDIA	O	M	R	W		O	M	R	W
Kapil Dev	39	3	149	2		8	2	27	0
Madan Lal	27	2	101	3		5	1	10	0
Amarnath	23	5	60	0		3	1	5	0
Doshi	32.5	6	90	5		15	2	57	1
Shastri	22	3	81	0		14	1	33	0
Gavaskar						1	1	0	0

PAKISTAN	O	M	R	W		O	M	R	W
Imran Khan	27	8	68	3					
Sarfraz Nawaz	31.5	11	63	4					
Jalaluddin	34	10	93	2					
Tahir Naqqash	29	6	114	0					
Mudassar Nazar	3	1	10	0					

FALL OF WICKETS	PAK	IND	PAK			PAK	IND	PAK	
1st	85	105	55		6th	367	305		
2nd	100	111			7th	438	322		
3rd	126	123			8th	447	348		
4th	238	188			9th	478	375		
5th	250	294			10th	485	379		

PAKISTAN vs INDIA

at Karachi on 23/12/1982
Pakistan won by an innings and 86 runs

INDIA

S.M.Gavaskar *	run out	8	b Imran Khan	42
Arun Lal	lbw b Sarfraz Nawaz	35	lbw b Abdul Qadir	11
D.B.Vengsarkar	c Mohsin Khan b Imran Khan	0	c Wasim Bari b Imran Khan	79
G.R.Viswanath	c Wasim Bari b Abdul Qadir	24	b Imran Khan	0
M.Amarnath	lbw b Imran Khan	5	lbw b Imran Khan	3
S.M.Patil	c Javed Miandad b Abdul Qadir	4	b Imran Khan	0
Kapil Dev	c & b Sarfraz Nawaz	73	(8) b Imran Khan	1
S.M.H.Kirmani +	c Mohsin Khan b Abdul Qadir	11	(7) c Salim Malik b Abdul Qadir	1
Madan Lal	not out	3	not out	52
Maninder Singh	b Abdul Qadir	0	b Imran Khan	0
D.R.Doshi	b Imran Khan	0	b Imran Khan	0
	Extras (lb 4,nb 2)	6	(b 1,lb 3,w 1,nb 3)	8
	TOTAL	169		197

PAKISTAN

Mohsin Khan	c Amarnath b Madan Lal	12
Mansoor Akhtar	c Kirmani b Madan Lal	0
Salim Malik	c Kirmani b Madan Lal	3
Javed Miandad	b Amarnath	39
Zaheer Abbas	lbw b Kapil Dev	186
Mudassar Nazar	c Kirmani b Kapil Dev	119
Imran Khan *	c Amarnath b Kapil Dev	33
Wasim Bari +	c Arun Lal b Doshi	30
Abdul Qadir	b Kapil Dev	0
Sarfraz Nawaz	lbw b Kapil Dev	13
Jalaluddin	not out	0
	Extras (b 2,lb 6,w 2,nb 7)	17
	TOTAL	452

PAKISTAN	O	M	R	W		O	M	R	W
Imran Khan	12.1	6	19	3		20.1	4	60	8
Jalaluddin	10	2	28	0		7	2	31	0
Sarfraz Nawaz	16	2	49	2		10	2	23	0
Abdul Qadir	15	3	67	4		23	3	75	2

INDIA	O	M	R	W		O	M	R	W
Kapil Dev	28.5	3	102	5					
Madan Lal	23	1	129	3					
Maninder Singh	23	2	67	0					
Amarnath	17	1	69	1					
Doshi	18	1	68	1					

FALL OF WICKETS	IND	PAK	IND			IND	PAK	IND	
1st	10	6	28		6th	130	397	113	
2nd	10	15	102		7th	165	427	114	
3rd	48	18	108		8th	168	427	197	
4th	55	128	112		9th	168	452	197	
5th	70	341	112		10th	169	452	197	

PAKISTAN vs INDIA
at Faisalabad on 03/01/1983
Pakistan won by 10 wickets

INDIA

S.M.Gavaskar *	c Salim Malik b Imran Khan	12	not out	127
Arun Lal	b Sarfraz Nawaz	0	c Zaheer Abbas b Sarfraz Nawaz	3
D.B.Vengsarkar	lbw b Imran Khan	6	b Imran Khan	1
G.R.Viswanath	b Mudassar Nazar	53	c Javed Miandad b Sarfraz Nawaz	9
M.Amarnath	b Mudassar Nazar	22	b Imran Khan	78
S.M.Patil	c Wasim Bari b Imran Khan	84	b Imran Khan	6
Kapil Dev	lbw b Imran Khan	41	c Sikander Bakht b Sarfraz Nawaz	16
S.M.H.Kirmani +	b Imran Khan	66	c Wasim Bari b Sikander Bakht	6
Madan Lal	c Salim Malik b Imran Khan	54	lbw b Sarfraz Nawaz	10
Maninder Singh	c Mohsin Khan b Abdul Qadir	6	lbw b Imran Khan	2
D.R.Doshi	not out	2	b Imran Khan	4
	Extras (b 6,lb 8,w 4,nb 8)	26	(b 1,lb 9,nb 14)	24
	TOTAL	372		286

PAKISTAN

Mohsin Khan	c Kirmani b Kapil Dev	4	not out	8
Mudassar Nazar	c Kirmani b Kapil Dev	38	not out	2
Mansoor Akhtar	c Kirmani b Kapil Dev	23		
Javed Miandad	c Gavaskar b Madan Lal	126		
Zaheer Abbas	c Kirmani b Madan Lal	168		
Salim Malik	b Kapil Dev	107		
Imran Khan *	c Madan Lal b Maninder Singh	117		
Wasim Bari +	c Kirmani b Kapil Dev	6		
Sarfraz Nawaz	c Gavaskar b Kapil Dev	4		
Abdul Qadir	not out	38		
Sikander Bakht	b Kapil Dev	9		
	Extras (lb 10,nb 2)	12		0
	TOTAL	652	(for 0 wkts)	10

PAKISTAN

	O	M	R	W		O	M	R	W
Imran Khan	25	3	98	6		30.5	12	82	5
Sarfraz Nawaz	23	4	95	1		33	11	79	4
Sikander Bakht	13	1	66	0		9	3	41	1
Mudassar Nazar	12	2	39	2		11	3	27	0
Abdul Qadir	12.3	1	48	1		11	1	33	0

INDIA

	O	M	R	W		O	M	R	W
Kapil Dev	38.4	3	220	7					
Madan Lal	28	5	109	2					
Doshi	29	2	130	0					
Amarnath	16	1	68	0					
Maninder Singh	29	3	103	1					
Gavaskar	2	0	10	0					
Arun Lal						1.1	0	6	0
Vengsarkar						1	0	4	0

FALL OF WICKETS

	IND	PAK	IND	PAK		IND	PAK	IND	PAK
1st	6	4	27		6th	220	574	227	
2nd	17	66	28		7th	235	595	236	
3rd	22	79	48		8th	357	599	261	
4th	82	366	193		9th	370	612	282	
5th	122	367	201		10th	372	652	286	

PAKISTAN vs INDIA
at Hyderabad on 14/01/1983
Pakistan won by an innings and 119 runs

PAKISTAN

Mohsin Khan	lbw b Sandhu	24
Mudassar Nazar	c Maninder Singh b Doshi	231
Haroon Rashid	b Sandhu	0
Javed Miandad	not out	280
Zaheer Abbas	not out	25
Salim Malik		
Imran Khan *		
Wasim Bari +		
Sarfraz Nawaz		
Abdul Qadir		
Iqbal Qasim		
	Extras (b 9,lb 12)	21
	TOTAL (for 3 wkts dec)	581

INDIA

S.M.Gavaskar *	c Wasim Bari b Imran Khan	17	c & b Iqbal Qasim	60
K.Srikkanth	lbw b Sarfraz Nawaz	2	c Salim Malik b Imran Khan	5
M.Amarnath	st Wasim Bari b Iqbal Qasim	61	c Imran Khan b Iqbal Qasim	64
G.R.Viswanath	lbw b Imran Khan	0	lbw b Sarfraz Nawaz	37
D.B.Vengsarkar	c Wasim Bari b Imran Khan	4	not out	58
Kapil Dev	b Imran Khan	3	b Sarfraz Nawaz	2
S.M.H.Kirmani +	b Imran Khan	1	lbw b Sarfraz Nawaz	0
S.M.Patil	c Imran Khan b Sarfraz Nawaz	2	c Imran Khan b Abdul Qadir	9
B.S.Sandhu	b Sarfraz Nawaz	71	c Imran Khan b Abdul Qadir	12
Maninder Singh	not out	12	lbw b Sarfraz Nawaz	4
D.R.Doshi	lbw b Imran Khan	1	b Imran Khan	14
	Extras (b 1,lb 7,nb 7)	15	(b 1,lb 1,nb 6)	8
	TOTAL	189		273

INDIA

	O	M	R	W		O	M	R	W
Kapil Dev	27	2	111	0					
Sandhu	33	7	107	2					
Amarnath	15	0	64	0					
Maninder Singh	50	10	135	0					
Doshi	41	9	143	1					

PAKISTAN

	O	M	R	W		O	M	R	W
Imran Khan	17.2	4	35	6		24.4	14	45	2
Sarfraz Nawaz	19	5	56	3		30	4	85	4
Abdul Qadir	11	2	35	0		26	7	77	2
Iqbal Qasim	9	3	48	1		31	9	58	2

FALL OF WICKETS

	PAK	IND	IND			PAK	IND	IND	
1st	60	3	8		6th	65	203		
2nd	60	44	133		7th	72	223		
3rd	511	44	134		8th	131	249		
4th		52	201		9th	184	254		
5th		61	203		10th	189	273		

PAKISTAN vs INDIA
at Lahore on 23/01/1983
Match drawn

PAKISTAN

Mohsin Khan	c Srikkanth b Kapil Dev	7
Mudassar Nazar	not out	152
Majid Khan	c Kirmani b Kapil Dev	0
Javed Miandad	c Viswanath b Maninder Singh	85
Zaheer Abbas	c Kirmani b Kapil Dev	13
Salim Malik	b Maninder Singh	6
Imran Khan *	c Kirmani b Kapil Dev	20
Wasim Bari +	c Amarnath b Kapil Dev	8
Sarfraz Nawaz	c Yashpal Sharma b Kapil Dev	26
Abdul Qadir	b Kapil Dev	0
Iqbal Qasim	lbw b Kapil Dev	0
	Extras (lb 6)	6
	TOTAL	323

INDIA

S.M.Gavaskar *	lbw b Imran Khan	13
K.Srikkanth	b Abdul Qadir	21
M.Amarnath	c Wasim Bari b Imran Khan	120
Yashpal Sharma	not out	63
D.B.Vengsarkar	not out	1
G.R.Viswanath		
Kapil Dev		
S.M.H.Kirmani +		
B.S.Sandhu		
Maninder Singh		
T.A.P.Sekhar		
	Extras (b 6,lb 5,w 1,nb 5)	17
	TOTAL (for 3 wkts)	235

INDIA

	O	M	R	W		O	M	R	W
Kapil Dev	30.5	7	82	8					
Sandhu	21	2	56	0					
Sekhar	20	2	86	0					
Maninder Singh	32	7	90	2					

PAKISTAN

	O	M	R	W		O	M	R	W
Imran Khan	18	5	45	2					
Sarfraz Nawaz	23.2	9	46	0					
Abdul Qadir	16	1	63	1					
Majid Khan	1	0	4	0					
Mudassar Nazar	11	1	41	0					
Iqbal Qasim	12	3	19	0					

FALL OF WICKETS

	PAK	IND			PAK	IND
1st	22	29		6th	244	
2nd	26	41		7th	276	
3rd	174	231		8th	323	
4th	191			9th	323	
5th	202			10th	323	

PAKISTAN vs INDIA
at Karachi on 30/01/1983
Match drawn

INDIA

S.M.Gavaskar *	c Wasim Bari b Tahir Naqqash	5	b Imran Khan	67
R.J.Shastri	st Wasim Bari b Abdul Qadir	128	c Wasim Bari b Imran Khan	17
M.Amarnath	c Wasim Bari b Imran Khan	19	not out	103
Yashpal Sharma	c Wasim Bari b Imran Khan	9	not out	19
D.B.Vengsarkar	c & b Tahir Naqqash	89		
G.R.Viswanath	b Mudassar Nazar	10		
S.M.H.Kirmani +	c Zaheer Abbas b Sarfraz Nawaz	18		
Kapil Dev	lbw b Imran Khan	33		
B.S.Sandhu	not out	32		
T.A.P.Sekhar	not out	0		
Maninder Singh				
	Extras (b 13,lb 9,nb 28)	50	(b 10,w 3,nb 5)	18
	TOTAL (for 8 wkts dec)	393	(for 2 wkts)	224

PAKISTAN

Mohsin Khan	lbw b Kapil Dev	91
Mudassar Nazar	lbw b Kapil Dev	152
Javed Miandad	c Kirmani b Sandhu	47
Zaheer Abbas	c Amarnath b Shastri	43
Wasim Raja	run out	10
Imran Khan *	not out	32
Wasim Bari +	c Kirmani b Sandhu	12
Sarfraz Nawaz	not out	6
Salim Malik		
Abdul Qadir		
Tahir Naqqash		
	Extras (b 5,lb 12,w 1,nb 9)	27
	TOTAL (for 6 wkts dec)	420

PAKISTAN

	O	M	R	W		O	M	R	W
Imran Khan	32	11	65	3		16	3	41	2
Sarfraz Nawaz	41	10	92	1		14	4	45	0
Tahir Naqqash	24	7	69	2		8	1	28	0
Abdul Qadir	23	3	86	1		14	2	42	0
Mudassar Nazar	15	4	30	1					
Wasim Raja	1	0	1	0		5	2	12	0
Zaheer Abbas						8	2	24	0
Mohsin Khan						1	0	3	0
Javed Miandad						2	0	11	0

INDIA

	O	M	R	W		O	M	R	W
Kapil Dev	33	2	137	2					
Sandhu	28.2	4	87	2					
Sekhar	14	1	43	0					
Maninder Singh	16	3	49	0					
Shastri	22	1	62	1					
Amarnath	4	1	15	0					

FALL OF WICKETS

	IND	PAK	IND			IND	PAK	IND
1st	47	157	43		6th	267	411	
2nd	86	269	150		7th	316		
3rd	109	342			8th	393		
4th	178	363			9th			
5th	218	371			10th			

INDIA vs PAKISTAN
at Bangalore on 14th September 1983
Match drawn

INDIA

S.M.Gavaskar	lbw b Tahir Naqqash	42	not out	103
A.D.Gaekwad	b Mudassar Nazar	11	not out	66
M.Amarnath	b Mudassar Nazar	4		
Yashpal Sharma	c Wasim Bari b Mudassar Nazar	16		
S.M.Patil	c Javed Miandad b Tahir Naqqash	6		
Kapil Dev *	c Mohsin Khan b Azeem Hafeez	0		
R.M.H.Binny	not out	83		
Madan Lal	c Wasim Bari b Azeem Hafeez	74		
S.M.H.Kirmani +	c Wasim Bari b Tahir Naqqash	14		
S.Venkataraghavan	c Salim Malik b Tahir Naqqash	5		
D.R.Doshi	lbw b Tahir Naqqash	0		
Extras	(b 1,lb 8,w 6,nb 5)	20	(lb 4,w 1,nb 2)	7
TOTAL		275	(for 0 wkts)	176

PAKISTAN

Mohsin Khan	c Kirmani b Madan Lal	17
Mudassar Nazar	c Kirmani b Kapil Dev	25
Salim Malik	c Amarnath b Kapil Dev	5
Javed Miandad	c sub b Madan Lal	99
Zaheer Abbas *	c Kapil Dev b Madan Lal	22
Wasim Raja	b Doshi	39
Wasim Bari +	b Kapil Dev	64
Tahir Naqqash	b Kapil Dev	1
Iqbal Qasim	c Gaekwad b Venkataraghavan	9
Azeem Hafeez	b Kapil Dev	0
Mohammad Nazir	not out	0
Extras	(b 1,lb 4,nb 2)	7
TOTAL		288

PAKISTAN	O	M	R	W	O	M	R	W
Tahir Naqqash	34.5	11	76	5	17	2	54	0
Azeem Hafeez	39	11	102	2	8	2	20	0
Mohammad Nazir	10	2	26	0	21	4	47	0
Mudassar Nazar	23	6	44	3	2.1	0	19	0
Iqbal Qasim	13	7	18	0	12	2	29	0
Zaheer Abbas					1	0	3	0

INDIA	O	M	R	W	O	M	R	W
Kapil Dev	29	6	68	5				
Madan Lal	24	5	72	3				
Binny	18	3	42	0				
Venkataraghavan	21.1	4	49	1				
Doshi	20	5	52	1				

FALL OF WICKETS	IND	PAK	IND		IND	PAK	IND
1st	38	32		6th	85	243	
2nd	42	37		7th	240	244	
3rd	72	58		8th	269	288	
4th	80	99		9th	275	288	
5th	81	187		10th	275	288	

INDIA vs PAKISTAN
at Jullundur on 24th September 1983
Match drawn

PAKISTAN

Mohsin Khan	lbw b Kapil Dev	0	not out	7
Shoaib Mohammad	c Kirmani b Kapil Dev	6	not out	6
Qasim Omar	c Kirmani b Binny	15		
Zaheer Abbas *	b Shastri	49		
Javed Miandad	c Shastri b Kapil Dev	66		
Mudassar Nazar	c sub b Shastri	24		
Wasim Raja	c Kirmani b Shastri	125		
Wasim Bari +	c Kirmani b Kapil Dev	0		
Tahir Naqqash	b Binny	37		
Mohammad Nazir	run out	2		
Azeem Hafeez	not out	2		
Extras	(b 3,lb 6,w 1,nb 1)	11	(nb 3)	3
TOTAL		337	(for 0 wkts)	16

INDIA

S.M.Gavaskar	b Azeem Hafeez	5
A.D.Gaekwad	c & b Wasim Raja	201
M.Amarnath	c Wasim Bari b Azeem Hafeez	7
Yashpal Sharma	lbw b Tahir Naqqash	7
S.M.Patil	c Wasim Bari b Tahir Naqqash	26
R.J.Shastri	c Wasim Bari b Azeem Hafeez	26
R.M.H.Binny	b Zaheer Abbas	54
Kapil Dev *	lbw b Wasim Raja	4
Madan Lal	c Wasim Bari b Wasim Raja	11
S.M.H.Kirmani +	not out	8
S.Venkataraghavan	b Wasim Raja	6
Extras	(b 2,lb 4,w 9,nb 4)	19
TOTAL		374

INDIA	O	M	R	W	O	M	R	W
Kapil Dev	32	8	80	4	2	0	9	0
Madan Lal	20	4	61	0	1	0	1	0
Binny	16	1	69	2				
Shastri	37.2	12	63	3	3	2	1	0
Venkataraghavan	28	5	55	0				
Patil					2	1	2	0
Gavaskar					1	0	3	0

PAKISTAN	O	M	R	W	O	M	R	W
Tahir Naqqash	27	3	74	2				
Azeem Hafeez	23	3	65	3				
Mudassar Nazar	28	6	80	0				
Mohammad Nazir	52	16	76	0				
Wasim Raja	28.5	5	50	4				
Mohsin Khan	5	2	9	0				
Zaheer Abbas	6	1	14	1				

FALL OF WICKETS	PAK	IND	PAK		PAK	IND	PAK
1st	0	5		6th	169	330	
2nd	7	20		7th	169	345	
3rd	55	73		8th	264	353	
4th	101	131		9th	309	368	
5th	154	209		10th	337	374	

INDIA vs PAKISTAN
at Nagpur on 5th October 1983
Match drawn

INDIA

S.M.Gavaskar	c Mudassar Nazar b Azeem Hafeez	50	c Mudassar Nazar b Mohammad Nazir	64
A.D.Gaekwad	c Wasim Bari b Tahir Naqqash	6	c Wasim Raja b Mohammad Nazir	29
D.B.Vengsarkar	c Wasim Bari b Salim Malik	21	c Mohsin Khan b Mohammad Nazir	40
Yashpal Sharma	lbw b Mohammad Nazir	13	c Wasim Bari b Azeem Hafeez	15
S.M.Patil	c Wasim Raja b Azeem Hafeez	6	lbw b Wasim Raja	26
Kapil Dev *	c Wasim Bari b Mudassar Nazar	32	(8) st Wasim Bari b Wasim Raja	10
R.J.Shastri	c Mudassar Nazar b Azeem Hafeez	52	(6) c Mudassar Nazar b Mohammad Nazir	0
K.Azad	c Mohsin Khan b Azeem Hafeez	11	(7) c Zaheer Abbas b Mohammad Nazir	0
Madan Lal	c Salim Malik b Mohammad Nazir	5	not out	32
S.M.H.Kirmani +	run out	30	not out	31
A.R.Bhat	not out	0		
Extras	(b 9,lb 6,w 1,nb 3)	19	(b 7,lb 7,nb 1)	15
TOTAL		245	(for 8 wkts dec)	262

PAKISTAN

Mohsin Khan	c Kirmani b Shastri	44		
Shoaib Mohammad	c Yashpal Sharma b Kapil Dev	9		
Salim Malik	lbw b Kapil Dev	0	not out	0
Javed Miandad	lbw b Bhat	60		
Zaheer Abbas *	c Kirmani b Kapil Dev	85		
Mudassar Nazar	st Kirmani b Bhat	78		
Wasim Raja	c Yashpal Sharma b Shastri	16		
Wasim Bari +	c Patil b Shastri	1		
Tahir Naqqash	c Gaekwad b Shastri	6	(1) not out	18
Mohammad Nazir	not out	13		
Azeem Hafeez	c Patil b Shastri	4	(2) b Kirmani	18
Extras	(b 1,lb 1,nb 4)	6	(b 4,lb 1,nb 1)	6
TOTAL		322	(for 1 wkt)	42

PAKISTAN	O	M	R	W	O	M	R	W
Azeem Hafeez	27	10	58	4	19	1	67	1
Tahir Naqqash	19.3	3	72	1	23	7	55	0
Mudassar Nazar	14	2	43	1				
Salim Malik	3	0	7	1				
Mohammad Nazir	22	5	50	2	50	19	72	5
Zaheer Abbas					1	1	0	0
Wasim Raja					10	1	46	2
Mohsin Khan					3	1	7	0
Javed Miandad					1	0	1	0

INDIA	O	M	R	W	O	M	R	W
Kapil Dev	27	8	68	3	1	1	0	0
Madan Lal	13	2	44	0				
Bhat	39	16	65	2				
Azad	25	7	68	0				
Shastri	30.4	7	75	5				
Vengsarkar					2	0	15	0
Yashpal Sharma					1	0	10	0
Kirmani					2	0	9	1
Gaekwad					1	0	3	0
Gavaskar					1	1	0	0

FALL OF WICKETS	IND	PAK	IND	PAK		IND	PAK	IND	PAK
1st	27	20	78	42	6th	171	287	188	
2nd	66	26	125		7th	190	289	188	
3rd	96	83	148		8th	205	305	207	
4th	103	153	172		9th	242	309		
5th	103	254	172		10th	245	322		

AUSTRALIA vs PAKISTAN
at Perth on 11th November 1983
Australia won by an innings and 9 runs

AUSTRALIA

K.C.Wessels	c Wasim Bari b Azeem Hafeez	12
W.B.Phillips	c Tahir Naqqash b Mohammad Nazir	159
G.N.Yallop	b Azeem Hafeez	141
K.J.Hughes *	b Abdul Qadir	16
A.R.Border	c Wasim Raja b Azeem Hafeez	32
G.S.Chappell	c Azeem Hafeez b Abdul Qadir	17
R.W.Marsh +	c Wasim Bari b Azeem Hafeez	24
G.F.Lawson	c Mohammad Nazir b Abdul Qadir	9
D.K.Lillee	c Wasim Raja b Azeem Hafeez	0
R.M.Hogg	not out	7
C.G.Rackemann		
Extras	(lb 9,w 3,nb 7)	19
TOTAL	(for 9 wkts dec)	436

PAKISTAN

Mohsin Khan	c Marsh b Hogg	8	c Border b Rackemann	24
Mudassar Nazar	c Phillips b Lillee	1	c Chappell b Rackemann	27
Qasim Omar	c Yallop b Rackemann	48	c Marsh b Rackemann	65
Javed Miandad	c Phillips b Hogg	0	lbw b Rackemann	46
Zaheer Abbas *	c Phillips b Hogg	0	c Marsh b Rackemann	30
Wasim Raja	c Chappell b Rackemann	14	c Marsh b Lawson	4
Wasim Bari +	c Chappell b Rackemann	0	c Marsh b Lawson	7
Tahir Naqqash	not out	29	c Marsh b Rackemann	26
Abdul Qadir	b Rackemann	5	run out	18
Mohammad Nazir	c Chappell b Rackemann	16	c Border b Hogg	18
Azeem Hafeez	c Border b Lawson	1	not out	0
Extras	(lb 3,nb 4)	7	(b 4,lb 7,w 2,nb 20)	33
TOTAL		129		298

PAKISTAN	O	M	R	W	O	M	R	W
Tahir Naqqash	22	6	76	0				
Azeem Hafeez	27.3	5	100	5				
Mudassar Nazar	15	1	39	0				
Mohammad Nazir	29	5	91	1				
Abdul Qadir	32	4	121	3				

AUSTRALIA	O	M	R	W	O	M	R	W
Lillee	13	3	26	1	29	6	56	0
Hogg	12	4	20	3	21.1	2	72	1
Rackemann	8	0	32	5	26	6	86	6
Lawson	7.2	0	48	1	13	1	53	2
Chappell					9	1	20	0

FALL OF WICKETS	AUS	PAK	PAK		AUS	PAK	PAK
1st	34	7	62	6th	404	68	218
2nd	293	13	63	7th	424	90	257
3rd	321	15	188	8th	424	105	267
4th	369	15	197	9th	436	124	281
5th	386	65	206	10th		129	298

AUSTRALIA vs PAKISTAN
at Brisbane on 25th November 1983
Match drawn

PAKISTAN

Mohsin Khan	c Chappell b Lawson	2	b Lawson		37
Mudassar Nazar	c Marsh b Lawson	24	c Wessels b Rackemann		18
Qasim Omar	c Hughes b Lawson	17	not out		11
Javed Miandad	c Marsh b Hogg	6	c Phillips b Rackemann		5
Zaheer Abbas *	c Border b Lawson	56	not out		3
Wasim Raja	c Hughes b Rackemann	27			
Wasim Bari +	c Border b Rackemann	2			
Abdul Qadir	b Rackemann	0			
Rashid Khan	not out	13			
Mohammad Nazir	c Marsh b Hogg	1			
Azeem Hafeez	b Lawson	2			
Extras	(lb 3,w 1,nb 2)	6	(lb 6,nb 2)		8
TOTAL		156	(for 3 wkts)		82

AUSTRALIA

K.C.Wessels	c Qasim Omar b Azeem Hafeez	35
W.B.Phillips	b Rashid Khan	46
G.N.Yallop	c Wasim Bari b Rashid Khan	33
K.J.Hughes *	c Mohammad Nazir b Azeem Hafeez	53
A.R.Border	c Wasim Bari b Rashid Khan	118
G.S.Chappell	not out	150
R.W.Marsh +	b Azeem Hafeez	1
G.F.Lawson	b Abdul Qadir	49
D.K.Lillee		
R.M.Hogg		
C.G.Rackemann		
Extras	(b 2,lb 6,w 1,nb 15)	24
TOTAL	(for 7 wkts dec)	509

AUSTRALIA	O	M	R	W		O	M	R	W
Lawson	17.1	1	49	5		10	3	24	1
Hogg	15	2	43	2		3	0	11	0
Rackemann	10	3	28	3		8	1	31	2
Lillee	8	1	33	0		2	0	10	0

PAKISTAN	O	M	R	W		O	M	R	W
Azeem Hafeez	37	7	152	3					
Rashid Khan	43	10	129	3					
Mudassar Nazar	16	2	47	0					
Abdul Qadir	32	5	112	1					
Mohammad Nazir	24	6	50	0					
Wasim Raja	3	0	11	0					

FALL OF WICKETS	PAK	AUS	PAK			PAK	AUS	PAK
1st	10	56	57		6th	128	406	
2nd	39	120	59		7th	128	509	
3rd	46	124	74		8th	146		
4th	62	232			9th	147		
5th	124	403			10th	156		

AUSTRALIA vs PAKISTAN
at Adelaide on 9th December 1983
Match drawn

AUSTRALIA

K.C.Wessels	c Zaheer Abbas b Abdul Qadir	179	c Wasim Bari b Sarfraz Nawaz		2
W.B.Phillips	c Wasim Bari b Azeem Hafeez	12	c Mudassar Nazar b Abdul Qadir		54
G.N.Yallop	c Qasim Omar b Sarfraz Nawaz	68	c Javed Miandad b Abdul Qadir		14
K.J.Hughes *	c Wasim Bari b Azeem Hafeez	30	c Mudassar Nazar b Azeem Hafeez		106
A.R.Border	not out	117	lbw b Azeem Hafeez		66
G.S.Chappell	c Wasim Bari b Sarfraz Nawaz	6	run out		4
R.W.Marsh +	c Mohsin Khan b Sarfraz Nawaz	2	retired hurt/ill		33
T.G.Hogan	run out	2	c Qasim Omar b Salim Malik		8
G.F.Lawson	c Wasim Bari b Azeem Hafeez	4	not out		7
D.K.Lillee	c Sarfraz Nawaz b Azeem Hafeez	25	not out		4
R.M.Hogg	c Javed Miandad b Azeem Hafeez	5			
Extras	(lb 7,w 4,nb 4)	15	(b 3,lb 4,w 1,nb 4)		12
TOTAL		465	(for 7 wkts)		310

PAKISTAN

Mohsin Khan	c Phillips b Lawson	149
Mudassar Nazar	c Marsh b Lillee	44
Qasim Omar	c Marsh b Lillee	113
Javed Miandad	lbw b Lawson	131
Zaheer Abbas *	c Yallop b Hogg	46
Salim Malik	c Lawson b Hogan	77
Sarfraz Nawaz	c Yallop b Lillee	32
Abdul Qadir	b Lillee	10
Wasim Bari +	c Marsh b Lillee	0
Mohammad Nazir	not out	5
Azeem Hafeez	c Wessels b Lillee	5
Extras	(b 1,lb 4,nb 7)	12
TOTAL		624

PAKISTAN	O	M	R	W		O	M	R	W
Azeem Hafeez	38.2	8	167	5		19	4	50	2
Sarfraz Nawaz	42	7	105	3		30	8	69	1
Abdul Qadir	20	1	96	1		47	9	132	2
Mudassar Nazar	10	2	45	0					
Mohammad Nazir	9	0	37	0		27	14	39	0
Mohsin Khan	3	0	8	0		1	1	0	0
Javed Miandad						3	0	10	0
Salim Malik						1	0	3	1
Qasim Omar						1	1	0	0

AUSTRALIA	O	M	R	W		O	M	R	W
Lawson	37	7	127	2					
Hogg	34	3	123	1					
Lillee	50.2	8	171	6					
Hogan	37	8	107	1					
Chappell	32	6	82	0					
Border	1	0	9	0					

FALL OF WICKETS	AUS	PAK	AUS			AUS	PAK	AUS
1st	21	73	3		6th	378	590	293
2nd	163	306	44		7th	383	604	305
3rd	219	314	121		8th	394	612	
4th	353	371	216		9th	451	613	
5th	376	557	228		10th	465	624	

AUSTRALIA vs PAKISTAN
at Melbourne on 26th December 1983
Match drawn

PAKISTAN

Mohsin Khan	lbw b Lillee	152	c Hughes b Lillee		3
Mudassar Nazar	c Marsh b Lawson	7	lbw b Matthews		35
Qasim Omar	b Maguire	23	b Lawson		9
Javed Miandad	c Marsh b Maguire	27	lbw b Lillee		11
Zaheer Abbas	run out	44	(6) b Matthews		50
Salim Malik	c Maguire b Lawson	35	(8) b Lillee		14
Imran Khan *	c Marsh b Lillee	83	not out		72
Sarfraz Nawaz	c Hughes b Maguire	22	(9) not out		11
Abdul Qadir	c Lawson b Matthews	45	(5) b Lawson		12
Wasim Bari +	not out	6			
Azeem Hafeez	c Maguire b Matthews	7			
Extras	(lb 11,nb 8)	19	(b 10,lb 9,w 2)		21
TOTAL		470	(for 7 wkts)		238

AUSTRALIA

K.C.Wessels	c Wasim Bari b Azeem Hafeez	11
W.B.Phillips	lbw b Azeem Hafeez	35
G.N.Yallop	c Wasim Bari b Sarfraz Nawaz	268
K.J.Hughes *	lbw b Azeem Hafeez	94
A.R.Border	lbw b Abdul Qadir	32
G.S.Chappell	c Salim Malik b Abdul Qadir	5
R.W.Marsh +	c Mudassar Nazar b Abdul Qadir	0
G.R.J.Matthews	lbw b Sarfraz Nawaz	75
G.F.Lawson	c Mudassar Nazar b Abdul Qadir	0
J.N.Maguire	c Wasim Bari b Abdul Qadir	4
D.K.Lillee	not out	0
Extras	(b 15,lb 9,w 2,nb 3)	29
TOTAL		555

AUSTRALIA	O	M	R	W		O	M	R	W
Lawson	38	8	125	2		21	8	47	2
Lillee	38	11	113	2		29	7	71	3
Maguire	29	7	111	3		12	3	26	0
Matthews	28.4	7	95	2		21	8	48	2
Chappell	7	3	15	0		8	3	13	0
Border						5	3	9	0
Marsh						2	0	3	0
Wessels						2	1	2	0

PAKISTAN	O	M	R	W		O	M	R	W
Sarfraz Nawaz	51	12	106	2					
Azeem Hafeez	35	8	115	3					
Abdul Qadir	54.3	12	166	5					
Mudassar Nazar	20	0	76	0					
Javed Miandad	5	0	16	0					
Zaheer Abbas	22	5	42	0					
Salim Malik	2	1	10	0					

FALL OF WICKETS	PAK	AUS	PAK			PAK	AUS	PAK
1st	13	21	3		6th	321	354	160
2nd	64	70	18		7th	349	539	213
3rd	112	273	37		8th	457	540	
4th	244	342	73		9th	459	553	
5th	294	354	81		10th	470	555	

AUSTRALIA vs PAKISTAN
at Sydney on 2nd January 1984
Australia won by 10 wickets

PAKISTAN

Mohsin Khan	c Border b Lillee	14	c Chappell b Lawson		1
Mudassar Nazar	c Chappell b Lawson	84	b Lawson		21
Qasim Omar	c Border b Lillee	15	c Marsh b Lawson		26
Abdul Qadir	c Hughes b Lawson	4	(9) c Marsh b Lillee		5
Javed Miandad	c Lillee b Matthews	16	(4) c Marsh b Lawson		60
Zaheer Abbas	c Yallop b Lawson	61	(5) c Marsh b Hogg		33
Imran Khan *	c Yallop b Lawson	5	(6) c Marsh b Hogg		10
Salim Malik	c Lillee b Lawson	54	(7) c Chappell b Lillee		7
Sarfraz Nawaz	lbw b Lillee	5	(8) c Phillips b Lillee		20
Wasim Bari +	not out	7	c Phillips b Lillee		20
Azeem Hafeez	c Marsh b Lillee	4	not out		2
Extras	(b 2,lb 7)	9	(lb 4,nb 1)		5
TOTAL		278			210

AUSTRALIA

K.C.Wessels	c Wasim Bari b Azeem Hafeez	3	not out		14
W.B.Phillips	c Salim Malik b Sarfraz Nawaz	37	not out		19
G.N.Yallop	c Wasim Bari b Mudassar Nazar	30			
G.S.Chappell	lbw b Mudassar Nazar	182			
K.J.Hughes *	lbw b Sarfraz Nawaz	76			
A.R.Border	c Wasim Bari b Mudassar Nazar	64			
G.R.J.Matthews	not out	22			
R.W.Marsh +	not out	15			
G.F.Lawson					
R.M.Hogg					
D.K.Lillee					
Extras	(lb 15,w 1,nb 9)	25	(nb 2)		2
TOTAL	(for 6 wkts dec)	454	(for 0 wkts)		35

AUSTRALIA	O	M	R	W		O	M	R	W
Lillee	31.2	10	65	4		29.5	5	88	4
Hogg	18	1	61	0		14	2	53	2
Chappell	8	0	25	0					
Lawson	25	5	59	5		20	7	48	4
Matthews	18	4	59	1		7	4	17	0

PAKISTAN	O	M	R	W		O	M	R	W
Sarfraz Nawaz	53	13	132	2		3	1	7	0
Azeem Hafeez	36	7	121	1		2.4	0	28	0
Mudassar Nazar	31	9	81	3					
Abdul Qadir	34	9	105	0					

FALL OF WICKETS	PAK	AUS	PAK	AUS		PAK	AUS	PAK	AUS
1st	18	11	5		6th	158	436	163	
2nd	57	66	47		7th	254		163	
3rd	67	83	56		8th	267		173	
4th	131	254	104		9th	267		191	
5th	150	407	132		10th	278		210	

PAKISTAN vs ENGLAND
at Karachi on 2nd March 1984
Pakistan won by 3 wickets

ENGLAND

C.L.Smith	c Wasim Raja b Sarfraz Nawaz	28	lbw b Sarfraz Nawaz	5
M.W.Gatting	b Tauseef Ahmed	26	lbw b Sarfraz Nawaz	4
D.I.Gower	lbw b Abdul Qadir	58	c Mohsin Khan b Tauseef Ahmed	57
A.J.Lamb	c Ramiz Raja b Sarfraz Nawaz	4	c Anil Dalpat b Abdul Qadir	20
D.W.Randall	b Abdul Qadir	8	b Abdul Qadir	16
I.T.Botham	c Ramiz Raja b Abdul Qadir	22	b Tauseef Ahmed	10
V.J.Marks	c Ramiz Raja b Sarfraz Nawaz	5	lbw b Abdul Qadir	1
R.W.Taylor +	lbw b Abdul Qadir	4	c Mohsin Khan b Tauseef Ahmed	19
N.G.B.Cook	c Salim Malik b Abdul Qadir	9	c Mohsin Khan b Wasim Raja	5
R.G.D.Willis *	c Wasim Raja b Sarfraz Nawaz	6	c Tauseef Ahmed b Wasim Raja	2
N.G.Cowans	not out	1	not out	0
	Extras (lb 6,nb 5)	11	(b 6,lb 6,nb 8)	20
	TOTAL	**182**		**159**

PAKISTAN

Mohsin Khan	c Botham b Cook	54	b Cook	10
Qasim Omar	lbw b Cook	29	c Botham b Cook	7
Ramiz Raja	c Smith b Cook	1	c Botham b Marks	1
Zaheer Abbas *	c Lamb b Botham	0	lbw b Cook	8
Salim Malik	lbw b Willis	74	run out	11
Wasim Raja	c Cowans b Cook	3	c Cowans b Cook	0
Anil Dalpat +	c Taylor b Willis	12	not out	16
Abdul Qadir	c Lamb b Botham	40	b Cook	7
Sarfraz Nawaz	c Botham b Cook	8	not out	4
Tauseef Ahmed	not out	17		
Azeem Hafeez	c Willis b Cook	24		
	Extras (lb 5,nb 10)	15	(b 1,nb 1)	2
	TOTAL	**277**	**(for 7 wkts)**	**66**

PAKISTAN	O	M	R	W		O	M	R	W
Azeem Hafeez	11	3	21	0		8	3	14	0
Sarfraz Nawaz	25.5	8	42	4		15	1	27	2
Tauseef Ahmed	24	11	33	1		21	6	37	3
Wasim Raja	3	2	1	0		3.3	1	2	2
Abdul Qadir	31	12	74	5		31	4	59	3

ENGLAND	O	M	R	W		O	M	R	W
Willis	17	6	33	2		2	0	13	0
Cowans	12	3	34	0		2.3	1	10	0
Botham	30	5	90	2					
Cook	30	12	65	6		14	8	18	5
Marks	13	4	40	0		12	5	23	1

FALL OF WICKETS	ENG	PAK	ENG	PAK		ENG	PAK	ENG	PAK
1st	41	67	6	17	6th	159	138	128	40
2nd	90	79	21	18	7th	164	213	128	59
3rd	94	80	63	26	8th	165	229	157	
4th	108	96	94	38	9th	180	240	159	
5th	154	105	121	38	10th	182	277	159	

PAKISTAN vs ENGLAND
at Lahore on 19th March 1984
Match drawn

ENGLAND

C.L.Smith	c Salim Malik b Sarfraz Nawaz	18	(2) run out	15
M.W.Gatting	lbw b Sarfraz Nawaz	0	(3) run out	53
D.I.Gower *	c Anil Dalpat b Mohsin Kamal	9	(4) not out	173
A.J.Lamb	c Ramiz Raja b Abdul Qadir	29	(5) c & b Abdul Qadir	6
D.W.Randall	c Salim Malik b Abdul Qadir	14	(6) c Salim Malik b Abdul Qadir	0
G.Fowler	c Qasim Omar b Abdul Qadir	58	(1) c Anil Dalpat b Mohsin Kamal	19
V.J.Marks	c Mohsin Khan b Abdul Qadir	74	c sub b Abdul Qadir	55
R.W.Taylor +	lbw b Sarfraz Nawaz	1	(10) b Sarfraz Nawaz	5
N.A.Foster	lbw b Abdul Qadir	6	(8) lbw b Abdul Qadir	0
N.G.B.Cook	c Anil Dalpat b Sarfraz Nawaz	3		
N.G.Cowans	not out	3	(9) st Anil Dalpat b Abdul Qadir	3
	Extras (b 4,lb 5,w 9,nb 8)	26	(b 6,lb 3,w 1,nb 5)	15
	TOTAL	**241**	**(for 9 wkts dec)**	**344**

PAKISTAN

Mohsin Khan	lbw b Foster	1	c Smith b Cowans	104
Shoaib Mohammad	lbw b Cowans	7	c Gatting b Cowans	80
Qasim Omar	c Fowler b Foster	73	run out	0
Salim Malik	b Marks	38	c Gatting b Cowans	7
Ramiz Raja	c Smith b Foster	26	(8) not out	6
Wasim Raja	c Gower b Cowans	12	lbw b Cowans	0
Zaheer Abbas *	not out	82	(5) c Gatting b Cowans	5
Abdul Qadir	c Taylor b Foster	3		
Anil Dalpat +	c Gower b Foster	2		
Sarfraz Nawaz	c Gatting b Smith	90	(7) not out	10
Mohsin Kamal	c Gower b Cook	0		
	Extras (lb 9)	9	(lb 5)	5
	TOTAL	**343**	**(for 6 wkts)**	**217**

PAKISTAN	O	M	R	W		O	M	R	W
Mohsin Kamal	15	0	66	1		17	3	59	1
Sarfraz Nawaz	22.5	5	49	4		27.4	1	112	1
Abdul Qadir	30	7	84	5		42	5	110	5
Wasim Raja	11	4	16	0		21	5	48	0

ENGLAND	O	M	R	W		O	M	R	W
Cowans	29	5	89	2		14	2	42	5
Foster	32	8	67	5		15	4	44	0
Cook	46	12	117	1		18.3	2	73	0
Marks	20	4	59	1		10	0	53	0
Smith	1	0	2	1		1	1	0	0

FALL OF WICKETS	ENG	PAK	ENG	PAK		ENG	PAK	ENG	PAK
1st	5	9	35	173	6th	203	166	308	199
2nd	20	13	38	175	7th	205	175	309	
3rd	47	99	175	187	8th	222	181	327	
4th	77	138	189	197	9th	237	342	344	
5th	83	151	189	199	10th	241	343		

PAKISTAN vs ENGLAND
at Faisalabad on 12th March 1984
Match drawn

PAKISTAN

Mohsin Khan	c Lamb b Dilley	20	b Dilley	2
Mudassar Nazar	c Gatting b Cook	12	lbw b Foster	4
Qasim Omar	c Gatting b Foster	16	c Taylor b Dilley	17
Salim Malik	c Lamb b Cook	116	c sub b Marks	76
Zaheer Abbas *	lbw b Gatting	68	not out	32
Wasim Raja	b Marks	112	not out	5
Abdul Qadir	c Foster b Dilley	50		
Anil Dalpat +	lbw b Dilley	8		
Sarfraz Nawaz	not out	16		
Tauseef Ahmed	not out	1		
Azeem Hafeez				
	Extras (lb 11,w 2,nb 17)	30	(lb 1)	1
	TOTAL (for 8 wkts dec)	**449**	**(for 4 wkts)**	**137**

ENGLAND

C.L.Smith	b Sarfraz Nawaz	66
M.W.Gatting	c Salim Malik b Tauseef Ahmed	75
D.W.Randall	b Sarfraz Nawaz	65
A.J.Lamb	c Anil Dalpat b Azeem Hafeez	19
D.I.Gower *	st Anil Dalpat b Mudassar Nazar	152
G.Fowler	c Qasim Omar b Wasim Raja	57
R.W.Taylor +	c Salim Malik b Abdul Qadir	0
V.J.Marks	b Sarfraz Nawaz	83
G.R.Dilley	not out	2
N.G.B.Cook	not out	1
N.A.Foster		
	Extras (b 10,lb 4,nb 12)	2
	TOTAL (for 8 wkts dec)	**546**

ENGLAND	O	M	R	W		O	M	R	W
Foster	30	7	109	1		5	1	10	1
Dilley	28	6	101	3		9	0	41	2
Cook	54	14	133	2		16	6	38	0
Marks	27	9	59	1		8	2	26	1
Gatting	3	0	17	1		2	0	18	0
Fowler						1	0	3	0

PAKISTAN	O	M	R	W		O	M	R	W
Azeem Hafeez	19	3	71	1					
Sarfraz Nawaz	50	11	129	3					
Wasim Raja	26	6	61	1					
Abdul Qadir	51	14	124	1					
Tauseef Ahmed	30	8	96	1					
Mudassar Nazar	13	1	39	1					

FALL OF WICKETS	PAK	ENG	PAK		PAK	ENG	PAK
1st	35	127	6	6th	416	361	
2nd	53	163	6	7th	430	528	
3rd	70	214	56	8th	433	545	
4th	200	245	123	9th			
5th	323	361		10th			

PAKISTAN vs INDIA
at Lahore on 17th October 1984
Match drawn

PAKISTAN

Mohsin Khan	b Sharma	4
Mudassar Nazar	c Gavaskar b Sharma	15
Qasim Omar	c Amarnath b Shastri	4
Javed Miandad	c Amarnath b Sharma	134
Zaheer Abbas *	not out	168
Salim Malik	c & b Shastri	45
Wasim Raja	c Amarnath b Kapil Dev	3
Ashraf Ali +	c Gavaskar b Gaekwad	65
Tauseef Ahmed	c Gavaskar b Maninder Singh	10
Jalaluddin	lbw b Shastri	2
Azeem Hafeez	not out	17
	Extras (lb 7,w 1,nb 11)	19
	TOTAL (for 9 wkts dec)	**428**

INDIA

S.M.Gavaskar *	c Salim Malik b Azeem Hafeez	48	lbw b Jalaluddin	37
A.D.Gaekwad	b Jalaluddin	4	c Salim Malik b Tauseef Ahmed	60
D.B.Vengsarkar	c Ashraf Ali b Azeem Hafeez	41	c Mudassar Nazar b Azeem Hafeez	28
M.Amarnath	b Wasim Raja	36	not out	101
S.M.Patil	c Salim Malik b Azeem Hafeez	0	lbw b Jalaluddin	7
R.J.Shastri	lbw b Azeem Hafeez	0	lbw b Salim Malik	71
Kapil Dev	lbw b Azeem Hafeez	3	(8) not out	33
R.M.H.Binny	lbw b Mudassar Nazar	0	(7) lbw b Wasim Raja	13
S.M.H.Kirmani +	c sub b Mudassar Nazar	2		
C.Sharma	b Azeem Hafeez	4		
Maninder Singh	not out	4		
	Extras (b 2,lb 7,w 1,nb 4)	14	(b 6,lb 7,w 4,nb 4)	21
	TOTAL	**156**	**(for 6 wkts)**	**371**

INDIA	O	M	R	W		O	M	R	W
Kapil Dev	30	4	104	1					
Sharma	29	2	94	3					
Binny	8	1	20	0					
Maninder Singh	40	10	90	1					
Shastri	46	13	90	3					
Amarnath	4	0	19	0					
Gaekwad	1	0	4	1					

PAKISTAN	O	M	R	W		O	M	R	W
Jalaluddin	16.3	5	40	1		24	3	61	2
Azeem Hafeez	23	7	46	6		43	12	114	1
Mudassar Nazar	16.3	2	32	2		14	3	34	0
Tauseef Ahmed	13	3	19	0		50	19	93	1
Wasim Raja	3.5	0	10	1		19	4	46	1
Salim Malik						5	2	6	1
Javed Miandad						1	0	4	0

FALL OF WICKETS	PAK	IND	IND		PAK	IND	IND
1st	6	7	85	6th	212	119	315
2nd	54	94	114	7th	354	120	
3rd	100	112	147	8th	394	130	
4th	110	114	164	9th	397	135	
5th	195	114	290	10th		156	

PAKISTAN vs INDIA
at Faisalabad on 24th October 1984
Match drawn

INDIA

S.M.Gavaskar *	c Qasim Omar b Abdul Qadir	35
A.D.Gaekwad	c & b Manzoor Elahi	74
D.B.Vengsarkar	c Mohsin Khan b Abdul Qadir	5
M.Amarnath	hit wicket b Azeem Hafeez	37
S.M.Patil	c Zaheer Abbas b Mudassar Nazar	127
R.J.Shastri	c Ashraf Ali b Abdul Qadir	139
Kapil Dev	c Manzoor Elahi b Azeem Hafeez	16
Madan Lal	c Ashraf Ali b Azeem Hafeez	0
S.M.H.Kirmani +	c sub b Azeem Hafeez	6
N.S.Yadav	c Salim Malik b Abdul Qadir	29
C.Sharma	not out	18
	Extras (b 1,lb 6,nb 7)	14
	TOTAL	**500**

PAKISTAN

Mohsin Khan	c Gavaskar b Sharma	59
Mudassar Nazar	c Kirmani b Yadav	199
Qasim Omar	c Yadav b Gaekwad	210
Javed Miandad	st Kirmani b Shastri	16
Zaheer Abbas *	c Kirmani b Madan Lal	26
Salim Malik	not out	102
Manzoor Elahi	run out	26
Ashraf Ali +	not out	9
Abdul Qadir		
Jalaluddin		
Azeem Hafeez		
	Extras (b 7,lb 6,w 1,nb 13)	27
	TOTAL (for 6 wkts)	**674**

PAKISTAN	O	M	R	W		O	M	R	W
Jalaluddin	34	5	103	0					
Azeem Hafeez	44	9	137	4					
Mudassar Nazar	25	5	74	1					
Manzoor Elahi	21	3	74	1					
Abdul Qadir	38	8	104	4					
Salim Malik	1	0	1	0					

INDIA	O	M	R	W		O	M	R	W
Kapil Dev	4.5	0	22	0					
Sharma	32	0	139	1					
Madan Lal	27	3	94	1					
Yadav	75	18	196	1					
Shastri	50.1	17	99	1					
Gaekwad	27	5	75	1					
Amarnath	8.5	0	36	0					

FALL OF WICKETS	IND	PAK				IND	PAK
1st	88	141			6th	412	650
2nd	100	391			7th	420	
3rd	148	430			8th	441	
4th	170	494			9th	461	
5th	370	608			10th	500	

PAKISTAN vs NEW ZEALAND
at Lahore on 16th November 1984
Pakistan won by 6 wickets

NEW ZEALAND

J.J.Crowe	c Anil Dalpat b Mudassar Nazar	0	(5) b Iqbal Qasim	43
B.A.Edgar	b Mudassar Nazar	3	lbw b Azeem Hafeez	26
M.D.Crowe	c Qasim Omar b Abdul Qadir	55	c sub b Iqbal Qasim	33
J.G.Wright	c Anil Dalpat b Azeem Hafeez	1	(1) run out	65
J.F.Reid	lbw b Mudassar Nazar	7	(4) b Abdul Qadir	6
J.V.Coney *	c Mohsin Khan b Iqbal Qasim	12	c Anil Dalpat b Azeem Hafeez	26
E.J.Gray	c sub b Iqbal Qasim	12	(8) c Mudassar Nazar b Abdul Qadir	6
I.D.S.Smith +	c Iqbal Qasim b Azeem Hafeez	41	(9) not out	11
D.A.Stirling	b Iqbal Qasim	16	(10) c Anil Dalpat b Iqbal Qasim	10
S.L.Boock	c Javed Miandad b Iqbal Qasim	13	(7) c Javed Miandad b Abdul Qadir	0
E.J.Chatfield	not out	1	c Qasim Omar b Iqbal Qasim	15
	Extras (b 1)	1	(b 8,lb 2,w 1,nb 4)	15
	TOTAL	**157**		**241**

PAKISTAN

Mudassar Nazar	c Reid b Stirling	26	b Boock	16
Mohsin Khan	c Reid b Gray	58	c & b Gray	38
Qasim Omar	c Crowe J.J. b Boock	13	lbw b Stirling	20
Javed Miandad	c Reid b Gray	11	not out	48
Zaheer Abbas *	c Crowe M.D. b Boock	43	c Smith b Gray	31
Salim Malik	lbw b Stirling	10	not out	24
Abdul Qadir	c Coney b Chatfield	14		
Anil Dalpat +	b Crowe M.D.	11		
Iqbal Qasim	c Coney b Chatfield	22		
Azeem Hafeez	c Boock b Chatfield	11		
Tauseef Ahmed	not out	0		
	Extras (nb 2)	2	(lb 4)	4
	TOTAL	**221**	**(for 4 wkts)**	**181**

PAKISTAN	O	M	R	W		O	M	R	W
Mudassar Nazar	11	5	8	3		10	1	30	0
Azeem Hafeez	18	9	40	2		13	5	37	2
Abdul Qadir	21	6	58	1		26	4	82	
Iqbal Qasim	22.4	10	41	4		30	10	65	4
Tauseef Ahmed	2	0	9	0		4	0	17	0

NEW ZEALAND	O	M	R	W		O	M	R	W
Stirling	27	7	71	2		15.1	2	60	1
Crowe M.D.	7	1	21	1					
Gray	8	1	19	2		18	0	45	2
Chatfield	27.2	7	57	3		13	7	12	0
Boock	24	7	53	2		17	2	56	1
Coney						2	1	4	0

FALL OF WICKETS	NZ	PAK	NZ	PAK		NZ	PAK	NZ	PAK
1st	0	54	66	33	6th	76	165	210	
2nd	11	84	123	77	7th	120	188	220	
3rd	28	103	138	77	8th	124	189	220	
4th	31	114	140	138	9th	146	212	235	
5th	50	144	208		10th	157	221	241	

PAKISTAN vs NEW ZEALAND
at Hyderabad on 25th November 1984
Pakistan won by 7 wickets

NEW ZEALAND

J.G.Wright	c Anil Dalpat b Iqbal Qasim	18	c Anil Dalpat b Iqbal Qasim	22
B.A.Edgar	c Salim Malik b Abdul Qadir	11	lbw b Mudassar Nazar	1
M.D.Crowe	b Abdul Qadir	19	(4) st Anil Dalpat b Iqbal Qasim	21
J.F.Reid	lbw b Azeem Hafeez	106	(3) lbw b Abdul Qadir	21
J.V.Coney *	c Manzoor Elahi b Abdul Qadir	6	b Iqbal Qasim	5
J.J.Crowe	c Salim Malik b Zaheer Abbas	39	lbw b Iqbal Qasim	57
I.D.S.Smith +	c Iqbal Qasim b Zaheer Abbas	6	c Mudassar Nazar b Azeem Hafeez	34
E.J.Gray	lbw b Mudassar Nazar	25	c Qasim Omar b Iqbal Qasim	5
J.G.Bracewell	c Mudassar Nazar b Abdul Qadir	0	c & b Abdul Qadir	0
D.A.Stirling	not out	11	b Abdul Qadir	11
S.L.Boock	lbw b Abdul Qadir	12	not out	4
	Extras (b 13,nb 1)	14	(b 1,lb 4,nb 3)	8
	TOTAL	**267**		**189**

PAKISTAN

Mudassar Nazar	c Crowe M.D. b Bracewell	28	c Coney b Boock	106
Mohsin Khan	c Gray b Boock	9	b Crowe M.D.	2
Qasim Omar	c Coney b Boock	45	lbw b Crowe M.D.	0
Javed Miandad	c Crowe J.J. b Boock	104	not out	103
Anil Dalpat +	b Bracewell	1		
Zaheer Abbas *	st Smith b Boock	2		
Salim Malik	b Boock	1		
Manzoor Elahi	c Crowe J.J. b Boock	19	(5) not out	4
Abdul Qadir	lbw b Boock	11		
Iqbal Qasim	c Crowe J.J. b Bracewell	8		
Azeem Hafeez	not out	0		
	Extras (lb 2)	2	(b 5,lb 7,nb 3)	15
	TOTAL	**230**	**(for 3 wkts)**	**230**

PAKISTAN	O	M	R	W		O	M	R	W
Mudassar Nazar	7	4	14	1		5	2	8	1
Azeem Hafeez	18	4	29	1		8	2	34	1
Iqbal Qasim	33	6	80	1		24.1	7	78	5
Abdul Qadir	40.3	11	108	5		18	3	59	3
Manzoor Elahi	2	1	2	0					
Zaheer Abbas	8	1	21	2		1	0	5	0

NEW ZEALAND	O	M	R	W		O	M	R	W
Stirling	3	0	11	0		4	0	26	0
Crowe M.D.	3	0	8	0		8	1	29	2
Coney	10	4	8	0		4	1	9	0
Boock	37	12	87	7		23.4	4	69	1
Bracewell	16.1	3	44	3		14	3	36	0
Gray	22	4	70	0		11	0	49	0

FALL OF WICKETS	NZ	PAK	NZ	PAK		NZ	PAK	NZ	PAK
1st	30	26	2	14	6th	164	169	125	
2nd	30	50	34	14	7th	238	191	149	
3rd	74	153	58	226	8th	239	215	149	
4th	88	154	71		9th	243	230	167	
5th	150	159	80		10th	267	230	189	

PAKISTAN vs NEW ZEALAND
at Karachi on 10th December 1984
Match drawn

PAKISTAN

Mudassar Nazar	c Smith b Stirling	5	c McEwan b Stirling	0
Shoaib Mohammad	c Smith b Stirling	31	c McEwan b Boock	34
Qasim Omar	lbw b Boock	45	c & b Crowe M.D.	17
Javed Miandad	c Smith b Crowe M.D.	13	c Crowe J.J. b Boock	58
Zaheer Abbas *	c Smith b Stirling	14	c Smith b Bracewell	3
Salim Malik	c & b Crowe M.D.	50	not out	119
Wasim Raja	lbw b Stirling	51	not out	60
Abdul Qadir	c Wright b Boock	7		
Anil Dalpat +	b Boock	52		
Iqbal Qasim	not out	45		
Azeem Hafeez	lbw b Boock	0		
	Extras (b 5,lb 6,w 1,nb 3)	15	(b 2,lb 8,nb 7)	17
	TOTAL	**328**	**(for 5 wkts)**	**308**

NEW ZEALAND

J.G.Wright	c Anil Dalpat b Iqbal Qasim	107
B.A.Edgar	run out	15
J.F.Reid	c Iqbal Qasim b Azeem Hafeez	97
M.D.Crowe	lbw b Wasim Raja	45
J.J.Crowe	c Javed Miandad b Azeem Hafeez	62
J.V.Coney *	c & b Iqbal Qasim	16
P.E.McEwan	not out	40
I.D.S.Smith +	c Salim Malik b Iqbal Qasim	0
D.A.Stirling	c Qasim Omar b Iqbal Qasim	7
J.G.Bracewell	c Anil Dalpat b Azeem Hafeez	30
S.L.Boock	c Anil Dalpat b Azeem Hafeez	0
	Extras (b 1,lb 5,nb 1)	7
	TOTAL	**426**

NEW ZEALAND	O	M	R	W		O	M	R	W
Stirling	29	5	88	4		14	1	82	1
Crowe M.D.	21	4	81	2		10	3	26	1
McEwan	4	1	6	0		2	0	7	0
Boock	41	19	83	4		30	10	83	2
Coney	5	3	5	0					
Bracewell	20	5	54	0		33	11	83	1
Crowe J.J.						2	0	9	0
Wright						1	0	1	0
Reid						2	0	7	0

PAKISTAN	O	M	R	W		O	M	R	W
Mudassar Nazar	15.4	2	45	0					
Azeem Hafeez	46.4	9	132	4					
Iqbal Qasim	57	13	133	4					
Wasim Raja	33	8	97	1					
Zaheer Abbas	5.2	1	13	0					

FALL OF WICKETS	PAK	NZ	PAK			PAK	NZ	PAK
1st	14	83	5		6th	204	352	
2nd	80	163	37		7th	226	353	
3rd	92	258	119		8th	315	361	
4th	102	292	126		9th	319	426	
5th	124	338	130		10th	328	426	

NEW ZEALAND vs PAKISTAN

at Wellington on 18th January 1985
Match drawn

NEW ZEALAND

G.P.Howarth *	run out	33	c Anil Dalpat b Azeem Hafeez	17
J.G.Wright	c Shoaib Mohammad b Azeem Hafeez	11	lbw b Mudassar Nazar	11
J.F.Reid	b Azeem Hafeez	148	c Abdul Qadir b Iqbal Qasim	3
M.D.Crowe	c Anil Dalpat b Iqbal Qasim	37	c Abdul Qadir b Iqbal Qasim	33
J.J.Crowe	c Shoaib Mohammad b Iqbal Qasim	4	not out	19
J.V.Coney	b Abdul Qadir	48	not out	18
R.J.Hadlee	c Javed Miandad b Azeem Hafeez	89		
I.D.S.Smith +	c & b Mudassar Nazar	65		
B.L.Cairns	b Azeem Hafeez	36		
S.L.Boock	c Anil Dalpat b Azeem Hafeez	0		
E.J.Chatfield	not out	3		
	Extras (b 5,lb 12,nb 1)	18	(lb 2)	2
	TOTAL	492	(for 4 wkts)	103

PAKISTAN

Mudassar Nazar	c & b Boock	38
Mohsin Khan	c Wright b Boock	40
Shoaib Mohammad	run out	7
Qasim Omar	b Boock	8
Javed Miandad *	c Smith b Boock	30
Salim Malik	c Cairns b Haclee	66
Wasim Raja	c Crowe M.D. b Boock	14
Abdul Qadir	c Smith b Hadlee	54
Anil Dalpat +	c Smith b Chatfield	15
Iqbal Qasim	not out	27
Azeem Hafeez	c Boock b Cairns	3
	Extras (b 9,lb 9,nb 2)	20
	TOTAL	322

PAKISTAN	O	M	R	W		O	M	R	W
Mudassar Nazar	29	5	80	1		6	3	13	1
Azeem Hafeez	48	12	127	5		15	3	51	1
Abdul Qadir	51	13	142	1		8	1	18	0
Iqbal Qasim	41	5	105	2		16	8	19	2
Wasim Raja	2	0	10	0					
Shoaib Mohammad	1	0	4	0					
Javed Miandad	3	1	7	0					

NEW ZEALAND	O	M	R	W		O	M	R	W
Hadlee	32	11	70	2					
Cairns	27.4	5	65	1					
Chatfield	25	10	52	1					
Boock	45	18	117	5					

FALL OF WICKETS	NZ	PAK	NZ			NZ	PAK	NZ
1st	24	62	24		6th	375	187	
2nd	61	85	30		7th	414	223	
3rd	126	95	42		8th	488	288	
4th	138	102	73		9th	488	309	
5th	230	161			10th	492	322	

NEW ZEALAND vs PAKISTAN

at Auckland on 25th January 1985
New Zealand won by an innings and 99 runs

PAKISTAN

Mudassar Nazar	lbw b Hadlee	12	b Cairns	89
Mohsin Khan	c Coney b Cairns	26	c Coney b Hadlee	1
Qasim Omar	c Crowe M.D. b Cairns	33	c Cairns b Chatfield	22
Javed Miandad *	c Smith b Chatfield	26	(5) c Smith b Chatfield	1
Zaheer Abbas	c Crowe J.J. b Cairns	6	(6) c sub b Hadlee	12
Salim Malik	not out	41	(4) c Cairns b Chatfield	0
Wasim Raja	c Smith b Chatfield	4	c Wright b Boock	11
Abdul Qadir	run out	0	lbw b Cairns	10
Anil Dalpat +	c Crowe J.J. b Hadlee	7	lbw b Cairns	6
Wasim Akram	c Crowe M.D. b Hadlee	0	(11) not out	0
Azeem Hafeez	c Boock b Hadlee	6	(10) lbw b Cairns	17
	Extras (lb 5,nb 3)	8	(lb 11,nb 3)	14
	TOTAL	169		183

NEW ZEALAND

G.P.Howarth *	c Javed Miandad b Mudassar Nazar	13
J.G.Wright	c Salim Malik b Wasim Akram	66
J.F.Reid	not out	158
M.D.Crowe	c sub b Abdul Qadir	84
S.L.Boock	c Wasim Raja b Azeem Hafeez	10
J.J.Crowe	run out	30
J.V.Coney	c Anil Dalpat b Mudassar Nazar	25
R.J.Hadlee	c Mohsin Khan b Azeem Hafeez	13
I.D.S.Smith +	c Javed Miandad b Wasim Akram	7
B.L.Cairns	b Azeem Hafeez	23
E.J.Chatfield	not out	1
	Extras (b 6,lb 9,nb 6)	21
	TOTAL (for 9 wkts dec)	451

NEW ZEALAND	O	M	R	W		O	M	R	W
Hadlee	19.5	3	60	4		17	1	66	2
Cairns	29	10	73	3		19.4	8	49	4
Chatfield	14	5	24	2		19	5	47	3
Coney	4	1	7	0					
Boock						4	2	10	1

PAKISTAN	O	M	R	W		O	M	R	W
Azeem Hafeez	47	10	157	3					
Wasim Akram	34.4	4	105	2					
Mudassar Nazar	34	5	85	2					
Abdul Qadir	22	5	52	1					
Wasim Raja	1	0	3	0					
Salim Malik	8.2	2	34	0					

FALL OF WICKETS	PAK	NZ	PAK			PAK	NZ	PAK
1st	33	60	13		6th	115	366	122
2nd	58	108	54		7th	123	387	140
3rd	93	245	54		8th	147	411	152
4th	105	278	57		9th	151	447	178
5th	111	359	79		10th	169		183

NEW ZEALAND vs PAKISTAN

at Dunedin on 9th February 1985
New Zealand won by 2 wickets

PAKISTAN

Mudassar Nazar	c Crowe J.J. b Hadlee	18	c Coney b Bracewel	5
Mohsin Khan	run out	39	c Crowe M.D. b Hadlee	27
Qasim Omar	c Crowe J.J. b Coney	96	c Smith b Chatfield	89
Javed Miandad *	c Smith b Hadlee	79	c Reid b Hadlee	2
Zaheer Abbas	c Reid b Hadlee	6	lbw b Cairns	0
Rashid Khan	c Crowe M.D. b Hadlee	0	(9) b Bracewel	37
Anil Dalpat +	b Bracewel	16	b Chatfield	21
Salim Malik	lbw b Hadlee	0	(6) b Cairns	9
Tahir Naqqash	c Wright b Hadlee	0	(8) run out	1
Azeem Hafeez	c Smith b Bracewel	4	b Chatfield	7
Wasim Akram	not out	1	not out	8
	Extras (b 1,lb 2,nb 12)	15	(b 1,lb 9,nb 7)	17
	TOTAL	274		223

NEW ZEALAND

G.P.Howarth *	b Wasim Akram	23	c Mohsin Khan b Wasim Akram	17
J.G.Wright	c Qasim Omar b Azeem Hafeez	32	c Mohsin Khan b Hadlee	1
J.F.Reid	b Wasim Akram	24	c Anil Dalpat b Wasim Akram	0
M.D.Crowe	c Javed Miandad b Wasim Akram	57	c Mudassar Nazar b Tahir Naqqash	84
J.J.Crowe	lbw b Wasim Akram	6	lbw b Wasim Akram	0
J.V.Coney	c Anil Dalpat b Rashid Khan	24	not out	111
R.J.Hadlee	c Anil Dalpat b Rashid Khan	18	b Azeem Hafeez	11
I.D.S.Smith +	lbw b Tahir Naqqash	12	c Javed Miandad b Wasim Akram	6
B.L.Cairns	c Anil Dalpat b Wasim Akram	6	retired hurt/ill	0
B.P.Bracewell	c Rashid Khan b Tahir Naqqash	3	c Tahir Naqqash b Wasim Akram	4
E.J.Chatfield	not out	2	not out	21
	Extras (b 7,lb 5,nb 1)	13	(b 5,lb 6,w 1,nb 11)	23
	TOTAL	220	(for 8 wkts)	278

NEW ZEALAND	O	M	R	W		O	M	R	W
Hadlee	24	5	51	6		26	9	59	2
Bracewel	18.2	1	81	2		14.4	2	48	2
Cairns	22	0	77	0		22	5	41	2
Chatfield	24	6	46	0		26	5	65	3
Coney	6	1	16	1					

PAKISTAN	O	M	R	W		O	M	R	W
Rashid Khan	23	7	64	2		9	2	33	0
Azeem Hafeez	20	6	65	1		32	9	84	2
Wasim Akram	26	7	56	5		33	10	72	5
Tahir Naqqash	16.4	4	23	2		16.4	1	58	1
Mudassar Nazar						9	2	20	0

FALL OF WICKETS	PAK	NZ	PAK	NZ			PAK	NZ	PAK	NZ
1st	25	41	5	4		6th	251	185	157	208
2nd	100	81	72	5		7th	251	203	166	217
3rd	241	84	75	23		8th	255	205	169	228
4th	243	92	76	23		9th	273	216	181	
5th	245	149	103	180		10th	274	220	223	

PAKISTAN vs SRI LANKA

at Faisalabad on 16th October 1985
Match drawn

SRI LANKA

S.Wettimuny	lbw b Abdul Qadir	52
S.A.R.Silva +	c Shoaib Mohammad b Imran Khan	17
R.S.Madugalle	b Mudassar Nazar	5
R.L.Dias	c Ashraf Ali b Jalaluddin	48
L.R.D.Mendis *	lbw b Imran Khan	15
A.Ranatunga	c Shoaib Mohammad b Abdul Qadir	79
P.A.de Silva	c Ashraf Ali b Imran Khan	122
J.R.Ratnayeke	run out	34
A.L.F.de Mel	c Ashraf Ali b Wasim Akram	17
R.J.Ratnayake	lbw b Abdul Qadir	56
R.G.C.E.Wijesuriya	not out	7
	Extras (b 4,lb 11,w 2,nb 10)	27
	TOTAL	479

PAKISTAN

Mudassar Nazar	lbw b Ratnayake	78
Shoaib Mohammad	c Silva b Ratnayeke	33
Qasim Omar	b Ratnayeke	206
Javed Miandad *	not out	203
Zaheer Abbas		
Salim Malik		
Imran Khan		
Ashraf Ali +		
Abdul Qadir		
Wasim Akram		
Jalaluddin		
	Extras (b 6,lb 17,w 1,nb 11)	35
	TOTAL (for 3 wkts)	555

PAKISTAN	O	M	R	W		O	M	R	W
Imran Khan	49	15	112	3					
Wasim Akram	42.3	12	98	1					
Jalaluddin	39	12	89	1					
Mudassar Nazar	13.3	3	29	1					
Abdul Qadir	54.3	17	132	3					
Shoaib Mohammad	2	1	4	0					

SRI LANKA	O	M	R	W		O	M	R	W
de Mel	27	3	106	0					
Ratnayake	32	4	93	2					
Ratnayeke	29.5	3	117	1					
Wijesuriya	44	13	102	0					
Ranatunga	18	1	74	0					
Madugalle	7	1	18	0					
de Silva	5	0	22	0					

FALL OF WICKETS	SRI	PAK			SRI	PAK
1st	23	86		6th	286	
2nd	40	158		7th	352	
3rd	125	555		8th	391	
4th	129			9th	443	
5th	165			10th	479	

PAKISTAN vs SRI LANKA
at Sialkot on 27th October 1985
Pakistan won by 8 wickets

SRI LANKA

Batsman	Dismissal	R	Dismissal 2	R2
S.Wettimuny	c Salim Yousuf b Imran Khan	45	lbw b Imran Khan	0
S.A.R.Silva +	c Qasim Omar b Mudassar Nazar	12	c Wasim Akram b Mudassar Nazar	35
R.S.Madugalle	c Salim Yousuf b Mohsin Kamal	0	c Javed Miandad b Mohsin Kamal	65
R.L.Dias	c Qasim Omar b Mohsin Kamal	21	lbw b Mudassar Nazar	7
L.R.D.Mendis *	c Mudassar Nazar b Mohsin Kamal	20	c Salim Yousuf b Wasim Akram	3
A.Ranatunga	not out	25	c Salim Malik b Imran Khan	28
P.A.de Silva	hit wicket b Imran Khan	2	c Salim Yousuf b Wasim Akram	8
J.R.Ratnayeke	c Salim Yousuf b Imran Khan	0	not out	17
A.L.F.de Mel	lbw b Wasim Akram	1	b Imran Khan	0
R.J.Ratnayake	b Imran Khan	1	c sub b Imran Khan	2
R.G.C.E.Wijesuriya	lbw b Wasim Akram	8	lbw b Imran Khan	0
Extras	(b 6,lb 2,w 3,nb 11)	22	(b 9,lb 10,nb 16)	35
TOTAL		157		200

PAKISTAN

Batsman	Dismissal	R	Dismissal 2	R2
Mudassar Nazar	c Silva b Ratnayake	78	not out	24
Mohsin Khan	lbw b Ratnayake	50	run out	44
Qasim Omar	c Wijesuriya b Ratnayake	1	c Ranatunga b de Mel	3
Javed Miandad *	lbw b Ratnayeke	40		
Zaheer Abbas	b Ratnayeke	4		
Salim Malik	lbw b Ratnayeke	22		
Imran Khan	c sub b Ratnayeke	6		
Salim Yousuf +	lbw b Ratnayeke	23	(4) not out	13
Abdul Qadir	c Silva b Ratnayeke	10		
Wasim Akram	c Silva b Ratnayeke	4		
Mohsin Kamal	not out	4		
Extras	(b 5,lb 3,w 1,nb 8)	17	(b 4,lb 4,nb 8)	16
TOTAL		259	(for 2 wkts)	100

PAKISTAN	O	M	R	W		O	M	R	W
Imran Khan	19	3	55	4		18.3	5	40	5
Wasim Akram	14.2	4	38	2		19	4	74	2
Mohsin Kamal	17	3	50	3		12	2	38	1
Mudassar Nazar	6	1	6	1		11.5	1	28	2
Abdul Qadir						1.1	0	1	0

SRI LANKA	O	M	R	W		O	M	R	W
de Mel	15	3	63	0		10	1	43	1
Ratnayake	18	2	77	2		6	0	24	0
Ratnayeke	23.2	5	83	8		7.4	1	25	0
Ranatunga	3	0	18	0					
Wijesuriya	4	1	10	0					

FALL OF WICKETS	SRI	PAK	SRI	PAK		SRI	PAK	SRI	PAK
1st	41	88	0	76	6th	101	216	163	
2nd	41	93	98	82	7th	110	216	188	
3rd	81	181	111		8th	130	245	188	
4th	99	185	121		9th	131	252	200	
5th	101	209	147		10th	157	259	200	

PAKISTAN vs SRI LANKA
at Karachi on 7th November 1985
Pakistan won by 10 wickets

SRI LANKA

Batsman	Dismissal	R	Dismissal 2	R2
S.Wettimuny	b Wasim Akram	17	c Salim Yousuf b Imran Khan	10
J.R.Ratnayeke	b Abdul Qadir	36	c Salim Yousuf b Imran Khan	3
R.S.Madugalle	lbw b Wasim Akram	0	(8) b Tauseef Ahmed	5
R.L.Dias	c Salim Yousuf b Imran Khan	7	c Salim Malik b Abdul Qadir	4
L.R.D.Mendis *	c Javed Miandad b Abdul Qadir	15	(7) b Imran Khan	2
A.Ranatunga	c Javed Miandad b Tauseef Ahmed	12	(5) c Salim Yousuf b Wasim Akram	25
P.A.de Silva	c & b Abdul Qadir	13	(3) c Salim Yousuf b Tauseef Ahmed	105
A.P.Gurusinha +	lbw b Imran Khan	17	(6) c Salim Yousuf b Tauseef Ahmed	12
A.L.F.de Mel	st Salim Yousuf b Abdul Qadir	3	b Tauseef Ahmed	18
R.J.Ratnayake	not out	21	c Qasim Omar b Tauseef Ahmed	22
R.G.C.E.Wijesuriya	lbw b Abdul Qadir	2	not out	2
Extras	(b 5,lb 10,w 1,nb 3)	19	(b 5,lb 11,nb 6)	22
TOTAL		162		230

PAKISTAN

Batsman	Dismissal	R	Dismissal 2	R2
Mudassar Nazar	c Gurusinha b de Mel	16	not out	57
Mohsin Khan	c Gurusinha b de Mel	13	not out	36
Qasim Omar	c Ranatunga b de Mel	8		
Javed Miandad *	lbw b de Mel	63		
Salim Malik	b de Mel	4		
Ramiz Raja	c & b de Mel	52		
Imran Khan	c Ratnayeka b Ratnayeke	63		
Salim Yousuf +	lbw b Ratnayeke	27		
Abdul Qadir	c Wettimuny b Wijesuriya	19		
Tauseef Ahmed	b Ratnayeke	1		
Wasim Akram	not out	5		
Extras	(b 13,lb 8,w 2,nb 1)	24	(b 1,lb 3,nb 1)	5
TOTAL		295	(for 0 wkts)	98

PAKISTAN	O	M	R	W		O	M	R	W
Imran Khan	20	9	36	2		14.1	5	28	3
Wasim Akram	14	7	17	2		14	4	24	1
Tauseef Ahmed	22	10	50	1		23.2	8	54	5
Abdul Qadir	20.5	5	44	5		25.5	4	102	1
Mudassar Nazar						3	0	6	0

SRI LANKA	O	M	R	W		O	M	R	W
de Mel	22	1	109	6		3	0	28	0
Ratnayake	15	2	48	2		4	0	33	0
Ratnayeke	15	2	48	1		6	1	24	0
Wijesuriya	22	5	68	1		3.4	1	9	0
Ranatunga	1	0	1	0					

FALL OF WICKETS	SRI	PAK	SRI	PAK		SRI	PAK	SRI	PAK
1st	27	27	14		6th	106	228	139	
2nd	28	43	15		7th	122	259	157	
3rd	60	60	57		8th	125	288	191	
4th	89	68	104		9th	151	290	221	
5th	90	153	132		10th	162	295	230	

SRI LANKA vs PAKISTAN
at Kandy on 23rd February 1986
Pakistan won by an innings and 20 runs

SRI LANKA

Batsman	Dismissal	R	Dismissal 2	R2
S.Wettimuny	lbw b Imran Khan	0	c Ramiz Raja b Wasim Akram	8
S.A.R.Silva +	c Zulqarnain b Wasim Akram	3	absent hurt/ill	
P.A.de Silva	c Zulqarnain b Imran Khan	11	b Tauseef Ahmed	5
R.L.Dias	b Tauseef Ahmed	11	b Tauseef Ahmed	26
L.R.D.Mendis *	c Mudassar Nazar b Imran Khan	6	c Mudassar Nazar b Tauseef Ahmed	4
A.Ranatunga	b Tauseef Ahmed	18	st Zulqarnain b Tauseef Ahmed	33
J.R.Ratnayeke	b Abdul Qadir	4	(2) b Imran Khan	7
A.L.F.de Mel	b Tauseef Ahmed	23	(7) b Tauseef Ahmed	0
R.J.Ratnayake	c Salim Malik b Abdul Qadir	4	(8) st Zulqarnain b Tauseef Ahmed	4
E.A.R.De Silva	not out	10	(9) not out	4
K.P.J.Warnaweera	c Imran Khan b Abdul Qadir	3	(10) b Imran Khan	0
Extras	(lb 2,w 2,nb 7)	16	(lb 3.w 6,nb 1)	10
TOTAL		109		101

PAKISTAN

Mudassar Nazar	c Mendis b Ratnayeke	81
Mohsin Khan	lbw b de Mel	1
Qasim Omar	lbw b Ratnayeke	11
Javed Miandad	lbw b De Silva E.A.R.	4
Ramiz Raja	lbw b Warnaweera	3
Salim Malik	c de Silva P.A. b de Mel	54
Imran Khan *	c sub b Ranatunga	7
Abdul Qadir	b Ratnayeke	11
Zulqarnain +	b de Mel	5
Tauseef Ahmed	not out	23
Wasim Akram	run out	19
Extras	(b 4,w 7)	11
TOTAL		230

PAKISTAN	O	M	R	W		O	M	R	W
Imran Khan	9	0	20	3		16	5	29	2
Wasim Akram	8	3	21	1		5	3	5	1
Tauseef Ahmed	13	4	32	3		15	7	45	6
Abdul Qadir	12.4	3	29	3		7	1	19	0

SRI LANKA	O	M	R	W		O	M	R	W
de Mel	16.2	5	50	3					
Ratnayeke	10	1	26	0					
Ratnayake	23	2	57	3					
Warnaweera	8.3	2	26	1					
De Silva E.A.R.	18	7	37	1					
Ranatunga	14.3	6	30	1					

FALL OF WICKETS	SRI	PAK	SRI		SRI	PAK	SRI
1st	0	1	14	6th	59	167	74
2nd	14	28	19	7th	69	173	80
3rd	25	49	31	8th	78	181	100
4th	37	52	43	9th	100	191	101
5th	44	154	74	10th	109	230	

SRI LANKA vs PAKISTAN
at Colombo on 14th March 1986
Sri Lanka won by 8 wickets

PAKISTAN

Batsman	Dismissal	R	Dismissal 2	R2
Mudassar Nazar	c de Alwis b Kuruppuarachchi	3	lbw b Kuruppuarachchi	1
Mohsin Khan	lbw b Kuruppuarachchi	35	c de Silva b de Mel	2
Qasim Omar	lbw b de Mel	3	c de Alwis b Ratnayeke	52
Javed Miandad	c de Alwis b de Mel	0	(5) lbw b Ratnayeke	36
Ramiz Raja	lbw b de Mel	32	(4) c de Alwis b Ratnayeke	21
Salim Malik	c Mahanama b Kuruppuarachchi	42	c Wettimuny b Ratnayeke	30
Imran Khan *	c Mendis b Ratnayeke	8	c de Silva b de Mel	0
Tauseef Ahmed	b Ratnayeke	0	(9) lbw b Ratnayeke	1
Wasim Akram	c de Mel b Kuruppuarachchi	0	(8) c Ranatunga b de Mel	0
Zulqarnain +	c de Silva b Kuruppuarachchi	1	lbw b Kuruppuarachchi	5
Mohsin Kamal	not out	1	not out	13
Extras	(lb 4,w 2,nb 1)	7	(b 1,lb 6,nb 4)	11
TOTAL		132		172

SRI LANKA

Batsman	Dismissal	R	Dismissal 2	R2
S.Wettimuny	c Zulqarnain b Mudassar Nazar	37	c Salim Malik b Imran Khan	7
R.S.Mahanama	run out	10	c Zulqarnain b Imran Khan	8
A.P.Gurusinha	c Imran Khan b Wasim Akram	23	not out	9
P.A.de Silva	c sub b Mohsin Kamal	37	not out	1
A.Ranatunga	c Qasim Omar b Wasim Akram	77		
L.R.D.Mendis *	c Mohsin Khan b Imran Khan	5		
J.R.Ratnayeke	c Imran Khan b Wasim Akram	38		
R.G.de Alwis +	c Javed Miandad b Mohsin Kamal	10		
A.L.F.de Mel	c Zulqarnain b Imran Khan	11		
S.D.Anurasiri	c Ramiz Raja b Wasim Akram	4		
A.K.Kuruppuarachchi	not out	0		
Extras	(b 7,lb 3,w 4,nb 7)	21	(b 2,lb 2,w 1,nb 2)	7
TOTAL		273	(for 2 wkts)	32

SRI LANKA	O	M	R	W		O	M	R	W
de Mel	16	6	39	3		16	1	79	3
Kuruppuarachchi	14.5	2	44	5		10.3	1	41	2
Ratnayeke	17.4	8	29	2		17	3	37	5
Ranatunga	1	0	12	0					
Anurasiri	2	1	4	0		2	0	8	0

PAKISTAN	O	M	R	W		O	M	R	W
Imran Khan	27	5	78	2		7	2	18	2
Wasim Akram	27.3	9	55	4		6	1	10	0
Mohsin Kamal	15	0	52	2					
Mudassar Nazar	14	2	36	1					
Tauseef Ahmed	11	2	40	0					
Salim Malik	1	0	2	0					

FALL OF WICKETS	PAK	SRI	PAK	SRI		PAK	SRI	PAK	SRI
1st	3	40	6	19	6th	124	227	136	
2nd	12	69	6	31	7th	124	248	136	
3rd	12	82	72		8th	130	265	145	
4th	74	130	93		9th	131	272	154	
5th	78	147	131		10th	132	273	172	

SRI LANKA vs PAKISTAN
at Colombo on 22nd March 1986
Match drawn

SRI LANKA

S.Wettimuny	c Ramiz Raja b Wasim Akram	0	c Ramiz Raja b Wasim Akram	14
R.S.Mahanama	c Zulqarnain b Abdul Qadir	41	b Imran Khan	4
A.P.Gurusinha	c Zulqarnain b Imran Khan	39	not out	116
A.Ranatunga	c Imran Khan b Zakir Khan	53	(5) not out	135
P.A.de Silva	c Mohsin Khan b Zakir Khan	16	(4) c Javed Miandad b Imran Khan	25
L.R.D.Mendis *	c Zulqarnain b Imran Khan	58		
J.R.Ratnayeke	c Javed Miandad b Zakir Khan	7		
R.G.de Alwis +	b Imran Khan	18		
A.L.F.de Mel	not out	14		
S.D.Anurasiri	b Imran Khan	8		
K.N.Amalean	lbw b Abdul Qadir	2		
Extras	(b 7,lb 9,w 6,nb 3)	25	(b 19,lb 7,w 1,nb 2)	29
TOTAL		281	(for 3 wkts)	323

PAKISTAN

Mudassar Nazar	c de Alwis b de Mel	8
Mohsin Khan	lbw b Amalean	12
Qasim Omar	c de Alwis b Ratnayeke	19
Javed Miandad	lbw b Amalean	23
Ramiz Raja	lbw b Ratnayeke	122
Salim Malik	c sub b Ratnayeke	29
Imran Khan *	c de Alwis b Ranatunga	33
Abdul Qadir	b Amalean	20
Zulqarnain +	c de Alwis b Ratnayeke	13
Wasim Akram	run out	11
Zakir Khan	not out	0
Extras	(b 10,lb 7,w 1,nb 10)	28
TOTAL		318

PAKISTAN

	O	M	R	W		O	M	R	W
Imran Khan	32	11	69	4		25	4	56	2
Wasim Akram	22	8	41	1		29	11	72	1
Zakir Khan	24	6	80	3		21	4	70	0
Mudassar Nazar	7	2	19	0		10	2	29	0
Abdul Qadir	23.5	3	56	2		22	5	70	0
Salim Malik						1	1	0	0

SRI LANKA

	O	M	R	W		O	M	R	W
de Mel	27	3	91	1					
Amalean	18.2	1	59	3					
Ratnayeke	30	4	116	4					
Anurasiri	15	11	9	0					
Ranatunga	11	5	26	1					

FALL OF WICKETS	SRI	PAK	SRI			SRI	PAK	SRI
1st	12	24	18		6th	218	234	
2nd	79	32	18		7th	251	278	
3rd	109	49	83		8th	260	305	
4th	149	87			9th	272	318	
5th	202	158			10th	281	318	

PAKISTAN vs WEST INDIES
at Faisalabad on 24th October 1986
Pakistan won by 186 runs

PAKISTAN

Mohsin Khan	lbw b Marshall	2	c Haynes b Walsh	40
Mudassar Nazar	c Richardson b Marshall	26	c Haynes b Marshall	2
Ramiz Raja	lbw b Marshall	0	c Gray b Patterson	13
Javed Miandad	c Dujon b Patterson	1	(6) c sub b Gray	30
Qasim Omar	hit wicket b Gray	3	lbw b Walsh	48
Salim Malik	retired hurt/ill	21	(11) not out	3
Imran Khan *	c & b Gray	61	c Harper b Marshall	23
Abdul Qadir	c & b Patterson	14	lbw b Gray	2
Salim Yousuf +	lbw b Gray	0	(4) c Greenidge b Harper	61
Wasim Akram	c Richardson b Gray	0	(9) st Dujon b Harper	66
Tauseef Ahmed	not out	9	(10) b Walsh	8
Extras	(b 1,lb 11,nb 10)	22	(b 7,lb 8,w 2,nb 15)	32
TOTAL		159		328

WEST INDIES

C.G.Greenidge	lbw b Wasim Akram	10	lbw b Imran Khan	12
D.L.Haynes	lbw b Imran Khan	40	lbw b Imran Khan	0
R.B.Richardson	b Tauseef Ahmed	54	c Ramiz Raja b Abdul Qadir	14
H.A.Gomes	c sub b Abdul Qadir	33	b Abdul Qadir	2
P.J.L.Dujon +	c Ramiz Raja b Tauseef Ahmed	0	(6) lbw b Imran Khan	0
R.A.Harper	c Salim Yousuf b Wasim Akram	28	(7) c sub b Abdul Qadir	2
M.D.Marshall	c Salim Yousuf b Wasim Akram	5	(8) c & b Abdul Qadir	10
I.V.A.Richards *	c Salim Yousuf b Wasim Akram	33	(5) c Ramiz Raja b Abdul Qadir	0
A.H.Gray	not out	12	b Abdul Qadir	5
C.A.Walsh	lbw b Wasim Akram	4	b Imran Khan	0
B.P.Patterson	lbw b Wasim Akram	0	not out	6
Extras	(b 9,lb 8,nb 12)	29	(lb 2)	2
TOTAL		248		53

WEST INDIES

	O	M	R	W		O	M	R	W
Marshall	10	2	48	3		26	3	83	2
Patterson	12	1	38	2		19	3	63	1
Gray	11.5	3	39	4		22	4	82	2
Walsh	5	0	22	0		23	6	49	3
Harper						27.5	9	36	2

PAKISTAN

	O	M	R	W		O	M	R	W
Wasim Akram	25	3	91	6		3	0	5	0
Imran Khan	21	8	32	1		13	5	30	4
Abdul Qadir	15	1	58	1		9.3	1	16	6
Tauseef Ahmed	22	5	50	2					

FALL OF WICKETS	PAK	WI	PAK	WI		PAK	WI	PAK	WI
1st	12	12	2	5	6th	119	192	218	23
2nd	12	103	19	16	7th	120	223	224	36
3rd	19	124	113	19	8th	120	243	258	42
4th	37	124	124	19	9th	159	247	296	43
5th	37	178	208	20	10th		248	328	53

PAKISTAN vs WEST INDIES
at Lahore on 7th November 1986
West Indies won by an innings and 10 runs

PAKISTAN

Mohsin Khan	b Marshall	0	lbw b Gray	1
Rizwan-uz-Zaman	c Richardson b Marshall	2	b Marshall	1
Qasim Omar	lbw b Marshall	4	retired hurt/ill	10
Javed Miandad	c Greenidge b Walsh	46	b Walsh	19
Ramiz Raja	b Gray	15	lbw b Gray	1
Asif Mujtaba	b Marshall	8	lbw b Richards	6
Salim Yousuf +	lbw b Walsh	8	(8) lbw b Gray	13
Abdul Qadir	run out	12	(9) b Walsh	2
Wasim Akram	lbw b Marshall	1	(11) c Harper b Walsh	0
Imran Khan *	not out	13	(7) c Dujon b Walsh	2
Tauseef Ahmed	c Dujon b Walsh	0	(10) not out	6
Extras	(b 9,lb 4,nb 9)	22	(b 4,lb 9,w 1,nb 2)	16
TOTAL		131		77

WEST INDIES

C.G.Greenidge	lbw b Abdul Qadir	75
D.L.Haynes	b Tauseef Ahmed	18
R.B.Richardson	lbw b Abdul Qadir	4
H.A.Gomes	b Imran Khan	9
I.V.A.Richards *	c Salim Yousuf b Abdul Qadir	44
P.J.L.Dujon +	b Imran Khan	2
R.A.Harper	lbw b Abdul Qadir	6
M.D.Marshall	not out	13
C.G.Butts	c Salim Yousuf b Imran Khan	6
A.H.Gray	b Imran Khan	10
C.A.Walsh	b Imran Khan	8
Extras	(b 15,lb 5,nb 3)	23
TOTAL		218

WEST INDIES

	O	M	R	W		O	M	R	W
Marshall	18	5	33	5		8	3	14	1
Gray	13	0	28	1		17	7	20	3
Walsh	21.4	3	56	3		14.5	5	21	4
Harper	1	0	1	0					
Richards						5	2	9	1

PAKISTAN

	O	M	R	W		O	M	R	W
Imran Khan	30.5	4	59	5					
Wasim Akram	9	2	16	0					
Abdul Qadir	32	5	96	4					
Tauseef Ahmed	19	8	27	1					

FALL OF WICKETS	PAK	WI	PAK			PAK	WI	PAK
1st	0	49	3		6th	97	172	63
2nd	6	71	3		7th	98	179	69
3rd	9	107	33		8th	99	189	71
4th	46	153	44		9th	129	204	77
5th	75	160	54		10th	131	218	

PAKISTAN vs WEST INDIES
at Karachi on 20th November 1986
Match drawn

WEST INDIES

C.G.Greenidge	c Salim Yousuf b Mudassar Nazar	27	b Abdul Qadir	8
D.L.Haynes	lbw b Imran Khan	3	not out	88
R.B.Richardson	c Asif Mujtaba b Salim Jaffer	44	c Ramiz Raja b Abdul Qadir	32
H.A.Gomes	lbw b Abdul Qadir	18	lbw b Abdul Qadir	5
I.V.A.Richards *	c Ramiz Raja b Tauseef Ahmed	70	c Salim Yousuf b Imran Khan	28
P.J.L.Dujon +	c Salim Yousuf b Abdul Qadir	19	c Salim Yousuf b Salim Jaffer	6
R.A.Harper	lbw b Imran Khan	9	b Imran Khan	4
M.D.Marshall	b Tauseef Ahmed	4	lbw b Imran Khan	0
C.G.Butts	lbw b Abdul Qadir	17	c Mohsin Khan b Imran Khan	12
A.H.Gray	c Imran Khan b Abdul Qadir	1	b Imran Khan	0
C.A.Walsh	not out	0	b Imran Khan	0
Extras	(b 14,lb 11,w 1,nb 3)	29	(b 7,lb 13,w 1,nb 7)	28
TOTAL		240		211

PAKISTAN

Mudassar Nazar	b Gray	16	(6) lbw b Butts	25
Mohsin Khan	c Richards b Marshall	1	c Greenidge b Marshall	4
Ramiz Raja	c Harper b Butts	62	(4) b Butts	29
Javed Miandad	run out	76	(5) b Marshall	4
Imran Khan *	lbw b Butts	1	(8) not out	15
Asif Mujtaba	c Dujon b Marshall	12	(7) c Dujon b Walsh	6
Qasim Omar	c Richardson b Butts	5	(1) c Dujon b Gray	1
Salim Yousuf +	c Walsh b Butts	22	(3) c Haynes b Marshall	10
Tauseef Ahmed	c Richardson b Gray	3	not out	7
Salim Jaffer	b Gray	9		
Abdul Qadir	not out	8		
Extras	(b 9,lb 12,w 1,nb 2)	24	(b 17,lb 6,w 1)	24
TOTAL		239	(for 7 wkts)	125

PAKISTAN

	O	M	R	W		O	M	R	W
Imran Khan	19	4	32	2		22.3	2	46	6
Salim Jaffer	15	5	34	1		14	4	23	1
Mudassar Nazar	4	0	15	1					
Abdul Qadir	31.5	3	107	4		44	9	84	3
Tauseef Ahmed	17	7	27	2		12	2	36	0
Asif Mujtaba						3	2	2	0

WEST INDIES

	O	M	R	W		O	M	R	W
Marshall	33	9	57	2		19	5	31	3
Gray	21.1	6	40	3		14	7	18	1
Harper	7	0	31	0		1	0	1	0
Walsh	11	2	17	0		22	11	30	1
Butts	38	15	73	4		22	9	22	2

FALL OF WICKETS	WI	PAK	WI	PAK		WI	PAK	WI	PAK
1st	14	19	36	3	6th	204	179	185	95
2nd	55	29	107	16	7th	210	215	185	95
3rd	94	140	128	19	8th	227	218	209	
4th	110	145	159	25	9th	234	222	211	
5th	172	172	171	73	10th	240	239	211	

INDIA vs PAKISTAN
at Madras on 3rd February 1987
Match drawn

PAKISTAN

Rizwan-uz-Zaman	c More b Kulkarni	1	(3) not out	54
Shoaib Mohammad	lbw b Maninder Singh	101	c Vengsarkar b Maninder Singh	45
Ramiz Raja	c Srikkanth b Maninder Singh	24	(1) c Azharuddin b Kulkarni	14
Javed Miandad	run out	94	st More b Maninder Singh	54
Salim Malik	b Maninder Singh	19	not out	6
Ijaz Ahmed	c Vengsarkar b Maninder Singh	3		
Abdul Qadir	c Azharuddin b Shastri	21		
Imran Khan *	not out	135		
Wasim Akram	c Gavaskar b Yadav	62		
Salim Yousuf +	c Kulkarni b Maninder Singh	1		
Tauseef Ahmed	not out	13		
Extras	(lb 11,w 1,nb 1)	13	(lb 3,nb 6)	9
TOTAL	(for 9 wkts dec)	487	(for 3 wkts)	182

INDIA

S.M.Gavaskar	c Tauseef Ahmed b Abdul Qadir	91
K.Srikkanth	c Wasim Akram b Tauseef Ahmed	123
M.Amarnath	run out	89
D.B.Vengsarkar	st Salim Yousuf b Tauseef Ahmed	96
M.Azharuddin	st Salim Yousuf b Tauseef Ahmed	20
R.J.Shastri	c Salim Yousuf b Imran Khan	41
Kapil Dev *	c Ramiz Raja b Abdul Qadir	5
K.S.More +	lbw b Wasim Akram	28
R.R.Kulkarni	c Salim Yousuf b Imran Khan	2
N.S.Yadav	not out	6
Maninder Singh	not out	7
Extras	(b 9,lb 5,nb 5)	19
TOTAL	(for 9 wkts dec)	527

INDIA	O	M	R	W		O	M	R	W
Kapil Dev	18	1	68	0		9	1	36	0
Kulkarni	7	0	41	1		5	0	15	1
Maninder Singh	59	16	135	5		26	10	47	2
Yadav	41	3	127	1		15	4	29	0
Shastri	38	8	105	1		18	5	42	0
Srikkanth						3	0	6	0
Gavaskar						1	0	4	0

PAKISTAN	O	M	R	W		O	M	R	W
Wasim Akram	34	10	78	1					
Imran Khan	27	4	103	2					
Abdul Qadir	39	4	130	2					
Tauseef Ahmed	67	6	189	3					
Shoaib Mohammad	3	0	13	0					

FALL OF WICKETS	PAK	IND	PAK		PAK	IND	PAK
1st	2	200	17	6th	257	453	
2nd	60	220	70	7th	273	494	
3rd	215	405	160	8th	385	498	
4th	237	424		9th	406	515	
5th	244	429		10th			

INDIA vs PAKISTAN
at Calcutta on 11th February 1987
Match drawn

INDIA

K.Srikkanth	c Salim Malik b Wasim Akram	22	lbw b Imran Khan	21
Arun Lal	c Tauseef Ahmed b Salim Jaffer	52	c Wasim Akram b Imran Khan	70
M.Amarnath	run out	9	b Tauseef Ahmed	31
D.B.Vengsarkar	c Salim Yousuf b Wasim Akram	38	not out	41
M.Azharuddin	b Wasim Akram	141		
R.J.Shastri	b Abdul Qadir	5		
Kapil Dev *	c Javed Miandad b Salim Jaffer	66		
R.M.H.Binny	not out	52		
K.S.More +	run out	0		
R.R.Kulkarni	lbw b Wasim Akram	0		
Maninder Singh	b Wasim Akram	3		
Extras	(b 1,lb 8,w 1,nb 5)	15	(b 4,lb 12,nb 2)	18
TOTAL		403	(for 3 wkts dec)	181

PAKISTAN

Shoaib Mohammad	run out	24	lbw b Binny	5
Ramiz Raja	c sub b Shastri	69	c More b Binny	29
Rizwan-uz-Zaman	b Kapil Dev	60	(4) b Shastri	8
Javed Miandad	c More b Binny	17	(5) not out	63
Salim Malik	lbw b Binny	0	(6) lbw b Kapil Dev	20
Imran Khan *	c Kapil Dev b Binny	1	(7) not out	5
Salim Yousuf +	lbw b Kapil Dev	33	(3) b Maninder Singh	43
Wasim Akram	b Binny	1		
Abdul Qadir	b Binny	2		
Tauseef Ahmed	c Vengsarkar b Binny	0		
Salim Jaffer	not out	0		
Extras	(b 4,lb 4,w 1,nb 13)	22	(b 1,lb 2,w 2,nb 1)	6
TOTAL		229	(for 5 wkts)	179

PAKISTAN	O	M	R	W		O	M	R	W
Imran Khan	27	2	93	0		7.1	0	28	2
Wasim Akram	31	6	96	5		18	4	46	0
Salim Jaffer	36	2	115	2		7	0	33	0
Tauseef Ahmed	10	1	39	0		18	2	50	1
Abdul Qadir	14	3	51	1		2	0	8	0

INDIA	O	M	R	W		O	M	R	W
Kapil Dev	29	5	88	2		19	7	41	1
Binny	25.1	8	56	6		21	4	45	2
Maninder Singh	20.1	11	21	0		16	6	30	1
Shastri	20.5	9	18	1		24	6	41	1
Kulkarni	13	1	38	0		7	2	19	0

FALL OF WICKETS	IND	PAK	IND	PAK		IND	PAK	IND	PAK
1st	30	57	37	12	6th	292	195		
2nd	73	136	100	37	7th	393	207		
3rd	104	178	181	73	8th	393	215		
4th	144	178		116	9th	395	229		
5th	149	191		170	10th	403	229		

INDIA vs PAKISTAN
at Jaipur on 21st February 1987
Match drawn

INDIA

S.M.Gavaskar	c Javed Miandad b Imran Khan	0	c Ramiz Raja b Tauseef Ahmed	24
K.Srikkanth	lbw b Wasim Akram	45	c sub b Iqbal Qasim	51
M.Amarnath	b Imran Khan	49	not out	15
D.B.Vengsarkar	c Iqbal Qasim b Shoaib Mohammad	30	not out	21
M.Azharuddin	c Salim Yousuf b Tauseef Ahmed	110		
R.J.Shastri	c Ramiz Raja b Iqbal Qasim	125		
Kapil Dev *	c Salim Yousuf b Rizwan-uz-Zaman	50		
K.S.More +	c Javed Miandad b Tauseef Ahmed	22		
R.M.H.Binny	not out	6		
N.S.Yadav	not out	8		
G.Sharma				
Extras	(b 2,lb 10,w 1,nb 7)	20	(lb 2,nb 1)	3
TOTAL	(for 8 wkts dec)	465	(for 2 wkts)	114

PAKISTAN

Ramiz Raja	b Kapil Dev	114
Shoaib Mohammad	c Gavaskar b Amarnath	0
Rizwan-uz-Zaman	c More b Kapil Dev	10
Javed Miandad	lbw b Shastri	50
Younis Ahmed	c sub b Sharma	14
Salim Malik	c Srikkanth b Sharma	10
Imran Khan *	c Kapil Dev b Sharma	66
Salim Yousuf +	run out	14
Wasim Akram	c Kapil Dev b Yadav	11
Iqbal Qasim	c Srikkanth b Sharma	20
Tauseef Ahmed	not out	10
Extras	(b 8,lb 2,nb 12)	22
TOTAL		341

PAKISTAN	O	M	R	W		O	M	R	W
Imran Khan	35	7	93	2		5	2	8	0
Wasim Akram	36.3	5	88	1		5	1	17	0
Iqbal Qasim	44	5	149	1		13	4	34	1
Tauseef Ahmed	38	5	97	2		13	3	47	1
Shoaib Mohammad	5	0	19	1		1	1	0	0
Rizwan-uz-Zaman	5	2	7	1					
Younis Ahmed						1	0	6	0

INDIA	O	M	R	W		O	M	R	W
Kapil Dev	27	7	84	2					
Amarnath	8	4	15	1					
Shastri	36	12	79	1					
Yadav	25	7	65	1					
Sharma	32.5	8	84	4					

FALL OF WICKETS	IND	PAK	IND		IND	PAK	IND
1st	0	0	72	6th	384	228	
2nd	74	28	88	7th	444	282	
3rd	114	122		8th	451	302	
4th	156	162		9th		318	
5th	286	174		10th		341	

INDIA vs PAKISTAN
at Ahmedabad on 4th March 1987
Match drawn

PAKISTAN

Ramiz Raja	b Kapil Dev	41	c Azharuddin b Maninder Singh	21
Salim Yousuf +	st More b Amarnath	2		
Rizwan-uz-Zaman	c Kapil Dev b Maninder Singh	5	(2) c Azharuddin b Sharma	58
Younis Ahmed	st More b Yadav	40	(3) not out	34
Salim Malik	c More b Yadav	20	(4) not out	14
Manzoor Elahi	c Kapil Dev b Yadav	52		
Imran Khan *	b Sharma	72		
Ijaz Faqih	lbw b Kapil Dev	105		
Abdul Qadir	b Kapil Dev	25		
Wasim Akram	not out	4		
Iqbal Qasim	c More b Yadav	0		
Extras	(b 6,lb 20,nb 3)	29	(nb 8)	8
TOTAL		395	(for 2 wkts)	135

INDIA

S.M.Gavaskar	lbw b Imran Khan	63
K.Srikkanth	b Ijaz Faqih	22
M.Amarnath	c & b Iqbal Qasim	7
D.B.Vengsarkar	c Salim Malik b Wasim Akram	109
K.S.More +	c Iqbal Qasim b Abdul Qadir	23
M.Azharuddin	b Imran Khan	12
R.J.Shastri	c Iqbal Qasim b Manzoor Elahi	15
Kapil Dev *	not out	50
N.S.Yadav	b Wasim Akram	0
G.Sharma	lbw b Wasim Akram	30
Maninder Singh	b Wasim Akram	0
Extras	(b 11,lb 6,nb 5)	22
TOTAL		323

INDIA	O	M	R	W		O	M	R	W
Kapil Dev	27	9	46	3		10	3	19	0
Amarnath	9	3	14	1		2	0	6	0
Maninder Singh	54	21	106	1		23	16	13	1
Sharma	36	8	62	1		26	5	36	1
Yadav	48.3	13	109	4		14	4	18	0
Shastri	11	3	26	0		18	6	23	0
Srikkanth	2	0	6	0		2	0	5	0
Gavaskar						4	1	15	0

PAKISTAN	O	M	R	W		O	M	R	W
Imran Khan	17	6	41	2					
Wasim Akram	21.5	2	60	4					
Ijaz Faqih	27	3	81	1					
Iqbal Qasim	30	11	63	1					
Abdul Qadir	13	1	53	1					
Manzoor Elahi	3	2	8	1					

FALL OF WICKETS	PAK	IND	PAK		PAK	IND	PAK
1st	2	34	43	6th	176	246	
2nd	23	46	107	7th	330	306	
3rd	62	157		8th	391	322	
4th	99	204		9th	394	322	
5th	149	218		10th	395	323	

INDIA vs PAKISTAN
at Bangalore on 13th March 1987
Pakistan won by 16 runs

PAKISTAN

Ramiz Raja	c Vengsarkar b Kapil Dev	22	b Yadav	47
Rizwan-uz-Zaman	b Kapil Dev	0	(3) b Shastri	1
Salim Malik	b Maninder Singh	33	(4) b Kapil Dev	33
Javed Miandad	c Shastri b Maninder Singh	7	(2) c Srikkanth b Shastri	17
Manzoor Elahi	c Azharuddin b Maninder Singh	0	(7) c More b Maninder Singh	8
Imran Khan *	c Amarnath b Maninder Singh	6	c Srikkanth b Shastri	39
Wasim Akram	b Maninder Singh	0	(8) lbw b Maninder Singh	11
Salim Yousuf +	c & b Shastri	0	(9) not out	41
Iqbal Qasim	b Maninder Singh	19	(5) c Srikkanth b Yadav	26
Tauseef Ahmed	not out	15	c Yadav b Shastri	10
Salim Jaffer	c Vengsarkar b Maninder Singh	8	c Gavaskar b Maninder Singh	0
	Extras (b 2,lb 1,nb 3)	6	(b 7,lb 8,nb 1)	16
	TOTAL	**116**		**249**

INDIA

S.M.Gavaskar	b Tauseef Ahmed	21	c Rizwan-uz-Zaman b Iqbal Qasim	96
K.Srikkanth	b Tauseef Ahmed	21	lbw b Wasim Akram	6
M.Amarnath	b Tauseef Ahmed	13	c Salim Yousuf b Wasim Akram	0
D.B.Vengsarkar	c Manzoor Elahi b Tauseef Ahmed	50	b Tauseef Ahmed	19
M.Azharuddin	c Manzoor Elahi b Iqbal Qasim	6	(6) c & b Iqbal Qasim	26
R.J.Shastri	c Salim Malik b Tauseef Ahmed	7	(7) c & b Iqbal Qasim	4
Kapil Dev *	c Salim Malik b Iqbal Qasim	9	(8) b Iqbal Qasim	2
R.M.H.Binny	c Tauseef Ahmed b Iqbal Qasim	1	(9) c Salim Yousuf b Tauseef Ahmed	15
K.S.More +	not out	9	(5) lbw b Tauseef Ahmed	3
N.S.Yadav	b Iqbal Qasim	0	b Tauseef Ahmed	4
Maninder Singh	c Salim Yousuf b Iqbal Qasim	0	not out	2
	Extras (b 4,lb 4)	8	(b 22,lb 5)	27
	TOTAL	**145**		**204**

INDIA	O	M	R	W	O	M	R	W
Kapil Dev	11	2	23	2	12	2	25	1
Binny	3	0	25	0				
Amarnath	3	1	7	0				
Maninder Singh	18.2	8	27	7	43.5	8	99	3
Shastri	11	1	19	1	24	3	69	4
Yadav	3	0	12	0	15	3	41	2

PAKISTAN	O	M	R	W	O	M	R	W
Imran Khan	5	0	26	0				
Wasim Akram	2	0	9	0	11	3	19	2
Iqbal Qasim	30	15	48	5	37	11	73	4
Tauseef Ahmed	27	7	54	5	45.5	12	85	4

FALL OF WICKETS	PAK	IND	PAK	IND		PAK	IND	PAK	IND
1st	3	39	45	15	6th	68	130	166	155
2nd	39	56	57	15	7th	73	135	184	161
3rd	60	71	89	64	8th	74	137	198	180
4th	60	102	121	80	9th	98	143	249	185
5th	68	126	142	123	10th	116	145	249	204

ENGLAND vs PAKISTAN
at Old Trafford on 4th June 1987
Match drawn

ENGLAND

C.W.J.Athey	b Wasim Akram	19
R.T.Robinson	c Salim Yousuf b Mohsin Kamal	166
M.W.Gatting *	b Mohsin Kamal	42
N.H.Fairbrother	lbw b Mohsin Kamal	0
B.N.French +	c Imran Khan b Wasim Akram	59
D.I.Gower	c Salim Yousuf b Wasim Akram	22
I.T.Botham	c Wasim Akram b Tauseef Ahmed	48
J.E.Emburey	c Shoaib Mohammad b Mohsin Kamal	19
P.A.J.DeFreitas	b Wasim Akram	11
N.A.Foster	b Tauseef Ahmed	8
P.H.Edmonds	not out	23
	Extras (b 9,lb 15,w 1,nb 5)	30
	TOTAL	**447**

PAKISTAN

Shoaib Mohammad	c French b Foster	0
Ramiz Raja	c Emburey b DeFreitas	15
Mansoor Akhtar	c Fairbrother b Edmonds	75
Javed Miandad	c French b Botham	21
Salim Malik	run out	6
Imran Khan *	not out	10
Mudassar Nazar	not out	0
Salim Yousuf +		
Wasim Akram		
Tauseef Ahmed		
Mohsin Kamal		
	Extras (b 9,lb 2,w 1,nb 1)	13
	TOTAL (for 5 wkts)	**140**

PAKISTAN	O	M	R	W	O	M	R	W
Wasim Akram	46	11	111	4				
Mohsin Kamal	39	4	127	4				
Tauseef Ahmed	21.4	4	52	2				
Mudassar Nazar	37	8	133	0				

ENGLAND	O	M	R	W	O	M	R	W
Foster	15	3	34	1				
DeFreitas	12	4	36	1				
Botham	14	7	29	1				
Emburey	16	3	28	0				
Edmonds	7	5	2	1				

FALL OF WICKETS	ENG	PAK		ENG	PAK
1st	50	9	6th	373	
2nd	133	21	7th	397	
3rd	133	74	8th	413	
4th	246	100	9th	413	
5th	284	139	10th	447	

ENGLAND vs PAKISTAN
at Lord's on 18th June 1987
Match drawn

ENGLAND

B.C.Broad	b Mudassar Nazar	55
R.T.Robinson	c Salim Yousuf b Mohsin Kamal	7
C.W.J.Athey	b Imran Khan	123
D.I.Gower	c Salim Yousuf b Mudassar Nazar	8
M.W.Gatting *	run out	43
B.N.French +	b Wasim Akram	42
I.T.Botham	c Javed Miandad b Wasim Akram	6
J.E.Emburey	run out	12
N.A.Foster	b Abdul Qadir	21
P.H.Edmonds	not out	17
G.R.Dilley	c Salim Yousuf b Imran Khan	17
	Extras (lb 12,w 1,nb 4)	17
	TOTAL	**368**

PAKISTAN

Mudassar Nazar		
Shoaib Mohammad		
Mansoor Akhtar		
Javed Miandad		
Salim Malik		
Imran Khan		
Ijaz Ahmed *		
Salim Yousuf +		
Wasim Akram		
Abdul Qadir		
Mohsin Kamal		
	Extras	
	TOTAL	

PAKISTAN	O	M	R	W	O	M	R	W
Imran Khan	34.5	7	90	2				
Wasim Akram	28	1	98	2				
Mohsin Kamal	9	2	42	1				
Abdul Qadir	25	1	100	1				
Mudassar Nazar	16	6	26	2				

ENGLAND	O	M	R	W	O	M	R	W

FALL OF WICKETS	ENG		ENG
1st	29	6th	294
2nd	118	7th	305
3rd	128	8th	329
4th	230	9th	340
5th	272	10th	368

ENGLAND vs PAKISTAN
at Headingley on 2nd July 1987
Pakistan won by an innings and 18 runs

ENGLAND

B.C.Broad	c Salim Yousuf b Wasim Akram	8	c Salim Yousuf b Imran Khan	4
R.T.Robinson	lbw b Imran Khan	0	c Salim Malik b Imran Khan	2
C.W.J.Athey	c Salim Yousuf b Imran Khan	4	lbw b Imran Khan	26
D.I.Gower	b Imran Khan	10	b Imran Khan	55
M.W.Gatting *	lbw b Wasim Akram	8	c Javed Miandad b Wasim Akram	9
I.T.Botham	c Salim Yousuf b Mudassar Nazar	26	(8) c Mudassar Nazar b Mohsin Kamal	24
D.J.Capel	c & b Mohsin Kamal	53	(6) c Ijaz Ahmed b Imran Khan	28
C.J.Richards +	lbw b Wasim Akram	6	(7) c Ijaz Ahmed b Imran Khan	2
N.A.Foster	c Salim Malik b Mohsin Kamal	9	b Wasim Akram	22
P.H.Edmonds	c Salim Yousuf b Mohsin Kamal	0	not out	0
G.R.Dilley	not out	1	b Imran Khan	0
	Extras (b 1,lb 8,w 1,nb 1)	11	(b 5,lb 12,w 7,nb 3)	27
	TOTAL	**136**		**199**

PAKISTAN

Mudassar Nazar	lbw b Foster	24
Shoaib Mohammad	c Richards b Foster	15
Mansoor Akhtar	lbw b Foster	29
Salim Yousuf +	c Athey b Foster	37
Javed Miandad	c Gatting b Foster	0
Salim Malik	c Gower b Edmonds	99
Imran Khan *	c Richards b Foster	26
Ijaz Ahmed	c Athey b Foster	50
Wasim Akram	c Edmonds b Foster	43
Abdul Qadir	b Dilley	2
Mohsin Kamal	not out	3
	Extras (b 5,lb 13,w 1,nb 5)	24
	TOTAL	**353**

PAKISTAN	O	M	R	W	O	M	R	W
Imran Khan	19	3	37	3	19.1	5	40	7
Wasim Akram	14	4	36	3	21	5	55	2
Abdul Qadir	5	0	14	0	27	5	60	0
Mudassar Nazar	14	5	18	1	2	0	8	0
Mohsin Kamal	8.4	2	22	3	9	4	19	1

ENGLAND	O	M	R	W	O	M	R	W
Dilley	33	7	89	1				
Foster	46.2	15	107	8				
Capel	18	1	64	0				
Edmonds	25	10	59	1				
Gatting	9	3	16	0				

FALL OF WICKETS	ENG	PAK	ENG		ENG	PAK	ENG
1st	1	22	4	6th	85	208	122
2nd	13	60	9	7th	113	280	160
3rd	13	86	60	8th	133	318	197
4th	31	86	94	9th	133	328	197
5th	31	152	120	10th	136	353	199

ENGLAND vs PAKISTAN
at Edgbaston on 23rd July 1987
Match drawn

PAKISTAN

Mudassar Nazar	lbw b Dilley	124	b Dilley		10
Shoaib Mohammad	c Foster b Edmonds	18	lbw b Foster		50
Mansoor Akhtar	b Foster	26	lbw b Foster		17
Javed Miandad	lbw b Dilley	75	c Emburey b Foster		4
Salim Malik	c French b Dilley	24	lbw b Botham		17
Ijaz Ahmed	lbw b Botham	20	lbw b Botham		11
Imran Khan *	c Emburey b Dilley	0	lbw b Foster		37
Salim Yousuf +	not out	91	c Gatting b Edmonds		17
Wasim Akram	c Botham b Foster	26	c Edmonds b Dilley		6
Abdul Qadir	c Edmonds b Dilley	6	run out		20
Mohsin Kamal	run out	10	not out		0
	Extras (b 4,lb 11,w 1,nb 3)	19	(lb 13,w 1,nb 2)		16
	TOTAL	**439**			**205**

ENGLAND

B.C.Broad	c Salim Yousuf b Imran Khan	54	c Mudassar Nazar b Imran Khan		30
R.T.Robinson	c Salim Yousuf b Wasim Akram	80	c Imran Khan b Wasim Akram		4
C.W.J.Athey	b Imran Khan	0	(6) not out		14
D.I.Gower	c Salim Yousuf b Imran Khan	61	(3) b Imran Khan		18
M.W.Gatting *	c Wasim Akram b Imran Khan	124	run out		8
B.N.French +	b Imran Khan	0	(9) not out		1
I.T.Botham	c & b Wasim Akram	37	(4) c Mohsin Kamal b Wasim Akram		6
J.E.Emburey	lbw b Wasim Akram	58	(7) run out		20
N.A.Foster	run out	29			
P.H.Edmonds	not out	24	(8) not out		0
G.R.Dilley	b Imran Khan	2			
	Extras (b 1,lb 24,w 11,nb 16)	52	(lb 7,w 1)		8
	TOTAL	**521**	**(for 7 wkts)**		**109**

ENGLAND	O	M	R	W		O	M	R	W
Dilley	35	6	92	5		18	3	53	2
Foster	37	8	107	2		27	5	59	4
Emburey	26	7	48	0		4	1	3	0
Edmonds	24.3	12	50	1		4	1	11	1
Botham	48	13	121	1		20.3	3	66	2
Gatting	3	0	6	0					

PAKISTAN	O	M	R	W		O	M	R	W
Imran Khan	41.5	8	129	6		9	0	61	2
Wasim Akram	43	13	83	3		8.4	0	41	2
Abdul Qadir	21	4	65	0					
Mudassar Nazar	35	7	97	0					
Mohsin Kamal	29	2	122	0					

FALL OF WICKETS	PAK	ENG	PAK	ENG		PAK	ENG	PAK	ENG
1st	44	119	47	37	6th	289	300	116	108
2nd	83	132	80	39	7th	317	443	156	108
3rd	218	157	85	53	8th	360	484	165	
4th	284	251	104	72	9th	384	512	204	
5th	289	251	104	73	10th	439	521	205	

ENGLAND vs PAKISTAN
at The Oval on 6th August 1987
Match drawn

PAKISTAN

Mudassar Nazar	c Moxon b Botham	73
Ramiz Raja	b Botham	14
Mansoor Akhtar	c French b Dilley	5
Javed Miandad	c & b Dilley	260
Salim Malik	c Gower b Botham	102
Imran Khan *	run out	118
Ijaz Ahmed	c Moxon b Dilley	69
Salim Yousuf +	c & b Dilley	42
Wasim Akram	c Botham b Dilley	5
Abdul Qadir	c Moxon b Dilley	0
Tauseef Ahmed	not out	0
	Extras (b 2,lb 18)	20
	TOTAL	**708**

ENGLAND

B.C.Broad	c Salim Yousuf b Imran Khan	0	c Ijaz Ahmed b Abdul Qadir		42
M.D.Moxon	c Javed Miandad b Abdul Qadir	8	c Salim Yousuf b Tauseef Ahmed		15
R.T.Robinson	b Abdul Qadir	30	c Wasim Akram b Abdul Qadir		10
D.I.Gower	b Tauseef Ahmed	28	c Mudassar Nazar b Abdul Qadir		34
M.W.Gatting *	c Imran Khan b Abdul Qadir	61	not out		150
I.T.Botham	b Abdul Qadir	34	not out		51
J.E.Emburey	c Salim Malik b Abdul Qadir	53			
B.N.French +	c Salim Malik b Abdul Qadir	1			
N.A.Foster	c Ijaz Ahmed b Tauseef Ahmed	4			
P.H.Edmonds	lbw b Abdul Qadir	2			
G.R.Dilley	not out	0			
	Extras (b 4,lb 3,w 1,nb 3)	11	(b 4,lb 5,w 1,nb 3)		13
	TOTAL	**232**	**(for 4 wkts)**		**315**

ENGLAND	O	M	R	W		O	M	R	W
Dilley	47.3	10	154	6					
Foster	12	3	32	0					
Botham	52	7	217	3					
Emburey	61	10	143	0					
Edmonds	32	8	97	0					
Gatting	10	2	18	0					
Moxon	6	2	27	0					

PAKISTAN	O	M	R	W		O	M	R	W
Imran Khan	18	2	39	1		26.3	8	59	0
Wasim Akram	14	2	37	0		6	3	3	0
Abdul Qadir	44.4	15	96	7		53	21	115	3
Tauseef Ahmed	23	9	53	2		46.3	15	98	1
Mudassar Nazar						6	0	21	0
Javed Miandad						4	2	10	0

FALL OF WICKETS	PAK	ENG	PAK	ENG		PAK	ENG	ENG
1st	40	0	22		6th	601	166	
2nd	45	32	40		7th	690	184	
3rd	148	54	89		8th	707	198	
4th	382	78	139		9th	707	223	
5th	573	165			10th	708	232	

PAKISTAN vs ENGLAND
at Lahore on 25th November 1987
Pakistan won by an innings and 87 runs

ENGLAND

G.A.Gooch	b Abdul Qadir	12	c Ashraf Ali b Iqbal Qasim		15
B.C.Broad	c Asif Mujtaba b Abdul Qadir	41	c Ashraf Ali b Iqbal Qasim		13
R.T.Robinson	c Ashraf Ali b Abdul Qadir	6	b Abdul Qadir		1
M.W.Gatting *	lbw b Abdul Qadir	0	lbw b Abdul Qadir		23
C.W.J.Athey	lbw b Abdul Qadir	5	c Ashraf Ali b Tauseef Ahmed		2
D.J.Capel	c Asif Mujtaba b Tauseef Ahmed	0	(7) c Javed Miandad b Abdul Qadir		0
P.A.J.DeFreitas	lbw b Abdul Qadir	5	(8) c Tauseef Ahmed b Iqbal Qasim		15
J.E.Emburey	b Abdul Qadir	0	(9) not out		38
N.A.Foster	lbw b Abdul Qadir	39	(10) c sub b Tauseef Ahmed		1
B.N.French +	not out	38	(6) lbw b Abdul Qadir		9
N.G.B.Cook	c Javed Miandad b Abdul Qadir	10	b Tauseef Ahmed		5
	Extras (b 4,lb 14,nb 1)	19	(b 4,lb 4)		8
	TOTAL	**175**			**130**

PAKISTAN

Ramiz Raja	b Emburey	35
Mudassar Nazar	lbw b Foster	120
Salim Malik	b Emburey	0
Javed Miandad *	c Gooch b Cook	65
Ijaz Ahmed	b DeFreitas	44
Asif Mujtaba	b Foster	7
Ashraf Ali +	b Emburey	7
Wasim Akram	c Broad b Cook	40
Abdul Qadir	st French b Cook	38
Iqbal Qasim	run out	1
Tauseef Ahmed	not out	5
	Extras (b 18,lb 8,nb 4)	30
	TOTAL	**392**

PAKISTAN	O	M	R	W		O	M	R	W
Wasim Akram	14	4	32	0		2	0	6	0
Mudassar Nazar	5	3	9	0		1	0	4	0
Abdul Qadir	37	13	56	9		36	14	45	4
Tauseef Ahmed	23	9	38	1		20.2	7	28	3
Iqbal Qasim	4	0	22	0		20	10	39	3

ENGLAND	O	M	R	W		O	M	R	W
DeFreitas	29	7	84	1					
Foster	23	6	58	2					
Emburey	48	16	109	3					
Cook	31	10	87	3					
Capel	3	0	28	0					

FALL OF WICKETS	ENG	PAK	ENG			ENG	PAK	ENG
1st	22	71	23		6th	70	301	70
2nd	36	71	24		7th	81	328	73
3rd	36	213	38		8th	94	360	105
4th	44	272	43		9th	151	370	116
5th	55	290	66		10th	175	392	130

PAKISTAN vs ENGLAND
at Faisalabad on 7th December 1987
Match drawn

ENGLAND

G.A.Gooch	c Aamer Malik b Iqbal Qasim	28	lbw b Abdul Qadir		65
B.C.Broad	b Tauseef Ahmed	116	st Ashraf Ali b Abdul Qadir		14
C.W.J.Athey	c Aamer Malik b Abdul Qadir	27	b Mudassar Nazar		20
M.W.Gatting *	b Abdul Qadir	79	c Abdul Qadir b Iqbal Qasim		8
R.T.Robinson	c Ashraf Ali b Abdul Qadir	2	(8) not out		7
N.G.B.Cook	c Ashraf Ali b Iqbal Qasim	2			
D.J.Capel	c Aamer Malik b Abdul Qadir	1	lbw b Abdul Qadir		2
J.E.Emburey	st Ashraf Ali b Iqbal Qasim	15	(5) not out		10
N.A.Foster	c Aamer Malik b Iqbal Qasim	0	(6) c Javed Miandad b Abdul Qadir		0
B.N.French +	st Ashraf Ali b Iqbal Qasim	2			
E.E.Hemmings	not out	1			
	Extras (b 10,lb 5,w 1,nb 3)	19	(b 1,lb 9,nb 1)		11
	TOTAL	**292**	**(for 6 wkts dec)**		**137**

PAKISTAN

Mudassar Nazar	c French b Foster	1	b Cook		4
Ramiz Raja	c Gooch b Foster	12	not out		13
Salim Malik	b Cook	60	not out		28
Javed Miandad *	b Emburey	19			
Ijaz Ahmed	c Robinson b Emburey	11			
Shoaib Mohammad	b Emburey	0			
Aamer Malik	c French b Foster	5			
Ashraf Ali +	c French b Foster	4			
Abdul Qadir	c Gooch b Cook	38			
Iqbal Qasim	lbw b Hemmings	24			
Tauseef Ahmed	not out	5			
	Extras (lb 5,nb 7)	12	(b 4,lb 1,nb 1)		6
	TOTAL	**191**	**(for 1 wkt)**		**51**

PAKISTAN	O	M	R	W		O	M	R	W
Aamer Malik	5	0	19	0		3	0	20	0
Mudassar Nazar	3	0	8	0		12	1	33	1
Abdul Qadir	42	7	105	4		15	3	45	3
Tauseef Ahmed	28	9	62	1					
Iqbal Qasim	35.2	7	83	5		10	2	29	2
Shoaib Mohammad	1	1	0	0					

ENGLAND	O	M	R	W		O	M	R	W
Foster	18	4	42	4		3	0	4	0
Capel	7	1	23	0					
Hemmings	18	5	35	1		7	3	16	0
Emburey	21	8	49	3		2	0	3	0
Cook	20.3	10	37	2		9	3	15	1
Gooch						2	1	4	0
Broad						1	0	4	0

FALL OF WICKETS	ENG	PAK	ENG	PAK		ENG	PAK	ENG	PAK
1st	73	11	47	15	6th	259	115	120	
2nd	124	22	102		7th	288	122		
3rd	241	58	107		8th	288	123		
4th	249	77	115		9th	288	175		
5th	258	77	115		10th	292	191		

PAKISTAN vs ENGLAND
at Karachi on 16th December 1987
Match drawn

ENGLAND

G.A.Gooch	c Ashraf Ali b Wasim Akram	12	b Mudassar Nazar	93
B.C.Broad	lbw b Wasim Akram	7	lbw b Abdul Qadir	13
C.W.J.Athey	b Abdul Qadir	26	c Ashraf Ali b Salim Jaffer	12
M.W.Gatting *	b Abdul Qadir	18	lbw b Salim Jaffer	0
N.H.Fairbrother	c sub b Salim Jaffer	3	c sub b Abdul Qadir	1
D.J.Capel	b Abdul Qadir	98	c Iqbal Qasim b Abdul Qadir	24
P.A.J.DeFreitas	b Abdul Qadir	12	(9) lbw b Abdul Qadir	6
J.E.Emburey	c Abdul Qadir b Salim Jaffer	70	(7) not out	74
B.N.French +	c Javed Miandad b Salim Malik	31	(8) lbw b Salim Jaffer	0
N.G.B.Cook	lbw b Abdul Qadir	2	b Abdul Qadir	14
G.R.Dilley	not out	0	not out	0
Extras	(lb 8,w 1,nb 6)	15	(b 9,lb 5,w 1,nb 6)	21
TOTAL		294	(for 9 wkts)	258

PAKISTAN

Mudassar Nazar	lbw b DeFreitas	6
Ramiz Raja	c French b Cook	50
Salim Malik	c Gatting b DeFreitas	55
Javed Miandad *	lbw b Emburey	4
Ijaz Ahmed	run out	0
Aamer Malik	not out	98
Ashraf Ali +	c French b Dilley	12
Wasim Akram	c French b DeFreitas	37
Abdul Qadir	b Capel	61
Iqbal Qasim	c French b DeFreitas	11
Salim Jaffer	lbw b DeFreitas	0
Extras	(lb 11,nb 8)	19
TOTAL		353

PAKISTAN

	O	M	R	W		O	M	R	W
Wasim Akram	24.1	3	64	2					
Salim Jaffer	23.5	6	74	2		42	9	79	3
Abdul Qadir	49.4	15	88	5		55	16	98	5
Iqbal Qasim	18	4	51	0		27	10	44	0
Mudassar Nazar	1	1	0	0		4	3	2	1
Salim Malik	5	2	9	1		7	2	14	0
Aamer Malik						2	0	7	0

ENGLAND

	O	M	R	W		O	M	R	W
Dilley	21	2	102	1					
DeFreitas	23.5	3	86	5					
Emburey	53	24	90	1					
Cook	33	12	56	1					
Capel	3	0	8	1					

FALL OF WICKETS	ENG	PAK	ENG		ENG	PAK	ENG
1st	20	18	34	6th	85	146	175
2nd	41	105	54	7th	199	222	176
3rd	55	110	54	8th	274	316	187
4th	72	110	61	9th	291	349	246
5th	72	122	115	10th	294	353	

WEST INDIES vs PAKISTAN
at Port of Spain on 14th April 1988
Match drawn

WEST INDIES

C.G.Greenidge	c Ijaz Ahmed b Imran Khan	1	c sub b Imran Khan	29
D.L.Haynes	lbw b Wasim Akram	17	c Ijaz Ahmed b Imran Khan	0
R.B.Richardson	c Abdul Qadir b Wasim Akram	42	c Salim Yousuf b Imran Khan	40
A.L.Logie	c Javed Miandad b Abdul Qadir	18	b Imran Khan	1
I.V.A.Richards *	c Javed Miandad b Abdul Qadir	49	lbw b Wasim Akram	123
C.L.Hooper	c Salim Yousuf b Abdul Qadir	0	c Ijaz Ahmed b Imran Khan	26
P.J.L.Dujon +	c Salim Yousuf b Imran Khan	24	not out	106
M.D.Marshall	not out	10	b Abdul Qadir	2
C.E.L.Ambrose	lbw b Imran Khan	4	lbw b Abdul Qadir	9
W.K.M.Benjamin	b Abdul Qadir	0	lbw b Abdul Qadir	16
C.A.Walsh	b Imran Khan	5	st Salim Yousuf b Abdul Qadir	12
Extras	(lb 2,nb 2)	4	(b 9,lb 14,nb 4)	27
TOTAL		174		391

PAKISTAN

Mudassar Nazar	c Haynes b Marshall	14	c Dujon b Benjamin	13
Ramiz Raja	c Richardson b Marshall	1	c Richards b Marshall	44
Shoaib Mohammad	c Richards b Ambrose	12	b Benjamin	0
Javed Miandad	b Benjamin	18	c Richards b Ambrose	102
Ijaz Ahmed	c Logie b Benjamin	3	(10) st Dujon b Richards	43
Ijaz Faqih	c Richards b Benjamin	0	(5) not out	10
Salim Malik	c Logie b Hooper	66	lbw b Walsh	30
Imran Khan *	c Logie b Marshall	4	(6) c Dujon b Benjamin	1
Salim Yousuf +	c Dujon b Marshall	39	(8) lbw b Richards	35
Wasim Akram	run out	7	(9) c Hooper b Marshall	2
Abdul Qadir	not out	17	not out	0
Extras	(b 1,lb 4,nb 8)	13	(b 17,lb 17,w 2,nb 25)	61
TOTAL		194	(for 9 wkts)	341

PAKISTAN

	O	M	R	W		O	M	R	W
Imran Khan	16.3	2	38	4		45	8	115	5
Wasim Akram	14	4	35	2		25	1	75	1
Ijaz Faqih	3	0	13	0		4	0	22	0
Mudassar Nazar	1	0	3	0					
Abdul Qadir	19	2	83	4		47.4	6	148	4
Shoaib Mohammad						3	0	8	0

WEST INDIES

	O	M	R	W		O	M	R	W
Marshall	20	4	55	4		30	4	85	2
Ambrose	14	3	44	1		30	7	62	1
Walsh	8	1	23	0		29	8	52	1
Benjamin	8	0	32	3		32	9	73	3
Hooper	9.1	1	35	1		4	1	18	0
Richards						4	1	17	2

FALL OF WICKETS	WI	PAK	WI	PAK		WI	PAK	WI	PAK
1st	2	3	1	60	6th	147	62	272	282
2nd	25	25	55	62	7th	157	68	284	288
3rd	80	46	66	67	8th	166	162	301	311
4th	89	49	81	153	9th	167	170	357	341
5th	89	50	175	169	10th	174	194	391	

WEST INDIES vs PAKISTAN
at Georgetown on 2nd April 1988
Pakistan won by 9 wickets

WEST INDIES

D.L.Haynes	c Salim Yousuf b Imran Khan	1	b Ijaz Faqih	5
P.V.Simmons	b Ijaz Faqih	16	b Abdul Qadir	11
R.B.Richardson	c Shoaib Mohammad b Imran Khan	75	c Salim Yousuf b Abdul Qadir	16
C.G.Greenidge *	c Salim Malik b Wasim Akram	17	b Imran Khan	43
A.L.Logie	lbw b Abdul Qadir	80	c Salim Yousuf b Imran Khan	24
C.L.Hooper	c Wasim Akram b Imran Khan	33	c Salim Malik b Abdul Qadir	30
P.J.L.Dujon +	lbw b Imran Khan	15	c Imran Khan b Shoaib Mohammad	11
W.K.M.Benjamin	lbw b Imran Khan	2	c Javed Miandad b Shoaib Mohammad	0
C.A.Walsh	b Imran Khan	7	c Salim Yousuf b Imran Khan	14
C.E.L.Ambrose	not out	25	not out	1
B.P.Patterson	b Imran Khan	10	b Imran Khan	0
Extras	(b 2,lb 3,nb 6)	11	(b 4,lb 8,nb 5)	17
TOTAL		292		172

PAKISTAN

Mudassar Nazar	b Ambrose	29	lbw b Patterson	0
Ramiz Raja	c Haynes b Patterson	5	not out	18
Shoaib Mohammad	c Greenidge b Walsh	46	not out	13
Javed Miandad	b Patterson	114		
Salim Malik	c Greenidge b Patterson	27		
Ijaz Ahmed	c Haynes b Ambrose	31		
Imran Khan *	c Simmons b Benjamin	24		
Salim Yousuf +	lbw b Walsh	62		
Ijaz Faqih	b Hooper	5		
Abdul Qadir	b Walsh	19		
Wasim Akram	not out	2		
Extras	(b 21,lb 8,w 4,nb 38)	71	(nb 1)	1
TOTAL		435	(for 1 wkt)	32

PAKISTAN

	O	M	R	W		O	M	R	W
Imran Khan	22.4	2	80	7		14.4	0	41	4
Wasim Akram	14	5	41	1		6	1	7	0
Ijaz Faqih	14	0	60	1		15	4	38	1
Abdul Qadir	24	2	91	1		25	5	66	3
Salim Malik	1	0	6	0					
Mudassar Nazar	5	2	9	0					
Shoaib Mohammad						2	0	8	2

WEST INDIES

	O	M	R	W		O	M	R	W
Patterson	24	2	82	3		2	0	19	1
Ambrose	28	5	108	2		1.3	0	13	0
Walsh	27	4	80	3					
Benjamin	31	3	99	1					
Hooper	12	0	37	1					

FALL OF WICKETS	WI	PAK	WI	PAK		WI	PAK	WI	PAK
1st	7	20	18	0	6th	244	300	145	
2nd	41	57	34		7th	248	364	145	
3rd	95	127	44		8th	249	383	166	
4th	144	217	109		9th	258	423	172	
5th	220	297	120		10th	292	435	172	

WEST INDIES vs PAKISTAN
at Bridgetown on 22nd April 1988
West Indies won by 2 wickets

PAKISTAN

Mudassar Nazar	b Ambrose	18	c Greenidge b Hooper	41
Ramiz Raja	c Greenidge b Benjamin	54	c Logie b Marshall	4
Shoaib Mohammad	c Greenidge b Ambrose	54	c & b Richards	64
Javed Miandad	c Richardson b Marshall	14	c Dujon b Marshall	34
Salim Malik	b Marshall	15	lbw b Benjamin	9
Aamer Malik	c Hooper b Benjamin	32	c Logie b Marshall	2
Imran Khan *	c Dujon b Benjamin	18	not out	43
Salim Yousuf +	retired hurt/ill	32	(9) c Richards b Benjamin	28
Wasim Akram	c Benjamin b Marshall	38	(8) lbw b Marshall	0
Abdul Qadir	c Walsh b Marshall	17	c Greenidge b Marshall	2
Salim Jaffer	not out	1	b Ambrose	4
Extras	(lb 7,nb 9)	16	(b 3,lb 14,nb 14)	31
TOTAL		309		262

WEST INDIES

C.G.Greenidge	lbw b Imran Khan	10	c Shoaib Mohammad b Salim Jaffer	35
D.L.Haynes	c Aamer Malik b Mudassar Nazar	48	c Salim Malik b Wasim Akram	4
R.B.Richardson	c Aamer Malik b Wasim Akram	3	st Aamer Malik b Abdul Qadir	64
C.L.Hooper	b Wasim Akram	54	run out	13
I.V.A.Richards *	c Mudassar Nazar b Wasim Akram	67	b Wasim Akram	39
A.L.Logie	c Javed Miandad b Mudassar Nazar	0	b Abdul Qadir	3
P.J.L.Dujon +	run out	0	(8) not out	29
M.D.Marshall	c Aamer Malik b Imran Khan	48	(9) lbw b Wasim Akram	15
C.E.L.Ambrose	lbw b Imran Khan	7	(7) c Salim Jaffer b Wasim Akram	1
W.K.M.Benjamin	run out	31	not out	40
C.A.Walsh	not out	14		
Extras	(b 5,lb 11,nb 8)	24	(b 9,lb 6,nb 10)	25
TOTAL		306	(for 8 wkts)	268

WEST INDIES

	O	M	R	W		O	M	R	W
Marshall	18.4	3	79	4		23	3	65	5
Ambrose	14	0	64	2		26.5	3	74	1
Benjamin	14	3	52	3		15	1	37	2
Walsh	10	1	53	0		12	1	22	0
Richards	6	0	19	0		7	3	8	1
Hooper	12	3	35	0		10	1	39	1

PAKISTAN

	O	M	R	W		O	M	R	W
Imran Khan	25	3	108	3		6	0	34	0
Wasim Akram	27	1	88	3		31	7	73	4
Abdul Qadir	15	1	35	0		32	5	115	2
Salim Jaffer	7	1	35	0		5	0	25	1
Mudassar Nazar	10	4	24	2					
Shoaib Mohammad						3	1	6	0

FALL OF WICKETS	PAK	WI	PAK	WI		PAK	WI	PAK	WI
1st	46	18	6	21	6th	215	199	169	159
2nd	99	21	100	78	7th	218	201	182	180
3rd	128	100	153	118	8th	297	225	234	207
4th	155	198	165	128	9th	309	283	245	
5th	186	198	167	150	10th		306	262	

PAKISTAN vs AUSTRALIA
at Karachi on 15th September 1988
Pakistan won by an innings and 188 runs

PAKISTAN

Mudassar Nazar	b Reid	0
Ramiz Raja	c Healy b Reid	9
Shoaib Mohammad	b Waugh	94
Javed Miandad *	c Boon b Reid	211
Tauseef Ahmed	c Boon b May	35
Salim Malik	c Boon b May	45
Ijaz Ahmed	c Boon b Reid	12
Aamer Malik	not out	17
Abdul Qadir +	c Marsh b May	8
Iqbal Qasim		
Salim Yousuf	c Wood b May	5
	Extras (b 16,lb 12,nb 5)	33
	TOTAL (for 9 wkts dec)	469

AUSTRALIA

G.R.Marsh	b Iqbal Qasim	8	lbw b Tauseef Ahmed	17
D.C.Boon	b Abdul Qadir	14	(3) b Iqbal Qasim	4
D.M.Jones	lbw b Iqbal Qasim	3	(4) c Ijaz Ahmed b Abdul Qadir	4
G.M.Wood	c Iqbal Qasim b Tauseef Ahmed	23	(5) lbw b Iqbal Qasim	15
A.R.Border *	c Aamer Malik b Abdul Qadir	4	(6) b Iqbal Qasim	18
S.R.Waugh	lbw b Iqbal Qasim	0	(7) st Salim Yousuf b Iqbal Qasim	13
P.L.Taylor	not out	54	(2) c Ijaz Ahmed b Aamer Malik	2
I.A.Healy +	c Ijaz Ahmed b Mudassar Nazar	26	c Shoaib Mohammad b Abdul Qadir	21
A.I.C.Dodemaide	c Ijaz Ahmed b Salim Malik	8	st Salim Yousuf b Tauseef Ahmed	2
T.B.A.May	c Salim Yousuf b Abdul Qadir	6	lbw b Abdul Qadir	0
B.A.Reid	lbw b Iqbal Qasim	0	not out	8
	Extras (b 12,lb 7)	19	(b 6,lb 6)	12
	TOTAL	165		116

AUSTRALIA	O	M	R	W	O	M	R	W
Reid	41	10	109	4				
Dodemaide	29	13	35	0				
Waugh	26	3	94	1				
May	40.5	10	97	4				
Taylor	16	2	73	0				
Border	17	7	33	0				

PAKISTAN	O	M	R	W	O	M	R	W
Mudassar Nazar	10	3	15	1	3	0	5	0
Aamer Malik	2	0	6	0	2	2	0	1
Iqbal Qasim	39	24	35	5	25	14	49	4
Abdul Qadir	37	16	54	2	13	4	34	3
Tauseef Ahmed	26	15	28	1	21.4	13	16	2
Shoaib Mohammad	2	1	1	0				
Salim Malik	6	4	7	1				

FALL OF WICKETS	1st	2nd	3rd	4th	5th	6th	7th	8th	9th	10th
PAK	0	21	217	284	398	428	444	457	469	
AUS	19	23	40	48	54	64	106	139	162	165
AUS	4	10	15	46	50	80	93	104	104	116

PAKISTAN vs AUSTRALIA
at Lahore on 7th October 1988
Match drawn

AUSTRALIA

D.C.Boon	c Shoaib Mohammad b Salim Jaffer	43	c Javed Miandad b Salim Jaffer	28
G.R.Marsh	st Salim Yousuf b Iqbal Qasim	64	not out	84
D.M.Jones	lbw b Tauseef Ahmed	0	lbw b Salim Jaffer	0
A.R.Border *	c Salim Yousuf b Tauseef Ahmed	75	c Salim Yousuf b Tauseef Ahmed	20
G.M.Wood	lbw b Mudassar Nazar	15		
P.L.Taylor	st Salim Yousuf b Abdul Qadir	29	(5) not out	25
S.R.Waugh	c Ijaz Ahmed b Iqbal Qasim	59		
I.A.Healy +	lbw b Abdul Qadir	0		
A.I.C.Dodemaide	c Iqbal Qasim b Abdul Qadir	14		
T.B.A.May	not out	13		
B.A.Reid	c Mudassar Nazar b Tauseef Ahmed	8		
	Extras (b 4,lb 12,nb 4)	20	(lb 4)	4
	TOTAL	340	(for 3 wkts dec)	161

PAKISTAN

Mudassar Nazar	c Boon b May	27	c Border b Taylor	49
Ramiz Raja	c Healy b Reid	64	c Boon b May	21
Shoaib Mohammad	run out	13	lbw b May	3
Javed Miandad *	c Healy b Reid	27	c Border b May	24
Salim Malik	c & b Dodemaide	26	c Healy b Taylor	13
Ijaz Ahmed	lbw b Dodemaide	23	c Taylor b Dodemaide	15
Salim Yousuf +	c Healy b Reid	1	c Waugh b Taylor	6
Abdul Qadir	lbw b Dodemaide	18	st Healy b Taylor	10
Iqbal Qasim	lbw b May	14	not out	10
Tauseef Ahmed	c Boon b May	3	not out	1
Salim Jaffer	not out	0		
	Extras (lb 6,nb 11)	17	(b 6,lb 1,nb 2)	9
	TOTAL	233	(for 8 wkts)	153

PAKISTAN	O	M	R	W	O	M	R	W
Salim Jaffer	33	9	82	1	14	2	60	2
Mudassar Nazar	15	6	23	1	3	0	8	0
Abdul Qadir	37	10	88	3	4	1	26	0
Tauseef Ahmed	50	20	85	3	17	2	48	1
Iqbal Qasim	22	6	42	2	3	0	15	0
Shoaib Mohammad	1	0	4	0				

AUSTRALIA	O	M	R	W	O	M	R	W
Reid	23	3	53	3				
Waugh	18	4	34	0	5	1	8	0
Dodemaide	26	6	56	3	12	5	20	1
May	27.2	6	73	3	35	20	39	3
Taylor	4	2	11	0	28	9	78	4
Border					4	3	1	0

FALL OF WICKETS	1st	2nd	3rd	4th	5th	6th	7th	8th	9th	10th
AUS	87	88	155	200	231	241	241	294	331	340
PAK	80	104	118	172	172	173	206	228	232	233
AUS	71	71	108							
PAK	36	48	86	107	123	125	131	147		

PAKISTAN vs AUSTRALIA
at Faisalabad on 23rd September 1988
Match drawn

PAKISTAN

Mudassar Nazar	c Marsh b Reid	9	c Border b May	27
Ramiz Raja	lbw b Dodemaide	0	c Boon b Waugh	32
Shoaib Mohammad	b Dodemaide	11	st Healy b May	74
Javed Miandad *	c Boon b May	43	lbw b Reid	107
Salim Malik	b Dodemaide	0	c Border b Reid	10
Ijaz Ahmed	b Reid	122	c Healy b Reid	0
Salim Yousuf +	c Boon b Dodemaide	62	not out	66
Abdul Qadir	b Reid	6	(10) c Reid b May	13
Tauseef Ahmed	not out	35	(8) c Waugh b Dodemaide	2
Iqbal Qasim	c & b Sleep	16	(9) lbw b Reid	28
Salim Jaffer	lbw b Sleep	0		
	Extras (b 2,lb 6,nb 4)	12	(lb 6,nb 13)	19
	TOTAL	316	(for 9 wkts dec)	378

AUSTRALIA

D.C.Boon	b Mudassar Nazar	13	c Mudassar Nazar b Tauseef Ahmed	15
G.R.Marsh	b Tauseef Ahmed	51	b Abdul Qadir	9
D.M.Jones	lbw b Abdul Qadir	16	not out	21
G.M.Wood	lbw b Salim Jaffer	32	(5) not out	2
A.I.C.Dodemaide	c Ijaz Ahmed b Mudassar Nazar	19		
A.R.Border *	not out	113		
S.R.Waugh	st Salim Yousuf b Tauseef Ahmed	1	(4) c & b Shoaib Mohammad	19
P.R.Sleep	b Tauseef Ahmed	12		
I.A.Healy +	c Iqbal Qasim b Salim Jaffer	27		
T.B.A.May	c sub b Abdul Qadir	14		
B.A.Reid	c Salim Yousuf b Iqbal Qasim	1		
	Extras (b 4,lb 15,w 1,nb 2)	22	(b 1)	1
	TOTAL	321	(for 3 wkts)	67

AUSTRALIA	O	M	R	W	O	M	R	W
Reid	31	8	92	3	30	6	100	4
Dodemaide	34	6	87	4	20	4	48	1
Waugh	11	3	36	0	18	4	44	1
Sleep	5.5	1	24	2	13	4	51	0
May	19	3	58	1	34.4	7	126	3
Border	6	1	11	0	1	0	3	0

PAKISTAN	O	M	R	W	O	M	R	W
Salim Jaffer	29	7	69	2	2	0	8	0
Mudassar Nazar	17	4	39	2	2	0	5	0
Abdul Qadir	34	5	84	2	10	1	34	1
Tauseef Ahmed	35	10	73	3	11	4	17	1
Iqbal Qasim	14.5	4	37	1				
Shoaib Mohammad					1	0	2	1

FALL OF WICKETS	1st	2nd	3rd	4th	5th	6th	7th	8th	9th	10th
PAK	4	20	24	25	144	255	255	267	316	316
AUS	24	65	122	122	167	170	204	256	318	321
PAK	64	64	236	264	265	269	274	344	378	
AUS	18	30	65							

NEW ZEALAND vs PAKISTAN
at Wellington on 10th February 1989
Match drawn

NEW ZEALAND

R.H.Vance	c Salim Yousuf b Mudassar Nazar	5	lbw b Imran Khan	44
J.G.Wright *	c Salim Yousuf b Mudassar Nazar	7	c Javed Miandad b Imran Khan	19
A.H.Jones	c Shoaib Mohammad b Salim Jaffer	86	c sub b Salim Jaffer	39
M.D.Crowe	c Javed Miandad b Salim Jaffer	174	lbw b Salim Jaffer	0
D.N.Patel	lbw b Imran Khan	10	c Salim Yousuf b Salim Jaffer	2
J.J.Crowe	b Abdul Qadir	39	b Salim Jaffer	23
J.G.Bracewell	b Imran Khan	15	lbw b Salim Jaffer	0
R.J.Hadlee	c Rizwan-uz-Zaman b Salim Jaffer	32	c sub b Imran Khan	7
I.D.S.Smith +	not out	40	not out	29
D.K.Morrison	lbw b Imran Khan	0	not out	1
E.J.Chatfield	run out	14		
	Extras (b 10,lb 14,nb 11)	35	(b 10,lb 6,nb 6)	22
	TOTAL	447	(for 8 wkts)	186

PAKISTAN

Mudassar Nazar	c & b Morrison	6
Rizwan-uz-Zaman	lbw b Hadlee	18
Shoaib Mohammad	b Hadlee	163
Javed Miandad	lbw b Hadlee	118
Salim Malik	c Smith b Bracewell	38
Imran Khan *	b Chatfield	71
Aamer Malik	not out	8
Salim Yousuf +	c Jones b Hadlee	4
Abdul Qadir	not out	0
Salim Jaffer		
Aqib Javed		
	Extras (b 1,lb 8,nb 3)	12
	TOTAL (for 7 wkts dec)	438

PAKISTAN	O	M	R	W	O	M	R	W
Imran Khan	46.4	18	75	3	17	8	34	3
Salim Jaffer	34	5	94	3	17	4	40	5
Mudassar Nazar	22	5	59	2				
Aqib Javed	34	5	103	0	13	1	57	0
Abdul Qadir	29	4	83	1	14	3	39	0
Aamer Malik	4	1	9	0				

NEW ZEALAND	O	M	R	W	O	M	R	W
Hadlee	54	14	101	4				
Morrison	36	10	96	1				
Chatfield	53	21	82	1				
Patel	12	3	27	0				
Bracewell	40	8	123	1				

FALL OF WICKETS	1st	2nd	3rd	4th	5th	6th	7th	8th	9th	10th
NZ	13	18	167	168	282	321	389	398	399	447
PAK	14	54	274	325	422	430	437			
NZ	36	107	108	117	128	132	140	180		

NEW ZEALAND vs PAKISTAN
at Auckland on 24th February 1989
Match drawn

PAKISTAN

Mudassar Nazar	lbw b Hadlee	5			
Rizwan-uz-Zaman	c Crowe J.J. b Boock	15			
Shoaib Mohammad	run out	112			
Javed Miandad	c Smith b Chatfield	271			
Aamer Malik	c Crowe J.J. b Bracewell	56			
Salim Malik	not out	80			
Imran Khan *	not out	69			
Salim Yousuf +					
Abdul Qadir					
Tauseef Ahmed					
Salim Jaffer					
	Extras (lb 7,nb 1)	8			
	TOTAL (for 5 wkts dec)	616			

NEW ZEALAND

R.H.Vance	c Shoaib Mohammad b Abdul Qadir	68	c Salim Yousuf b Mudassar Nazar	31	
J.G.Wright *	c Rizwan-uz-Zaman b Tauseef Ahmed	2	c Salim Yousuf b Abdul Qadir	36	
A.H.Jones	run out	47	c Salim Yousuf b Mudassar Nazar	0	
M.D.Crowe	c Salim Yousuf b Salim Jaffer	78	not out	9	
S.L.Boock	c Mudassar Nazar b Abdul Qadir	8			
M.J.Greatbatch	b Abdul Qadir	76	(5) not out	13	
J.J.Crowe	c Javed Miandad b Abdul Qadir	33			
J.G.Bracewell	b Abdul Qadir	0			
I.D.S.Smith +	c Mudassar Nazar b Imran Khan	58			
R.J.Hadlee	not out	14			
E.J.Chatfield	c Aamer Malik b Abdul Qadir	0			
	Extras (b 7,lb 2,nb 10)	19	(nb 10)	10	
	TOTAL	403	(for 3 wkts)	99	

NEW ZEALAND	O	M	R	W		O	M	R	W
Hadlee	28	7	68	1					
Chatfield	65	14	158	1					
Boock	70	10	229	1					
Bracewell	37	4	138	1					
Jones	3	0	16	0					

PAKISTAN	O	M	R	W		O	M	R	W
Salim Jaffer	18	6	44	1		8	4	18	0
Imran Khan	34	9	76	1		5.4	1	13	0
Tauseef Ahmed	69	28	106	1		12	4	23	0
Abdul Qadir	58.1	18	160	6		16	7	27	1
Shoaib Mohammad	2	1	1	0		1	0	5	0
Mudassar Nazar	3	1	7	0		8	2	13	2

FALL OF WICKETS	1st	2nd	3rd	4th	5th	6th	7th	8th	9th	10th
PAK	10	44	292	439	480					
NZ	13	122	123	132	286	294	294	288	388	403
NZ	68	71	76							

PAKISTAN vs INDIA
at Karachi on 15th November 1989
Match drawn

PAKISTAN

Aamer Malik	c Azharuddin b Kapil Dev	0	c Manjrekar b Kapil Dev	15	
Ramiz Raja	c Shastri b Prabhakar	44	b Prabhakar	2	
Shoaib Mohammad	c Azharuddin b Kapil Dev	67	lbw b Kapil Dev	95	
Javed Miandad	c Azharuddin b Kapil Dev	78	b Kapil Dev	36	
Salim Malik	c Azharuddin b Ankola	36	(6) not out	102	
Imran Khan *	not out	109	(7) not out	28	
Shahid Saeed	c More b Kapil Dev	12			
Salim Yousuf +	c More b Prabhakar	36	(5) c More b Ankola	4	
Wasim Akram	c Azharuddin b Prabhakar	0			
Abdul Qadir	c More b Prabhakar	4			
Waqar Younis	c More b Prabhakar	0			
	Extras (b 4,lb 9,w 3,nb 7)	23	(b 3,lb 11,nb 9)	23	
	TOTAL	409	(for 5 wkts dec)	305	

INDIA

K.Srikkanth *	lbw b Wasim Akram	4	lbw b Wasim Akram	31	
N.S.Sidhu	b Wasim Akram	0	c Ramiz Raja b Imran Khan	85	
S.V.Manjrekar	c Salim Yousuf b Waqar Younis	3	not out	113	
M.Azharuddin	lbw b Imran Khan	35	c Aamer Malik b Abdul Qadir	35	
M.Prabhakar	b Waqar Younis	9			
S.R.Tendulkar	b Waqar Younis	15			
R.J.Shastri	c Imran Khan b Abdul Qadir	45	(5) not out	22	
Kapil Dev	c Javed Miandad b Waqar Younis	55			
K.S.More +	not out	58			
Arshad Ayub	lbw b Wasim Akram	1			
S.A.Ankola	b Wasim Akram	6			
	Extras (b 5,lb 10,w 5,nb 11)	31	(b 9,lb 4,w 1,nb 3)	17	
	TOTAL	262	(for 3 wkts)	303	

INDIA	O	M	R	W		O	M	R	W
Kapil Dev	24	5	69	4		36	15	82	3
Prabhakar	34.5	6	104	5		30	4	107	1
Ankola	19	1	93	1		11	6	35	1
Shastri	10	1	37	0		5	0	15	0
Arshad Ayub	27	3	81	0		10	1	37	0
Srikkanth	1	0	2	0					
Tendulkar	1	0	10	0		4	0	15	0

PAKISTAN	O	M	R	W		O	M	R	W
Wasim Akram	26.2	4	83	4		25	7	68	1
Waqar Younis	19	1	80	4		2	0	11	0
Imran Khan	15	4	44	1		28	10	56	1
Shahid Saeed	2	0	7	0		13	0	36	0
Abdul Qadir	10	1	33	1		28	3	119	1

FALL OF WICKETS	1st	2nd	3rd	4th	5th	6th	7th	8th	9th	10th
PAK	4	83	158	233	271	307	398	398	409	409
IND	1	13	13	41	73	85	163	220	241	262
PAK	2	24	92	109	250					
IND	43	178	256							

PAKISTAN vs INDIA
at Faisalabad on 23rd November 1989
Match drawn

INDIA

K.Srikkanth *	lbw b Wasim Akram	36	b Wasim Akram	13	
N.S.Sidhu	c Nadeem Abbasi b Wasim Akram	20	run out	51	
S.V.Manjrekar	c Salim Malik b Naved Anjum	76	lbw b Naved Anjum	83	
M.Azharuddin	lbw b Wasim Akram	0	b Naved Anjum	109	
R.J.Shastri	c Nadeem Abbasi b Salim Jaffer	11	c Nadeem Abbasi b Wasim Akram	5	
S.R.Tendulkar	lbw b Imran Khan	59	run out	8	
M.Prabhakar	not out	24	not out	54	
Kapil Dev	lbw b Naved Anjum	0	c Ramiz Raja b Abdul Qadir	49	
K.S.More +	lbw b Imran Khan	4	not out	2	
Maninder Singh	c Ramiz Raja b Imran Khan	3			
V.Razdan	c sub b Imran Khan	0			
	Extras (b 2,lb 16,w 15,nb 22)	55	(b 7,lb 7,w 7,nb 3)	24	
	TOTAL	288	(for 7 wkts)	398	

PAKISTAN

Aamer Malik	c & b Prabhakar	117	
Ramiz Raja	c Srikkanth b Prabhakar	58	
Shoaib Mohammad	lbw b Kapil Dev	24	
Javed Miandad	lbw b Prabhakar	13	
Salim Malik	lbw b Prabhakar	63	
Imran Khan *	c Azharuddin b Prabhakar	34	
Naved Anjum	c More b Kapil Dev	12	
Nadeem Abbasi +	c More b Kapil Dev	36	
Wasim Akram	c Tendulkar b Prabhakar	28	
Abdul Qadir	not out	5	
Salim Jaffer	not out	0	
	Extras (b 2,lb 9,w 8,nb 14)	33	
	TOTAL (for 9 wkts dec)	423	

PAKISTAN	O	M	R	W		O	M	R	W
Imran Khan	26.1	7	45	4		27	5	100	0
Wasim Akram	38	4	107	3		31	6	86	2
Salim Jaffer	17	4	54	1					
Naved Anjum	29	6	57	2		22	4	92	2
Abdul Qadir	3	1	7	0		31	3	90	1
Aamer Malik						2	0	9	0
Shoaib Mohammad						3	0	7	0

INDIA	O	M	R	W		O	M	R	W
Kapil Dev	45	11	106	3					
Prabhakar	42.3	4	132	6					
Razdan	13	1	62	0					
Maninder Singh	21	4	70	0					
Shastri	9	0	29	0					
Srikkanth	2	0	13	0					

FALL OF WICKETS	1st	2nd	3rd	4th	5th	6th	7th	8th	9th	10th
IND	68	74	85	101	244	252	253	278	284	288
PAK	105	157	193	289	307	331	368	409	419	
IND	33	91	249	258	274	290	385			

PAKISTAN vs INDIA
at Lahore on 1st December 1989
Match drawn

INDIA

K.Srikkanth *	b Wasim Akram	0	
N.S.Sidhu	lbw b Imran Khan	4	
S.V.Manjrekar	run out	218	
M.Azharuddin	c Nadeem Abbasi b Shahid Mahboob	77	
R.J.Shastri	c Javed Miandad b Shahid Mahboob	61	
M.Prabhakar	run out	45	
S.R.Tendulkar	b Abdul Qadir	41	
Kapil Dev	b Abdul Qadir	1	
K.S.More +	not out	26	
Arshad Ayub	c sub b Abdul Qadir	10	
Maninder Singh	c Akram Raza b Imran Khan	0	
	Extras (b 4,lb 19,w 1,nb 2)	26	
	TOTAL	509	

PAKISTAN

Aamer Malik	c sub b Maninder Singh	113	
Ramiz Raja	c More b Prabhakar	63	
Salim Malik	c Manjrekar b Maninder Singh	55	
Javed Miandad	b Shastri	145	
Shoaib Mohammad	not out	203	
Imran Khan *	c Manjrekar b Shastri	66	
Abdul Qadir	not out	39	
Wasim Akram			
Akram Raza			
Nadeem Abbasi +			
Shahid Mahboob			
	Extras (b 3,lb 4,nb 8)	15	
	TOTAL (for 5 wkts)	699	

PAKISTAN	O	M	R	W		O	M	R	W
Imran Khan	50.2	13	130	2					
Wasim Akram	24	6	65	1					
Shahid Mahboob	49	12	131	2					
Akram Raza	18	3	58	0					
Abdul Qadir	35	8	97	3					
Salim Malik	1	0	2	0					
Aamer Malik	1	0	3	0					

INDIA	O	M	R	W		O	M	R	W
Kapil Dev	28	2	77	0					
Prabhakar	34	2	107	1					
Maninder Singh	61	7	191	2					
Arshad Ayub	49	4	182	0					
Srikkanth	3	0	18	0					
Shastri	26.4	2	105	2					
More	2	0	12	0					

FALL OF WICKETS	1st	2nd	3rd	4th	5th	6th	7th	8th	9th	10th
IND	1	5	154	340	375	466	466	469	508	509
PAK	100	223	248	494	628					

PAKISTAN vs INDIA
at Sialkot on 9th December 1989
Match drawn

INDIA

K.Srikkanth *	lbw b Wasim Akram	10	c Wasim Akram b Imran Khan	3
N.S.Sidhu	c Ramiz Raja b Wasim Akram	12	c Imran Khan b Zakir Khan	97
S.V.Manjrekar	lbw b Waqar Younis	72	lbw b Imran Khan	4
M.Azharuddin	run out	52	c Shoaib Mohammad b Wasim Akram	4
R.J.Shastri	c & b Imran Khan	20	lbw b Wasim Akram	0
S.R.Tendulkar	lbw b Wasim Akram	35	c Nadeem Abbasi b Imran Khan	57
Kapil Dev	b Wasim Akram	27	lbw b Zakir Khan	27
M.Prabhakar	c Shoaib Mohammad b Imran Khan	25	not out	11
K.S.More +	c Zakir Khan b Waqar Younis	15	not out	17
Maninder Singh	c Nadeem Abbasi b Wasim Akram	8		
V.Razdan	not out	6		
	Extras (b 6,lb 14,w 8,nb 14)	42	(b 5,lb 7,nb 2)	14
	TOTAL	324	(for 7 wkts)	234

PAKISTAN

Aamer Malik	lbw b Prabhakar	9
Ramiz Raja	b Razdan	56
Shoaib Mohammad	b Razdan	23
Javed Miandad	c More b Kapil Dev	7
Salim Malik	c Shastri b Razdan	34
Imran Khan *	c More b Prabhakar	25
Nadeem Abbasi +	b Prabhakar	10
Wasim Akram	b Razdan	30
Abdul Qadir	c Azharuddin b Razdan	7
Zakir Khan	not out	9
Waqar Younis	c More b Kapil Dev	4
	Extras (b 7,lb 24,w 1,nb 4)	36
	TOTAL	250

PAKISTAN

	O	M	R	W		O	M	R	W
Wasim Akram	28.2	6	101	5		32	17	41	2
Waqar Younis	21	2	83	2		16	1	63	0
Zakir Khan	16	3	59	0		13	0	50	2
Imran Khan	17	3	61	2		22	4	68	3
Abdul Qadir	2	2	0	0					
Shoaib Mohammad						1	1	0	0

INDIA

	O	M	R	W		O	M	R	W
Kapil Dev	35.4	17	44	2					
Prabhakar	40	10	92	3					
Razdan	27	5	79	5					
Maninder Singh	1	0	4	0					

FALL OF WICKETS

	1st	2nd	3rd	4th	5th	6th	7th	8th	9th	10th
IND	20	39	167	181	225	251	270	296	314	324
PAK	11	76	87	133	170	185	194	222	233	250
IND	10	33	38	38	139	198	207			

AUSTRALIA vs PAKISTAN
at Melbourne on 12th January 1990
Australia won by 92 runs

AUSTRALIA

G.R.Marsh	c Salim Yousuf b Wasim Akram	30	(2) c Wasim Akram b Aqib Javed	24
M.A.Taylor	c Aqib Javed b Imran Khan	52	(1) c Aamer Malik b Tauseef Ahmed	101
D.C.Boon	lbw b Wasim Akram	0	run out	21
A.R.Border *	c Javed Miandad b Wasim Akram	24	not out	62
D.M.Jones	c Salim Yousuf b Imran Khan	0	lbw b Wasim Akram	10
S.R.Waugh	c Salim Yousuf b Aqib Javed	20	c Salim Yousuf b Wasim Akram	3
P.R.Sleep	lbw b Wasim Akram	23	b Wasim Akram	0
I.A.Healy +	c Shoaib Mohammad b Aqib Javed	48	c Ijaz Ahmed b Wasim Akram	25
M.G.Hughes	c Mansoor Akhtar b Wasim Akram	8	c Mansoor Akhtar b Wasim Akram	32
T.M.Alderman	c Aamer Malik b Wasim Akram	0	not out	1
C.G.Rackemann	not out	0		
	Extras (lb 9,nb 9)	18	(b 2,lb 10,w 1,nb 20)	33
	TOTAL	223	(for 8 wkts dec)	312

PAKISTAN

Aamer Malik	lbw b Alderman	7	c Taylor b Hughes	0
Shoaib Mohammad	c Healy b Alderman	6	(3) c Boon b Alderman	10
Mansoor Akhtar	c Taylor b Rackemann	5	(2) lbw b Alderman	14
Javed Miandad	c Healy b Alderman	3	lbw b Waugh	65
Ijaz Ahmed	c Taylor b Hughes	19	c Marsh b Hughes	121
Imran Khan *	c Alderman b Rackemann	3	lbw b Alderman	45
Salim Yousuf +	c Taylor b Hughes	16	lbw b Alderman	38
Wasim Akram	c Healy b Hughes	6	c Taylor b Sleep	6
Tauseef Ahmed	not out	9	not out	14
Waqar Younis	lbw b Sleep	18	lbw b Alderman	4
Aqib Javed	c Healy b Rackemann	0	lbw b Alderman	0
	Extras (b 1,lb 4,nb 10)	15	(b 1,lb 7,w 2,nb 9)	19
	TOTAL	107	TOTAL	336

PAKISTAN

	O	M	R	W		O	M	R	W
Imran Khan	18	6	53	2		8	2	21	0
Wasim Akram	30	9	62	6		41.4	12	98	5
Aqib Javed	22.1	7	47	2		21	1	55	1
Waqar Younis	12	3	27	0		22	4	68	0
Tauseef Ahmed	8	1	25	0		16	3	58	1

AUSTRALIA

	O	M	R	W		O	M	R	W
Alderman	19	6	30	3		33.5	6	105	5
Rackemann	21.5	8	32	3		38	13	67	0
Hughes	17	7	34	3		42	14	79	3
Sleep	8	5	6	1		21	7	64	1
Waugh						3	0	13	1

FALL OF WICKETS

	1st	2nd	3rd	4th	5th	6th	7th	8th	9th	10th
AUS	90	90	98	98	131	148	201	223	223	223
PAK	12	20	20	44	44	65	71	71	106	107
AUS	73	116	204	216	220	220	260	305		
PAK	4	23	31	134	218	291	303	328	333	336

AUSTRALIA vs PAKISTAN
at Adelaide on 19th January 1990
Match drawn

PAKISTAN

Shoaib Mohammad	lbw b Hughes	43	c Healy b Hughes	0
Ramiz Raja	c Taylor P.L. b Campbell	9	c Waugh b Hughes	2
Salim Yousuf +	lbw b Rackemann	38	c Taylor M.A. b Hughes	1
Javed Miandad	c Healy b Campbell	52	(6) c Taylor P.L. b Hughes	21
Ijaz Ahmed	c Marsh b Border	28	(4) c Taylor P.L. b Hughes	4
Salim Malik	c Healy b Hughes	11	(8) not out	65
Imran Khan *	c Healy b Campbell	13	(5) b Taylor P.L.	136
Wasim Akram	c Border b Campbell	52	(7) b Campbell	123
Tauseef Ahmed	c Healy b Rackemann	0	c Healy b Rackemann	18
Mushtaq Ahmed	c Healy b Rackemann	0	b Taylor P.L.	4
Waqar Younis	not out	1		
	Extras (b 4,lb 4,w 1,nb 1)	10	(b 4,lb 5,w 1,nb 3)	13
	TOTAL	257	(for 9 wkts dec)	387

AUSTRALIA

G.R.Marsh	c Salim Yousuf b Wasim Akram	13		
M.A.Taylor	lbw b Imran Khan	77	(1) c sub b Mushtaq Ahmed	59
D.C.Boon	lbw b Wasim Akram	29	(2) c Ramiz Raja b Wasim Akram	5
A.R.Border *	b Waqar Younis	13	(3) c Salim Yousuf b Waqar Younis	8
D.M.Jones	c Wasim Akram b Imran Khan	116	(4) not out	121
S.R.Waugh	lbw b Wasim Akram	17	(5) b Tauseef Ahmed	4
I.A.Healy +	c sub b Waqar Younis	12	(6) c sub b Tauseef Ahmed	27
P.L.Taylor	run out	33	(7) c Shoaib Mohammad b Tauseef Ahmed	1
M.G.Hughes	not out	6	(8) not out	2
G.D.Campbell	lbw b Wasim Akram	0		
C.G.Rackemann	b Wasim Akram	0		
	Extras (lb 12,nb 13)	25	(lb 3,nb 3)	6
	TOTAL	341	(for 6 wkts)	233

AUSTRALIA

	O	M	R	W		O	M	R	W
Hughes	18	5	63	2		32	9	111	5
Campbell	21.3	2	79	3		29	5	83	1
Taylor P.L.	12	0	57	0		41.5	13	94	2
Rackemann	21	3	40	4		37	11	85	1
Border	4	0	10	1		4	0	5	0

PAKISTAN

	O	M	R	W		O	M	R	W
Wasim Akram	43	10	100	5		11	3	29	1
Waqar Younis	26	4	66	2		14	4	42	1
Mushtaq Ahmed	23	4	69	0		25	5	72	1
Imran Khan	27	6	61	2					
Tauseef Ahmed	14	1	33	0		32	6	80	3
Shoaib Mohammad						1	0	7	0

FALL OF WICKETS

	1st	2nd	3rd	4th	5th	6th	7th	8th	9th	10th
PAK	27	91	95	166	187	187	241	251	251	257
AUS	82	113	156	188	216	328	328	341	341	341
PAK	0	2	7	22	90	281	316	380	387	
AUS	9	33	106	129	213	229				

AUSTRALIA vs PAKISTAN
at Sydney on 3rd February 1990
Match drawn

PAKISTAN

Aamer Malik	c Healy b Alderman	7
Ramiz Raja	c & b Hughes	0
Shoaib Mohammad	lbw b Alderman	9
Javed Miandad	c Jones b Hughes	49
Ijaz Ahmed	c Taylor M.A. b Rackemann	8
Imran Khan *	not out	82
Wasim Akram	c Taylor M.A. b Alderman	10
Salim Yousuf +	c Jones b Rackemann	6
Tauseef Ahmed	b Alderman	0
Waqar Younis	c Veletta b Hughes	16
Nadeem Ghauri	b Alderman	0
	Extras (b 1,lb 7,nb 4)	12
	TOTAL	199

AUSTRALIA

M.A.Taylor	not out	101
M.R.J.Veletta	lbw b Waqar Younis	9
T.M.Moody	c Aamer Malik b Tauseef Ahmed	26
A.R.Border *	not out	27
D.M.Jones		
S.R.Waugh		
I.A.Healy +		
P.L.Taylor		
M.G.Hughes		
C.G.Rackemann		
T.M.Alderman		
	Extras (b 4,lb 5,nb 4)	13
	TOTAL (for 2 wkts)	176

AUSTRALIA

	O	M	R	W		O	M	R	W
Alderman	33.5	10	65	5					
Hughes	31	16	70	3					
Rackemann	22	8	33	2					
Taylor P.L.	8	1	23	0					

PAKISTAN

	O	M	R	W		O	M	R	W
Wasim Akram	10	3	29	0					
Imran Khan	17	2	32	0					
Tauseef Ahmed	19	3	62	1					
Nadeem Ghauri	8	1	20	0					
Waqar Younis	9	4	21	1					
Ijaz Ahmed	2	0	3	0					

FALL OF WICKETS

	1st	2nd	3rd	4th	5th	6th	7th	8th	9th	10th
PAK	2	15	20	51	106	128	154	160	191	199
AUS	33	106								

PAKISTAN vs NEW ZEALAND
at Karachi on 11th October 1990
Pakistan won by an innings and 43 runs

NEW ZEALAND

T.J.Franklin	c Salim Yousuf b Waqar Younis	16	b Wasim Akram	0
D.J.White	c Salim Yousuf b Wasim Akram	9	b Wasim Akram	18
M.J.Greatbatch	c & b Ijaz Ahmed	43	lbw b Aqib Javed	21
M.D.Crowe *	c Ramiz Raja b Waqar Younis	7	not out	68
K.R.Rutherford	b Aqib Javed	79	b Aqib Javed	0
D.N.Patel	lbw b Waqar Younis	2	lbw b Wasim Akram	19
D.K.Morrison	lbw b Wasim Akram	4	(9) b Wasim Akram	0
G.E.Bradburn	not out	11	(7) c Salim Yousuf b Waqar Younis	2
I.D.S.Smith +	lbw b Wasim Akram	4	(8) b Waqar Younis	14
C.Pringle	b Waqar Younis	0	lbw b Abdul Qadir	20
W.Watson	lbw b Wasim Akram	0	lbw b Waqar Younis	11
	Extras (b 5,lb 11,w 2,nb 3)	21	(b 7,lb 9,nb 5)	21
	TOTAL	196		194

PAKISTAN

Ramiz Raja	c Crowe b Bradburn	78
Shoaib Mohammad	not out	203
Salim Malik	c Rutherford b Pringle	43
Javed Miandad *	lbw b Morrison	27
Wasim Akram	run out	28
Ijaz Ahmed	b Watson	9
Salim Yousuf +	c Crowe b Morrison	13
Abdul Qadir	not out	6
Tauseef Ahmed		
Aqib Javed		
Waqar Younis		
	Extras (b 3,lb 11,w 1,nb 11)	26
	TOTAL (for 6 wkts dec)	433

PAKISTAN

	O	M	R	W		O	M	R	W
Wasim Akram	29.5	12	44	4		24	5	60	4
Waqar Younis	22	7	40	4		15.4	4	39	3
Aqib Javed	16	4	37	1		12	1	45	2
Abdul Qadir	7	1	32	0		10	2	32	1
Tauseef Ahmed	5	0	18	0		1	0	2	0
Ijaz Ahmed	5	0	9	1					

NEW ZEALAND

	O	M	R	W		O	M	R	W
Morrison	28.3	5	86	2					
Pringle	25	3	68	1					
Watson	40	8	125	1					
Bradburn	17	3	56	1					
Patel	24	6	62	0					
Crowe	6	1	22	0					

FALL OF WICKETS

	1st	2nd	3rd	4th	5th	6th	7th	8th	9th	10th
NZ	28	34	51	167	174	181	181	194	195	196
PAK	172	239	288	360	384	413				
NZ	4	23	56	57	96	103	119	120	173	194

PAKISTAN vs NEW ZEALAND
at Lahore on 19th October 1990
Pakistan won by 9 wickets

NEW ZEALAND

T.J.Franklin	c Wasim Akram b Salim Jaffer	11	c Salim Yousuf b Salim Jaffer	25
D.J.White	c Salim Yousuf b Wasim Akram	3	b Waqar Younis	1
M.J.Greatbatch	b Waqar Younis	11	b Waqar Younis	6
M.D.Crowe *	c Salim Malik b Aqib Javed	20	not out	108
K.R.Rutherford	lbw b Wasim Akram	23	(6) lbw b Waqar Younis	60
D.N.Patel	b Waqar Younis	4	(7) c Salim Yousuf b Salim Jaffer	7
G.E.Bradburn	lbw b Salim Jaffer	8	(8) c sub b Waqar Younis	14
I.D.S.Smith +	c Salim Yousuf b Abdul Qadir	33	(9) c Salim Jaffer b Abdul Qadir	8
C.Pringle	c Ramiz Raja b Waqar Younis	9	(10) b Waqar Younis	7
D.K.Morrison	c Salim Yousuf b Abdul Qadir	0	(5) b Waqar Younis	7
W.Watson	not out	0	lbw b Waqar Younis	0
	Extras (b 5,lb 13,w 5,nb 15)	38	(b 17,lb 10,nb 17)	44
	TOTAL	160		287

PAKISTAN

Ramiz Raja	c Greatbatch b Watson	48	c Crowe b Morrison	11
Shoaib Mohammad	b Morrison	105	not out	42
Salim Malik	lbw b Watson	6	not out	19
Javed Miandad *	c Smith b Bradburn	43		
Ijaz Ahmed	c Greatbatch b Watson	86		
Salim Yousuf +	c Rutherford b Pringle	33		
Wasim Akram	c Bradburn b Watson	1		
Waqar Younis	b Watson	17		
Salim Jaffer	not out	10		
Aqib Javed	c Crowe b Watson	7		
Abdul Qadir				
	Extras (b 4,lb 1,w 1,nb 12)	17	(lb 1,w 1,nb 3)	5
	TOTAL (for 9 wkts dec)	373	(for 1 wkt)	77

PAKISTAN

	O	M	R	W		O	M	R	W
Wasim Akram	16	3	43	2		9	4	15	0
Waqar Younis	15	6	20	3		37.5	11	86	7
Salim Jaffer	12	2	37	2		25	8	62	2
Aqib Javed	13	2	37	1		21	9	40	0
Abdul Qadir	3	1	5	2		19	4	43	1
Shoaib Mohammad						2	0	8	0
Ijaz Ahmed						2	0	6	0

NEW ZEALAND

	O	M	R	W		O	M	R	W
Morrison	29	9	103	1		8	2	36	1
Pringle	31	6	112	1		7	4	10	0
Watson	36	10	78	6		2	0	12	0
Patel	16	5	43	0		3	0	13	0
Bradburn	13	4	32	1					
White						0.3	0	5	0

FALL OF WICKETS

	1st	2nd	3rd	4th	5th	6th	7th	8th	9th	10th
NZ	7	30	39	79	99	103	143	147	154	160
PAK	98	117	192	246	317	337	342	363	373	
NZ	10	18	57	74	206	228	264	277	287	287
PAK	27									

PAKISTAN vs NEW ZEALAND
at Faisalabad on 26th October 1990
Pakistan won by 65 runs

PAKISTAN

Ramiz Raja	c Smith b Pringle	20	lbw b Watson	16
Shoaib Mohammad	c Crowe b Pringle	15	c sub b Pringle	142
Salim Malik	c Smith b Pringle	4	(4) c & b Crowe	71
Javed Miandad *	c Smith b Pringle	25	(5) c Bradburn b Pringle	55
Ijaz Ahmed	c Horne b Watson	5	(6) c Horne b Pringle	6
Salim Yousuf +	c Morrison b Watson	14	(3) c Crowe b Pringle	13
Naved Anjum	c Smith b Pringle	10	b Morrison	22
Tauseef Ahmed	c Rutherford b Pringle	1	not out	12
Waqar Younis	b Pringle	0	c Rutherford b Morrison	0
Salim Jaffer	lbw b Watson	0	b Morrison	2
Aqib Javed	not out	0	c sub b Morrison	4
	Extras (b 3,nb 5)	8	(b 1,lb 8,nb 5)	14
	TOTAL	102		357

NEW ZEALAND

T.J.Franklin	b Waqar Younis	25	c Ijaz Ahmed b Aqib Javed	12
P.A.Horne	c Ramiz Raja b Salim Jaffer	0	lbw b Waqar Younis	12
M.J.Greatbatch	c Salim Yousuf b Waqar Younis	8	(4) b Aqib Javed	0
M.D.Crowe *	c Tauseef Ahmed b Salim Jaffer	31	(5) c Salim Yousuf b Waqar Younis	10
K.R.Rutherford	b Waqar Younis	0	(6) c Salim Yousuf b Salim Jaffer	25
D.N.Patel	lbw b Waqar Younis	0	(7) c Salim Yousuf b Salim Jaffer	45
D.K.Morrison	c Shoaib Mohammad b Waqar Younis	25	(3) c Salim Yousuf b Aqib Javed	0
I.D.S.Smith +	c Salim Malik b Tauseef Ahmed	61	(9) c & b Waqar Younis	21
G.E.Bradburn	c Salim Yousuf b Waqar Younis	18	(8) not out	30
C.Pringle	not out	24	c Salim Yousuf b Waqar Younis	0
W.Watson	lbw b Waqar Younis	2	lbw b Waqar Younis	2
	Extras (b 12,lb 8,nb 3)	23	(b 10,lb 5,w 1,nb 4)	20
	TOTAL	217		177

NEW ZEALAND

	O	M	R	W		O	M	R	W
Morrison	9	3	18	0		29.5	3	105	4
Pringle	16	5	52	7		43	12	100	4
Watson	15.3	5	29	3		44	23	77	1
Patel						6	0	21	0
Crowe						11	5	22	1
Bradburn						6	1	23	0

PAKISTAN

	O	M	R	W		O	M	R	W
Waqar Younis	30.2	13	76	7		24	9	54	5
Aqib Javed	10	5	24	0		17	1	57	3
Naved Anjum	6	4	13	0					
Salim Jaffer	20	5	47	2		18	4	51	2
Tauseef Ahmed	10	2	37	1					

FALL OF WICKETS

	1st	2nd	3rd	4th	5th	6th	7th	8th	9th	10th
PAK	35	37	42	65	82	92	98	102	102	102
NZ	36	37	37	37	89	166	171	178	207	217
PAK	33	61	192	300	314	321	349	349	353	357
NZ	23	25	28	31	45	64	148	171	171	177

PAKISTAN vs WEST INDIES
at Karachi on 15th November 1990
Pakistan won by 8 wickets

WEST INDIES

C.G.Greenidge	lbw b Waqar Younis	3	st Salim Yousuf b Abdul Qadir	11
D.L.Haynes *	lbw b Wasim Akram	117	c Salim Yousuf b Waqar Younis	47
R.B.Richardson	st Salim Yousuf b Mushtaq Ahmed	26	lbw b Waqar Younis	11
C.A.Best	c Ramiz Raja b Mushtaq Ahmed	1	lbw b Mushtaq Ahmed	8
C.L.Hooper	lbw b Waqar Younis	8	lbw b Wasim Akram	0
A.L.Logie	c Salim Yousuf b Wasim Akram	25	not out	58
P.J.L.Dujon +	c Javed Miandad b Waqar Younis	17	b Shoaib Mohammad	1
M.D.Marshall	b Waqar Younis	13	b Wasim Akram	21
C.E.L.Ambrose	lbw b Waqar Younis	2	lbw b Waqar Younis	0
I.R.Bishop	c Salim Yousuf b Wasim Akram	22	b Waqar Younis	0
C.A.Walsh	not out	6	b Wasim Akram	4
	Extras (b 6,lb 6,nb 9)	21	(b 10,lb 8,nb 6)	24
	TOTAL	261		181

PAKISTAN

Shoaib Mohammad	c Richardson b Marshall	86	(2) not out	32
Ramiz Raja	b Bishop	0	(1) lbw b Walsh	7
Zahid Fazal	c Logie b Ambrose	7	c Richardson b Walsh	12
Javed Miandad	c Dujon b Bishop	7		
Salim Malik	c Dujon b Marshall	102	(4) not out	30
Imran Khan *	not out	73		
Salim Yousuf +	b Ambrose	5		
Wasim Akram	c Richardson b Walsh	9		
Mushtaq Ahmed	c Richardson b Ambrose	3		
Abdul Qadir	c Dujon b Ambrose	0		
Waqar Younis	c Hooper b Bishop	5		
	Extras (b 7,lb 14,w 1,nb 26)	48	(lb 8,nb 9)	17
	TOTAL	345	(for 2 wkts)	98

PAKISTAN

	O	M	R	W		O	M	R	W
Wasim Akram	23.3	7	61	3		20.3	6	39	3
Waqar Younis	22	0	76	5		17	3	44	4
Abdul Qadir	20	2	56	0		8	1	22	1
Mushtaq Ahmed	18	3	56	2		15	5	38	1
Shoaib Mohammad						6	1	15	1
Salim Malik						1	0	5	0

WEST INDIES

	O	M	R	W		O	M	R	W
Ambrose	34	7	78	4		2	0	4	0
Bishop	27.2	3	81	3		7	0	21	0
Marshall	24	5	48	2		5	1	8	0
Walsh	19	0	50	1		12	2	27	2
Hooper	28	6	65	0		11	2	30	0
Best	1	0	2	0					

FALL OF WICKETS

	1st	2nd	3rd	4th	5th	6th	7th	8th	9th	10th
WI	4	77	81	96	151	178	200	204	243	261
PAK	2	16	27	201	281	298	313	318	318	345
WI	47	85	86	90	111	127	166	174	174	181
PAK	15	56								

PAKISTAN vs WEST INDIES
at Faisalabad on 23rd November 1990
West Indies won by 7 wickets

PAKISTAN

Batsman	Dismissal	R	Dismissal 2	R2
Saeed Anwar	c Best b Ambrose	0	lbw b Bishop	0
Shoaib Mohammad	c Dujon b Bishop	7	b Ambrose	15
Zahid Fazal	run out	32	b Bishop	5
Javed Miandad	c Dujon b Walsh	7	(6) c Dujon b Ambrose	9
Salim Malik	c Richardson b Bishop	74	(4) b Marshall	71
Imran Khan *	lbw b Walsh	3	(7) c Dujon b Marshall	0
Wasim Akram	run out	4	(8) run out	0
Moin Khan +	c Greenidge b Ambrose	24	(5) c Logie b Walsh	32
Akram Raza	b Bishop	5	b Marshall	0
Mushtaq Ahmed	not out	2	not out	5
Waqar Younis	c Dujon b Bishop	1	c Dujon b Marshall	3
Extras	(lb 3,nb 8)	11	(lb 4,nb 10)	14
TOTAL		170		154

WEST INDIES

Batsman	Dismissal	R	Dismissal 2	R2
C.G.Greenidge	lbw b Waqar Younis	12	(4) lbw b Wasim Akram	10
D.L.Haynes *	lbw b Akram Raza	19	(1) c Akram Raza b Wasim Akram	0
R.B.Richardson	c Saeed Anwar b Akram Raza	44	not out	70
C.A.Best	c Moin Khan b Waqar Younis	6	(2) b Wasim Akram	7
C.L.Hooper	lbw b Waqar Younis	5	not out	33
A.L.Logie	c Moin Khan b Waqar Younis	12		
P.J.L.Dujon +	lbw b Wasim Akram	9		
M.D.Marshall	b Wasim Akram	20		
C.E.L.Ambrose	b Waqar Younis	15		
I.R.Bishop	lbw b Wasim Akram	14		
C.A.Walsh	not out	14		
Extras	(b 8,lb 20,nb 11)	39	(lb 6,nb 4)	10
TOTAL		195	(for 3 wkts)	130

WEST INDIES	O	M	R	W		O	M	R	W
Bishop	17.2	6	47	4		11	1	53	2
Ambrose	17	3	47	2		13	4	32	2
Walsh	10	1	38	2		9	0	32	1
Marshall	8	1	30	0		4.2	0	24	4
Hooper	2	1	5	0		3	1	9	0

PAKISTAN	O	M	R	W		O	M	R	W
Wasim Akram	17	1	63	3		12	0	46	3
Waqar Younis	16	3	46	5		9	2	41	0
Akram Raza	19	4	52	2		7.2	1	37	0
Mushtaq Ahmed	4	1	6	0		1	1	0	0

FALL OF WICKETS	1st	2nd	3rd	4th	5th	6th	7th	8th	9th	10th
PAK	1	15	29	76	91	99	146	157	169	170
WI	26	78	101	101	108	121	143	162	162	195
PAK	0	10	38	127	145	146	146	146	146	154
WI	0	11	34							

PAKISTAN vs WEST INDIES
at Lahore on 6th December 1990
Match drawn

WEST INDIES

Batsman	Dismissal	R	Dismissal 2	R2
C.G.Greenidge	lbw b Imran Khan	21	c Zahid Fazal b Waqar Younis	1
D.L.Haynes *	c Moin Khan b Imran Khan	3	c Shoaib Mohammad b Masood Anwar	12
R.B.Richardson	lbw b Wasim Akram	5	c Aamer Malik b Imran Khan	6
B.C.Lara	c Aamer Malik b Abdul Qadir	44	c Salim Malik b Imran Khan	5
C.L.Hooper	c Zahid Fazal b Masood Anwar	134	run out	49
A.L.Logie	lbw b Waqar Younis	16	lbw b Wasim Akram	59
P.J.L.Dujon +	st Moin Khan b Masood Anwar	0	c Moin Khan b Wasim Akram	3
M.D.Marshall	b Wasim Akram	27	b Wasim Akram	11
C.E.L.Ambrose	lbw b Wasim Akram	0	lbw b Wasim Akram	0
I.R.Bishop	c Moin Khan b Wasim Akram	9	not out	1
C.A.Walsh	not out	5	lbw b Wasim Akram	0
Extras	(b 8,lb 12,nb 10)	30	(b 14,lb 4,nb 8)	26
TOTAL		294		173

PAKISTAN

Batsman	Dismissal	R	Dismissal 2	R2
Aamer Malik	b Bishop	3	c Logie b Ambrose	0
Shoaib Mohammad	b Bishop	0	(3) b Bishop	49
Zahid Fazal	c Haynes b Ambrose	13	(7) b Walsh	6
Ramiz Raja	c Logie b Ambrose	6	(2) b Walsh	41
Salim Malik	c Greenidge b Bishop	8	b Bishop	0
Imran Khan *	c Logie b Ambrose	17	not out	58
Wasim Akram	b Ambrose	38	(8) not out	21
Moin Khan +	c Logie b Ambrose	7		
Masood Anwar	c Logie b Bishop	2	(4) c Lara b Hooper	37
Abdul Qadir	lbw b Bishop	1		
Waqar Younis	not out	0		
Extras	(b 4,lb 12,w 1,nb 10)	27	(lb 4,nb 26)	30
TOTAL		122	(for 6 wkts)	242

PAKISTAN	O	M	R	W		O	M	R	W
Imran Khan	6	0	22	2		13	5	32	2
Wasim Akram	21	4	61	4		9	0	28	5
Waqar Younis	17	0	57	1		8	0	32	1
Abdul Qadir	18	1	75	1		4	0	19	0
Masood Anwar	13.5	3	59	2		13	1	43	1
Shoaib Mohammad						1	0	1	0

WEST INDIES	O	M	R	W		O	M	R	W
Ambrose	20	5	35	5		20.4	0	43	1
Bishop	19.2	7	41	5		23	6	59	2
Marshall	5	2	8	0		19	5	48	0
Walsh	5	1	22	0		19	3	53	2
Hooper						15	4	35	1

FALL OF WICKETS	1st	2nd	3rd	4th	5th	6th	7th	8th	9th	10th
WI	13	24	37	132	185	186	247	249	278	294
PAK	2	11	33	34	48	93	108	120	121	122
WI	1	13	27	47	154	155	172	172	173	173
PAK	0	90	107	110	177	187				

PAKISTAN vs SRI LANKA
at Sialkot on 12th, 13th, 14th, 16th, 17th December 1991
Match drawn

SRI LANKA

Batsman	Dismissal	R	Dismissal 2	R2
M.A.R.Samarakekera	c Moin Khan b Waqar Younis	19	b Waqar Younis	6
U.C.Hathurusinghe	c Akram Raza b Aqib Javed	17	c Ramiz Raja b Wasim Akram	7
A.P.Gurusinha	b Aqib Javed	33	lbw b Aqib Javed	23
P.A.de Silva *	b Waqar Younis	31	c sub b Akram Raza	19
A.Ranatunga	lbw b Aqib Javed	0	c Moin Khan b Waqar Younis	0
S.T.Jayasuriya	b Akram Raza	77	not out	35
H.P.Tillekeratne +	c Akram Raza b Waqar Younis	49	not out	42
R.J.Ratnayake	b Waqar Younis	13		
C.P.H.Ramanayake	b Akram Raza	0		
S.D.Anurasiri	not out	3		
G.P.Wickremasinghe	b Waqar Younis	0		
Extras	(b 5,lb 11,nb 12)	28	(nb 5)	5
TOTAL		270	(for 5 wkts)	137

PAKISTAN

Ramiz Raja	c Tillekeratne b Anurasiri	98
Shoaib Mohammad	c & b Wickremasinghe	43
Zahid Fazal	c & b Ratnayake	36
Salim Malik	c Gurusinha b Anurasiri	101
Javed Miandad	c Jayasuriya b Anurasiri	1
Imran Khan *	not out	93
Wasim Akram	not out	20
Moin Khan +		
Akram Raza		
Waqar Younis		
Aqib Javed		
Extras	(lb 6,nb 25)	31
TOTAL	(for 5 wkts dec)	423

PAKISTAN	O	M	R	W		O	M	R	W
Wasim Akram	32	7	47	0		13	4	31	1
Waqar Younis	30.5	5	84	5		14.4	1	43	2
Akram Raza	24	10	37	2		11	3	34	1
Aqib Javed	23	4	70	3		7	3	22	1
Imran Khan	9	1	16	0					
Salim Malik						1	0	7	0

SRI LANKA	O	M	R	W		O	M	R	W
Ratnayake	31	4	100	1					
Ramanayake	33	9	75	0					
Wickremasinghe	27	3	120	1					
Hathurusinghe	1	0	3	0					
Anurasiri	61	21	106	3					
de Silva	4	0	13	0					

FALL OF WICKETS	1st	2nd	3rd	4th	5th	6th	7th	8th	9th	10th
SRI	21	70	89	89	128	229	244	249	269	270
PAK	128	169	232	233	365					
SRI	6	33	58	58	58					

PAKISTAN vs SRI LANKA
at Gujranwala on 20th, 21st, 22nd, 24th, 25th December 1991
Match drawn

PAKISTAN

Ramiz Raja	not out	51
Shoaib Mohammad	c Tillekeratne b Ratnayake	1
Zahid Fazal	c Tillekeratne b Wickremasinghe	21
Javed Miandad	not out	20
Salim Malik		
Imran Khan *		
Moin Khan +		
Wasim Akram		
Waqar Younis		
Salim Jaffer		
Aqib Javed		
Extras	(lb 10,nb 6)	16
TOTAL	(for 2 wkts)	109

SRI LANKA

R.S.Mahanama
U.C.Hathurusinghe
A.P.Gurusinha
P.A.de Silva *
A.Ranatunga
S.T.Jayasuriya
H.P.Tillekeratne +
R.J.Ratnayake
C.P.H.Ramanayake
S.D.Anurasiri
G.P.Wickremasinghe

Extras
TOTAL

SRI LANKA	O	M	R	W		O	M	R	W
Ratnayake	13	3	39	1					
Ramanayake	10	2	16	0					
Wickremasinghe	7	2	27	1					
Hathurusinghe	2	1	6	0					
Anurasiri	1	0	2	0					
Gurusinha	2	0	9	0					
Ranatunga	1	1	0	0					

PAKISTAN	O	M	R	W		O	M	R	W

FALL OF WICKETS	1st	2nd	3rd	4th	5th	6th	7th	8th	9th	10th
PAK	3	59								

PAKISTAN vs SRI LANKA
at Faisalabad on 2nd, 3rd, 4th, 6th, 7th January 1992
Pakistan won by 3 wickets

SRI LANKA

R.S.Mahanama	c Moin Khan b Salim Jaffer	58	lbw b Waqar Younis	8
U.C.Hathurusinghe	b Waqar Younis	49	c Zahid Fazal b Waqar Younis	20
A.P.Gurusinha	c Zahid Fazal b Waqar Younis	3	lbw b Aqib Javed	14
P.A.de Silva *	c Moin Khan b Salim Jaffer	12	lbw b Waqar Younis	38
A.Ranatunga	lbw b Salim Jaffer	0	(8) c Javed Miandad b Wasim Akram	6
S.T.Jayasuriya	run out	81	c Salim Malik b Waqar Younis	45
H.P.Tillekeratne +	c Shoaib Mohammad b Waqar Younis	11	c Moin Khan b Aqib Javed	14
R.J.Ratnayake	lbw b Waqar Younis	4	(9) not out	5
S.D.Anurasiri	c Shoaib Mohammad b Waqar Younis	0	(10) b Wasim Akram	0
K.I.W.Wijegunawardene	lbw b Wasim Akram	2	(5) b Waqar Younis	2
G.P.Wickremasinghe	not out	1	b Wasim Akram	0
	Extras (b 3,lb 6,w 2,nb 8)	19	(lb 3,nb 10)	13
	TOTAL	240		165

PAKISTAN

Ramiz Raja	lbw b Wickremasinghe	63	lbw b Wickremasinghe	8
Shoaib Mohammad	lbw b Wickremasinghe	30	(7) b Ratnayake	7
Zahid Fazal	lbw b Wijegunawardene	13	(2) c Anurasiri b Gurusinha	78
Javed Miandad	c Gurusinha b Wickremasinghe	14	(4) c Gurusinha b Wijegunawardene	2
Salim Malik	c Tillekeratne b Gurusinha	4	(4) c Gurusinha b Wijegunawardene	4
Imran Khan *	b Wijegunawardene	22	(5) lbw b Wijegunawardene	0
Wasim Akram	lbw b Gurusinha	13	(6) c de Silva b Wijegunawardene	54
Moin Khan +	lbw b Wickremasinghe	3	not out	22
Waqar Younis	lbw b Wickremasinghe	6	not out	1
Salim Jaffer	not out	8		
Aqib Javed	c sub b Wijegunawardene	10		
	Extras (lb 8,w 1,nb 26)	35	(b 2,lb 3,nb 7)	12
	TOTAL	221	(for 7 wkts)	188

PAKISTAN	O	M	R	W		O	M	R	W
Wasim Akram	22	8	62	2		18	2	71	3
Salim Jaffer	17	4	36	3		8	2	19	0
Waqar Younis	21	1	87	4		17	3	65	5
Aqib Javed	12.1	3	46	0		8	4	7	2

SRI LANKA	O	M	R	W		O	M	R	W
Ratnayake	13	2	40	0		9.3	0	43	1
Wijegunawardene	31.2	13	47	3		17.2	1	52	4
Wickremasinghe	32	9	73	5		26	5	52	1
Anurasiri	10	2	28	0		6	1	18	0
Gurusinha	15	9	19	2		12	5	18	1
Ranatunga	3	2	2	0					
Hathurusinghe	2	0	4	0					

FALL OF WICKETS	1st	2nd	3rd	4th	5th	6th	7th	8th	9th	10th
SRI	81	89	130	130	150	179	185	193	205	240
PAK	102	110	141	146	162	186	196	197	205	221
SRI1	28	43	67	72	105	136	146	160	165	165
PAK	31	52	60	60	149	156	179			

ENGLAND vs PAKISTAN
at Lord's on 18th, 19th, 20th, 21st June 1992
Pakistan won by 2 wickets

ENGLAND

G.A.Gooch *	b Wasim Akram	69	lbw b Aqib Javed	13
A.J.Stewart	c Javed Miandad b Asif Mujtaba	74	not out	69
G.A.Hick	c Javed Miandad b Waqar Younis	13	(4) c Moin Khan b Mushtaq Ahmed	11
R.A.Smith	c sub b Wasim Akram	9	(5) b Mushtaq Ahmed	8
A.J.Lamb	b Waqar Younis	30	(6) lbw b Mushtaq Ahmed	12
I.T.Botham	b Waqar Younis	2	(7) lbw b Waqar Younis	6
C.C.Lewis	lbw b Waqar Younis	2	(8) b Waqar Younis	15
R.C.Russell +	not out	22	(9) b Wasim Akram	0
P.A.J.DeFreitas	c Inzamam-ul-Haq b Waqar Younis	3	(10) c Inzamam-ul-Haq b Wasim Akram	0
I.D.K.Salisbury	hit wicket b Mushtaq Ahmed	4	(3) lbw b Wasim Akram	12
D.E.Malcolm	lbw b Mushtaq Ahmed	0	b Wasim Akram	0
	Extras (b 6,lb 12,nb 9)	27	(b 5,lb 8,nb 15)	28
	TOTAL	255		175

PAKISTAN

Aamir Sohail	c Russell b DeFreitas	73	b Salisbury	39
Ramiz Raja	b Lewis	24	c Hick b Lewis	0
Asif Mujtaba	c Smith b Malcolm	59	c Russell b Lewis	0
Javed Miandad *	c Botham b Salisbury	9	c Russell b Lewis	0
Salim Malik	c Smith b Malcolm	55	c Lewis b Salisbury	12
Inzamam-ul-Haq	c & b Malcolm	0	run out	8
Wasim Akram	b Salisbury	24	not out	45
Moin Khan +	c Botham b DeFreitas	12	c Smith b Salisbury	3
Mushtaq Ahmed	c Russell b DeFreitas	4	c Hick b Malcolm	5
Waqar Younis	b Malcolm	14	not out	20
Aqib Javed	not out	5		
	Extras (b 4,lb 3,nb 7)	14	(b 2,lb 5,w 1,nb 1)	9
	TOTAL	293	(for 8 wkts)	141

PAKISTAN	O	M	R	W		O	M	R	W
Wasim Akram	19	5	49	2		17.4	2	66	4
Aqib Javed	14	3	40	0		12	3	23	1
Waqar Younis	21	4	91	5		13	3	40	2
Mushtaq Ahmed	19.1	5	57	2		9	1	32	3
Asif Mujtaba	3	3	0	1		1	0	1	0

ENGLAND	O	M	R	W		O	M	R	W
DeFreitas	26	8	58	3					
Malcolm	15.5	1	70	4		15	2	42	1
Lewis	29	7	76	1		16	3	43	3
Salisbury	23	3	73	2		14.1	0	49	3
Botham	5	2	9	0					

FALL OF WICKETS	1st	2nd	3rd	4th	5th	6th	7th	8th	9th	10th
ENG	123	153	172	197	213	221	232	242	247	255
PAK	43	123	143	228	228	235	263	271	276	293
ENG	40	73	108	120	137	148	174	175	175	175
PAK	6	10	18	41	62	68	81	95		

ENGLAND vs PAKISTAN
at Edgbaston on 4th, 5th, 6th, 7th, 8th June 1992
Match drawn

PAKISTAN

Aamir Sohail	c Stewart b DeFreitas	18
Ramiz Raja	lbw b DeFreitas	47
Asif Mujtaba	c Russell b DeFreitas	29
Javed Miandad *	not out	153
Salim Malik	lbw b DeFreitas	165
Inzamam-ul-Haq	not out	8
Moin Khan +		
Mushtaq Ahmed		
Waqar Younis		
Aqib Javed		
Ata-ur-Rehman		
	Extras (b 2,lb 5,nb 19)	26
	TOTAL (for 4 wkts dec)	446

ENGLAND

G.A.Gooch *	c Asif Mujtaba b Aqib Javed	8
A.J.Stewart	c Salim Malik b Ata-ur-Rehman	190
G.A.Hick	c Javed Miandad b Waqar Younis	51
R.A.Smith	lbw b Mushtaq Ahmed	127
M.R.Ramprakash	c Moin Khan b Ata-ur-Rehman	0
A.J.Lamb	c Javed Miandad b Ata-ur-Rehman	12
C.C.Lewis	b Mushtaq Ahmed	24
R.C.Russell +	not out	29
D.R.Pringle	not out	0
I.T.Botham		
P.A.J.DeFreitas		
	Extras (b 5,lb 5,w 1,nb 7)	18
	TOTAL (for 7 wkts dec)	459

ENGLAND	O	M	R	W		O	M	R	W
DeFreitas	33	6	121	4					
Lewis	33	3	116	0					
Pringle	28	2	92	0					
Botham	19	6	52	0					
Hick	13	1	46	0					
Gooch	10	5	9	0					
Ramprakash	1	0	3	0					

PAKISTAN	O	M	R	W		O	M	R	W
Waqar Younis	24	2	96	1					
Aqib Javed	16	3	86	1					
Mushtaq Ahmed	50	8	156	2					
Ata-ur-Rehman	18	5	69	3					
Asif Mujtaba	8	1	29	0					
Aamir Sohail	2	0	8	0					
Salim Malik	1	0	5	0					

FALL OF WICKETS	1st	2nd	3rd	4th	5th	6th	7th	8th	9th	10th
PAK	33	96	110	432						
ENG	28	121	348	348	378	415	446			

ENGLAND vs PAKISTAN
at Old Trafford on 2nd, 3rd, 4th, 6th, 7th July 1992
Match drawn

PAKISTAN

Aamir Sohail	b Lewis	205	c Smith b Lewis	1
Ramiz Raja	c Russell b Malcolm	54	c Hick b Lewis	88
Asif Mujtaba	c Atherton b Lewis	57	c Atherton b Lewis	40
Javed Miandad *	c Hick b Munton	88	not out	45
Moin Khan +	c Gower b Malcolm	15	(7) not out	11
Salim Malik	b Gooch	34	(5) b Gooch	16
Inzamam-ul-Haq	c Gooch b Malcolm	26		
Wasim Akram	st Russell b Gooch	0	(6) c Atherton b Gooch	13
Waqar Younis	not out	2		
Mushtaq Ahmed	c Lewis b Gooch	6		
Aqib Javed				
	Extras (b 9,lb 4,w 2,nb 3)	18	(b 8,lb 5,w 5,nb 7)	25
	TOTAL (for 9 wkts dec)	505	(for 5 wkts dec)	239

ENGLAND

G.A.Gooch *	c Moin Khan b Waqar Younis	78
A.J.Stewart	c Inzamam-ul-Haq b Wasim Akram	15
M.A.Atherton	c Moin Khan b Wasim Akram	0
R.A.Smith	lbw b Aqib Javed	11
D.I.Gower	c Moin Khan b Wasim Akram	73
G.A.Hick	b Aqib Javed	22
C.C.Lewis	c Moin Khan b Wasim Akram	55
R.C.Russell +	c Aamir Sohail b Aqib Javed	4
I.D.K.Salisbury	c Aamir Sohail b Wasim Akram	50
T.A.Munton	not out	25
D.E.Malcolm	b Aqib Javed	4
	Extras (b 8,lb 8,w 2,nb 35)	53
	TOTAL	390

ENGLAND	O	M	R	W		O	M	R	W
Malcolm	31	3	117	3		12	2	57	0
Lewis	24	5	90	2		17	5	46	3
Munton	30	6	112	1		17	6	26	0
Salisbury	20	0	117	0		13	0	67	0
Gooch	18	2	39	3		16	5	30	2
Hick	3	0	17	0		2	2	0	0

PAKISTAN	O	M	R	W		O	M	R	W
Wasim Akram	36	4	128	5					
Waqar Younis	32	6	96	1					
Aqib Javed	21.4	1	100	4					
Asif Mujtaba	1	1	0	0					
Mushtaq Ahmed	10	1	50	0					

FALL OF WICKETS	1st	2nd	3rd	4th	5th	6th	7th	8th	9th	10th
PAK	115	241	378	428	432	492	497	497	505	
ENG	41	42	93	186	200	252	256	315	379	390
PAK	1	143	148	195	217					

ENGLAND vs PAKISTAN
at Headingley on 23rd, 24th, 25th, 26th July 1992
England won by 6 wickets

PAKISTAN

Aamir Sohail	c Atherton b Mallender	23	c Stewart b Mallender		1
Ramiz Raja	b Pringle	17	c Atherton b Munton		63
Asif Mujtaba	b Mallender	7	c Hick b Mallender		11
Javed Miandad *	c Smith b Pringle	6	c Stewart b Mallender		4
Salim Malik	not out	82	not out		84
Inzamam-ul-Haq	c Hick b Munton	5	c Smith b Pringle		19
Wasim Akram	run out	12	c Ramprakash b Pringle		17
Moin Khan +	c Hick b Lewis	2	c Hick b Mallender		3
Waqar Younis	c Hick b Mallender	6	(10) b Mallender		3
Mushtaq Ahmed	b Lewis	11	(9) lbw b Pringle		0
Aqib Javed	c Hick b Munton	0	run out		0
	Extras (b 1,lb 2,w 7,nb 16)	26	(b 4,lb 1,w 2,nb 9)		16
	TOTAL	197			221

ENGLAND

G.A.Gooch *	b Mushtaq Ahmed	135	c Asif Mujtaba b Mushtaq Ahmed		37
M.A.Atherton	b Wasim Akram	76	lbw b Waqar Younis		5
R.A.Smith	c Javed Miandad b Aqib Javed	42	c sub b Waqar Younis		0
A.J.Stewart +	lbw b Waqar Younis	8	(5) c Moin Khan b Mushtaq Ahmed		2
D.I.Gower	not out	18	(4) not out		31
M.R.Ramprakash	lbw b Mushtaq Ahmed	0	not out		12
G.A.Hick	b Wasim Akram	1			
C.C.Lewis	lbw b Waqar Younis	0			
D.R.Pringle	b Wasim Akram	0			
N.A.Mallender	b Waqar Younis	1			
T.A.Munton	c Inzamam-ul-Haq b Mushtaq Ahmed	0			
	Extras (b 1,lb 14,w 1,nb 23)	39	(b 5,lb 3,nb 4)		12
	TOTAL	320	(for 4 wkts)		99

ENGLAND	O	M	R	W		O	M	R	W
Lewis	23	6	48	2		16	3	55	0
Mallender	23	7	72	3		23	7	50	5
Pringle	17	6	41	2		19	2	66	3
Munton	10.3	3	22	2		10	0	40	1
Gooch	6	3	11	0		1	0	5	0

PAKISTAN	O	M	R	W		O	M	R	W
Wasim Akram	36	12	80	1		17	4	36	0
Aqib Javed	16	3	48	1					
Waqar Younis	30	3	117	5		12	2	28	2
Mushtaq Ahmed	29.5	6	60	3		13.4	3	27	2
Aamir Sohail	2	2	0	0					

FALL OF WICKETS	1st	2nd	3rd	4th	5th	6th	7th	8th	9th	10th
PAK	34	54	60	68	80	111	117	128	192	197
ENG	168	270	292	298	298	303	305	305	313	320
PAK	11	53	64	96	147	177	205	206	213	221
ENG	27	27	61	65						

ENGLAND vs PAKISTAN
at The Oval on 6th, 7th, 8th, 9th August 1992
Pakistan won by 10 wickets

ENGLAND

G.A.Gooch *	c Asif Mujtaba b Aqib Javed	20	c Aamir Sohail b Waqar Younis		24
A.J.Stewart +	c Ramiz Raja b Wasim Akram	31	lbw b Waqar Younis		8
M.A.Atherton	c Rashid Latif b Waqar Younis	60	c Rashid Latif b Waqar Younis		4
R.A.Smith	b Mushtaq Ahmed	33	not out		84
D.I.Gower	b Aqib Javed	27	b Waqar Younis		1
M.R.Ramprakash	lbw b Wasim Akram	2	c Asif Mujtaba b Mushtaq Ahmed		17
C.C.Lewis	lbw b Wasim Akram	4	st Rashid Latif b Mushtaq Ahmed		14
D.R.Pringle	b Wasim Akram	1	b Wasim Akram		1
N.A.Mallender	b Wasim Akram	4	c Mushtaq Ahmed b Wasim Akram		3
P.C.R.Tufnell	not out	0	b Wasim Akram		0
D.E.Malcolm	b Wasim Akram	2	b Waqar Younis		0
	Extras (b 4,lb 8,w 1,nb 10)	23	(b 1,lb 8,nb 9)		18
	TOTAL	207			174

PAKISTAN

Aamir Sohail	c Stewart b Malcolm	49	not out		4
Ramiz Raja	b Malcolm	19	not out		0
Shoaib Mohammad	c & b Tufnell	55			
Javed Miandad *	c & b Lewis	59			
Salim Malik	b Malcolm	40			
Asif Mujtaba	run out	50			
Wasim Akram	c Stewart b Malcolm	7			
Rashid Latif +	c Smith b Mallender	50			
Waqar Younis	c Gooch b Malcolm	6			
Mushtaq Ahmed	c Lewis b Mallender	9			
Aqib Javed	not out	0			
	Extras (b 2,lb 6,w 4,nb 24)	36	(w 1)		1
	TOTAL	380	(for 0 wkts)		5

PAKISTAN	O	M	R	W		O	M	R	W
Wasim Akram	22.1	3	67	6		21	6	36	3
Waqar Younis	16	4	37	1		18	5	52	5
Aqib Javed	16	6	44	2		9	2	25	0
Mushtaq Ahmed	24	7	47	1		23	6	46	2
Aamir Sohail						1	0	6	0

ENGLAND	O	M	R	W		O	M	R	W
Mallender	28.5	6	93	2					
Malcolm	29	6	94	5					
Lewis	30	8	70	1					
Tufnell	34	9	87	1					
Pringle	6	0	28	0					
Ramprakash						0.1	0	5	0

FALL OF WICKETS	1st	2nd	3rd	4th	5th	6th	7th	8th	9th	10th
ENG	39	57	138	182	190	196	199	203	205	207
PAK	64	86	197	214	278	292	332	342	359	380
ENG	29	47	55	59	92	153	159	173	173	174
PAK										

NEW ZEALAND vs PAKISTAN
at Hamilton on 2nd, 3rd, 4th, 5th January 1993
Pakistan won by 33 runs

PAKISTAN

Ramiz Raja	c Rutherford b Su'a	4	(2) c Parore b Morrison		8
Aamir Sohail	c Owens b Morrison	0	(1) b Morrison		0
Asif Mujtaba	c Owens b Su'a	0	lbw b Morrison		11
Javed Miandad *	b Su'a	92	lbw b Su'a		12
Salim Malik	c Parore b Morrison	14	c Su'a b Morrison		0
Inzamam-ul-Haq	c Morrison b Su'a	23	lbw b Owens		75
Wasim Akram	c Greatbatch b Patel	27	b Patel		15
Rashid Latif +	not out	32	(7) c Rutherford b Su'a		33
Waqar Younis	run out	13	not out		4
Mushtaq Ahmed	lbw b Su'a	2	c Rutherford b Morrison		10
Aqib Javed	c Greatbatch b Morrison	1	c Hartland b Patel		2
	Extras (w 4,nb 4)	8	(lb 2,nb 2)		4
	TOTAL	216			174

NEW ZEALAND

M.J.Greatbatch	lbw b Waqar Younis	133	(2) c Aamir Sohail b Wasim Akram		8
B.R.Hartland	st Rashid Latif b Mushtaq Ahmed	43	(1) b Wasim Akram		9
A.H.Jones *	lbw b Wasim Akram	2	c Asif Mujtaba b Waqar Younis		19
R.T.Latham	lbw b Wasim Akram	2	(6) b Waqar Younis		0
K.R.Rutherford	c Rashid Latif b Mushtaq Ahmed	14	(7) c Aamir Sohail b Wasim Akram		9
C.Z.Harris	lbw b Waqar Younis	6	(8) b Waqar Younis		9
D.N.Patel	lbw b Mushtaq Ahmed	12	(9) b Waqar Younis		4
A.C.Parore +	lbw b Wasim Akram	16	(5) c Rashid Latif b Wasim Akram		13
M.L.Su'a	c Rashid Latif b Waqar Younis	0	(10) lbw b Waqar Younis		0
D.K.Morrison	not out	3	(4) lbw b Wasim Akram		0
M.B.Owens	b Waqar Younis	0	not out		0
	Extras (b 1,lb 15,w 1,nb 16)	33	(b 1,lb 11,nb 10)		22
	TOTAL	264			93

NEW ZEALAND	O	M	R	W		O	M	R	W
Morrison	19.3	4	42	3		15	2	41	5
Su'a	24	2	73	5		13	1	47	2
Owens	12	3	48	0		7	0	19	1
Patel	14	2	53	1		20.1	5	65	2

PAKISTAN	O	M	R	W		O	M	R	W
Wasim Akram	31	9	66	3		22	4	45	5
Waqar Younis	28	11	59	4		13.3	4	22	5
Mushtaq Ahmed	38	10	87	3					
Aqib Javed	7	2	24	0		8	2	14	0
Aamir Sohail	5	2	12	0					

FALL OF WICKETS	1st	2nd	3rd	4th	5th	6th	7th	8th	9th	10th
PAK	4	4	12	45	87	158	176	202	208	216
NZ	108	111	117	147	164	193	254	256	257	264
PAK	0	20	25	25	39	119	158	158	171	174
NZ	19	31	32	65	67	71	88	88	88	93

WEST INDIES vs PAKISTAN
at Queen's Park Oval, Port of Spain on 16th, 17th, 18th April 1993
West Indies won by 204 runs

WEST INDIES

D.L.Haynes	c Moin Khan b Ata-ur-Rehman	31	not out		143
P.V.Simmons	c Moin Khan b Ata-ur-Rehman	27	c Asif Mujtaba b Aamir Sohail		22
R.B.Richardson *	b Mushtaq Ahmed	7	c Wasim Akram b Waqar Younis		68
B.C.Lara	c Aamir Sohail b Waqar Younis	6	b Asif Mujtaba		96
K.L.T.Arthurton	run out	3	(6) lbw b Wasim Akram		1
C.L.Hooper	lbw b Waqar Younis	9	(7) lbw b Waqar Younis		0
J.R.Murray +	lbw b Waqar Younis	0	(8) lbw b Waqar Younis		0
I.R.Bishop	c Inzamam-ul-Haq b Ata-ur-Rehman	4	(5) c Moin Khan b Wasim Akram		3
C.E.L.Ambrose	lbw b Wasim Akram	4	lbw b Wasim Akram		5
A.C.Cummins	not out	14	lbw b Wasim Akram		6
C.A.Walsh	b Wasim Akram	0	run out		0
	Extras (b 6,lb 3,w 2,nb 11)	22	(b 1,lb 18,w 2,nb 17)		38
	TOTAL	127			382

PAKISTAN

Aamir Sohail	c Hooper b Bishop	55	lbw b Walsh		15
Ramiz Raja	lbw b Bishop	9	lbw b Ambrose		11
Inzamam-ul-Haq	lbw b Walsh	10	lbw b Walsh		6
Javed Miandad	lbw b Ambrose	20	c Murray b Bishop		4
Basit Ali	lbw b Bishop	0	c Richardson b Hooper		37
Asif Mujtaba	c Lara b Bishop	10	lbw b Hooper		20
Wasim Akram *	c Richardson b Ambrose	2	st Murray b Hooper		4
Moin Khan +	c Murray b Ambrose	0	c Bishop b Hooper		18
Waqar Younis	c Lara b Ambrose	16	lbw b Walsh		1
Mushtaq Ahmed	c Hooper b Bishop	3	not out		12
Ata-ur-Rehman	not out	3	c Ambrose b Hooper		19
	Extras (lb 6,nb 6)	12	(lb 10,nb 8)		18
	TOTAL	140			165

PAKISTAN	O	M	R	W		O	M	R	W
Wasim Akram	10.2	2	32	2		27	6	75	4
Waqar Younis	11	3	37	3		23	2	88	3
Ata-ur-Rehman	9	1	28	3		19	0	82	0
Mushtaq Ahmed	8	1	21	1		13	1	45	0
Aamir Sohail						5	1	30	1
Asif Mujtaba						10	1	43	1

WEST INDIES	O	M	R	W		O	M	R	W
Ambrose	17	6	34	4		13	3	37	1
Bishop	15.5	6	43	5		11	2	28	1
Walsh	7	4	13	1		12	3	29	3
Cummins	5	0	19	0		5	1	16	0
Hooper	4	0	25	0		11.5	3	40	5
Simmons						1	0	5	0

FALL OF WICKETS	1st	2nd	3rd	4th	5th	6th	7th	8th	9th	10th
WI	63	76	85	85	95	95	102	102	127	127
PAK	17	52	100	100	102	104	108	120	136	140
WI	57	160	329	342	356	358	358	371	371	382
PAK	17	35	41	42	109	111	114	127	134	165

WEST INDIES vs PAKISTAN

at Kensington Oval, Bridgetown on 23rd, 24th, 25th, 27th April 1993
West Indies won by 10 wickets

WEST INDIES

D.L.Haynes	b Aamir Nazir	125	not out	16
P.V.Simmons	c Moin Khan b Ata-ur-Rehman	87	not out	8
R.B.Richardson *	lbw b Waqar Younis	31		
B.C.Lara	c Moin Khan b Ata-ur-Rehman	51		
K.L.T.Arthurton	b Wasim Akram	56		
C.L.Hooper	c Moin Khan b Waqar Younis	15		
J.R.Murray +	st Moin Khan b Aamir Sohail	35		
I.R.Bishop	c Moin Khan b Aamir Nazir	11		
C.E.L.Ambrose	not out	12		
W.K.M.Benjamin	b Waqar Younis	0		
C.A.Walsh	c & b Waqar Younis	3		
	Extras (b 1,lb 1,nb 27)	29	(w 3,nb 2)	5
	TOTAL	455	(for 0 wkts)	29

PAKISTAN

Aamir Sohail	c Murray b Ambrose	10	c Benjamin b Ambrose	4
Ramiz Raja	c Haynes b Ambrose	37	c Haynes b Ambrose	25
Asif Mujtaba	c Richardson b Walsh	13	lbw b Benjamin	41
Javed Miandad	c Richardson b Benjamin	22	c Arthurton b Hooper	43
Inzamam-ul-Haq	lbw b Bishop	7	(7) lbw b Benjamin	26
Basit Ali	not out	92	lbw b Walsh	37
Wasim Akram *	c Simmons b Hooper	29	(8) b Benjamin	0
Moin Khan +	c Murray b Walsh	0	(5) c Murray b Hooper	17
Waqar Younis	c Murray b Walsh	0	c Lara b Hooper	29
Ata-ur-Rehman	c Benjamin b Walsh	0	c Simmons b Walsh	13
Aamir Nazir	c Arthurton b Benjamin	1	not out	6
	Extras (lb 3,nb 7)	10	(b 12,lb 5,nb 4)	21
	TOTAL	221		262

PAKISTAN

	O	M	R	W	O	M	R	W
Wasim Akram	32	2	95	1	2.3	0	18	0
Waqar Younis	25.5	2	132	4				
Aamir Nazir	20	1	79	2	2	0	11	0
Ata-ur-Rehman	21	1	103	2				
Asif Mujtaba	3	0	30	0				
Aamir Sohail	4	1	14	1				

WEST INDIES

	O	M	R	W	O	M	R	W
Ambrose	16	5	42	2	26	10	55	1
Bishop	16	5	43	1	4	1	13	0
Walsh	18	2	56	4	24	7	51	3
Benjamin	19	5	55	2	17	7	30	3
Hooper	7	0	22	1	32.3	6	96	3

FALL OF WICKETS

	1st	2nd	3rd	4th	5th	6th	7th	8th	9th	10th
WI	122	200	303	337	363	426	440	440	445	455
PAK	12	31	62	79	109	189	190	190	200	221
PAK	4	47	113	133	141	207	207	215	238	262
WI										

WEST INDIES vs PAKISTAN

at Antigua Recreation Ground, St John's on 1st, 2nd, 4th, 5th, 6th May 1993
Match drawn

WEST INDIES

D.L.Haynes	c Rashid Latif b Nadim Khan	23	not out	64
P.V.Simmons	c Wasim Akram b Ata-ur-Rehman	28	b Waqar Younis	17
R.B.Richardson *	c Wasim Akram b Waqar Younis	52	lbw b Waqar Younis	0
B.C.Lara	st Rashid Latif b Nadim Khan	44	lbw b Waqar Younis	19
K.L.T.Arthurton	lbw b Waqar Younis	30	lbw b Waqar Younis	0
C.L.Hooper	not out	178	not out	29
J.R.Murray +	lbw b Waqar Younis	1		
C.E.L.Ambrose	lbw b Wasim Akram	1		
A.C.Cummins	lbw b Waqar Younis	14		
W.K.M.Benjamin	c Wasim Akram b Waqar Younis	12		
C.A.Walsh	c Asif Mujtaba b Wasim Akram	30		
	Extras (lb 5,nb 17)	22	(b 11,lb 5,nb 8)	24
	TOTAL	438	(for 4 wkts)	153

PAKISTAN

Shakeel Ahmed	lbw b Ambrose	0
Ramiz Raja	c Murray b Walsh	0
Asif Mujtaba	c Haynes b Hooper	59
Javed Miandad	lbw b Benjamin	31
Basit Ali	b Cummins	56
Inzamam-ul-Haq	c Haynes b Cummins	123
Rashid Latif +	lbw b Cummins	4
Wasim Akram *	c Hooper b Benjamin	6
Waqar Younis	c Hooper b Benjamin	4
Nadim Khan	c Murray b Cummins	25
Ata-ur-Rehman	not out	1
	Extras (lb 6,nb 11)	17
	TOTAL	326

PAKISTAN

	O	M	R	W	O	M	R	W
Wasim Akram	26.2	5	108	2	10	2	30	0
Waqar Younis	28	4	105	5	11	1	23	4
Ata-ur-Rehman	17	1	66	1	9	1	21	0
Nadim Khan	38	5	147	2	14	0	48	0
Asif Mujtaba	1	0	7	0	4	1	9	0
Basit Ali					1	0	6	0

WEST INDIES

	O	M	R	W	O	M	R	W
Ambrose	23	9	40	1				
Walsh	19	3	58	1				
Benjamin	20	4	53	3				
Cummins	20	4	54	4				
Hooper	28	2	98	1				
Simmons	5	0	17	0				

FALL OF WICKETS

	1st	2nd	3rd	4th	5th	6th	7th	8th	9th	10th
WI	35	77	153	159	218	241	252	312	332	438
PAK	0	4	85	108	196	206	221	227	323	326
WI	36	36	68	68						

PAKISTAN vs ZIMBABWE

at Defence Cricket Club, Karachi on 1st, 2nd, 3rd, 5th, 6th December 1993
Pakistan won by 131 runs

PAKISTAN

Aamir Sohail	b Peall	63	run out	29
Shoaib Mohammad	c Flower A. b Rennie	81		
Inzamam-ul-Haq	c Flower A. b Brandes	21	(2) not out	57
Javed Miandad	lbw b Brandes	70	run out	12
Basit Ali	c Flower A. b Whittal	36	(3) c & b Brandes	13
Asif Mujtaba	c Dekker b Brandes	4	(5) not out	10
Rashid Latif +	not out	68		
Waqar Younis *	c Peall b Flower G.W.	13		
Mushtaq Ahmed	c Flower A. b Peall	18		
Tauseef Ahmed	run out	21		
Ata-ur-Rehman				
	Extras (b 15,lb 12,nb 1)	28	(b 6,lb 2,w 1,nb 1)	10
	TOTAL (for 8 wkts dec)	423	(for 3 wkts dec) 131	

ZIMBABWE

G.W.Flower	b Waqar Younis	24	b Ata-ur-Rehman	25
M.H.Dekker	lbw b Waqar Younis	5	lbw b Waqar Younis	0
A.D.R.Campbell	lbw b Mushtaq Ahmed	53	c Inzamam-ul-Haq b Mushtaq Ahmed	8
D.L.Houghton	lbw b Waqar Younis	46	lbw b Waqar Younis	18
A.Flower * +	lbw b Ata-ur-Rehman	63	c Inzamam-ul-Haq b Mushtaq Ahmed	21
G.J.Whittal	run out	33	b Ata-ur-Rehman	2
G.Bruk-Jackson	b Waqar Younis	31	lbw b Waqar Younis	4
S.G.Peall	c Aamir Sohail b Waqar Younis	1	b Waqar Younis	0
H.H.Streak	b Waqar Younis	0	not out	19
E.A.Brandes	not out	0	b Waqar Younis	17
J.A.Rennie	lbw b Waqar Younis	3	lbw b Waqar Younis	0
	Extras (b 5,lb 24,w 1,nb 1)	31	(b 12,lb 5,nb 3)	20
	TOTAL	289		134

ZIMBABWE

	O	M	R	W	O	M	R	W
Brandes	35	4	106	3	13	0	59	1
Streak	29	6	77	0	10	1	40	0
Rennie	32	6	90	1	3	0	24	0
Whittal	12	4	26	1				
Peall	41	10	89	2				
Flower G.W.	6	2	8	1				

PAKISTAN

	O	M	R	W	O	M	R	W
Waqar Younis	34.1	8	91	7	21.5	7	44	6
Ata-ur-Rehman	15	5	28	1	16	6	20	2
Mushtaq Ahmed	39	11	89	1	17	7	24	2
Tauseef Ahmed	23	7	49	0	6	2	13	0
Shoaib Mohammad	1	0	1	0				
Aamir Sohail	1	0	1	0	2	0	16	0
Asif Mujtaba	3	2	1	0				

FALL OF WICKETS

	1st	2nd	3rd	4th	5th	6th	7th	8th	9th	10th
PAK	95	134	217	268	280	305	332	363		
ZIM	16	71	132	153	230	280	284	284	285	289
PAK	47	76	108							
ZIM	1	17	61	63	65	78	80	92	130	134

PAKISTAN vs ZIMBABWE

at Rawalpindi on 9th, 10th, 11th, 13th, 14th December 1993
Pakistan won by 52 runs

PAKISTAN

Aamir Sohail	c Houghton b Streak	8	lbw b Streak	9
Shoaib Mohammad	lbw b Brain	18	c Flower A. b Streak	13
Inzamam-ul-Haq	b Brain	38	b Brandes	14
Javed Miandad	b Streak	20	(5) b Streak	10
Basit Ali	c Streak b Brandes	25	(6) lbw b Brandes	40
Asif Mujtaba	not out	54	(7) c Flower A. b Brain	51
Rashid Latif +	lbw b Brain	33	(8) c Houghton b Streak	61
Wasim Akram *	c Campbell b Brandes	11	(9) lbw b Brandes	15
Waqar Younis	lbw b Brandes	1	(10) c Campbell b Streak	17
Ata-ur-Rehman	lbw b Brain	10	(4) lbw b Brain	0
Ashfaq Ahmed	c Flower A. b Streak	0	not out	1
	Extras (b 4,lb 12,w 2,nb 3)	21	(b 1,lb 11,w 3,nb 2)	17
	TOTAL	245		248

ZIMBABWE

G.W.Flower	c Inzamam-ul-Haq b Wasim Akram	0	b Wasim Akram	0
M.H.Dekker	c Inzamam-ul-Haq b Waqar Younis	68	not out	68
A.D.R.Campbell	lbw b Ata-ur-Rehman	63	c Aamir Sohail b Ata-ur-Rehman	75
D.L.Houghton	c Asif Mujtaba b Ashfaq Ahmed	5	lbw b Waqar Younis	4
A.Flower * +	c Wasim Akram b Waqar Younis	12	c Rashid Latif b Waqar Younis	0
G.J.Whittal	c Inzamam-ul-Haq b Ashfaq Ahmed	29	lbw b Wasim Akram	0
H.H.Streak	c Inzamam-ul-Haq b Waqar Younis	2	(8) b Waqar Younis	0
G.Bruk-Jackson	c Aamir Sohail b Waqar Younis	0	(7) c Rashid Latif b Wasim Akram	4
D.H.Brain	c Ata-ur-Rehman b Waqar Younis	16	b Waqar Younis	2
E.A.Brandes	c Basit Ali b Wasim Akram	18	lbw b Wasim Akram	1
S.G.Peall	not out	11	c Inzamam-ul-Haq b Wasim Akram	10
	Extras (b 9,lb 10,w 1,nb 10)	30	(b 1,lb 11,w 1,nb 10)	23
	TOTAL	254		187

ZIMBABWE

	O	M	R	W	O	M	R	W
Brandes	32	5	82	3	31	9	71	3
Brain	32	9	41	4	34	6	73	2
Streak	23.2	5	58	3	20.3	3	56	5
Whittal	17	6	39	0	4	1	10	0
Peall	6	3	9	0	8	4	13	0
Flower G.W.					4	0	13	0

PAKISTAN

	O	M	R	W	O	M	R	W
Wasim Akram	21	4	68	2	23.2	3	65	5
Waqar Younis	19	3	88	5	21	4	50	4
Ata-ur-Rehman	14	4	40	1	8	1	22	1
Ashfaq Ahmed	17	8	31	2	6	1	22	0
Aamir Sohail	3	0	8	0				
Shoaib Mohammad					4	1	16	0

FALL OF WICKETS

	1st	2nd	3rd	4th	5th	6th	7th	8th	9th	10th
PAK	29	33	99	101	131	187	209	225	241	245
ZIM	0	102	110	126	131	203	203	204	225	254
PAK	25	38	39	54	58	132	209	219	240	248
ZIM	0	135	140	144	147	152	153	164	168	187

PAKISTAN vs ZIMBABWE
at Lahore on 16th, 17th, 18th, 20th, 21st December 1993
Match drawn

PAKISTAN

Aamir Sohail	c Campbell b Brain	2	c James b Brain	32
Shoaib Mohammad	c Brandes b Rennie	14	not out	53
Inzamam-ul-Haq	b Brandes	33		
Javed Miandad	lbw b Brain	31		
Basit Ali	b Brain	29		
Asif Mujtaba	c James b Brain	0	(3) not out	65
Rashid Latif +	c Houghton b Brandes	7		
Wasim Akram *	not out	16		
Waqar Younis	b Brain	0		
Mushtaq Ahmed	b Brandes	1		
Ata-ur-Rehman	c James b Rennie	0		
Extras	(b 4,lb 6,nb 4)	14	(b 7,lb 13,w 1,nb 3)	24
TOTAL		147	(for 1 wkt)	174

ZIMBABWE

G.W.Flower	c Rashid Latif b Ata-ur-Rehman	30
M.H.Dekker	c Rashid Latif b Wasim Akram	2
A.D.R.Campbell	c Rashid Latif b Waqar Younis	6
D.L.Houghton	c Rashid Latif b Waqar Younis	50
A.Flower *	not out	62
G.J.Whittal	c Asif Mujtaba b Wasim Akram	2
W.R.James +	c Shoaib Mohammad b Waqar Younis	8
H.H.Streak	b Waqar Younis	0
D.H.Brain	c Aamir Sohail b Wasim Akram	28
E.A.Brandes	lbw b Wasim Akram	9
J.A.Rennie	c Rashid Latif b Waqar Younis	2
Extras	(b 10,lb 13,w 1,nb 7)	31
TOTAL		230

ZIMBABWE

	O	M	R	W		O	M	R	W
Brandes	14	3	45	3		16	5	31	0
Brain	15	3	42	5		14	6	28	1
Streak	12	3	28	0		16	4	25	0
Rennie	10.4	3	22	2		14	6	35	0
Flower G.W.						10	2	15	0
Whittal						10.5	4	17	0
Campbell						1	0	3	0
Flower A.						0.1	0	0	0

PAKISTAN

	O	M	R	W		O	M	R	W
Wasim Akram	32	7	70	4					
Waqar Younis	34.4	9	100	5					
Ata-ur-Rehman	13	6	24	1					
Mushtaq Ahmed	5	1	13	0					

FALL OF WICKETS	1st	2nd	3rd	4th	5th	6th	7th	8th	9th	10th
PAK	3	50	54	107	111	130	1301	135	140	147
ZIM	17	35	88	121	126	141	141	181	215	230
PAK	56									

NEW ZEALAND vs PAKISTAN
at Auckland on 10th, 11th, 12th February 1994
Pakistan won by 5 wickets

NEW ZEALAND

B.A.Young	c Rashid Latif b Waqar Younis	29	c Rashid Latif b Wasim Akram	0
B.A.Pocock	c Rashid Latif b Wasim Akram	0	c Asif Mujtaba b Wasim Akram	10
A.H.Jones	c Rashid Latif b Mushtaq Ahmed	66	c Rashid Latif b Wasim Akram	6
K.R.Rutherford *	b Waqar Younis	14	b Waqar Younis	18
M.J.Greatbatch	c Salim Malik b Mushtaq Ahmed	48	c Inzamam-ul-Haq b Wasim Akram	0
S.A.Thomson	c Rashid Latif b Waqar Younis	29	c Rashid Latif b Waqar Younis	0
C.L.Cairns	c Salim Malik b Mushtaq Ahmed	6	c Asif Mujtaba b Ata-ur-Rehman	31
T.E.Blain +	c Mushtaq Ahmed b Wasim Akram	26	c Rashid Latif b Ata-ur-Rehman	4
S.B.Doull	c & b Waqar Younis	2	c Salim Malik b Wasim Akram	29
R.P.de Groen	c Mushtaq Ahmed b Wasim Akram	2	not out	0
M.B.Owens	not out	2	c Rashid Latif b Wasim Akram	0
Extras	(b 4,lb 8,w 1,nb 7)	20	(b 4,lb 5,nb 3)	12
TOTAL		242		110

PAKISTAN

Saeed Anwar	c Blain b Cairns	16	c Young b de Groen	7
Aamir Sohail	c Jones b de Groen	16	c Young b Thomson	78
Asif Mujtaba	c Blain b Doull	8	c & b Doull	0
Mushtaq Ahmed	c Young b Doull	0		
Salim Malik *	c Young b Doull	18	(4) c Young b de Groen	11
Basit Ali	b Cairns	25	(5) c & b Doull	7
Inzamam-ul-Haq	c Young b de Groen	43	(6) not out	20
Rashid Latif +	lbw b Doull	30	(7) not out	13
Wasim Akram	c Blain b de Groen	35		
Waqar Younis	c Cairns b Doull	11		
Ata-ur-Rehman	not out	2		
Extras	(lb 6,nb 5)	11	(lb 3,nb 2)	5
TOTAL		215	(for 5 wkts)	141

PAKISTAN

	O	M	R	W		O	M	R	W
Wasim Akram	22.3	9	50	3		16.1	4	43	6
Waqar Younis	15	2	46	4		10	3	35	2
Ata-ur-Rehman	14	3	55	0		6	1	23	2
Mushtaq Ahmed	17	1	79	3					

NEW ZEALAND

	O	M	R	W		O	M	R	W
Cairns	18	2	75	2		6	1	15	0
Owens	7	1	28	0		2	0	10	0
Doull	15	2	66	5		16	0	48	2
de Groen	17.4	5	40	3		13	3	48	2
Thomson						4	1	17	1

FALL OF WICKETS	1st	2nd	3rd	4th	5th	6th	7th	8th	9th	10th
NZ	3	67	95	170	175	185	228	228	233	242
PAK	17	36	48	50	87	93	141	176	207	215
NZ	0	8	31	35	40	44	67	103	110	110
PAK	21	25	56	73	119					

NEW ZEALAND vs PAKISTAN
at Wellington on 17th, 18th, 19th, 20th February 1994
Pakistan won by an innings and 12 runs

NEW ZEALAND

B.A.Young	lbw b Wasim Akram	0	(2) b Wasim Akram	4
B.A.Pocock	b Ata-ur-Rehman	16	(1) b Waqar Younis	0
A.H.Jones	lbw b Ata-ur-Rehman	43	b Wasim Akram	76
K.R.Rutherford *	c Akram Raza b Ata-ur-Rehman	7	c Akram Raza b Ata-ur-Rehman	63
M.J.Greatbatch	c Rashid Latif b Waqar Younis	45	c Rashid Latif b Wasim Akram	10
S.A.Thomson	b Wasim Akram	7	c Ata-ur-Rehman b Wasim Akram	47
T.E.Blain +	c Saeed Anwar b Waqar Younis	8	c Basit Ali b Wasim Akram	78
M.N.Hart	not out	12	b Wasim Akram	7
D.K.Morrison	c Rashid Latif b Wasim Akram	5	(10) lbw b Waqar Younis	42
S.B.Doull	c Basit Ali b Waqar Younis	17	(9) c Salim Malik b Wasim Akram	15
R.P.de Groen	b Wasim Akram	4	not out	1
Extras	(lb 7,nb 4)	11	(b 1,lb 5,nb 12)	18
TOTAL		175		361

PAKISTAN

Saeed Anwar	run out	169
Aamir Sohail	lbw b Morrison	2
Akram Raza	c Blain b Morrison	0
Basit Ali	b Thomson	85
Salim Malik *	c & b Hart	140
Inzamam-ul-Haq	not out	135
Asif Mujtaba		
Rashid Latif +		
Wasim Akram		
Waqar Younis		
Ata-ur-Rehman		
Extras	(b 5,lb 6,nb 6)	17
TOTAL	(for 5 wkts dec)	548

PAKISTAN

	O	M	R	W		O	M	R	W
Wasim Akram	24	10	60	4		37	7	119	7
Waqar Younis	22	5	51	3		25.2	4	111	2
Ata-ur-Rehman	15	4	50	3		18	1	86	1
Akram Raza	6	4	7	0		12	4	25	0
Aamir Sohail						1	0	1	0
Salim Malik						2	0	13	0

NEW ZEALAND

	O	M	R	W		O	M	R	W
Morrison	31	4	139	2					
de Groen	31	8	104	0					
Doull	27	6	112	0					
Hart	31.2	9	102	1					
Thomson	17	3	80	1					

FALL OF WICKETS	1st	2nd	3rd	4th	5th	6th	7th	8th	9th	10th
NZ	0	40	49	100	126	128	140	149	170	175
PAK	34	36	223	290	548					
NZ	3	6	120	143	209	216	244	276	350	361

NEW ZEALAND vs PAKISTAN
at Christchurch on 24th, 25th, 26th, 27th, 28th February 1994
New Zealand won by 5 wickets

PAKISTAN

Saeed Anwar	c Young b Doull	69	c Blain b Morrison	0
Aamir Sohail	c Hartland b Doull	60	c Young b Doull	3
Atif Rauf	c Greatbatch b Morrison	16	c Young b Doull	9
Salim Malik *	b Hart	18	(5) c Pringle b Morrison	23
Basit Ali	c Hartland b Pringle	103	(6) run out	67
Inzamam-ul-Haq	c Greatbatch b Doull	5	(7) c sub b Morrison	20
Rashid Latif +	c Hartland b Thomson	27	(8) c & b Hart	3
Wasim Akram	c Greatbatch b Morrison	5	(9) b Hart	17
Akram Raza	not out	29	st Blain b Hart	26
Waqar Younis	c Doull b Morrison	2	c Blain b Morrison	10
Aamir Nazir	b Morrison	0	not out	0
Extras	(lb 6,w 1,nb 3)	10	(nb 1)	1
TOTAL		344		179

NEW ZEALAND

B.R.Hartland	c Basit Ali b Waqar Younis	3	(2) c Inzamam-ul-Haq b Wasim Akram	10
B.A.Young	lbw b Aamir Nazir	38	(1) b Wasim Akram	120
A.H.Jones	run out	81	run out	26
K.R.Rutherford *	c Inzamam-ui-Haq b Waqar Younis	7	lbw b Wasim Akram	13
M.J.Greatbatch	lbw b Wasim Akram	1	c Inzamam-ul-Haq b Waqar Younis	1
S.A.Thomson	c Rashid Latif b Waqar Younis	3	not out	120
T.E.Blain +	lbw b Waqar Younis	0	not out	11
M.N.Hart	lbw b Wasim Akram	6		
S.B.Doull	lbw b Waqar Younis	17		
D.K.Morrison	not out	6		
C.Pringle	b Waqar Younis	0		
Extras	(b 5,lb 9,nb 24)	38	(lb 5,nb 18)	23
TOTAL		200	(for 5 wkts)	324

NEW ZEALAND

	O	M	R	W		O	M	R	W
Morrison	24	3	105	4		21.3	5	66	4
Doull	25	3	93	3		5	0	13	2
Pringle	33	6	83	1		17	3	41	0
Hart	9	2	37	1		18	5	47	3
Thomson	6	0	20	1		4	0	12	0

PAKISTAN

	O	M	R	W		O	M	R	W
Wasim Akram	22	5	54	2		38	6	105	3
Waqar Younis	19	1	78	6		27	6	84	1
Aamir Nazir	15	2	54	1		16	0	59	0
Akram Raza						19	5	49	0
Aamir Sohail						2	1	5	0
Salim Malik						4	1	13	0
Saeed Anwar						1	0	4	0

FALL OF WICKETS	1st	2nd	3rd	4th	5th	6th	7th	8th	9th	10th
PAK	125	147	159	195	206	254	261	339	344	344
NZ	12	109	134	139	147	147	171	186	198	200
PAK	0	4	26	53	77	133	152	154	171	179
NZ	22	76	119	133	287					

SRI LANKA vs PAKISTAN
at Colombo on 9th, 10th, 11th, 13th August 1994
Pakistan won by 301 runs

PAKISTAN

Saeed Anwar	c Jayasuriya b Warnaweera	94	c Dassanayake b Warnaweera	136
Aamir Sohail	b Dharmasena	41	c Jayasuriya b Dharmasena	65
Asif Mujtaba	c Dassanayake b Dharmasena	44	c Dassanayake b Warnaweera	31
Salim Malik *	c Tillekeratne b Dharmasena	1	not out	50
Basit Ali	lbw b Warnaweera	27	b Dharmasena	11
Inzamam-ul-Haq	c Tillekeratne b Dharmasena	81	not out	7
Rashid Latif +	c Dharmasena b Muralitharan	0		
Wasim Akram	c Jayasuriya b Dharmasena	37		
Akram Raza	c Tillekeratne b Warnaweera	25		
Mushtaq Ahmed	not out	5		
Waqar Younis	c Gurusinha b Dharmasena	2		
Extras	(b 11,lb 6,nb 16)	33	(lb 6,nb 12)	18
TOTAL		390	(for 4 wkts dec)	318

SRI LANKA

R.S.Mahanama	b Mushtaq Ahmed	21	c sub b Akram Raza	37
S.T.Jayasuriya	c Aamir Sohail b Wasim Akram	9	c Rashid Latif b Wasim Akram	1
A.P.Gurusinha	c Rashid Latif b Mushtaq Ahmed	11	c Asif Mujtaba b Waqar Younis	8
P.A.de Silva	c Aamir Sohail b Akram Raza	127	c & b Waqar Younis	5
A.Ranatunga *	c & b Mushtaq Ahmed	9	(6) st Rashid Latif b Akram Raza	41
H.P.Tillekeratne	lbw b Waqar Younis	34	(5) c & b Akram Raza	8
P.B.Dassanayake +	c Rashid Latif b Wasim Akram	3	b Wasim Akram	24
H.D.P.K.Dharmasena	c Aamir Sohail b Wasim Akram	1	lbw b Wasim Akram	30
G.P.Wickremasinghe	not out	0	b Wasim Akram	4
M.Muralitharan	c Asif Mujtaba b Akram Raza	0	not out	20
K.P.J.Warnaweera	c & b Akram Raza	4	b Wasim Akram	0
Extras	(b 1,lb 5,nb 1)	7	(lb 2,nb 1)	3
TOTAL		226		181

SRI LANKA

	O	M	R	W		O	M	R	W
Wickremasinghe	12	0	59	0		5	0	25	0
Gurusinha	4	1	24	0					
Dharmasena	45.2	13	99	6		31	2	84	2
Muralitharan	36	6	123	1		11	0	42	0
Warnaweera	28	5	63	3		31	1	108	2
de Silva	1	0	5	0					
Jayasuriya						13	0	53	0

PAKISTAN

	O	M	R	W		O	M	R	W
Wasim Akram	17	4	30	3		18	4	43	5
Waqar Younis	16	1	84	1		7	0	28	2
Mushtaq Ahmed	14	2	57	3		6	1	25	0
Akram Raza	19	7	46	3		16	3	83	3
Aamir Sohail	2	0	3	0					

FALL OF WICKETS	1st	2nd	3rd	4th	5th	6th	7th	8th	9th	10th
PAK	65	180	181	221	247	260	345	354	387	390
SRI	13	41	42	60	179	215	218	222	222	226
PAK	128	202	273	298						
SRI	1	30	38	52	59	118	135	160	18	181

SRI LANKA vs PAKISTAN
at Kandy on 26th, 27th, 28th August 1994
Pakistan won by an innings and 52 runs

SRI LANKA

R.S.Mahanama	c Rashid Latif b Waqar Younis	2	c Inzamam-ul-Haq b Waqar Younis	10
D.P.Samaraweera	c Rashid Latif b Wasim Akram	6	lbw b Waqar Younis	13
S.Ranatunga	c Rashid Latif b Waqar Younis	5	(4) c Wasim Akram b Waqar Younis	4
P.A.de Silva	lbw b Wasim Akram	7	(5) c Rashid Latif b Wasim Akram	5
A.Ranatunga *	c Saeed Anwar b Waqar Younis	0	(6) c Rashid Latif b Waqar Younis	34
H.P.Tillekeratne	b Waqar Younis	9	(7) not out	83
R.S.Kalpage	c Aamir Sohail b Wasim Akram	6	(8) c sub b Kabir Khan	62
P.B.Dassanayake +	not out	19	(3) lbw b Waqar Younis	1
H.D.P.K.Dharmasena	lbw b Waqar Younis	0	c sub b Mushtaq Ahmed	3
U.C.J.Vaas	c Wasim Akram b Waqar Younis	1	lbw b Mushtaq Ahmed	4
K.R.Pushpakumara	c Aamir Sohail b Wasim Akram	6	lbw b Mushtaq Ahmed	0
Extras	(b 1,lb 4,w 5,nb 1)	11	(lb 6,nb 9)	15
TOTAL		71		234

PAKISTAN

Saeed Anwar	lbw b Pushpakumara	31
Aamir Sohail	c Tillekeratne b Pushpakumara	74
Mushtaq Ahmed	run out	0
Asif Mujtaba	c Dassanayake b Pushpakumara	17
Salim Malik *	c Dassanayake b Dharmasena	22
Basit Ali	c & b Dharmasena	53
Inzamam-ul-Haq	not out	100
Rashid Latif +	c Samaraweera b Dharmasena	7
Wasim Akram	c de Silva b Pushpakumara	12
Waqar Younis	c Kalpage b Dharmasena	20
Kabir Khan		
Extras	(b 4,lb 3,w 1,nb 13)	21
TOTAL	(for 9 wkts dec)	357

PAKISTAN

	O	M	R	W		O	M	R	W
Wasim Akram	14.2	4	32	4		26	12	70	1
Waqar Younis	14	4	34	6		18	1	85	5
Kabir Khan						10	1	39	1
Mushtaq Ahmed						7.3	1	34	3

SRI LANKA

	O	M	R	W		O	M	R	W
Vaas	22	2	80	0					
Pushpakumara	26	3	145	4					
Dharmasena	28.5	7	75	4					
Kalpage	11	0	50	0					

FALL OF WICKETS	1st	2nd	3rd	4th	5th	6th	7th	8th	9th	10th
SRI	12	20	22	28	28	43	45	46	46	71
PAK	94	94	117	158	158	256	264	297	357	
SRI	11	13	17	22	42	78	209	221	234	234

PAKISTAN vs AUSTRALIA
at Karachi on 28th, 29th, 30th September, 1st, 2nd October 1994
Pakistan won by 1 wicket

AUSTRALIA

M.J.Slater	lbw b Wasim Akram	36	(2) lbw b Mushtaq Ahmed	23
M.A.Taylor *	c & b Wasim Akram	0	(1) c Rashid Latif b Waqar Younis	0
D.C.Boon	b Mushtaq Ahmed	19	not out	114
M.E.Waugh	c Zahid Fazal b Mushtaq Ahmed	20	b Waqar Younis	61
M.G.Bevan	c Aamir Sohail b Mushtaq Ahmed	82	b Wasim Akram	0
S.R.Waugh	b Waqar Younis	73	lbw b Wasim Akram	0
I.A.Healy +	c Rashid Latif b Waqar Younis	57	c Rashid Latif b Wasim Akram	8
S.K.Warne	c Rashid Latif b Aamir Sohail	22	lbw b Waqar Younis	0
J.Angel	b Wasim Akram	5	c Rashid Latif b Wasim Akram	8
T.B.A.May	not out	1	b Wasim Akram	1
G.D.McGrath	b Wasim Akram	0	b Waqar Younis	1
Extras	(b 2,lb 12,nb 8)	22	(b 7,lb 4,nb 5)	16
TOTAL		337		232

PAKISTAN

Saeed Anwar	c Waugh M.E. b May	85	c & b Angel	77
Aamir Sohail	c Bevan b Warne	36	run out	34
Zahid Fazal	c Boon b May	27	c Boon b Warne	3
Salim Malik *	lbw b Angel	26	c Taylor b Angel	43
Basit Ali	c Bevan b McGrath	0	(6) lbw b Warne	12
Inzamam-ul-Haq	c Taylor b Warne	9	(8) not out	58
Rashid Latif +	c Taylor b Warne	2	(9) lbw b Waugh S.R.	35
Wasim Akram	c Healy b Angel	39	(7) c & b Warne	4
Akram Raza	b McGrath	13	(5) lbw b Warne	2
Waqar Younis	c Healy b Angel	6	c Healy b Warne	7
Mushtaq Ahmed	not out	2	not out	20
Extras	(lb 7,nb 4)	11	(b 4,lb 13,nb 3)	20
TOTAL		256	(for 9 wkts)	315

PAKISTAN

	O	M	R	W		O	M	R	W
Wasim Akram	25	4	75	3		22	3	63	5
Waqar Younis	19.2	2	75	3		18	2	69	4
Mushtaq Ahmed	24	2	97	3		21	3	51	1
Akram Raza	14	1	50	0		10	1	19	0
Aamir Sohail	5	2	19	1		7	0	19	0
Salim Malik	1	0	7	0					

AUSTRALIA

	O	M	R	W		O	M	R	W
McGrath	25	6	70	2		6	2	18	0
Angel	13.1	0	54	3		28	8	92	2
May	20	5	55	2		18	4	67	0
Warne	27	10	61	3		36.1	12	89	5
Waugh S.R.	2	0	9	0		15	3	28	1
Waugh M.E.						3	1	4	0

FALL OF WICKETS	1st	2nd	3rd	4th	5th	6th	7th	8th	9th	10th
AUS	12	41	75	95	216	281	325	335	335	337
PAK	90	153	157	157	175	181	200	234	253	256
AUS	1	49	171	174	174	213	218	227	229	232
PAK	45	64	148	157	174	179	184	236	258	

PAKISTAN vs AUSTRALIA
at Rawalpindi on 5th, 6th, 7th, 8th, 9th October 1994
Match drawn

AUSTRALIA

M.A.Taylor *	lbw b Mohsin Kamal	69	not out	6
M.J.Slater	c Inzamam-ul-Haq b Mohsin Kamal	110	b Waqar Younis	1
D.C.Boon	b Mushtaq Ahmed	4	not out	7
M.E.Waugh	c Aamir Sohail b Mohsin Kamal	68		
M.G.Bevan	lbw b Waqar Younis	70		
S.R.Waugh	b Waqar Younis	98		
I.A.Healy +	c Mohsin Kamal b Aamir Sohail	58		
S.K.Warne	c & b Aamir Sohail	14		
J.Angel	b Wasim Akram	7		
C.J.McDermott	not out	9		
D.W.Fleming				
Extras	(b 3,lb 3,w 3,nb 5)	14		0
TOTAL	(for 9 wkts dec)	521	(for 1 wkt)	14

PAKISTAN

Saeed Anwar	c Waugh S.R. b McDermott	15	c Healy b Waugh M.E.	75
Aamir Sohail	b Fleming	80	c Healy b McDermott	72
Zahid Fazal	b Fleming	10	c Healy b Waugh M.E.	1
Salim Malik *	b McDermott	33	c Healy b Fleming	237
Aamer Malik	lbw b McDermott	11	c Bevan b Fleming	65
Inzamam-ul-Haq	lbw b Warne	14	lbw b Fleming	0
Rashid Latif +	c Slater b Fleming	18	c Bevan b Taylor	38
Wasim Akram	not out	45	c Healy b Angel	5
Mushtaq Ahmed	c Warne b McDermott	0	c Waugh S.R. b McDermott	0
Waqar Younis	lbw b Fleming	13	lbw b Slater	10
Mohsin Kamal	run out	2	not out	0
Extras	(b 10,lb 7,nb 2)	19	(b 17,lb 13,w 1,nb 3)	34
TOTAL		260		537

PAKISTAN

	O	M	R	W		O	M	R	W
Wasim Akram	23.5	2	62	1					
Waqar Younis	32	5	112	2		5	3	2	1
Mohsin Kamal	26	3	109	3					
Mushtaq Ahmed	36	2	145	1		1	0	1	0
Aamir Sohail	21	3	67	2					
Aamer Malik	5	2	16	0					
Salim Malik	1	0	4	0					
Rashid Latif						2	0	11	0
Saeed Anwar						2	2	0	0

AUSTRALIA

	O	M	R	W		O	M	R	W
McDermott	22	8	74	4		33	3	86	2
Fleming	22	3	75	4		26	2	86	3
Warne	21.4	8	58	1		25	6	56	0
Angel	11	2	36	0		28	1	124	1
Waugh M.E.						16	1	63	2
Bevan						4	0	27	0
Waugh S.R.						13	2	41	0
Slater						1.1	0	4	1
Boon						3	1	9	0
Taylor						3	1	11	1

FALL OF WICKETS	1st	2nd	3rd	4th	5th	6th	7th	8th	9th	10th
AUS	176	181	198	323	347	456	501	511	521	
PAK	28	90	119	152	155	189	189	198	253	260
PAK	79	227	336	469	469	478	495	496	537	537
AUS	2									

PAKISTAN vs AUSTRALIA
at Lahore on 1st, 2nd, 3rd, 4th, 5th November 1994
Match drawn

PAKISTAN

Saeed Anwar	b Warne	30	(2) c Emery b McGrath	32
Aamir Sohail	c Emery b McGrath	1	(7) st Emery b Warne	105
Inzamam-ul-Haq	lbw b May	66	c Emery b McDermott	3
Salim Malik *	c Bevan b May	75	b Bevan	143
Ijaz Ahmed	c Boon b Warne	48	lbw b McGrath	6
Basit Ali	c Waugh b Warne	0	(1) c Emery b McGrath	2
Moin Khan +	not out	115	(6) c McDermott b May	16
Akram Raza	b Warne	0	lbw b Warne	32
Mushtaq Ahmed	b May	14	c Emery b McGrath	27
Aqib Javed	c Waugh b Warne	2	lbw b Warne	0
Mohsin Kamal	lbw b Warne	4	not out	0
Extras	(b 5,lb 7,nb 6)	18	(b 8,lb 16,w 4,nb 8)	36
TOTAL		373		404

AUSTRALIA

M.J.Slater	c Moin Khan b Mohsin Kamal	74
M.A.Taylor *	c Saeed Anwar b Mushtaq Ahmed	32
D.C.Boon	c Moin Khan b Akram Raza	5
P.A.Emery +	not out	8
M.E.Waugh	c Moin Khan b Mohsin Kamal	71
M.G.Bevan	c Moin Khan b Mushtaq Ahmed	91
J.L.Langer	c Ijaz Ahmed b Mohsin Kamal	69
S.K.Warne	c & b Mohsin Kamal	33
C.J.McDermott	c & b Mushtaq Ahmed	29
T.B.A.May	c Moin Khan b Akram Raza	10
G.D.McGrath	b Mushtaq Ahmed	3
Extras	(b 3,lb 17,w 2,nb 8)	30
TOTAL		455

AUSTRALIA	O	M	R	W	O	M	R	W
McDermott	24	4	87	0	19	2	81	1
McGrath	24	6	65	1	25.1	1	92	4
Warne	41.5	12	136	6	30	2	104	3
May	29	7	69	3	25	4	60	1
Waugh	2	0	4	0	6	0	22	0
Bevan					4	0	21	1

PAKISTAN	O	M	R	W	O	M	R	W
Aqib Javed	31	9	75	0				
Mohsin Kamal	28	2	116	4				
Mushtaq Ahmed	45.1	6	121	4				
Akram Raza	45	9	123	2				

FALL OF WICKETS	1st	2nd	3rd	4th	5th	6th	7th	8th	9th	10th
PAK	8	34	157	204	209	294	294	294	355	373
AUS	97	106	126	248	318	402	406	443	450	455
PAK	20	28	60	74	107	303	363	384	394	404

SOUTH AFRICA vs PAKISTAN
at Johannesburg on 19th, 20th, 21st, 22nd, 23rd Jan. 1995
South Africa won by 324 runs

SOUTH AFRICA

G.Kirsten	c Aamir Sohail b Kabir Khan	62	b Wasim Akram	42
P.J.R.Steyn	c Moin Khan b Wasim Akram	1	c Moin Khan b Aamir Nazir	17
J.B.Commins	b Aqib Javed	13	(6) run out	0
D.J.Cullinan	c Moin Khan b Aqib Javed	0	not out	69
W.J.Cronje *	c Asif Mujtaba b Kabir Khan	41	(3) c Aamir Sohail b Aqib Javed	48
J.N.Rhodes	c Inzamam-ul-Haq b Aamir Nazir	72	(5) c Moin Khan b Wasim Akram	16
B.M.McMillan	c Moin Khan b Aqib Javed	113	c Salim Malik b Kabir Khan	33
D.J.Richardson +	b Aamir Nazir	0	lbw b Aqib Javed	0
C.E.Eksteen	c Moin Khan b Wasim Akram	13	not out	2
P.S.de Villiers	not out	66		
A.A.Donald	c Inzamam-ul-Haq b Aamir Sohail	15		
Extras	(b 4,lb 18,w 6,nb 36)	64	(b 6,lb 5,w 15,nb 6)	32
TOTAL		460	(for 7 wkts dec)	259

PAKISTAN

Aamir Sohail	c Richardson b de Villiers	23	c McMillan b de Villiers	0
Saeed Anwar	c Cullinan b de Villiers	2	c de Villiers b Donald	1
Asif Mujtaba	c Richardson b de Villiers	0	c Richardson b McMillan	26
Salim Malik *	c Eksteen b Donald	99	lbw b de Villiers	1
Ijaz Ahmed	b de Villiers	19	(6) c Richardson b McMillan	1
Inzamam-ul-Haq	b McMillan	19	(5) c Richardson b de Villiers	95
Moin Khan +	c de Villiers b McMillan	9	c Rhodes b Eksteen	0
Wasim Akram	b de Villiers	41	c Kirsten b Eksteen	11
Kabir Khan	c Richardson b Donald	4	c Eksteen b Donald	10
Aqib Javed	not out	0	c Richardson b de Villiers	0
Aamir Nazir	b de Villiers	0	not out	1
Extras	(lb 5,nb 9)	14	(b 8,lb 7,w 1,nb 3)	19
TOTAL		230		165

PAKISTAN	O	M	R	W	O	M	R	W
Wasim Akram	36	11	113	2	23	4	53	2
Aqib Javed	29.4	6	102	3	26	2	82	2
Kabir Khan	19.1	4	60	2	18	0	58	1
Aamir Nazir	13.1	1	67	2	13	1	55	1
Aamir Sohail	14.2	2	47	1				
Salim Malik	8	0	49	0				

SOUTH AFRICA	O	M	R	W	O	M	R	W
Donald	17	2	63	2	15	3	53	2
de Villiers	20.5	4	81	6	19.3	11	27	4
McMillan	12	3	46	2	11	1	33	2
Eksteen	7	1	16	0	19	7	34	2
Cronje	9	5	19	0	5	3	5	0

FALL OF WICKETS	1st	2nd	3rd	4th	5th	6th	7th	8th	9th	10th
SA	1	55	59	138	168	325	325	367	389	460
PAK	20	20	44	106	134	158	193	207	230	230
SA	69	96	155	185	185	251	255			
PAK	3	3	5	98	100	101	124	164	164	165

ZIMBABWE vs PAKISTAN
at Harare on 1st, 2nd, 3rd, 4th February 1995
Zimbabwe won by an innings and 64 runs

ZIMBABWE

M.H.Dekker	c Rashid Latif b Aqib Javed	2
G.W.Flower	not out	201
A.D.R.Campbell	lbw b Wasim Akram	1
D.L.Houghton	c Aamir Sohail b Aqib Javed	23
A.Flower *+	c Wasim Akram b Kabir Khan	156
G.J.Whittal	not out	113
S.Carlisle		
H.H.Streak		
P.A.Strang		
D.H.Brain		
H.Olonga		
Extras	(b 4,lb 19,w 3,nb 22)	48
TOTAL	(for 4 wkts dec)	544

PAKISTAN

Aamir Sohail	c Houghton b Brain	61	c Campbell b Brain	5
Saeed Anwar	c Flower A. b Olonga	8	lbw b Whittal	7
Akram Raza	c Whittal b Streak	19	(9) not out	2
Asif Mujtaba	c Carlisle b Streak	2	(3) b Brain	4
Salim Malik *	c Carlisle b Whittal	32	(4) c Flower A. b Brain	6
Ijaz Ahmed	c Flower G.W. b Streak	65	(5) c Brain b Streak	2
Rashid Latif +	c Campbell b Whittal	6	(6) c Houghton b Whittal	38
Inzamam-ul-Haq	c Flower G.W. b Streak	71	(7) c Flower A. b Streak	65
Wasim Akram	c Carlisle b Streak	27	(8) c Dekker b Strang	19
Kabir Khan	not out	2	b Streak	0
Aqib Javed	lbw b Streak	0	b Streak	2
Extras	(b 3,lb 4,w 9,nb 13)	29	(w 2,nb 6)	8
TOTAL		322		158

PAKISTAN	O	M	R	W	O	M	R	W
Wasim Akram	39.5	12	95	1				
Aqib Javed	34.1	8	73	2				
Kabir Khan	35	5	142	1				
Salim Malik	9	0	42	0				
Akram Raza	34	6	112	0				
Asif Mujtaba	7	0	30	0				
Aamir Sohail	6	1	27	0				

ZIMBABWE	O	M	R	W	O	M	R	W
Streak	39	11	90	6	11	4	15	3
Brain	27	4	94	1	16	4	50	3
Olonga	10	0	27	1				
Whittal	29	10	49	2	16	3	58	3
Strang	15	5	45	0	19	7	35	1
Dekker	4	0	10	0				

FALL OF WICKETS	1st	2nd	3rd	4th	5th	6th	7th	8th	9th	10th
ZIM	4	9	42	311						
PAK	36	82	88	131	135	151	271	317	322	322
PAK	13	16	26	29	35	131	142	156	156	158

ZIMBABWE vs PAKISTAN
at Bulawayo on 7th, 8th, 9th February 1995
Pakistan won by 8 wickets

ZIMBABWE

M.H.Dekker	c Shakeel Ahmed b Aamir Nazir	0	c Aamir Sohail b Wasim Akram	9
G.W.Flower	b Wasim Akram	6	b Manzoor Elahi	22
A.D.R.Campbell	c Ijaz Ahmed b Manzoor Elahi	60	c Shakeel Ahmed b Wasim Akram	0
D.L.Houghton	b Wasim Akram	11	lbw b Wasim Akram	25
A.Flower *+	c Ijaz Ahmed b Kabir Khan	14	lbw b Wasim Akram	8
G.J.Whittal	c Aamir Sohail b Manzoor Elahi	7	c sub b Aamir Nazir	5
S.Carlisle	c Kabir Khan b Wasim Akram	1	not out	46
P.A.Strang	b Aamir Nazir	32	c Aamir Sohail b Kabir Khan	3
H.H.Streak	st Rashid Latif b Aamir Sohail	13	c Manzoor Elahi b Kabir Khan	11
D.H.Brain	c Rashid Latif b Aamir Sohail	5	b Kabir Khan	0
B.Strang	not out	0	lbw b Wasim Akram	0
Extras	(b 1,lb 9,nb 15)	25	(lb 6,nb 11)	17
TOTAL		174		146

PAKISTAN

Aamir Sohail	lbw b Streak	26	c Campbell b Strang B.	46
Shakeel Ahmed	lbw b Streak	5	lbw b Strang B.	7
Rashid Latif +	lbw b Streak	17	not out	1
Basit Ali	c Flower A. b Streak	0		
Salim Malik *	b Streak	44		
Ijaz Ahmed	b Strang B.	76		
Inzamam-ul-Haq	lbw b Whittal	47		
Wasim Akram	c Dekker b Strang B.	1		
Manzoor Elahi	c Flower A. b Strang B.	13	(4) not out	1
Kabir Khan	not out	8		
Aamir Nazir	b Brain	7		
Extras	(b 2,lb 5,w 2,nb 7)	16	(lb 2,w 1,nb 3)	6
TOTAL		260	(for 2 wkts)	61

PAKISTAN	O	M	R	W	O	M	R	W
Wasim Akram	22	9	40	3	22.3	7	43	5
Aamir Nazir	18	4	36	2	11	1	39	1
Kabir Khan	16	2	45	1	11	3	26	3
Manzoor Elahi	21	8	38	2	14	6	32	1
Aamir Sohail	2.1	1	5	2				

ZIMBABWE	O	M	R	W	O	M	R	W
Streak	26	5	70	5	6	1	18	0
Brain	15	4	49	1	2	0	35	0
Strang B.	23	10	44	3	3.4	2	6	2
Whittal	15	3	42	1				
Strang P.A.	15	4	48	0				

FALL OF WICKETS	1st	2nd	3rd	4th	5th	6th	7th	8th	9th	10th
ZIM	3	7	23	56	73	86	134	167	174	174
PAK	9	47	52	63	133	212	226	231	246	260
ZIM	14	16	58	73	77	93	106	145	145	146
PAK	56	60								

ZIMBABWE vs PAKISTAN

at Harare on 15th, 16th, 18th, 19th February 1995
Pakistan won by 99 runs

PAKISTAN				
Aamir Sohail	c Strang P.A. b Streak	21	(6) c Flower G.W. b Whittal	19
Shakeel Ahmed	c Flower A. b Whittal	29	c Flower A. b Strang B.	33
Saeed Anwar	c Butchart b Streak	4	(1) c Carlisle b Streak	26
Salim Malik *	c Flower G.W. b Streak	20	c Carlisle b Whittal	5
Ijaz Ahmed	lbw b Streak	41	c Whittal b Streak	55
Inzamam-ul-Haq	c Strang P.A. b Brain	101	(3) c Flower G.W. b Whittal	83
Rashid Latif +	c Strang P.A. b Strang B.	6	c Flower A. b Streak	6
Wasim Akram	b Strang B.	0	c Campbell b Brain	4
Manzoor Elahi	c Streak b Strang B.	0	c Flower A. b Streak	0
Aqib Javed	run out	0	c Flower A. b Brain	3
Aamir Nazir	not out	0	not out	0
	Extras (lb 3,w 3,nb 3)	9	(lb 3,w 3,nb 10)	16
	TOTAL	**231**		**250**

ZIMBABWE				
G.W.Flower	b Aamir Nazir	6	b Aamir Nazir	2
S.Carlisle	c Salim Malik b Aqib Javed	31	b Aamir Nazir	0
A.D.R.Campbell	c Manzoor Elahi b Aamir Nazir	14	c Rashid Latif b Aamir Nazir	18
D.L.Houghton	c Rashid Latif b Wasim Akram	19	(6) c Rashid Latif b Aamir Nazir	5
A.Flower *+	c Aamir Sohail b Manzoor Elahi	37	(4) c Aamir Nazir b Manzoor Elahi	35
G.J.Whittal	b Aqib Javed	34	(5) c Shakeel Ahmed b Wasim Akram	2
I.P.Butchart	c Inzamam-ul-Haq b Wasim Akram	15	c & b Aamir Nazir	8
P.A.Strang	c Aamir Sohail b Aamir Nazir	28	c Ijaz Ahmed b Aqib Javed	5
H.H.Streak	lbw b Aqib Javed	0	not out	30
D.H.Brain	not out	22	c Inzamam-ul-Haq b Wasim Akram	8
B.Strang	b Aqib Javed	6	c Shakeel Ahmed b Aqib Javed	0
	Extras (lb 4,w 1,nb 26)	31	(b 5,lb 5,nb 16)	26
	TOTAL	**243**		**139**

ZIMBABWE	O	M	R	W	O	M	R	W
Streak	18	4	53	4	18	5	52	4
Brain	12.3	1	48	1	16.1	2	61	2
Strang B.	32	15	43	3	26	16	27	1
Whittal	18	3	73	1	22	3	66	3
Butchart	3	0	11	0				
Strang P.A.					13	3	41	0

PAKISTAN	O	M	R	W	O	M	R	W
Wasim Akram	28	2	90	2	20	1	45	2
Aqib Javed	25	5	64	4	17.4	3	26	2
Aamir Nazir	13	3	50	3	19	3	46	5
Manzoor Elahi	10	3	28	1	3	0	12	1
Aamir Sohail	2	0	7	0				

FALL OF WICKETS	**1st**	**2nd**	**3rd**	**4th**	**5th**	**6th**	**7th**	**8th**	**9th**	**10th**
PAK	42	46	64	83	159	180	180	183	203	231
ZIM	20	51	79	95	145	175	193	193	233	243
PAK	58	72	88	204	230	233	246	247	250	250
ZIM	2	12	37	68	72	85	95	95	122	139

PAKISTAN vs SRI LANKA

At Arbab Niaz Stadium, Peshawar, on 8, 9, 10, 11, September 1995.
Toss: Pakistan. Result: Pakistan won by an innings and 40 runs.
Debuts: Pakistan - Ijaz Ahmed II, Saqlain Mushtaq

PAKISTAN		
Saeed Anwar	c A Ranatunga b Muralitharan	50
Aamir Sohail	c Dunusinghe b Vaas	28
Ramiz Raja *	c Pushpakumara b Vaas	78
Inzamam-ul-Haq	lbw b Vaas	95
Shoaib Mohammad	c A Ranatunga b Vaas	57
Ijaz Ahmed II	c Gurusinha b Muralitharan	5
Wasim Akram	c and b Muralitharan	36
Moin Khan +	c Hathurusinghe b Vaas	51
Waqar Younis	c Mahanama b Muralitharan	0
Aqib Javed	not out	28
Saqlain Mushtaq not out		8
	Extras (b1, lb4, w1, nb17)	23
	Total (9 wickets declared)	**459**

SRI LANKA				
R S Mahanama	c Moin b Waqar	29	lbw b Aqib	2
U C Hathurusinghe	c Inzamam b Saqlain	23	c Saeed b Wasim	53
A P Gurusinha	c Wasim b Saqlain	24	c Saeed b Aamir	10
S Ranatunga	lbw b Wasim	33	c Moin b Aqib	18
A Ranatunga *	lbw b Aqib	8	c Inzamam b Aamir	76
H P Tillekeratne	not out	44	c Ramiz b Wasim	48
C I Dunusinghe +	lbw b Wasim	0	c Inzamam b Aamir	0
W P U C J Vaas	b Wasim	4	c Ramiz b Saqlain	4
G P Wickremasinghe	b Wasim	0	c Ramiz b Saqlain	6
M Muralitharan	c Saqlain b Wasim	8	st Moin b Aamir	0
K R Pushpakumara	run out	1	not out	0
	Extras (b1, lb6, nb5)	12	(b1, lb6,nb9)	16
	Total	**186**		**233**

SRI LANKA	O	M	R	W	O	M	R	W
Wickremasinghe	32	5	98	0				
Vaas	29	3	99	5				
Pushpakumara	17	2	89	0				
Muralitharan	50	9	134	4				
Hathurusinghe	18	10	29	0				
Gurusinha	3	1	5	0				
PAKISTAN								
Wasim	20	3	55	5	10	3	24	2
Waqar	11	2	47	1	9	1	39	0
Saqlain	18	4	49	2	26	10	58	2
Aqib	11.1	2	27	1	13	1	50	2
Aamir	2	1	1	0	21	4	54	4
Ijaz					1	0	1	0

FALL OF WICKETS	**P**	**SL**	**SL**		**P**	**SL**	**SL**
1st	59	39	8	6th	340	134	222
2nd	102	76	36	7th	422	142	222
3rd	234	83	86	8th	422	143	232
4th	285	102	89	9th	425	184	233
5th	318	132	214	10th	-	186	233

PAKISTAN vs SRI LANKA

At Iqbal Stadium, Faisalabad, on 15, 16, 17, 18, 19, September 1995.
Toss: Pakistan. Result: Sri Lanka won by 42 runs.
Debuts: Pakistan - Mohammad Akram + (D P Samaraweera)

SRI LANKA				
R S Mahanama	lbw b Wasim	0	lbw b Mohammad Akram	10
U C Hathurusinghe	c Saeed b M Akram	47	c Ijaz b Aqib	83
A P Gurusinha	c Wasim b Aqib	9	lbw b Aqib	12
P A de Silva	c and b Saqlain	0	lbw Saqlain	105
A Ranatunga *	c Ijaz b Saqlain	0	(6) c and b Aamir	2
H P Tillekeratne	c Moin b Saqlain	115	(5) lbw b Aqib	0
H D P K Dharmasena	run out	0	c Moin b Mohammad Akram	49
C I Dunusinghe +	lbw b Wasim	12	c M Akram b Saqlain	27
W P U C J Vaas	c Ijaz b Aqib	21	b Aqib	40
G P Wickremasinghe	c Moin b Aqib	1	(11) b Aqib	2
M Muralitharan	not out	8	(10) not out	10
	Extras (b3, lb1, nb6)	10	(b4, lb10, nb7)	21
	Total	**223**		**361**
PAKISTAN				
Saeed Anwar	c De Silva b Muralitharan	54	b Dharmasena	50
Aamir Sohail	b Muralitharan	20	lbw b Vaas	0
Saqlain Mushtaq	c Mahanama b Muralitharan	34	(9) c Ranatunga b Vaas	7
Ramiz Raja *	c sub+ b De Silva	75	(3) c Tillekeratne b Muralitharan	25
Inzamam-ul-Haq	b Gurusinha	50	(4) c and b Muralitharan	26
Shoaib Mohammad	run out	12	(5) lbw b Wickremasinghe	5
Ijaz Ahmed II	c Dunusinghe b Wickremasinghe	16	(6) c Dharmasena b Vaas	8
Wasim Akram	c Mahanama b Gurusinha	2	b Dharmasena	26
Moin Khan +	st Dunusinghe b Muralitharan	30	(7) c Muralitharan b Vaas	50
Aqib Javed	b Muralitharan	8	not out	1
Mohammad Akram	not out	0	c Mahanama b Dharmasena	0
	Extras (b4, lb15, nb13)	32	(nb11)	11
	Total	**333**		**209**

PAKISTAN	O	M	R	W	O	M	R	W
Wasim	13	6	31	2				
Mohammad Akram	14	4	42	1	27	5	78	2
Aqib	13	5	34	3	32.3	6	84	5
Saqlain	20	3	74	3	36	12	84	2
Aamir	7	2	28	0	44	12	87	1
Shoaib	3	2	10	0	4	2	9	0
Ijaz					3	0	5	0
SRI LANKA								
Wickremasinghe	23	6	53	1	11	1	23	1
Vaas	14	4	35	0	15	2	45	4
Gurusinha	8	1	30	2				
Dharmasena	30	4	79	0	22.1	6	43	3
Muralitharan	23.3	6	68	5	20	2	83	2
Hathurusinghe	6	1	10	0				
De Silva	13.3	3	39	1	4	0	15	0

FALL OF WICKETS	**SL**	**P**	**SL**	**P**		**SL**	**P**	**SL**	**P**
1st	0	42	11	6	6th	117	288	240	129
2nd	32	109	24	58	7th	149	288	279	175
3rd	33	168	200	99	8th	213	291	346	206
4th	34	213	212	108	9th	213	324	354	207
5th	117	248	225	119	10th	223	333	361	209

PAKISTAN vs SRI LANKA

At Jinnah Stadium, Sialkot, on 22, 23, 24, 25, 26 September 1995.
Toss: Sri Lanka. Result: Sri Lanka won by 144 runs

SRI LANKA				
R S Mahanama	c Mohammad Akram b Aqib	21	lbw b Aqib	20
U C Hathurusinghe	c Inzamam b Aamir Nazir	12	c Moin b Aqib	73
A P Gurusinha	run out	45	c Ramiz b Rehman	18
P A de Silva	c Shoaib b Rehman	0	lbw b Aamir Nazir	8
A Ranatunga *	b Aamir Sohail	24	c Inzamam b M Akram	87
H P Tillekerante	c Inzamam b M Akram	24	(7) b Aamir Sohail	50
H D P K Dharmasena	not out	62	(8) c Inzamam b M Akram	7
C I Dunusinghe +	lbw b Aqib	1	(6) b Mohammad Akram	7
W P U C J Vaas	b Aqib	16	run out	27
M Muralitharan	c Aamir Sohail b Aamir Nazir	4	not out	0
G P Wickremasinghe	run out	1		
	Extras (b1, lb12, nb9)	22	(b23, lb10, nb8)	41
	Total	**232**	**(9 wickets declared)**	**338**
PAKISTAN				
Aamir Sohail	b Dharmasena	48	c Hathu'singhe b Wickremasinghe	5
Soaib Mohammad	lbw b Muralitharan	8	c and b Vaas	1
Ramiz Raja *	lbw b Muralitharan	26	c Mahanama b Wickremasinghe	4
Inzamam-ul-Haq	b Wickremasinghe	21	c Mahanama b Vaas	0
Basit Ali	lbw b Muralitharan	4	(7) c Dharmasena b Vaas	27
Zahid Fazal	st Dunusinghe b De Silva	23	(5) c Gurusinha b Vaas	1
Moin Khan +	c Dunusinghe b Wickremasinghe	26	(6) not out	117
Aqib Javed	c Dunusinghe b Dharmasena	19	run out	6
Ata-ur-Rehman	c Mahanama b De Silva	9	c Dunusinghe b Wickremasinghe	4
Mohammad Akram	b Muralitharan	5	b Wickremasinghe	2
Aamir Nazir	not out	5	c Tillekerante b De Silva	11
	Extras (b3, lb4, nb13)	20	(b13, lb10, nb11)	34
	Total	**214**		**212**

PAKISTAN	O	M	R	W	O	M	R	W
Aqib	19.3	6	47	3	24	2	71	2
Mohammad Akram	17	4	37	1	20	5	39	3
Aamir Nazir	19	6	46	2	17	2	55	1
Rehman	19	4	42	1	23	5	66	1
Aamir Sohail	17	4	45	1	25.3	7	55	1
Shoaib	1	0	2	0	11	3	19	0
SRI LANKA								
Wickremasinghe	13	2	29	2	18	4	55	4
Vaas	14	0	38	0	24	9	37	4
Gurusingha	1	0	6	0	3	0	16	0
Muralitharan	27.1	6	72	4	17	3	53	0
De Silva	10	1	29	2	4	2	5	1
Dharmasena	16	5	33	2	10	2	23	0

FALL OF WICKETS	**SL**	**P**	**SL**	**P**		**SL**	**P**	**SL**	**P**
1st	32	39	37	7	6th	158	173	265	79
2nd	36	72	71	7	7th	171	173	279	106
3rd	41	111	97	7	8th	216	196	330	132
4th	108	119	175	13	9th	225	204	330	147
5th	118	122	206	15	10th	232	214	-	212

AUSTRALIA vs PAKISTAN

At Woolloongabba, Brisbane, on 9, 10, 11, 13, November 1995.
Toss; Australia: Result: Australia won by an innings and 126 runs.
Debuts: Pakistan - Salim Elahi. **(Mushtaq Ahmed)

AUSTRALIA

M A Taylor *	c Salim Malik b Saqlain	69
M J Slater	c Mohammad Akram b Wasim	42
D C Boon	c Inzamam b Wasim	54
M E Waugh	c Salim Elahi b saqlain	59
S R Waugh	not out	112
G S Blewett	lbw b Waqar	57
L A Healy +	c sub** b Mohammad Akram	18
P R Reiffel	lbw b Waqar	9
S K Warne	c Moin b Aamir	5
C J McDermott	b Waqar	8
G D McGrath	st Moin b Aamir	5
	Extras (b2, lb6, w4, nb13)	25
	Total	**463**

PAKISTAN

Aamir Sohail	st Healy b Warne	32	b McGrath	99	
Salim Elahi	c Taylor b McDermott	11	c Healy b McGrath	2	
Ramiz Raja	c Taylor b Warne	8	c Healy b McGrath	16	
Saqlain Mushtaq	lbw b McGrath	0	(9) not out	2	
Inzamam-ul-Haq	c S R Waugh b Warne	5	(4) c McDermott b M E Waugh	62	
Basit Ali	c Taylor b Warne	1	(5) lbw b McGrath	26	
Moin Khan +	c McDermott b Warne	4	(6) c Healy b Reiffel	9	
Wasim Akram *	c Boon b Warne	1	(7) c Slater b Warne	6	
Waqar Younis	not out	19	(10) lbw b Warne	0	
Mohammad Akram	c Blewett b Warne	1	(11) b Warne	0	
Salim Malik	absent hurt	0	(8) c McDermott b Warne	0	
	Extras (b4, lb5, nb6)	15	(lb7, nb11)	18	
	Total	**97**		**240**	

PAKISTAN	O	M	R	W		O	M	R	W
Wasim	38	9	84	2					
Waqar	29.5	7	101	3					
Mohammad Akram	33.1	4	97	1					
Saqlain	44	12	130	2					
Aamir	16.5	2	43	2					

AUSTRALIA	O	M	R	W		O	M	R	W
McDermott	11	4	32	1		11	0	47	0
McGrath	14	3	33	1		25	7	76	4
Warne	16.1	9	23	7		27.5	10	54	4
Reiffel						15	4	47	1
S R Waugh						2	1	3	0
M E Waugh						5	2	6	1

FALL OF WICKETS	A	P	P			A	P	P
1st	107	20	30	6th		411	70	233
2nd	119	37	88	7th		434	70	233
3rd	213	40	167	8th		441	80	239
4th	250	62	217	9th		452	97	240
5th	385	66	218	10th		463	-	240

AUSTRALIA vs PAKISTAN

At Bellerive Oval, Hobart, on 17, 18, 19, 20 November 1995.
Toss: Australia. Result: Australia won by 155 runs.

AUSTRALIA

M J Slater	lbw b Wasim	0	(2) lbw b Mushtaq	73	
M A Taylor *	b Wasim	40	(1) b Waqar	123	
D C Boon	run out	34	c Waqar b Mushtaq	0	
M E Waugh	c Ramiz b Mushtaq	88	b Wasim	3	
S R Waugh	c Moin b Mushtaq	7	c Moin b Mohammad Akram	29	
G S Blewett	b Mushtaq	0	c Basit b Wasim	11	
I A Healy +	c Basit b Mushtaq	37	c Inzamam b Wasim	24	
P R Reiffel	c Mohammad Akram b Mushtaq	14	b Mushtaq	0	
S K Warne	not out	27	absent hurt		
C J McDermott	b Waqar	0	(9) c Wasim b Mushtaq	20	
G D McGrath	b Wasim	3	(10) not out	2	
	Extras (b3, lb9, nb5)	17	(b6, lb5, w1, nb9)	21	
	Total	**267**		**306**	

PAKISTAN

Aamir Sohail	c Healy b Reiffel	32	c sub (B P Julian) b Blewett	57	
Salim Elahi	b McGrath	13	c Boon b McGrath	17	
Mushtaq Ahmed	lbw b McGrath	0	(9) b McGrath	8	
Ramiz Raja	c and b Reiffel	59	(3) lbw b Reiffel	25	
Inzamam-ul-Haq	c Healy b S R Waugh	27	(4) lbw b Reiffel	40	
Ijaz Ahmed	not out	34	(5) lbw b Blewett	4	
Basit Ali	lbw b McGrath	2	(6) b Reiffel	5	
Moin Khan +	b McDermott	12	(7) c M E Waugh b McGrath	16	
Wasim Akram *	c Taylor B Mc Dermott	2	(8) c Blewett b McGrath	33	
Waqar Younis	c sub (B P Julian) b Reiffel	10	c Blewett b McGrath	4	
Mohammad Akram	lbw b Reiffel	0	not out	0	
	Extras (lb1, nb6)	7	(lb11)	11	
	Total	**198**		**220**	

PAKISTAN	O	M	R	W		O	M	R	W
Wasim	18.3	7	42	3		26.1	7	72	3
Waqar	17	3	54	1		20	4	67	1
Mohammad Akram	10	1	41	0		10	1	58	0
Mushtaq	30	5	115	5		38	8	83	4
Aamir	3	1	3	0		8	2	15	0

AUSTRALIA	O	M	R	W		O	M	R	W
McDermott	18	2	72	2		16	7	38	0
McGrath	19	4	46	3		24.3	7	61	5
Reiffel	15.5	4	38	4		14	6	42	3
M E Waugh	8	0	23	0		12	2	24	0
S R Waugh	6	0	18	1		8	1	19	0
Blewett						10	4	25	2

FALL OF WICKETS	A	P	A	P		A	P	A	P
1st	0	24	120	27	6th	209	155	255	157
2nd	68	24	125	62	7th	235	173	256	205
3rd	111	79	132	132	8th	238	183	296	210
4th	156	126	189	142	9th	244	198	306	220
5th	156	150	233	152	10th	267	198	306	220

AUSTRALIA vs PAKISTAN

At Sydney Cricket Ground, on 30 November, 1, 2, 3, December 1995.
Toss: Pakistan. Result: Pakistan won by 74 runs.
Debuts: None. +(Moin Khan)

PAKISTAN

Aamir Sohail	c M E Waugh b McDermott	4	c Boon b McDermott	9	
Ramiz Raja	c Slater b Warne	33	c M E Waugh b Warne	39	
Ijaz Ahmed	c McGrath b Warne	137	lbw b Warne	15	
Inzamam-ul-Haq	c Healy b Warne	39	(6) c Taylor b McDermott	59	
Salim Malik	lbw b McGrath	36	(4) lbw b M E Waugh	45	
Basit Ali	c Slater b McDermott	17	(5) b Warne	14	
Rashid Latif +	c Healy b McDermott	1	(8) lbw b Warne	3	
Wasim Akram *	c and b McGrath	21	(7) lbw b McDermott	5	
Saqlain Mushtaq	run out	0	c M E Waugh b McDermott	2	
Mushtaq Ahmed	c McDermott b Warne	0	lbw b McDermott	2	
Waqar Younis	not out	0	not out	1	
	Extras (lb3, w2, nb6)	11	(b1, lb5, nb4)	10	
	Total	**299**		**204**	

AUSTRALIA

M J Slater	b Wasim	1	(2) lbw b Mushtaq	23	
M A Taylor *	c Rashid b Saqlain Mushtaq	47	(1) st Rashid b Mushtaq Ahmed	59	
D C Boon	c Rashid b Mushtaq Ahmed	16	c sub++ b Saqlain Mushtaq	6	
M E Waugh	c Mushtaq b Wasim	116	c Rashid b Wasim	34	
S R Waugh	st Rashid b Mushtaq Ahmed	38	(6) b Mushaq Ahmed	14	
G S Blewett	b Mushtaq Ahmed	5	(7) b Waqar	14	
I A Healy +	c Rashid b Mushtaq Ahmed	6	(5) c Rashid b Wasim	7	
P R Reiffel	not out	10	(10) not out	2	
S K Warne	c Rashid b Wasim	2	(8) c Saqlain b Mushtaq Ahmed	5	
C J McDermott	b Wasim	0	(9) b Waqar	0	
G D McGrath	c Wasim b Mushtaq Ahmed	0	b Waqar	0	
	Extras (lb6, nb10)	16	(lb5, nb3)	8	
	Total	**257**		**172**	

AUSTRALIA	O	M	R	W		O	M	R	W
McDermott	21	6	62	3		15.3	0	49	5
McGrath	22.2	1	79	2		17	3	47	0
Reiffel	22	5	71	0		8.3	2	15	0
Warne	34	20	55	4		37	13	66	4
M E Waugh	10	4	23	0		14	4	21	1
Blewett	4	2	6	0		2	2	0	0

PAKISTAN	O	M	R	W		O	M	R	W
Wasim	24	4	50	4		16	5	25	2
Waqar	11	4	26	0		6.1	2	15	3
Mushtaq Ahmed	36.2	7	95	5		30	6	91	4
Saqlain Mushtaq	22	2	62	1		13	5	35	1
Aamir						1	0	1	0

FALL OF WICKETS	P	A	P	A		P	A	P	A
1st	4	2	18	42	6th	269	228	185	152
2nd	64	44	58	69	7th	297	240	188	170
3rd	141	91	82	82	8th	299	249	198	170
4th	210	174	101	126	9th	299	249	203	172
5th	263	182	163	182	10th	299	257	204	172

NEW ZEALAND vs PAKISTAN

At Lancaster Park, Christchurch on 8, 9, 10, 11, 12 December 1995.
Toss: New Zealand. Result: Pakistan won by 161 runs.
Debuts: New Zealand - C M Spearman.

PAKISTAN

Aamir Sohail	hit wicket b Cairns	88	b Patel	30	
Ramiz Raja	lbw b Cairns	54	lbw b Morrison	62	
Ijaz Ahmed	c Morrison b Larsen	30	c Germon b Nash	103	
Inzamam-ul-Haq	lbw b Cairns	0	c Fleming b Nash	82	
Salim Malik	c Germon b Nash	0	c Germon b Morrison	21	
Basit Ali	c Germon b Larsen	0	lbw b Cairns	0	
Rashid Latif +	c Spearman b Morrison	2	c Germon b Cairns	39	
Wasim Akram *	c Young b Morrison	2	c Fleming b Cairns	19	
Mushtaq Ahmed	lbw b Nash	5	c Germon b Larsen	24	
Waqar Younis	not out	12	lbw b Larsen	34	
Ata-ur-Rehman	c and b Cairns	5	not out	0	
	Extras (lb1, w1, nb3)	5	(b5, lb6, w4, nb5)	20	
	Total	**208**		**434**	

NEW ZEALAND

B A Young	c Rashid b Rehman	16	c Rashid b Mushtaq	18	
C M Spearman	b Mushtaq	40	c Aamir b Mushtaq	33	
A C Parore	c Rashid b Rehman	9	lbw b Mushtaq	5	
S P Fleming	st Rashid b Mushtaq	25	lbw b Rehman	0	
R G Twose	lbw b Wasim	59	not out	51	
C L Cairns	b Wasim	76	c Salim b Mushtaq	8	
L K Germon *+	c Rashid b Wasim	21	run out	12	
D N Patel	c Aamir b Wasim	3	b Mushtaq	15	
G R Larsen	not out	5	c Aamir b Mushtaq	13	
D J Nash	c Rashid b Wasim	11	b Waqar	22	
D K Morrison	b Mushtaq	0	c Salim b Mushtaq	1	
	Extras (lb4, nb17)	21	(b3, lb9, w1, nb4)	17	
	Total	**286**		**195**	

NEW ZELAND	O	M	R	W		O	M	R	R
Morrison	14	0	57	2		27	5	99	2
Cairns	11.1	2	51	4		35	6	114	3
Larsen	15	2	44	2		29	10	58	2
Nash	11	3	43	2		30	6	91	2
Patel	3	1	12	0		24	8	61	1

PAKISTAN	O	M	R	W		O	M	R	W
Wasim	24.5	4	53	5		11	3	31	0
Waqar	16	2	60	0		26	6	73	1
Rehman	17.1	4	47	2		9	1	23	1
Mushtaq	30.4	4	115	3		34.4	13	56	7
Aamir	3	0	7	0					

FALL OF WICKETS	P	NZ	P	NZ		P	NZ	P	NZ
1st	135	48	55	50	6th	184	262	339	101
2nd	148	65	195	57	7th	184	265	363	131
3rd	148	73	224	60	8th	187	269	384	163
4th	149	119	260	60	9th	203	283	425	192
5th	177	221	265	75	10th	208	286	434	195

ENGLAND vs PAKISTAN

at Lord's on July 25, 26, 27, 28, 29, 1996. Pakistan won by 164 runs.
Toss: Pakistan. Debut: Shadab Kabir, S.J.E. Brown.

PAKISTAN

Aamir Sohail	lbw b Brown	2	(1) c Russell b Mullally	88
Saeed Anwar	c Russel b Hick	74	lbw b Cork	76
Ijaz Ahmed	b Cork	1	(5) c Ealham b Cork	70
Inzamam-ul-Haq	b Mullally	148	(6) not out	27
Salim Malik	run out (Salisbury)	7	(2) c Russell b Cork	33
Shadab Kabir	lbw b Cork	17	not out	34
Wasim Akram*	lbw b Ealham	10		
Rashid Latif+	c Hick b Salisbury	45		
Mushtaq Ahmed	c Russell b Mullally	11	(4) c Thorpe b Brown	5
Waqar Younis	c Brown b Mullally	4		
Ata-ur-Rehman	not out	10		
Extras	(b3, lb5, nb3)	11	(b4, lb14, nb1)	19
Total	**(108.2 overs)**	**340**	**(5 wkts dec)**	**352**
			(113.2 overs)	

ENGLAND

N V Knight	lbw b Waqar	51	lbw b Waqar	1
M A Atherton*	lbw b Wasim	12	c sub (Mujtaba) b Mustaq	64
A J Stewart	lbw b Mushtaq	39	c sub (M. Khan) b Mustaq	89
G P Thorpe	b Ata-ur-Rehman	77	lbw b Mushtaq	3
G A Hick	b Waqar	4	b Waqar	4
M A Ealham	c Latif b Ata-ur-Rehman	25	b Mushtaq	5
R C Russell+	not out	41	c Latif b Waqar	1
D G Cork	c Anwar b Ata-ur-Rehman	3	b Waqar	3
I D K Salisbury	lbw b Waqar	5	c Latif b Wasim	40
A D Mullally	b Waqar	0	c sub (M. Khan) b Mustaq	6
S J E Brown	b Ata-ur-Rehman	1	not out	10
Extras	(b9, lb13, w1, nb4)	27	(b6, lb7, nb4)	17
Total	**(102.4 overs)**	**285**	**(97.1 overs)**	**243**

ENGLAND

	O	M	R	W		O	M	R	W
Cork	28	6	100	2		24	4	86	3
Brown	17	2	78	1		16	2	60	1
Mullally	24	8	44	3		30.2	9	70	1
Salisbury	12.2	1	42	1		20	4	63	0
Ealham	21	4	42	1		16	4	39	0
Hick	6	0	26	1		7	2	16	0

PAKISTAN

	O	M	R	W		O	M	R	W
Wasim	22	4	49	1		21.1	5	45	1
Waqar	24	6	69	4		25	3	85	4
Mushtaq	38	5	92	1		38	15	57	5
Ata-ur-Rehman	15.4	3	50	4		11	2	33	0
Aamir Sohail	3	1	3	0		-	-	-	-
Salim Malik	-	-	-	-		1	0	1	0
Shadab Kabir	-	-	-	-		1	0	9	0

FALL OF WICKETS

	P	E	P	E		P	E	P	E
1st	7	27	136	14	6th	257	260	-	182
2nd	12	107	136	168	7th	267	264	-	186
3rd	142	107	161	171	8th	280	269	-	186
4th	153	116	279	176	9th	290	269	-	208
5th	209	180	308	181	10th	340	285	-	243

ENGLAND vs PAKISTAN

Played at The Oval on August 22, 23, 24, 25, 26, 1996.
Pakistan won by 9 wickets. Toss: England. Debut: R.D.B. Croft.

ENGLAND

M A Atherton*	b Waqar	31	c Inzamam b Mushtaq	43
A J Stewart+	b Mushtaq	44	c Asif Mujtaba b Mushtaq	54
N Hussain	c Saeed Anwar b Waqar	12	lbw b Mushtaq	51
G P Thorpe	lbw b Mohammad	54	c Wasim b Mushtaq	9
J P Crawley	b Waqar	106	c Sohail b Wasim	19
N V Knight	b Mushtaq	17	c and b Mushtaq	8
C C Lewis	b Wasim	5	lbw b Waqar	4
I D K Salisbury	c Inzamam b Wasim	5	(10) not out	0
D G Cork	c Moin b Waqar	0	(8) b Mushtaq	26
R D B Croft	not out	5	(9) c Ijaz b Wasim	6
A D Mullally	b Wasim	24	b Wasim	0
Extras	(lb12, w1, nb10)	23	(b6, lb2, w1, nb13)	22
Total	**(99.2 overs)**	**326**	**(82.4 overs)**	**242**

PAKISTAN

Saeed Anwar	c Croft b Cork	176	c Knight b Mullally	1
Aamir Sohail	c Cork b Croft	46	not out	29
Ijaz Ahmed	c Stewart b Mullally	61	not out	13
Inzamam-ul-Haq	c Hussain b Mullally	35		
Salim Malik	not out	100		
Asif Mujtaba	run out (Lewis/Stewart)	13		
Wasim Akram*	st Stewart b Croft	40		
Moin Khan+	b Salisbury	23		
Mushtaq Ahmed	c Crawley b Mullally	2		
Waqar Younis	not out	0		
Mohammad Akram	did not bat			
Extras	(b4, lb5, nb16)	25	(nb5)	5
Total	**(8 wkts dec)**	**521**	**(1 wicket)**	**48**
	(159.1 overs)		**(6.4 overs)**	

PAKISTAN

	O	M	R	W		O	M	R	W
Wasim Akram	29.2	9	83	3		15.4	1	67	3
Waqar Younis	25	6	95	4		18	3	55	1
Mohammad	12	1	41	1		10	3	30	0
Mushtaq	27	5	78	2		37	10	78	6
Sohail	6	1	17	0		2	1	4	0

ENGLAND

	O	M	R	W		O	M	R	W
Lewis	23	3	112	0		-	-	-	-
Mullally	37.1	7	97	3		3	0	24	1
Croft	47	10	116	2		0.4	0	9	0
Cork	23	5	71	1		3	0	15	0
Salisbury	29	3	116	1		-	-	-	-

FALL OF WICKETS

	E	P	E	P		E	P	E	P
1st	64	106	96	7	6th	273	440	205	-
2nd	85	239	136	-	7th	283	502	220	-
3rd	116	334	166	-	8th	284	519	238	-
4th	205	334	179	-	9th	295	-	242	-
5th	248	365	187	-	10th	326	-	242	-

ENGLAND v PAKISTAN

Played at Headingley on August 8, 9, 10, 11, 12, 1996
Toss: England. Match drawn.

PAKISTAN

Saeed Anwar	c Atherton b Mullally	1	c Russell b Cork	22
Shadab Kabir	lbw b Caddick	35	c and b Lewis	2
Ijaz Ahmed	c Russell b Cork	141	c Russell b Caddick	52
Inzamam-ul-Haq	c Atherton b Mullally	2	c Stewart b Caddick	65
Salim Malik	b Cork	55	c Cork b Caddick	6
Asif Mujtaba	c Thorpe b Cork	51	run out (Atherton)	26
Wasim Akram*	c Russell b Caddick	7	lbw b Atherton	7
Moin Khan+	c Russell b Cork	105	not out	30
Mushtaq Ahmed	c Atherton b Caddick	20	not out	6
Waqar Younis	c and b Cork	7		
Ata-ur-Rehman	not out	0		
Extras	(b4, lb10, nb10)	24	(b4, lb12, nb10)	26
TOTAL	**(153.2 overs)**	**448**	**(7 wkts dec)**	**242**
			(81 overs)	

ENGLAND

M A Atherton*	c Moin b Wasim	12
A J Stewart	c and b Mushtaq	170
N Hussain	c and b Waqar	48
G P Thorpe	c Shadab b Mushtaq	16
J P Crawley	c Moin b Rehman	53
N V Knight	c Mushtaq b Waqar	113
R C Russell+	b Wasim	9
C C Lewis	b Mushtaq	9
D G Cork	c Shadab b Wasim	26
A R Caddick	b Waqar	4
A D Mullally	not out	9
Extras	(b7, lb23, nb2)	32
Total	**(156.5 overs)**	**501**

ENGLAND

	O	M	R	W		O	M	R	W
Caddick	40.2	6	113	3		17	4	52	3
Mulilally	41	10	99	2		15	2	43	0
Lewis	32	4	100	0		16	3	52	1
Cork	37	6	113	5		16	2	49	1
Thorpe	3	1	9	0		10	3	10	0
Atherton	-	-	-	-		7	1	20	1

PAKISTAN

	O	M	R	W
Wasim	39.5	10	106	3
Waqar	33	7	127	3
Ata-ur-Rehman	22	1	90	1
Mushtaq	55	17	142	3
Mujtaba	7	5	6	0

FALL OF WICKETS

	P	E	P		P	E	P
1st	1	14	16	6th	266	402	201
2nd	98	121	34	7th	378	441	221
3rd	103	168	132	8th	434	465	-
4th	233	257	142	9th	444	471	-
5th	252	365	188	10th	448	501	-

Test Averages

TEST BATTING AVERAGES - Including fielding

Name	Matches	Inns	NO	Runs	HS	Avge	100s	50s	Ct	St
Aamer Malik	14	19	3	565	117	35.31	2	3	15	1
Aamir Nazir	6	11	6	31	11	6.20	-	-	2	-
Aamir Sohail	34	62	3	2103	205	35.64	2	13	31	-
Abdul Kadir	4	8	0	272	95	34.00	-	2	-	1
Abdul Qadir	67	77	11	1029	61	15.59	-	3	15	-
Afaq Hussain	2	4	4	66	35*	-	-	-	2	-
Aftab Baloch	2	3	1	97	60*	48.50	-	1	-	-
Aftab Gul	6	8	0	182	33	22.75	-	-	3	-
Agha Saadat Ali	1	1	1	8	8*	-	-	-	3	-
Agha Zahid	1	2	0	15	14	7.50	-	-	-	-
Akram Raza	9	12	2	153	32	15.30	-	-	8	-
Alimuddin	25	45	2	1091	109	25.37	2	7	8	-
Amir Elahi	5	7	1	65	47	10.83	-	-	-	-
Anil Dalpat	9	12	1	167	52	15.18	-	1	22	3
Anwar Hussain	4	6	0	42	17	7.00	-	-	-	-
Anwar Khan	1	2	1	15	12	15.00	-	-	-	-
Aqib Javed	21	25	6	100	28*	5.26	-	-	2	-
Arif Butt	3	5	0	59	20	11.80	-	-	-	-
Ashfaq Ahmed	1	2	1	1	1*	1.00	-	-	-	-
Ashraf Ali	8	8	3	229	65	45.80	-	2	17	5
Asif Iqbal	58	99	7	3575	175	38.85	11	12	36	-
Asif Masood	16	19	10	93	30*	10.33	-	-	5	-
Asif Mujtaba	23	38	3	852	65*	24.34	-	8	18	-
Ata-ur-Rehman	13	15	6	76	19	8.44	-	-	2	-
Atif Rauf	1	2	0	25	16	12.50	-	-	-	-
Azam Khan	1	1	0	14	14	14.00	-	-	-	-
Azeem Hafeez	18	21	5	134	24	8.37	-	-	1	-
Azhar Khan	1	1	0	14	14	14.00	-	-	-	-
Azmat Rana	1	1	0	49	49	49.00	-	-	-	-
Basit Ali	19	33	1	858	103	26.81	1	5	6	-
A.D'Souza	6	10	8	76	23*	38.00	-	-	3	-
Ehteshamuddin	5	3	1	2	2	1.00	-	-	2	-
Farooq Hamid	1	2	0	3	3	1.50	-	-	-	-
Farrukh Zaman	1	0	0	0	0	-	-	-	-	-
Fazal Mahmood	34	50	6	620	60	14.09	-	1	11	-
M.E.Z.Ghazali	2	4	0	32	18	8.00	-	-	-	-
Ghulam Abbas	1	2	0	12	12	6.00	-	-	-	-
Gul Mahomed	1	2	1	39	27*	39.00	-	-	-	-
Hanif Mohammad	55	97	8	3915	337	43.98	12	15	40	-
Haroon Rashid	23	36	1	1217	153	34.77	3	5	16	-
Hasan Raza	1	1	0	27	27	27.00	-	-	-	-
Haseeb Ahsan	12	16	7	61	14	6.77	-	-	1	-
Muhammad Hussain	1	1	0	0	0	0.00	-	-	1	-
Khalid Ibadulla	4	8	0	253	166	31.62	1	-	3	-
Ijaz Ahmed	32	48	2	1734	141	37.69	5	9	21	-
Ijaz Ahmed jr	2	3	0	29	16	9.66	-	-	3	-
Ijaz Butt	8	16	2	279	58	19.92	-	1	5	-
Ijaz Faqih	5	8	1	183	105	26.14	1	-	-	-
Imran Khan	88	126	25	3807	136	37.69	6	18	28	-
Imtiaz Ahmed	41	72	1	2079	209	29.28	3	11	77	16
Intikhab Alam	47	77	10	1493	138	22.28	1	8	20	-
Inzamam-ul-Haq	33	57	7	2367	148	47.34	5	16	34	-
Iqbal Qasim	50	57	15	549	56	13.07	-	1	42	-
Israr Ali	4	8	1	33	10	4.71	-	-	1	-
Jalaluddin	6	3	2	3	2	3.00	-	-	-	-
Javed Akhtar	1	2	1	4	2*	4.00	-	-	-	-
Javed Burki	25	48	4	1341	140	30.47	3	4	7	-
Javed Miandad	124	189	21	8832	280*	52.57	23	43	93	1
Kabir Khan	4	5	2	24	10	8.00	-	-	1	-
A.H.Kardar	23	37	3	847	93	24.91	-	5	15	-
Khalid Hassan	1	2	1	17	10	17.00	-	-	-	-
Khalid Wazir	2	3	1	14	9*	7.00	-	-	-	-
Khan Mohammad	13	17	7	100	26*	10.00	-	-	4	-
Liaqat Ali	5	7	3	28	12	7.00	-	-	1	-
Mahmood Hussain	27	39	6	336	35	10.18	-	-	5	-
Majid Khan	63	106	5	3931	167	38.92	8	19	70	-
Mansoor Akhtar	19	29	3	655	111	25.19	1	3	9	-
Manzoor Elahi	6	10	2	123	52	15.37	-	1	7	-
Maqsood Ahmed	16	27	1	507	99	19.50	-	2	13	-
Masood Anwar	1	2	0	39	37	19.50	-	-	-	-
W.Mathias	21	36	3	783	77	23.72	-	3	22	-
Miran Bux	2	3	2	1	1*	1.00	-	-	-	-
Mohammad Akram	5	8	2	8	5	1.33	-	-	4	-
Mohammad Aslam	1	2	0	34	18	17.00	-	-	-	-
Mohammad Farooq	7	9	4	85	47	17.00	-	-	1	-
Mohammad Ilyas	10	19	0	441	126	23.21	1	2	6	-
Mohammad Munaf	4	7	2	63	19	12.60	-	-	-	-
Mohammad Nazir	14	18	10	144	29*	18.00	-	-	4	-
Mohsin Kamal	9	11	7	37	13*	9.25	-	-	4	-
Mohsin Khan	48	79	6	2709	200	37.10	7	9	34	-
Moin Khan	22	33	5	858	117*	30.64	3	3	49	4
Mudassar Nazar	76	116	8	4114	231	38.09	10	17	48	-
Mufasir-ul-Haq	1	1	1	8	8*	-	-	-	1	-
Munir Malik	3	4	1	7	4	2.33	-	-	1	-
Mushtaq Ahmed	24	37	7	246	27	8.20	-	-	9	-
Mushtaq Mohammad	57	100	7	3643	201	39.17	10	19	42	-
Nadeem Abbasi	3	2	0	46	36	23.00	-	-	6	-
Nadeem Ghauri	1	1	0	0	0	0.00	-	-	-	-
Nadim Khan	1	1	0	25	25	25.00	-	-	-	-
Nasim-ul-Ghani	29	50	5	747	101	16.60	1	2	11	-
Naushad Ali	6	11	0	156	39	14.18	-	-	9	-
Naved Anjum	2	3	0	44	22	14.66	-	-	-	-
Nazar Mohammad	5	8	1	277	124*	39.57	1	1	7	-

Name	Matches	Inns	NO	Runs	HS	Avge	100s	50s	Ct	St
Shahid Nazir	2	2	0	1	1	0.50	-	-	-	-
Niaz Ahmed	2	3	3	17	16*	-	-	-	1	-
Pervez Sajjad	19	20	11	123	24	13.66	-	-	9	-
Qasim Omar	26	43	2	1502	210	36.63	3	5	15	-
Ramiz Raja	55	91	5	2747	122	31.94	2	21	32	-
Rashid Khan	4	6	3	155	59	51.66	-	1	2	-
Rashid Latif	19	29	4	623	68*	24.92	-	3	58	8
S.F.Rehman	1	2	0	10	8	5.00	-	-	1	-
Rizwan-uz-Zaman	11	19	1	345	60	19.16	-	3	4	-
Sadiq Mohammad	41	74	2	2579	166	35.81	5	10	28	-
Saeed Ahmed	41	78	4	2991	172	40.41	5	16	13	-
Saeed Anwar	19	34	1	1582	176	47.93	3	13	10	-
Salahuddin	5	8	2	117	34*	19.50	-	-	3	-
Salim Altaf	21	31	12	276	53*	14.52	-	1	3	-
Salim Elahi	2	4	0	43	17	10.75	-	-	1	-
Salim Jaffer	14	14	6	42	10*	5.25	-	-	2	-
Salim Malik	92	136	21	5171	237	44.96	14	26	59	-
Salim Yousuf	32	44	5	1055	91*	27.05	-	5	91	13
Saqlain Mushtaq	6	9	3	147	79	24.50	-	1	3	-
Sarfraz Nawaz	55	72	13	1045	90	17.71	-	4	26	-
Shadab Kabir	3	5	0	89	35	17.80	-	-	4	-
Shafiq Ahmed	6	10	1	99	27*	11.00	-	-	-	-
Shafqat Rana	5	7	0	221	95	31.57	-	2	5	-
Shahid Israr	1	1	1	7	7*	-	-	-	2	-
Shahid Mahboob	1	0	0	0	0	-	-	-	-	-
Shahid Mahmood	1	2	0	25	16	12.50	-	-	-	-
Shahid Saeed	1	1	0	12	12	12.00	-	-	-	-
Shakeel Ahmed	3	5	0	74	33	14.80	-	-	4	-
D.Sharpe	3	6	0	134	56	22.33	-	1	2	-
Shoaib Mohammad	45	68	7	2705	203*	44.34	7	13	22	-
Shujauddin	19	32	6	395	47	15.19	-	-	8	-
Sikander Bakht	26	35	12	146	22*	6.34	-	-	7	-
Tahir Naqqash	15	19	5	300	57	21.42	-	1	3	-
Talat Ali	10	18	2	370	61	23.12	-	2	4	-
Taslim Arif	6	10	2	501	210*	62.62	1	2	6	3
Tauseef Ahmed	34	38	20	318	35*	17.66	-	-	9	-
Waqar Hassan	21	35	1	1071	189	31.50	1	6	10	-
Waqar Younis	43	55	11	426	34	9.68	-	-	6	-
Wasim Akram	72	100	13	1944	257*	22.34	2	4	27	-
Wasim Bari	81	112	26	1366	85	15.88	-	6	201	27
Wasim Raja	57	92	14	2821	125	36.16	4	18	20	-
Wazir Mohammad	20	33	4	801	189	27.62	2	3	5	-
Younis Ahmed	4	7	1	177	62	29.50	-	1	-	-
Zaheer Abbas	78	124	11	5062	274	44.79	12	20	34	-
Zahid Fazal	9	16	0	288	78	18.00	-	1	5	-
Zakir Khan	2	2	2	9	9*	-	-	-	1	-
Zulfiqar Ahmed	9	10	4	200	63*	33.33	-	1	5	-
Zulqarnain	3	4	0	24	13	6.00	-	-	8	2

BOWLING AVERAGES

Name	Balls	Runs	Wkts	Avge	Best	5wI	10wM
Aamer Malik	156	89	1	89.00	1-0	-	-
Aamir Nazir	1057	597	20	29.85	5-46	1	-
Aamir Sohail	1613	710	17	41.76	4-54	-	-
Abdul Kadir							
Abdul Qadir	17126	7742	236	32.80	9-56	15	5
Afaq Hussain	240	106	1	106.00	1-40	-	-
Aftab Baloch	44	17	0	-	-	-	-
Aftab Gul	6	4	0	-	-	-	-
Agha Saadat Ali							
Agha Zahid							
Akram Raza	1526	732	13	56.30	3-46	-	-
Alimuddin	84	75	1	75.00	1-17	-	-
Amir Elahi	400	248	7	35.42	4-134	-	-
Anil Dalpat							
Anwar Hussain	36	29	1	29.00	1-25	-	-
Anwar Khan	32	12	0	-	-	-	-
Aqib Javed	3754	1786	54	33.07	5-84	1	-
Arif Butt	666	288	14	20.57	6-89	1	-
Ashfaq Ahmed	138	53	2	26.50	2-31	-	-
Ashraf Ali							
Asif Iqbal	3864	1502	53	28.33	5-48	2	-
Asif Masood	3038	1568	38	41.26	5-111	1	-
Asif Mujtaba	306	158	2	79.00	1-0	-	-
Ata-ur-Rehman	1973	1071	31	34.54	4-50	-	-
Atif Rauf							
Azam Khan							
Azeem Hafeez	4351	2204	63	34.98	6-46	4	-
Azhar Khan	18	2	1	2.00	1-1	-	-
Azmat Rana							
Basit Ali	6	6	0	-	-	-	-
A.D'Souza	1587	745	17	43.82	5-112	1	-
Ehteshamuddin	940	375	16	23.43	5-47	1	-
Farooq Hamid	184	107	1	107.00	1-82	-	-
Farrukh Zaman	80	15	0	-	-	-	-
Fazal Mahmood	9834	3434	139	24.70	7-42	13	4
M.E.Z.Ghazali	48	18	0	-	-	-	-
Ghulam Abbas							
Gul Mahomed							
Hanif Mohammad	206	95	1	95.00	1-1	-	-
Haroon Rashid	8	3	0	-	-	-	-
Hasan Raza							
Haseeb Ahsan	2835	1330	27	49.25	6-202	2	-
Muhammad Hussain	60	21	1	21.00	1-7	-	-
Khalid Ibadulla	336	99	1	99.00	1-42	-	-
Ijaz Ahmed	54	18	1	18.00	1-9	-	-

TEST BOWLING AVERAGES

Name	Balls	Runs	Wkts	Avge	Best	5wI	10wM
Ijaz Ahmed jr	24	6	0			-	-
Ijaz Butt							
Ijaz Faqih	534	299	4	74.75	1-38	-	-
Imran Khan	19458	8258	362	22.81	8-58	23	6
Imtiaz Ahmed	6	0	0			-	-
Intikhab Alam	10474	4494	125	35.95	7-52	5	2
Inzamam-ul-Haq							
Iqbal Qasim	13019	4807	171	28.11	7-49	8	2
Israr Ali	318	165	6	27.50	2-29	-	-
Jalaluddin	1197	537	11	48.81	3-77	-	-
Javed Akhtar	96	52	0			-	-
Javed Burki	42	23	0			-	-
Javed Miandad	1470	682	17	40.11	3-74	-	-
Kabir Khan	655	370	9	41.11	3-26	-	-
A.H.Kardar	2712	954	21	45.42	3-35	-	-
Khalid Hassan	126	116	2	58.00	2-116	-	-
Khalid Wazir							
Khan Mohammad	3157	1292	54	23.92	6-21	4	-
Liaqat Ali	808	359	6	59.83	3-80	-	-
Mahmood Hussain	5910	2628	68	38.64	6-67	2	-
Majid Khan	3584	1456	27	53.92	4-45	-	-
Mansoor Akhtar							
Manzoor Elahi	444	194	7	27.71	2-38	-	-
Maqsood Ahmed	462	191	3	63.66	2-12	-	-
Masood Anwar	161	102	3	34.00	2-59	-	-
W.Mathias	24	20	0			-	-
Miran Bux	348	115	2	57.50	2-82	-	-
Mohammad Akram	919	463	10	46.30	3-39	-	-
Mohammad Aslam							
Mohammad Farooq	1422	682	21	32.47	4-70	-	-
Mohammad Ilyas	84	63	0			-	-
Mohammad Munaf	769	341	11	31.00	4-42	-	-
Mohammad Nazir	3262	1124	34	33.05	7-99	3	-
Mohsin Kamal	1348	822	24	34.25	4-116	-	-
Mohsin Khan	86	30	0			-	-
Moin Khan							
Mudassar Nazar	5967	2532	66	38.36	6-32	1	-
Mufasir-ul-Haq	222	84	3	28.00	2-50	-	-
Munir Malik	684	358	9	39.77	5-128	1	-
Mushtaq Ahmed	5706	2607	89	29.29	7-56	5	1
Mushtaq Mohammad	5260	2309	79	29.22	5-28	3	-
Nadeem Abbasi							
Nadeem Ghauri	48	20	0			-	-
Nadim Khan	312	195	2	97.50	2-147	-	-
Nasim-ul-Ghani	4406	1959	52	37.67	6-67	2	-
Naushad Ali							
Naved Anjum	342	162	4	40.50	2-57	-	-
Nazar Mohammad	12	4	0			-	-
Shahid Nazir	351	146	10	14.60	5-53	1	-
Niaz Ahmed	294	94	3	31.33	2-72	-	-
Pervez Sajjad	4145	1410	59	23.89	7-74	3	-
Qasim Omar	6	0	0			-	-
Ramiz Raja							
Rashid Khan	738	360	8	45.00	3-129	-	-
Rashid Latif	12	10	0			-	-
S.F.Rehman	204	99	1	99.00	1-43	-	-
Rizwan-uz-Zaman	132	46	4	11.50	3-26	-	-
Sadiq Mohammad	200	98	0			-	-
Saeed Ahmed	1980	802	22	36.45	4-64	-	-
Saeed Anwar	18	4	0			-	-
Salahuddin	546	187	7	26.71	2-36	-	-
Salim Altaf	4001	1710	46	37.17	4-11	-	-
Salim Elahi							
Salim Jaffer	2531	1139	36	31.63	5-40	1	-
Salim Malik	470	267	5	53.40	1-3	-	-
Salim Yousuf							
Saqlain Mushtaq	1668	755	21	35.95	4-75	-	-
Sarfraz Nawaz	13951	5798	177	32.75	9-86	4	1
Shadab Kabir	6	9	0			-	-
Shafiq Ahmed	8	1	0			-	-
Shafqat Rana	36	9	1	9.00	1-2	-	-
Shahid Israr							
Shahid Mahboob	294	131	2	65.50	2-131	-	-
Shahid Mahmood	36	23	0			-	-
Shahid Saeed	90	43	0			-	-
Shakeel Ahmed							
D.Sharpe							
Shoaib Mohammad	396	170	5	34.00	2-8	-	-
Shujauddin	2313	801	20	40.05	3-18	-	-
Sikander Bakht	4870	2412	67	36.00	8-69	3	1
Tahir Naqqash	2800	1398	34	41.11	5-40	2	-
Talat Ali	20	7	0			-	-
Taslim Arif	30	28	1	28.00	1-28	-	-
Tauseef Ahmed	7778	2950	93	31.72	6-45	3	-
Waqar Hassan	6	10	0			-	-
Waqar Younis	8891	4770	222	21.48	7-76	19	4
Wasim Akram	16464	7054	311	22.68	7-119	21	4
Wasim Bari	8	2	0			-	-
Wasim Raja	4082	1826	51	35.80	4-50	-	-
Wazir Mohammad	24	15	0			-	-
Younis Ahmed	6	6	0			-	-
Zaheer Abbas	370	132	3	44.00	2-21	-	-
Zahid Fazal							
Zakir Khan	444	259	5	51.80	3-80	-	-
Zulfiqar Ahmed	1285	366	20	18.30	6-42	2	1
Zulqarnain							

One-Day Averages

ONE-DAY BATTING AVERAGES - Including fielding

Name	Matches	Inns	NO	Runs	HS	Avge	100s	50s	Ct	St
Aamer Hameed	2	0	0	0	0	-	-	-	1	-
Aamer Hanif	5	4	2	89	36*	44.50	-	-	-	-
Aamer Malik	24	23	1	556	90	25.27	-	5	13	3
Aamir Nazir	9	3	2	13	9*	13.00	-	-	-	-
Aamir Sohail	112	111	2	3672	134	33.68	5	23	33	-
Abdul Qadir	104	68	26	641	41*	15.26	-	-	21	-
Akram Raza	49	25	14	193	33*	17.54	-	-	19	-
Anil Dalpat	15	10	3	87	37	12.42	-	-	13	2
Shahid Anwar	1	1	0	37	37	37.00	-	-	-	-
Aqib Javed	133	42	24	237	45*	13.16	-	-	19	-
Arshad Khan	5	4	3	15	9*	15.00	-	-	3	-
Arshad Pervez	2	2	0	11	8	5.50	-	-	-	-
Ashfaq Ahmed	3	0	0	0	0	-	-	-	-	-
Ashraf Ali	16	9	5	69	19*	17.25	-	-	17	3
Asif Iqbal	10	8	2	330	62	55.00	-	5	7	-
Asif Masood	7	3	1	10	6	5.00	-	-	1	-
Asif Mujtaba	66	55	14	1068	113*	26.04	1	6	18	-
Ata-ur-Rehman	30	13	6	34	11*	4.85	-	-	-	-
Azam Khan	5	4	0	113	72	28.25	-	1	-	-
Azeem Hafeez	15	10	7	45	15	15.00	-	-	3	-
Azhar Mahmood	7	7	1	41	15	6.83	-	-	1	-
Azmat Rana	2	2	1	42	22*	42.00	-	-	-	-
Basit Ali	49	43	6	1265	127*	34.18	1	9	15	-
Zahoor Elahi	1	1	0	1	1	1.00	-	-	-	-
Ghulam Ali	3	3	0	53	38	17.66	-	-	-	-
Haafiz Shahid	3	3	2	11	7*	11.00	-	-	1	-
Haroon Rashid	12	10	2	166	63*	20.75	-	1	3	-
Hasan Jamil	6	5	0	111	28	22.20	-	-	1	-
Ijaz Ahmed	153	137	20	3499	124*	29.90	5	17	52	-
Ijaz Faqih	27	19	3	197	42*	12.31	-	-	2	-
Imran Khan	175	151	40	3709	102*	33.41	1	19	37	-
Intikhab Alam	4	2	0	17	10	8.50	-	-	-	-
Inzamam-ul-Haq	115	110	16	3725	137*	39.62	4	26	30	-
Iqbal Qasim	15	7	1	39	13	6.50	-	-	3	-
Iqbal Sikander	4	1	1	1	1*	-	-	-	-	-
Irfan Bhatti	1	0	0	0	0	-	-	-	1	-
Jalaluddin	8	2	0	5	5	2.50	-	-	1	-
Javed Miandad	233	218	41	7381	119*	41.70	8	50	71	2
Javed Qadeer	1	1	0	12	12	12.00	-	-	1	-
Kabir Khan	2	0	0	0	0	-	-	-	-	-
Liaqat Ali	3	1	0	7	7	7.00	-	-	-	-
Majid Khan	23	22	1	786	109	37.42	1	7	3	-
Mansoor Akhtar	41	35	1	593	47	17.44	-	-	14	-
Mansoor Rana	2	2	0	15	10	7.50	-	-	-	-
Manzoor Elahi	54	46	13	741	50*	22.45	-	1	21	-
Maqsood Rana	1	1	0	5	5	5.00	-	-	-	-
Masood Iqbal	1	1	0	2	2	2.00	-	-	-	-
Mehmood Hamid	1	1	0	1	1	1.00	-	-	-	-
Mohammad Akram	7	5	3	11	7*	5.50	-	-	2	-
Mohammad Nazir	4	3	3	4	2*	-	-	-	-	-
Mohsin Kamal	19	6	3	27	11*	9.00	-	-	4	-
Mohsin Khan	75	75	5	1877	117*	26.81	2	8	13	-
Moin Khan	59	44	10	629	50*	18.50	-	1	62	22
Moin-ul-Atiq	5	5	0	199	105	39.80	1	-	-	-
Mudassar Nazar	122	115	10	2653	95	25.26	-	16	21	-
Mushtaq Ahmed	110	54	21	291	26	8.81	-	-	24	-
Mushtaq Mohammad	10	9	3	209	55	34.83	-	1	3	-
Nadeem Ghauri	6	3	2	14	7*	14.00	-	-	-	-
Nadeem Khan	2	1	0	2	2	2.00	-	-	-	-
Naeem Ahmed	1	1	0	0	0*	-	-	-	1	-
Naeem Ashraf	2	2	0	24	16	24.00	-	-	-	-
Naseer Malik	3	1	1	0	0*	-	-	-	-	-
Nasim-ul-Ghani	1	1	0	1	1	1.00	-	-	-	-
Naved Anjum	13	12	3	113	30	12.55	-	-	-	-
Parvez Mir	3	3	1	26	18	13.00	-	-	2	-
Qasim Omar	31	31	3	642	69	22.92	-	4	3	-
Ramiz Raja	180	179	14	5396	119*	32.70	9	29	28	-
Rashid Khan	29	15	7	110	17	13.75	-	-	3	-
Rashid Latif	84	57	16	664	50	16.19	-	1	81	22
Hassan Raza	5	4	0	29	12	7.25	-	-	1	-
Abdul Razzak	2	1	1	0	0*	-	-	-	-	-
Rizwan-uz-Zaman	3	3	0	20	14	6.66	-	-	2	-
Saadat Ali	8	7	1	184	78*	30.66	-	1	1	-
Sadiq Mohammad	19	19	1	383	74	21.27	-	2	5	-
Saeed Anwar	114	113	11	3998	131	39.19	11	16	25	-
Saeed Azad	4	4	0	65	31	16.25	-	-	2	-
Sajid Ali	10	9	0	83	16	9.22	-	-	1	-
Sajjad Akbar	2	1	0	5	5	5.00	-	-	-	-
Salim Altaf	6	2	1	25	21	25.00	-	-	1	-
Salim Elahi	14	14	1	437	102*	33.61	1	3	4	-
Salim Jaffer	39	13	11	36	10*	18.00	-	-	3	-
Salim Malik	246	221	34	6266	102	33.50	5	40	74	-
Salim Pervez	1	1	0	18	18	18.00	-	-	-	-
Salim Yousuf	86	62	19	768	62	17.86	-	4	81	22
Saqlain Mushtaq	32	21	7	143	30	10.21	-	-	12	-
Sarfraz Nawaz	45	31	8	221	34*	9.60	-	-	8	-
Shadab Kabir	3	3	0	0	0	0.00	-	-	1	-
Shafiq Ahmed	3	3	0	41	29	13.66	-	-	1	-
Shahid Afridi	11	9	0	261	102	29.00	1	1	6	-
Shahid Mahboob	10	6	1	119	77	23.80	-	1	1	-
Shahid Nazir	9	4	4	17	6*	-	-	-	3	-
Shahid Saeed	10	10	0	141	50	14.10	-	1	2	-

ONE-DAY BATTING AVERAGES - Including fielding

Name	Matches	Inns	NO	Runs	HS	Avge	100s	50s	Ct	St
Shakil Ahmed	2	2	0	61	36	30.50	-	-	-	-
Shakil Khan	1	1	0	0	0	0.00	-	-	-	-
Shoaib Mohammad	63	58	6	1269	126*	24.40	1	8	13	-
Sikander Bakht	27	11	7	31	16*	7.75	-	-	4	-
Sohail Fazal	2	2	0	56	32	28.00	-	-	-	-
Tahir Naqqash	40	23	9	210	61	15.00	-	1	11	-
Tanvir Mehdi	1	1	0	0	0	0.00	-	-	-	-
Taslim Arif	2	2	0	28	24	14.00	-	-	1	1
Tausif Ahmed	70	25	14	116	27*	10.54	-	-	10	-
Waqar Younis	142	68	25	423	37	9.83	-	-	15	-
Wasim Akram	214	164	31	1952	86	14.67	-	2	49	-
Wasim Bari	51	26	13	221	34	17.00	-	-	52	10
Wasim Haider	3	2	0	26	13	13.00	-	-	-	-
Wasim Raja	54	45	10	782	60	22.34	-	2	24	-
Younis Ahmed	2	2	0	84	58	42.00	-	1	1	-
Zafar Iqbal	8	6	0	48	18	8.00	-	-	1	-
Zaheer Abbas	62	60	6	2572	123	47.62	7	13	16	-
Zahid Ahmed	2	2	1	3	3*	3.00	-	-	-	-
Zahid Fazal	19	18	3	348	98*	23.20	-	2	2	-
Zakir Khan	17	5	4	27	11*	27.00	-	-	-	-
Zulqarnain	16	6	3	18	11*	6.00	-	-	18	5

ONE-DAY BOWLING AVERAGES

Name	Balls	Runs	Wkts	Avge	Best	5wl
Aamer Hameed	88	38	1	38.00	1-32	-
Aamer Hanif	130	122	4	30.50	3-36	-
Aamer Malik	120	86	3	28.66	2-35	-
Aamir Nazir	417	346	11	31.45	3-43	-
Aamir Sohail	3805	2849	67	42.52	4-22	-
Abdul Qadir	5100	3453	132	26.15	5-44	2
Akram Raza	2601	1611	38	42.39	3-18	-
Anil Dalpat						
Shahid Anwar						
Aqib Javed	6673	4637	146	31.76	7-37	2
Arshad Khan	233	159	2	79.50	1-29	-
Arshad Pervez						
Ashfaq Ahmed	102	84	0	-	-	-
Ashraf Ali						
Asif Iqbal	592	378	16	23.62	4-56	-
Asif Masood	402	234	5	46.80	2-9	-
Asif Mujtaba	756	658	7	94.00	2-38	-
Ata-ur-Rehman	1492	1186	27	43.92	3-27	-
Azam Khan						
Azeem Hafeez	719	586	15	39.06	4-22	-
Azhar Mahmood	252	245	2	122.50	2-38	-
Azmat Rana						
Basit Ali	30	21	1	21.00	1-17	-
Zahoor Elahi						
Ghulam Ali						
Haafiz Shahid	127	112	3	37.33	2-56	-
Haroon Rashid						
Hasan Jamil	232	154	8	19.25	3-18	-
Ijaz Ahmed	432	324	3	108.00	2-31	-
Ijaz Faqih	1116	819	13	63.00	4-43	-
Imran Khan	7461	4845	182	26.62	6-14	1
Intikhab Alam	158	118	4	29.50	2-36	-
Inzamam-ul-Haq	40	52	2	26.00	1-4	-
Iqbal Qasim	664	500	12	41.66	3-13	-
Iqbal Sikander	210	147	3	49.00	1-30	-
Irfan Bhatti	48	22	2	11.00	2-22	-
Jalaluddin	306	211	14	15.07	4-32	-
Javed Miandad	436	297	7	42.42	2-22	-
Javed Qadeer						
Kabir Khan	116	66	3	22.00	2-32	-
Liaqat Ali	188	111	2	55.50	1-41	-
Majid Khan	658	374	13	28.76	3-27	-
Mansoor Akhtar	138	110	2	55.00	1-7	-
Mansoor Rana	6	7	0	-	-	-
Manzoor Elahi	1743	1262	29	43.51	3-22	-
Maqsood Rana	12	11	0	-	-	-
Masood Iqbal						
Mehmood Hamid						
Mohammad Akram	342	307	9	34.11	2-36	-
Mohammad Nazir	222	156	3	52.00	2-37	-
Mohsin Kamal	881	760	21	36.19	4-47	-
Mohsin Khan	12	5	1	5.00	1-2	-
Moin Khan						
Moin-ul-Atiq						
Mudassar Nazar	4855	3432	111	30.91	5-28	1
Mushtaq Ahmed	5669	4111	129	31.86	5-36	1
Mushtaq Mohammad	42	23	0	-	-	-
Nadeem Ghauri	342	230	5	46.00	2-51	-
Nadeem Khan	96	81	0	-	-	-
Naeem Ahmed	60	43	0	-	-	-
Naeem Ashraf	42	52	0	-	-	-
Naseer Malik	180	98	5	19.60	2-37	-
Nasim-ul-Ghani						
Naved Anjum	472	344	8	43.00	2-27	-
Parvez Mir	122	77	3	25.66	1-17	-
Qasim Omar						
Ramiz Raja	6	10	0	-	-	-
Rashid Khan	1414	923	20	46.15	3-47	-
Rashid Latif						
Hassan Raza						
Abdul Razzak	75	53	3	17.66	2-29	-

ONE-DAY BOWLING AVERAGES

Name	Balls	Runs	Wkts	Avge	Best	5wl
Rizwan-uz-Zaman						
Saadat Ali	27	29	2	14.50	2-24	-
Sadiq Mohammad	38	26	2	13.00	2-20	-
Saeed Anwar	162	144	3	48.00	1-9	-
Saeed Azad						
Sajid Ali						
Sajjad Akbar	60	45	2	22.50	2-45	-
Salim Altaf	285	151	5	30.20	2-7	-
Salim Elahi						
Salim Jaffer	1900	1382	40	34.55	3-25	-
Salim Malik	2842	2348	69	34.02	5-35	1
Salim Pervez						
Salim Yousuf						
Saqlain Mushtaq	1670	1230	61	20.16	4-28	-
Sarfraz Nawaz	2412	1463	63	23.22	4-27	-
Shadab Kabir						
Shafiq Ahmed						
Shahid Afridi	557	372	10	37.20	3-48	-
Shahid Mahboob	540	382	7	54.57	1-23	-
Shahid Nazir	384	312	9	34.66	2-28	-
Shahid Saeed	222	159	3	53.00	2-20	-
Shakil Ahmed						
Shakil Khan	54	50	1	50.00	1-50	-
Shoaib Mohammad	919	725	20	36.25	3-20	-
Sikander Bakht	1277	860	33	26.06	4-34	-
Sohail Fazal	6	4	0	-	-	-
Tahir Naqqash	1596	1240	34	36.47	3-23	-
Tanvir Mehdi	66	72	1	72.00	1-72	-
Taslim Arif						
Tausif Ahmed	3250	2247	55	40.85	4-38	-
Waqar Younis	7115	5325	242	22.00	6-26	9
Wasim Akram	11044	6972	310	22.49	5-15	5
Wasim Bari						
Wasim Haider	114	79	1	79.00	1-36	-
Wasim Raja	1036	687	21	32.71	4-25	-
Younis Ahmed						
Zafar Iqbal	198	137	3	45.66	2-37	-
Zaheer Abbas	280	223	7	31.85	2-26	-
Zahid Ahmed	96	61	3	20.33	2-24	-
Zahid Fazal						
Zakir Khan	646	494	16	30.87	4-19	-
Zulqarnain						

Statistics accurate to October 1996 - includes series vs Zimbabwe, 1996

Bibliography

Ahmed, Shafiq. *An Artists impression of 25 Greats of Pakistan Cricket* (Deenar Design, 1991)
Allen, David Rayvern, Ed. *Arlott on Cricket* (Willow Books, 1984)
Bailey, Philip and Philip Thorn, Peter Wynne-Thomas. *Who's Who of Cricketers* (Hamlyn, 1993)
Botham, Ian. *Botham, My Autobiography* (Collins Willow, 1994)
Brearley, Mike. *The Art of Captaincy* (Hodder and Stoughton, 1985)
Chandrashekar, B.S and Rajan Bala. *The Winning Hand* (Rupa & Co, 1993)
Corbett, Ted and Joanne King. *The Wisden Book of Test Captain* (Stanley Paul, 1991)
Crace, John. *Wasim and Waqar* (Boxtree, 1992)
Frindall, Bill. *The Wisden Book of Test Cricket* (Book Club Associates, 1979)
Frindall, Bill. *The Wisden Book of Cricket Records* (Headline, 1993)
Gatting, Mike. *Leading from the Front* (Macdonald, Queen Anne Press, 1988)
Hadlee, Richard with Richard Becht. *Rhythm and Swing* (Collins Publishers, 1989)
Haynes, Des with Rob Steen. *The Lion of Barbados* (H.F. & G. Witherby, 1993)
Khan, Imran. *All Round View* (Chatto & Windus, 1988)
Khan, Imran with Patrick Murphy. *Imran, The Autobiography* (Pelham Books, 1983)
Lemmon, David. *The Guinness Book of Test Cricket Captains* (Guinness, 1992)
Lodge, Derek. *Figures on the Green* (George Allen & Unwin, 1982)
Martin-Jenkins, Christopher. *World Cricketers* (Oxford 1996)
Sproat, Iain, Ed. *The Cricketers' Who's Who* (Lennard Queen Anne Press, 1987-96)
Swanton, E.W., Ed. *Barclay's World of Cricket* (Collins Publishers, 1980)
Tennant, Ivo. *Imran Khan* (Witherby 1994)
Various. *Test Match Grounds of the World*, Mihir Bose on Pakistan (Collins Willow, 1990)
Wynne-Thomas, Peter. *The Complete History of Cricket Tours, at Home and Abroad* (Hamlyn, 1988)
Wisden Cricketers' Almanack, 1946-1995
Wisden Cricket Monthly
The Cricketer International
The Cricketer Quarterly